CONNORS ON ADVANCED TRADING STRATEGIES

Laurence A. Connors

M. GORDON PUBLISHING GROUP
Malibu, California

ISBN 0-9650461-5-X

Printed in the United States of America

To Karen

Disclaimer

It should not be assumed that the methods, techniques, or indicators presented in this book will be profitable or that they will not result in losses. Past results are not necessarily indicative of future results. Examples in this book are for educational purposes only. The author, publishing firm, and any affiliates assume no responsibility for your trading results. This is not a solicitation of any order to buy or sell.

CONTENTS

INTRODUCTION

· ·

This book was written with the me of 10 years ago in mind. My goal has been to produce the book I wish I had a decade ago when I made a full-time commitment to my trading.

Over the years I have read hundreds of books on investing and trading. The ones I learned the most from were written by individuals who removed their egos from their writing. Their books were written simply, and without the need to show the reader how smart the authors were. I hope to do the same here. I suspect, if I tried, I could bore you with 12-letter words, run-on sentences, and I could quote Nietzsche and Plutarch to show you how intelligent I am. I could drop names of some of the financial market celebrities I barely know, and I could fill the back of the book with a huge bibliography. But I will not, for as I mentioned earlier, I am writing the book as I would have wanted it myself, and I suspect my need to keep things simple and to the point are also yours.

This book is a compilation of two years of my monthly newsletter, the *Professional Traders Journal*. I have taken the best strategies and updated them for you. I have also added new strategies, concepts, and thoughts to hopefully bring the research to a new level.

The majority of the strategies presented were originally created by my research firm, Oceanview Financial Research. I have attempted to give reference and credit to those individuals from whom other strategies were derived. If I missed anyone, I give you my strongest apologies.

Good work must be acknowledged and only I am to blame for any oversights.

I would like to thank Mark Boucher, Fernando Diz, Jeff Cooper and Derek Gipson for their contributions. They have helped make a good publication better. I would also like to thank my editor Bill Masciarelli, Bob Pisani, Danilo Torres, Irene Golden, Judy Brown, David Landry, Joe Calandro, and Jeff Cox for their invaluable contributions in helping create this book.

Finally, I would like to thank my wife Karen for again lovingly putting up with my nonsense while writing a book. Thanks also to my daughter Brittany, who is now the only ten year old, who knows how to create historical volatility charts from a Bloomberg terminal, and my daughter Alexandra, who is, as far as I know, the first five-year-old to help collate a financial markets trading book. I marvel at both of you and can only wonder in amazement what the future will bring.

CHAPTER 1

THE BASE

■ ■

This first chapter is more important than the trading strategies chapters. It will provide you with a basis for understanding why a small handful of players make extraordinary money trading while the majority do not. This chapter will create the foundation you must have to maximize the effectiveness of the strategies which are the heart of the book.

I have traded the markets directly or indirectly since I was in college more than twenty years ago. I began, as most traders do, by searching for the perfect trading system. If I told you that I have outgrown this pie in the sky pursuit, I would be lying. I still wake up in the middle of the night and go to my home Bloomberg terminal to test something that I believe will change the course of trading history. I suspect that if I am still alive 50 years from now, I will be doing the same.

As I have grown older, I have learned to lessen my expectations. I have come to realize that it is good to think big, but success in trading is not dependent on finding the holy grail trading system. It is much more dependent upon having a trading method that meets the following three criteria:

1. The method must be conceptually correct.

2. It must provide you with a small "edge."

3. Most importantly, the method must be able to manage the "bad tail."

Let's look at each component in further depth.

COMPONENT 1—THE STRATEGY MUST BE CONCEPTUALLY CORRECT

If a strategy is not based upon inherently correct market principles, it is probably useless. I suspect that if I looked at the schedule of every Major League Baseball team over the past decade, I could find some sort of pattern that predicted market behavior. An example would be when the Seattle Mariners win by two runs or more on Tuesday night, and Randy Johnson doesn't pitch the game, soybeans rise 72 percent of the time the following day. You may laugh at this example (don't trade it), but I have seen methodologies and strategies sold to traders that make as much sense as the one above.

Markets have built-in characteristics. For example, strongly trending markets will pause, pullback, and then continue their original move; in bear markets, sessions tend to close below their opening; low volatility is preceded by high volatility, etc. Any middle level student of the game has come to know these and similar truths. When you read the upcoming chapters, you will see that the inherent market features I have just listed and others like them are the basis of my strategies.

I strongly believe that in order to improve upon your trading you must only trade strategies that exploit inherent market characteristics.

COMPONENT 2—THE EDGE

Over the past 100 years, which industry has been one of the most consistently profitable? The insurance industry. Why? Because insurance companies have a built-in "edge." They can statistically show that based on a normal distribution of events—mortality rates, average life span, etc.—they will profit in the long run. Casinos and bookmakers work from and profit from the same long-term statistical probabilities.

In sports betting, there is a 4.5 percent edge to the house. It is even higher on parlays, teasers, etc. Last year an acquaintance of mine used this edge to earn more than $12 million from his offshore sports betting establishment. Even though it is a bit more complicated than this, this gentleman needs only to match-up both sides of a game and he is assured a profit. The same type edge holds true for the casinos in craps, roulette, and any other game of chance. A well-know casino executive wasn't kidding when he said, "When a sheep is on the way to the slaughter, he *may* kill the butcher . . . but we always bet on the butcher!"

In trading, the edge immediately goes to players like the market makers who buy on the bid and sell on the offer. One does not need to be a genius to figure out that the guy who buys at 46 and can immediately sell it at 46 1/2 has the edge over guys like me who have to buy at 46 1/2 and can only immediately sell it at 46.

Your strategies must provide you with some sort of edge. It does not have to be big! The casino's edge is usually only a few percentage points and the edge for the market maker in the previous example is less than 1.5 percent. This small edge is enough to make one rich if the opportunity arises enough times and if you can conquer the third component which is . . .

COMPONENT 3—YOU MUST MANAGE THE BAD TAIL!

This is the single most important and critical point I will make in the book. It must be burned into your memory. Anyone can make money when things work out as they *normally* should. The majority of traders who blow-out, do so when they succumb to the "it-will-never-happen-to-me" syndrome.

Let's look at a bell curve to understand this further.

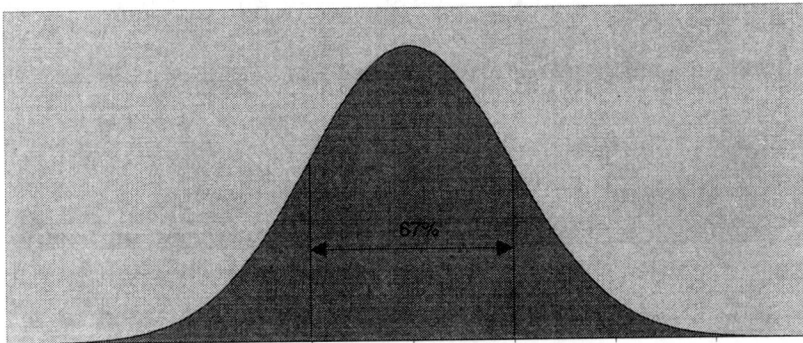

As you can see, normal events occur around 67 percent of the time. In market terms, this means that prices will fall within one standard deviation of their mean (average) 67 percent of the time within a specific time frame. When this happens, (approximately two-thirds of the days are like this) one's methodology makes some money and loses some money. As we move further and further away from the mean we get into the areas where the large profits or substantial losses occur. This is when our normal $200/trade edge makes $5,000 or loses $5,000. When our methodology makes $5,000, we are geniuses, and when it loses $5,000 it hurts badly, but usually not enough to wipe us out. It is when a trade occurs on the "very edge" of the tails that the rumor mill gets cranked up. When the trade lands on the **"good tail,"** it becomes the story of the trader who turns $10,000 into over $3 million in one option trade (a true event told to me by a friend who handled the trade) and on the other end of the spectrum, it is the well-known money manager who recently sold thousands of naked puts into a severe market decline and turned his client's money into dust after a decade of stellar performance **("the bad tail").**

My main concern for you (and for me) is how to manage the bad tail. The risk of ruin can never be eliminated but it can be greatly lessened when the bad tail occurs. It is mostly done with protective stops, it is done with spreads on options (instead of a naked position), and it is done with adjusting your trade size to reflect current volatility (see Chapter 5). As you will see, trading 1000 shares of a stock that has a current volatility of 10 percent is vastly different than trading the same stock when its volatility rises to 40 percent.

There are many unsuccessful traders who grind themselves to death because they do not have an edge. There are more traders, though, who die because of one reason: they did not manage the bad tail!

One more point: when creating market strategies, you must realize that market generalities are useless. A "market generality" is different from a conceptually correct market characteristic. For example, most traders believe that sustained TRIN readings under one are bearish and sustained TRIN readings above one are bullish. I have yet to see a money manager take this information and consistently make money from it. Other examples that you have heard include fade the morning move, buy the market after lunch, go long heating oil in the fall, buy the breakout-fade the test, etc. We can all name many more generalities, but I suspect you get the point.

Before you trade "market lore," ask yourself, "Why isn't everyone rich if something so simple is true?" In order to gain an edge over some of the smartest people in the world, you cannot trade generalities. You must step outside the box and think differently. This is easier said than done, but as you will see from the strategies in the upcoming chapters, the best ones were conceived by looking at things from a perspective that is decidedly different.

SECTION ONE

S&P AND STOCK MARKET TIMING

The strategies in this section identify when the stock market is at psychological extremes and likely to reverse. The strategies, "Connors VIX Reversal I, II, and III," "TRIN Thrusts," and the "Percent Advance/Decline Indicator" are among my favorites for trading the stock market and stocks. They identify times when fear or greed are at maximums and market reversals are likely to follow.

James Cramer, who is one of the best traders on Wall Street and oversees a terrific web site, TheStreet.com, is a master at instinctively identifying these periods. In a recent article he was quoted as saying "I'm neither bull nor bear. I try to take advantage of emotional swings in stocks that are probably unjustified by fundamentals." Though I do not personally know Cramer, based upon his track record, I suspect his abilities to identify market extremes—to smell the fear and punish the greed—are as good as they come.

I do not possess Cramer's magic touch. I need to rely on some sort of statistical evidence to confirm my instincts at these extremes. The following strategies are among my best and are the ones I use to "smell the fear and punish the greed." Before trading these strategies, you should be aware of the risks involved in trying to identify large market reversals. You are many times using your face to stop a runaway train and when you are wrong, you will be punished. Your largest profits, though, will come when you are correct. Therefore, I strongly recommend using some type of money management strategy combined with these signals.

One final note: The testing in the following chapters show the results using $500 per contract point on the S&P's. Due to a recent split, the value is now $250 per contract point. Also, even though I am publishing mechanical results, none of my methods are intended to be mechanical systems, nor do I trade them as mechanical systems. I use them only to help me identify a potential directional bias in upcoming days.

CHAPTER 2

CONNORS VIX REVERSALS

In 1994, when Blake Hayward and I wrote *Investment Secrets of a Hedge Fund Manager*, we included a chapter entitled, "New Markets, New Indicators." Among the strategies mentioned in that chapter was one which incorporated the VIX indicator. I mentioned that up to that point markets made very short-term tops when the VIX dropped under 11 percent and very short-term bottoms when the VIX traded above 15 percent. Because the indicator was so new, I felt it was too soon to blindly fix upon those levels, but the concept certainly had promise.

Since that time, and especially after 1995, the normal daily trading range for the VIX has greatly increased. In this chapter, I will show you how I have adjusted the parameters of the indicator to identify one- to three-day market tops and bottoms. I have also included more than four years of test results. We will also look at how to apply the readings to trade the S&P's and the stock market.

CONNORS VIX REVERSAL I

The VIX (CBOE, OEX, Volatility Index) reflects a market consensus estimate of future volatility based on "at-the-money" quotes of OEX index options. Periods of low volatility (a low VIX reading) basically reflect a quiet, rising market, whereas periods of high volatility (a high VIX reading) are associated with sharp market sell-offs.

The VIX is used as a contrary indicator. The higher its reading (and hence the more fear in the market), the more likely the market is reaching a short-term bottom, and the lower the reading, the more likely the market is reaching a short-term top. In my opinion, due to the increasingly speculative role that OEX options have assumed, *the significance and the reliability of the VIX as a market timing indicator have greatly increased over the past few years.*

Until now, most traders have used predetermined static bands (as I did in 1994) to identify what is a "high" reading and what is a "low" reading. Although this works, one never knows if those bands are truly reflective of today's market or if they really only reflect how markets reacted in the past. I endeavored to create a way to look at the VIX only within the context of its very recent price action and settled on the relative VIX action of the previous fifteen trading days. I then addressed the matter of the indicator reaching an overbought or oversold condition but continuing to become even more overbought or oversold. Finally, I added a feature that identifies when market sentiment has reversed intraday from an extreme reading. From these pieces comes the "Connors VIX Reversal I."

Here are the rules:

FOR BUYS

1.   Today the VIX must make a 15-day high.

2.   Today, the close of the VIX must be below the open.

3.   If Rules 1 and 2 are met, buy the S&P's (or the market) on the close of today. This will have to be done at the same time Rule 2 is met and in the last few minutes of trading.

4.   Hold the position at least one to three days.

FOR SELLS

1.   Today the VIX must make a 15-day low.

2.   Today the close of the VIX must be above the open.

3.   If Rules 1 and 2 are met, sell the S&P's (or the market) on the close of today. This will have to be done at the same time Rule 2 is met and in the last few minutes of trading.

4.   Hold the position at least one to three days.

FIGURE 2.1 CBOE OEX Volatility Index—Here Is What a Setup Looks Like

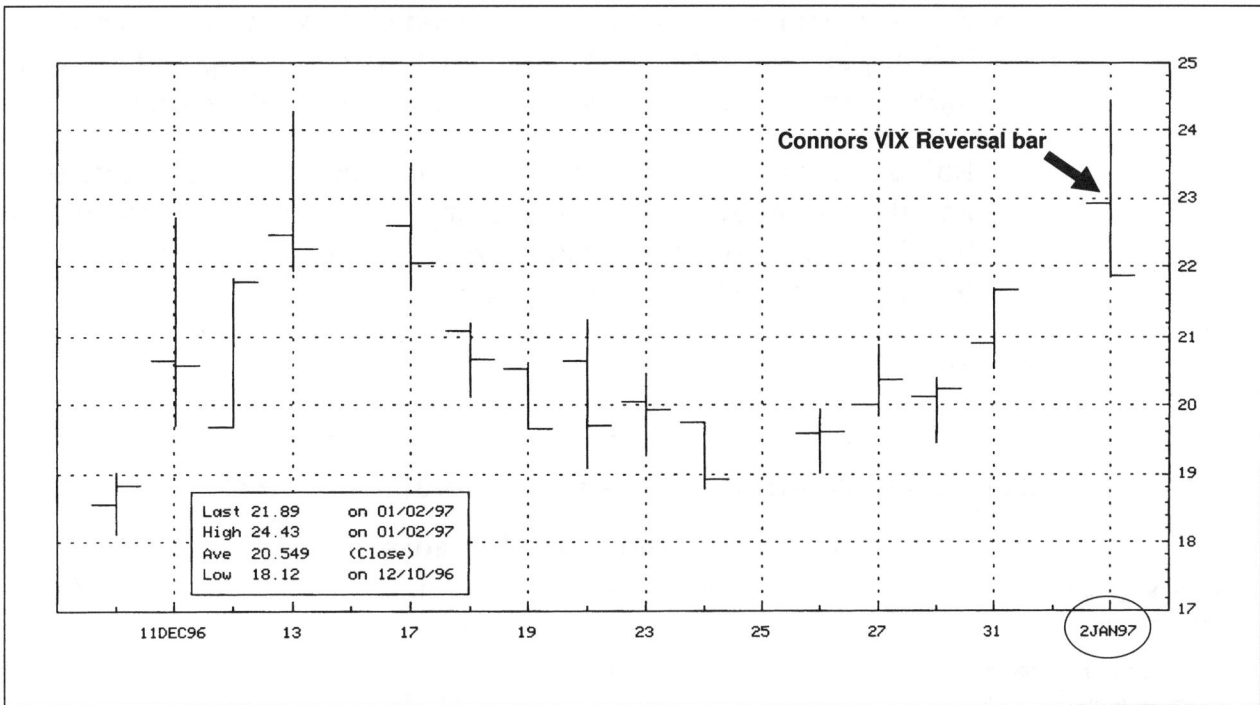

FIGURE 2.2 S&P 500 Futures

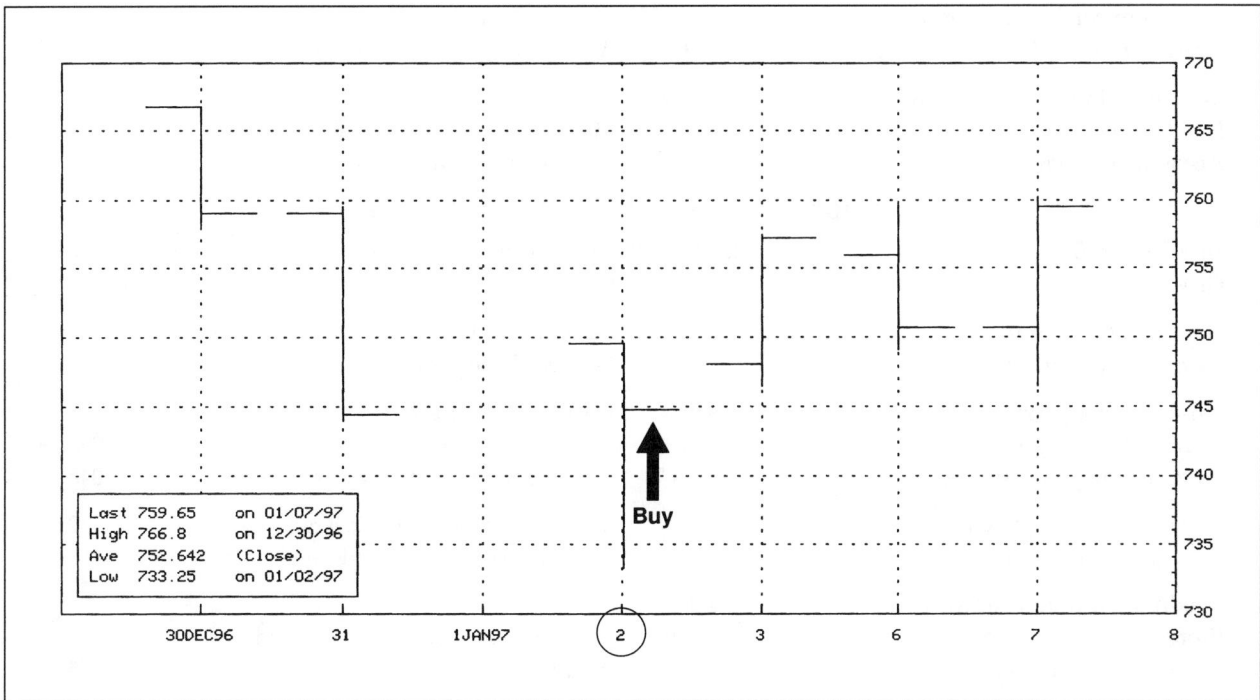

Before looking at the results, let's look at the basis of the rules:

- Rule 1 overcomes the weaknesses inherent in having a predetermined VIX buy and sell zone. We now have a dynamic (as opposed to static) indicator which is truly reflective of current market conditions.

- Rule 2 helps us avoid markets which become overbought/oversold and then continue to move further in that direction. By waiting for the VIX index to reverse intraday, we are identifying a definite *change in market sentiment* occurring at extreme levels.

Let's look at the results:

CVR I S&P 500 Index—CME—Daily—01/01/93–10/01/97

Performance Summary: All Trades

Total net profit	$	81,400.00	Open position P/L	$ 0.00
Gross profit	$	151,175.00	Gross loss	$ −69,775.00
Total number of trades		72	Percent profitable	65%
Number winning trades		47	Number losing trades	25
Largest winning trade	$	16,950.00	Largest losing trade	$ −9,275.00
Average winning trade	$	3,216.49	Average losing trade	$ −2,791.00
Ratio average win/average loss		1.15	Average trade (win and loss)	$ 1,130.56
Maximum consecutive winners		7	Maximum consecutive losers	3
Average number bars in winners		3	Average number bars in losers	3
Maximum intraday drawdown	$	−18,275.00		
Profit factor		2.17	Maximum number contracts held	1
Account size required	$	18,275.00	Return on account	445%

Performance Summary: Long Trades

Total net profit	$	52,425.00	Open position P/L	$ 0.00
Gross profit	$	110,175.00	Gross loss	$ −57,750.00
Total number of trades		50	Percent profitable	64%
Number winning trades		32	Number losing trades	18
Largest winning trade	$	16,950.00	Largest losing trade	$ −9,275.00
Average winning trade	$	3,442.97	Average losing trade	$ −3,208.33
Ratio average win/average loss		1.07	Average trade (win and loss)	$ 1,048.50
Maximum consecutive winners		6	Maximum consecutive losers	2
Average number bars in winners		3	Average number bars in losers	3
Maximum intraday drawdown	$	−18,225.00		
Profit factor		1.91	Maximum number contracts held	1
Account size required	$	18,225.00	Return on account	288%

Performance Summary: Short Trades

Total net profit	$	28,975.00	Open position P/L	$	0.00
Gross profit	$	41,000.00	Gross loss	$	–12,025.00
Total number of trades		22	Percent profitable		68%
Number winning trades		15	Number losing trades		7
Largest winning trade	$	12,100.00	Largest losing trade	$	–3,675.00
Average winning trade	$	2,733.33	Average losing trade	$	–1,717.86
Ratio average win/average loss		1.59	Average trade (win and loss)	$	1,317.05
Maximum consecutive winners		5	Maximum consecutive losers		2
Average number bars in winners		3	Average number bars in losers		3
Maximum intraday drawdown	$	–4,950.00			
Profit factor		3.41	Maximum number contracts held		1
Account size required	$	4,950.00	Return on account		585%

As you can see, I went back more than four years, from January 1, 1993 up through October 1, 1997. I did not include slippage and commission, as this is not a mechanical system, but $150 slippage and commission per trade won't greatly affect the results. Finally, I used no stops in the testing. This led to a few good hits, yet in spite of this the results were solid.

The daily signals for the Connors VIX Reversal I can be found in the Appendix.

SUMMARY

The Connors VIX Reversal I does a solid job of identifying short-term market tops and bottoms. What is also significant is that in spite of the fact that we had been in a raging bull market during the test period, the setup worked well to the short side.

Now, the question of how to trade the indicator. Obviously, if you are an S&P trader, you will trade the futures and implement some type of protective stop to avoid the 18-point drop that occurred in 1996. You can also use this indicator to derive directional bias to complement your other indicators. (If you trade stocks, and have a buy signal, it behooves you to take your profits in your short positions and reverse to the long side.)

I am not advocating using this as a mechanical system. I specifically use it to help identify short-term market tops and bottoms. Also, you may wish to adjust the look-back period and holding period to create more trades. I will many times look at less than 15-day highs/lows and if it is in confirmation with other indicators, I am quite likely to take the signal. Finally, to me, the most exciting and most profitable strategies for this indicator are in the options markets. On the long side alone (selling puts) you have a directional bias combined with implied volatility collapsing! This will be further discussed in the options section.

CONNORS VIX REVERSAL II

Here is another methodology that uses the VIX to measure overbought and oversold conditions. The "Connors VIX Reversal II" (CVR II) adds the use of the Relative Strength Index (RSI) of the VIX to provide insight into another way to time your entries more precisely.

"Common Wall Street wisdom" states that when the VIX is high, the market is likely to rise and when the VIX is low, the market is likely to drop. As far as I am aware, until the CVR I was introduced, no one could show where was the best high/low level to enter, and certainly no one has combined it with an intraday reversal. The CVR II takes the same concepts of the CVR I and uses an even more efficient way to measure overbought/oversold levels.

Here are the rules:

1. Take a five-period RSI of the closing VIX.

2a. When the five-period RSI gets to 70 or above, it signifies the VIX is overbought and the market is oversold.

2b. When the five-period RSI of the VIX gets to 30 or below, it signifies that the VIX is oversold and the market is overbought.

3. When a daily RSI reading above 70 is followed by a downtick in RSI, buy the market that day on the close. When an RSI reading below 30 is followed by an uptick in RSI, sell the market that day on the close.

4. Exit five to eight trading days later (or use some type of trailing stop exit).

Here are the results using an eight-day exit for the period January 1, 1993 through October 1, 1997. They are among the best of any strategy I have presented (a trade-by-trade summary is in the Appendix).

CVR II S&P 500 Index—CME—Daily—01/01/93–10/01/97

Performance Summary: All Trades

Total net profit	$ 179,100.00	Open position P/L	$ −4,500.00
Gross profit	$ 312,500.00	Gross loss	$ −133,400.00
Total number of trades	96	Percent profitable	61%
Number winning trades	59	Number losing trades	37
Largest winning trade	$ 30,700.00	Largest losing trade	$ −10,525.00
Average winning trade	$ 5,296.61	Average losing trade	$ −3,605.41
Ratio average win/average loss	1.47	Average trade (win and loss)	$ 1865.63
Maximum consecutive winners	5	Maximum consecutive losers	6
Average number bars in winners	7	Average number bars in losers	8
Maximum intraday drawdown	$ −44,450.00		
Profit factor	2.34	Maximum number contracts held	1
Account size required	$ 44,450.00	Return on account	403%

Performance Summary: Long Trades

Total net profit	$ 161,725.00	Open position P/L	$ 0.00
Gross profit	$ 214,400.00	Gross loss	$ −52,675.00
Total number of trades	55	Percent profitable	67%
Number winning trades	37	Number losing trades	18
Largest winning trade	$ 30,700.00	Largest losing trade	$ −10,525.00
Average winning trade	$ 5,794.59	Average losing trade	$ −2,926.39
Ratio average win/average loss	1.98	Average trade (win and loss)	$ 2,940.45
Maximum consecutive winners	7	Maximum consecutive losers	4
Average number bars in winners	8	Average number bars in losers	8
Maximum intraday drawdown	$ −24,475.00		
Profit factor	4.07	Maximum number contracts held	1
Account size required	$ 24,475.00	Return on account	661%

Performance Summary: Short Trades

Total net profit	$ 17,375.00	Open position P/L	$ −4,500.00
Gross profit	$ 98,100.00	Gross loss	$ −80,725.00
Total number of trades	41	Percent profitable	54%
Number winning trades	22	Number losing trades	19
Largest winning trade	$ 14,100.00	Largest losing trade	$ −9,900.00
Average winning trade	$ 4,459.09	Average losing trade	$ −4,248.68
Ratio average win/average loss	1.05	Average trade (win and loss)	$ 423.78
Maximum consecutive winners	7	Maximum consecutive losers	6
Average number bars in winners	7	Average number bars in losers	9
Maximum intraday drawdown	$ −50,550.00		
Profit factor	1.22	Maximum number contracts held	1
Account size required	$ 50,550.00	Return on account	34%

SUMMARY

The most significant aspects of the test are the percent correct and the total net profits. Also, the average profit per trade is about as solid as I have seen in my research. Please note that the above results reflect a mechanical system which used no stops. I, again, strongly recommend using some kind of protective stop with this methodology.

CONNORS VIX REVERSAL III

This is the third VIX Reversal strategy I follow. It was co-created by a member of my research staff, Dave Landry. Dave, who is also a CTA, is in my opinion, a top researcher. More importantly, he very much understands underlying market principles.

As many of you are aware, volatility is mean reverting. This means periods of high volatility are likely to revert back to their normal levels and periods of low volatility also revert back to their normal levels. I have found that this concept is an inherent feature of the VIX. Dave and I found that by applying the *reversion to the mean* principle, we could predict S&P behavior. We found that whenever the VIX closed 10 percent above or below its 10-day moving average, it had a tendency to revert back to its mean. At the same time stock market prices also reversed.

Here are the rules of the "Connors VIX Reversal III" (CVR III):

FOR BUYS

1.   Today, the low of the VIX must be above its 10-day moving average.

2.   Today, the VIX must close at least 10 percent above its 10-day moving average.

3.   If rules 1 and 2 are met, buy the market on the close.

4.   Exit (on the close) the day the VIX trades (intraday) below yesterday's 10-day moving average (reversion to the mean).

FOR SELLS

1.   Today, the high of the VIX must be below its 10-day moving average.

2.   Today, the VIX must close at least 10 percent below its 10-day moving average.

3.   If rules 1 and 2 are met, sell on the close.

4.   Exit (on the close) the day the VIX trades (intraday) above yesterday's 10-day moving average (reversion to the mean).

CVR III S&P 500 Index—CME—Daily—01/01/93–10/01/97

Performance Summary: All Trades

Total net profit	$ 120,675.00	Open position P/L	$ 0.00
Gross profit	$ 176,250.00	Gross loss	$ −55,575.00
Total number of trades	75	Percent profitable	72%
Number winning trades	54	Number losing trades	21
Largest winning trade	$ 14,425.00	Largest losing trade	$ −10,025.00
Average winning trade	$ 3,263.89	Average losing trade	$ −2,646.43
Ratio average win/average loss	1.23	Average trade (win and loss)	$ 1,609.00
Maximum consecutive winners	10	Maximum consecutive losers	3
Average number bars in winners	4	Average number bars in losers	5
Maximum intraday drawdown	$ −22,025.00		
Profit factor	3.17	Maximum number contracts held	1
Account size required	$ 22,025.00	Return on account	548%

Performance Summary: Long Trades

Total net profit	$ 74,450.00	Open position P/L	$ 0.00
Gross profit	$ 88,625.00	Gross loss	$ −14,175.00
Total number of trades	41	Percent profitable	78%
Number winning trades	32	Number losing trades	9
Largest winning trade	$ 14,425.00	Largest losing trade	$ −2,950.00
Average winning trade	$ 2,769.53	Average losing trade	$ −1,575.00
Ratio average win/average loss	1.76	Average trade (win and loss)	$ 1,815.85
Maximum consecutive winners	9	Maximum consecutive losers	3
Average number bars in winners	4	Average number bars in losers	5
Maximum intraday drawdown	$ −19,050.00		
Profit factor	6.25	Maximum number contracts held	1
Account size required	$ 19,050.00	Return on account	391%

Performance Summary: Short Trades

Total net profit	$ 46,225.00	Open position P/L	$ 0.00
Gross profit	$ 87,625.00	Gross loss	$ −41,400.00
Total number of trades	34	Percent profitable	65%
Number winning trades	22	Number losing trades	12
Largest winning trade	$ 14,400.00	Largest losing trade	$ −10,025.00
Average winning trade	$ 3,982.95	Average losing trade	$ −3,450.00
Ratio average win/average loss	1.15	Average trade (win and loss)	$ 1,359.56
Maximum consecutive winners	5	Maximum consecutive losers	4
Average number bars in winners	4	Average number bars in losers	6
Maximum intraday drawdown	$ −20,925.00		
Profit factor	2.12	Maximum number contracts held	1
Account size required	$ 20,925.00	Return on account	221%

SUMMARY

As you can see, the results are solid both to the long and short side. The average profit per trade is excellent and the percent profitable is also quite strong. Finally, as always, a protective stop helps avoid potentially large drawdowns.

In my opinion, and as you can see from the three CVR strategies, the VIX is a superior vehicle to the put/call ratio for using options to predict market direction. By combining the three reversal methods, you will be able to identify reversals in the stock market on a more efficient basis.

CHAPTER 3

TRIN THRUSTS

▪ ▪

This chapter focuses on another method to time the overall market. The "TRIN Thrust Strategy" is one that will be of special interest to S&P futures traders, mutual fund timers, and OEX traders.

As you probably know, the TRIN is the NYSE Short-Term Trading Index. It was originally called the ARMS Index in honor of its creator Dick Arms.

The TRIN measures a ratio of the number of advances and declines on the NYSE and relates those totals to the up-and-down volume activity in the stocks. Wall Street views extended periods above 1.00 as an indication of a weak market and extended periods below 1.00 as an indication of a strong market. The TRIN Thrust strategy does not look at the readings this way. It simply looks at the daily percentage change in the closing TRIN from yesterday to today to predict the market direction for the next two trading days.

As was just mentioned, the TRIN is used to identify strong and weak markets. Conventional wisdom (this term should now make you nervous) states that extended readings above 1.00 indicate the market is oversold and due to decline; extended readings below 1.00 signal the market is overbought and due to rise.

This arbitrary generalization in the selection of greater than 1.00 or less than 1.00 for the TRIN carries as little weight of evidence as someone telling us a VIX reading above a certain number means the market is oversold or an advance/decline reading above a certain number means the market is overbought. Such generalities are what cause traders to get hurt badly when overbought becomes *more* overbought and oversold becomes even more oversold.

Does this failure of absolute TRIN values to predict market turns mean it's a useless indicator? No, only that in my opinion and experience, it has been and is misused by the majority on Wall Street.

Instead of looking at the TRIN as an oscillator which varies between overbought and oversold, let's break it down to its core components, as we did with the VIX, and then see how it adds to our understanding of current market action.

- By measuring the flow of funds into and out of stocks relative to their volume, the TRIN does signal that a market has been strong or weak.

- We also know that many times the market moves to an area that is overbought and remains that way until some force causes it to revert to the mean and pulls it back into oversold territory.

- As we saw with the VIX, for this change in direction to take place, the market's momentum needs to be stopped and reversed.

Taking these pieces into consideration, I have found that sharp one-day reversals (thrusts) off the TRIN are often the beginning of a one- to two-day general market reversal. (That is, the sharp change in the percentage TRIN reading is indicative of a momentum change and this new momentum surge takes approximately two days to run its course.)

Before looking at the rules, you must know that I rarely use the TRIN Thrust signal as a stand-alone indicator. *It is much more effective when it is combined with another signal such as a VIX reversal or a short-term pattern.* This combination, many times, gives further confirmation to the pending move.

FOR BUYS

1.   If today's closing TRIN is 30 percent or more *below* yesterday's closing TRIN, buy the market on the close today. For example, yesterday's closing TRIN reading was 1.00. If today's closing TRIN reading is .70 or less, buy the market.

2.   Sell on the close two trading days later.

3.   For your protection, I strongly recommend using a 1 1/2 to 2 percent protective stop. This means if the S&P's are at 900, your stop should be in the 982 to 987 range.

FOR SELLS

1.   If today's closing TRIN is 30 percent or more above yesterday's closing TRIN, sell the market on the close today. For example, yesterday's closing TRIN reading was .70. If today's closing TRIN is .91 or higher, sell the market.

2.   Close the position two trading days later.

3.   Use a 1 1/2 to 2 percent protective stop.

Here are the mechanical results using a 1 1/2 percent stop.

TRIN Thrust S&P 500 Index—CME—Daily 01/03/90–10/01/97

Performance Summary: All Trades

Total net profit	$ 186,495.00	Open position P/L	$ –4,450.00
Gross profit	$ 851,195.00	Gross loss	$ –664,700.00
Total number of trades	764	Percent profitable	51%
Number winning trades	387	Number losing trades	377
Largest winning trade	$ 14,665.00	Largest losing trade	$ –12,875.00
Average winning trade	$ 2,199.47	Average losing trade	$ –1,763.13
Ratio average win/average loss	1.25	Average trade (win and loss)	$ 244.10
Maximum consecutive winners	9	Maximum consecutive losers	11
Average number bars in winners	2	Average number bars in losers	1
Maximum intraday drawdown	$ –37,350.00		
Profit factor	1.28	Maximum number contracts held	1
Account size required	$ 37,350.00	Return on account	499%

Performance Summary: Long Trades

Total net profit	$ 197,535.00	Open position P/L	$ 0.00
Gross profit	$ 439,055.00	Gross loss	$ –241,520.00
Total number of trades	342	Percent profitable	57%
Number winning trades	194	Number losing trades	148
Largest winning trade	$ 13,800.00	Largest losing trade	$ –12,875.00
Average winning trade	$ 2,263.17	Average losing trade	$ –1,631.89
Ratio average win/average loss	1.39	Average trade (win and loss)	$ 577.59
Maximum consecutive winners	9	Maximum consecutive losers	12
Average number bars in winners	2	Average number bars in losers	1
Maximum intraday drawdown	$ –29,175.00,		
Profit factor	1.82	Maximum number contracts held	1
Account size required	$ 29,175.00	Return on account	677%

Performance Summary: Short Trades

Total net profit	$ –11,040.00	Open position P/L	
Gross profit	$ 412,140.00	Gross loss	$ –423,180.00
Total number of trades	422	Percent profitable	46%
Number winning trades	193	Number losing trades	229
Largest winning trade	$ 14,665.00	Largest losing trade	$ –12,250.00
Average winning trade	$ 2,135.44	Average losing trade	$ –1,847.95
Ratio average win/average loss	1.16	Average trade (win and loss)	$ –26.16
Maximum consecutive winners	6	Maximum consecutive losers	8
Average number bars in winners	2	Average number bars in losers	2
Maximum intraday drawdown	$ –55,800.00		
Profit factor	0.97	Maximum number contracts held	1
Account size required	$ 55,800.00	Return on account	–20%

SUMMARY

As with the Connors VIX Reversal, the TRIN Thrust strategy shows good profits. Even though the per-trade profit is lower than the VIX strategies, it does provide us with a small edge. Also, as I mentioned, this strategy should not be used as a stand-alone indicator. Use it in conjunction with other signals. In addition, as you can see, the strategy did significantly better on the long side than on the short side. This is due to the seven-year run the market has had. In 1990 and 1994, the two weakest years of the period, TRIN Thrusts showed good profits on the short side. When a bear market occurs, the results on the long side will be less and the results on the short side should increase substantially.

With the new smaller S&P futures contract, and derivative products for the Dow Jones Index, the TRIN Thrust strategy, combined with other indicators, should be helpful in assisting you to successfully trade these new vehicles.

CHAPTER 4

PERCENT ADVANCE/ DECLINE INDICATOR (PADI)

▪ ▪

The "Percent Advance/Decline Indicator" (PADI), is one of the better advance/decline indicators I have developed. As you will see from the results, it does a good job of identifying short-term tops and bottoms in the stock market and in the S&P futures.

In my opinion, advance/decline indicators do a very good job of identifying overbought and oversold stock market conditions. Unfortunately, the overwhelming number of traders use them as a static indicator and instead of increasing profits, lose money trading with them. Why is this? Because, as I've written again and again, markets that are overbought can and will become more overbought, and markets that are oversold can and will become more oversold. The fact that an advance/decline indicator has reached some extreme number absolutely does *not* mean that the market cannot move to even more extreme levels. I have seen too many traders use these fixed static numbers as if they were the Holy Grail and eventually get killed as the market kept running against them.

To take full advantage of these indicators, the market itself must first signal a reversal. This means that even when the market is grossly oversold, until the indicator reverses, you must remain patient. By letting the market reverse, you are not putting yourself in front of a speeding train in an attempt to stop it. Therefore, we must use a method that shows the market is either overbought or oversold and then combine it with a methodology that signals a clear reversal. Also, I have found it to be even more advantageous to only trade advance/decline setups in the direction of the market's longer-term trend.

Here are the calculations and rules for the PADI:

1. Add the total number of shares traded today on the NYSE. This is done by adding the advances, declines, and unchanged.

2. Divide the number of advancing issues by the total issues traded (advances ÷ total) to get today's advancing percent.

3. Divide the number of declining issues by the total issues traded (declines ÷ total) to get today's declining percent.

4. Take the six-day average of the advancing percent and the six-day average of the declining percentage.

5. If yesterday's advancing average was 40 percent or higher and today's advancing average is less than yesterday's advancing average, sell on the close (only if the stock market is trading below its 100-day moving average).

6. If yesterday's declining average was 40 percent or higher and today's declining average is less than yesterday's declining average, we buy on the close (only if the market is trading above its 100-day moving average).

7. Exit in five to seven days or if there is a signal in the opposite direction.

As with the other strategies, I recommend using a protective stop. Here are the results using a 1 1/2 percent stop with a five-day exit.

PADI S&P 500 Index—CME—Daily 01/01/90–10/03/97

Performance Summary: All Trades

Total net profit	$ 142,932.50	Open position P/L	$	0.00
Gross profit	$ 285,525.00	Gross loss	$	−142,592.50
Total number of trades	109	Percent profitable		61%
Number winning trades	66	Number losing trades		43
Largest winning trade	$ 18,775.00	Largest losing trade	$	−7,725.00
Average winning trade	$ 4,326.14	Average losing trade	$	−3,316.10
Ratio average win/average loss	1.30	Average trade (win and loss)	$	1,311.31
Maximum consecutive winners	7	Maximum consecutive losers		4
Average number bars in winners	6	Average number bars in losers		5
Maximum intraday drawdown	$ −17,340.00			
Profit factor	2.00	Maximum number contracts held		1
Account size required	$ 17,340.00	Return on account		824%

Performance Summary: Long Trades

Total net profit	$ 125,912.50	Open position P/L	$	0.00
Gross profit	$ 238,300.00	Gross loss	$	−112,387.50
Total number of trades	83	Percent profitable		64%
Number winning trades	53	Number losing trades		30
Largest winning trade	$ 18,775.00	Largest losing trade	$	−7,725.00
Average winning trade	$ 4,496.23	Average losing trade	$	−3,746.25
Ratio average win/average loss	1.20	Average trade (win and loss)	$	1,517.02
Maximum consecutive winners	8	Maximum consecutive losers		3
Average number bars in winners	6	Average number bars in losers		4
Maximum intraday drawdown	$ −17,340.00			
Profit factor	2.12	Maximum number contracts held		1
Account size required	$ 17,340.00	Return on account		726%

Performance Summary: Short Trades

Total net profit	$ 17,020.00	Open position P/L	$	0.00
Gross profit	$ 47,225.00	Gross loss	$	−30,205.00
Total number of trades	26	Percent profitable		50%
Number winning trades	13	Number losing trades		13
Largest winning trade	$ 6,525.00	Largest losing trade	$	−6,067.50
Average winning trade	$ 3,632.69	Average losing trade	$	−2,323.46
Ratio average win/average loss	1.56	Average trade (win and loss)	$	654.62
Maximum consecutive winners	3	Maximum consecutive losers		3
Average number bars in winners	5	Average number bars in losers		6
Maximum intraday drawdown	$ −9,835.00			
Profit factor	1.56	Maximum number contracts held		1
Account size required	$ 9,835.00	Return on account		173%

SUMMARY

The reason I like the PADI is because it is continuously self-adjusting to the number of issues that are traded each day. This means that when there is an onslaught on new issues that flood the market, or when an abundance of takeovers occurs, the PADI will adjust itself to this new number. Another point should be made: If you lower the percentage, you will get more trades and, even though the profit per trade is lower, the results are favorable.

As I stated earlier, advances versus declines do a good job of identifying when markets become overbought and oversold. By waiting for the market to reverse, as we have done with our other timing indicators, we improve their performance significantly.

As we discussed earlier, we want to trade strategies that give us an edge. The five market timing strategies presented give a directional bias which, if traded correctly, leads to that edge.

SECTION TWO

VOLATILITY

■ ■

Volatility and its application to trading has been a favorite field of research for me. The subject is in its infancy stage and is fertile ground for traders looking to go beyond the many worn out concepts and strategies that exist today.

In the following few chapters I build upon the work I released in *Investment Secrets of a Hedge Fund Manager* and *Street Smarts*. For those of you who have not read these books, I will attempt to explain some of the ideas presented in those publications to help you further your understanding of the subject.

A friendly warning: The Volatility section is built upon years of research and is by far the most complex in the book. If it is difficult to grasp at first, don't despair. With repeated study it will come and the rewards will be worth the time spent.

CHAPTER 5

MODIFYING TRADE SIZE AND STOP PLACEMENT BASED ON VOLATILITY MEASUREMENT

When I was a junior in high school, I had a chemistry teacher by the name of Lenny Brown (I've changed his name to avoid any embarrassment to him). Some people felt Lenny had a screw loose (no argument here), but most also felt he was a great teacher. One of his quirks, though, was to announce our weekly test scores to the entire class as he passed them back to us. Whenever someone got zero answers correct (a common occurrence), Lenny would look at the paper, announce the student's name, put a stupid grin on his face, and then in a loud booming voice he would scream **"GOOSE EGG"** for the grade.[*]

---

[*] I was once on the receiving end of Lenny's wrath. In 1975 I was a food vendor for the Boston Red Sox. When the now famous sixth game of the World Series ended at nearly 1 A.M., it left little time to prepare for Lenny's test of the upcoming morning. To this day, I can still hear Lenny screaming **"GOOSE EGG"** after my name.

In the money management industry it is quite difficult to blow out and get a Lenny Brown goose egg. In 1997, Victor Niederhoffer did. Before I go on, I need to say that I have absolute respect for Niederhoffer's accomplishments, especially up through 1996. He put together one of the best performance track records of any CTA for over a decade. It was done with guts, brains, and great trading. This accomplishment can never be taken away from him.

How could a man with his smarts and ability completely blow out? It is impossible to know the full story, but it appears it was a direct result of not adjusting his position size and stops to *greatly increased* volatility during the late October 1997 stock market sell-off. This one mistake cost his investors 100 percent of their money and destroyed a terrific career. (I suspect though, if you are reading this book five years after it was published, Niederhoffer is probably at the top of the trading world again.)

Let's look at what adjusting your stop and position size to current volatility actually means. Every stock and commodity has its own volatility reading. For example, two stocks trade at $100 per share. If stock A has a historical volatility reading of 10 percent, this means its annualized trading range was between 90 and 110, two-thirds of the time (based on an assumptive normal distribution). If we assume that the volatility will remain at 10 percent, we can safely assume the stock will trade between 90 and 110 two-thirds of the time over the next year, and we can get a feel of what our risk will be and where we can safely place stops.

Stock B has a 100-day volatility reading of 25 percent. This means that its annualized range has been between 75 and 125 two-thirds of the time (based on an assumptive normal distribution). Looking back, stock B is more volatile than stock A.

Going forward, if the volatility of these stocks stays the same, our drawdowns (assuming we don't use stops) from stock B will be higher than stock A and our profits when we are correct are likely to be higher than with stock A. Therefore, if you go into a trade telling yourself you will risk 2 points, you are much more likely to be stopped out of stock B than stock A. Also, if you trade with 100 percent of your cash, you will be much more likely to be destroyed by stock B than stock A.

Now let's look at what happens when volatility drastically changes (as happened to Niederhoffer in October). Stock A, with the 10 percent volatility all of a sudden sees its volatility explode to 40 percent. This means there is a 67 percent chance that stock A's price will be within 60 and 140 at the end of one year and has put your risk level at new extremes. In Niederhoffer's case, he used a healthy portion of his investors' capital to sell puts when market volatility was under 30 percent. As you can see from the chart below, the short-term volatility exploded to above 50 percent. This means that his risk greatly increased and the increased volatility took what started as an "X" percent bet and brought it to a more than 100 percent of the portfolio size bet. Because he bet wrong, he wiped out his clients' assets.

Figure 5.1

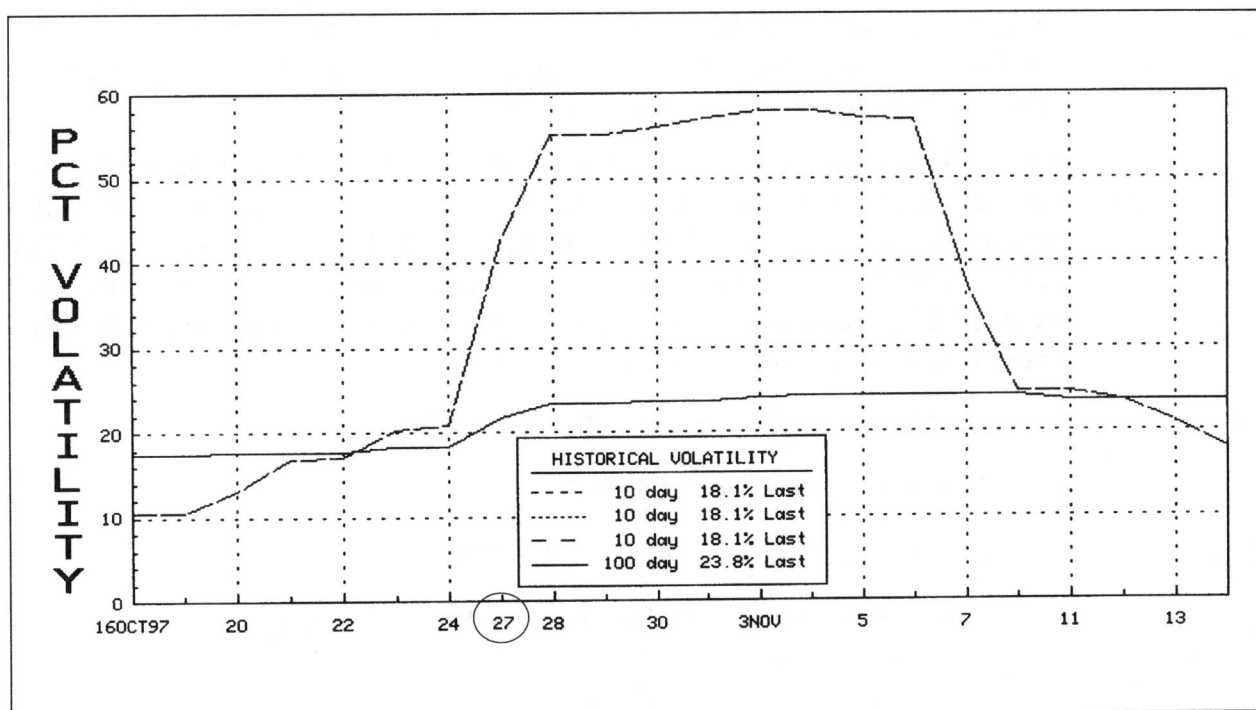

I can fully understand why Niederhoffer did what he did. I was *strongly* tempted to sell puts that same day (Monday, October 27). I had buy signals all over the place (one day too early!) and it seemed too good an opportunity to pass.* What ultimately stopped me from taking these signals was the increased volatility that continued to grow throughout the day. (On the negative side, it also stopped me from taking the trades on Tuesday, therefore completely missing the correct opportunity.) *What Niederhoffer failed to do was stop himself out as the risks grew throughout the*

---

* In fact, I picked up the phone three different times to call the trading desk and each time hung up without placing a trade.

day. What he also failed to do was adjust his position size down as the volatility increased. Sol Waksman, president of Barclay Trading Group, was quoted in Bloomberg as saying, "In this case, money management was entirely lacking. Any position can go against you and it is a manager's responsibility to guard against that."

How can we learn from this lesson? By being aware of the role that volatility plays in risk management. For example, if you normally trade 1000 shares of a $50 stock with a volatility reading of 20 percent, you should only trade 500 shares of the a $50 stock with a 40 percent volatility reading. The dollar risks for both are now approximately the same and even though you cannot predict what future volatility will bring, it's a good bet that it won't change drastically in the near future. If it does, you must adjust your position size to reflect the change.

As far as stop placement goes, you need to look at what the normal volatility is for the security you are trading. This will then tell you what the average likely range will be for the time period you are looking at. For example, let's assume you are buying a $100 stock with a volatility (100 days) of 20 percent and your system tells you to be in the trade for five days. You would take the following steps:

1.   Divide 260 trading days by 5 days = 52

2.   Take the square root of 52 = 7.2

3.   Divide the HV by #2. 20% ÷ 7.2 = 2.7%

4.   Take the stock price and add and subtract #3 from it.
      100 ± 2.7 = 97.3 and 102.7

This means that if the volatility remains at 20 percent, there is a two-thirds chance the stock price will be between 97.3 and 102.7 at the end of five days. Therefore, a stop placed at 99 is very likely to get hit, whereby a stop placed at 94 is unlikely to get hit.

To go further, if you then move into a $100 stock that has a volatility reading of 35, you should not be using the same stop placement as the example above.

In conclusion, there is no *exact science* to this. Because volatility is constantly changing, you must be constantly aware of these changes and act to adjust position size and stops in accordance with your risk tolerance.

CHAPTER 6

TRADING WHERE THE ACTION IS

As was mentioned in Chapter 1, one of the common traits of successful professional traders is that their strategies are usually based on conceptually correct principles. This means that they know how to exploit built-in characteristics that are fundamental to the markets they are trading. In this chapter I point to another factor which I believe is a major key to successfully and consistently profiting from the markets. *This principle is the role volatility plays in identifying the correct equities and commodities to trade.* Armed with this knowledge, you will know when and why to ignore nonmoving markets and will understand why you should trade only those markets that are moving.

I begin with the concept that *trading in sideways markets will chew you up.* As short-term traders, we do not have the luxury of waiting for a market to move. Because our profits tend to be small, we need to be trading those specific markets that provide us with the opportunity to maximize our profits on a daily basis.

This means that unless we are trading in active markets, our likelihood of locking in healthy profits is diminished. For example, the profit potential is always much higher in a volatile stock like Dell Computer (DELL) than it is in a lower priced, nonvolatile stock like the REIT, Simon Debartolo

Group (SPG). Dell Computer's average daily volatility is more than four times the average daily volatility of SPG and its price is more than three times the price of SPG. A winning setup on SPG may lead to, at most, a small profit, whereas the same setup on Dell will lead to a much greater profit. Even if the prices of these securities were equal, the higher volatility in Dell leads to larger moves than in the lower volatility stock.

This is just as true for the futures markets. *No matter how successful you are in predicting the direction of a move, a lack of meaningful day-to-day movement virtually guarantees that, as a short-term trader, you will be unable to make substantial profits.*

We therefore must identify the markets that will provide us with the most profit-making potential. How do we do this? There are a number of ways, but the measurement I use is historical volatility (HV). This can be measured with a period of as short as 25 days or as long as 200 days (for reference in this chapter, we will use a 50-day HV number). As you can see from Figure 6.1, as of December 1997, the most volatile commodity markets (hence the best markets to trade) are Natural Gas, Pork Bellies, and Coffee and the least volatile market (the worst market to trade) is the Canadian Dollar. The same holds true for equities. Figure 6.2 shows the best stocks to look at (as of December 1997) for setups and obviously, unless market characteristics change, you will want to avoid stocks such as utilities, REITs, etc.

Your volatility list should be adjusted on a weekly basis. This will assure you of consistently knowing which markets are likely to provide you with the best opportunities. Also, we must remember that there are over 10,000 stocks and more than 30 commodity markets available to trade. By using volatility to filter out the quiet markets, you will be able to focus on where the action is on a daily basis. I can't stress enough the importance of this concept.

Finally, you may ask, "Aren't I increasing my risk by trading in highly volatile markets?" The answer is yes, but if the setups you are trading are correct, your profits from these setups will be greatly increased because of the higher volatility.

Figure 6.1 50-Day Historical Volatility as of December 1997

Under 10%	*10–20%*	*20–30%*	*30+%*
Canadian Dollar	Gold	S&P's	Pork Bellies
DM	Yen	Silver	Coffee
	Swiss Franc	Corn	Natural Gas
	Cattle	Crude	
	Cocoa	Heating Oil	
	Hogs		
	Soybean		
	Wheat		
	Cotton		

For future reference, you should be aware that the Canadian Dollar is historically a less volatile entity than Pork Bellies, Coffee, and Natural Gas, which tend to have 50-day volatility reading predominately above 25 percent. Therefore, your position size and stop placement should reflect these inherent characteristics.

Figure 6.2 Highest 50-Day Historical Volatility Stocks as of December 1997

NYSE	*NASDAQ*
CA—Computer Associates	ALTR—Altera Corp.
CMB—Chase Manhattan	COMS—3 Com Corp.
CPQ—Compaq Computer	DELL—Dell Computer
CTX—Centrex Corp.	KLAC—KLA-Tencor Corp.
TER—Teradyne	LLTC—Linear Technology
BSX—Boston Scientific	TLAB—Tellabs, Inc.
PDX—Pediatrix Medical	SNPS—Synopsys Inc.
SCI—SCI Systems	PSFT—People Soft Corp.
MWD—Morgan Stanley/Dean Witter	

CHAPTER 7

ADDITIONAL VOLATILITY RESEARCH

In *Investments Secrets of a Hedge Fund Manager*, we showed what I still consider to be the best and most efficient way to correctly identify and measure the reversion to the mean principle as it applies to volatility. By using a 100-day period as the normalized base, we showed that whenever a 10-day period volatility was 50 percent or less than the 100-day period, a large market move was likely to occur (reversion to the mean). For example, if the 100-day historical volatility reading is 30 percent, a 10-day historical volatility reading under 15 percent is likely to be followed by a large market move.

Since the book was released a few years ago, I have published additional research on the subject. On the following pages you will learn some new and advanced volatility concepts which should assist you with your trading. Please note that most of the examples shown use a six-day lower trading period. As I stated earlier, almost any pairing of a shorter time period versus a longer time period will identify markets that are likely to explode. For the record then, any short-term versus long-term historical volatility reading under 50 percent will many times be followed by a larger than normal market move.

THE ADDED PROFIT FROM MULTIPLE-DAY SIGNALS

Our research has shown us that the longer the time frame a historical volatility ratio reading is under 50 percent, the larger the market move will be. Ideally, we would like to see the historical volatility ratio reading stay under 50 percent for more than one day. The more days it is under 50 percent, the more likely the market will explode.

Since I live in Southern California, an appropriate analogy would be that of an earthquake. The longer the build-up between quakes, the larger the resultant explosion will be. This principle holds true with volatility. The longer the period of low volatility, the larger the move will be to revert volatility to its longer-term mean.

Is this setup perfect? No! There will be times when the market has a change in overall volatility and is not accompanied by a large move. Over time though, this is a superior vehicle to use to identify potential market explosions.

Let's look at some examples.

FIGURE 7.1a March 96 S&P 500 Futures—Historical Volatility

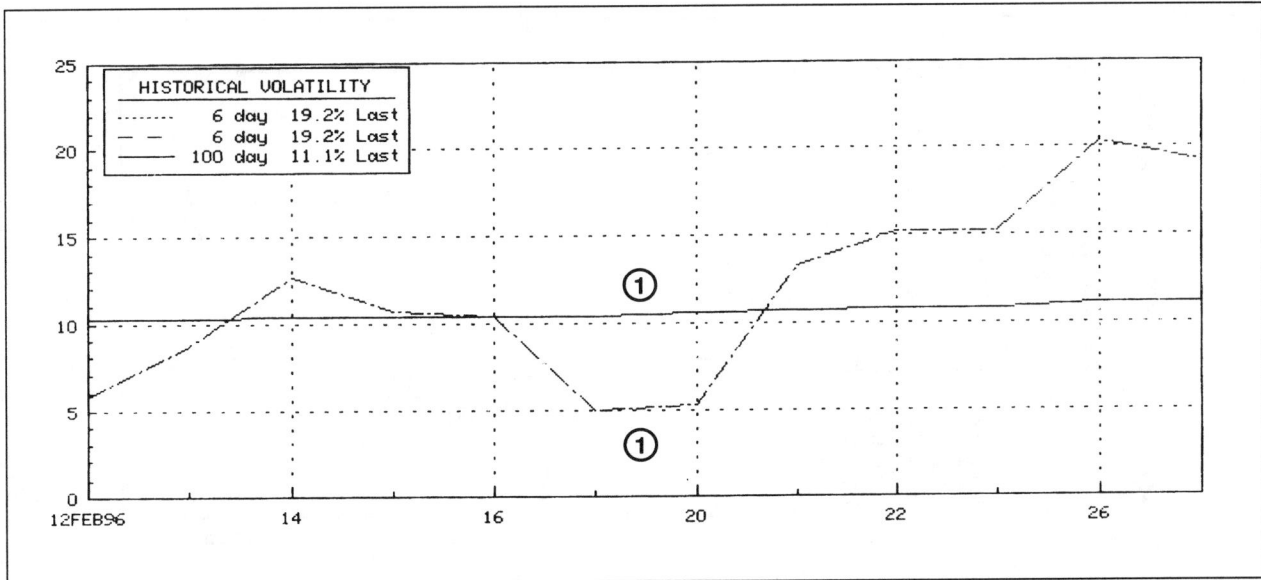

1. The 6-day/100-day historical volatility ratio reading is under 50 percent for two consecutive days (please refer to the values on the left-hand axis, not those in the box).

FIGURE 7.1b March 96 S&P Futures

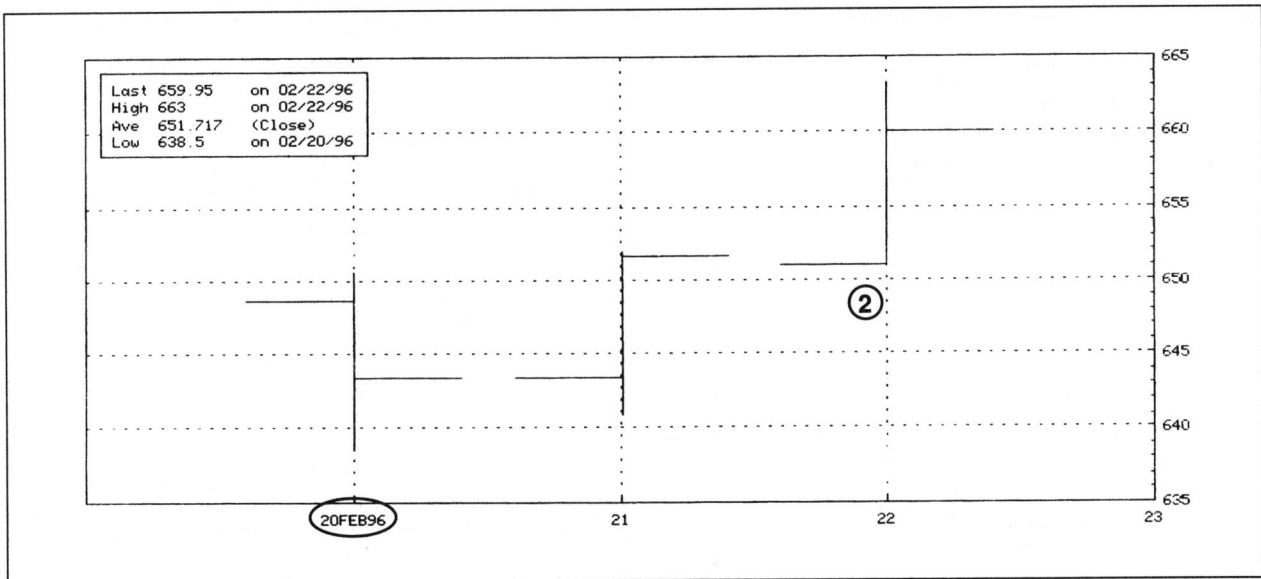

2. As you can see, after the multiple day historical volatility readings under 50 percent, the March S&P's explode more than 16 points to the upside over the next two trading sessions.

FIGURE 7.2a American Online

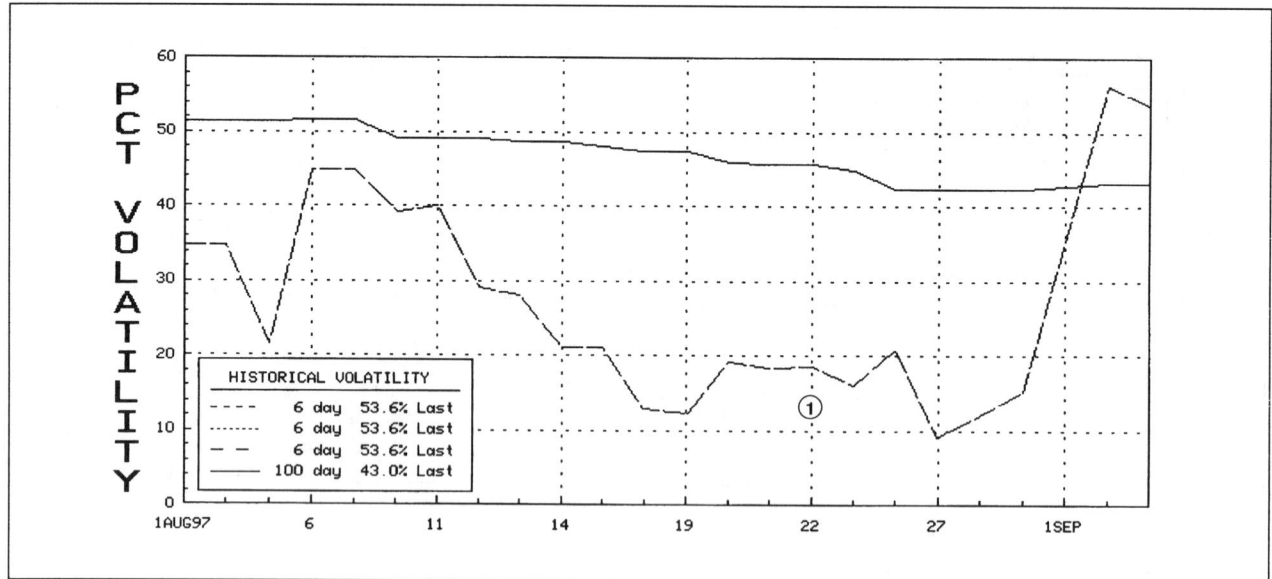

1.   Here we have American Online (AOL) with a multiple day histori-
      cal volatility reading under 50 percent. This signal remains for two
      weeks (!), thereby increasing the pressure on the market to explode.

FIGURE 7.2b American Online

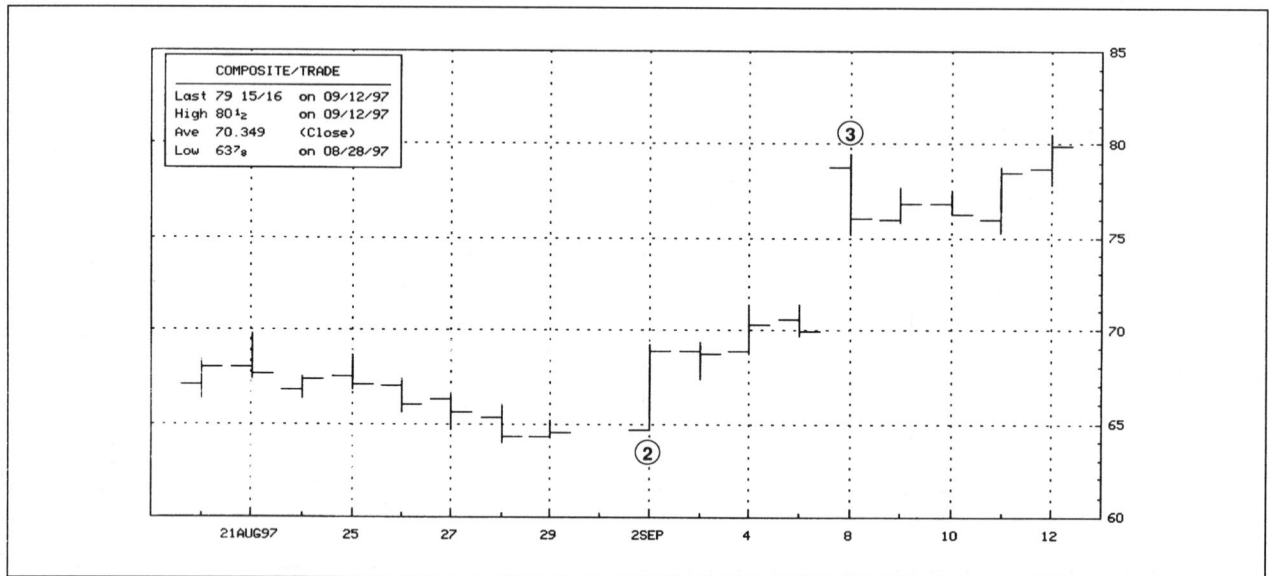

2.   On September 2, AOL moves 4 3/8 points higher on double its av-
      erage daily volume. The breakout holds and the stock rises more
      than 20 percent in a week.

FIGURE 7.3a December Corn

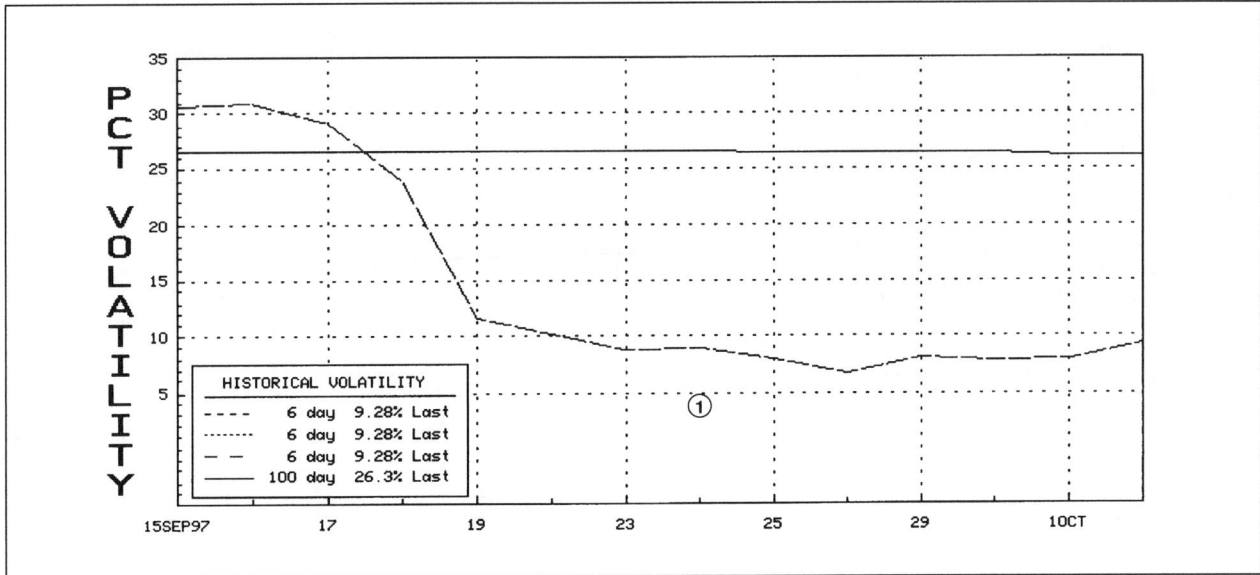

1. In mid to late September 1997, corn goes through a two-week ex-
    tremely low volatility period as measured by historical volatility.

FIGURE 7.3b December Corn

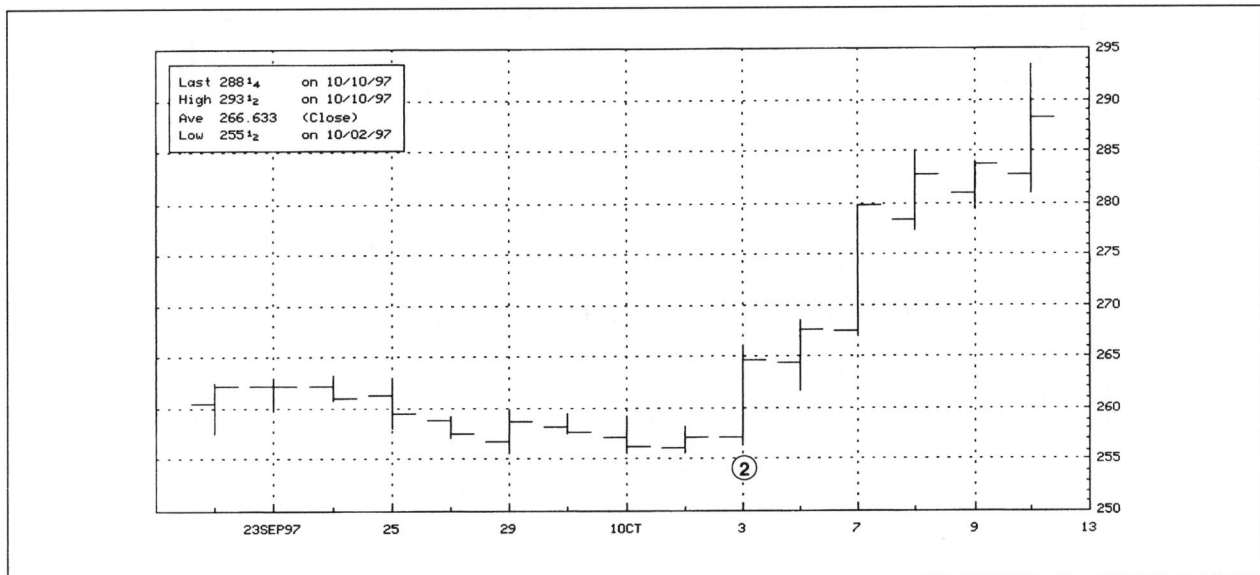

2. On October 3, the market wakes up as volatility reverts to its mean.
    December corn rises more than 30 cents in only six trading days.

FIGURE 7.4a British Pound

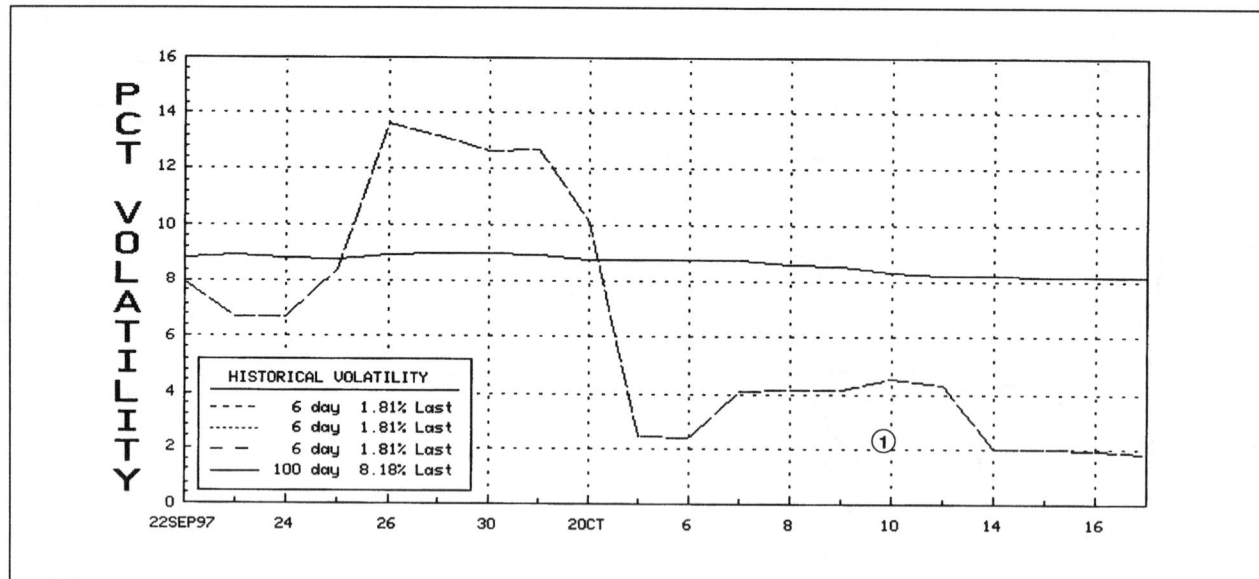

1.   A sustained period below normal volatility tells us a large move is near.

FIGURE 7.4b British Pound

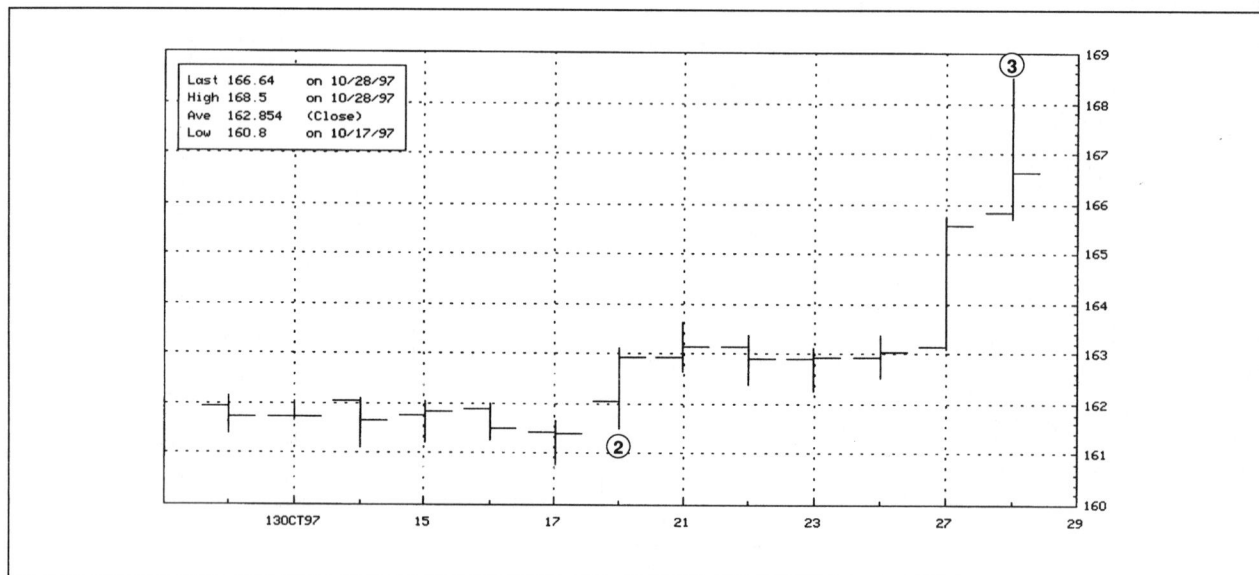

2.   The market moves 150 points higher.

3.   The British Pound explodes to a closing high of 166.66 in a week and a half.

FIGURE 7.5a American Online

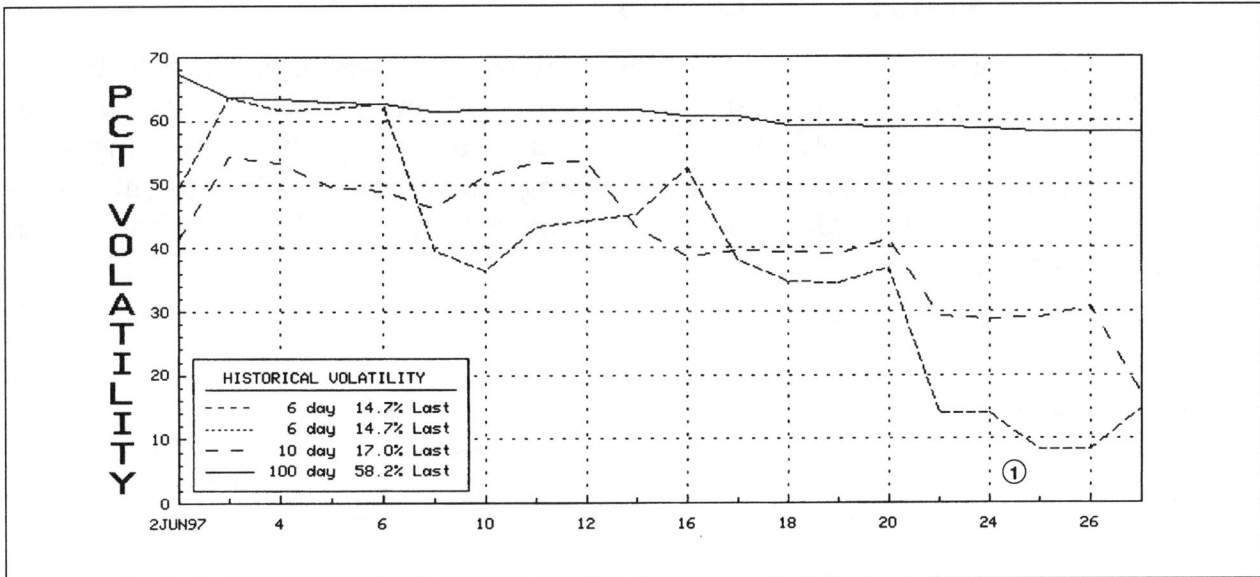

1. Here is AOL again, this time a few months earlier. For one week, the 6/100 historical volatility reading is under 50 percent.

FIGURE 7.5b American Online

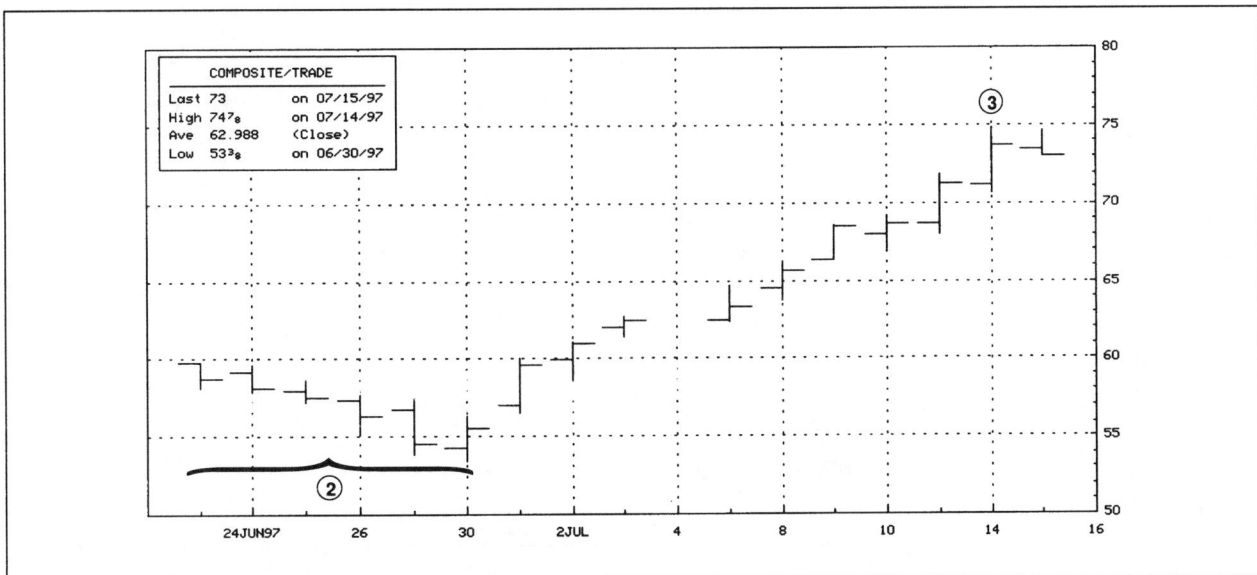

2. Signal period.

3. A better than 35 percent change in prices over a few weeks.

COMBINING MULTIPLE-PERIOD HISTORICAL VOLATILITY READINGS

One of the ways to closely pinpoint when a market is likely to have a large move is to look at multiple period historical volatility readings under 50 percent. My research and trading has found that combining a 10-period reading and a 6-period reading is a superior method to only using a 10-period reading. This holds true both on a daily basis and on an intraday basis.

Let's look at a few examples.

FIGURE 7.6   January Soybeans

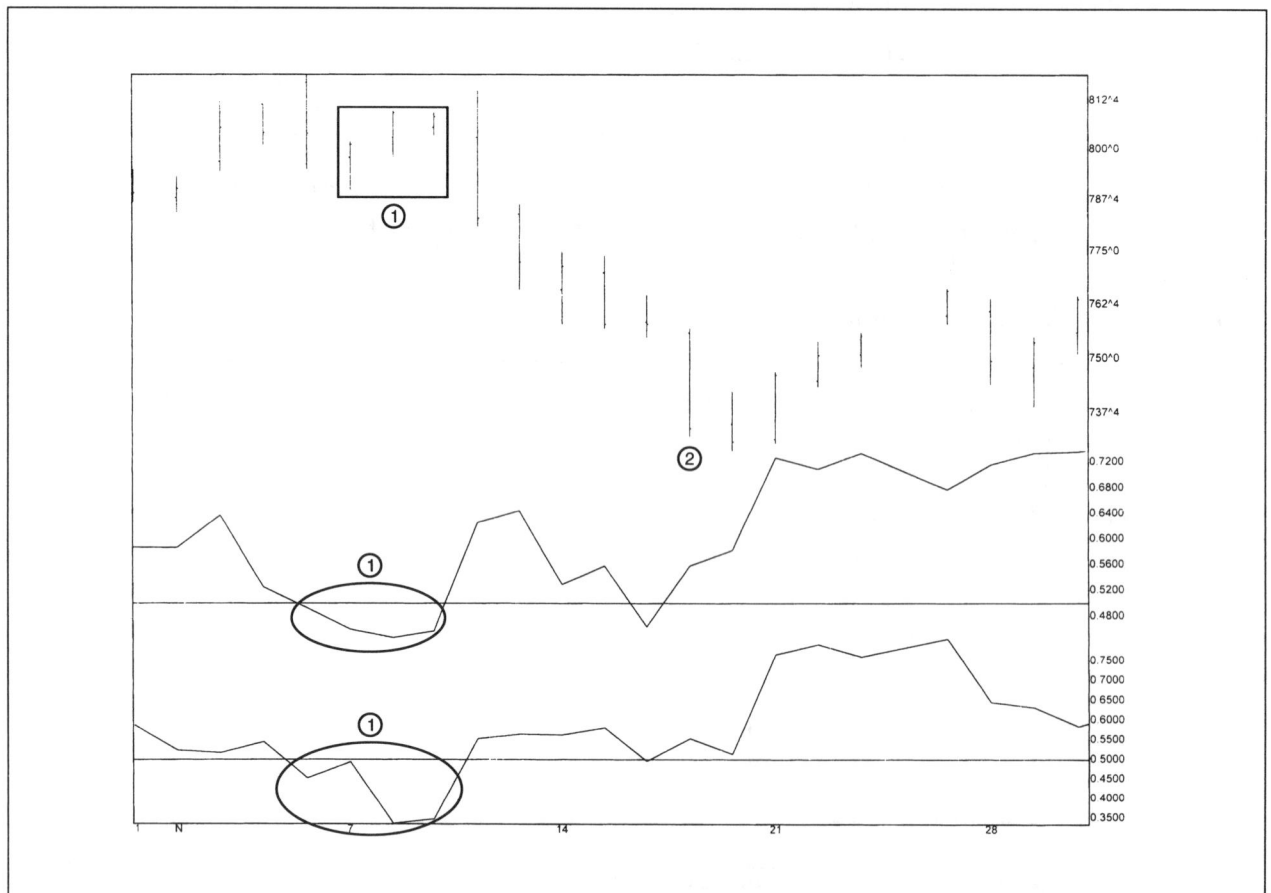

1.   Both the 10/100 historical volatility reading and the 6/100 historical volatility are under 50 percent, signaling a large move is near.

2.   Over a six-day period, beans drop more than 50 cents.

FIGURE 7.7 An Intraday S&P Setup Using 40-Minute Bars

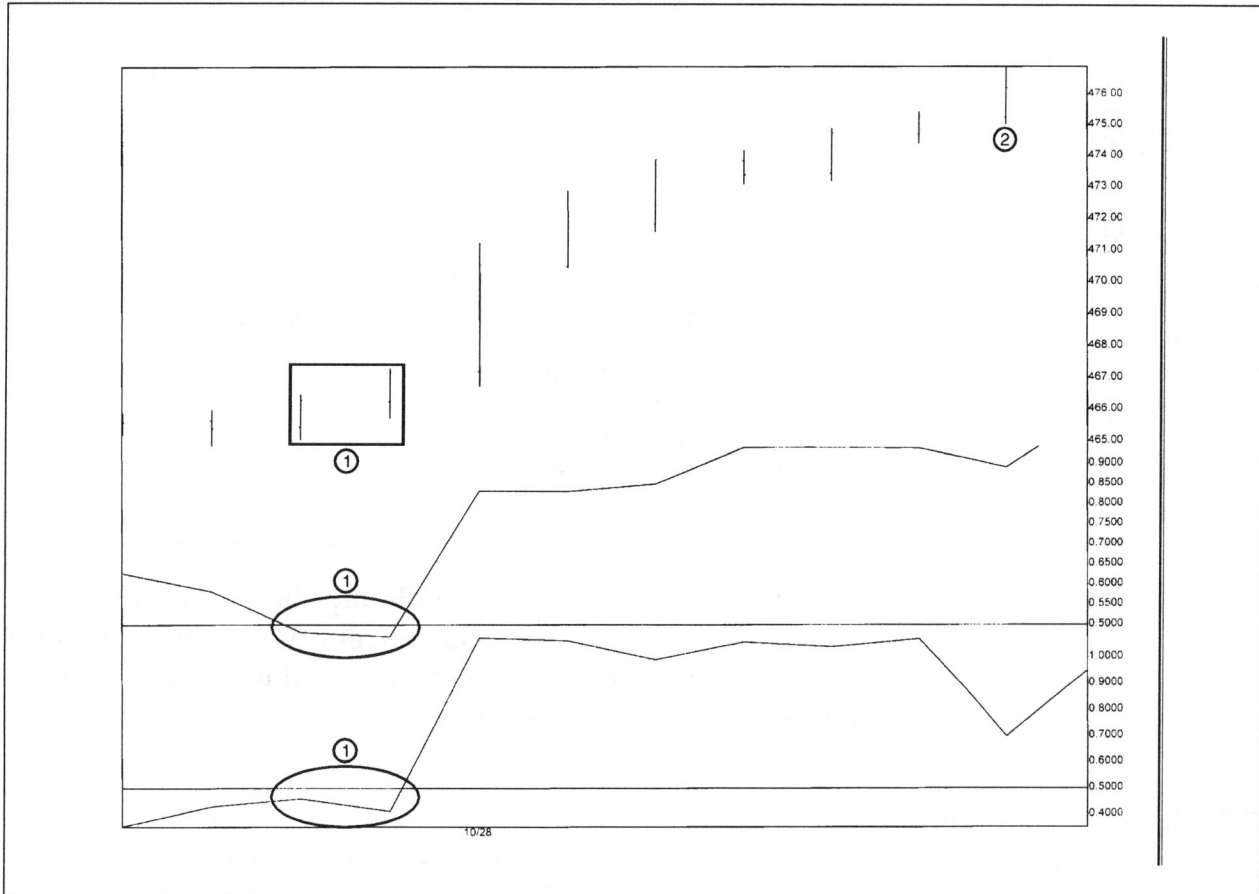

1. A 10/100 historical volatility reading combined with a 6/100 historical volatility reading under 50 percent.

2. The S&P's explode 8 points higher within a day.

FIGURE 7.8a Estee Lauder

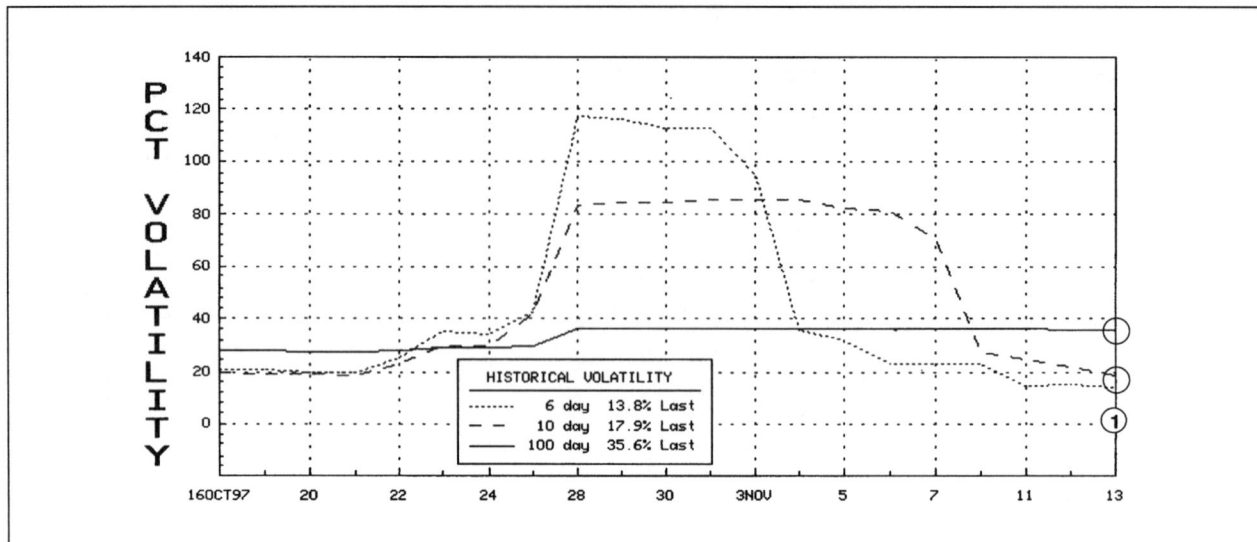

1.   In this example, the 6-day historical volatility is well under the 50 percent level and the 10-day is at 50.2 percent. When the number is this close, I will not stand on ceremony, as the reversion to the mean principle will certainly kick in.

FIGURE 7.8b Estee Lauder

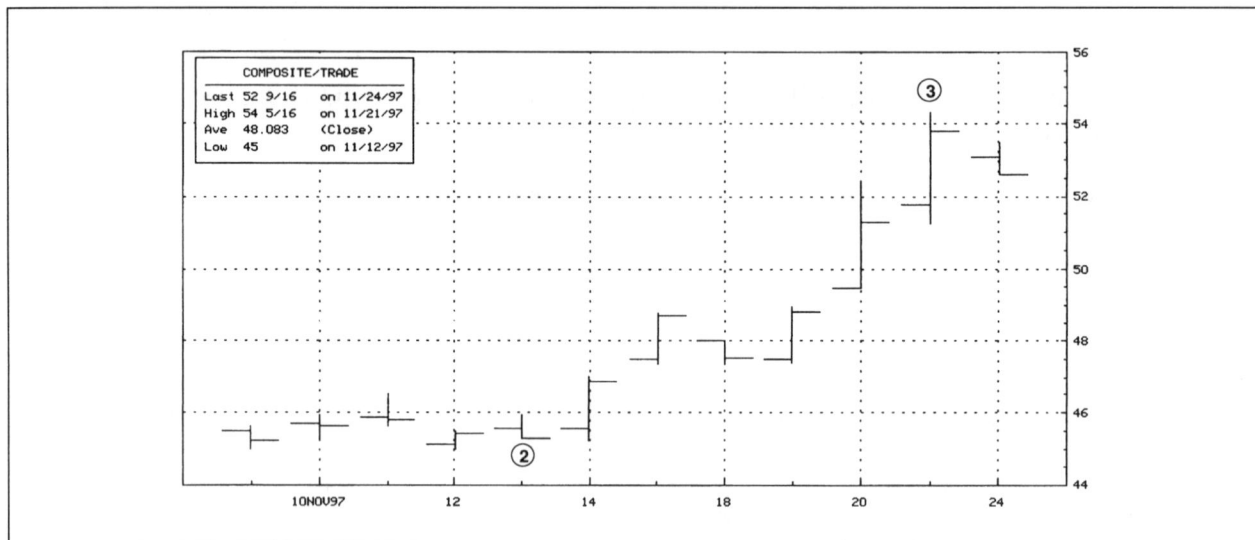

2.   Signal date.

3.   A nearly 20 percent move in prices six trading days later.

FIGURE 7.9a Viasoft

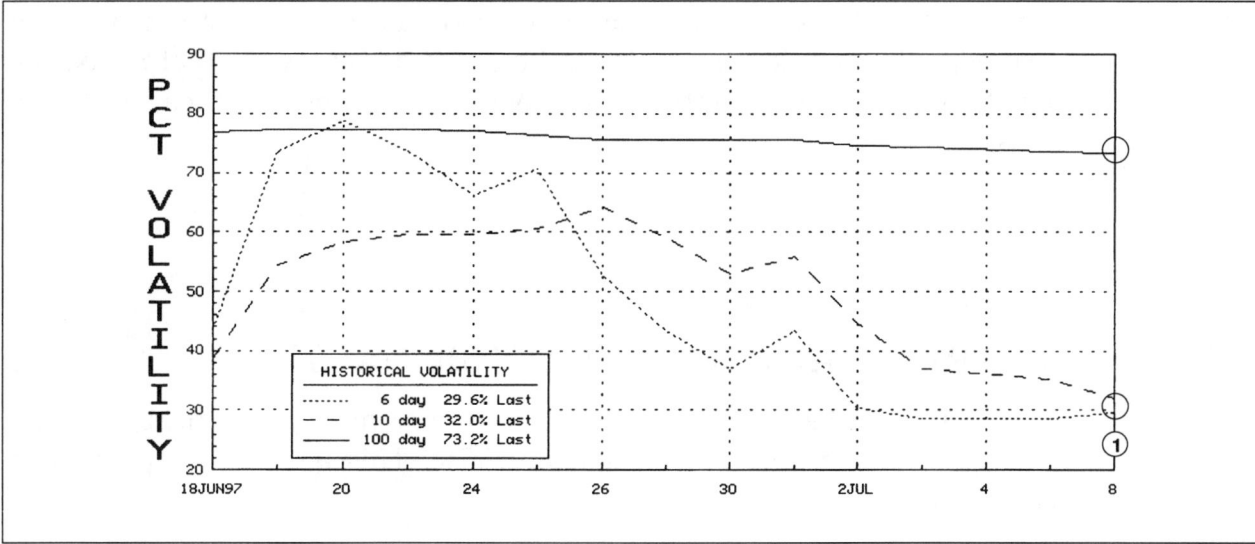

1.. Viasoft, an extremely volatile stock, has a 6-day and 10-day volatility reading more than 50 percent under its 100-day reading.

FIGURE 7.9b Viasoft

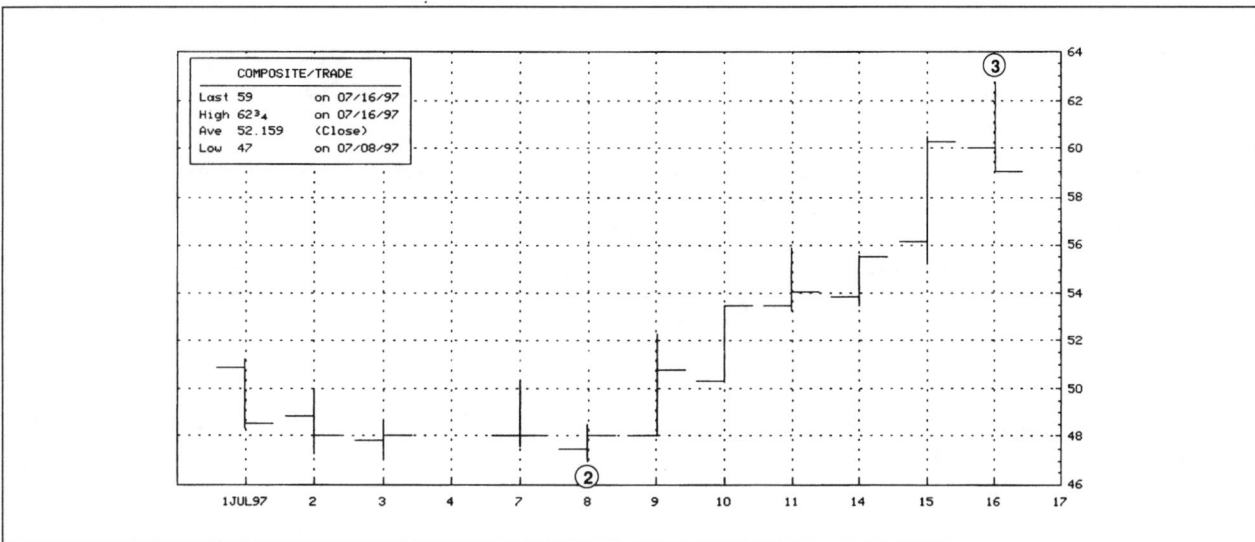

2. Signal date.

3. An explosion in price as the stock moves more than 20 percent
higher within six trading days.

SUMMARY

The one drawback to using multiple readings is that it gives a trader fewer signals than does a single reading. The advantage is that it does an even better job of pinpointing explosive opportunities that lead to larger gains.

FILTERING FALSE VOLATILITY SIGNALS

When a market has a very large, extraordinary move, historical volatility readings under 50 percent are usually false. This lesson is important to remember.

The extraordinary move causes the 100-day reading to increase drastically, thereby causing a long period of 6/100 and 10/100 readings under 50 percent. At these times we must wait for the 100-day reading to revert to its normal mean.

Let's look at the crash of 1987. As you can see from the Figure 7.10, the hundred day reading exploded from 20 percent to approximately 50 per-

FIGURE 7.10

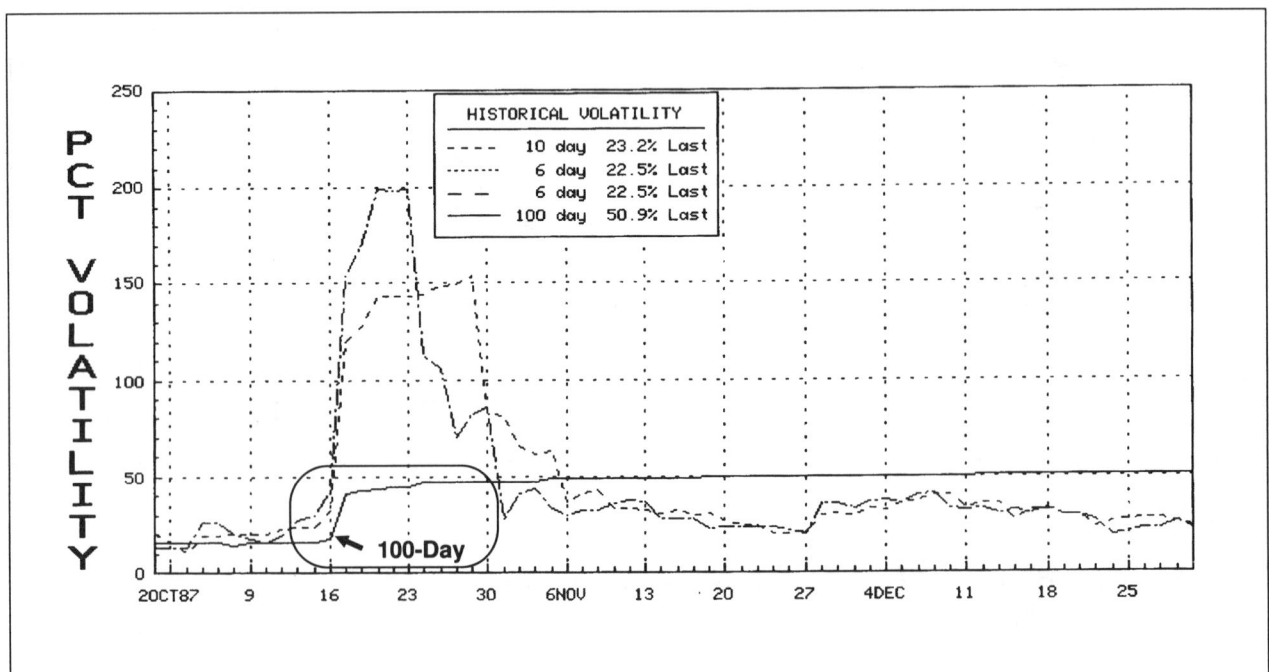

FIGURE 7.11

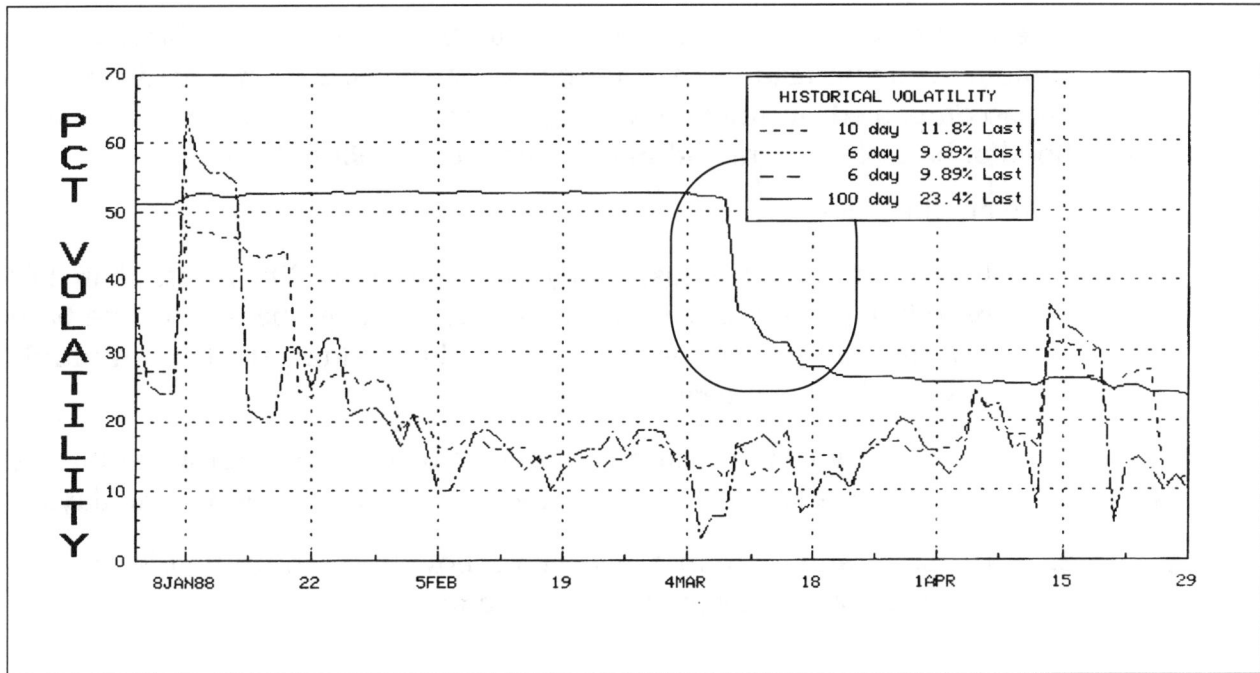

cent after the crash. During the months of November, December, January, and February, there were many 6/100 and 10/100 readings under the 50 percent ratio. These were false signals due to the volatility created during October.

By March 1988, the effects of the crash were no longer part of the 100-day calculation and the 100-day volatility began making its way back to the 20 percent level (*see* Figure 7.11). We therefore must wait a full 100 days to remove the extraordinary event from our calculations.

Among the events that have triggered this type of move have been the crash of 1987, the semi-crash of 1989 and the oil crisis in 1990. Obviously, these types of situations are rare but when they do occur historical volatility readings are skewed and must not be used until they become normalized.

HV THRUSTS

One of the filtering techniques I use to trade historical volatility is to combine extreme readings with range expansions. Extreme readings that are accompanied by single-day large moves tend to have a higher likelihood of both short-term and intermediate-term follow-through.

Here are the rules:

1. Identify a market whose 6-day or 10-day volatility is less than 1/2 its 100-day reading. As we discussed, it is even better to have both readings under 50 percent or for either reading to have multiple days under 50 percent.

2. On the day of the readings under 50 percent look for a daily price range that is larger than the daily range of the previous nine days.

3. If rules 1 and 2 are met, expect a follow-through in the direction of the large-range day for the next one to ten days.

FIGURE 7.12a June 96 British Pound

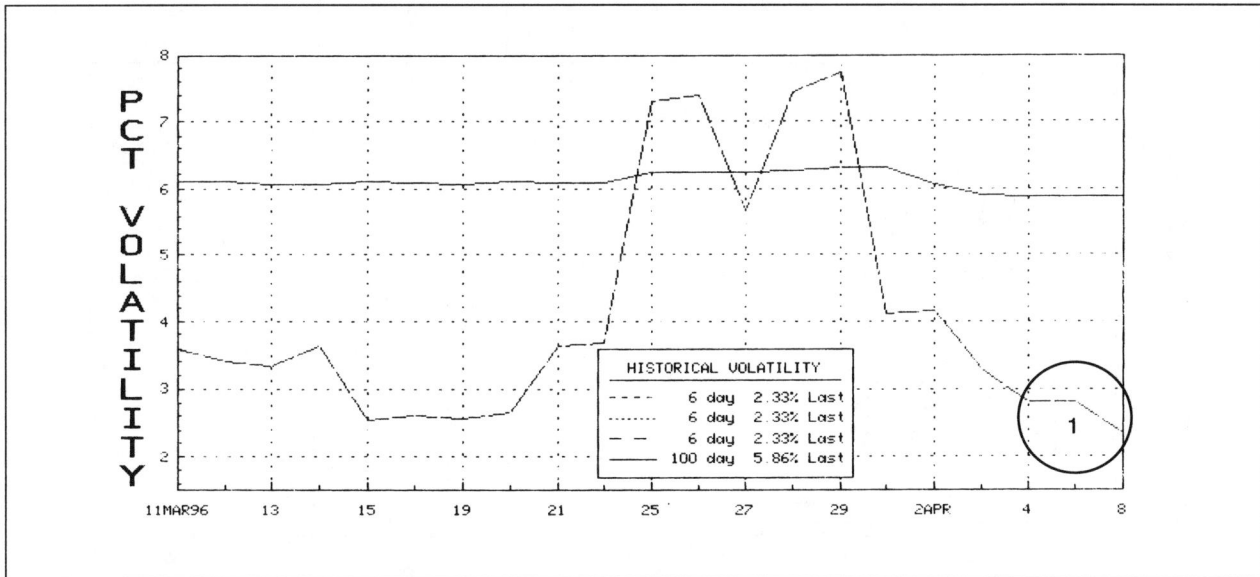

1. April 8—The six-day historical volatility reading has been less than half the 100-day reading for three consecutive days.

FIGURE 7.12b June 96 British Pound

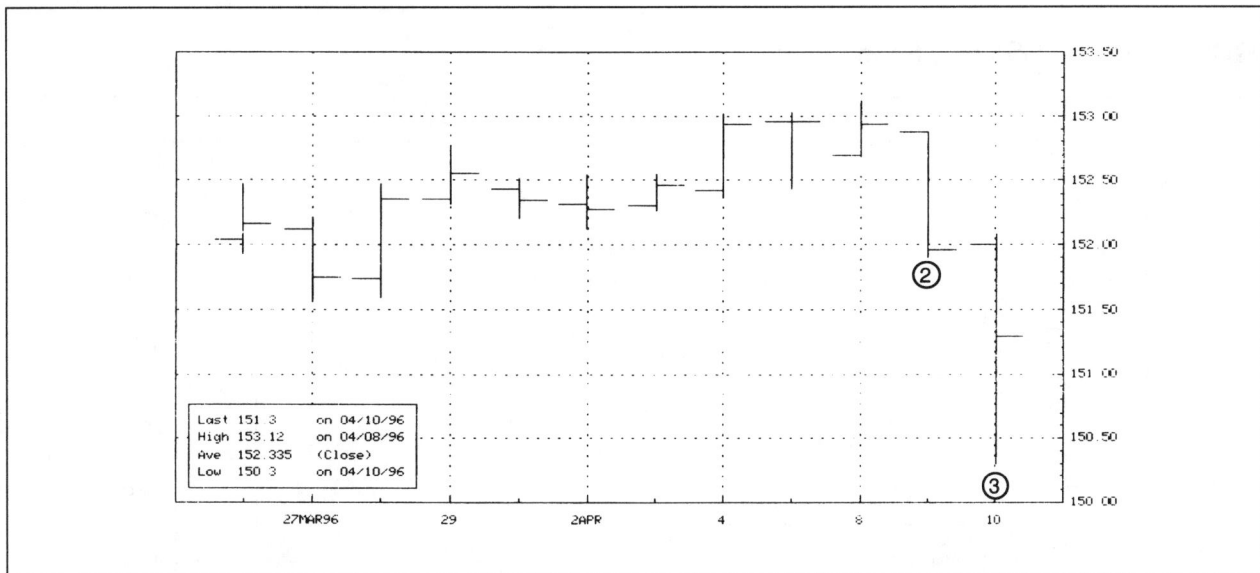

2. On April 9, the British pound breaks to the downside and its range is larger than the daily range of any of the previous nine days.

3. The next day the sell-off continues taking the pound to as low as 150.30 intraday.

FIGURE 7.13a US Long Bond

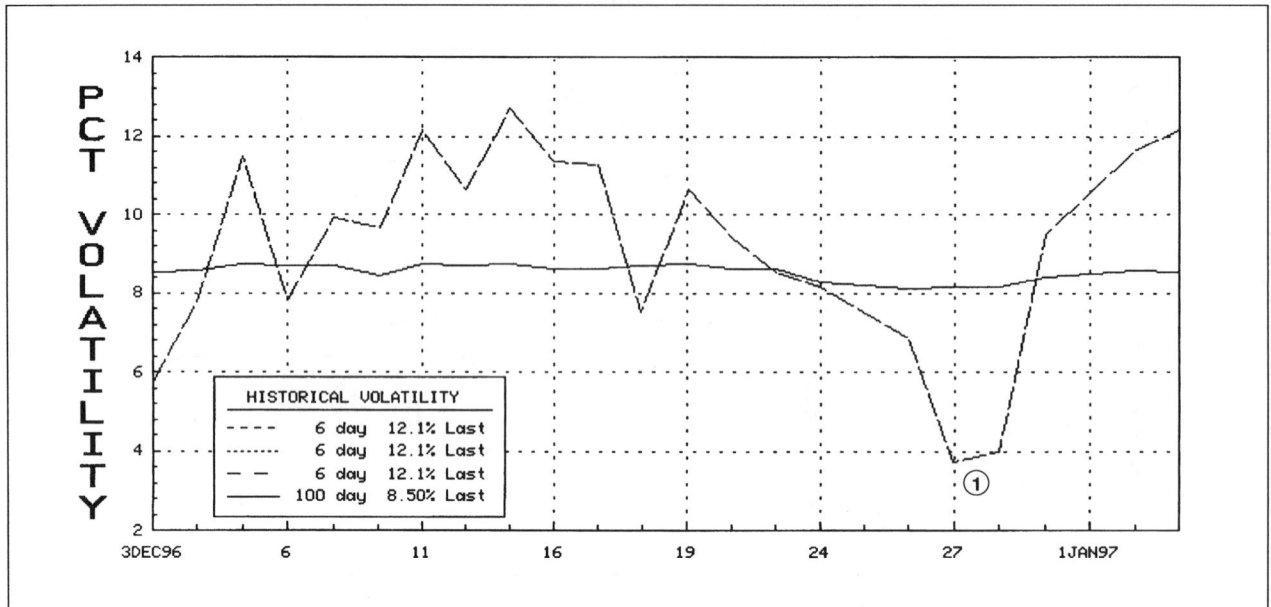

1.   The 6-day historical volatility is under 50 percent the 100-day historical volatility.

FIGURE 7.13b US Long Bond

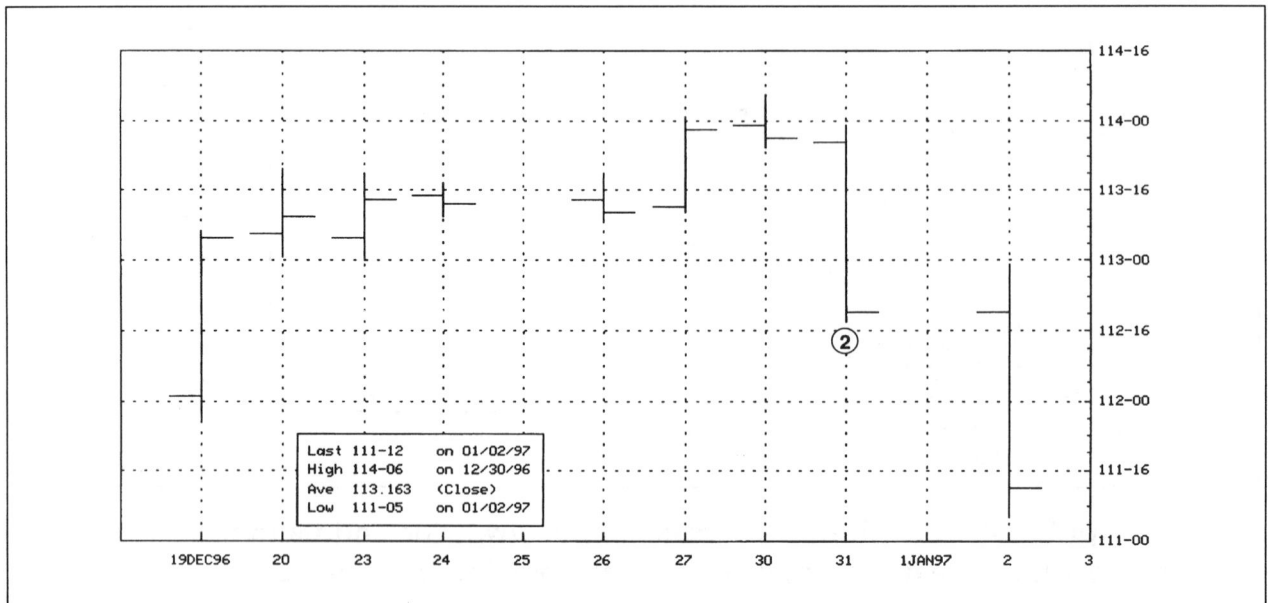

2.   Largest daily range of previous nine days.

SUMMARY

Measuring historical volatility as we do identifies tightly wound markets. The larger-range day confirms a breakout and many times these breakouts can be substantial.

SECTION THREE

NEW PATTERNS

＊ ＊

I have always been fascinated by bar patterns. To me, they tell a story of where a market has been and more importantly, where a market is likely to go.

The following three chapters are the easiest ones to understand in the book. They are simple chart patterns that provide an edge when triggered. The "8-Day High/Low Reversal Method" and the "Spent Market Trading Pattern" are setups that identify times when markets are likely to reverse. The "1-2-3-4" pattern is a wonderful setup which allows you to climb aboard strongly trending markets after they have had a brief pullback. All three patterns also combine good money management techniques by using tight protective stops.

CHAPTER 8

1-2-3-4

■ ■

Among the benefits I have received from writing two books are the traders I have met whom I now consider friends. One of these traders is Jeff Cooper. Jeff makes his living doing what most people only dream about—he mostly day trades momentum stocks.

Over the past few years Jeff and I have had long conversations on how to identify which stocks and commodities are likely to have large moves and how to properly climb aboard for these moves. Most traders (both stocks and futures) can identify markets that are in a runaway mode, but many do not have a proper method for climbing aboard as the move continues.

Here is a trading pattern Jeff and I developed which first was introduced to the trading world in his book *Hit and Run Trading*. Both he and I use the setup as a fundamental part of our strategy. We believe it solves the predicament of when and how to enter runaway markets.

By way of background, W. D. Gann, more than 65 years ago, observed an interesting phenomenon for extremely strong markets and extremely weak markets. He noted that very strong and very weak markets usually do not correct for more than three days.

As Jeff and I worked on our methodology to enter these markets, it became clear that Gann's analysis and insight were absolutely correct. It is amazing how often a runaway market will experience a *few days pause* and then resume its trend.

The "1-2-3-4" trading pattern is a specific short-term setup which combines:

- ADX

- Pattern recognition

- A specific price entry placement to give a trader the opportunity to profitably enter in the direction of the resumption of a longer-term trend.

Here are the rules:

FOR BUYS

1. Identify a market whose 14-day ADX is greater than 30. *The higher the ADX, the better.*

2. The 14-day +DI reading must be greater than the 14-day −DI reading. (If you do not understand ADX, please see either *Street Smarts* or *Hit and Run Trading*.)

3. Wait for the market to have a 1-2-3 correction. This means that the market must make three consecutive intraday lower lows or any combination of two lower lows and an inside day. The examples will clarify this further.

4. On day four only, buy 1 tick (1/8 for equities) above the day-three high.

5. When filled, your initial protective stop should be near the day-three low.

6. As the position moves in your favor, you should trail your stops. In this setup we tend to allow for a little more breathing room on our stops because of the upside potential of the move.

FOR SELLS

1. ADX > 30. The higher the ADX, the better.

2. The –DI must be greater than the +DI.

3. Wait for a 1-2-3 rally. Three higher highs or any combination or two higher highs and an inside day.

4. On day four only, sell (short for equities) 1 tick (1/8) below the day-three low.

5. Your initial protective stop should be near the day-three high.

6. As the position moves in your favor, trail your stops.

Let's look at some examples from the futures and equities.

FIGURE 8.1 May 96 Crude

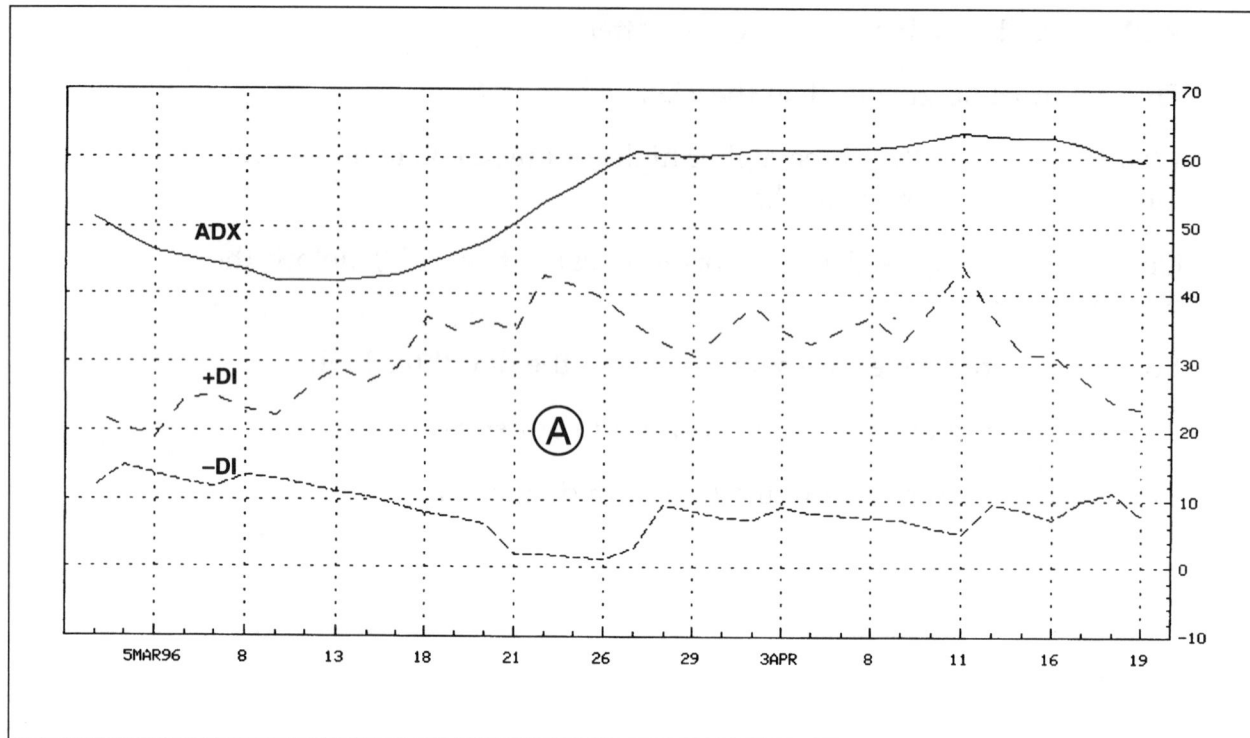

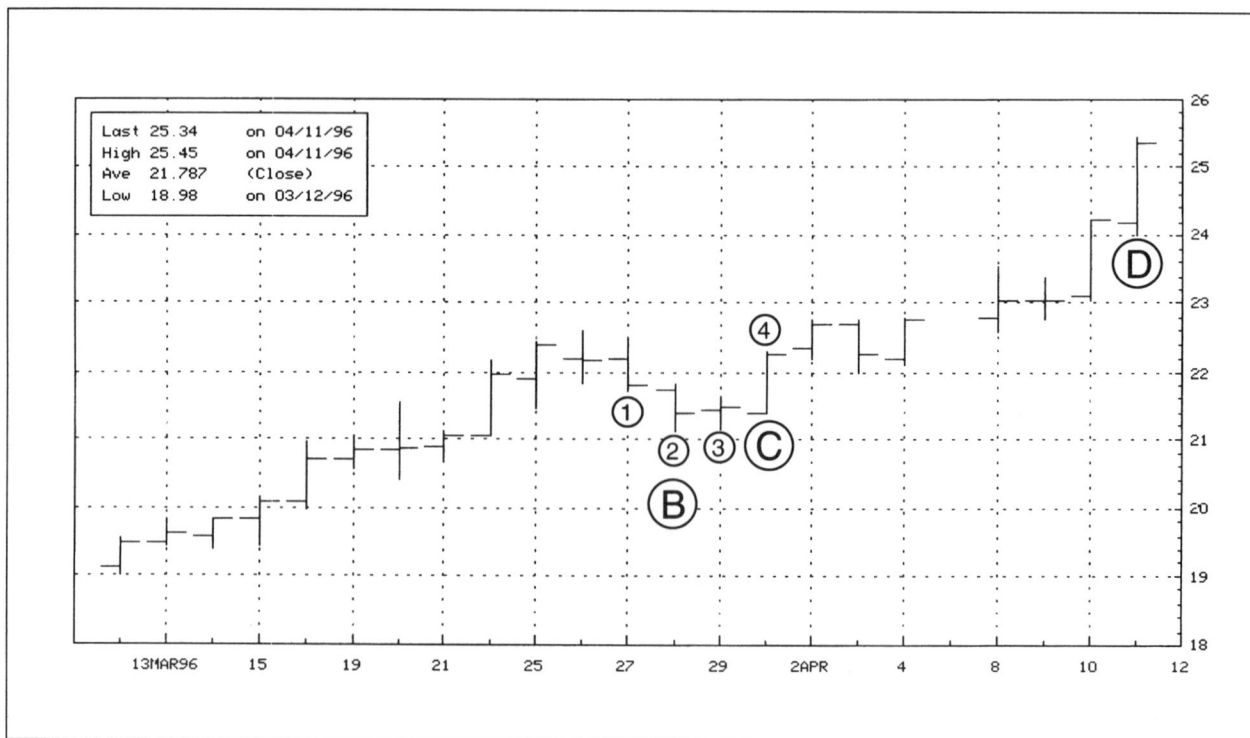

A.   In late March, the ADX for crude oil is well above 30 and the +DI is greater than the –DI, signifying an upward trend.

B.   **1.** March 27 has a lower low.

　　2. March 28 has a second lower low.

　　3. March 29 is an inside day. We will buy one tick above the March 29 high of 21.65 on April 1 only.

C.   The market explodes higher and we are long. Our initial protective stop is near the March 29 (day 3) low.

D.   The 1-2-3-4 trading pattern does a nice job of letting us participate in a better than $3,000 per contract upside move.

FIGURE 8.2 Gucci

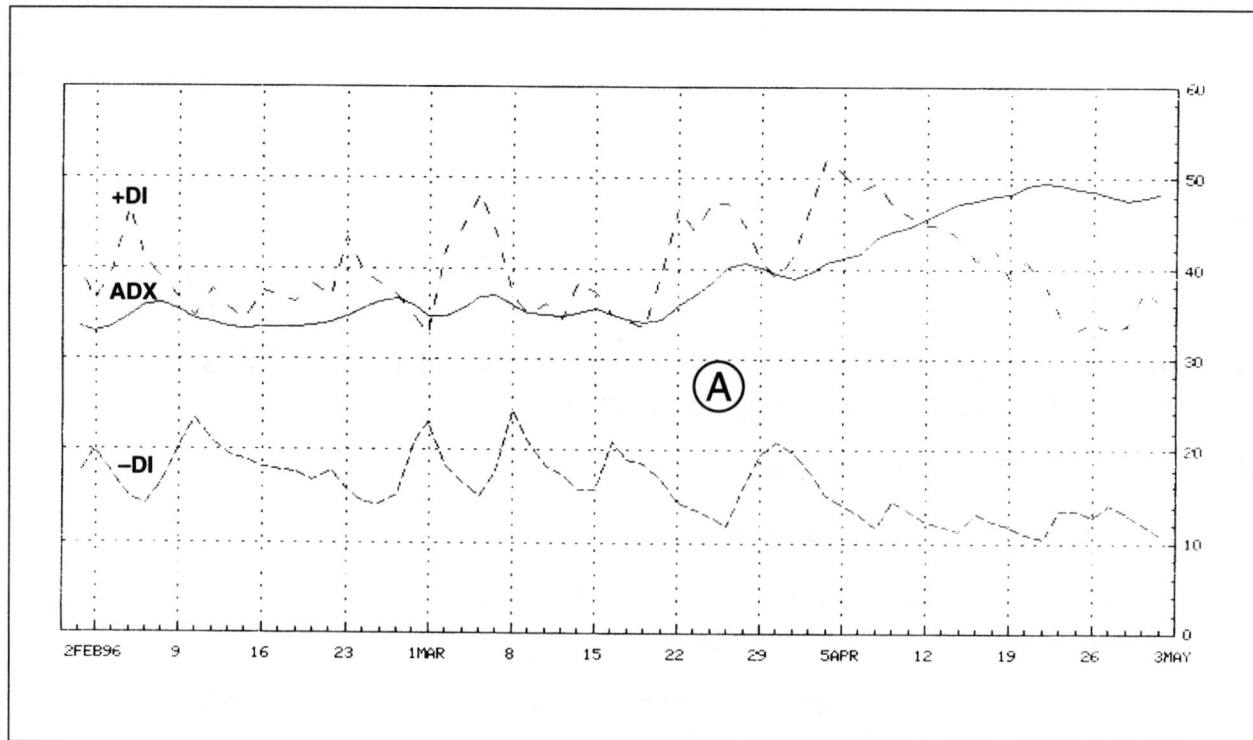

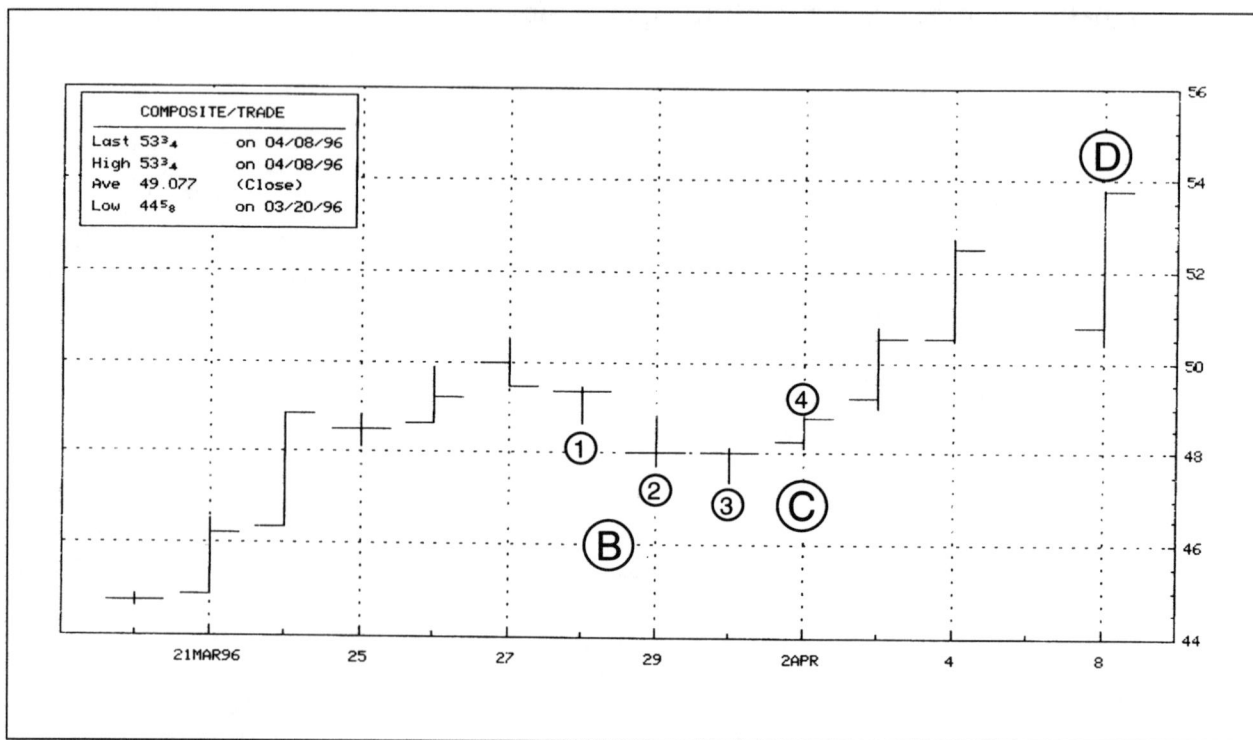

This strategy works especially well with higher priced momentum stocks.

A.   ADX is greater than 30 and +DI > –DI.

B.   **1.** A lower low.

     2. A second lower low.

     3. A third lower low.

C.   We buy on the opening as it is at least 1/8 point above the April 1 high of 48 1/8. Our initial protective stop is near the low of April 1 of 47 3/8.

D.   Gucci trades nearly 6 points higher (12 percent) in four trading sessions.

FIGURE 8.3 Pork Bellies

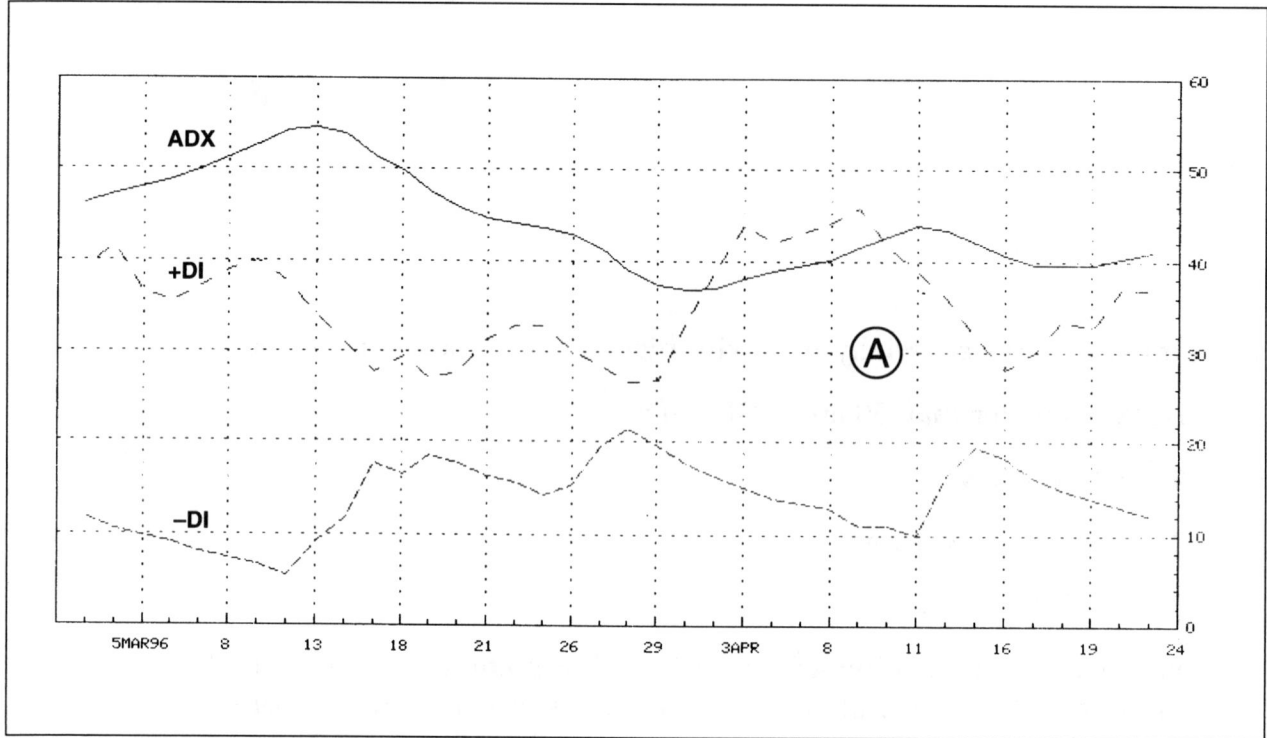

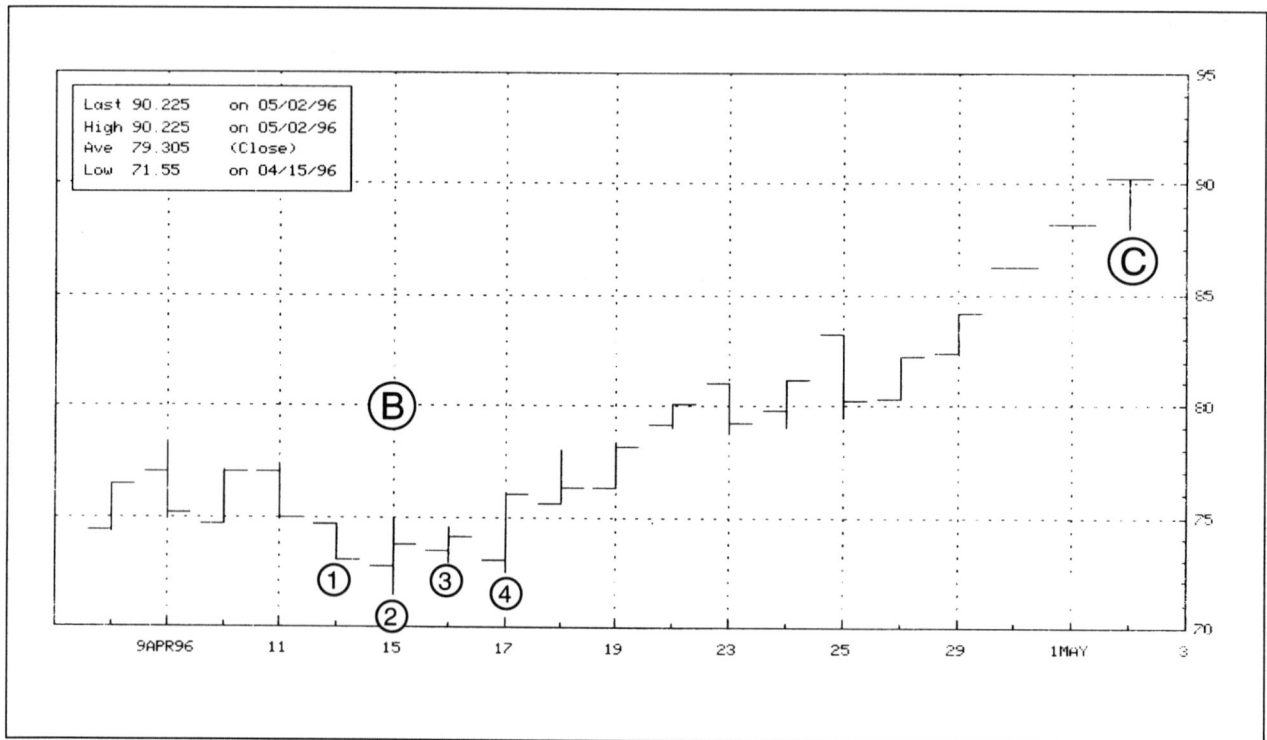

A.   As you can see from the top chart, May bellies are in a strong up-trend. In mid-April, the ADX is greater than 30 and the +DI is greater than the –DI.

B.   A 1-2-3-4 Setup

    1. A lower low.

    2. A second lower low.

    3. An inside day.

    4. Bellies trade lower in the morning and then begin an upward rise. We are filled at 74.52 and our initial protective stop is near the previous day's low.

C.   May Bellies trade more than 15 cents higher ($6,000 per contract) over the next two weeks.

FIGURE 8.4 Micron Technologies (MU)

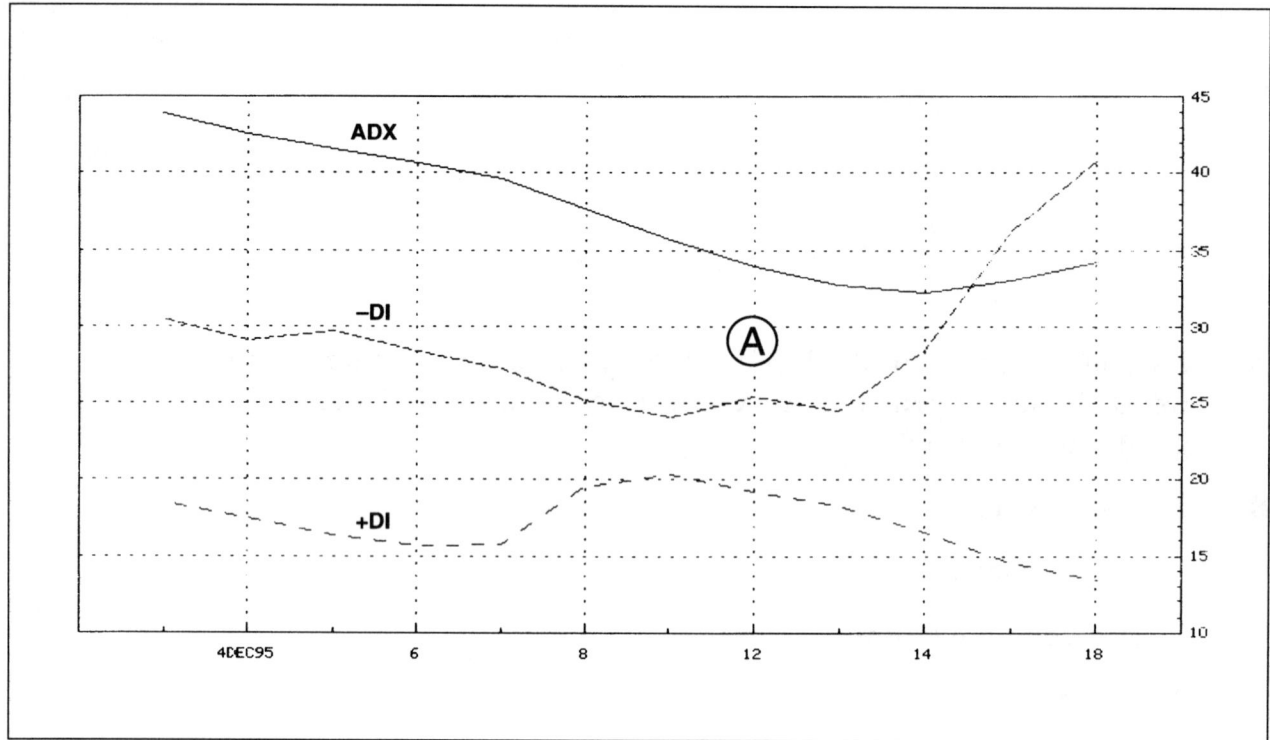

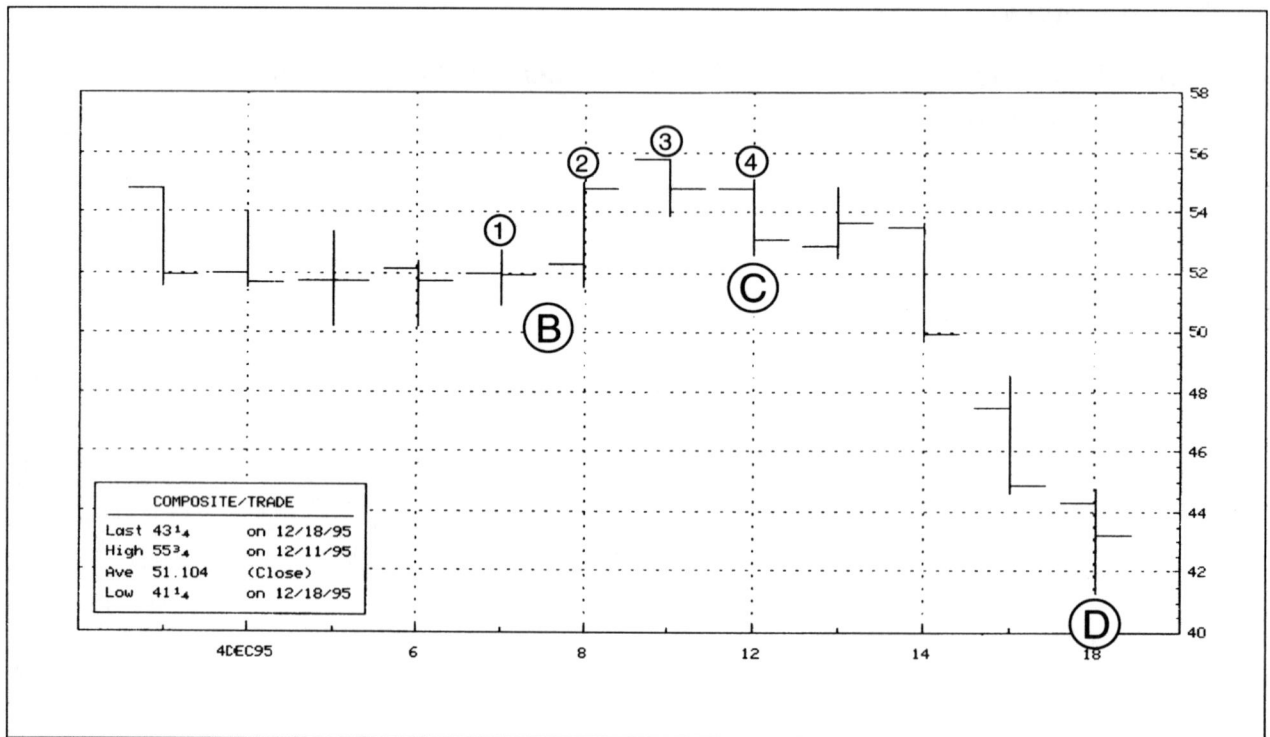

This strategy works equally well on the short-side for equities. Here is an example when the semiconductor stocks collapsed in late 1995.

A.   ADX > 30, –DI > +DI—A bear trend.

B.   **1.** First higher high.

       2. Second higher high.

       3. Third higher high.

C.   **4.** Sell short at 53 3/4.

D.   Micron drops 12 points in five trading sessions.

FIGURE 8.5 June Bonds

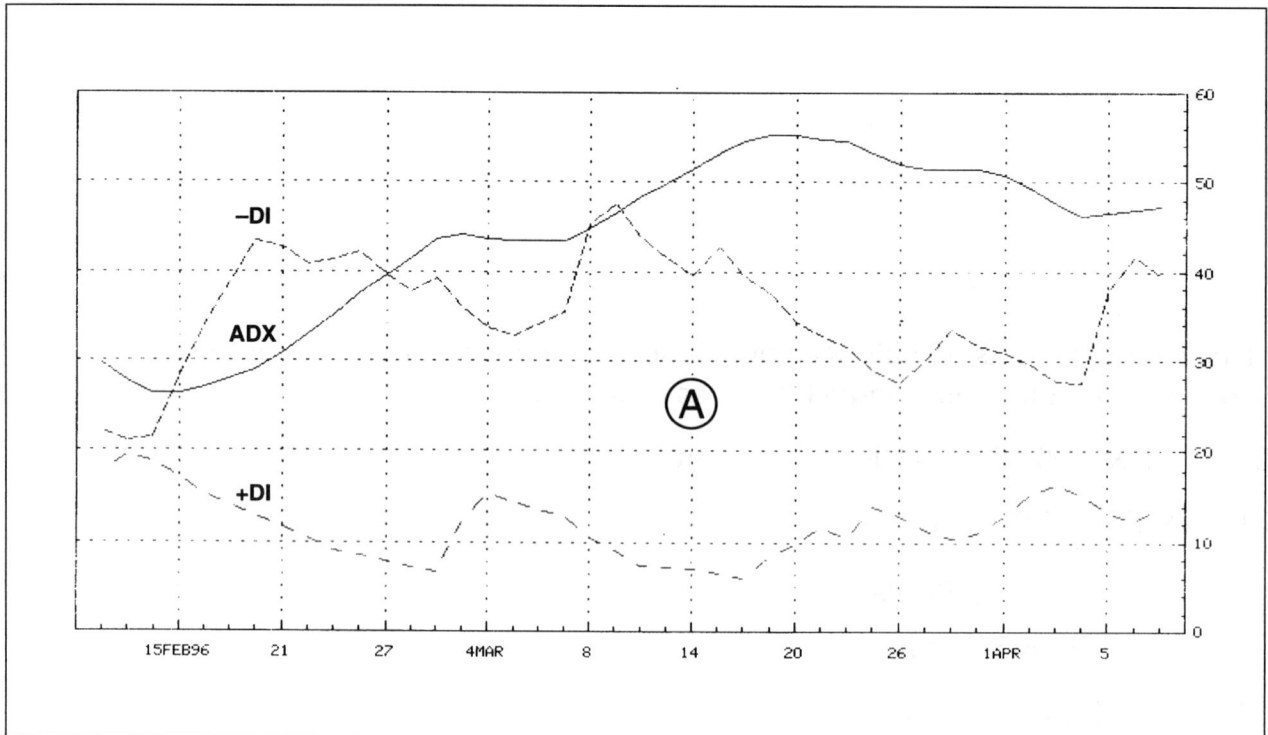

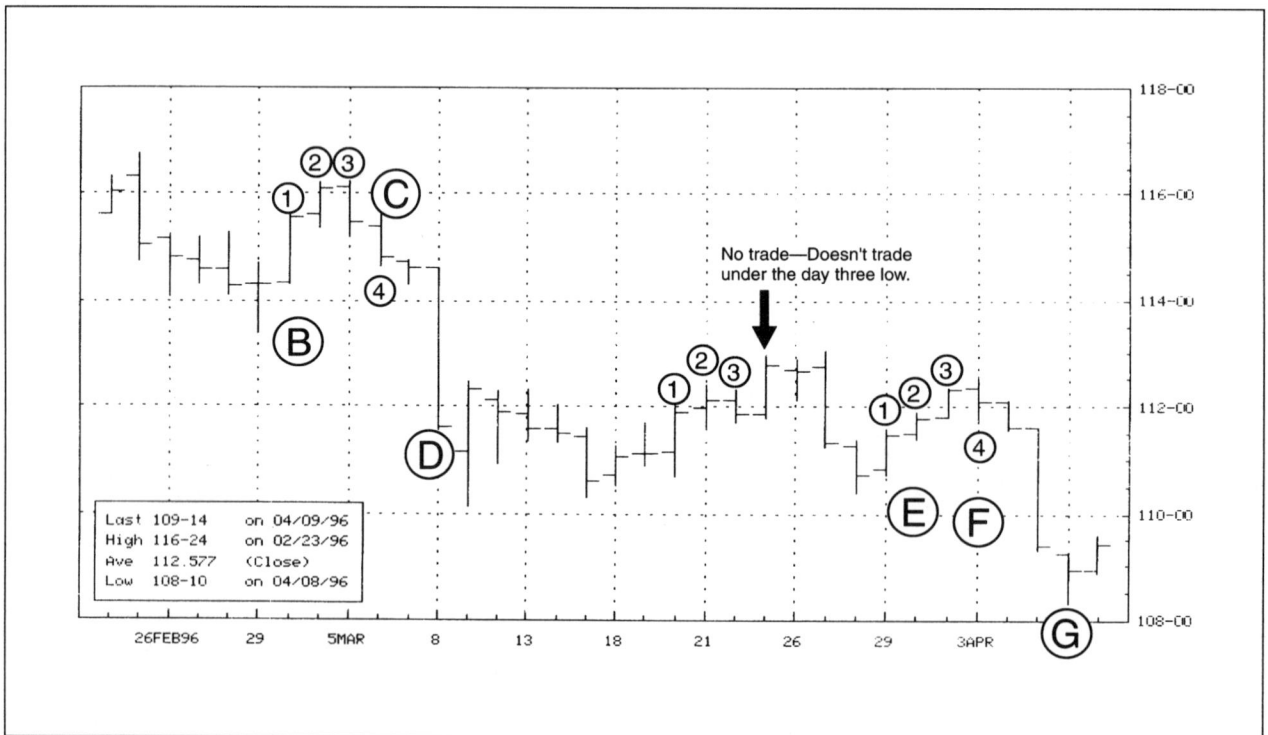

A. The ADX and DI confirm a strong downward trend.

B. Three consecutive higher highs.

C. Trades one tick under the March 5 low.

D. Bonds lose more than 3 points in three days.

E. Three consecutive higher highs.

F. Even though a fourth high is made intraday, we still trade today under the previous day's low and we are short.

G. Bonds again lose approximately 3 points, this time in four days.

SUMMARY

As you can see, this pattern works well in both futures and equities. An added benefit to trading this strategy with stocks is there are signals almost daily.

One of the hardest things to do is climb aboard a market that is in a run-away mode. As markets rapidly rise, the likelihood of entering near a top increases. By waiting for a pullback, which is a natural market phenomenon, and then climbing aboard as the trend resumes, you are looking at a lower risk entry for your trading. Also, by risking only a small amount (with your protective stops), you have an opportunity to participate in some potentially very large market moves.

Finally, even though I am not a fan of buying options, this setup obviously lends itself to call and put buying. From some of the moves that occurred in the examples, option traders surely benefited.

CHAPTER 9

THE 8-DAY HIGH/LOW REVERSAL METHOD

● ●

One of the earliest observations, made both by traders and academic researchers, is that markets go through various dominant cycles. These cycles range from decades to minutes. I suspect, the cycle many readers are most familiar with is the Taylor 3-Day Cycle: the Buy Day, Sell Day, Sell Short Day pattern discovered by George W. Taylor and described in *Street Smarts*.

Here is "The 8-Day High/Low Reversal Method," a longer-term cycle-trading methodology. The method is a distant cousin of Gerald Appel's 8-Day Action System which was introduced as an S&P scalping system approximately a decade ago. The 8-Day High/Low Reversal Method exploits the fact that normally markets go through three to four week cycles. Markets tend to rise for half this period and then decline for the other half. Instead of blindly trading the cycle and guessing at an entry, this methodology waits for a market to test its cycle's highs or lows and if the test is successful, we climb aboard for the reversal.

Markets tend to have dominant cycles. Too many of us, though, have been wrongly influenced by the prognosticators who attempt to predict market highs and lows based on these cycles. In reality, although markets do not strictly adhere to these cycle points, it does not mean we cannot take advantage of them.

The 8-Day High/Low Reversal Method works because it combines an observed market cycle with confirmed price action. The method is further enhanced with the use of tight money management.

Because it may be difficult to grasp at first, I have included additional examples. Before we go to the examples, let's look at the rules.

FOR BUYS

1.   Day one must be an eight-day low.

2.   Day two must trade above the day-one high.

3.   Days three or four or five or six must trade under the day-two low (this can be a new low).

4.   When condition three is satisfied, we buy one tick (1/8 for equities) above the day-two high as long as the one-tick breakout occurs within four trading days of condition three.

5.   Our stop goes one tick below the day-two low.

FOR SELLS

1.   Day one must be an eight-day high.

2.   Day two must trade below the day-one low.

3.   Days three, four, five, or six must trade above the day-two high (this can be a new high).

4.   When condition three is satisfied, we sell (short) one tick (1/8 for equities) below the day-two low as long as it occurs within four trading days.

5.   Our stop is placed one tick above the day-two high.

Let's look at a handful of examples.

FIGURE 9.1   S&P Dec 96

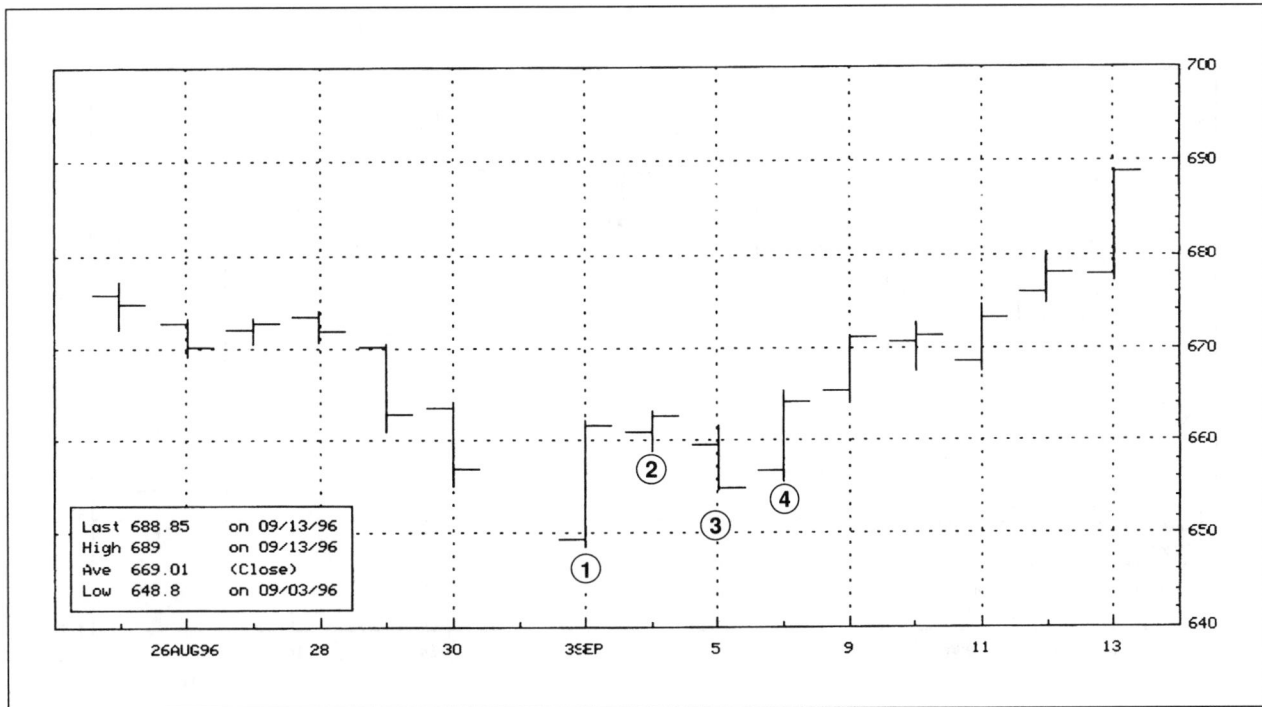

```
Last  688.85    on 09/13/96
High  689       on 09/13/96
Ave   669.01    (Close)
Low   648.8     on 09/03/96
```

1.   An eight-day low (day one)

2.   Day two trades above the day-one high.

3.   The next day trades under the day-two low. We will buy above the high (of day two) today (day three) or over the next four trading sessions only if the price trades one tick above the day-two high.

4.   We are triggered at 663.15 and our stop is one tick under the day-two low.

5.   The market explodes more than 25 points higher over six trading sessions.

FIGURE 9.2 July Copper

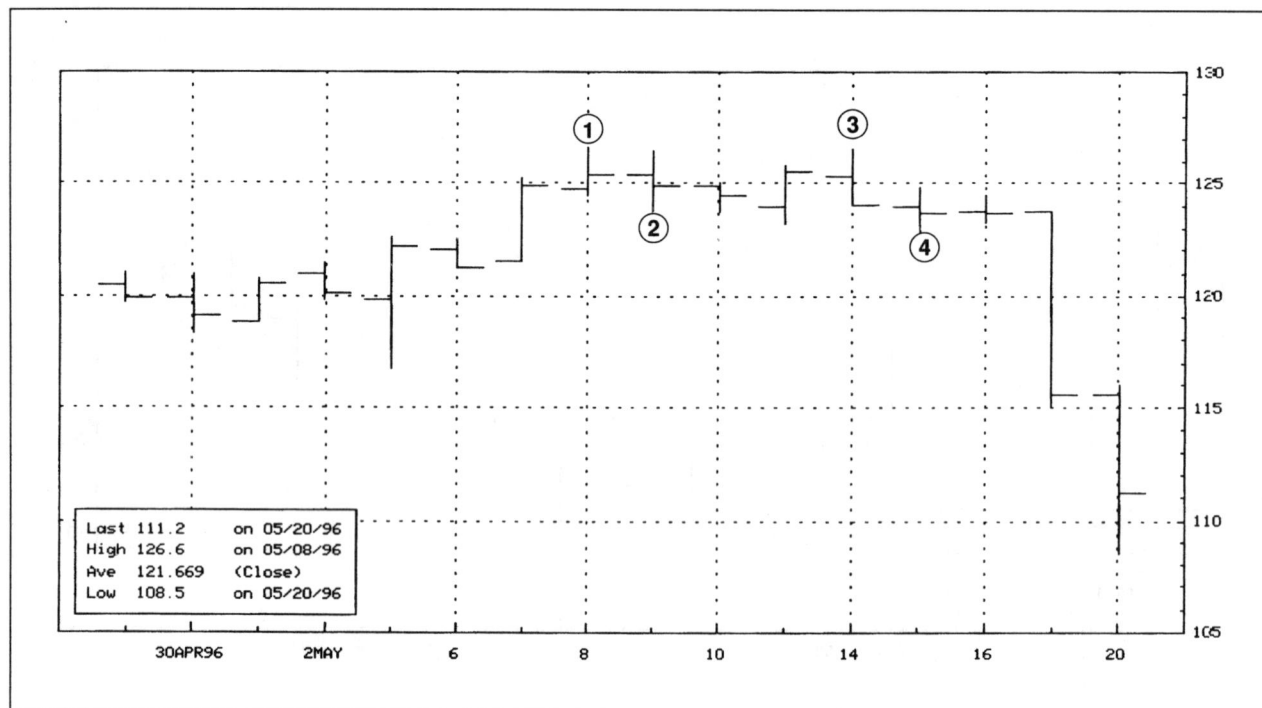

1. An eight-day high (day one)

2. The next day, we trade under the day-one low.

3. Three days later, we trade above the day-two high.

4. The attempted rally is short-lived and our sell signal under the day-two low is triggered. Our stop is one tick above the day-two high.

5. The market collapses over the next three days.

FIGURE 9.3 Microsoft

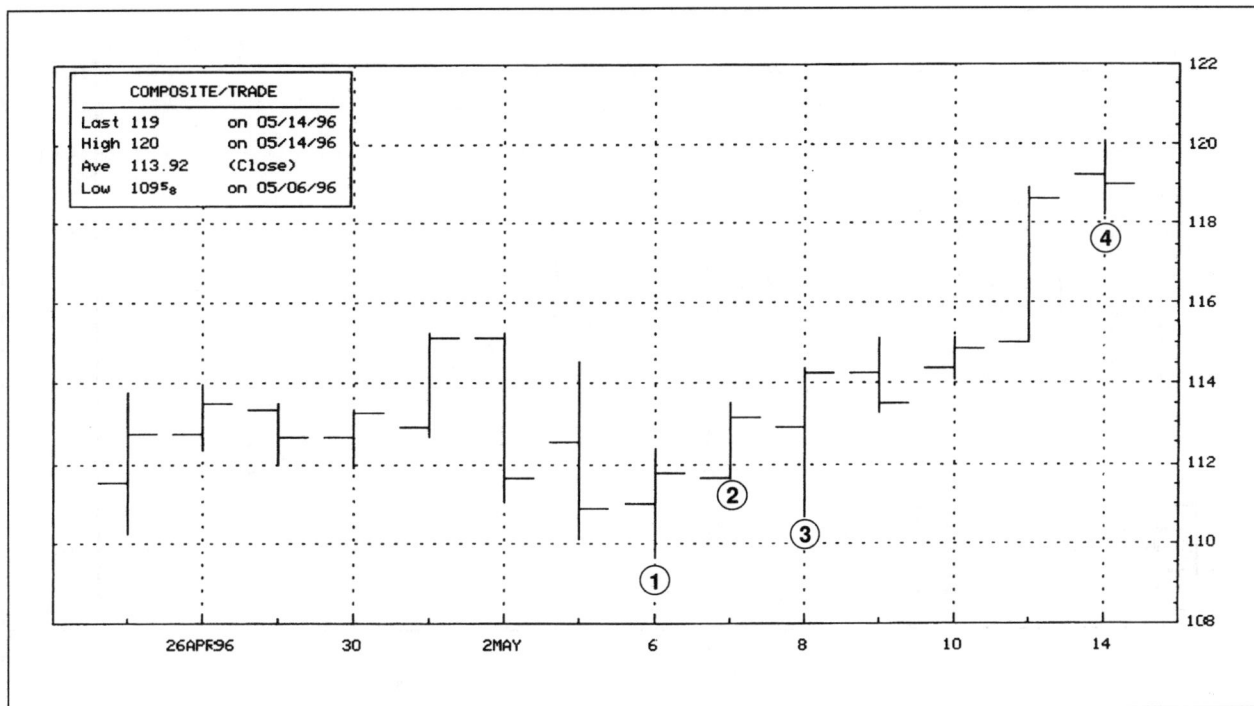

Here is a variation of the method. Notice how rules three and four are triggered the same day.

1.   An eight-day low (day one).

2.   The next day it trades above the previous day's high.

3.   We trade under the day-two low and immediately reverse to trade above the day-two high.

4.   Microsoft trades more than 6 points higher over the next week.

FIGURE 9.4   December Cocoa

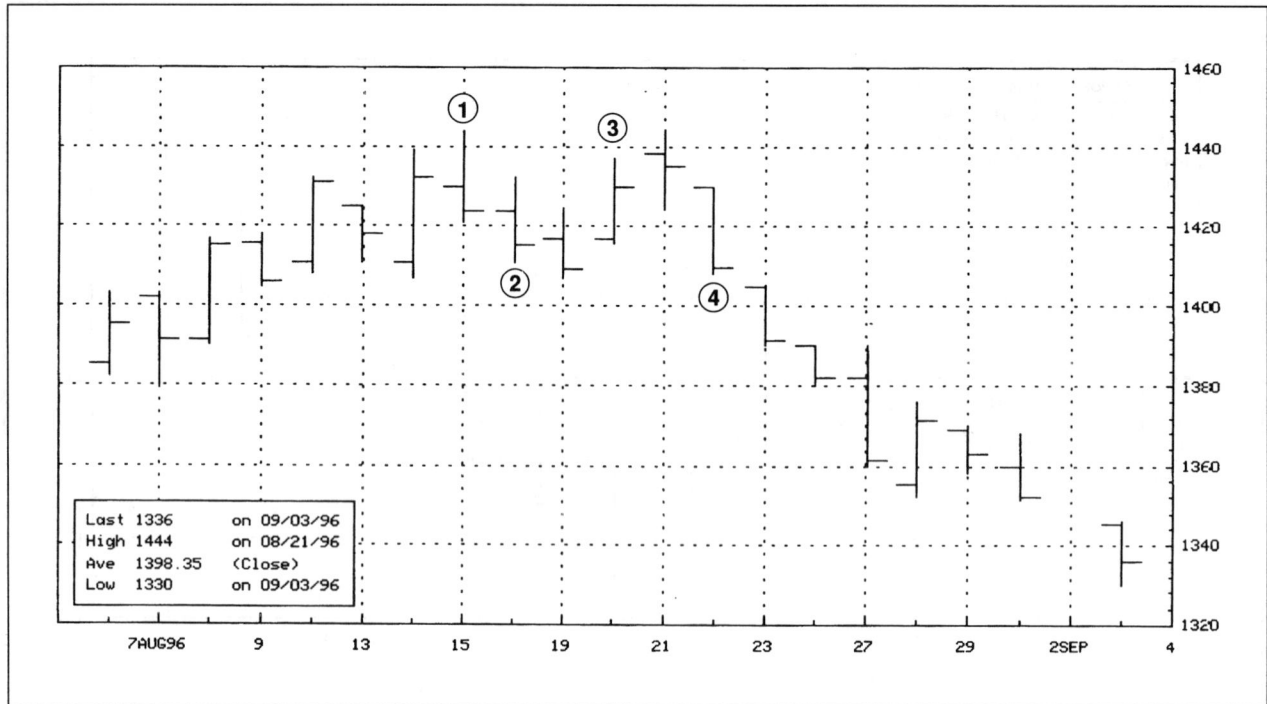

1.   An eight-day high.

2.   We trade under the day-one low.

3.   We trade above the day-two high and our sell stop is placed one tick under the day-two low.

4.   Our entry is triggered two days later and the 8-Day High/Low Reversal Method profits as cocoa sells off.

FIGURE 9.5   December Bonds

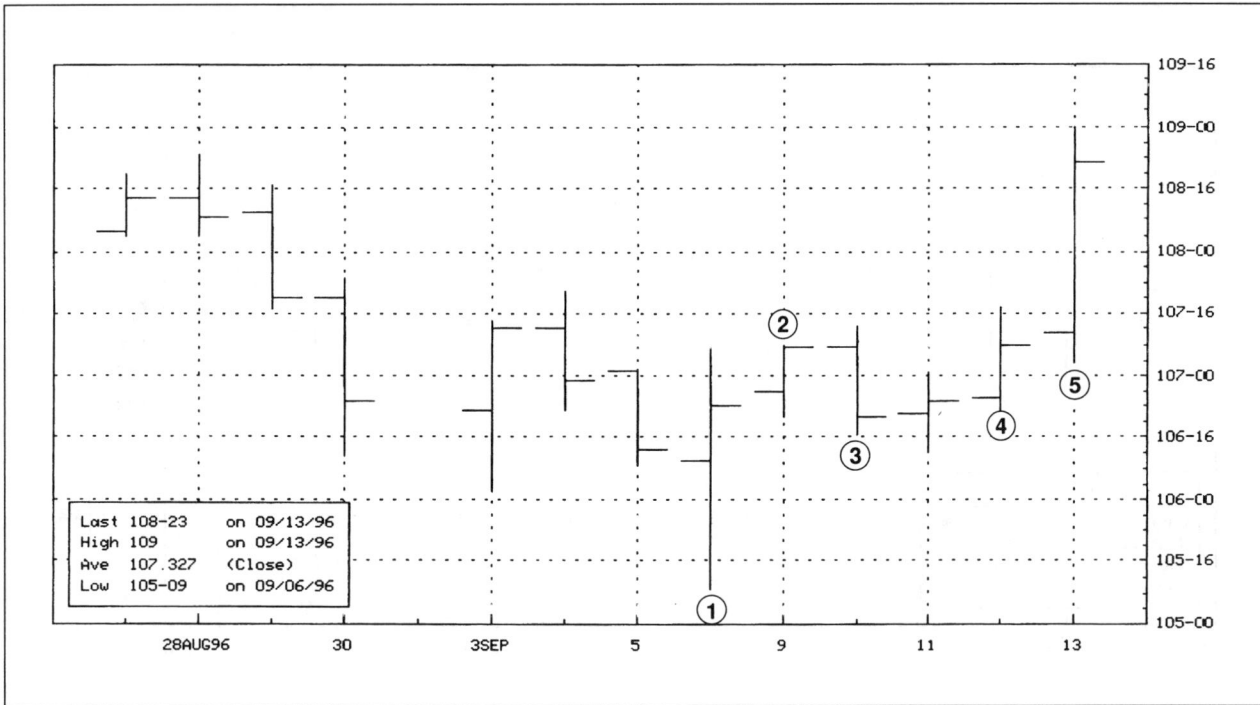

1. An eight-day low.

2. Trades above yesterday's high.

3. Trades under the day-two low.

4. The shorts are forced to scramble as a short-term bottom has been made.

FIGURE 9.6 IBM

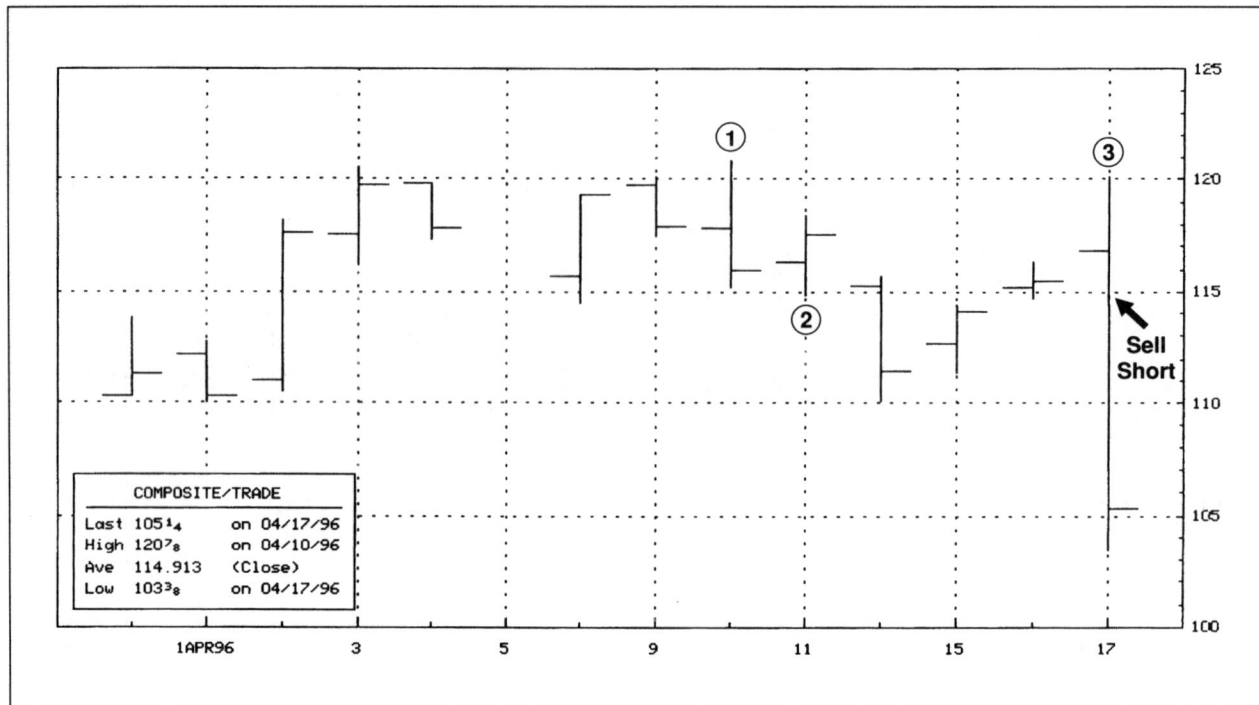

COMPOSITE/TRADE

Last 105$\frac{1}{4}$　on 04/17/96
High 120$^7_8$　on 04/10/96
Ave 114.913　(Close)
Low 103$^3_8$　on 04/17/96

1APR96　　3　　5　　9　　11　　15　　17

1. An eight-day high (day one).

2. The next day we trade under the day-one low.

3. Four days later (our time limit), IBM trades above the day-two high and then trades under the day-two low. We sell the stock short and by the end of the day, IBM is trading more than 12 points under our entry point.

FIGURE 9.7   December Coffee

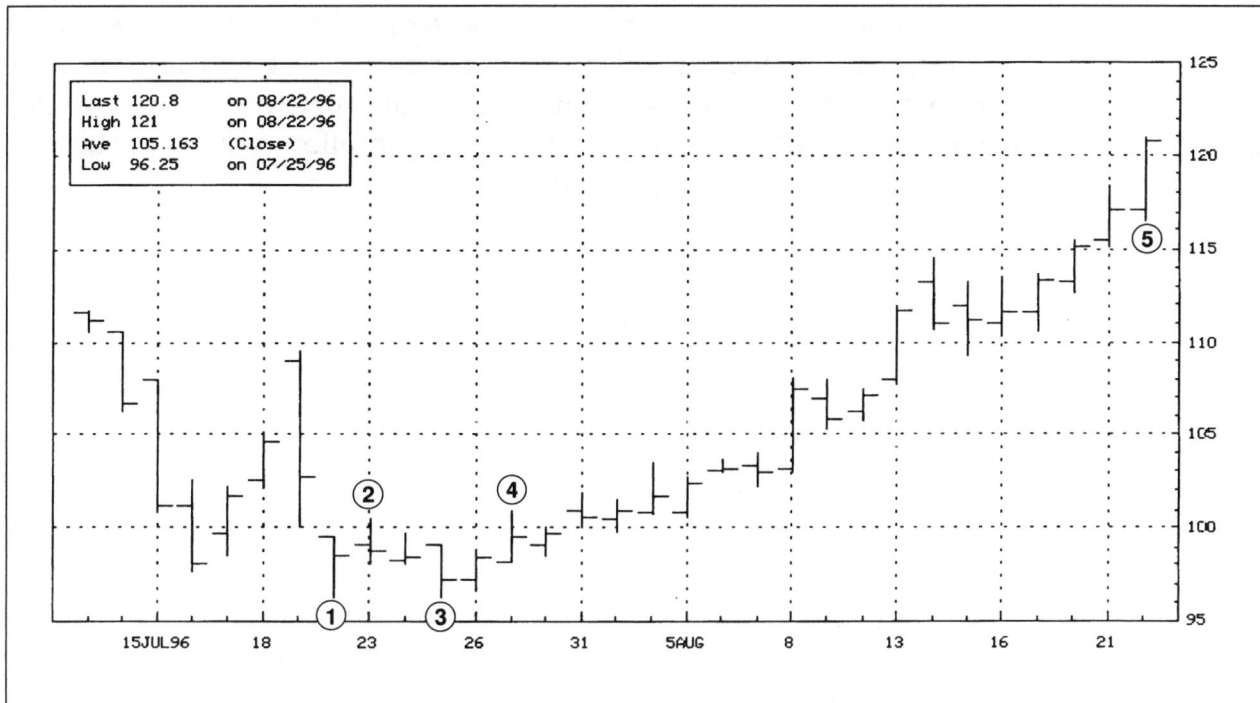

```
Last 120.8      on 08/22/96
High 121        on 08/22/96
Ave  105.163    (Close)
Low  96.25      on 07/25/96
```

Even though I mostly short-term trade, this setup did a nice job of getting into an intermediate term bottom in coffee.

1. An eight-day low.

2. We trade above the day-one high.

3. Trades under the day-two low.

4. We buy one lick above the day-two high.

5. A solid low-risk move over four weeks.

Notice the strength of this move. The market does not make two consecutive lower lows after the buy signal is triggered. This is fairly rare but it does show what markets will do when the selling is completed and legitimate bottoms are made.

SUMMARY

As you can see, this is a fairly low-risk setup that does a nice job of identifying markets that are likely to experience short and intermediate term reversals. Also, you may want to combine it with the Two-for-One money management method (*see* Chapter 28) to allow you to participate in those reversals that are substantial.

CHAPTER 10

SPENT MARKET TRADING PATTERN (SMTP)

▪ ▪

For years we have read about the virtues of trading reversal bars. Unfortunately, their track record is horrendous. I will quote Jack Schwager from his fine book, *Schwager on Futures: Technical Analysis,*

> "It can be said that reversal bars successfully call 100 out of every 10 highs . . . in my opinion, the standard definition of reversal days is so prone to generating false signals that it is worthless as an indicator."

I agree with Jack.

Fortunately though, the story doesn't end there. I have had very good success trading a variation of reversal days which I call the "Spent Market Trading Pattern." This strategy has structured rules that combine reversal days, spike bars, trends, and a specific entry method to provide a low-risk setup.

Here are the rules:

FOR BUYS (SELLS ARE REVERSED)

1.   Today the market must make a 10-period low.

2.   Today's range must be the largest range of the past 10 bars.

3.   Today's close must be in the top 25 percent of today's range.

4.   Tomorrow, or the trading day after tomorrow, buy one tick (1/8 for stocks) above today's high.

5.   If filled, place an initial protective sell stop at today's low and trail it appropriately to lock-in profits.

Let's look at three examples.

FIGURE 10.1 Compaq Computer

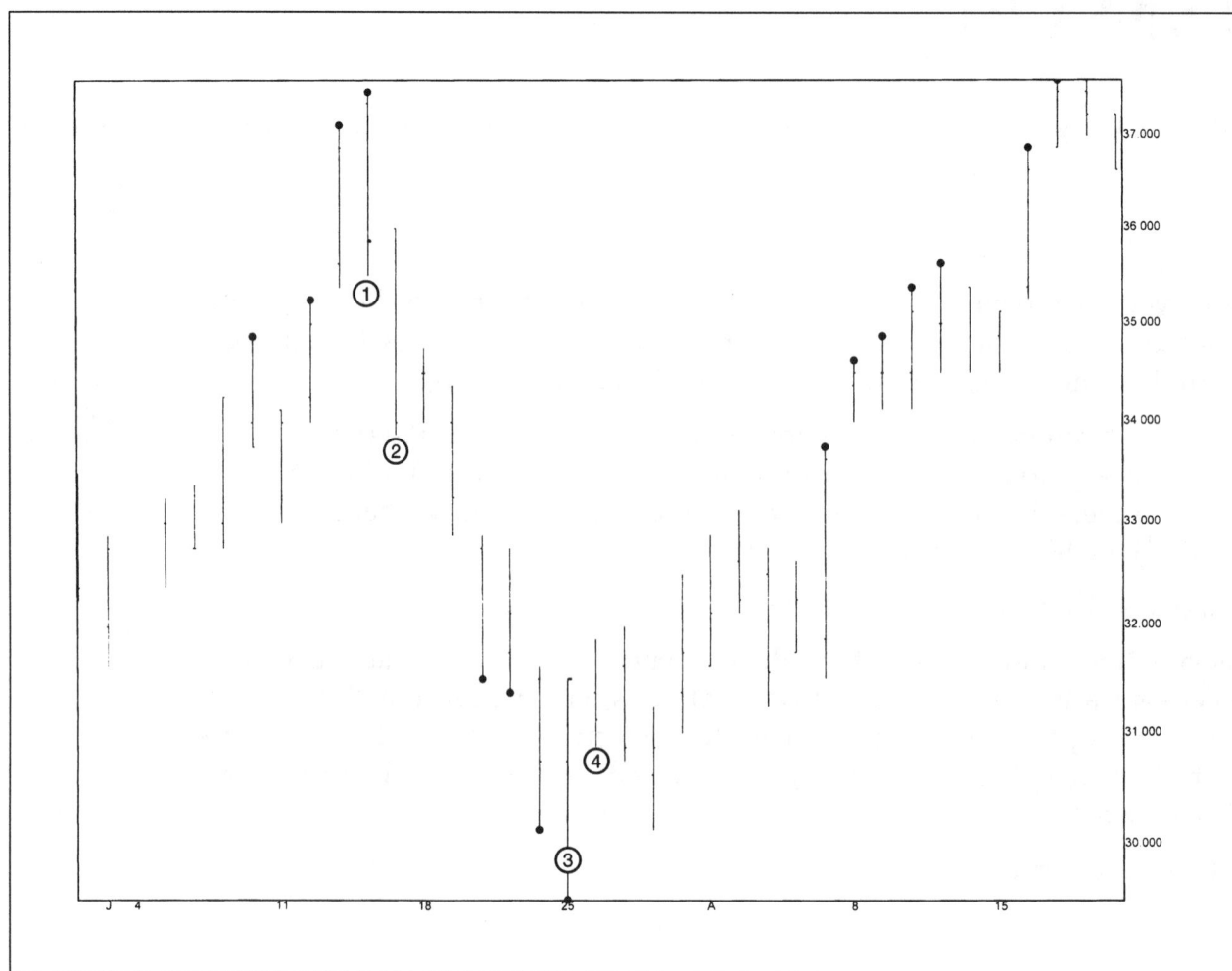

1.   Today's high is a 10-period high, the range is the largest of the past 10 trading sessions, and the close is in the bottom 25 percent of its range.

2.   A sell short stop is triggered 1/8 below yesterday's low of 35 1/2 and our protective stop is at yesterday's high of 37 1/2. The market proceeds to lose over 10 percent of its value over the next few trading sessions.

3.   A 10-period low, the largest range of the past 10 periods, and a close at the top 25 percent of the range.

4.   A buy is triggered at 31 5/8, one tick above yesterday's high and our protective stop is placed at yesterday's low of 29 1/2. The SMTP identifies an intermediate term low as Compaq rises nearly 20 percent over the next month.

FIGURE 10.2 US Bonds

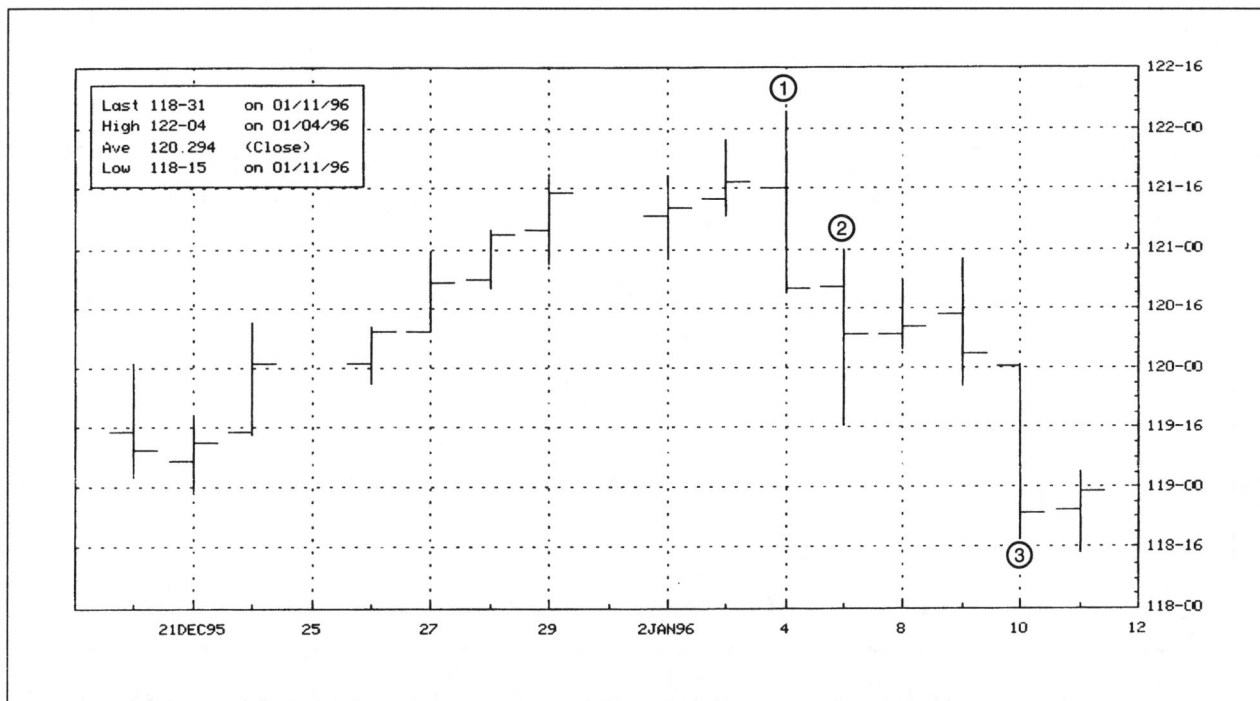

1.   A 10-bar high, the largest range of 10 days and a close in the bottom 25 percent of its daily range.

2.   Our sell stop is triggered one tick under yesterday's low of 120-25 and a protective buy stop is placed at 122-04.

3.   The setup identifies the life of the contract high for bonds and the market drops more than 2 points in four trading sessions. An additional strategy to look at with this setup is to sell options. In this example, both the 120 and 122 calls lost more than half their value in four days.

FIGURE 10.3 Biotechnology Index

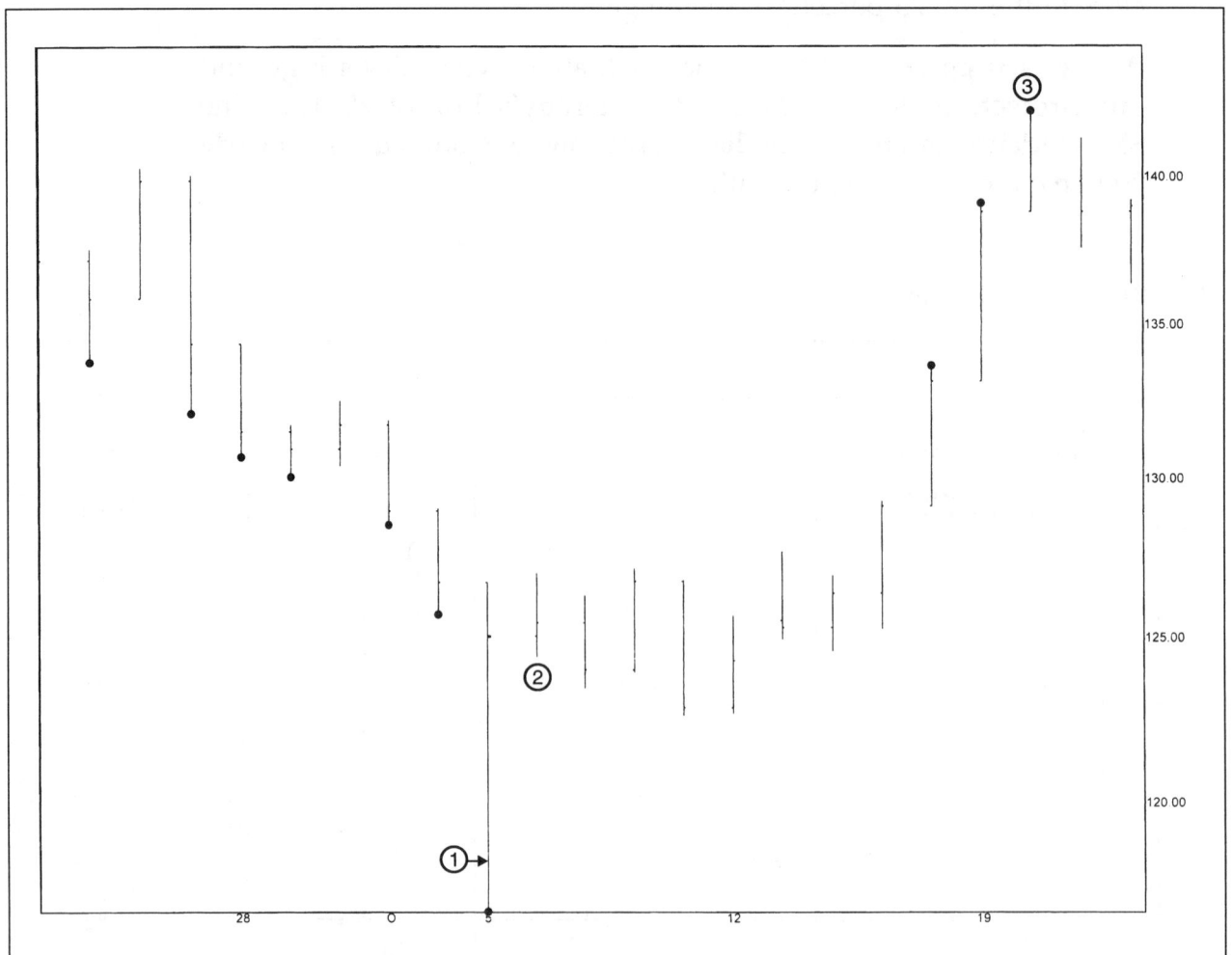

1.   A 10-bar low, the largest range of 10 days, and a close in the top 25 percent of the range.

2.   A buy stop is triggered.

3.   The market trades 15 points higher over the next few weeks.

FIGURE 10.4 December S&P 97 Futures

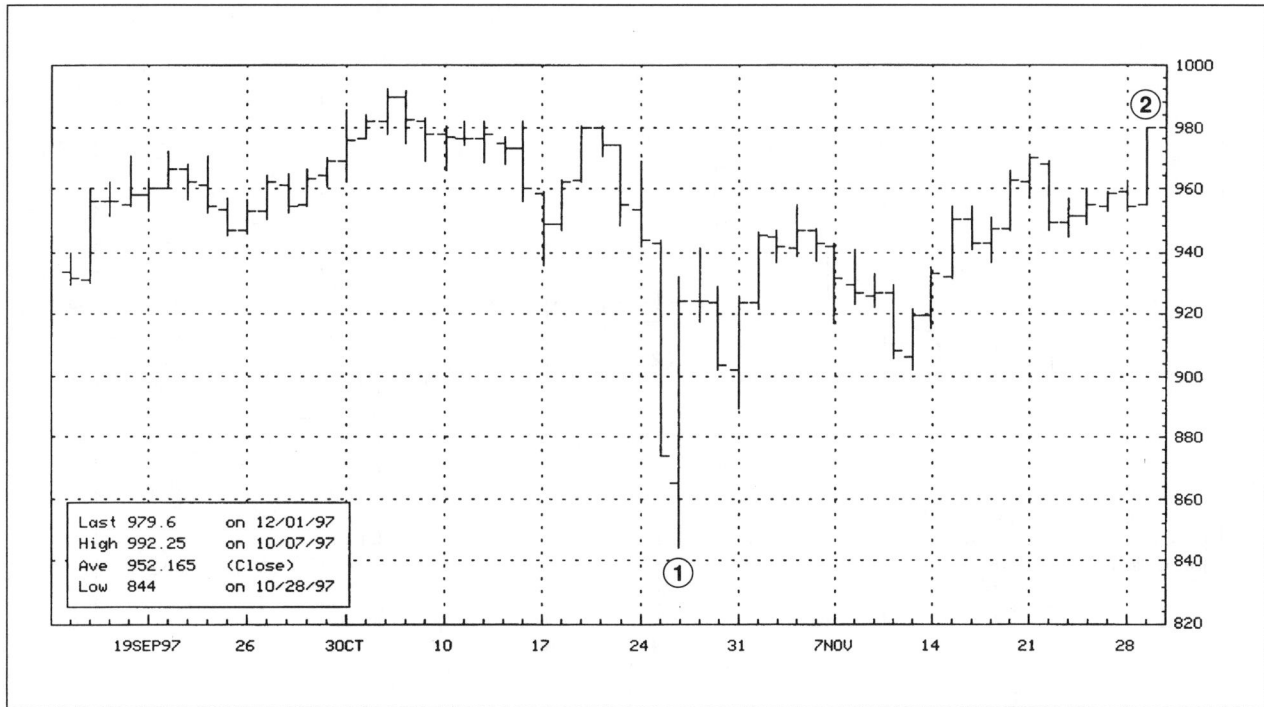

1.   A 10-period low, the largest range of the past 10 days, and a close in the top 25 percent of today's range.

2.   The sell-off exhausted itself and the market moves back to near all-time highs.

FIGURE 10.5 SLOT

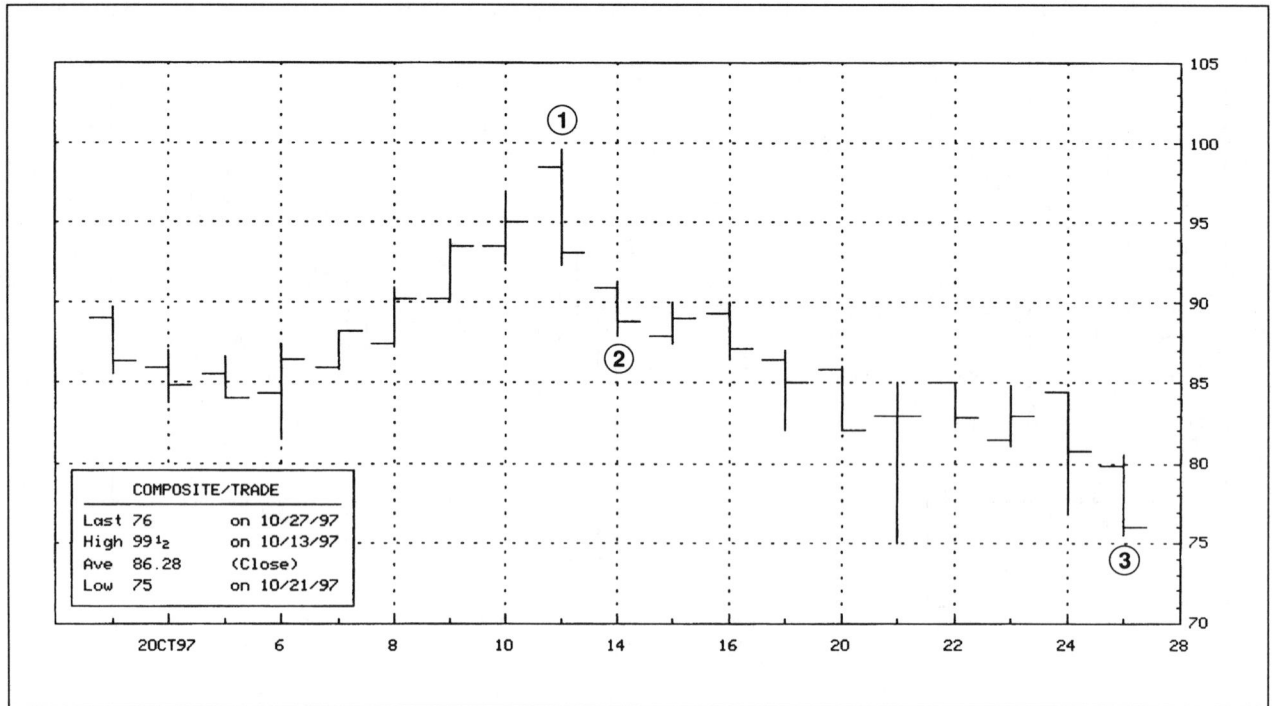

COMPOSITE/TRADE

Last	76	on 10/27/97
High	99 ½	on 10/13/97
Ave	86.28	(Close)
Low	75	on 10/21/97

1. The market makes a 10-period high, the range is the largest of the past 10 days, and the close in the bottom of its range.

2. Sell short at 91 3/4.

3. The stock drops 15 points in two weeks.

SUMMARY

In all time frames this setup indicates the exhaustion phase of a move and a short-term to intermediate-term reversal can be expected. Even though we only looked at daily examples, this setup works equally well with intraday and weekly time frames.

SECTION FOUR

EQUITY TRADING

The following five chapters will cover trading equities. The chapters "Crash, Burn, and Profit," "When They're Late They Are Probably Dead" and "The Double Volume Market Timing Method" are a short-seller's delight. In spite of what the mutual fund and brokerage house industries want you to believe, stocks actually do go down. As shocking as this news is I will top it; stocks drop much faster than they rise! This means traders who can properly identity and time stocks before they collapse can make substantial profits quickly.

The other two chapters are for very short-term traders who want to be in and out of a stock within a day or so. A couple of these strategies relate closely to other chapters and should be fairly simple to master.

CHAPTER 11

THE CRASH, BURN, AND PROFIT TRADING STRATEGY (CBP)

▪ ▪

If you look at the results of the major hedge funds from 1991 through 1997, you will see that the short-sellers have performed the worst. This is easily explained as the market more than doubled in value during that period. The one common characteristic of these short funds, though, is that when they are correct, they are very correct.

The majority of short sellers tend to focus on high flying stocks with hyped stories and then short them. Many times these short sellers are correct, but most times they are too early. Some of these stocks tend to go to stratospheric levels, moving 100 percent, 200 percent, and 300 percent above where they were shorted. Needless to say, most of these fund managers are long gone (stopped out) before the inevitable collapse.

I have studied these high-flying stocks and looked at the common characteristics they had before they collapsed. What invariably comes into the picture is that their weekly ADX reading reaches above 60 and then upon the ADX downticking, the stock also declines, at times never to see those price levels again.

Let's understand what is happening before moving onto the rules. For a stock to reach a level of 60 on its daily ADX, it must be climbing very strongly. For it to reach 60 on its *weekly* reading, it must be parabolic. Greed, fear (from the shorts), and volatility are at a maximum and it doesn't take much to make this bubble burst.

A word of warning needs to be given. *These stocks can and do go even higher and I highly recommend using some type of predetermined protective buy stop.* Because you will be looking to make larger gains on these setups, I recommend a 15 percent stop-out point. Also, deep in the money puts are a good choice instead of shorting the stock, as your loss will be limited if you are wrong and you avoid the difficulty of borrowing the stock. (The latter is a good tactic to keep in mind whenever a short sale is hampered by your broker's inability to find shares to borrow.)

Here are the rules for our short selling strategy:

1.   Identify a stock whose weekly ADX reading is above 60.

2.   The stocks price should be above 20, as I have found this setup to work even better on higher priced stocks.

3.   After the weekly ADX reading reaches 60, wait for the first lower ADX weekly reading to occur.

4.   When the above 3 rules are met, short the stock and risk no more than 15 percent.

5.   Cover one-half the position upon a 20 percent profit and use trailing stops on the other half.

Here are some examples:

FIGURE 11.1 Centennial Technologies

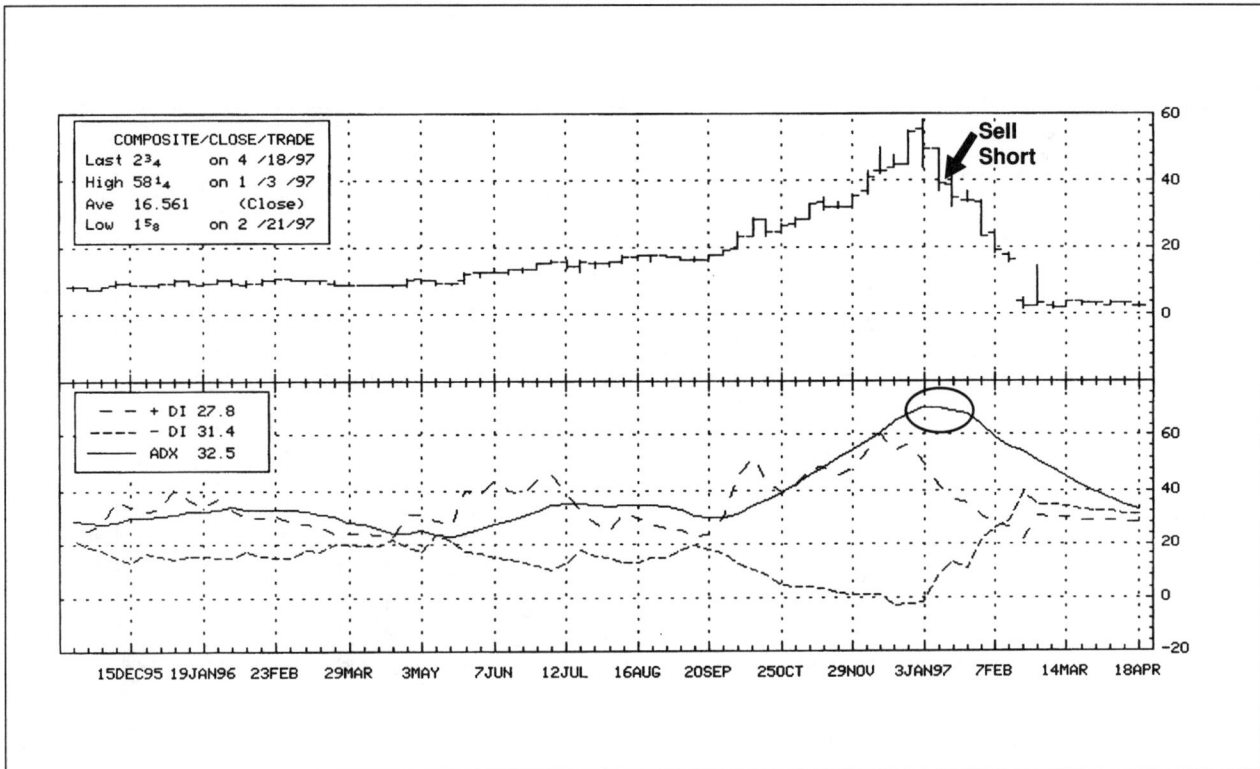

Centennial Technologies is a good CBP example. The PC solution company entered 1997 trading at more than 150 times stated earnings and promising investors the road to riches. On the week of January 10, 1997, the weekly ADX downticks for the first time since closing above 60. A short signal is triggered at 49 1/8 and the profit (as many times occurs when the bubble bursts) is immediate with the stock closing the week at 39 3/8. Six weeks later, the game is over as fraud has been uncovered and the company's chairman is indicted. The stock currently trades in the 2 1/2 range.

FIGURE 11.2 Diana Corp.

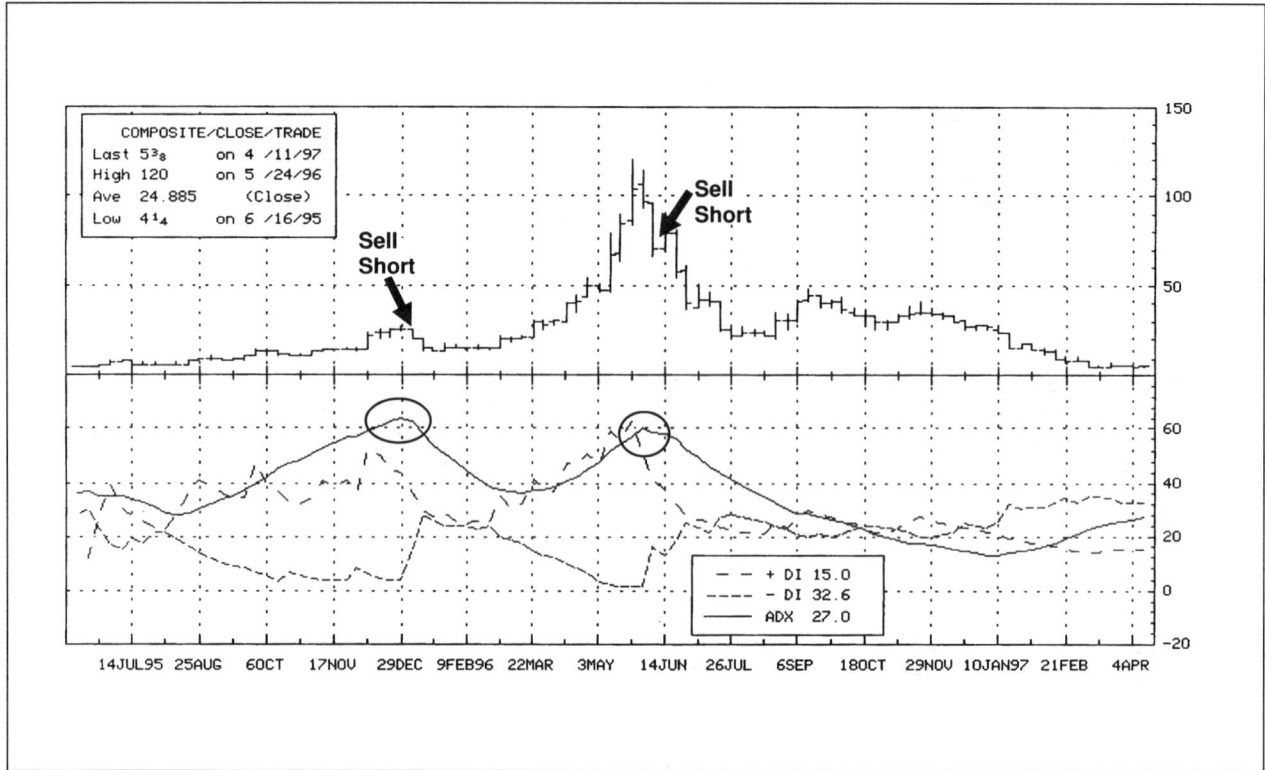

Diana Corp. (the symbol was DNA before the NYSE delisted them) is a telephone networking company. The stock had two CBP setups. The first occurred January 6, when the ADX downticked from its above-60 level. The next week, the stock lost 35 percent of its value. As you can see though, it's tough to keep a good story down and the stock rose another 100 points (!) triggering another CBP signal on June 7 at 67 3/8 (the stock had almost halved in the previous two weeks). Three weeks later, DNA was trading more than 30 points lower and as of April 22, 1997, it was changing hands at 4 3/8.

FIGURE 11.3 Wackenhut Corrections Corp.

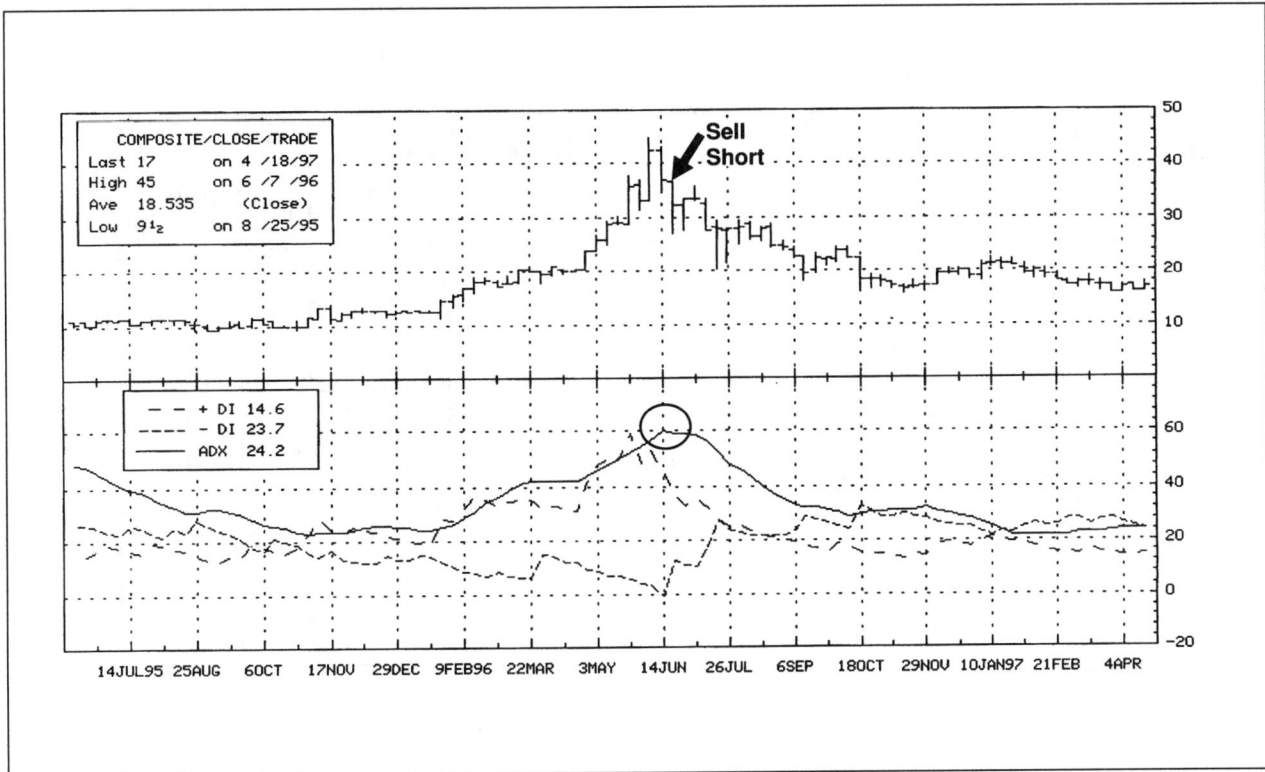

In the summer of 1996, momentum investors and money managers were tripping over themselves to buy Wackenhut Corrections Corp. On June 21, 1996, a CBP signal gets triggered at 32 1/8 and within one month the stock was nearly 40 percent lower.

FIGURE 11.4 Delta and Pine

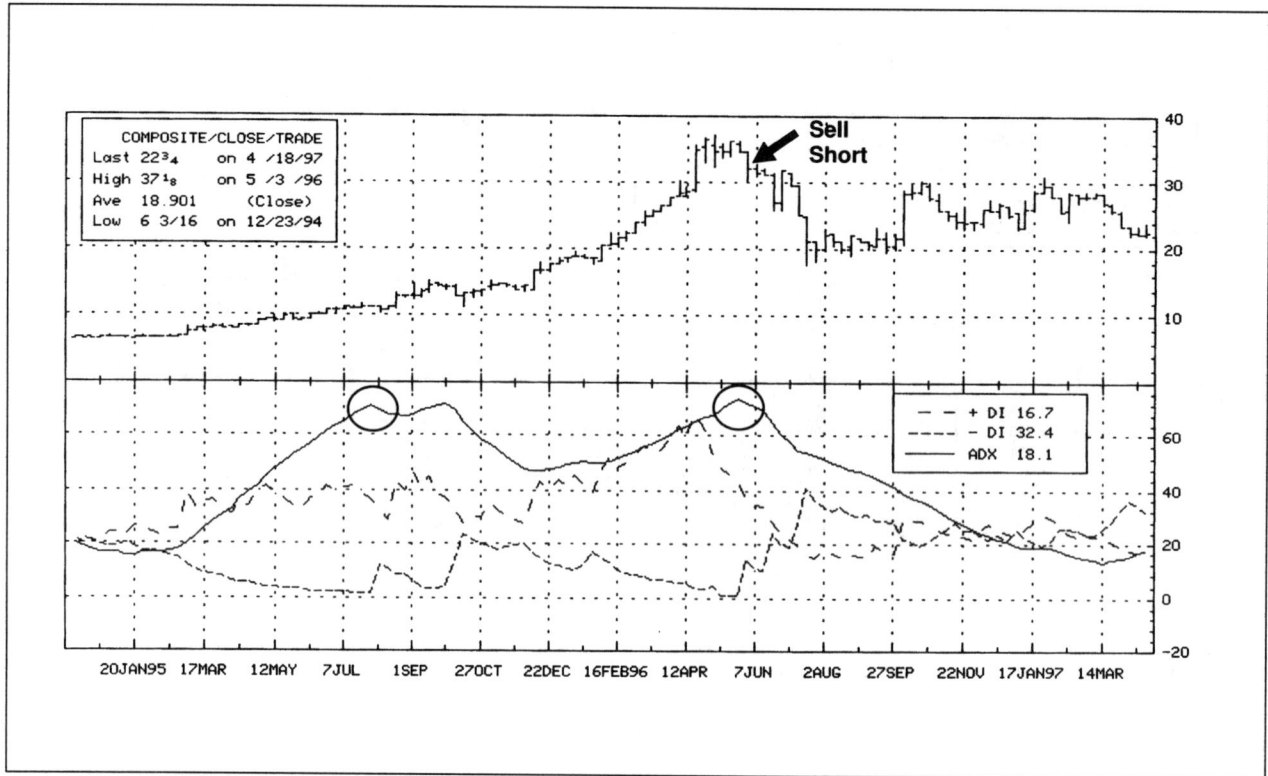

Delta and Pine breeds cotton seed. Here we have one unsuccessful setup in August 1995 and one very quick successful setup (eight weeks) last June leading to a 40 percent gain.

FIGURE 11.5 Micron Technologies

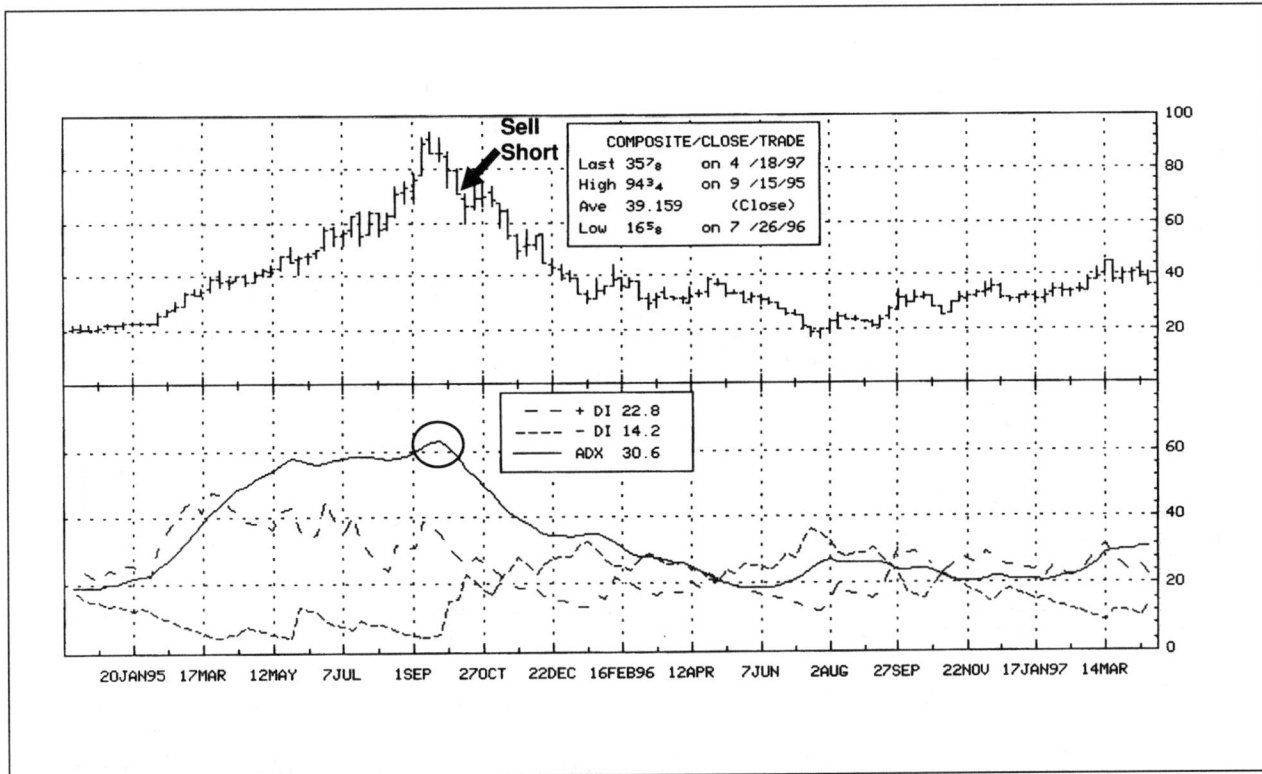

Micron Technologies was the darling of growth investors in 1995. Unfortunately for those investors who got caught owning the stock during its downturn, the sell-off that was triggered after the CBP signal was quite painful.

FIGURE 11.6 Fine Host Corporation

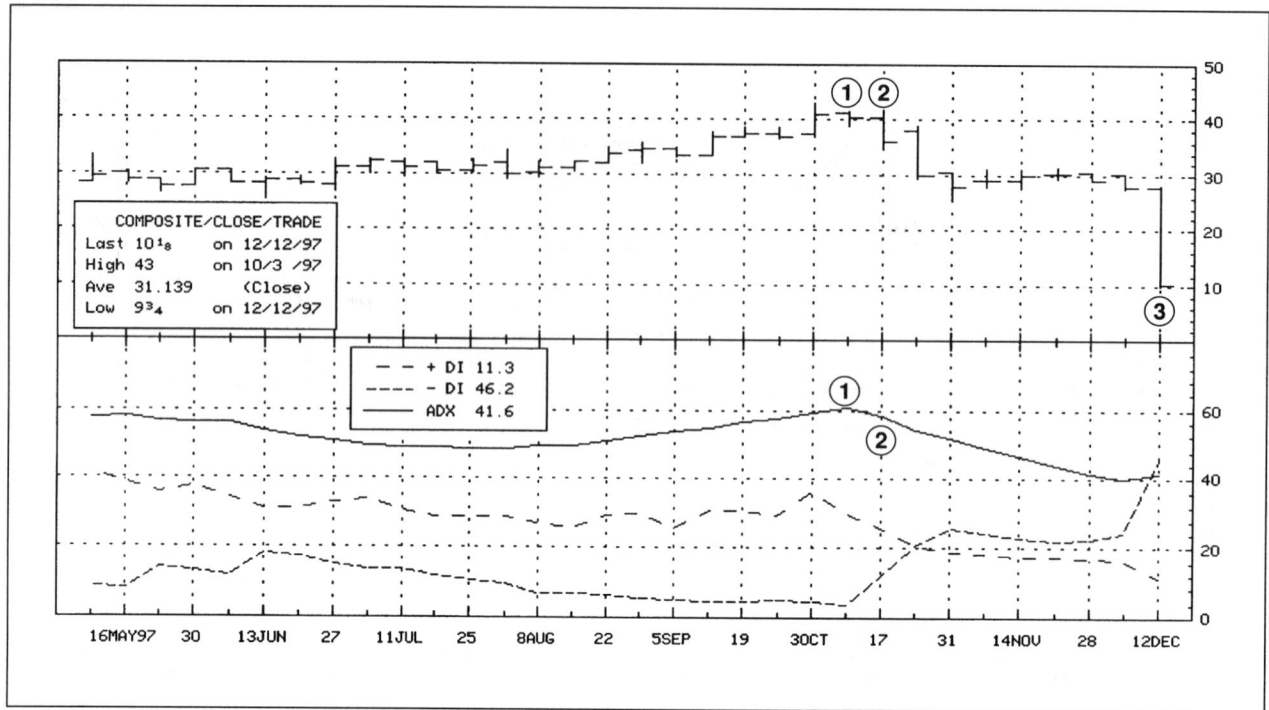

1.   Here is an example that occurred as the book was ready to go to the printers. Fine Host Corporation, a contract food service company, was reporting record earnings since going public. The stock rose five-fold in 14 months, bringing the weekly ADX above 60.

2.   A downtick in ADX and we are short.

3.   Two months later the company announces it would restate earnings due to "accounting irregularities" and it fired its CEO and treasurer. As I am writing this, the stock has been halted and may not resume trading for as long as a month.

SUMMARY

As the funds which short equities on fundamental analysis alone have learned, one needs to properly time when to short these highest-flying stocks. The ADX above 60 reversal method does a good job of doing this.

You need to be somewhat patient as this method is fairly rare, but with the proliferation of momentum-based money managers and investors, ample opportunities do occur over the course of a year. The best way to identify these opportunities is to do a weekly scan if you have the software, or to use Investor's Business Daily and identify those stocks whose Relative Strength is 98 or 99. This will keep you focused on the correct names to follow and allow you to participate when these crazy stocks collapse.

One final point should be made. Some of the examples showed companies whose stock completely collapsed. In reality, these are more the exception than the rule. Ideally, you should expect smaller moves, and when the home runs occur, view them as a gift.

CHAPTER 12

WHEN THEY'RE LATE, THEY'RE PROBABLY DEAD

▪ ▪

This strategy looks at a method to identify when companies will probably disappoint with their earnings. As you know, when a growth company has an earnings downfall, prices implode and those traders fortunate enough to be short are amply rewarded.

This is a method I have used over the years to exploit negative earnings surprises. Unfortunately, this strategy doesn't happen often but when it does the results are powerful.

The "When They're Late, They're Probably Dead" trading strategy targets companies:

1. That are late reporting their earnings.

2. Whose price trends lower before the earnings are due.

Let's look at an example.

FIGURE 12.1 Baby Superstores

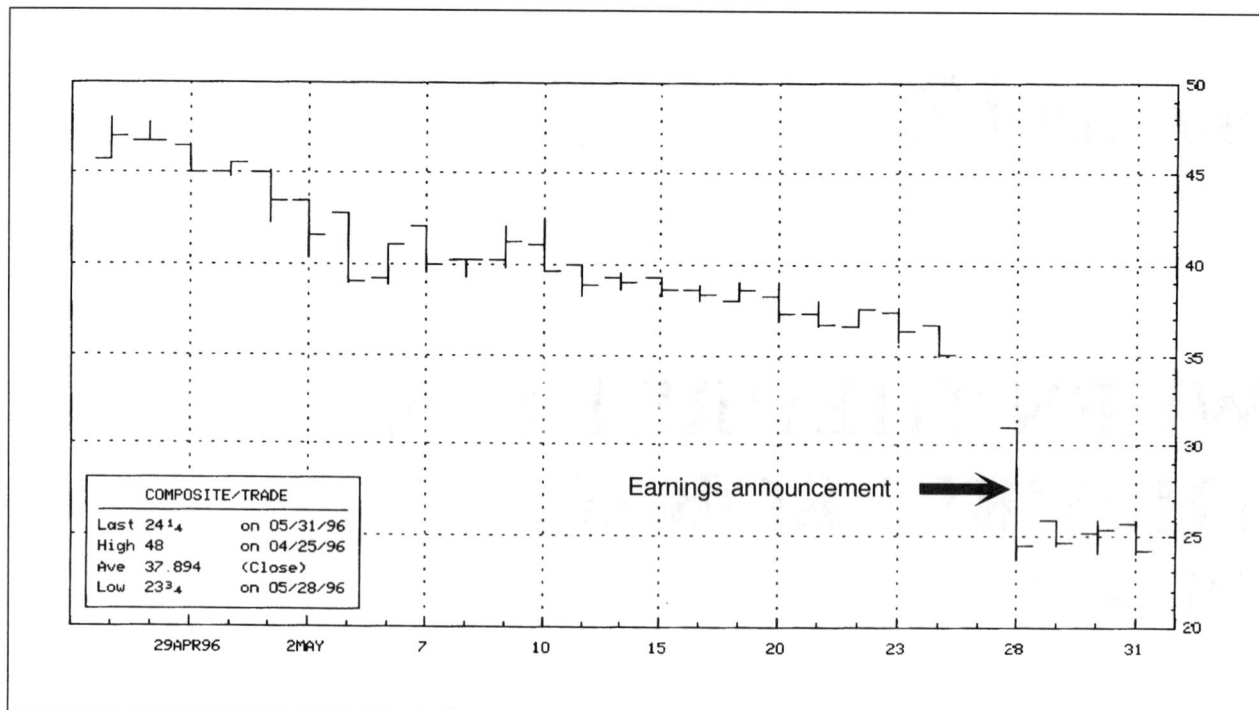

Baby Superstores,* a rapidly growing infant products company is expected to report earnings during the week of May 15, 1996. When the week comes to a close, the company still hasn't released their numbers and a red flag is triggered. We then look at the recent trend of the stock. As you can see, the stock is not only declining while the stock market is rising, but it is hovering around the year's lows.

We put these two pieces together and come to the conclusion that there is a potential problem. The safest strategy is to buy puts. If by chance we are wrong, this will limit our losses.

In this example, I paid 2 1/4 for the June 35 puts.

The company goes the entire next week again without reporting earnings! On Tuesday morning of the following week, Baby Superstores fi-

---

* When this trade occurred, I was in Washington, D.C., to listen to a friend speak at the Managed Futures Association annual meeting. The options desk I trade through called my office with the good news and I closed my position very near the high of the day from a pay phone in the hotel lobby. Sometimes you're better lucky than smart.

nally releases their numbers and they are terrible. The stock immediately collapses and the puts climb to above $10 intraday.

Why is the company late reporting earnings? My guess is that senior management is taken by surprise by the shortfall and it takes them a week or two to digest the problem and create a new "strategic plan" to announce to Wall Street.

A late earnings report alone though is only one piece of the puzzle. The other piece is the price action preceding the announcement. It is obvious by the trend that the so-called "smart money" was unloading its positions ahead of the report. There is no other way to explain a momentum stock like Baby Superstores trending downward in a climbing market.

Again, this situation does not happen everyday, but when it does, it pays to take a good close look at it.

CHAPTER 13

DOUBLE VOLUME MARKET TOP METHOD

- -

In the 1980s, there was a wonderful bookstore in West Los Angeles that sold nothing but investment books. In a one-room loft, it had copies (mostly photocopies) of nearly every book and course written over the previous 50 years on the markets. The owner unfortunately passed away six or seven years ago and the store was closed. On one of my last visits I was lucky enough to purchase a copy of Tubb's *Stock Market Correspondence Lessons,* written in the 1930s.

This book is one of the worst written treatises I have ever come across, but it is also one of the single best books published on how to trade the markets. Tubb's was decades ahead of everyone else in formulating "rules" and "laws" that dictate market behavior. One of his areas of expertise was how volume preceded and affected price. One of his concepts was that when the volume of a stock had a large spike relative to the previous 15 days, and the stock was near its highs, a reversal was likely.

For me this made sense but the rules were too vague and needed to be tightened and made more specific. Building on Tubb's observation, I created the "Double Volume Market Top Method" (DVMTM) which combines exact volume rules with an exact pattern to better pinpoint market tops.

Here are the rules:

1.   A stock must be trading near or at a three-month calendar-day high.

2.   Today's volume must be double its 15-day average volume. This means if the volume has averaged 1 million shares daily for the past 15 trading days, it must trade at least 2 million shares today.

3.   Either today, tomorrow, or the next day, the stock must close below its open.

4.   When Rule 3 is met, over the next two days sell 1/8 under the Rule 3 day low.

5.   Your initial protective stop should be the top of the Rule 3 day bar and trailing stops should be used to lock-in profits.

Let's look at a handful of examples to further understand this strategy.

FIGURE 13.1 Microsoft

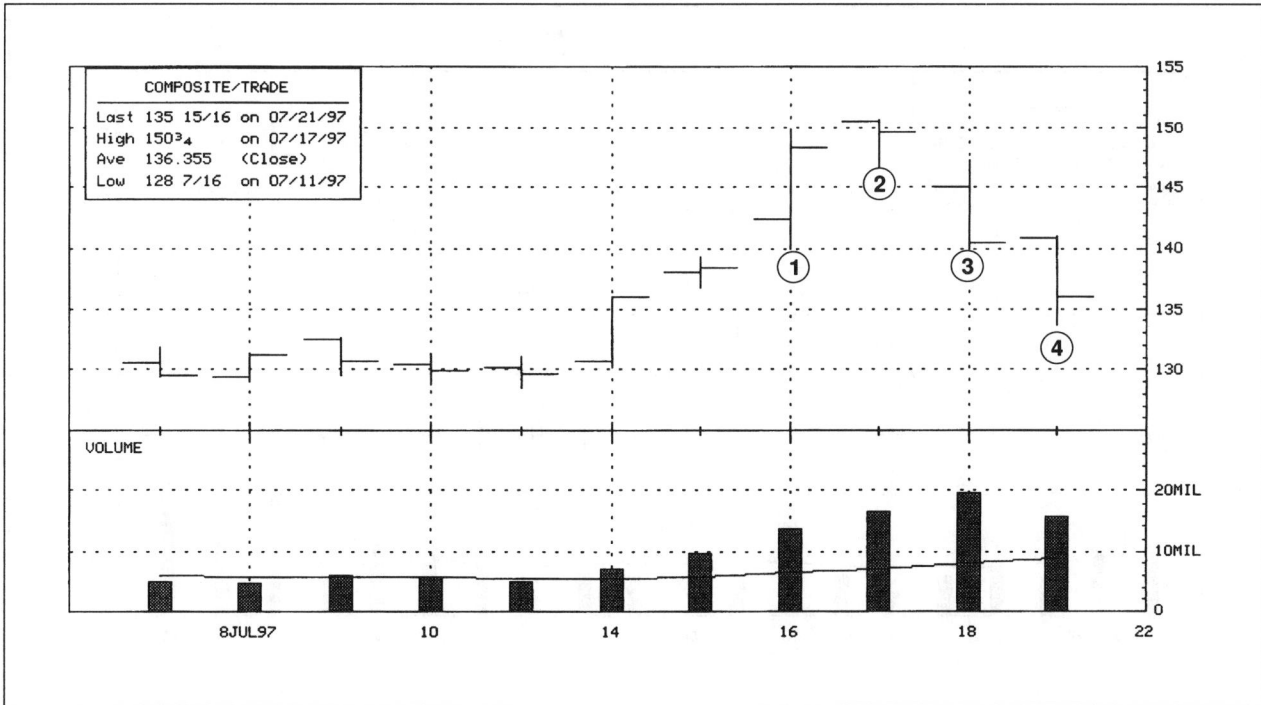

1. On July 16, 1997, Microsoft makes a new high on more than double its normal daily average volume.

2. Another new high and a close below its open.

3. Sell short at 145.

4. The stock closes 9 points below yesterday's fill.

FIGURE 13.2 Yahoo

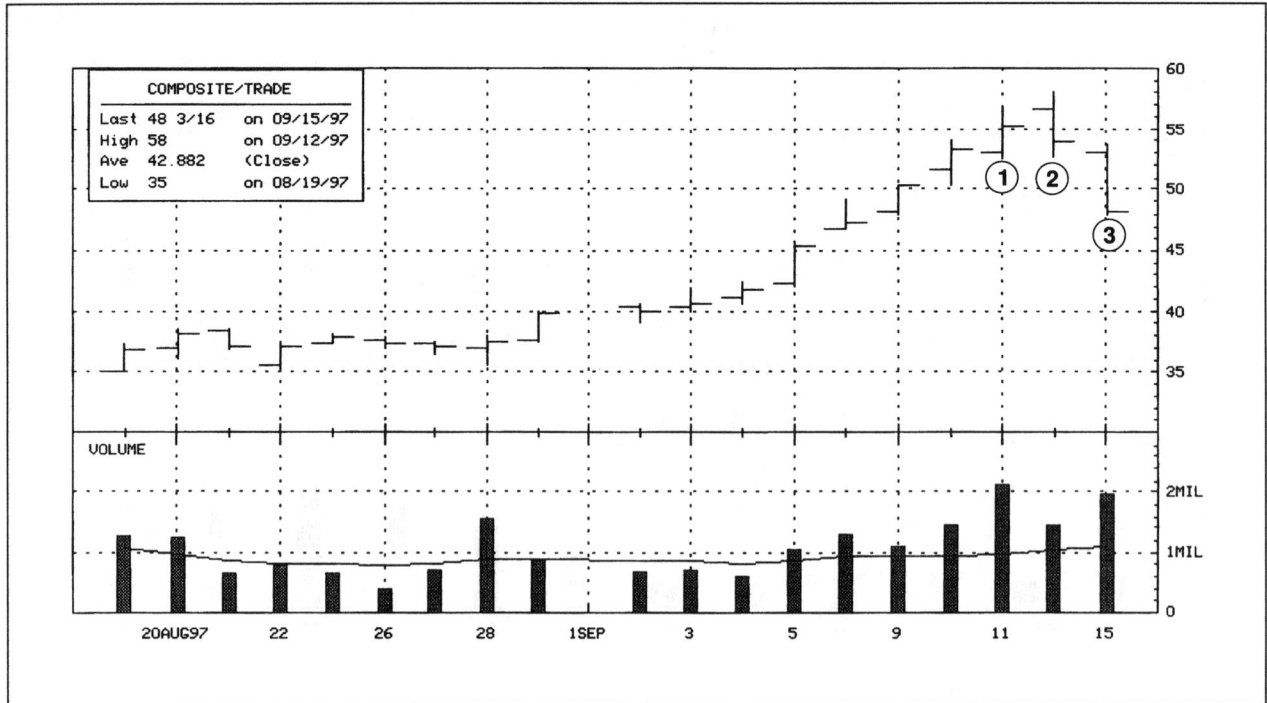

1.   A new high on double its average daily volume.

2.   Yahoo closes below its open.

3.   Sell short at 53 and it closes at 48 13/16.

FIGURE 13.3   Western Digital

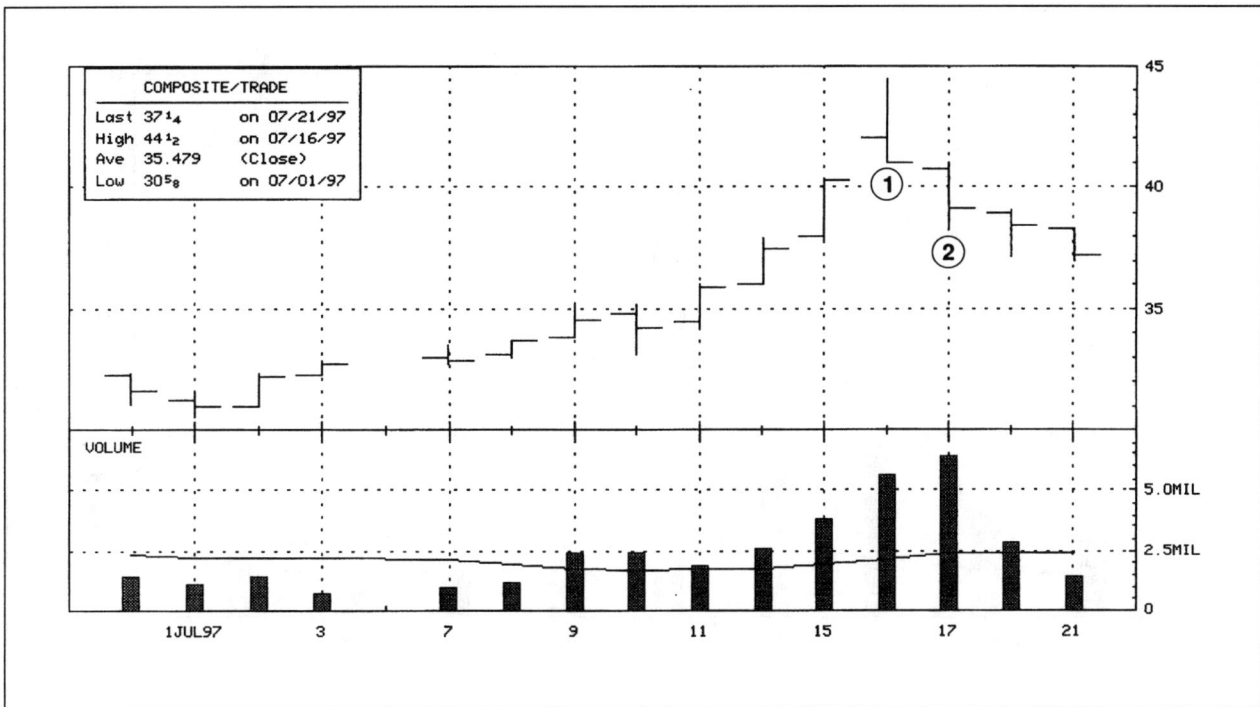

1.   On July 16, WDC makes a new high, has volume of double its daily average, and the close is below its open.

2.   We sell short on the opening at 40 3/4 and the stock closes 3 1/2 points lower two days later.

FIGURE 13.4   Fila

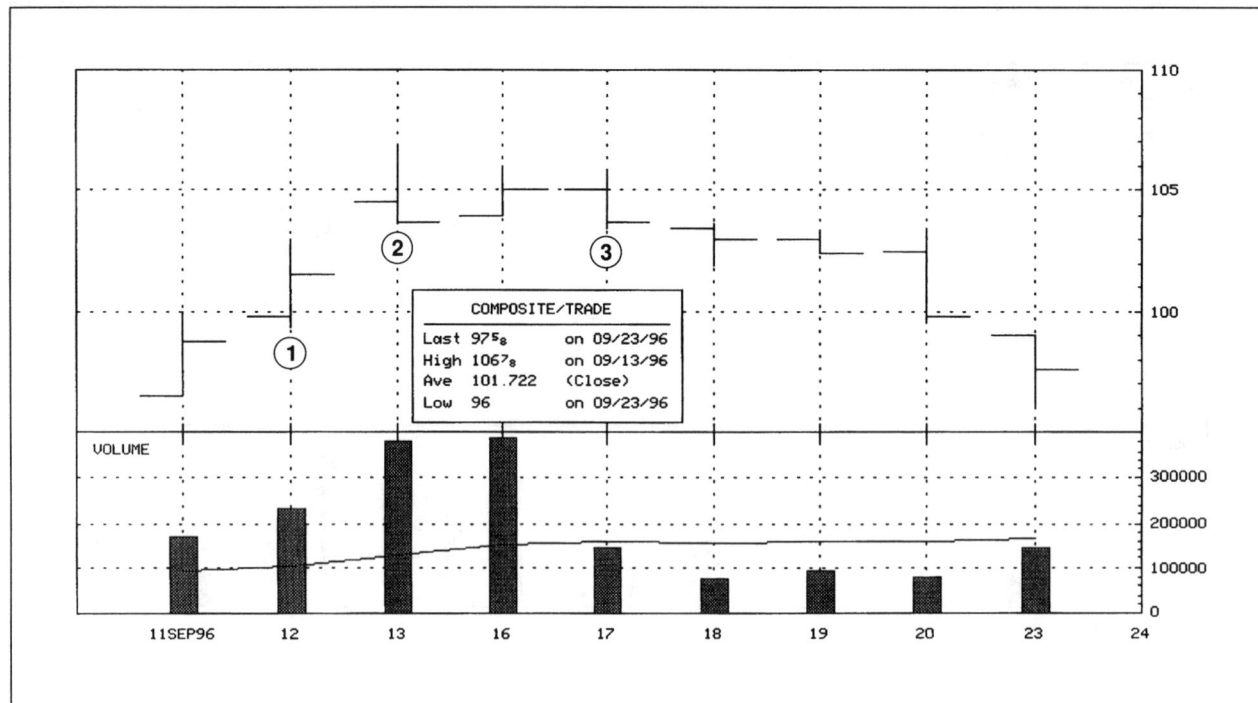

Here is an example of the DVMT catching the all-time high on Fila.

1.   A new high on double the average daily volume.

2.   A close below the open.

3.   Sell short at 103 3/8 and we catch the absolute top. In fact, a year later Fila traded under 30.

SUMMARY

If you have historical data going back into the 40s, 50s, 60s, and 70s, you will see this setup identify short-term tops over and over again. Tubb's observations of 60 years ago, when tightened with our rules, make this an excellent pattern with which to short stocks.

CHAPTER 14

TRADING EQUITIES WITH THE CONNORS VIX REVERSAL

With a methodology that does as good a job of identifying short-term highs and lows in the stock market as the three Connors VIX Reversal strategies do, it only makes sense to identify those stocks in the Dow and/or S&P 500 that are likely to lead the markets up or down.

In an upcoming chapter, "Maximizing Profits in Short-Term Market Declines," I highlight strategies to exploit declining markets. As you will see, the interest-sensitive stocks, brokerage stocks, and to a lesser extent technology stocks tend to lead the market both higher and lower.

In order to fully maximize our profits in equities when a CVR signal occurs, we want to be in these market leaders. In my opinion, the two best stocks to trade for this are Merrill Lynch and Intel. Both provide excellent, consistent market leadership at extreme market levels and both are weighted heavily in many of the indices.

Now, the answer to the question of how to best trade these stocks: exactly as you would trade the futures—buy (sell) on the close and hold for three days with some sort of protective stop in place. Because the VIX closes at

4:00 P.M., you will need to front-run the signal by a few minutes to assure getting filled.

Let's look at the results over a 15-month period using the CVR I for both Merrill Lynch and Intel. Please note that in the following results slippage and commission were not included, but the results should give you a rough guide to performance.

MERRILL LYNCH

Date	Signal	Entry Price	Exit Price	P	L
01/05/96	B	51 1/2	49 3/8		2 1/8
02/07/96	B	60 1/4	61 7/8	1 5/8	
02/14/96	B	60 7/8	57 3/4		3 1/8
02/29/96	B	57 5/8	60 1/4	2 5/8	
04/04/96	SS (1 DAY)	61 5/8	58 1/2	3 1/8	
04/08/96	B	58 1/2	56 1/4		2 1/4
04/22/96	SS	60 5/8	60	5/8	
06/07/96	B	64 7/8	63		1 7/8
07/16/96	B	58 3/8	59 1/2	1 1/8	
07/24/96	B	58 3/4	58 7/8	1/8	
09/03/96	B	62	61 3/8		5/8
09/27/96	B	65 1/4	69	3 3/4	
10/07/96	SS	71 5/8	68 3/8	3 1/4	
10/17/96	SS	69 1/4	67 5/8	1 5/8	
10/23/96	B	68 5/8	67 5/8		1
10/31/96	B	70 1/4	74 1/2	4 1/4	
11/15/96	SS	78 3/4	78 1/4	1/2	
12/04/96	B	79	79 3/4	3/4	
12/13/96	B	78 5/8	80 1/8	1 1/2	
01/02/97	B	79 3/4	80 3/8	5/8	
01/23/97	SS	84 1/8	80 1/8	4	
02/26/97	B	98 3/8	97 7/8		1/2
02/28/97	B	96	98 1/2	2 1/2	
03/20/97	B	91 3/4	91 7/8	1/8	
03/27/97	SS	87 1/2	85 7/8	1 5/8	

Total Results: **18 profitable**
                              7 unprofitable
                              + 22 1/4 points

INTEL

Date	Signal	Entry Price	Exit Price	P	L
				P/L	
01/05/96	B	57 1/2	54 1/8		3 3/8
02/07/96	B	58 1/4	58 1/4	—	—
02/14/96	B	58	57 7/8		1/8
02/29/96	B	58 7/8	55 3/8		3 1/2
04/04/96	SS (1 DAY)	59 1/4	60 5/8		1 3/8
04/08/96	B	60 5/8	60 1/2		1/8
04/22/96	SS	67 3/4	69 5/8		1 7/8
06/07/96	B	75 1/4	76 3/4	1 1/2	
07/16/96	B	70	72 3/4	2 3/4	
07/24/96	B	69	72 7/8	2 7/8	
09/03/96	B	81 5/8	81 1/4		3/8
09/27/96	B	96 7/8	99	2 1/8	
10/07/96	SS	104 3/4	99 7/8	4 7/8	
10/17/96	SS	110 3/4	105 1/2	5 1/4	
10/23/96	B	109 3/8	106		3 3/8
10/31/96	B	109 7/8	114	4 1/8	
11/15/96	SS	115 7/8	120 7/8		5
12/04/96	B	129 1/2	130 1/8	5/8	
12/13/96	B	132 3/8	135 3/4	3 3/8	
01/02/97	B	130 3/8	143 3/8	13	
01/23/97	SS	151 3/4	151	3/4	
02/20/97	B	149 7/8	148 7/8		1
02/28/97	B	141 7/8	149 1/2	7 5/8	
03/20/97	B	133 1/4	133 1/4	—	—
03/27/97	SS	139 1/8	137	2 1/8	

Total Results:

13 profitable
10 unprofitable
2 breakeven
+30 7/8 points

SUMMARY

You can select your own leaders to trade this strategy with but I believe that these two stocks move most consistently with the overall market. Also, as a reminder, always place protective stops to protect yourself!

CHAPTER 15

TORPEDOES

"Torpedoes" is an intraday strategy created by Jeff Cooper. Torpedoes are volatile, market-leading stocks which rise in spite of a sharply declining market. These stocks are on a mission of their own and tend to lead the rise most dramatically when the market bounces back.

Let's look at how to identify Torpedoes and how best to trade them.

FOR BUYS (THERE ARE NO SHORT-SALE TORPEDOES)

1. Identify the recent market leaders. These are usually higher priced, big cap names such as Microsoft, IBM, 3COM, Intel, Dell, etc. Another group of names to identify is the higher-priced, highly volatile names that can be screened using the "Trading Where The Action Is" chapter.

2. Wait for the stock market to be down at least 1 percent in the first hour of trading. At that time, look for any market leader or highly volatile stock that is defying the trend. This means stocks which are up for the day or down only a small amount.

3. Here is where it gets a bit subjective. If the overall market begins to bounce back, buy the strongest stock(s) from Rule 2. The key to this strategy is the initial protective stop you are using. *Your risk should*

be only one point from your entry. If you are stopped out, it is OK to re-enter if the stock begins rising again.

4.   When this strategy works, it often works big. On numerous occasions, I have seen Jeff make between 2 and 5 points within a few hours.

Here are three examples.

FIGURE 15.1   Vitesse Semiconductor

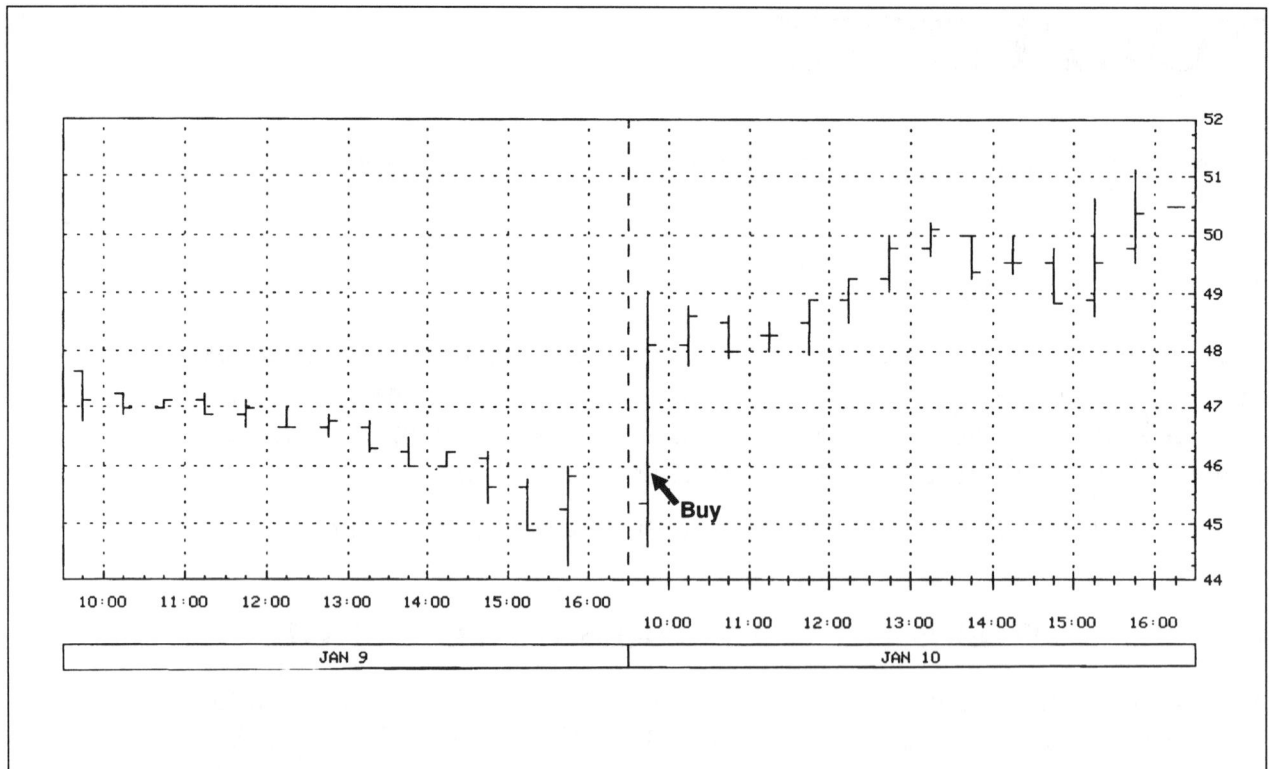

In January 1997, Vitesse Semiconductor, a *highly* volatile NASDAQ stock, opened down only 3/8 point in spite of the S&P's trading more than ten points lower near the opening. The stock immediately reversed and proceeded to trade 3 points higher with 30 minutes and 4 11/16 points higher for the day. This action is the epitome of the Perfect Torpedo.

FIGURE 15.2 Paccar

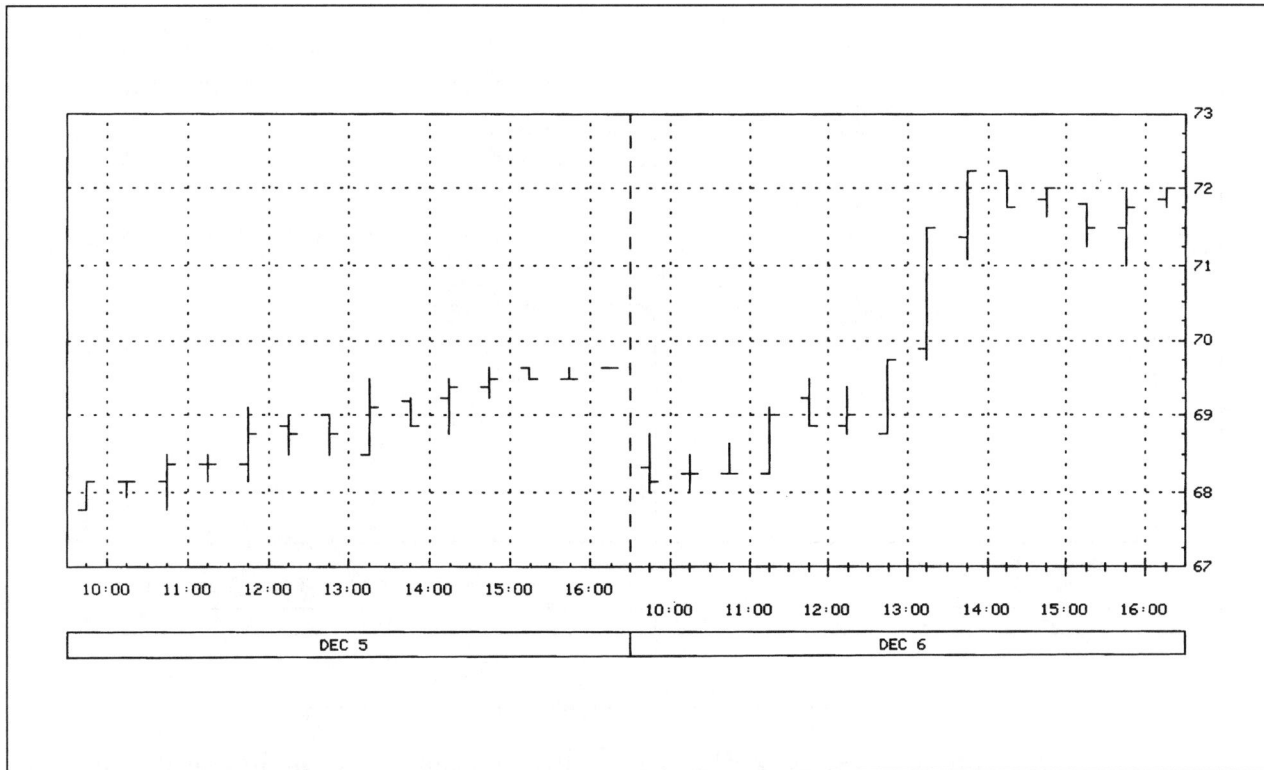

On December 6, 1996, the DOW trades 140 points lower but Paccar, a volatile NASDAQ stock, trades only 1 3/4 points lower. Within 90 minutes, the stock starts moving higher and proceeds to trade up for the day in spite of the market closing down approximately 60 points for the day.

FIGURE 15.3 Maxim

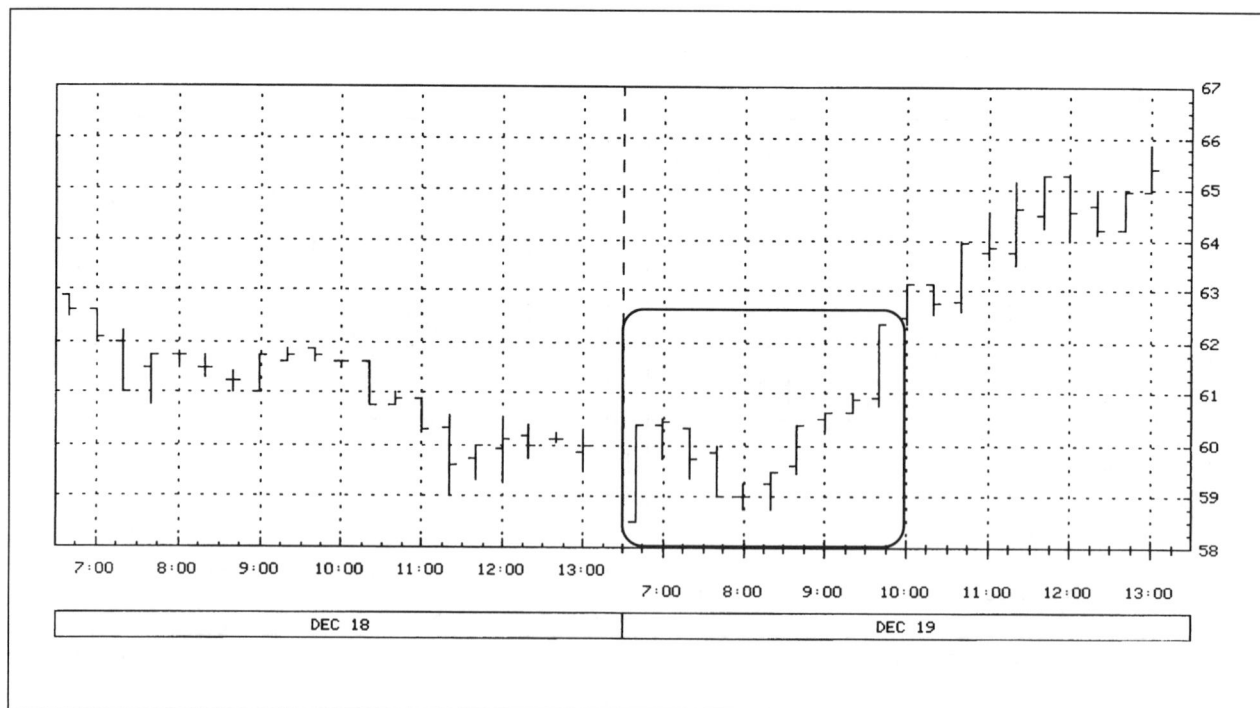

On December 19, 1997, the S&P's dropped as much as 30 points intraday while the Dow was down as much as 265 points.

Maxim (MXIM), after selling lower, shrugs off the market decline and begins rising quickly.

In spite of the day's sell-off, this Torpedo rises more than 5 3/8 points for the day.

SUMMARY

This is a volatile strategy and one that leads to quick profits. Remember to keep your initial stop tight and let your profits run when they occur.

SECTION FIVE

OPTIONS STRATEGIES

▪ ▪

A few years ago, the options columnist for Barrons ran a survey of its quarter million readers. He asked if any non-market maker could prove that he or she had made money trading options for the past three consecutive years. I am recalling this story from memory, but as I recollect, only one person (an elderly gentlemen) could prove he was a three-years-in-a-row profitable trader.

The odds are greatly stacked against your success in trading options. Most options (other than the OEX) trade with a 10 percent spread and with slippage and commission added in, the "take" is just too large.

With that said, I believe the option game can be beaten, but only by traders who are patient enough to wait for the few times when prices are out of line and can be exploited.

Three out of the following four chapters use my favorite topic, volatility, to identify options that are overpriced. Before using these strategies make sure you have the capital to not only handle the margin requirements, but also the drawdowns that are inherent in any option selling strategy.

CHAPTER 16

TRADING VOLATILITY WITH OPTIONS

* *

This chapter will focus on a strategy to capture option profits with volatility. It was created by a friend of mine, Professor Fernando Diz of Syracuse University. Unlike most financial market research generated from the academic world, Fernando's research is applicable in the real world. Not only is his volatility strategy conceptually correct, but just as important, he and I have both traded it successfully.

The following methodology is one of the most complicated in the book. Because it is such a strong strategy, though, I feel it is well worth the effort to learn and have as part of your overall trading arsenal.

Volatility is becoming one of the most useful areas of research for trading. There are two important reasons why this is true. First, most indicators used in technical analysis and pattern recognition can be reduced to different measures of volatility. Second, volatility has properties that make it an invaluable market timing tool. If you combine these two facts, the importance of volatility research for trading becomes readily apparent.

In this chapter we shall focus on the use of historical volatility as a market timing tool for trading options. To understand how volatility can be profitably used, we need to briefly describe two of its most important properties; *persistence,* and *mean-reversion.* Whenever we talk about volatility we shall refer to the annualized standard deviation of returns computed with daily closing prices.

Properties of Volatility Useful for Trading

The first important property of volatility is its *persistence.* Persistence means that a high volatility day tends to be followed by another high volatility day and that a low volatility day tends to be followed by a low volatility day. Another way of defining persistence is that when volatility starts moving in one direction, it keeps moving in that direction. *Trends in volatility are more predictable than trends in prices.* The degree of persistence in volatility is measured by its autocorrelation. Figure 16.1 contains a graph of the average autocorrelation for COMEX gold for the period 1994–96.

FIGURE 16.1 Autocorrelation of COMEX Gold Daily Volatility 1994–1996

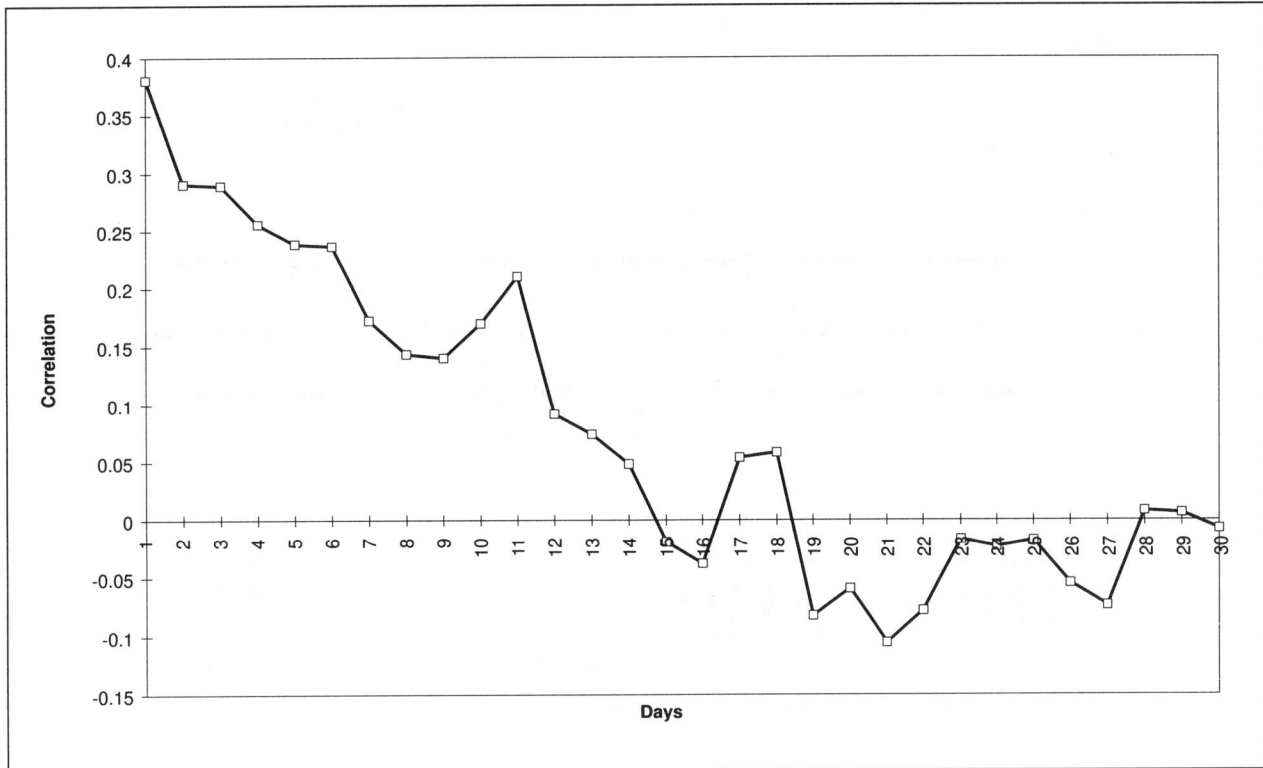

What Figure 16.1 tells you is how related is today's volatility to the volatility any number of days in the past. The higher level of correlation at lower lags indicates that today's volatility is more related to nearby volatility than distant volatility. Persistence is important because it makes volatility predictable. *Unlike price forecasts, one day ahead forecasts of volatility can be very accurate.*

The second important property of volatility is its tendency to oscillate around an average level. When volatility gets too far away from this average level it tends to go back to it. This is known as *mean-reversion. Once volatility starts moving in one direction it tends to keep moving in the same direction so that once reversion begins it tends to continue.* Figure 16.2 illustrates these points. The horizontal line in the middle of the graph is the level around which volatility oscillates. The two bands around this line indicate levels of volatility that are considered high or low.

FIGURE 16.2   10-Day Historical Volatility for COMEX Division Gold for 1994–95

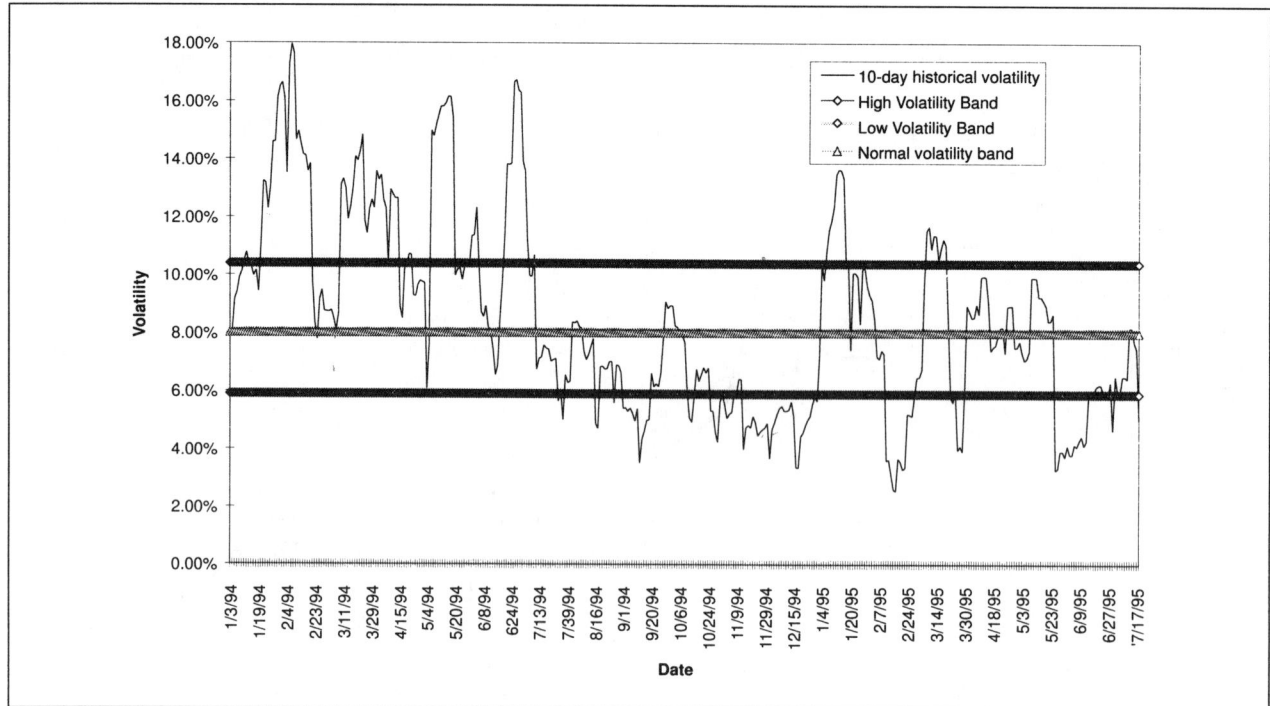

As you can see in Figure 16.2, when volatility reaches levels that are *too high* or *too low* it tends to go back to the average level. Note also that when volatility reaches high or low levels it tends to stay there for some-time before it returns to *normal* levels.

Using Volatility to Trade Options

Periods of volatility expansion eventually end and lead to mean-reversion and volatility contraction. *We have found that when short-term volatility (measured by the 10-day historical volatility) reaches 1.65 times the 100-day historical reading or higher, mean-reversion and volatility contraction are near.* How can mean-reversion be used profitably when it leads to volatility contraction? We have found that as mean-reversion begins and short-term volatility starts contracting two important things happen:

1.   Markets tend to move sideways for a period that can be as long as the full mean-reversion process.

2.   Under special conditions, option implied volatility will follow in the direction of the reversion or in the worst case will not expand.

FIGURE 16.3 10-Day versus 100-Day Historical Volatility for February 96 COMEX Gold 9/20/95–12/13/95

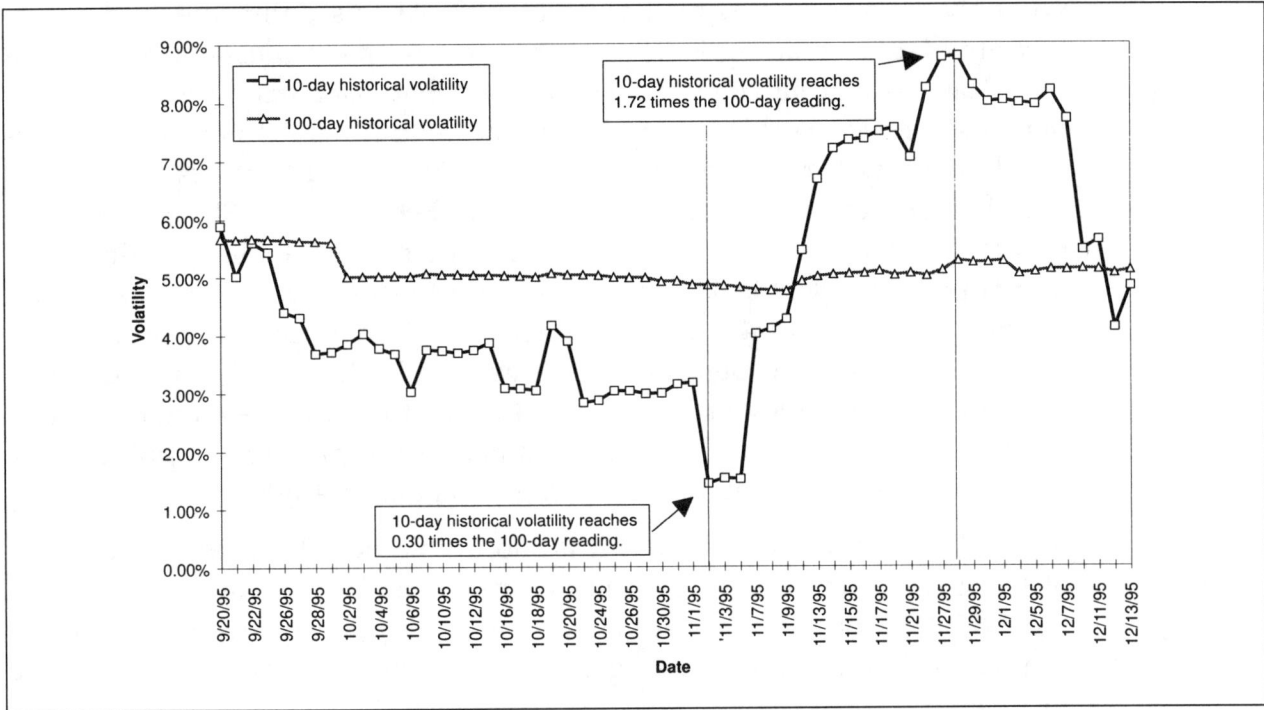

FIGURE 16.4 COMEX Division Gold February 1996—9/20/95–12/13/95

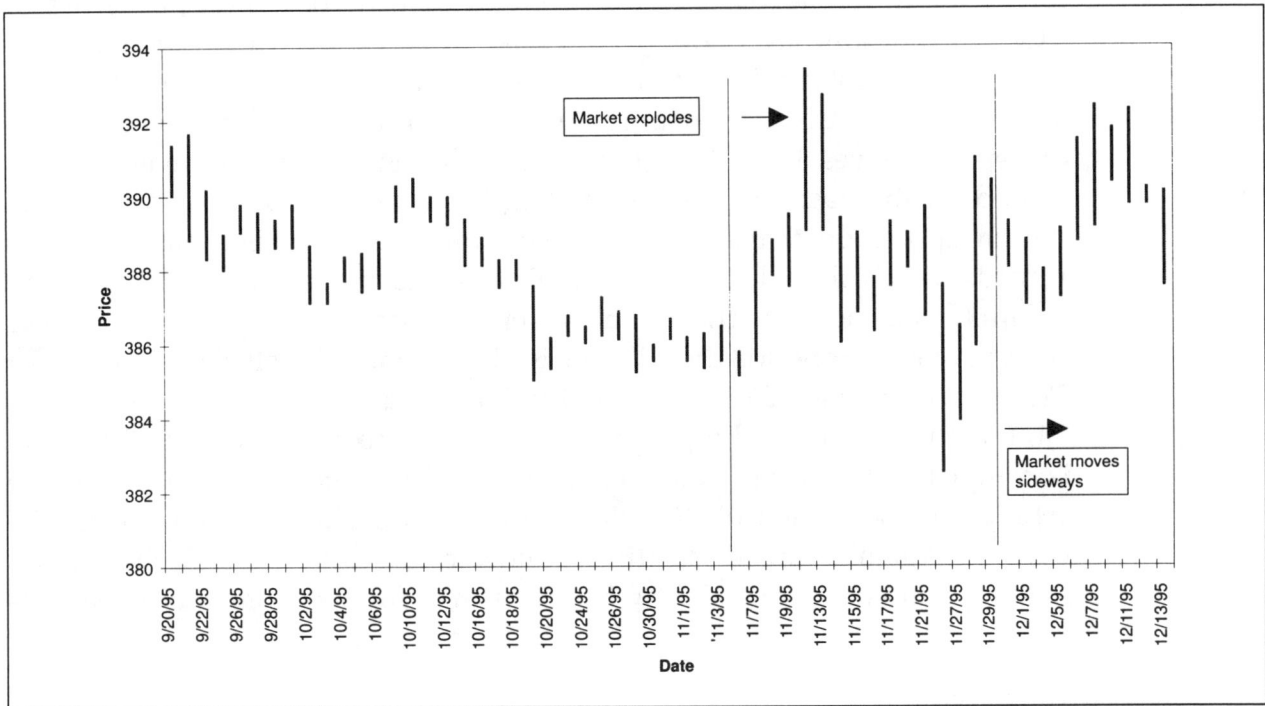

Figures 16.3 and 16.4 illustrate this phenomenon in COMEX gold. Short-term volatility continues to expand until the 10-day/100-day historical volatility ratio reaches a maximum of 1.72. At this point, the 10-day historical volatility reading is 8.7 percent. *We wait for two down-tick moves in the 10-day reading for confirmation that mean-reversion and volatility contraction have started.* At this point, the 10-day reading is 8.3 percent. The implied volatility for the February 96, 380 puts and 410 calls is 8.1 percent and 13.0 percent respectively. We sell the February 96, 380 put for 140 points and the February 410 call for 140 points for a total credit of 280 points per strangle. On December 12, nine trading days later, the 10-day reading collapsed to 4.1 percent and the option implied volatilities are 7.85 percent and 12.0 percent respectively. In both the call and put cases implied volatility moved in the direction of the mean-reversion. At this time we buy back the calls for 70 points and the puts for 80 points for a total profit before commissions of 130 points per strangle.

Silver differs from gold in that it is more volatile. The average volatility of COMEX silver was 29 percent compared to 18 percent for gold over the 1975-1995 period. One advantage of trading a more volatile contract is that option volatility strategies, like writing strangles, can be more profitable.

Figures 16.5 and 16.6 contain an example of the setup needed to initiate a volatility trade using options. On March 7, 1995 the 10-day historical volatility reading reaches 1.81. We have found that the reversion properties of COMEX division silver are very similar to those of gold. When the 10-day/100-day historical volatility ratio reaches about 1.65 or higher, the likelihood of mean-reversion is large. As with gold, we wait for two successive down-tick moves before we have confirmation that mean-reversion has started. In this case, the 10-day reading has a down-tick day on March 8, but an up-tick on March 9. On March 13 a mean-reversion signal is confirmed. At this time the 10-day volatility is 36.5 percent while the 100-day volatility is 23 percent. The volatility implied by the May 95, 525 call is 30.1 percent and the one for the 425 put is 25 percent. We sell the 525 calls for 370 points and the 425 puts for 160 points for a total credit of 530 points. On March 23, eight trading days later, reversion to a normal volatility level is complete. The 10-day volatility reading is 20.8 percent. The 525 calls are selling for an implied of 26 percent and the puts for an implied of 22.5 percent. Again, implied volatility followed the reversion of the 10-day reading and collapsed. We buy back the calls for 100 points and the puts

FIGURE 16.5 10-Day versus 100-Day Historical Volatility for COMEX Silver May 1995
2/23/95–3/21/95

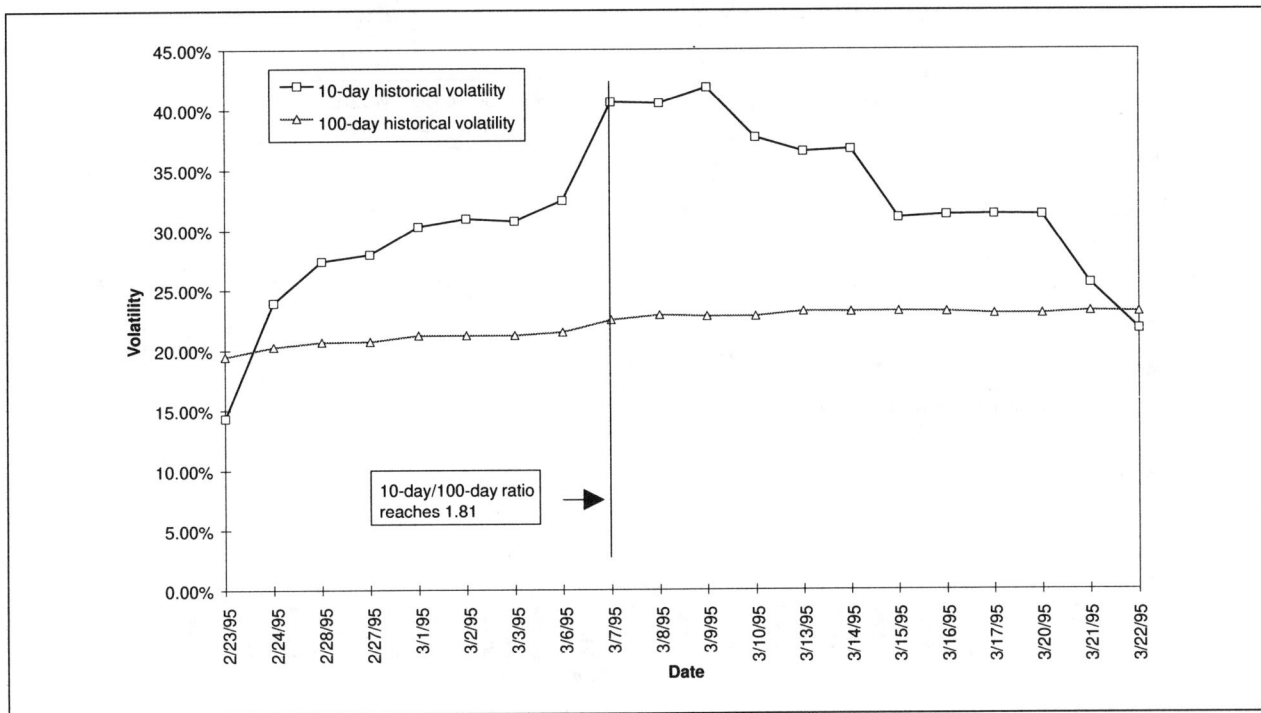

FIGURE 16.6 COMEX Division May 1995 Silver—2/23/95–3/22/95

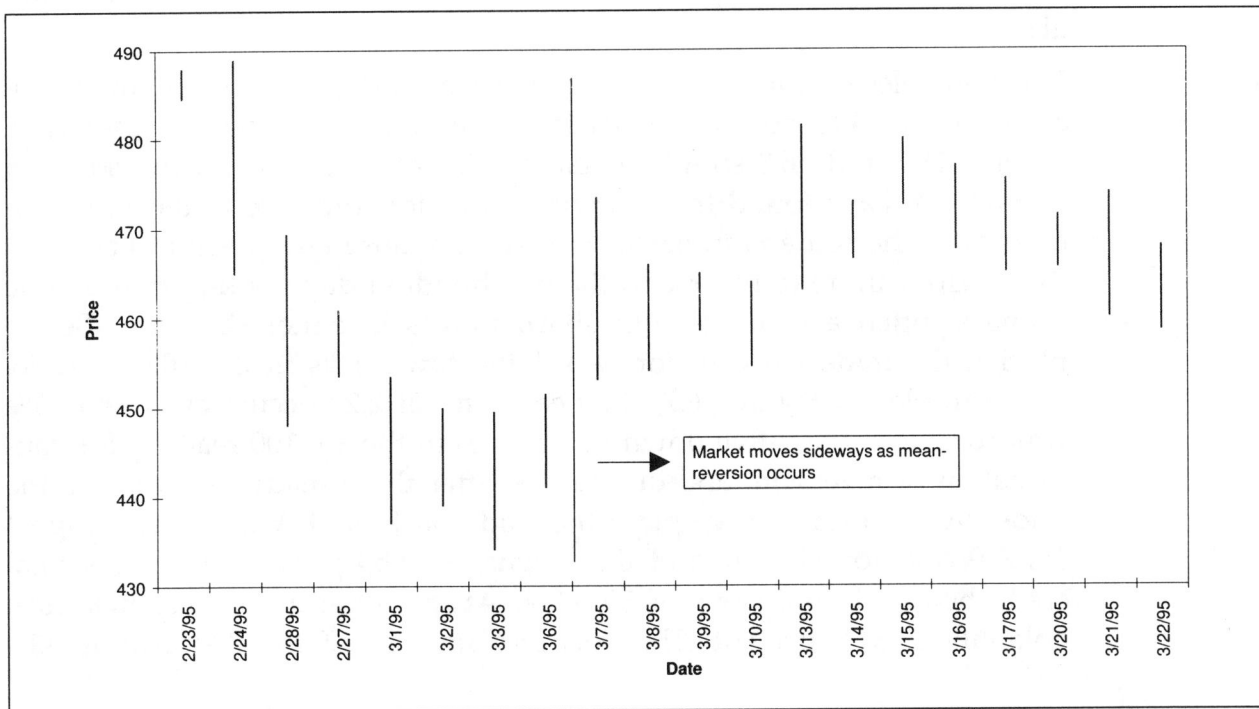

FIGURE 16.7   10-Day versus 100-Day Historical Volatility for August 1994 Soybeans
5/26/94–6/24/94

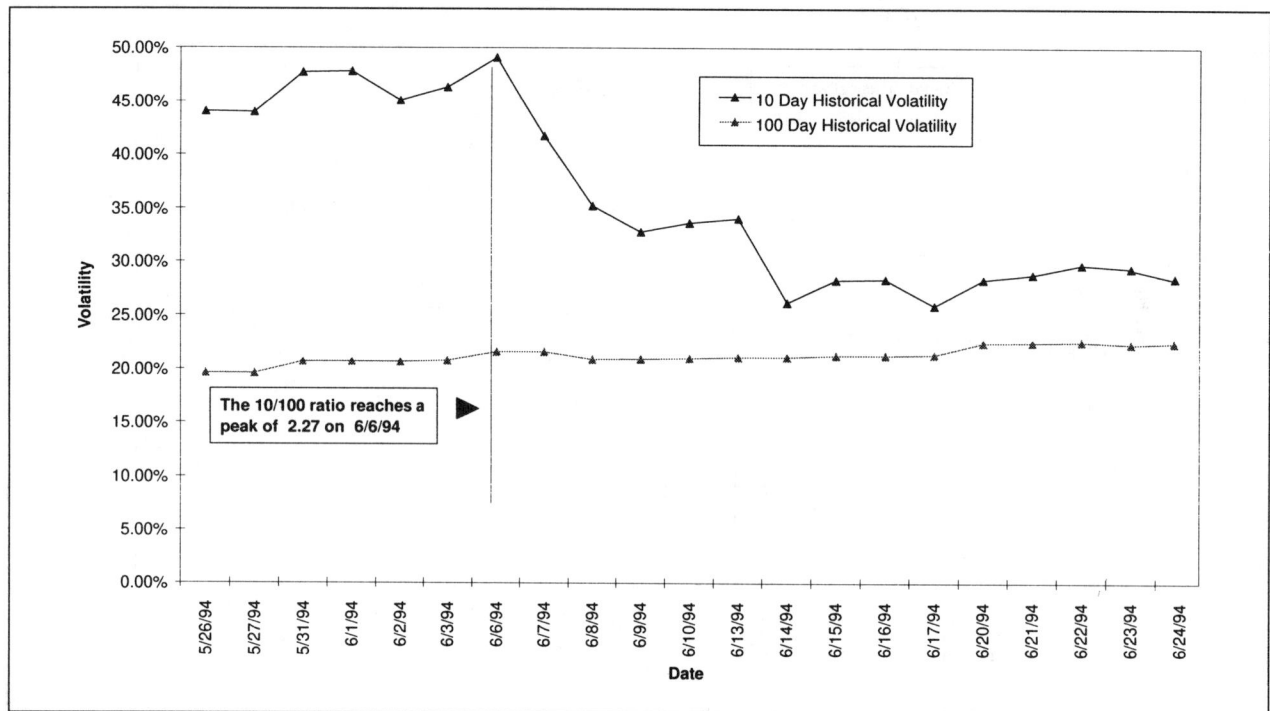

for 70 points for a total profit before commissions of 360 points per strangle.

The principles which these trades are based on depend only on the properties of volatility, not on the particular commodity under consideration.
Figures 16.7 and 16.8 show the same principles at work in the soybean
market. We have found that if reversion is not complete in ten to fifteen
days after the trade is initiated, one should close any position based on
this setup. Failure to reverse to the one hundred day reading in this time
frame is often associated with sharp moves in either direction. Before
placing the trade we wait for two daily down-ticks in the 10/100 ratio.
For example, on Figure 16.7, the peak ratio of 2.27 occurs on June 6. We
wait for two consecutive down-tick moves in the 10/100 reading for confirmation of reversion, and on the day after these readings we place the
trade. In this example we place the trade on June 9. We sell the August
94, 700 calls for 21 3/4¢ and the August 94, 650 puts for 18¢ for a total
credit before commissions of 39 3/4¢. At this time the 10-day historical
volatility is 32.8 percent. The volatility implied of the 700 calls is 42.4

FIGURE 16.8 August 1994 Soybeans—5/26/94–6/24/94

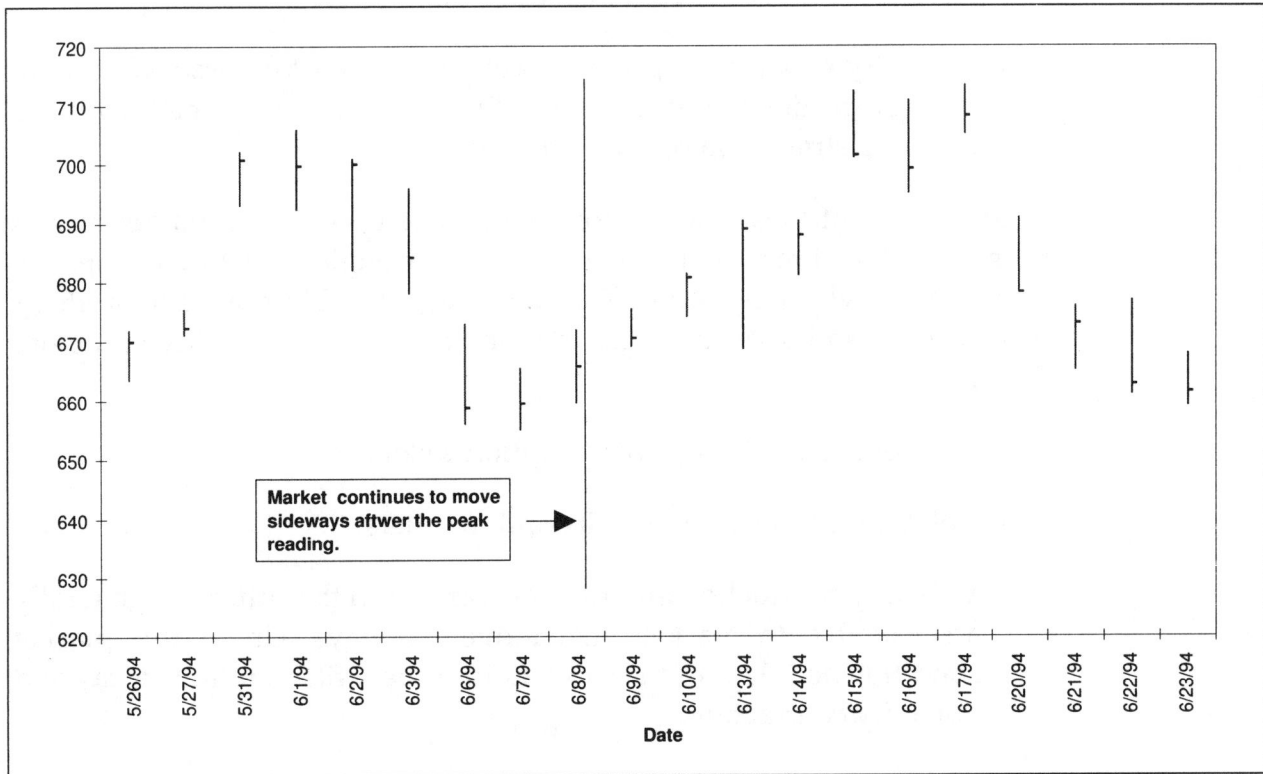

percent and the one implied by the 650 puts is 34 percent, both above the 10-day reading. Fourteen days after this trade was initiated (June 23), reversion to the 100-day reading has not been completed. We close the position by buying back the 650 puts for 13¢ and the 700 calls for 11 3/4¢ netting a profit before commissions of 15¢ per strangle. At this time the 10-day reading is 29.4 percent, while the volatility implied by the 650 puts and the 700 calls are 30.5 percent and 43.2 percent respectively.

At this point the reader may wonder why we have not talked about *buying* strangles when volatility reverts from a very low level. There are four reasons why, in general, buying strangles is not a profitable volatility strategy.

• Time decay works against option buyers.

• In periods of very low short-term volatility (measured by the 10-day historical volatility), implied volatility is often higher than the 10-day reading.

- Volatility expansion and time decay work in opposite directions on long positions somewhat offsetting each other.

- Volatility expansion and mean-reversion are often associated with strong directional moves. Strong directional moves affect the options in a long strangle in opposite directions.

The total effect of these four factors is that even when the market moves strongly in one direction the value of the strangle will not change by much. This is why long strangles are not a profitable volatility strategy. On the other hand short strangles are one of the best volatility strategies because:

- Time decay works in favor of option sellers.

- Volatility contraction benefits option sellers.

- Volatility contraction and mean-reversion in the futures is generally associated with markets that move sideways. Under this market condition both legs of the short strangle benefit from time decay and volatility contraction.

SUMMARY

Identifying periods of high volatility and waiting for the reversion to begin, can be a fairly low risk methodology to capture overpriced option premium. To ensure profitability however, it is necessary to understand the properties of volatility in the markets that you trade.

CHAPTER 17

TRADING OPTIONS WITH THE CONNORS VIX REVERSAL

....

Here we look at another application for the Connors VIX Reversal (CVR). In this chapter we will explore the best ways to use the method for trading S&P and OEX options.

As you are aware, the VIX is a measurement of expected future volatility (implied volatility) for the markets. When this expected future volatility is wrong and turns at extreme levels—hence our indicator—the prices of the underlying options adjust sharply. We will look at how to exploit these adjustments and how to best trade them.

In Chapter 2 we looked at the Connors VIX Reversal trading the S&P futures contract outright. There we saw that over the past four years, prices moved in our favor better than 60 percent of the time over a short-term period. We also discussed how the Connors VIX Reversal is a way to measure "extreme sentiment points" in the market. These extreme points are accompanied by over-priced options at high VIX readings and under-priced options at low VIX readings.

This next point is critical to understand if your goal is mastery of this subject: when the VIX rises in value, it means that the implied volatility is rising. When the implied volatility is rising, the value of the options is rising (we will leave time decay aside for the moment). On the other hand, when the VIX declines, the implied volatility is declining, and therefore the value of the options is also declining.

Now, let's put the above concept together with what we saw in the VIX chapters: *When the Connors VIX Reversal triggers a signal, we are not only predicting price movement, we are also predicting implied volatility movement.* When a buy signal is triggered, not only is there a solid chance that prices will move higher within a few trading sessions, but there is also a high probability that the implied volatility will be lower.

How do we combine these two factors and exploit them? *By selling puts!* Think of this conceptually. If we are correct, not only is time decay in our favor (three days), but more importantly, so are price and implied volatility. We have the best of all worlds—when the long CVR signal is correct, the price of the puts on the OEX and S&P will collapse.

Let's now look at the opposite signal: a Connors VIX Reversal sell signal. These signals occur less often, but they work nearly as well as the buy signals. Here our strategy is a bit different. Because a successful sell signal will be accompanied by a *rise* in implied volatility, we do not want to sell calls. It is more advisable to buy puts. The rise in implied volatility tends to offset the few days of time decay and we are therefore dealing only with price direction. When the signal is successful, prices will drop and our puts should rise in price.

The exit strategy on each should be consistent with the short-term hold recommended earlier. If, though, there is a sharp move in your favor earlier than this, I highly recommend taking profits on at least half the position.

As to which strike prices to trade, the answer is, "as near the money as possible" (within two to three strike prices). This is because the VIX measures the implied volatility of an at-the-money index option and these prices will move most in accordance with our theoretical concept.

Finally, stops or spreads must always be used, *especially* for naked puts. I recommend closing out the naked puts if prices reach your strike price, and recommend closing out the long puts if prices move 10 S&P points against you. This will allow you to maintain capital when the signal you've traded is a false one.

I realize the preceding is a lot of information to decipher, so please read and re-read it before applying it to the real world. The following examples should help make things easier to understand.

FIGURE 17.1 VIX—CBOE OEX Volatility Index

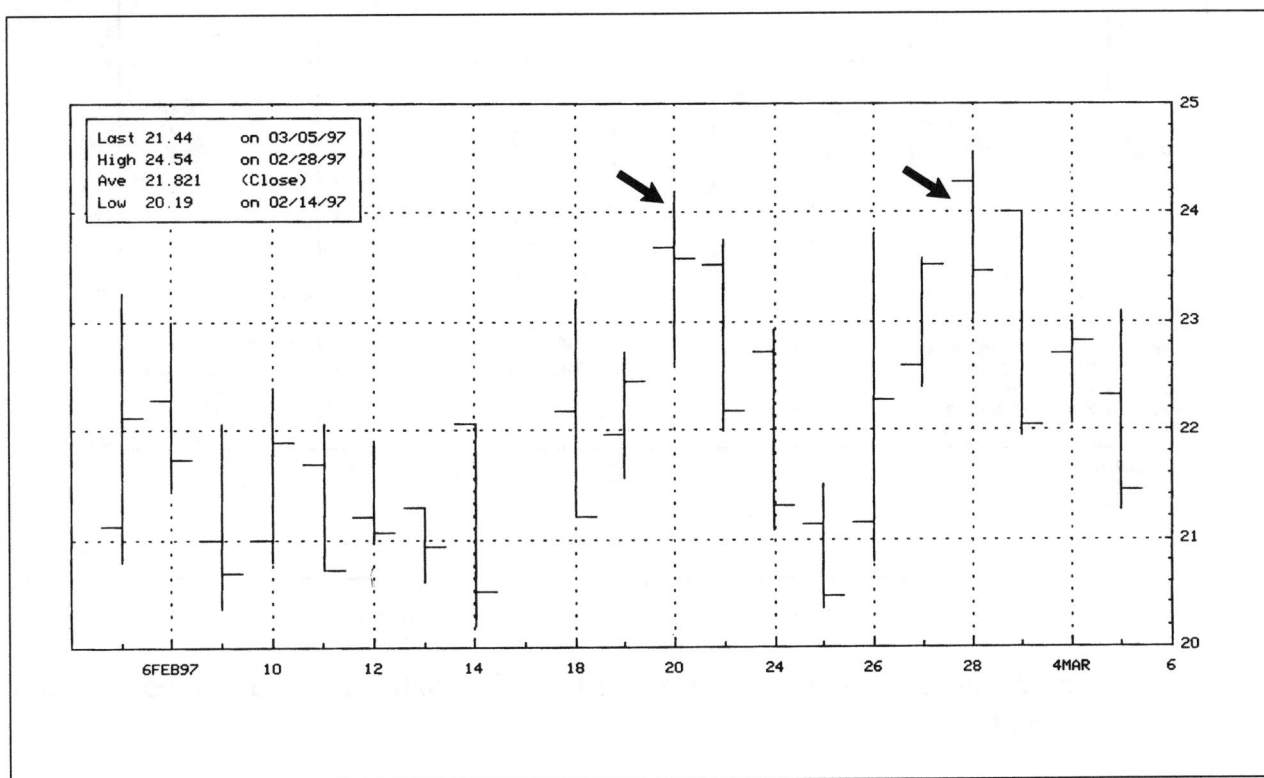

Here we have two Connors VIX Reversal I buy setups. The first occurs on the close on February 20 and the other on the close of February 28.

FIGURE 17.2   OEX—S&P 100 Index

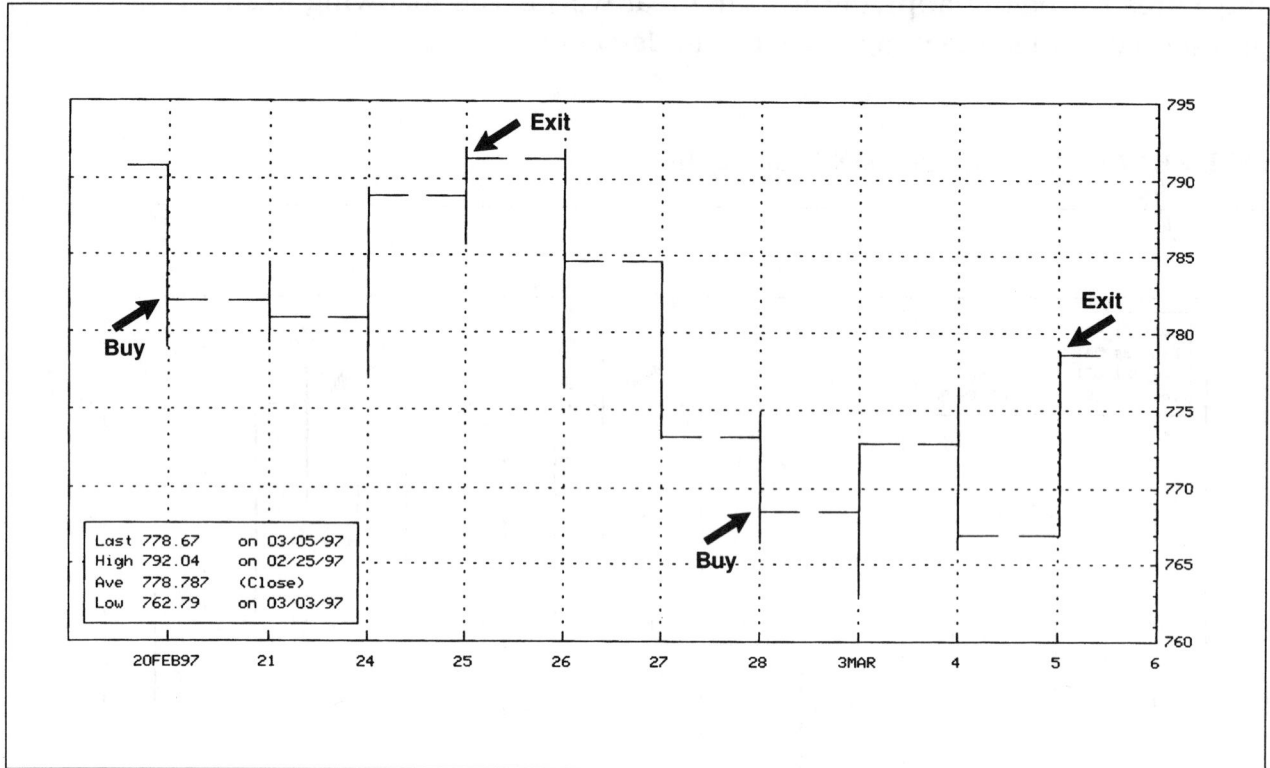

From the OEX market we can see how the cash index performed for each signal.

FIGURE 17.3   X1H7P 770—S&P 100 Index Options March 1997 770 Put

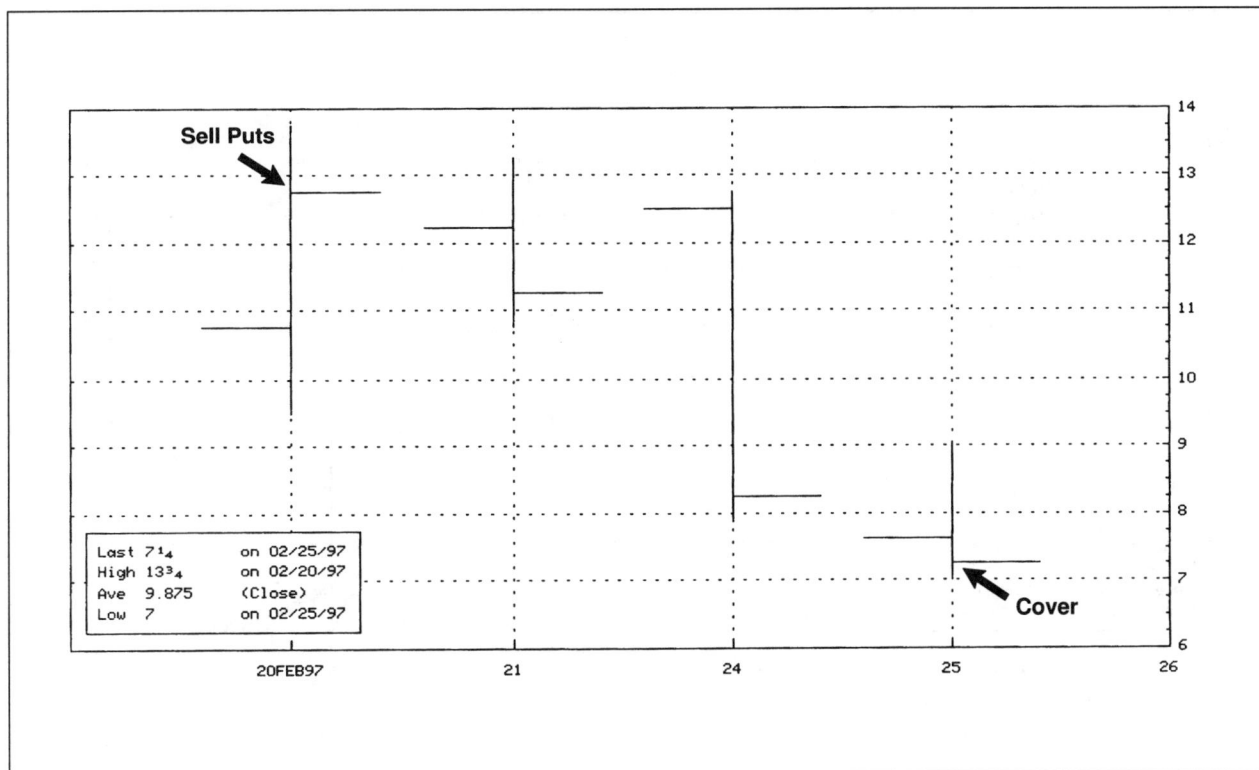

Now let's look at how our option strategies performed.

On the close of February 20, the OEX was trading at 781.98. We will look to sell the puts on the options that are two or three strike prices away. This means we will sell the closest month's 770 puts which close at 12 3/4. If the OEX index trades to under 770 within the next three days, we will close our position. On the first trading day (*see* Figure 17.2), prices move against us *but* the implied volatility drops (*see* Figure 17.1) and our short puts close at 11 1/4. On the second day, both prices and the implied volatility move in our favor and the puts lose another 3 points. Finally, on the third day, we again have implied volatility and prices move in our favor and the puts close at 7 1/4, 5 1/2 points under where we sold them.

FIGURE 17.4   X1H7P 760—S&P 100 Index Option March 1997 760 Put

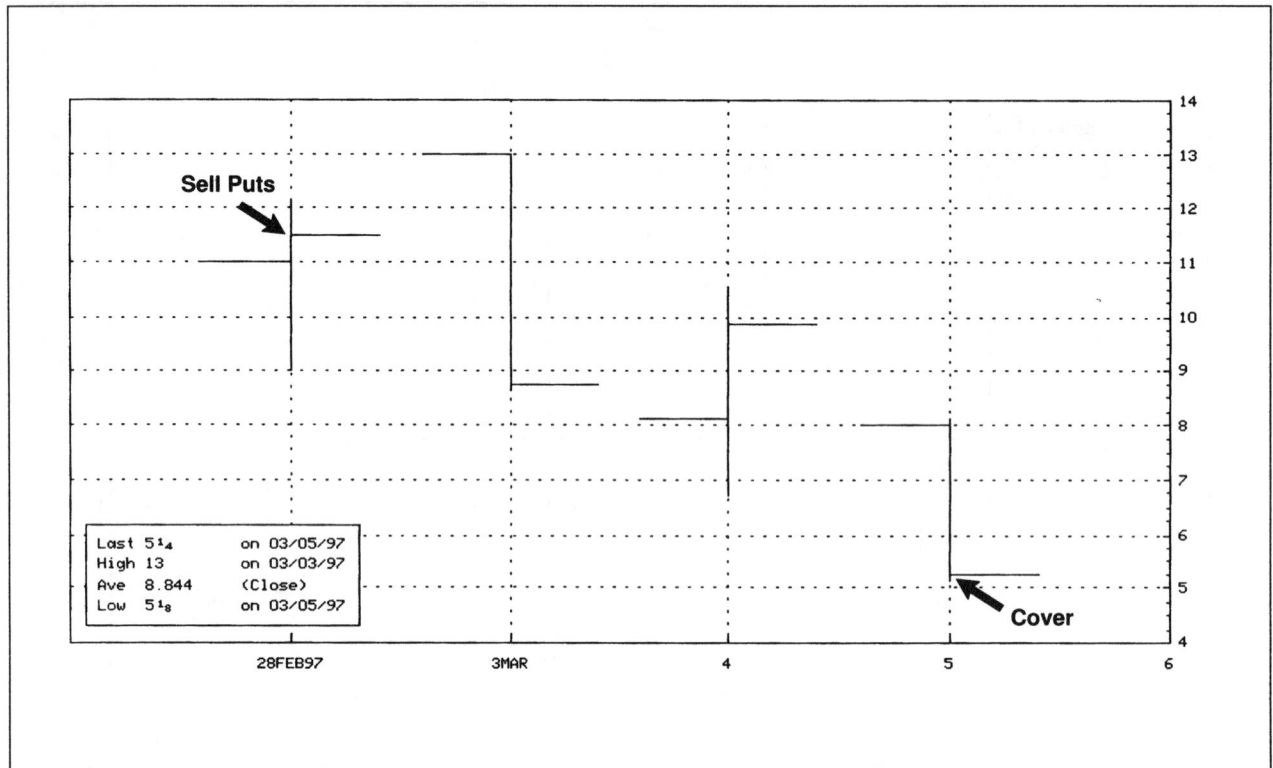

On February 28 (signal date) the OEX index closes at 768.54. We sell the March 760 puts on the close for 11 1/2. Should the index trade under 760 within the next three days, we will close out our position.

On the first day after initiating our position, we get the best of both worlds as prices rise and implied volatility drops. Our puts close at 8 3/4. The next day, both prices and implied volatility move sharply against us and our puts rise to 9 7/8, yet we are still profitable. On the third day, implied volatility drops and prices move strongly higher and the puts close at 5 1/4 for a 6 1/4 point profit.

SUMMARY

As solid as the results are trading the S&P futures contract outright, it is even better to use this indicator with options. One problem that may exist for some traders is the margin requirements needed to trade the OEX. Currently, (late 1997) it requires approximately $10,000 margin to trade one OEX contract. Unless you have a six-figure account, you are better served trading the S&P or Dow Jones futures and their underlying options. Even though the margin is approximately the same to trade the futures as it is the OEX, the value of each S&P contract point is much greater and therefore gives you greater leverage.

Finally, I of course need to remind you that there is unlimited risk in trading naked options and the possibility of a October 1987 scenario always exists. I suspect everyone knows their risk tolerance and will trade accordingly.

CHAPTER 18

OPTIONS ON STOCK SPLITS

▪ ▪

When P. T. Barnum coined the phrase "there is a sucker born every minute," he must have had in mind the unfortunate people who pay for beepers that alert them to buy stocks and options when a company announces a stock split. We will look at how you can exploit this phenomenon for your own personal gain.

Over the past few years, a handful of promoters have implored investors to buy stock whenever a company announces a stock split. Most recently I saw a "trainer" from one of these organizations on local television challenging viewers to name one stock which was trading lower one year after it was split (EFII had split seven months earlier and was down 65 percent, but I guess that's not a year).

Before I go on, I can tell you that looking back over the past fifty years, there is absolutely no built-in upward bias to stocks that split. Any recent bias is a direct result of the current bull market and it will be corrected in a bear market. Some of the services promoting this stock-split concept go further. They sell a monthly subscription service that "beeps" you and alerts you to a split. These services will tell you that the best way to take advantage of these splits is to buy calls.

Let's look at an example of what happens when hundreds of people get "beeped" at the same time.

FIGURE 18.1

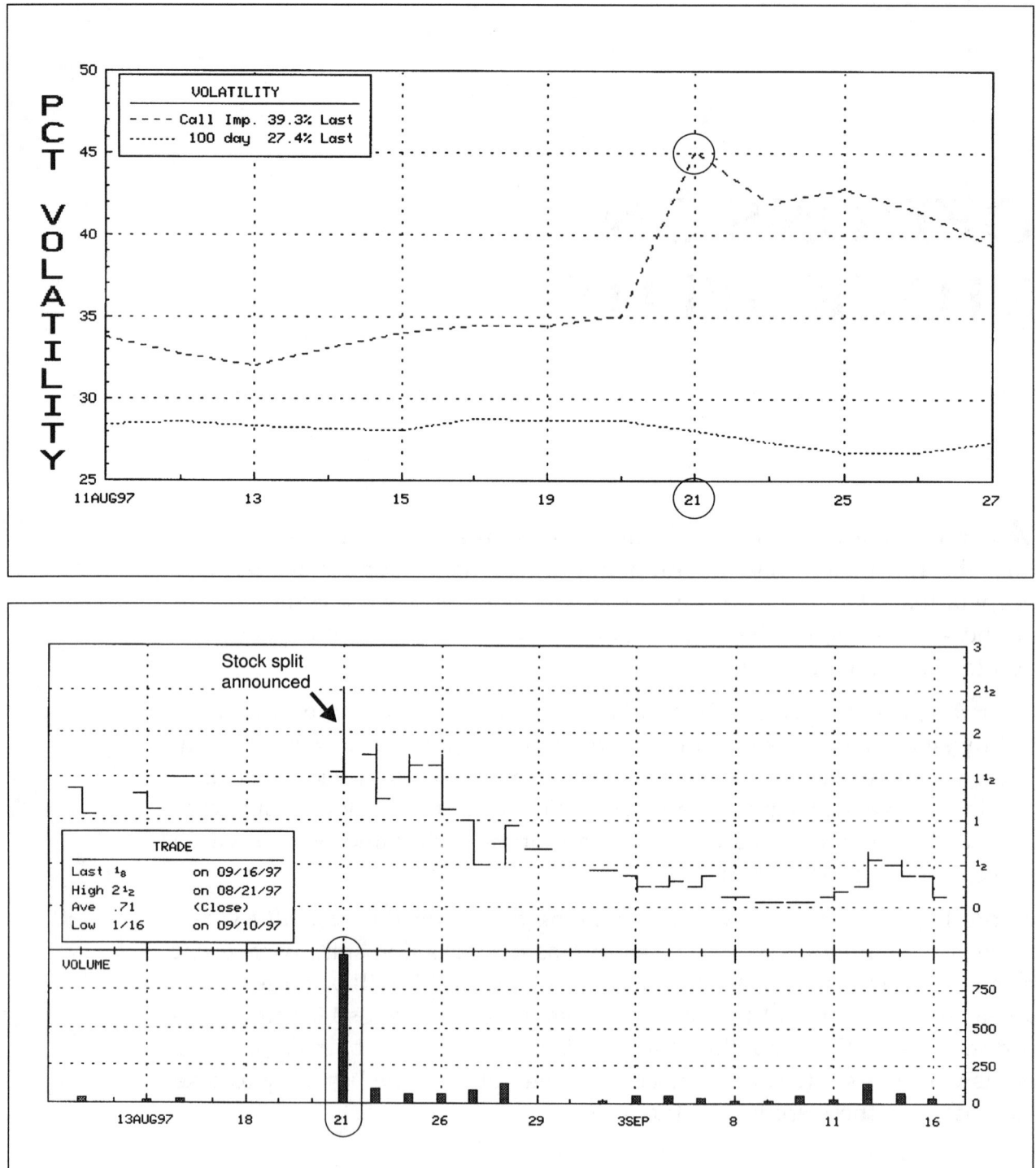

On August 21, 1997 Barnes and Noble announces a two-for-one stock split. Immediately the stock explodes higher, but what is more fascinating is what happens to the calls. The 100-day historical volatility reading for the stock was 27 percent. The implied volatility for the stock is high compared with the historical volatility from the very beginning, but when the split occurs, the prices of the calls explode and take the implied volatility to insane levels. The underlying stock would need to have a *much larger* than normal run to the upside just for the unsuspecting call buyers to break-even!

How can we best take advantage of this? By being kind enough to sell these beeper subscribers calls as they run up the price of the options. For those of you who cannot sit in front of a screen all day and look for these occurrences, don't despair. The options, as measured by implied volatility, tend to remain overvalued for a few days so you have an opportunity to do your homework at night.

SUMMARY

I do not know how long this phenomenon will last. Over time, most of the subscribers will lose money and quit. The strategy, though, is heavily marketed (via books and print ads) and I suspect it will be a while before the opportunity disappears.

A bigger picture point should be made. Even if this strategy disappears, history has shown that other irrational strategies will arise. *By being cognizant of underlying market principles, you will be able to identify and exploit these situations when they occur.*

CHAPTER 19

EXPLOITING OVER-PRICED STOCK SECTOR OPTIONS

Over the past few years there has been an explosion in the number of stock sectors available to trade options with. The options on most of these sectors are ignored and mispricing occurs quite frequently. Most of this mispricing tends to be on the overpriced side, thereby creating opportunities for option sellers. We can identify these opportunities with the following rules:

1. Identify a sector whose combined implied volatility on the near the money put and call strike price is three times the 50-day historical volatility reading. For example, a sector is trading at 197.02. Its 50-day historical volatility is 10 percent. If the implied volatility for the 195 put and the 200 call is over 30 percent (combined), sell these options.

2. Risk 30 percent to 45 percent of the combined price, which means if you sell the combined options for 4, you should stop yourself out at approximately 5 1/4–5 3/4.

Why does this work? Because historically, the sector has moved in a 10 percent volatility range. By selling the options with a 30 percent combined implied volatility, you are selling overpriced options. The odds are stacked in your favor that these options will erode quickly. Also, because we are using solid money management, we are protecting ourselves in case of a runaway market.

Let's look at an opportunity that occurs quite often. As you can see from Figure 19.1, the 50-day historical volatility for the Real Estate Index is 4.76 percent whereas the implied volatility reading for its calls (Figure 19.2) is in the 13 percent range and the implied volatility reading for the puts is in the 13.5 percent range. This provides an excellent profit opportunity for option sellers.

Can this be traded with futures and equities? The answer is yes, but it is a little riskier. Companies can be bought out, whereas sectors cannot. In the futures market, the options are notoriously thin and their spreads are wide, whereas the sector options have a fairly orderly market with stable spreads between the bid and ask. I therefore recommend you focus your energy more on the indices with this strategy than on the equity and futures markets.

FIGURE 19.1

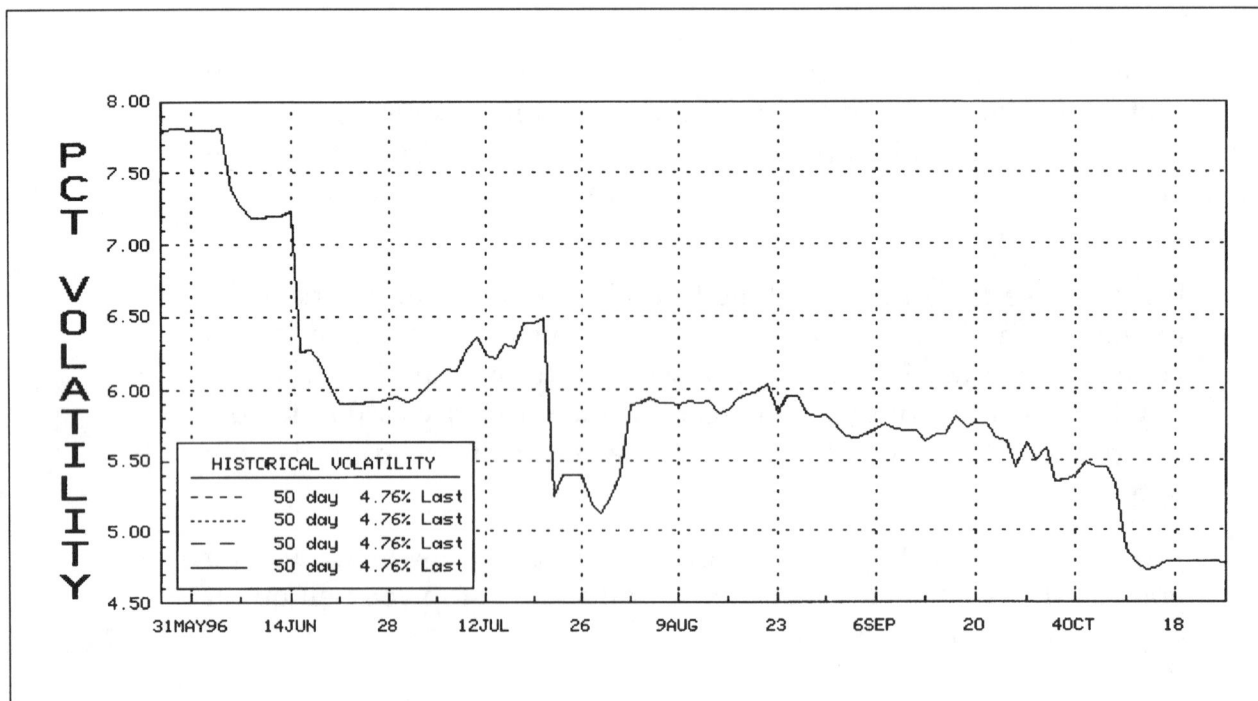

FIGURE 19.2

```
RIX Index OHT                                    DG26 Index  O H T
Screen printed.
11:59                          DISPLAY:  C  C-chg/%chg, D-delta/volat
Mon 10/28
Assume Index              O P T I O N   H O R I Z O N   A N A L Y S I S
$20.7/yr Div.                 NOV OPTIONS ON CBOE REIT INDEX
     R I X                         W O R K S H E E T

                         T O D A Y        |    7 D A Y S   L A T E R
 OPTION                    226.47         |         226.47   u n c h
  PRICING:                               | Volat=Same         Volat=Same
           C A L L S       P U T S       |    C A L L S        P U T S
  STRIKE  Prc  Del  I.Vol  Prc  Del I.Vol|  Prc   Chg %Chg    Prc    Chg %Chg
    210                                   |
    215                              ↓    |
    220                      3/4  .19 13.78|                    3/8   -3/8 -50%
    225    3 1/4 .57 13.15  2 1/4 .43 13.40|2 13/16 -7/16 -13% 1 5/8 -5/8 -28%
    230    1 3/16 .29 13.11               |  3/4   -7/16 -37%
    235
    240                              ↑    |
    245                                   |
        Mon 10/28/96 ( 19days Expr)  5.15 Fin | Mon 11/ 4/96 ( 12days Expr)  5.15 Fin

  OPTION      T -"Tickr" volatility       S -"Same" volatility
  PRICING:    M - Trade "Match" volatility 1 2 . 5 %  (or any other volat.)
```

Finally, if you have a directional bias, you can sell just one side. For example, if you believe the REIT index is going to move sideways or sell off, you can sell only the 230 calls. The options are priced to expect a 13 percent volatility until expiration. If volatility remains in line with its 50-day average or if prices drop, the premium you collected will be your reward.

SECTION SIX

DAY TRADING

▪ ▪

In 1994, I had my best year (in percentage terms) trading in the futures markets. I produced this performance predominantly by day trading.

In spite of having a solid year though, the mental strain was enormous (I was at the same time overseeing my private equities investment partnership). By the end of the year my brain was about as tired as it could be, and I knew that a few more years of day-trading would make me the only resident of the local nursing home who was under 40 years old.

This does not mean you should not day trade. Jeff Cooper has successfully done it in the equity markets for more than a decade. But the truth is that the wear and tear of day trading is tough and you should ask yourself how much torture you are willing to endure before you commit yourself to it.

With that said, the following are what I consider to be among my best day-trading strategies. I feel that if you only traded two, the "15-Minute ADX Breakout Method" combined with the "10% OOPS" strategy, you could make a comfortable living.

CHAPTER 20

15-MINUTE ADX BREAKOUT METHOD

In this chapter we will look at a day trading strategy I created a few years ago. This strategy is not for the faint of heart or for conservative traders. It is for *very aggressive traders* who are willing to take *larger than normal risks* in hopes of achieving larger than normal gains.

With the "15-Minute ADX Breakout Method," you will be trading the strongest moving and, many times, most volatile markets nearly every day. Profits come quickly, but so do losses. With that noted, this strategy, if harnessed correctly, has the potential to lend itself to some of the most spectacular day-trading moves you will ever experience.

Before looking at the rules, I want to make sure you understand conceptually the underlying forces that make it work.

Let's first look at the characteristics of a bull market. Bull markets are usually associated with daily closes higher than the daily opening. This means that in an ideal world you want to buy the market near the opening and sell it higher later in the day. Unfortunately, just blindly doing this does not work. One never knows when a strongly rising market will open at its high and then collapse. Therefore, to fully maximize the effectiveness of a bull market bias, we daily want to wait for the market to tip its hand early in the session. This is done by letting the market trade for 15 minutes and then, and only then, do we enter when the high of that first 15-minute bar is taken out. We will have entered what looks to be setting up as a typical bull market day with us buying low soon after the open and selling higher later in the session.

Let's look at the rules:

FOR BUYS (SELLS ARE REVERSED)

1. We will use this method only in the strongest trending markets! Therefore, we want the daily 14-period ADX reading to be above 30 and the 14-period +DI to be greater than the –DI.

2. Wait for the first 15 minutes of trading to pass.

3. Place a buy stop one tick above the first 15-minute bar high.

4. (This is critical.) Place a protective sell stop one tick below or at the first bar 15-minute low.

5. Hold onto your hats as you will probably experience more volatility than you ever have.

6. Where you take your profits is a personal choice. Ideally, you will use trailing stops to help lock in the gains. Also, please read the "Two-For-One Money Management Strategy" chapter. With a methodology as volatile as this one, it is important to be prepared to lock-in profits on half the position and let the other half run.

7. Close all positions out before the end of the day.

Let's look at a move in coffee to help understand how this strategy works. Please note these are the daily trades beginning April 29 and running through May 15, 1997.

FIGURE 20.1

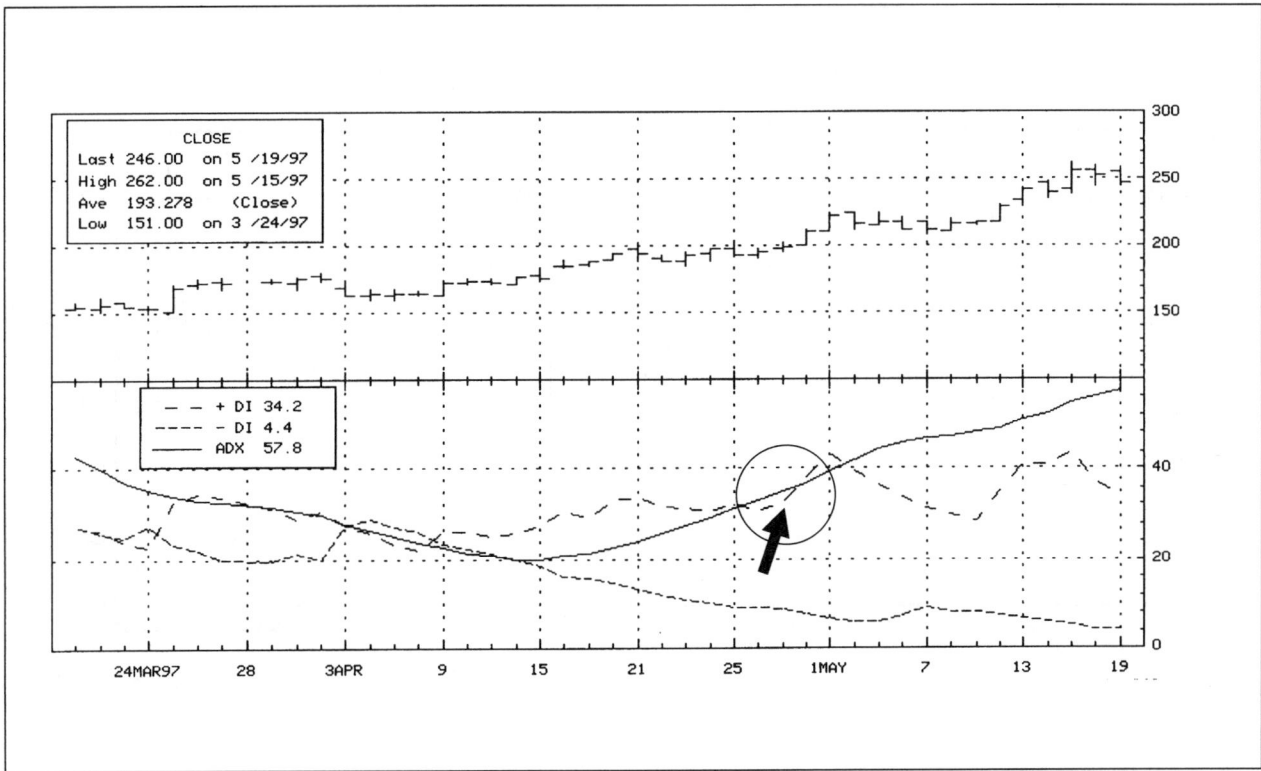

Here we see the ADX for July 97 Coffee crossing above the 30 level in late
April 1997.

FIGURE 20.2

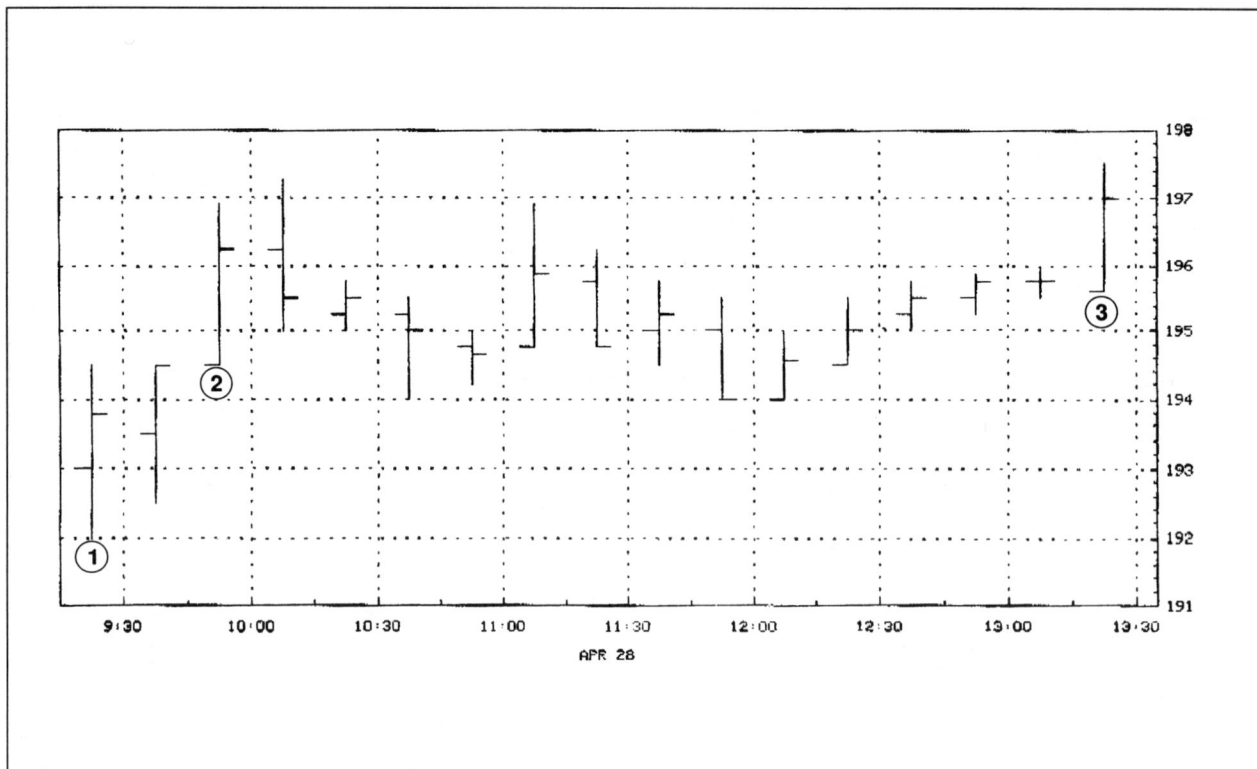

1.   The first 15-minute bar and our buy stop is placed one tick above it at 194.60.

2.   We are filled and the protective stop is near the first bar low of 192.00.

3.   The market closes 1.8 cents above our entry.

FIGURE 20.3

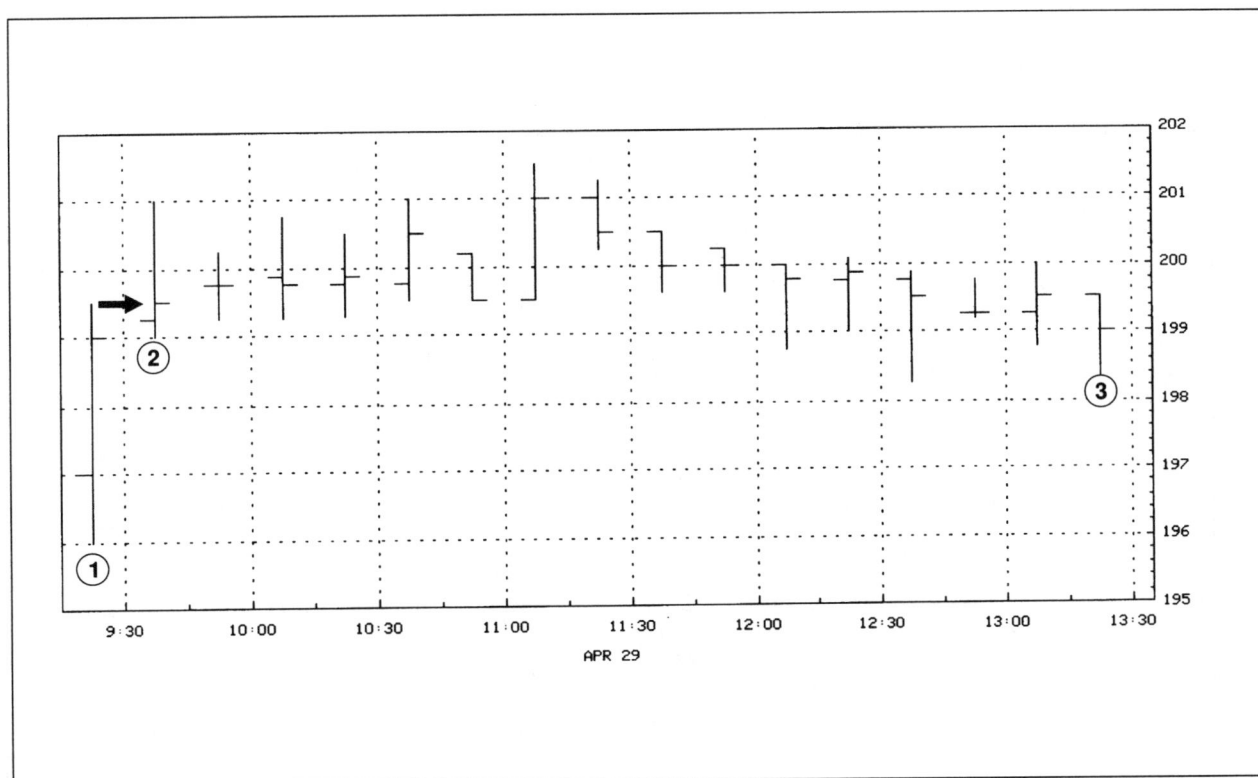

1.   The formation of the first 15-minute bar. Our buy stop is placed one tick above the bar.

2.   We buy at 199.70 and our stop is near the low of the first bar of 196.

3.   After a small rally, the position closes the day for a loss.

FIGURE 20.4

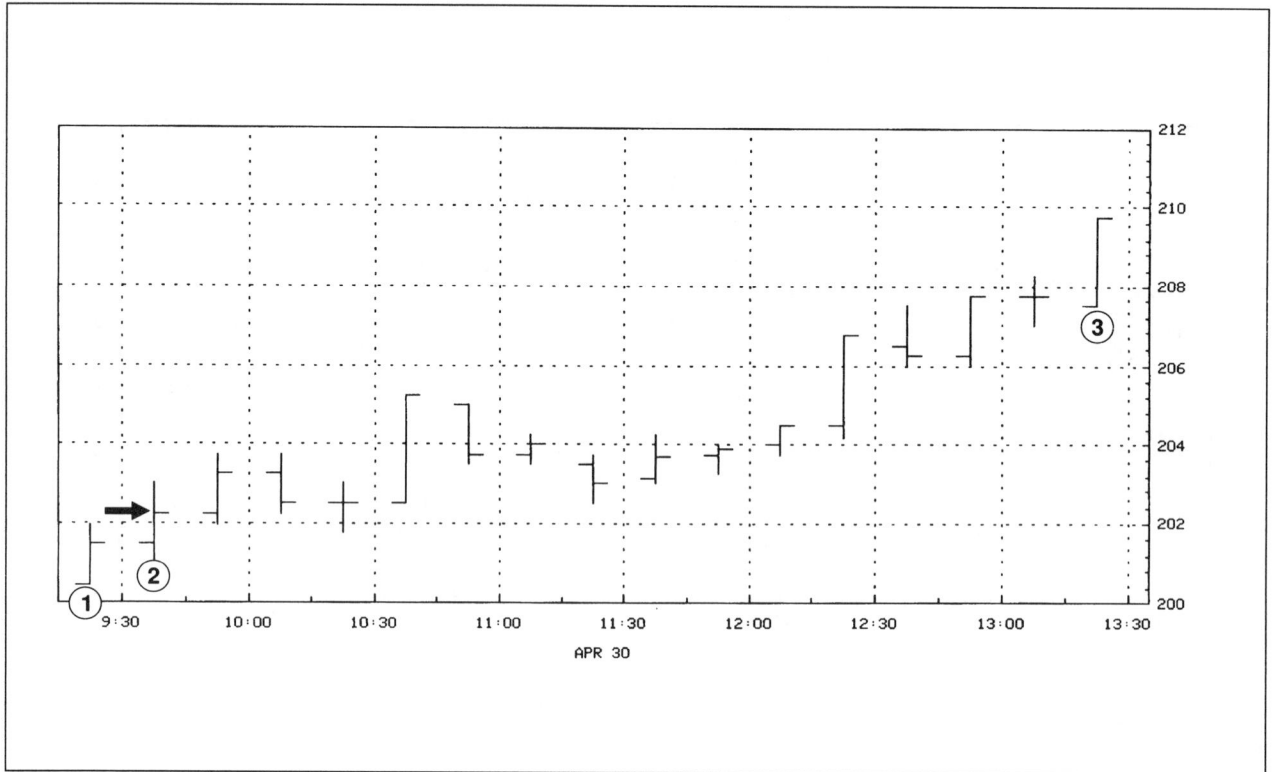

APR 30

1.   The opening 15-minute bar.

2.   The buy stop is filled at 202.10 and the sell stop is near 200.40.

3.   A better than eight-cent gain ($3,000/contract) if you held until the close. Multiple contract traders should certainly take profits on a piece as the day progresses.

FIGURE 20.5

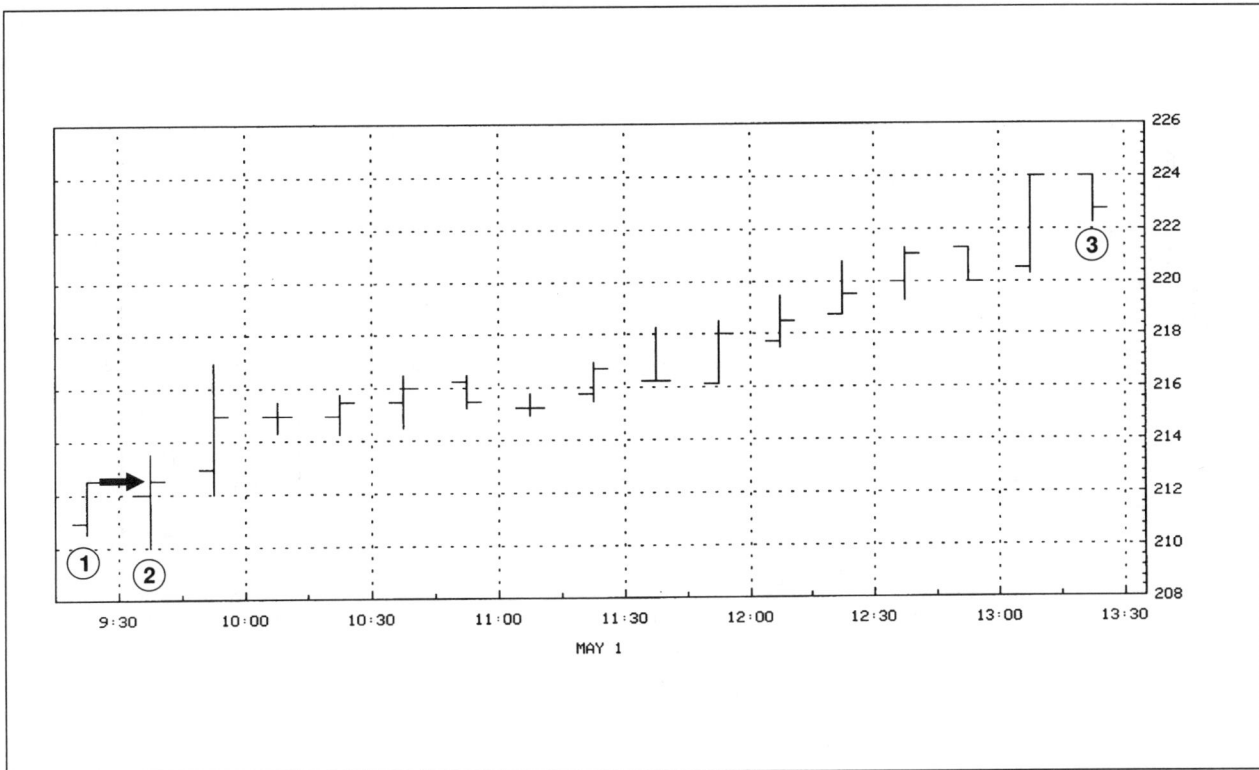

1. A buy stop is placed one tick above the bar.

2. We are filled and the market immediately collapses, stopping us out for an approximate two-cent loss. It then does what a good volatile market should do and re-rallies allowing us to re-enter (and giving us enormous stress!).

3. The trend is too powerful and the market rises approximately 10 cents from our initial entry.

FIGURE 20.6

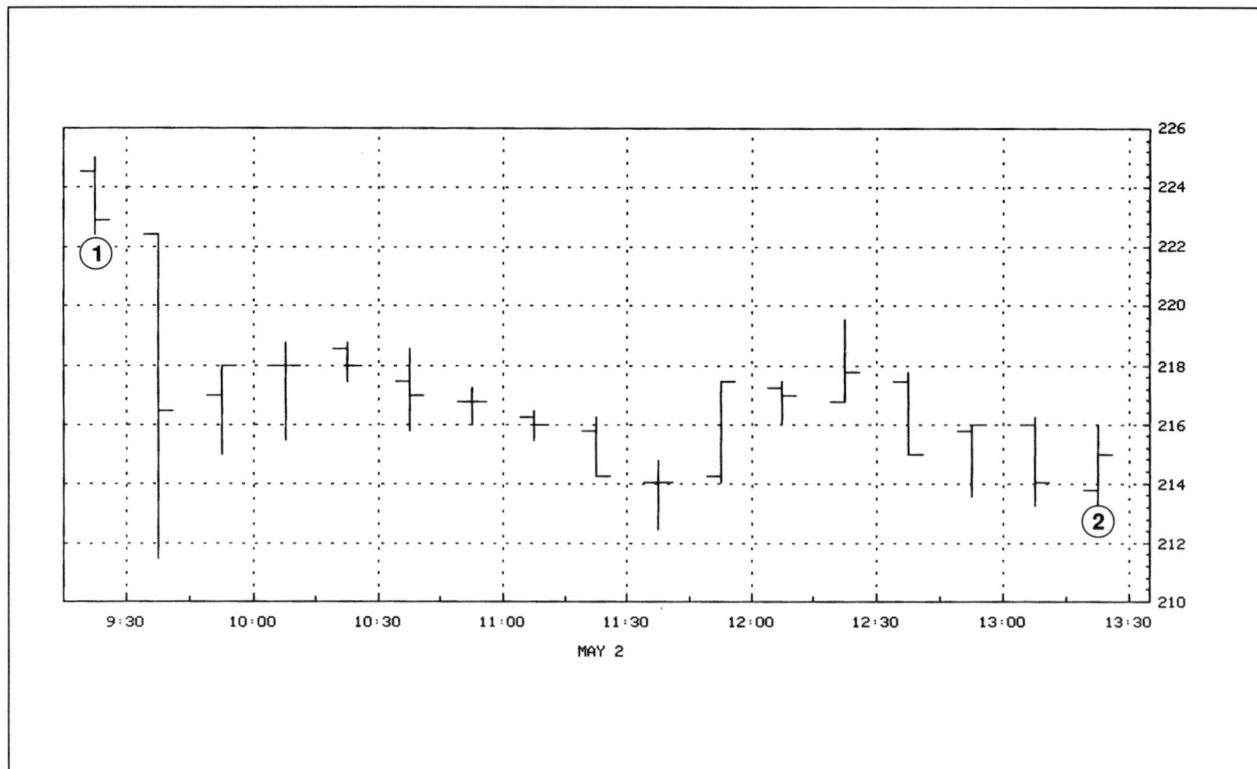

1.   15-minute opening bar.

2.   No trade for the day and we avoid the sell-off.

FIGURE 20.7

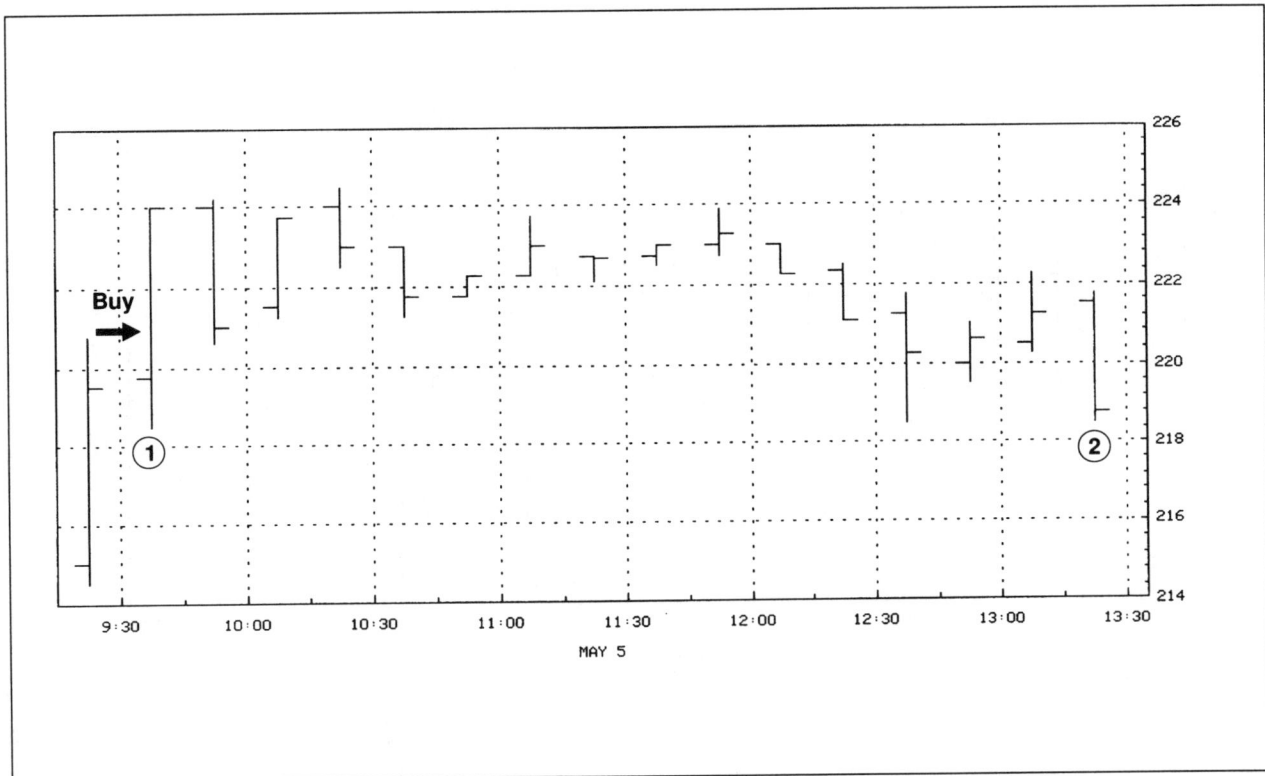

1.   A buy in the 221 range and . . .

2.   A loss of 3.5 cents for the day.

FIGURE 20.8

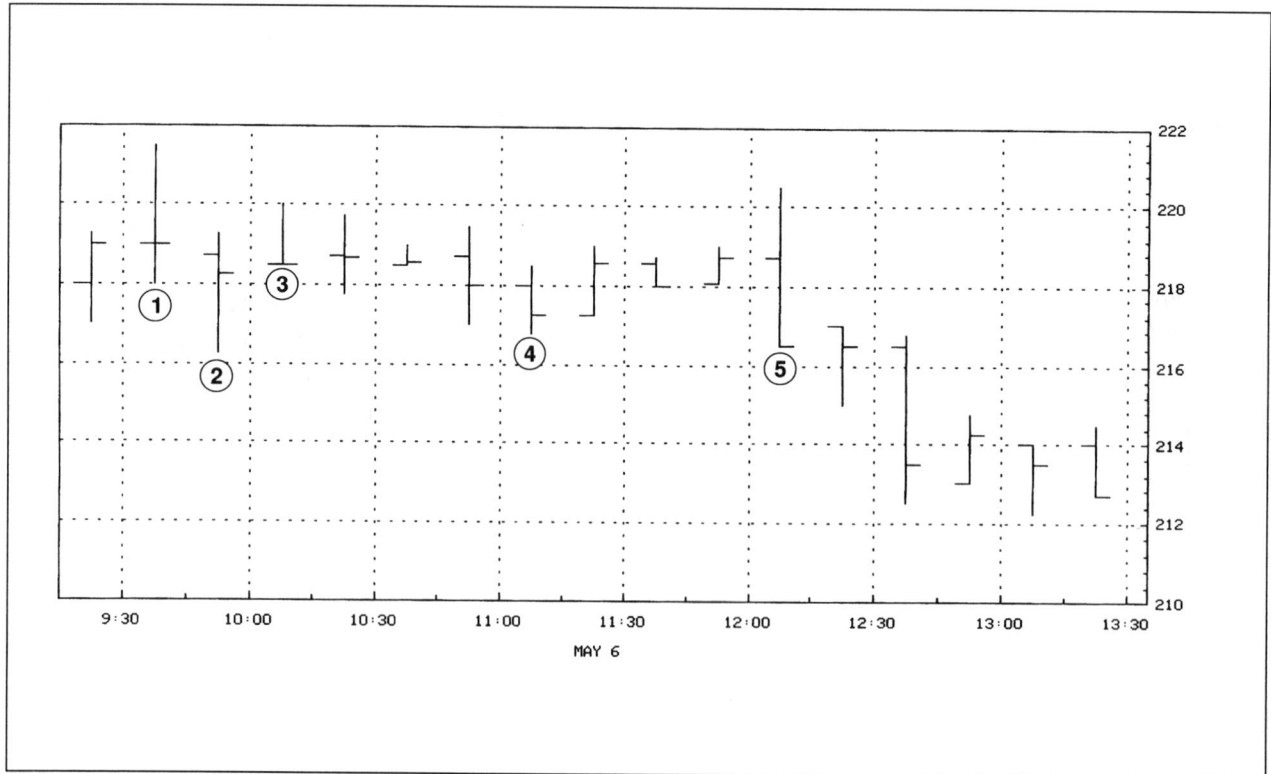

MAY 6

1.   Buy entry.

2.   A loss of two cents.

3.   Re-enter.

4.   Another loss of two cents.

5.   I will not enter a trade three times in a day. Two losses are my psychological limit.

FIGURE 20.9

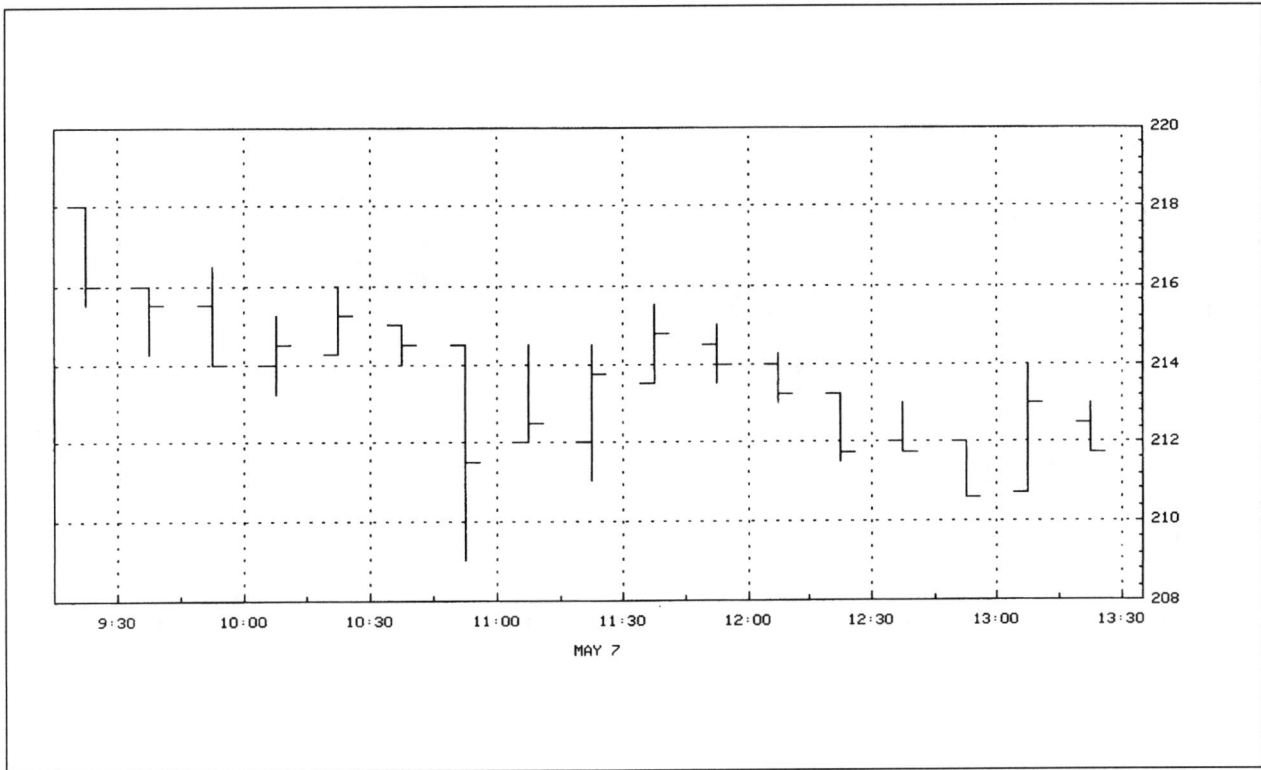

We avoid the sell-off as our buy stop is never triggered.

FIGURE 20.10

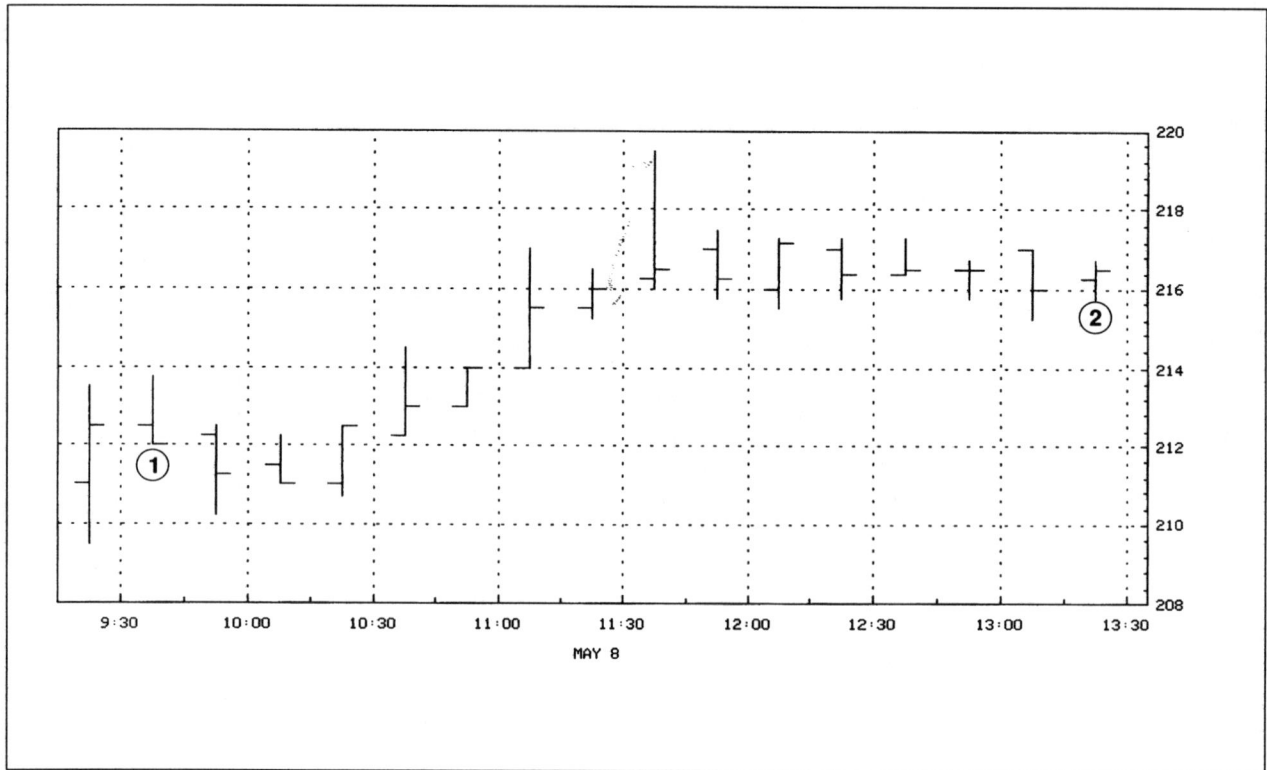

1.   Our buy stop is filled and our stop is near 209.50.

2.   A profitable trade.

FIGURE 20.11

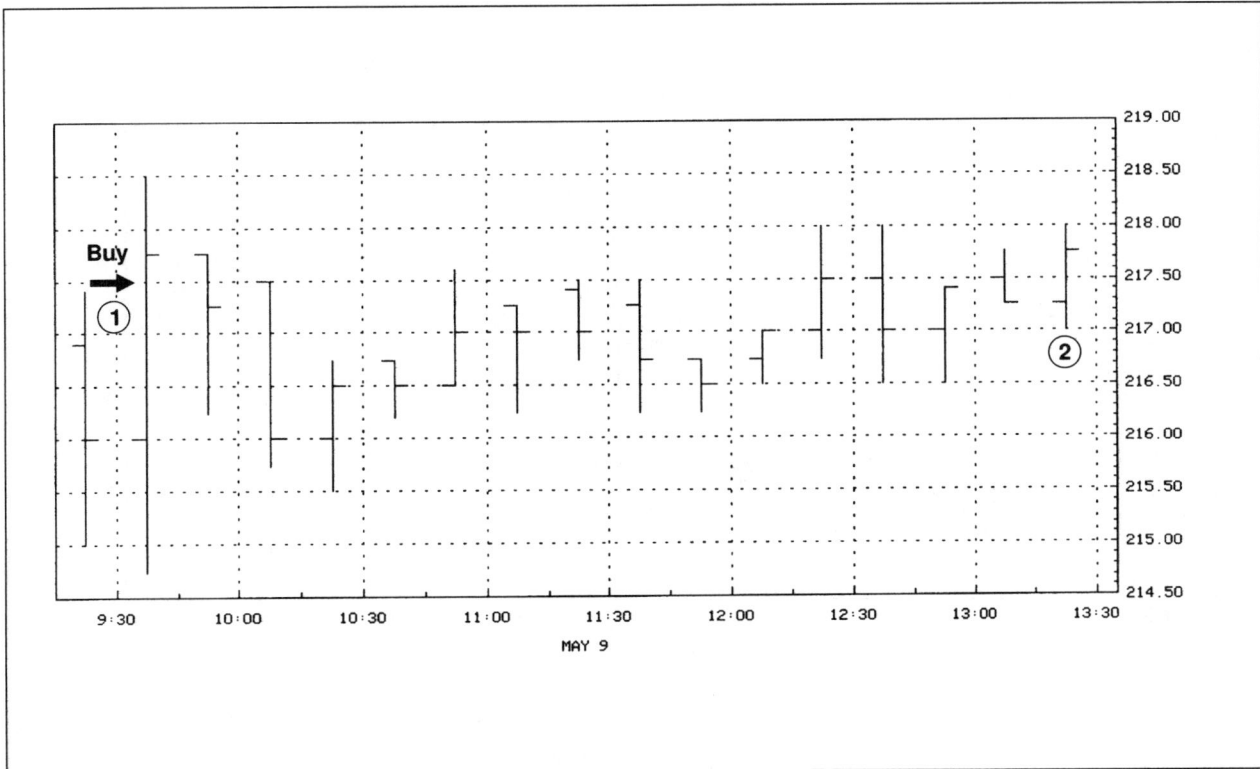

1.   We are filled at 217.50 (the second-bar low comes before our fill).

2.   The market closes at 217.90 and the trade is basically a scratch.

FIGURE 20.12

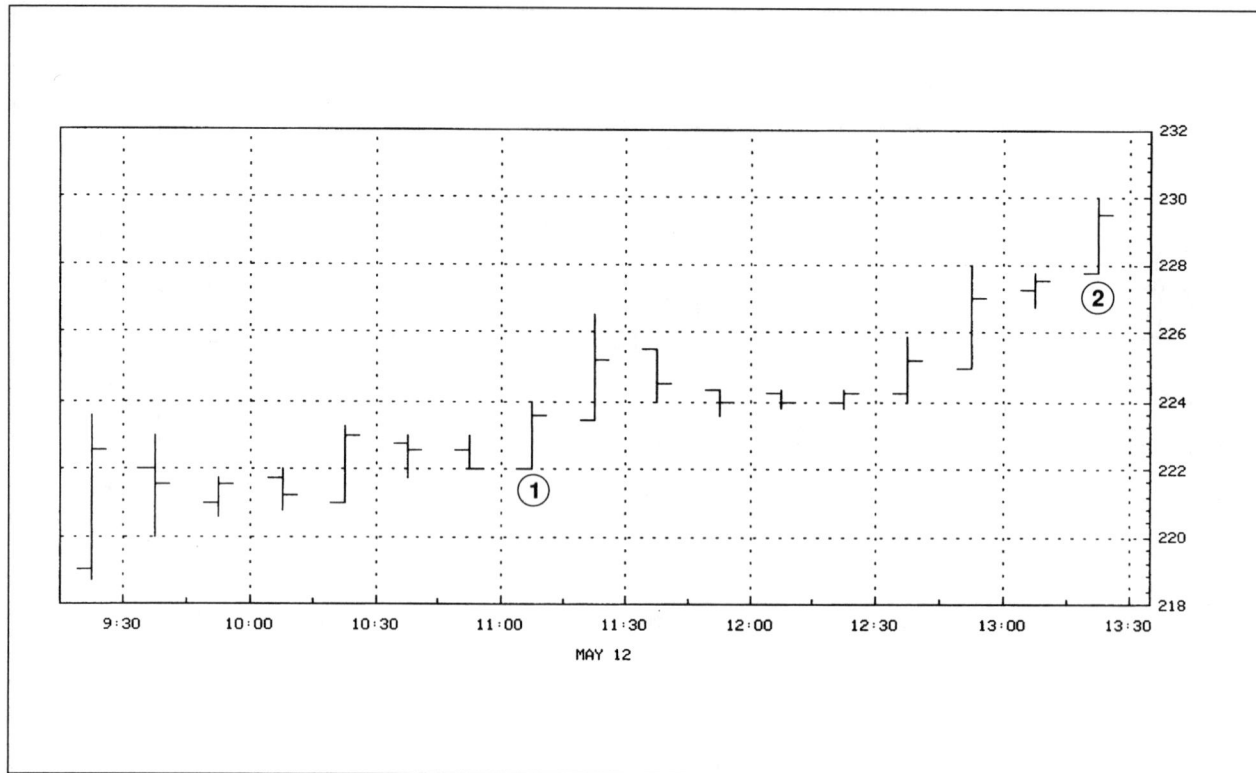

1.   Our buy stop is filled after 1.5 hours and it leads to . . .

2.   A better than five-cent gain.

FIGURE 20.13

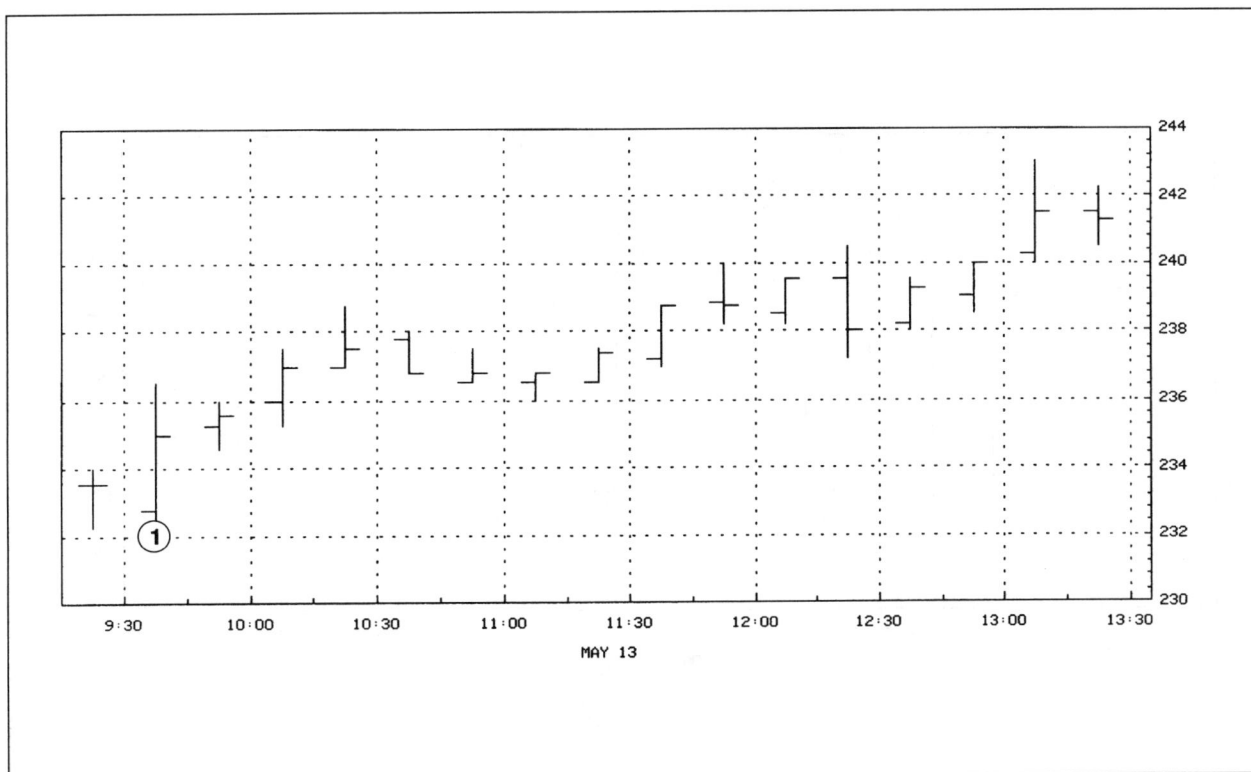

1.   Filled at 234.10 and it closes for a better than $2,600 profit.

FIGURE 20.14

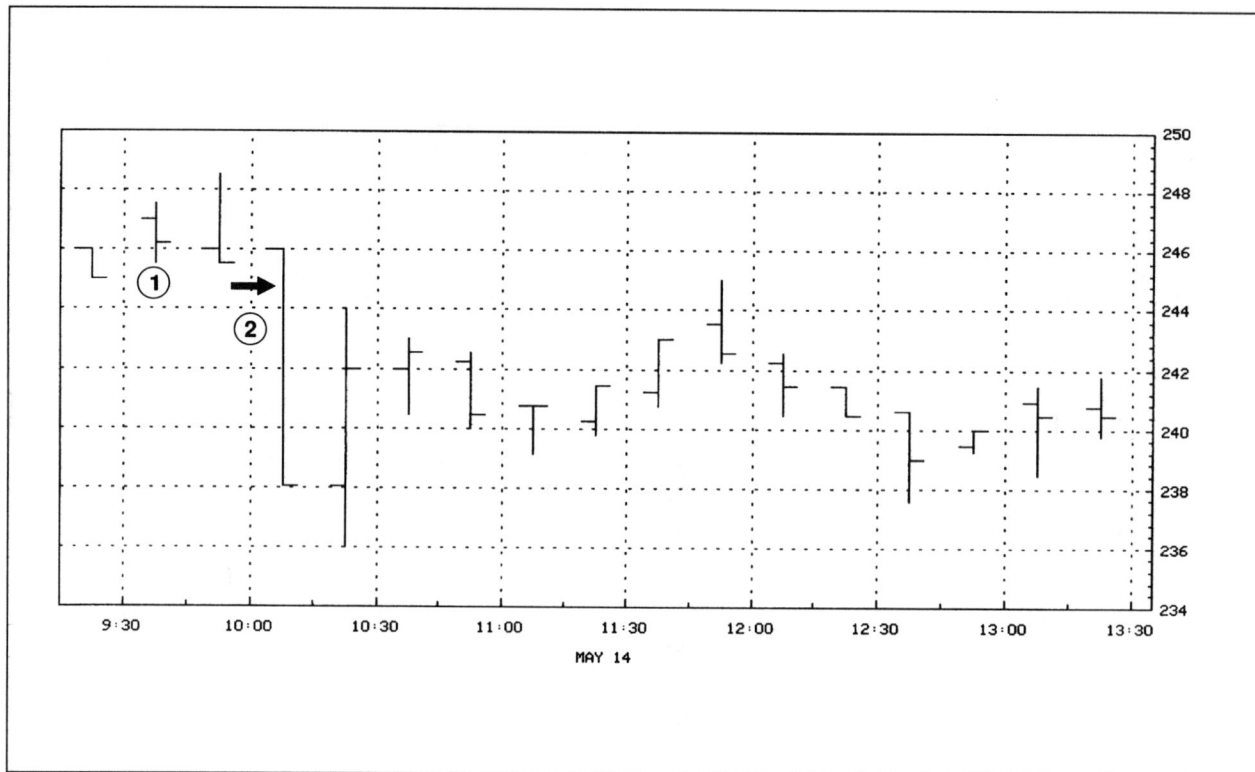

1.   Filled at 246.10

2.   Stopped out at 245 (and avoiding a sharp sell-off).

FIGURE 20.15

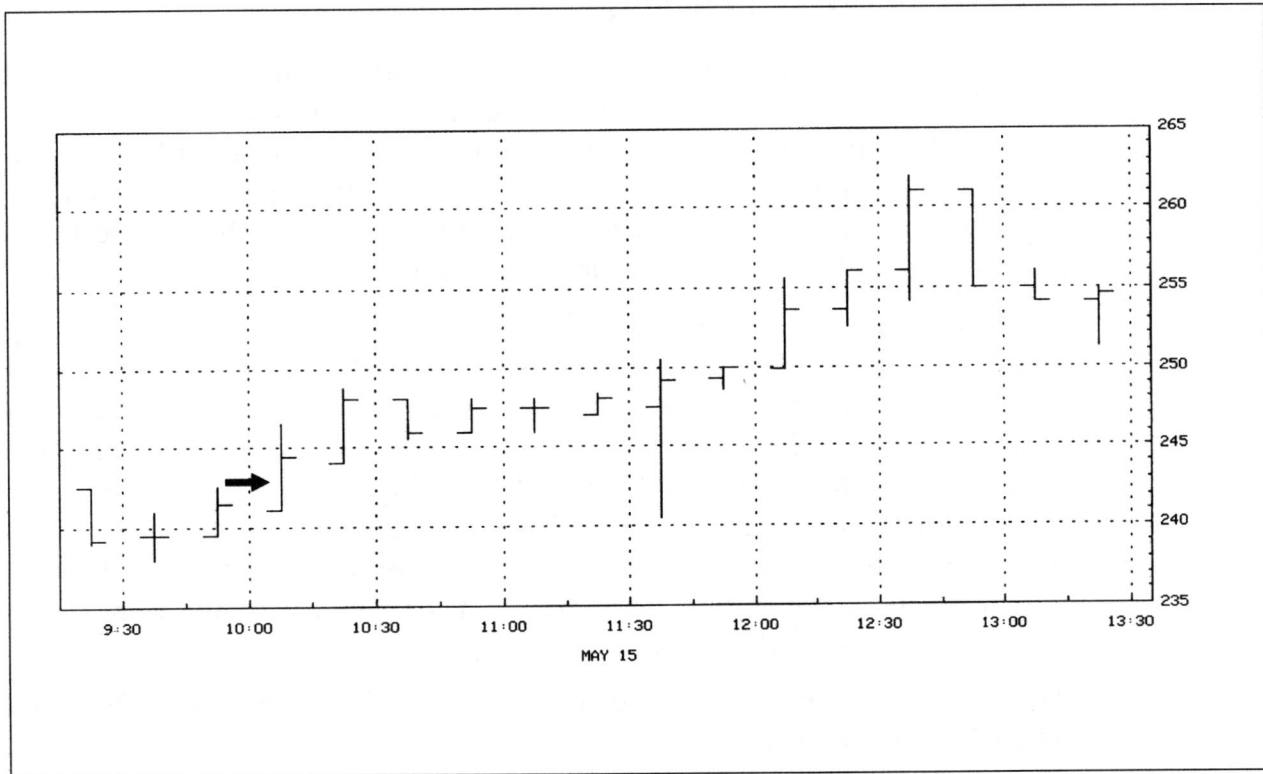

Bought near 244 and closed above 255. Notice also that at one point the gain is as much as 18 cents ($6,750/contract).

SUMMARY

The coffee examples replicate the pattern this strategy takes—small losses, sometimes three, four, or five in a row, and large, sometimes spectacular gains. Again, I encourage you to please be sure that you can handle this volatility both emotionally and financially before taking on this strategy.

TRADING THE 15-MINUTE ADX BREAKOUT METHOD WITH EQUITIES

This strategy provides more opportunities in the equities markets than it does the futures markets. This is because there are only 25–30 commodity markets to choose from but there are over 10,000 stocks. Unlike the futures markets, stocks as a whole do not provide large leveraged day-trading moves. Therefore, to maximize the effectiveness of this method, *you must trade volatile stocks that have large intraday ranges.*

To identify these stocks, please look again at the chapter entitled "Trading Where the Action Is" in the Volatility section. In it you learn how to select the most volatile stocks using what I consider to be the purest indicator to accomplish the job: historical volatility. The ideal situation is to trade those stocks whose 100-day historical volatility is above 40 percent *and* whose price is at least $40/share. These two criteria combined give you the stocks which have large daily ranges. The daily range is critical as you want the stock to be able to move at least a few points intraday in order to capture good profits.

Thus, the filter for the stocks to trade with the 15-Minute ADX Breakout Method is as follows:

FOR BUYS

1. ADX > 30, +DI > –DI

2. Price must be above $40/share.

3. 100-day historical volatility of 40 percent or higher.

FOR SHORT SALES

1. ADX > 30, –DI > +DI

2. Price must be above $40/share

3. 100-day historical volatility is 40 percent or higher.

Finally, I suggest you program the stock search in your computer. There are thousands of stocks to choose from and it is too time consuming to do by hand.

FURTHER INSIGHTS INTO THE 15-MINUTE ADX BREAKOUT METHOD

1. The higher the ADX, the stronger the trend and the higher the volatility.

2. Markets are correlated. If you have a high ADX reading in heating oil, you will most likely have one in unleaded gas. Trade only one correlated market at a time.

3. You should be in the position to watch the screen all day. This is a pro-active methodology which must be constantly monitored in order to maximize its effectiveness.

4. *Reminder:* If you are stopped out, it is correct to re-enter. These second entries tend to be the best trades.

5. 15-minutes is not the only time frame to use. I have traded this with 10-minute bars. This is a personal choice and you should use the time frame you are most comfortable with.

6. Be prepared for higher than normal slippage. Greed, fear, and panic are many times at their highest level in these markets.

7. One last caution—I have yet to trade a methodology that is this crazy. It is so wild that I cannot trade it unless I have absolutely no other positions and setups to look at. The 15-Minute ADX Breakout Method requires *total* concentration on the position.

CHAPTER 21

10% OOPS

■ ■

In the 1980s, Larry Williams introduced traders to his "Oops" strategy. The strategy stated that when a commodity gapped above (below) the previous day's high (low) and reversed, a sell (buy) signal is triggered near the previous day's high (low). In *Street Smarts*, I introduced a strategy that filtered the Oops strategy with ADX and traded only in the direction of the trend.

Here is another gap reversal strategy I use to very good effect. This strategy was originally mentioned in *Techniques of a Professional Commodity Chart Analyst*, written in 1980 by Arthur Sklarew. We will also look at one year's trades on the S&P's using this technique.

The "10% Oops" strategy is a derivative of the 80–20's strategy from *Street Smarts*. Briefly, an 80–20's sell setup occurs (buys are reversed) when a market opens in the bottom 20 percent of its daily range, closes in the top 20 percent of its range, trades higher the next day and then reverses back into the previous day's range. The 10% Oops applies the same principles as this strategy but includes a gap.

Here are the rules:

FOR BUYS

1.   Day one—A commodity or stock must close in the bottom 10 percent of its daily range.

2a.   Day two—The next morning, it must gap lower (night data is omitted).

2b.   If Rule 2a is met, buy at the day-one low. Your initial protective stop should be near the day-two opening.

3.   Lock in profits with a trailing stop or sell MOC.

FOR SELLS

1.   Day one—A commodity or stock must close in the top 10 percent of its range.

2a.   Day two—The next morning it must gap higher.

2b.   If Rule 2a is met, sell at day-one high. Your initial protective stop should be near the day-two opening.

3.   Buy MOC or take profits via a trailing stop.

Here are some examples of what the setup looks like:

FIGURE 21.1 December 96 Cotton

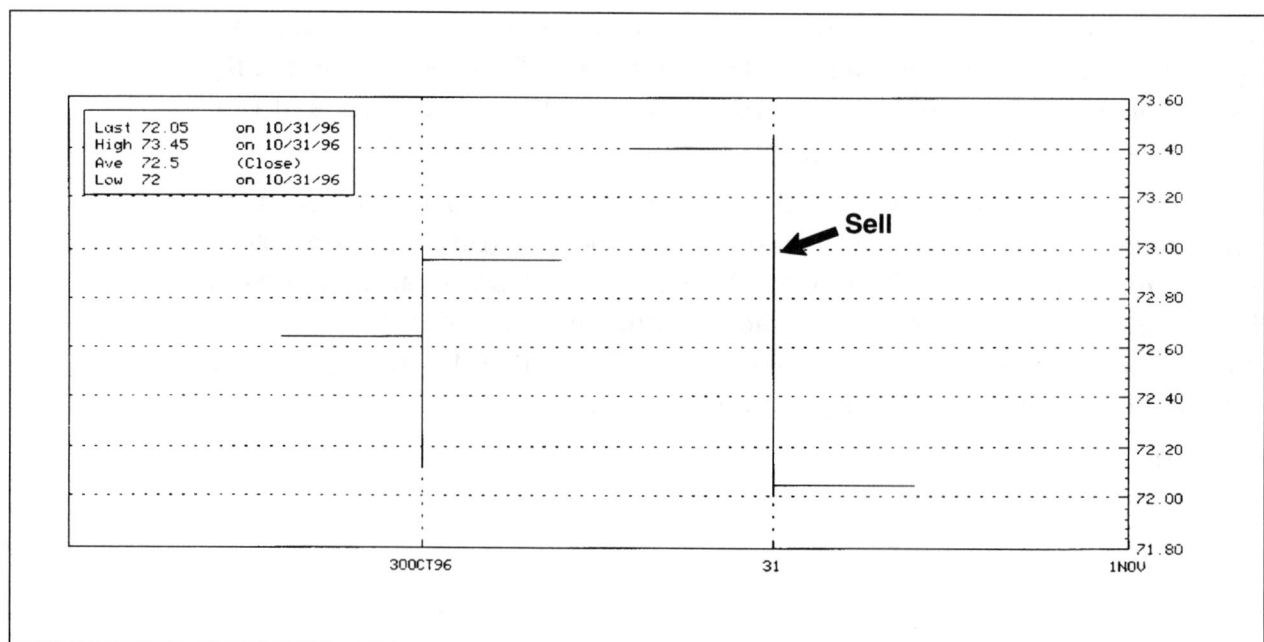

FIGURE 21.2 February 97 Pork Bellies

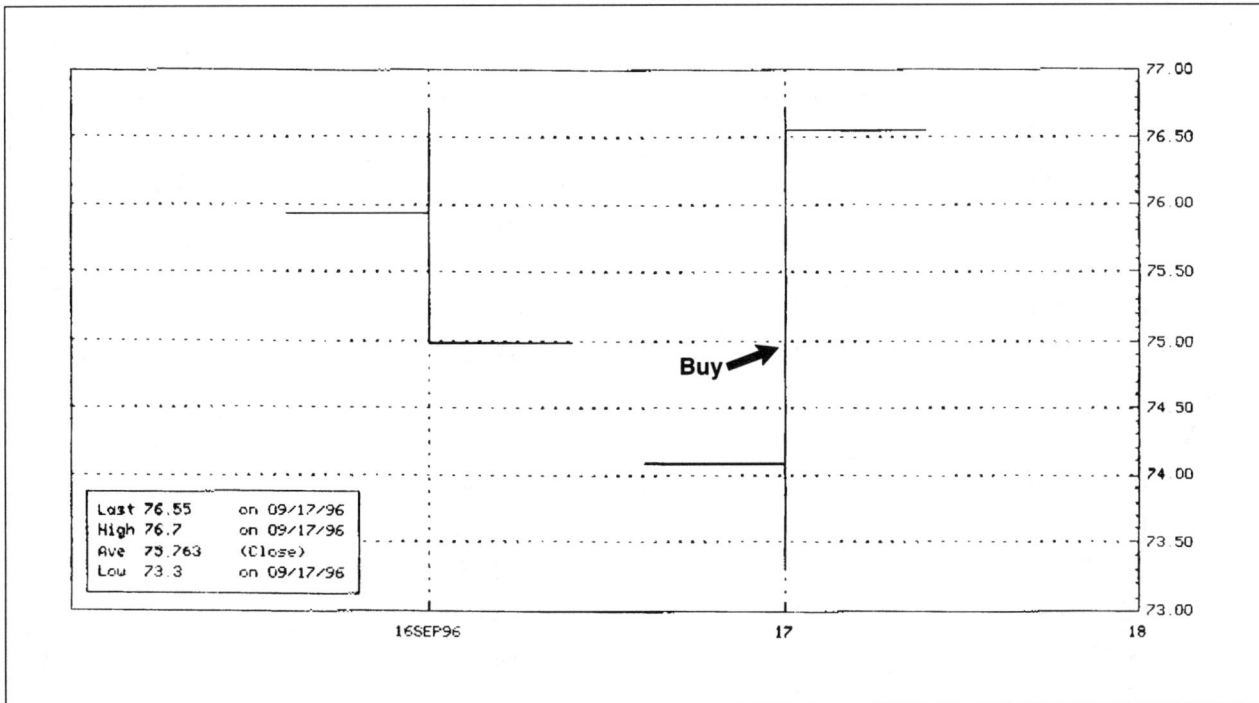

I am not recommending this as a mechanical system as I am a discretionary trader and prefer to use trailing stops to take profits. Finally, I recommend using this strategy with all commodities except bonds. Bonds have their big moves off the morning economic reports and the *Street Smarts* "Morning News Reversal" strategy works better on them.

Here is how the 10% Oops strategy fared in 1996 as a mechanical system with no stops.

S & P

1/1/96 to 12/31/96

Signal Date	Signal	P	L
01/03/96	S		(−1.65)
01/09/96	S	+14.10	
03/19/96	S	+2.30	
03/28/96	B	+3.85	
03/29/96	S	+3.65	
04/09/96	S	+2.60	
04/16/96	S		(−1.35)
04/24/96	S	+3.50	
05/23/96	S	+2.75	
06/07/96	B	+1.15	
06/10/96	S	+3.00	
06/27/96	B	+4.55	
07/24/96	B	+2.70	
08/09/96	S	+4.05	
11/15/96	S		(−1.45)

12 profitable

3 unprofitable

Total P & L includes $100 slippage and commission = $19,880

SUMMARY

This strategy is a good companion to the ADX Gapper strategy and the 80-20's strategy from *Street Smarts*. Those of you who also trade equities can use it to good advantage. My recommendation is to supplement it with the volatility filtering technique presented in this book's chapter, "Trading Where the Action Is." This will assure you of being in the stocks that will take best advantage of the setup.

CHAPTER 22

REVERSALS OFF THE MORNING CALL

■ ■

This strategy is a method you can use to profit from extreme overreactions off the opening. Even though the strategy works for both the buys and sells, the sell side usually leads to the larger gains.

Here are the rules:

FOR SELLS (BUYS ARE REVERSED)

1. Identify a market that is called to open significantly higher due to some fundamental event; i.e., weather for the futures, an earnings report for stocks (a gap is not needed). This information is available from most news services and your broker.

2. Monitor the call for any signs of weakness. For example, a stock is originally called to open at 57–59. The call is then lowered to 56–58 and the stock opens at the low end of the range. This is an obvious warning signal of overhead supply at higher levels.

3. After the opening, place a sell stop (sell-short stop for equities) at yesterday's closing price.

4.   On being filled, a protective buy stop should be placed one tick above the high reached thus far today.

Let's look at three examples:

FIGURE 22.1   General RE Corp.

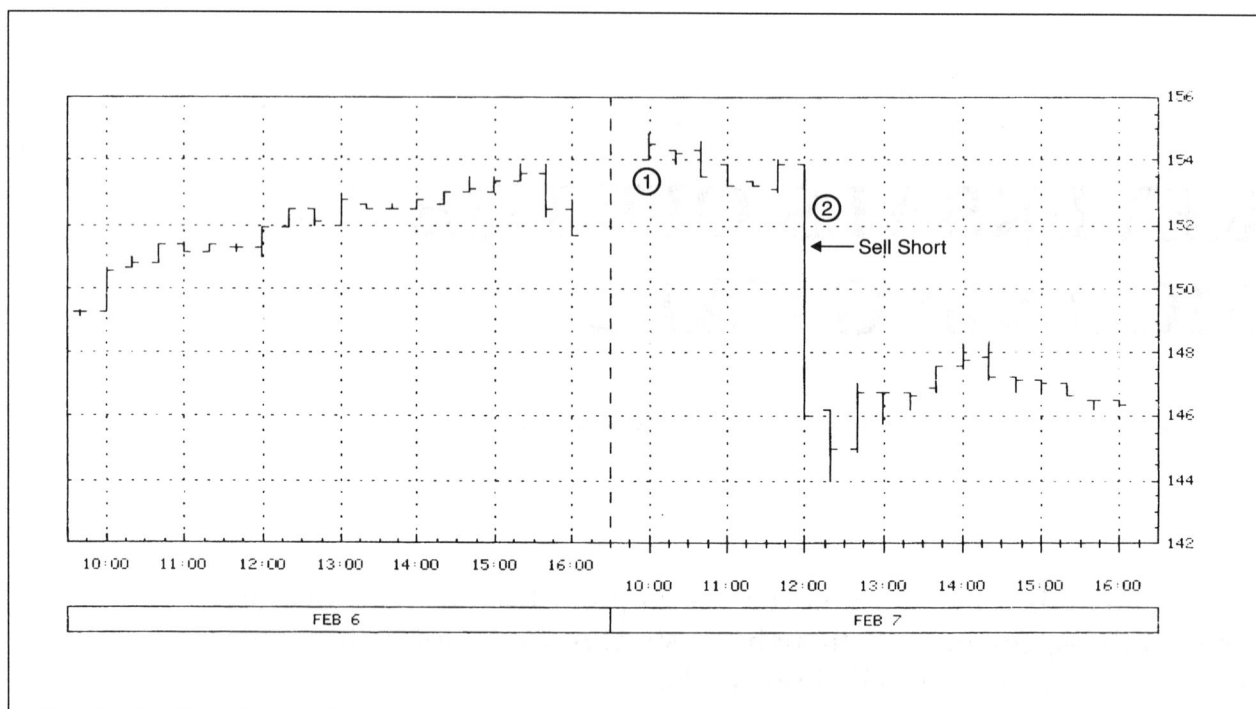

1.   The first example is General RE Corp. (GRN). On February 6, 1996, after the close, the reinsurance company announced better than expected earnings. The next morning, the stock was indicated to open at 156–158 (previous day's close was 151 5/8). The indication was then lowered to 154–156 and in fact opened at the low end of the range at 154. Because of the weakness off the morning call, a sell-short stop is placed at yesterday's close of 151 5/8.

2.   After trading sideways for a short time, the market collapses. As you can see, the stock closes more than five points under our short sell price.

FIGURE 22.2 Orange Juice

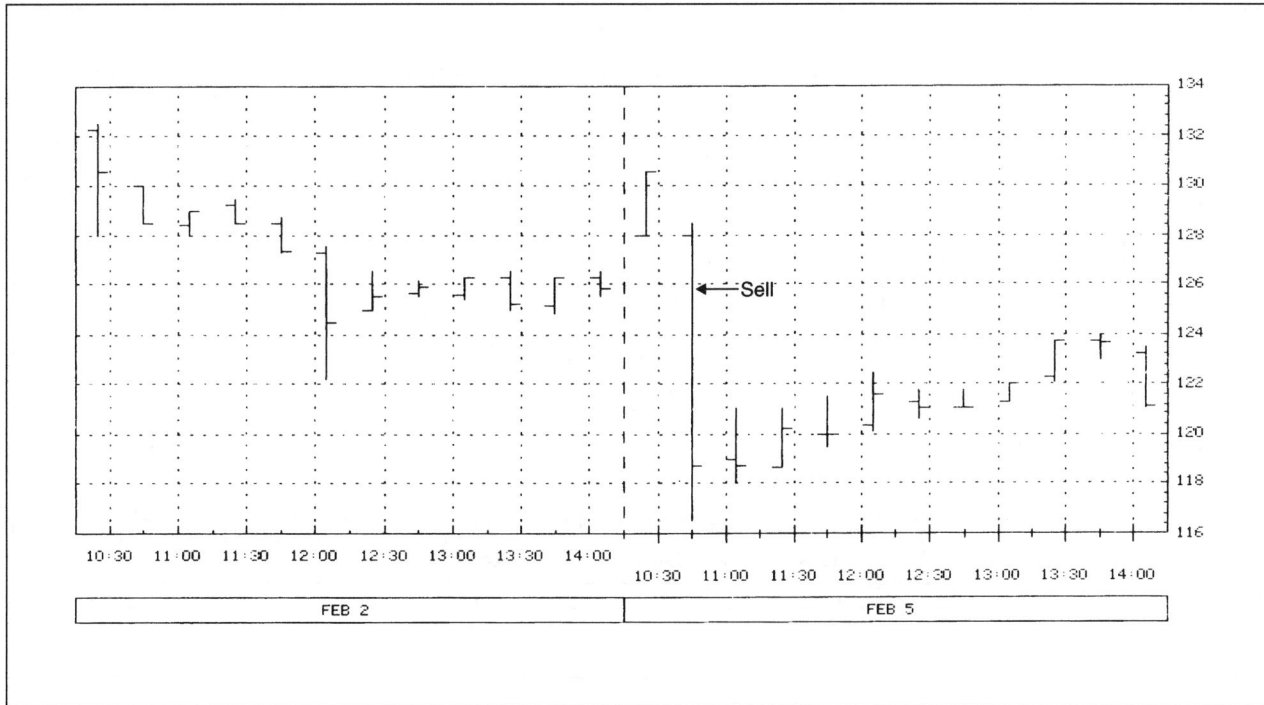

On February 5, March OJ is called to open 400–600 points higher due to cold weather. OJ in fact opens only 215 points higher and after a brief rally collapses. A sell stop in the 125.80 range is filled and a protective buy stop is placed at today's high of 130.50. The market proceeds to immediately lose over 900 points from our stop before gradually recovering.

FIGURE 22.3 Cigna Corp.

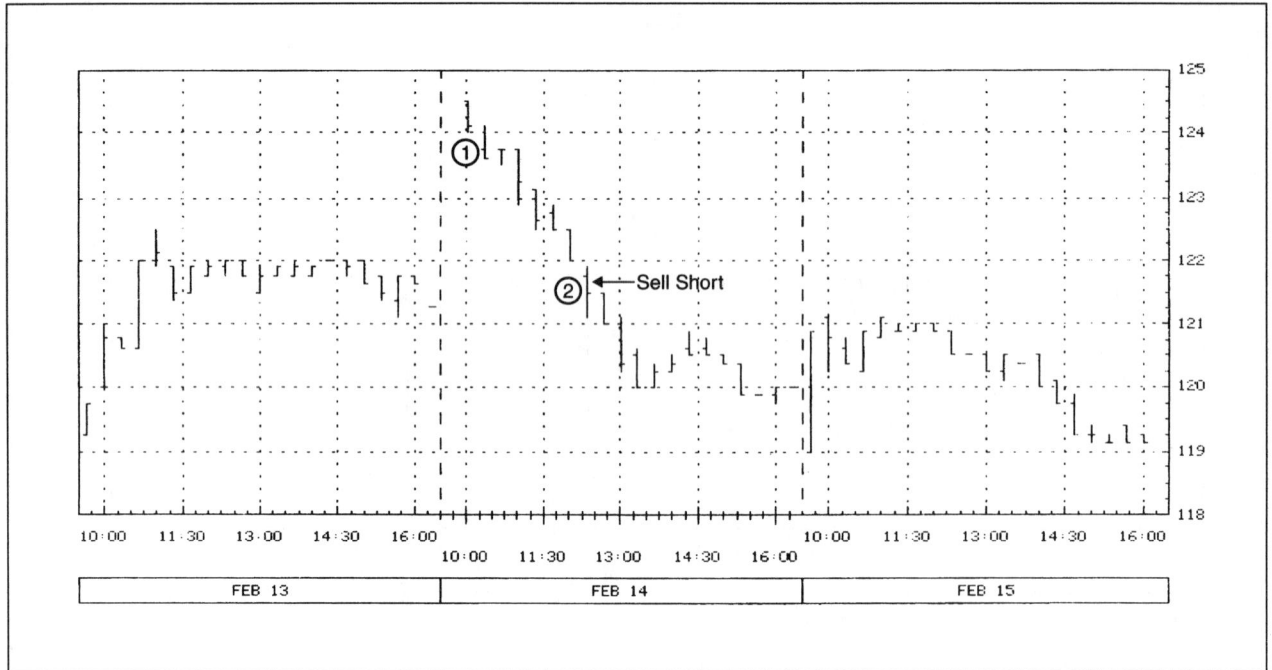

1.   Before the opening on February 14, 1996, Cigna Corp. reports better than expected earnings. The stock which is originally called to open as high as 126, opens only at 124 1/2 (an indication of overhead supply) and begins to immediately sell off.

2.   A sell-short stop is placed and filled at the previous day's close of 121 5/8 and Cigna closes the day at 120. The selling follows through the next morning with the stock opening at 119. Over the next few days, the sell-off continues taking the stock to as low as 115 1/8.

SUMMARY

The weakness off the morning call leads to potentially large gains. Obviously not all opening call reversal weakness follows through. However the ones that do lend themselves to significant profits.

The examples show that a reversal off the morning call can lead to panic selling. One drawback to the strategy is the number of times the reversals never take place. A trader must be patient and disciplined to fully take advantage of this phenomena. In the long run though, your patience will be rewarded.

CHAPTER 23

WIDE RANGE EXHAUSTION GAP REVERSALS

As you have seen, I am a fan of Larry Williams' Oops strategy. In reality though, it is impossible to identify and trade every potential gap setup on a daily basis. This is especially true in the equities markets with over 10,000 stocks now publicly traded. I have therefore, over the years, attempted to focus only on the potential gap reversals that have the highest profit possibility.

In the section "More Advanced Trading Strategies," in the chapter entitled "Large-Range Days," we will look at markets that have had a two standard deviation daily move. We will see that these markets tend to rest for three to four days after the move (the opposite of conventional wisdom). When these same markets have a large move (measured again by two standard deviations) and then gap the following day, there is a higher than average likelihood that this gap will be an *exhaustion gap*. This is tied into the reversion to the mean principle that is inherent in volatility and to a lesser (but just as important) degree, price. In these situations, both price and volatility have been pulled too far from the mean and from this condition the likelihood of reversals increases.

Let's look at the rules and then look at examples.

FOR BUYS (SELLS AND SHORT SALES ARE REVERSED)

Day 1

1.   Identify a market or stock that has had at least a two standard deviation daily move to the downside.

Day 2

2.   Tomorrow, if this market gaps lower (night data is omitted), place a buy stop near the previous day's *close* (not its low!). I use the close instead of the low to acknowledge the increased volatility period we are trading in.

3.   Your initial protective stop should be placed at the day-one low. Please note, if the day-one low and close are extremely close, give your stop some additional breathing room. *The key here is to risk a small amount in order to participate in those reversals that provide large moves.*

4.   If the position closes in the top 10 to 15 percent of its daily range, carry it into the next morning. Otherwise, lock in your profits near the close.

FIGURE 23.1   Zitel

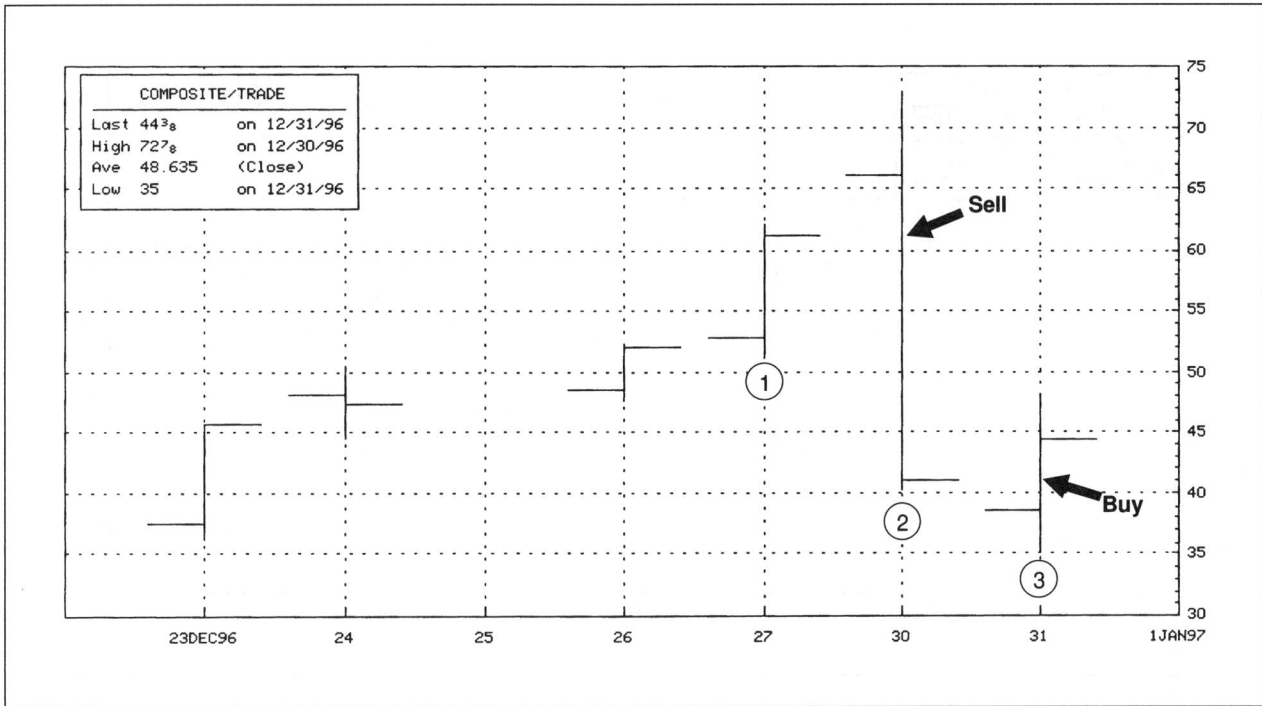

This is an extreme example but it does show what happens when markets pull too far.

1.   Zitel has a larger than two standard deviation move.

2.   This is followed by a large gap reversal and another two plus standard deviation move.

3.   This is then followed by another profitable wide range exhaustion gap reversal.

FIGURE 23.2   American Online

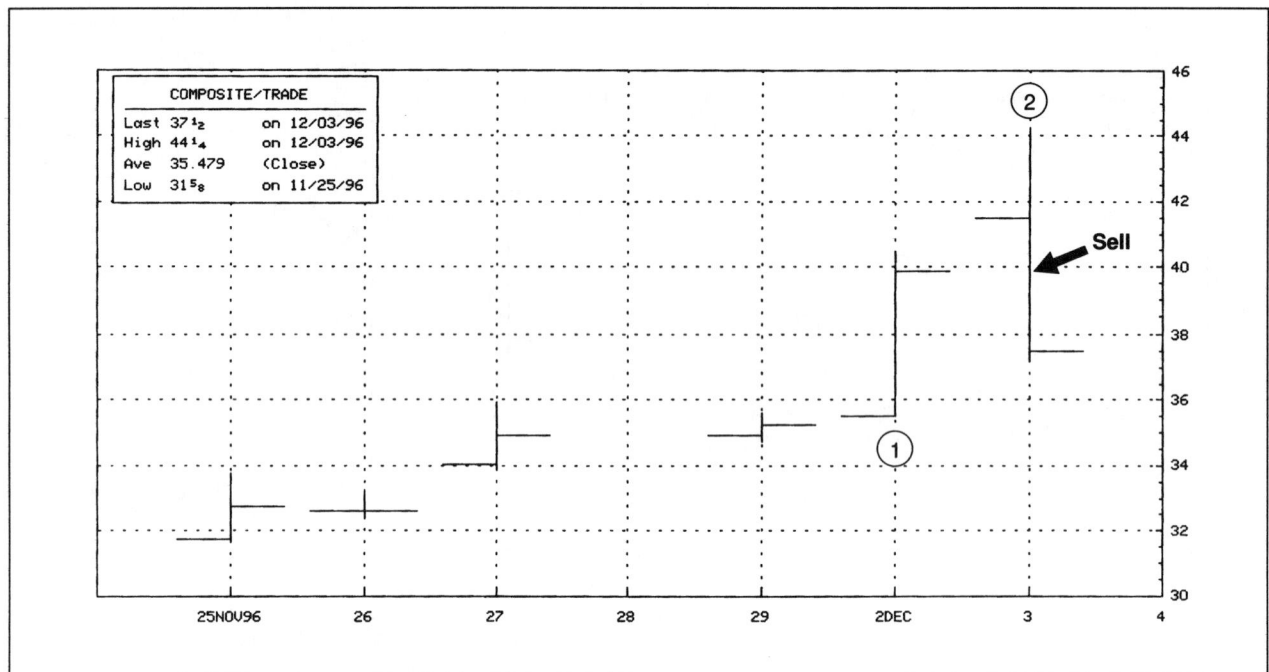

Here is an example from American Online:

1.   A two standard deviation move.

2.   The stock gaps to 41 3/4 and our short sale is triggered near yesterday's close at 39 7/8.

FIGURE 23.3 3COM

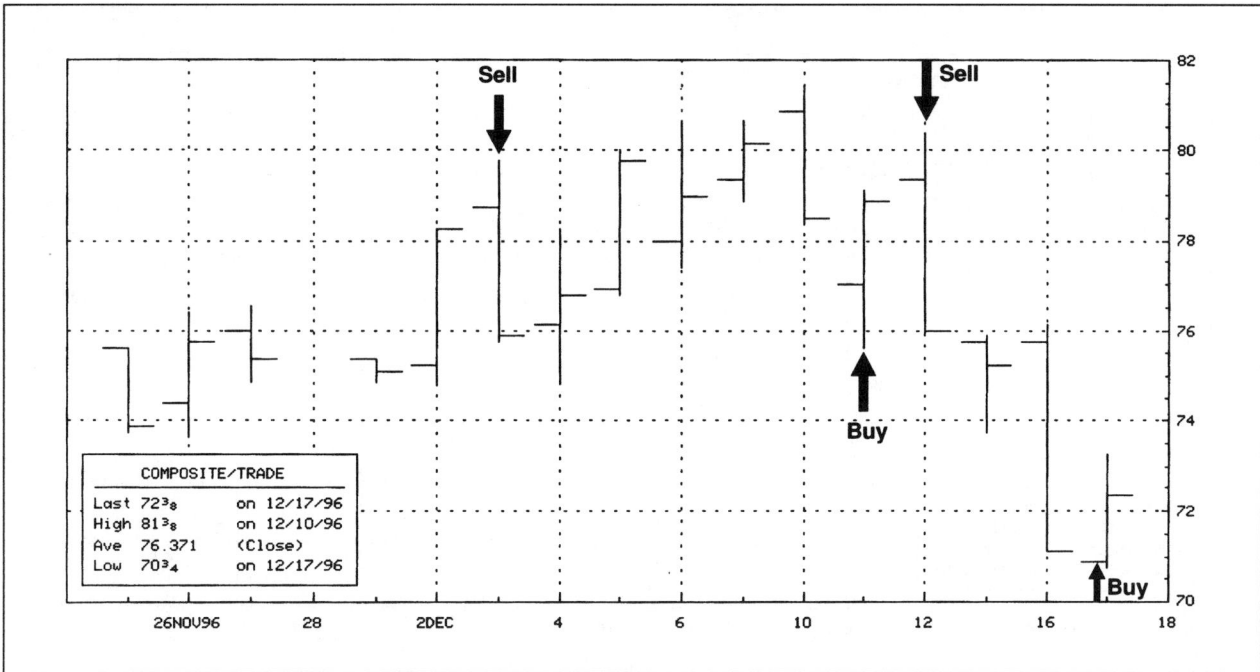

Here you see four setups over a two-week period in 3COM. Though this many setups over such a short period is rare, it does show the reality of "pulling the rubber band too far" and reversing.

FIGURE 23.4 Nikkei

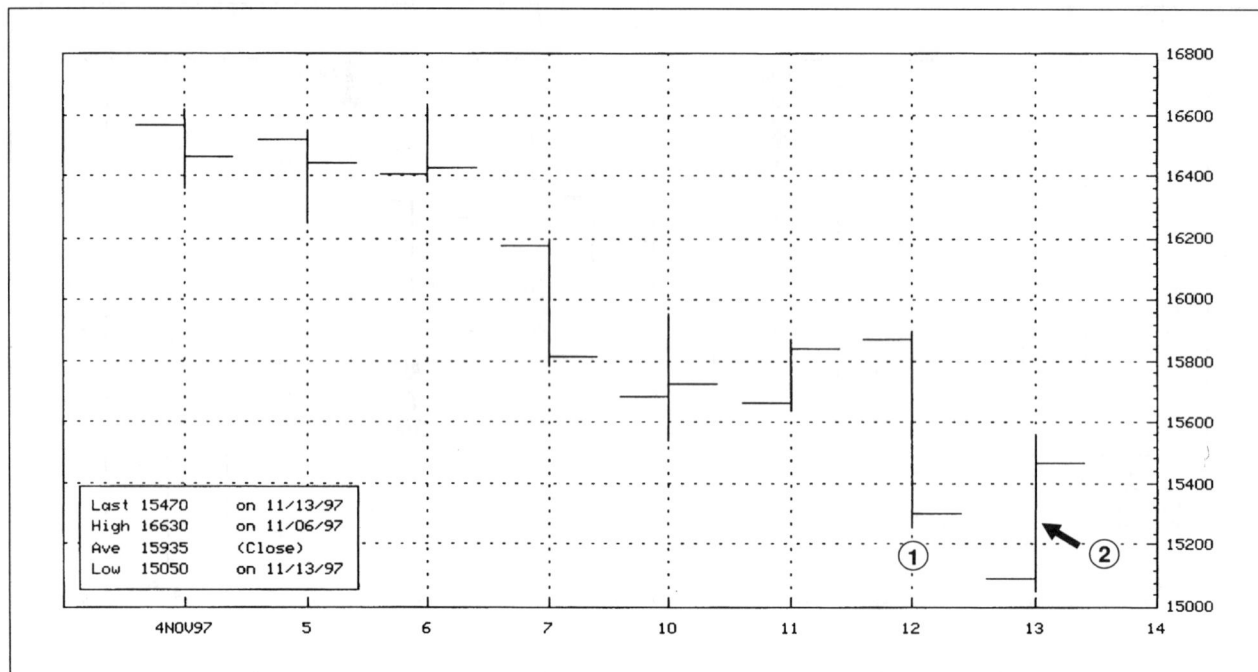

1.   A two standard deviation move.

2.   Buy.

SUMMARY

Even though I showed equity examples, this strategy works equally well on the futures markets. Wide Range Exhaustion Gap Reversals are fairly rare but when they do occur, they should be traded. By combining them with the other gap reversal strategies, you will have isolated what I believe to be the best gap setups to trade.

SECTION SEVEN

MORE ADVANCED TRADING STRATEGIES AND CONCEPTS

This section of the book covers a mixture of strategies. Two of the chapters are written by friends of mine, Mark Boucher and Derek Gipson, and reveal how to identify and enter strongly trending markets. I consider these strategies and the strategies presented by Fernando Diz and Jeff Cooper to be among the best presented in my *Professional Traders Journal*.

The next to last chapter covers a topic I have been fascinated with for many years. "How Superior Individuals Become" looks at whether great traders are made or born. As with most things in life, the study stresses the importance of hard work and the lack of importance of genetics.

CHAPTER **24**

TRADING RUNAWAY MOVES

■ ■

Mark Boucher is the author of the following. Mark is a long-time friend and a very successful hedge fund manager from Northern California. In 1990, I purchased one of Mark's original courses. To this day, I feel it has had a large and most profound effect on my trading. Mark has grown his fund using the techniques from his course into one of the most consistently performing funds in the country.

One of the most reliable and profitable situations a stock or futures contract can develop is after a strong breakout of a flag-type trading range. A flag trading range is a pattern in which a vehicle runs up strongly and then consolidates for a prolonged period of time before breaking out in the original direction again. Particularly in stocks, but also in futures, strong breakouts from flag trading ranges often lead to prolonged moves higher. In fact, simply trading flag trading ranges in their own time frame can be a very profitable endeavor.

However, for the purposes of short-term trading patterns, we will be discussing how to take advantage of these situations in order to position short-term by mixing time frames. In mixing time frames, one will often find that he or she is able to position with low, short-term bar risk distance between an open protective stop and entry, and yet participate in a move that is many, many times initial risk and which may develop into a longer than short-term move. This is how capital can be multiplied many-fold without significant risk—by finding low-risk trades that return many times that risk, and by finding short-term risk opportunities that have the potential to develop into longer-term moves than the original time frame one is looking at.

For our examples, and in our own use of this pattern, we first look at daily bars and then go to half-hourly bars for the pattern. In other words, we screen a half-hourly pattern with a longer-term bar chart. Even shorter-term traders could do the same thing on a shorter time frame. One could look at a half-hourly bar chart to screen 5- or 10-minute bar patterns for instance. The key point is that you are entering with entry points set on a shorter time frame—and may be able to capture a move that develops into a longer time-frame run-up in order to profit many multiples of your initial risk.

The pattern we are going to show you is called the "flag within a flag pattern."

As a brief side note, investors using these patterns should understand that they can achieve better results, both in terms of reliability and profitability, by concentrating on commodities that meet our runaway criteria and stocks that meet our runaway-up-with-fuel criteria as explained in our *Science of Trading* course and published monthly in our letter to clients, *Portfolio Strategy Letter*. Adding these filters is certainly not necessary to very profitably trade these patterns, but it does also enhance results rather dramatically.

Investors lacking a list of runaway-up-with-fuel stocks, as well as all those traders seeking as many investment opportunities as possible, should go through a daily process of reviewing all the stocks on the new high list. We're looking for stocks making new highs after having just broken out of at least a 17-day flag trading range pattern. Again, the flag pattern is a sharp run-up in price followed by a consolidation for 17+ days that does not retrace 38 percent of the initial sunup. We are looking for prices to break out on a gap from the prior close or on a large-range day.

Let's look at an example to clarify. Tuboscope, Inc. (symbol TUBO) began to make the 52 week new high list in mid June when it broke out of a

FIGURE 24.1a Tuboscope, Inc.

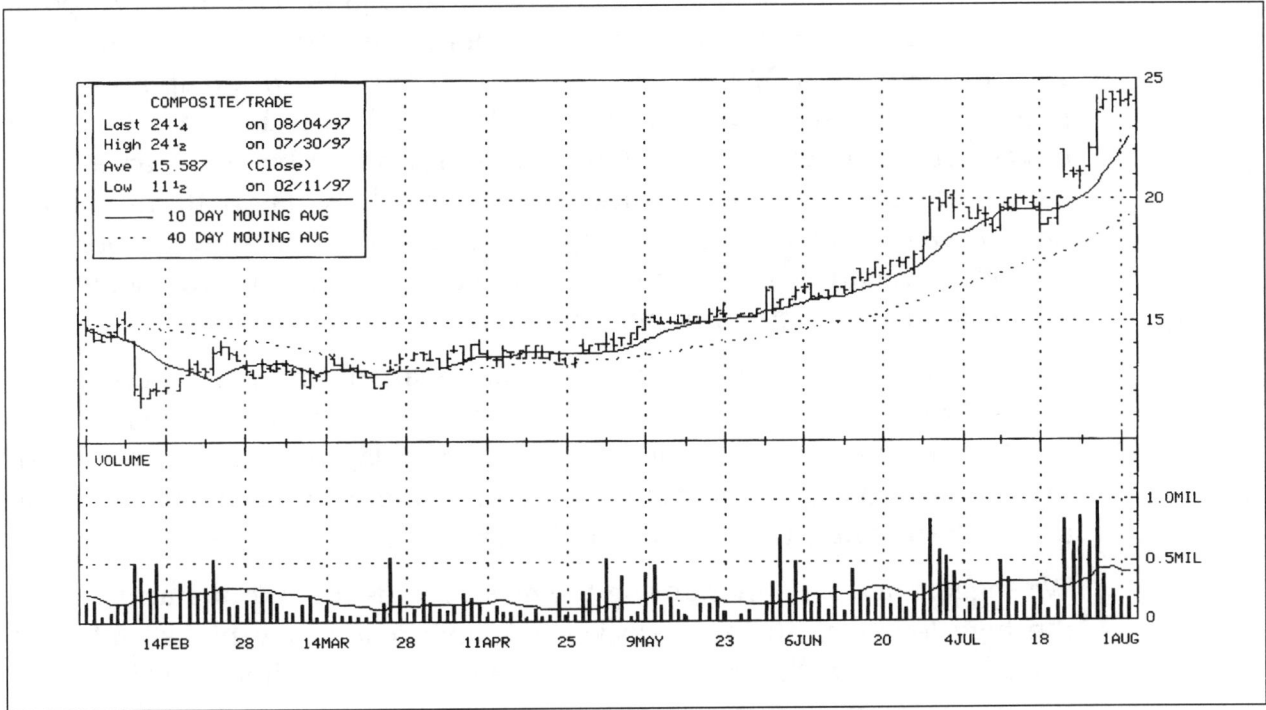

FIGURE 24.1b Tuboscope, Inc.

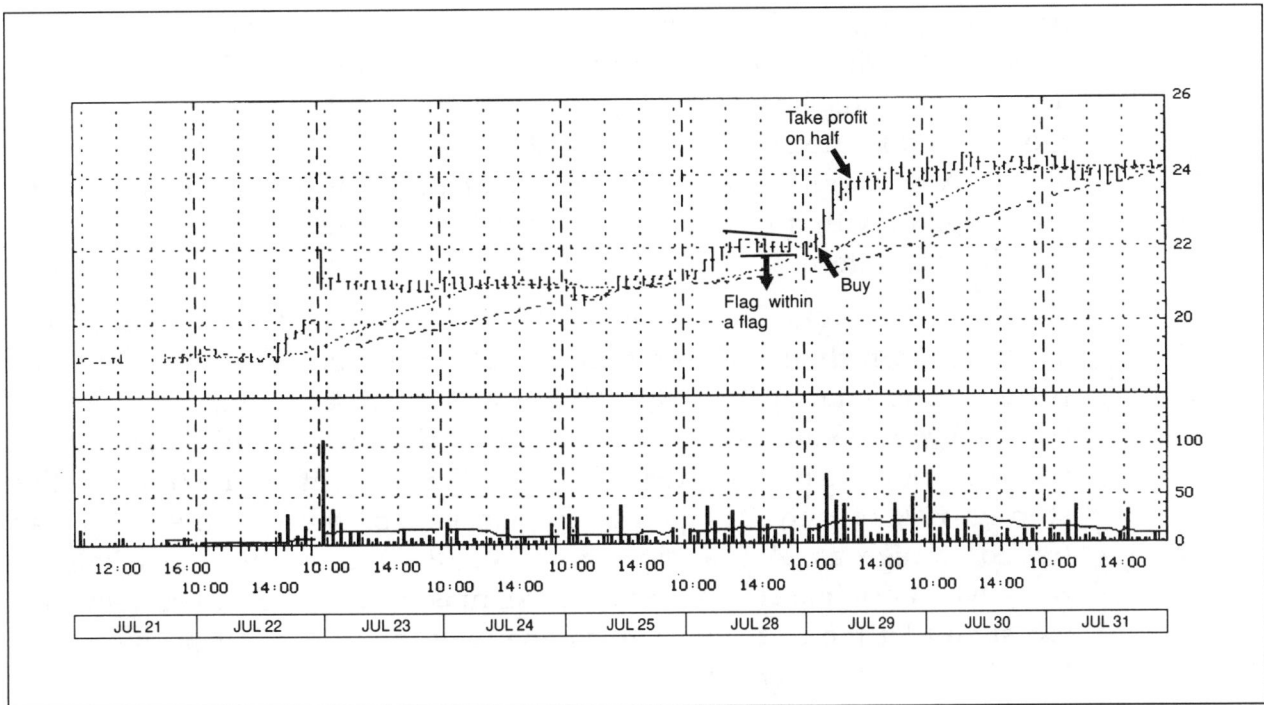

six-month trading range. (It also met our runaway-with-fuel criteria). It moved up from a low of 11 1/2 on 2/11 to 20 3/8 on 7/3, an 8 7/8 point move. From 20 3/8 it developed a consolidation pattern that declined to 18 5/8, a drop of 1 3/4 points, or 19.7 percent of the prior upmove (<38 percent). The consolidation lasted 17 days or longer before a breakout developed on a gap on 7/23. Our criteria for a flag breakout on a daily chart were met. Note that we need to first find daily flag patterns making new 52-week highs before looking for what will ultimately be our two shorter-term patterns. In this way we are adding a short-term element to an already explosively profitable situation.

Now an investor could certainly buy the breakout and use an open protective stop just below 18 5/8 with pretty low risk for a decent trade, meeting the criteria established in our courses flag pattern. But we're going to show you how you can get far more bang for your buck by adding a short-term pattern to this already lucrative setup.

We suggest investors monitoring the new high list daily put alarms above the high levels of all those stocks that have made new highs and have consolidated in a flag pattern for 17 days or more without retracing 38 percent of the prior upmove, so as not to miss an opportunity. One could use CQG, Bloomberg, TradeStation, Investigator, or even several sources on the internet (like Quote.com) to set these alarms.

The short-term flag within the longer-term breakout works as follows: once you get alerted of a breakout or a new high following a breakout, go to the half-hourly chart. Often, following an initial upthrust half hour, a stock will consolidate, making a short-term flag pattern of four bars or more that does not retrace 38 percent or more of the last half-hourly upswing. A breakout above the high bar of this half-hourly pattern is the entry signal, with a protective stop-loss (ops) below the low of this half-hourly flag pattern.

TUBO for example, broke out on 7/23, consolidated via a half-hourly stochastic correction and rose to new highs again on 7/28. It made a flag pattern consolidating between 22 1/4 and 21 3/4 for eight half-hourly bars before breaking to new highs again in the second half hour of 7/29, where it could be purchased at 22 3/8 to 22 5/16 with a 21 5/8 protective stop—a risk of only 3/4 points. By the end of the day the stock had traded as high as 24 1/4, closing at 23 5/8. Traders could exit half the trade when original risk is first covered, making the trade a break-even at worst and let the rest ride. This is one way to build a big position with low risk in a runaway stock.

A trader risking 1 percent of capital per trade (risk = distance between entry and protective stop) starting with $100,000 account could have risked $1,000 or if we allow a generous slippage and commission estimate of 1/4 point, could have purchased 1000 shares. Taking a quick 1/2 position profit at 23 3/8 to clear risk would have yielded $475 after commissions and open profits at the close were $625 on the remaining 1/2 position—a profit of 1.1 percent in a day with the strong possibility of being able to hang on to 500 shares of a stock that has just broken out of a trading range and is likely to move much higher with no more risk to original capital (at least theoretically) because the profit taken on the first 1/2 position more than covers the risk on the second 1/2. We have just locked in a large potential profit with very little risk—and a portfolio filled with several of these trades can return large amounts of profit with very little risk of capital, which is what we're trying to accomplish as traders.

Remember that once a stock or future emerges from its flag base it will go on our list to watch for this pattern each time it moves into new 52 week high territory until it gets overvalued (stock: PE its five-year growth rate or its current quarterly earnings growth rate), overowned institutionally (stock: 40 percent or higher institutional + bank ownership of capitalization), overbought (weekly, daily, and monthly RSI above 85), until the trend turns (below 50-day moving average is a good rule of thumb but I prefer the GTI trend method as explained in my *Science of Trading Course*), or until the Relative Strength drops below 65 on a reaction or below 80 on a new high. In other words, once a stock breaks out of a flag if it continues to not violate any of the above criteria we still watch for internal half-hourly flags on each new 52-week high because the stock still shows strong potential for a big move. The prime time to buy is just after a breakout, but one can continue to watch for this short-term pattern even if the stock has broken out recently and continues to be one of the strongest in the market as shown in the following example (*see* charts of CTS.).

CTS first broke out of a trading range flag in early April and traded sharply higher making the new high list almost daily into early June, where it formed another flag and broke out in early July. On July 23 it made a strong close to new highs on a wide half-hourly bar. It was still undervalued via its quarterly and five-year growth rate compared to PE, still owned less than 40 percent by institutions, not yet wildly overbought on a weekly, daily and monthly basis all at once, was definitely in a

FIGURE 24.2a CTS

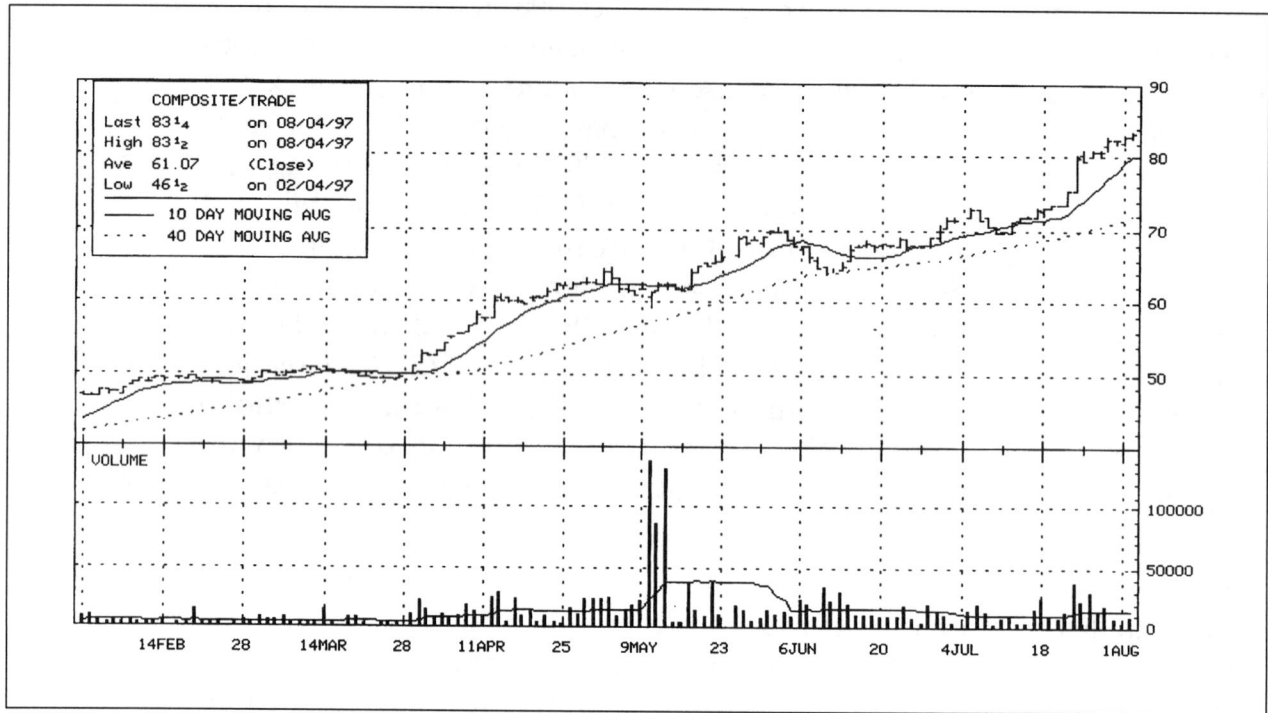

FIGURE 24.2b CTS

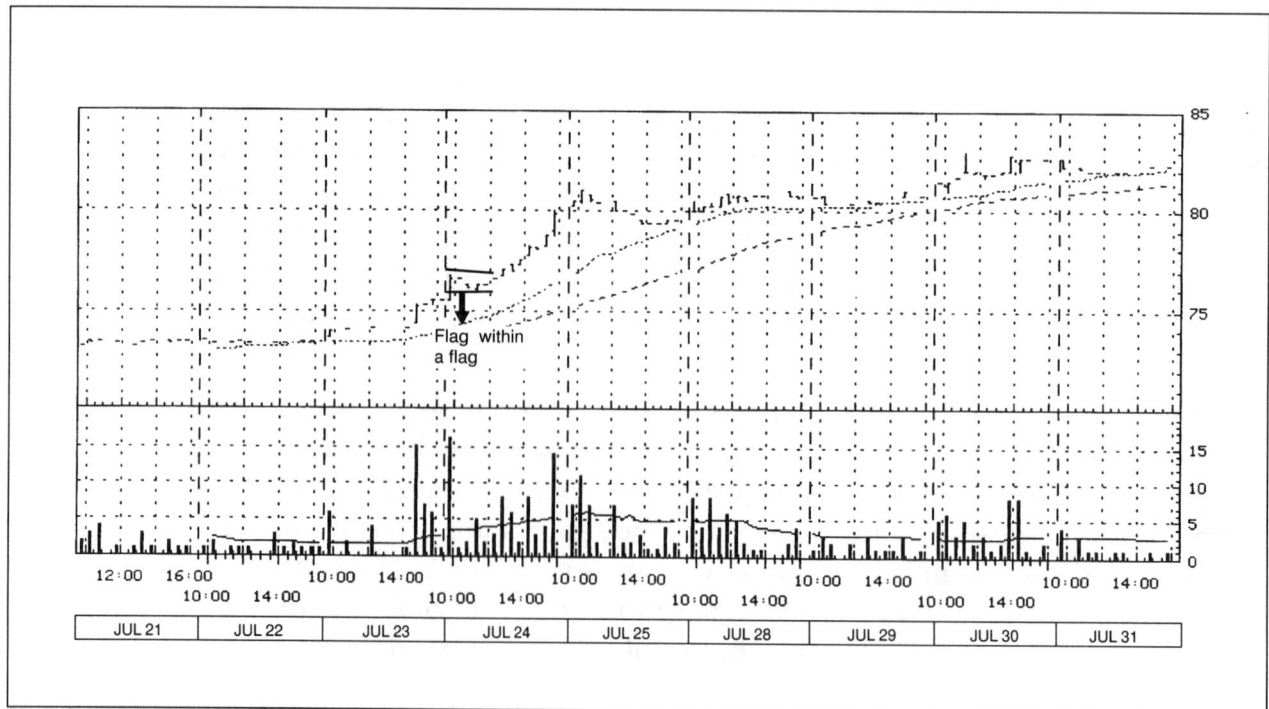

strong uptrend with RS above 90. And making new highs yet again. It clearly qualified for a potential short-term internal flag pattern.

The next morning it consolidated for five half-hourly bars below the highs of the last bar of July 23 (75 1/2) with a low of 75 1/8. When it broke above 75 1/2 if you bought the high of that half hour you got in at 75 5/8 and could have used a 75 protective sell stop—a risk of only 5/8 of a point. 1100 shares could be purchased with 1 percent risk. July 24 closed at 79 13/16 a profit of 4.19 points or almost five times your initial risk! If you took quick profits on 1/2 position at 76 5/8 you still ended up over $2,600 on the day (2.6 percent) and had no original capital at risk in a very explosive stock that has continued to move higher.

What about bear markets and what about futures? Surely if the pattern is robust it should hold up in runaway down vehicles as well as runaway up markets. Our next example should help answer those questions. If you run a relative strength analysis (O'Neil's RS) on futures contracts around the globe you can pinpoint the strongest and weakest futures just as you can in stocks. One of the weakest futures recently (RS < 5) has been the nearby D-Mark futures. There was a very recent flag within a flag pattern in this runaway bear market.

On June 30 (*see* D Mark charts), the D-Mark gapped down to a new low breaking out of a daily chart flag pattern. It continued to decline thereafter. On July 22 the D-Mark gapped down on the open to a new low—with a new low, clear very bearish runaway characteristics, and super low RS, traders should be on the lookout for bearish flags within a flag in this market. The D-mark consolidated and then made a big thrust to new lows on the seventh 1/2-hourly bar of the day. It then made a four-bar flag pattern on the 1/2-hourly chart off of 5515 low and a rally to 5528. Traders with a $100,000 account would have sold five contracts on a 5514 stop with a 5529 protective stop for a 15-tick risk, about $200 after commissions per contract risk. The market closed at 5502 and in order to cover risk traders would have taken a quick $400 profit after commissions on three contracts, keeping two open with risk more than covered by profits taken. With the D-Mark continuing to collapse, traders who took a 1 percent risk on 7/22 would now have $3,200 (3.2 percent) in open profit on those remaining two contracts with large potential profits on a break-even worst-case situation.

When a futures contract is especially bearish we can apply the exact same pattern in reverse for short signals. And when the stock market eventually turns lower in a bear market, we can do the same in stocks. Until

FIGURE 24.3a D-Mark

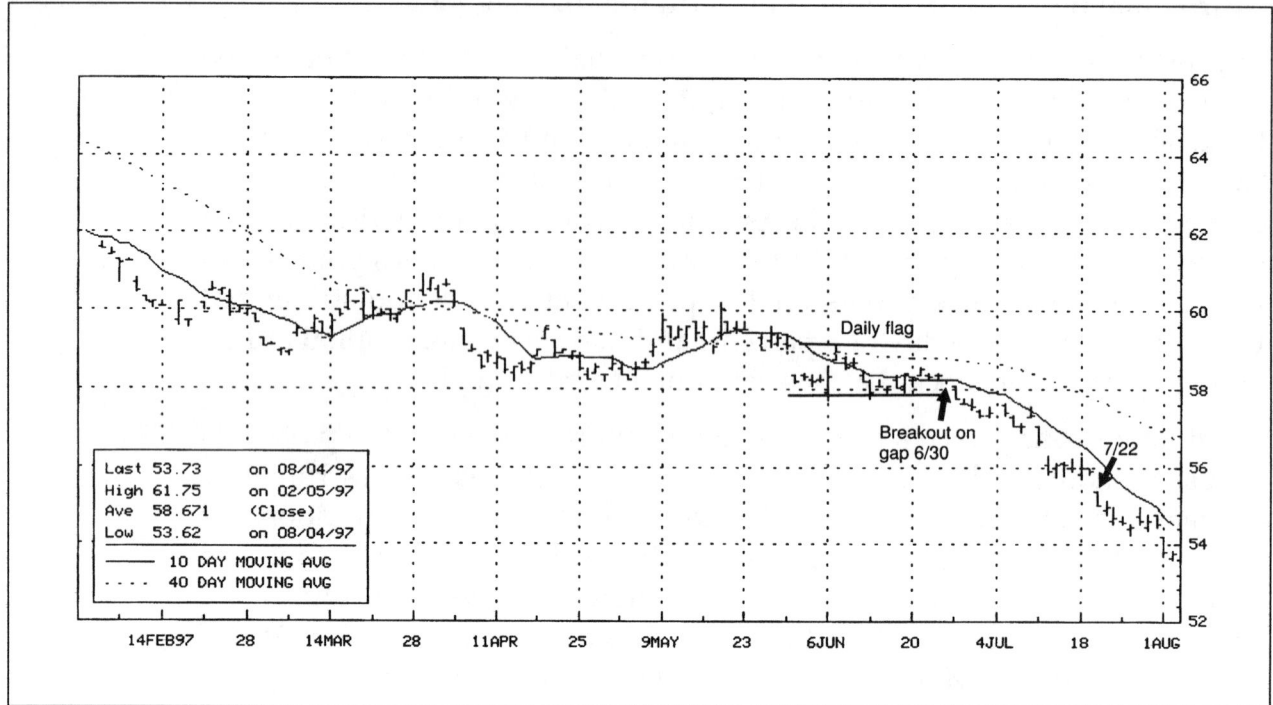

FIGURE 24.3b D-Mark

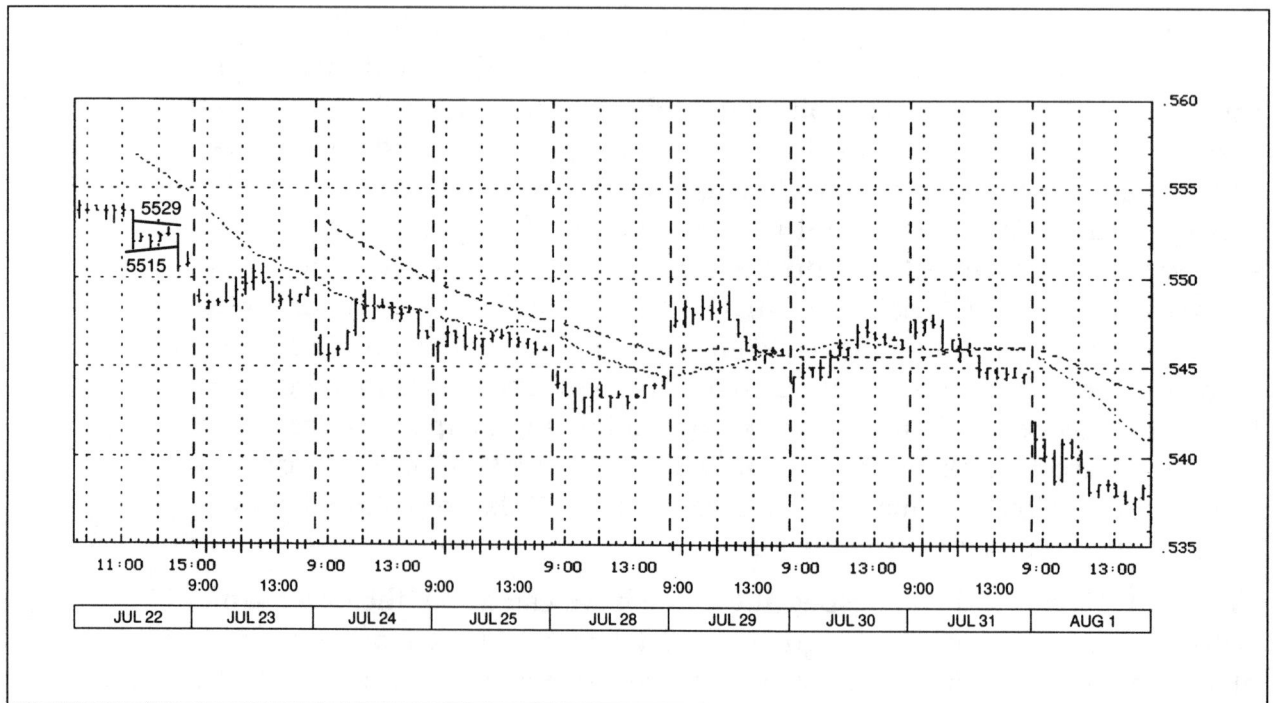

such time that new 52-week lows move above new 52-week highs, we recommend investors stick with bullish patterns in the U.S. stock market.

The bottom-line is that this simple pattern allows us to get in on a good short-term day-trade, and also leaves open the potential of a much more lucrative opportunity in the some of the most explosive stocks or futures available in the markets. It allows us to position heavily in the strongest stocks, but in a way that takes very small risk to original capital and yet still allows traders to profit at sometimes astronomical rates.

If you can't take enough profits the first day (or second day if it is entered in the second half of the day) on half the position to cover the risk on the remaining half then get out and wait for another opportunity. Cautious traders may only want to take trades in the first half of the day so that they don't have to take overnight risk unless they have large open profits and have booked profits on a day trade in the first half position. More cautious traders may also want to book the whole profit at the close unless the close is at least as far above your entry as your original protective stop was below it.

Traders should note that we are finding this simple pattern in new-high stocks at least twice a week—which should continue as long as the broad market remains strong. This is many more opportunities than any trader can exploit with limited capital. We hope you can watch and profit from such a pattern in the future, and that it becomes a key arrow in your quiver of short-term trades toward maximum profits. In addition, we hope short-term traders note that the huge upside potential of this trade comes from taking a risk on a short-time frame and getting into a move that can last much longer and move up many many times that small initial risk. Probably the biggest problem with short-term trading is that it is rare to get a reward 10 or 20 times risk because you have to get out at the end of the day. However by positioning in vehicles set to move up sharply on a daily basis, by taking quick day-trade 1/2 profits, and by only staying in overnight when a large profit exists at the close, short-term traders can not only book reliable trades consistently, but can often find a ten-bagger without taking very large risks—and without having to wait years to realize it by using this pattern.

CHAPTER 25

GIPSONS

∎ ∎

This strategy was created and written by Derek Gipson, a friend of mine and an extraordinary researcher. Derek will share with you his findings regarding predicting direction during times of low volatility. The academic world has claimed for 40 years that volatility and price direction are not correlated. Derek's findings of a directional-trend bias in low-volatility, high-ADX situations, appears to refute the academic assertion.

By way of personal background, Derek is a trader for a major investment firm. I have known him for more than seven years and have regularly relied on him to assist me with my research. What makes Derek's work special is that he begins with the premise that markets have inherent features which repeat themselves. He builds his models based on these features. You have heard me use the term "conceptually correct" in describing a strategy. By looking at the markets as he does, Derek's research leads to strategies that are both conceptually correct and profitable.

A built-in feature of all markets is the concept that periods of low volatility lead to periods of high volatility and vice versa. This has been shown true by academics for more than 40 years. The general consensus among academics is that even though volatility can be predicted, the price movement accompanying a change in volatility cannot be. In the following presentation, I will show you why I disagree and I will show you the method that identifies specific situations where there is a directional bias coming out of low-volatility situations.

Before going forward, let's review a few basic concepts that I will be using. The 6/100 historical volatility (H.V.) reading under 40 percent means that the six-day H.V. is .4 or less of the 100-day number. When this occurs, markets are poised to explode. ADX is a mathematical measurement which calculates the strength of a trend. The higher the ADX, the stronger the trend. +DI and –DI calculate the direction of the trend. +DI is greater than –DI means the market is rising and vice versa.

I have spent the last two years doing research uncovering specific situations when direction and volatility coincide. I have done this research to further my trading in the options market but the methodology I am about to reveal can and should be used in both the futures and equities.

Here are the rules:

1. Identify the markets or stocks which are trending most strongly. I use a 14 period ADX reading and I look for readings above 25. *The higher the reading, the better.* I also identify the trend with +DI and –DI. This is critical because we only trade in the direction of the trend.

2. If a market or equity qualifies with a high ADX reading, I then wait for its 6/100 day historical volatility reading to drop under .40. This means the six-day reading is less than 40 percent of the 100-day reading. I prefer a lower reading because it tells me the market is truly poised to explode.

3. When rules 1 and 2 are met, I then wait for the market to resume its move in the direction of the trend. I will not take signals opposite the trend. A long entry is triggered for uptrending markets when the high of the signal day is exceeded; a short entry is triggered for downtrending markets when the low of the signal day is taken out.

4. My initial protective stops are extremely tight. For uptrending markets, my initial protective stop is usually near the low of the signal day and for downtrending markets, my initial protective stop is near the high of the signal day.

5. Exits: There are three ways to exit profitable positions.

   a. Follow the price with a trailing stop until you are stopped out.

   b. Look to make a specific percentage return on your investment. That is, if you buy an option at 5, you might have a target exit at 7 1/2 to 10; for stocks you should look to exit at profit levels of at least 5 to 10 percent, etc.

   c. My recommendation: Exit half your position and tighten your stops on the other half when the 6-day H.V. reading reaches the 100-day reading. This shows that volatility has returned to normal.

Let's look at four examples to help better understand how to trade this methodology.

FIGURE 25.1a   IBM

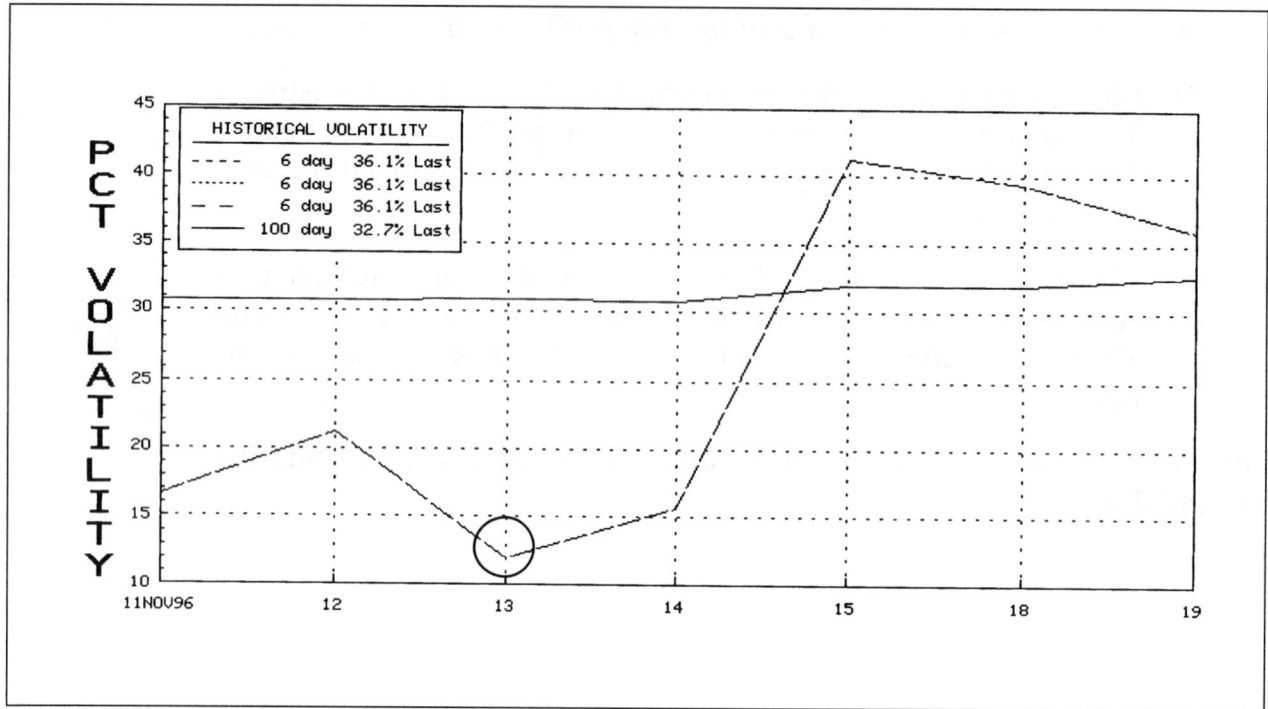

FIGURE 25.1b   IBM

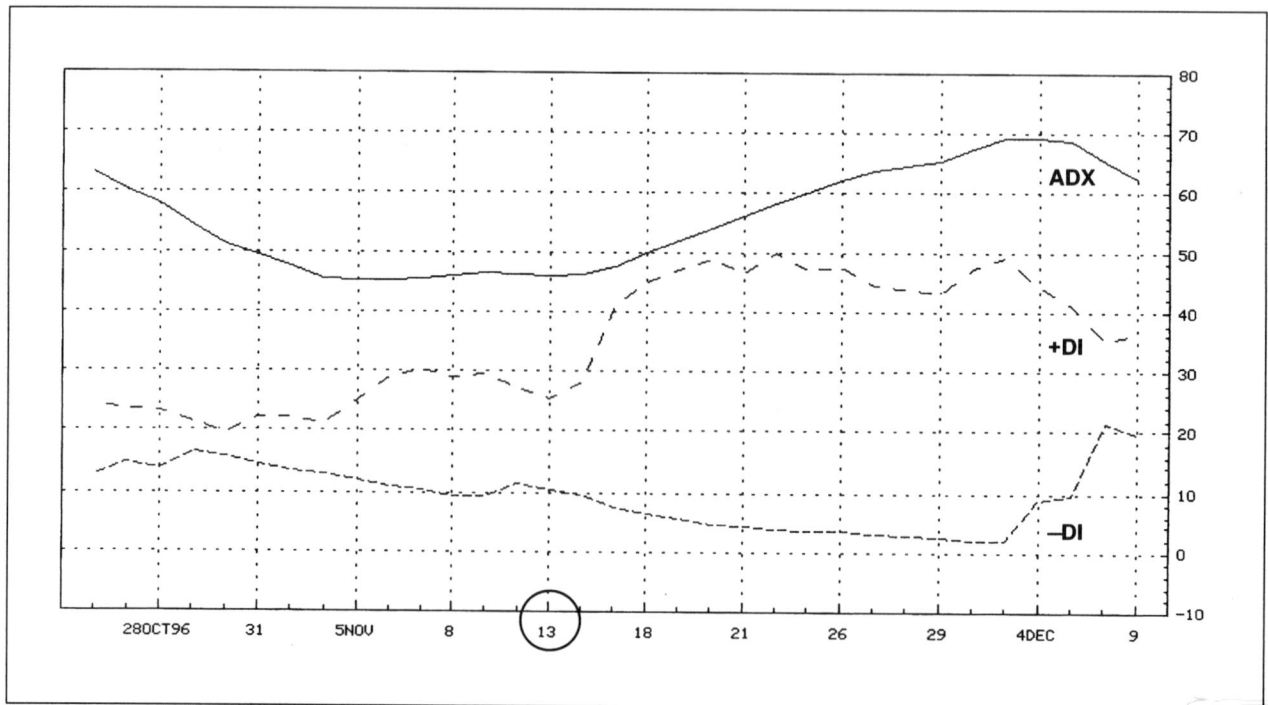

FIGURE 25.1c IBM

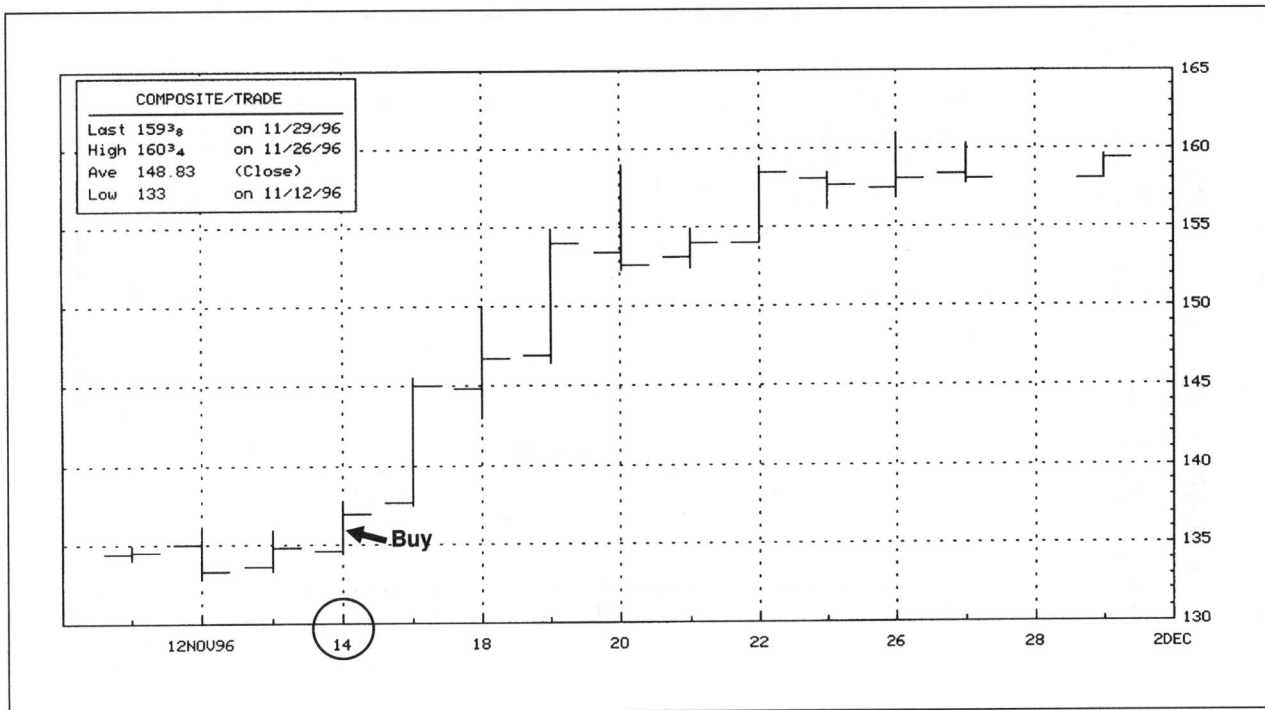

COMPOSITE/TRADE

Last	159³₈	on 11/29/96
High	160³₄	on 11/26/96
Ave	148.83	(Close)
Low	133	on 11/12/96

November 13, 1996—IBM has a six-day H.V. reading of 11.6 percent which is less than 40 percent of its 100-day reading of 30.9 37.5 percent). At the same time (Figure 25.1b) its ADX reading is well above 25 and its +DI > –DI signifying an uptrend. On November 14 (Figure 25.1c) it trades above its signal-day high triggering a buy signal and proceeds to explode nearly 19 points in four days.

FIGURE 25.2a Pediatrix Medical Group

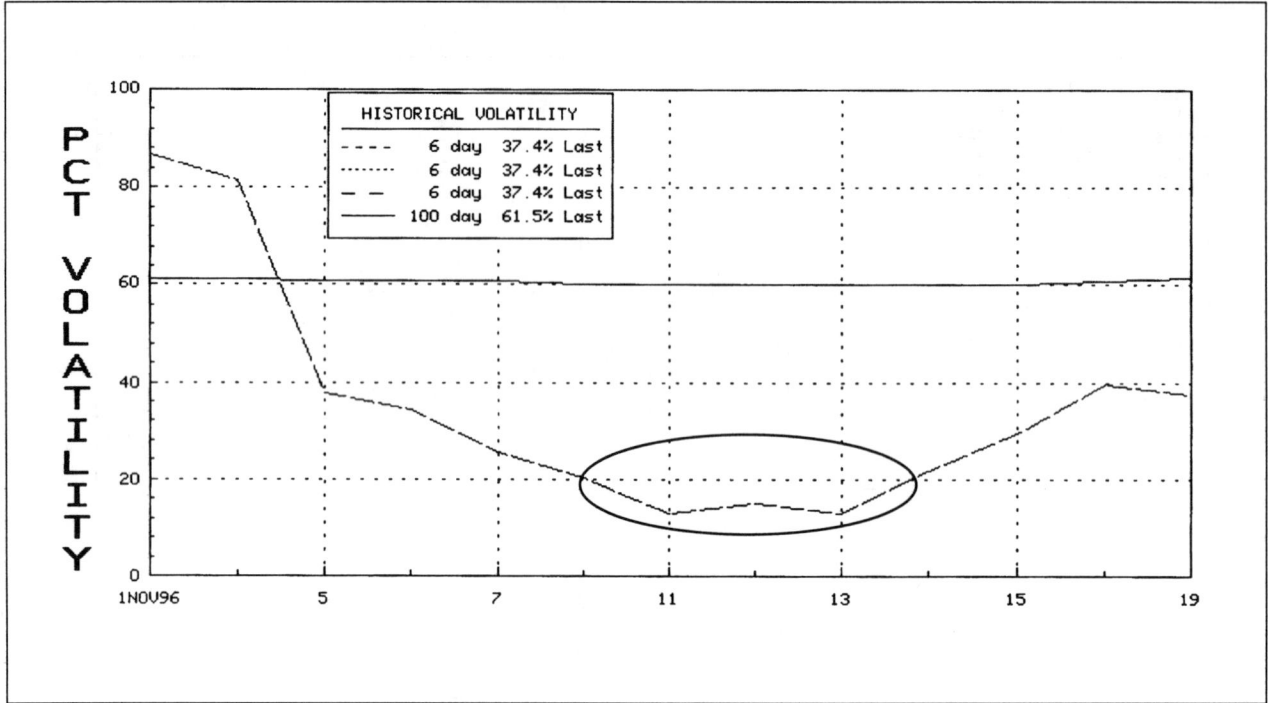

FIGURE 25.2b Pediatrix Medical Group

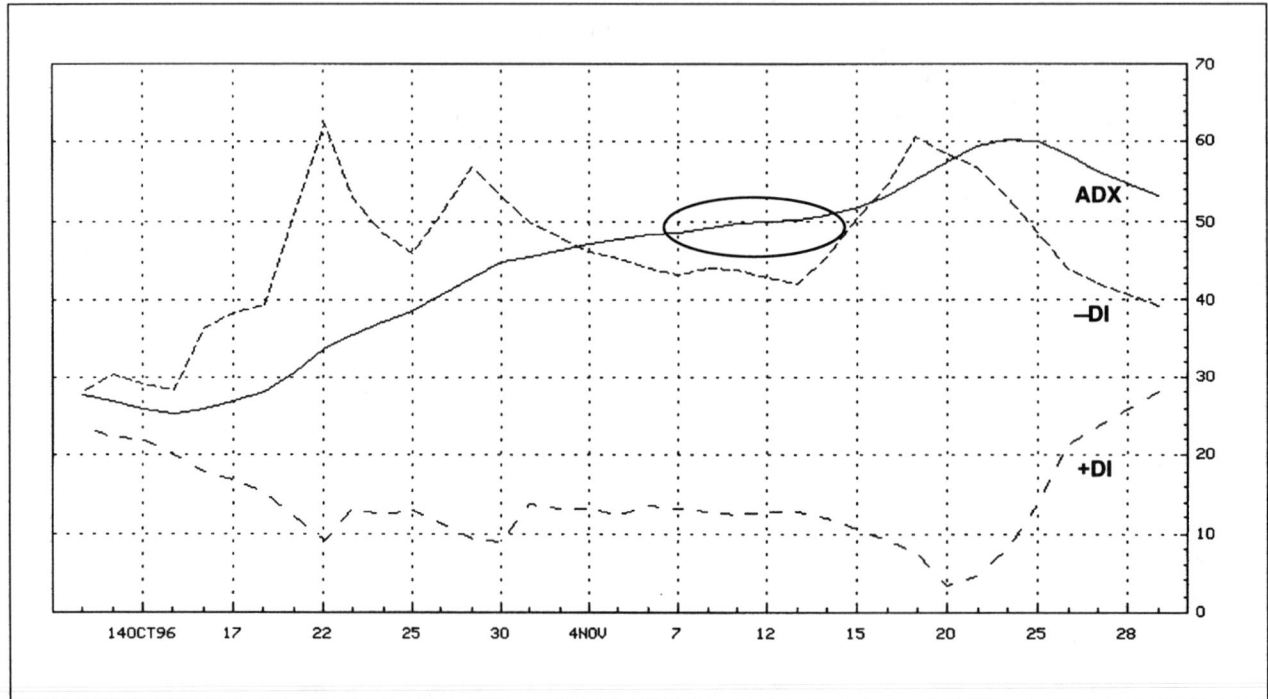

FIGURE 25.2c Pediatrix Medical Group

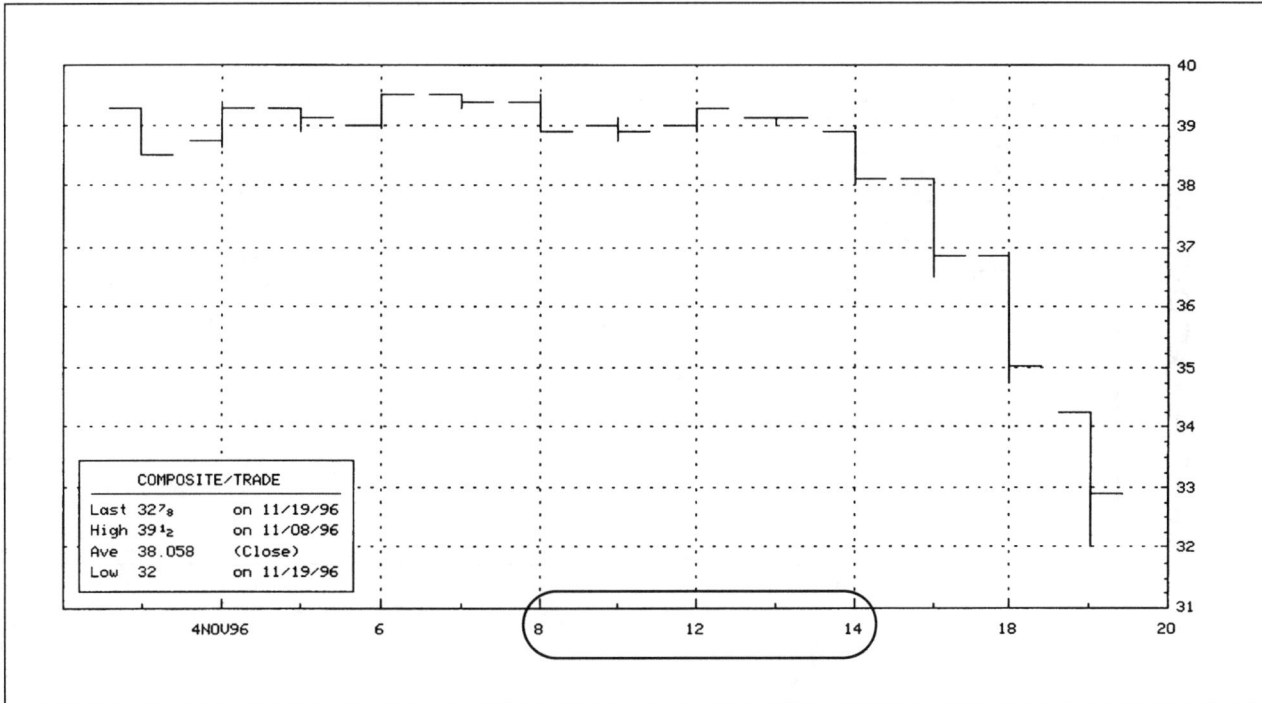

This is a terrific example because it shows a stock collapsing while there was a major uptrend in the overall stock market. November 8–13 (Figure 25.2a) shows a period of extreme low volatility combined with a down-trending market as defined by ADX (Figure 25.2b). November 11 (Figure 25.2c) shows a false move to the downside and when we again enter on November 14, we are amply rewarded with an almost 20 percent move to the downside.

FIGURE 25.3a   November Crude

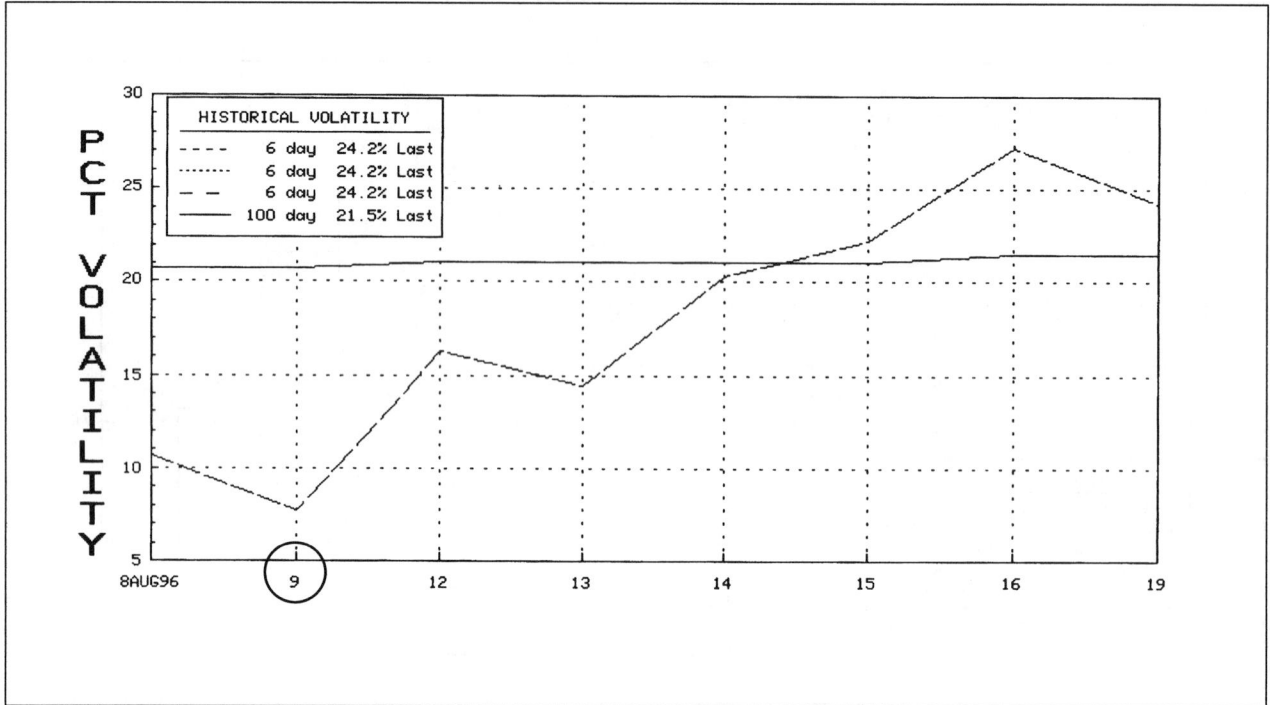

FIGURE 25.3b   November Crude

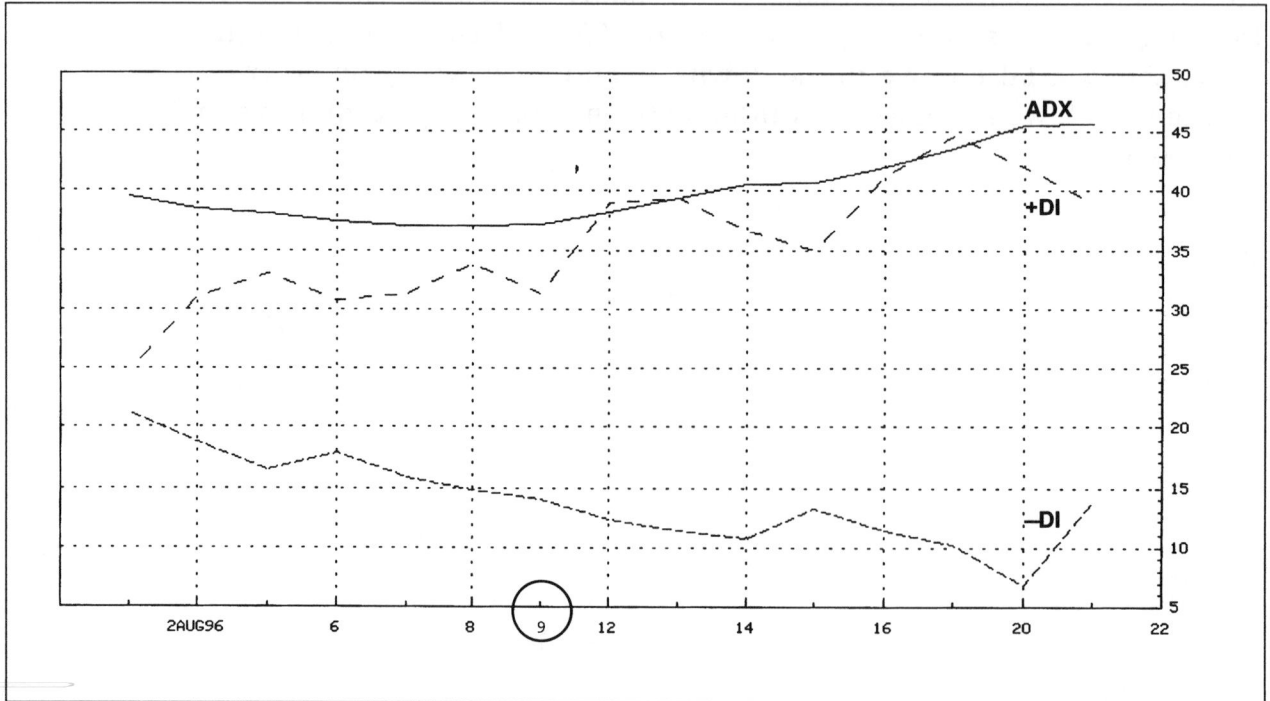

FIGURE 25.3c November Crude

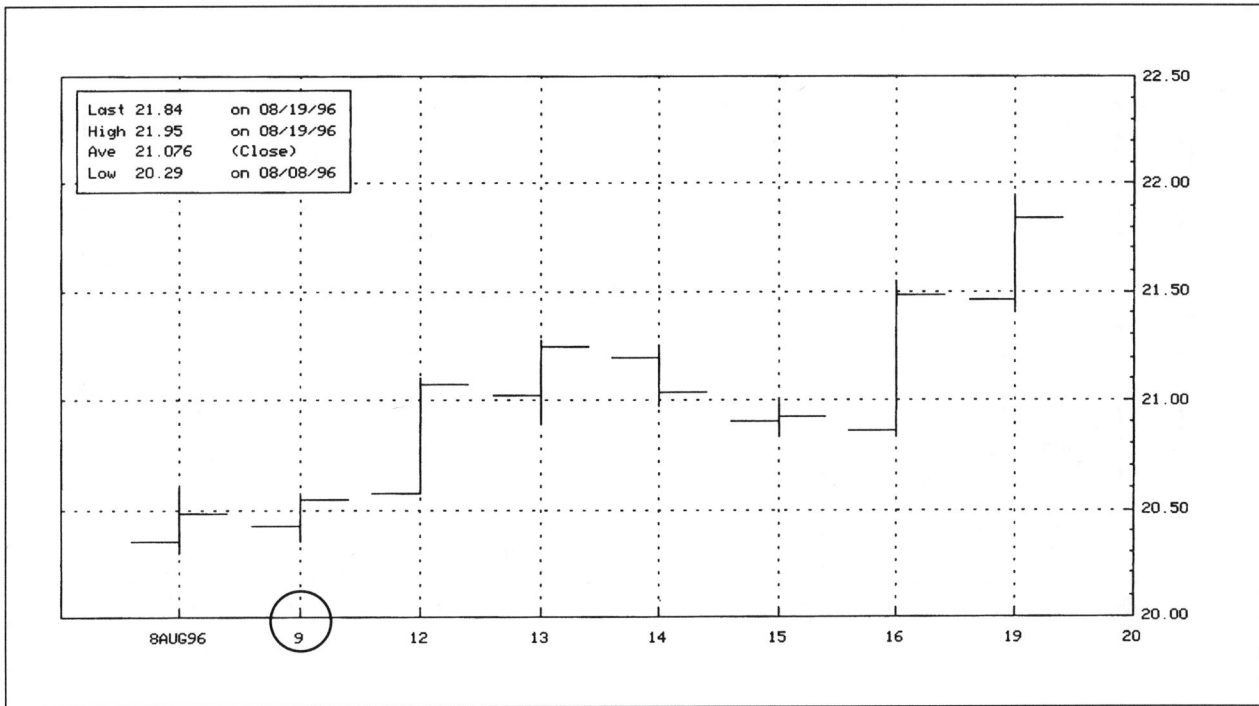

Figure 25.3a shows the 6-day reading at less than 40 percent the 100-day reading. At the same time, Figure 25.3b shows crude is clearly in an uptrend. We buy on the opening of August 12 as the trend resumes.

FIGURE 25.4a   December 96 S&P 500 Futures

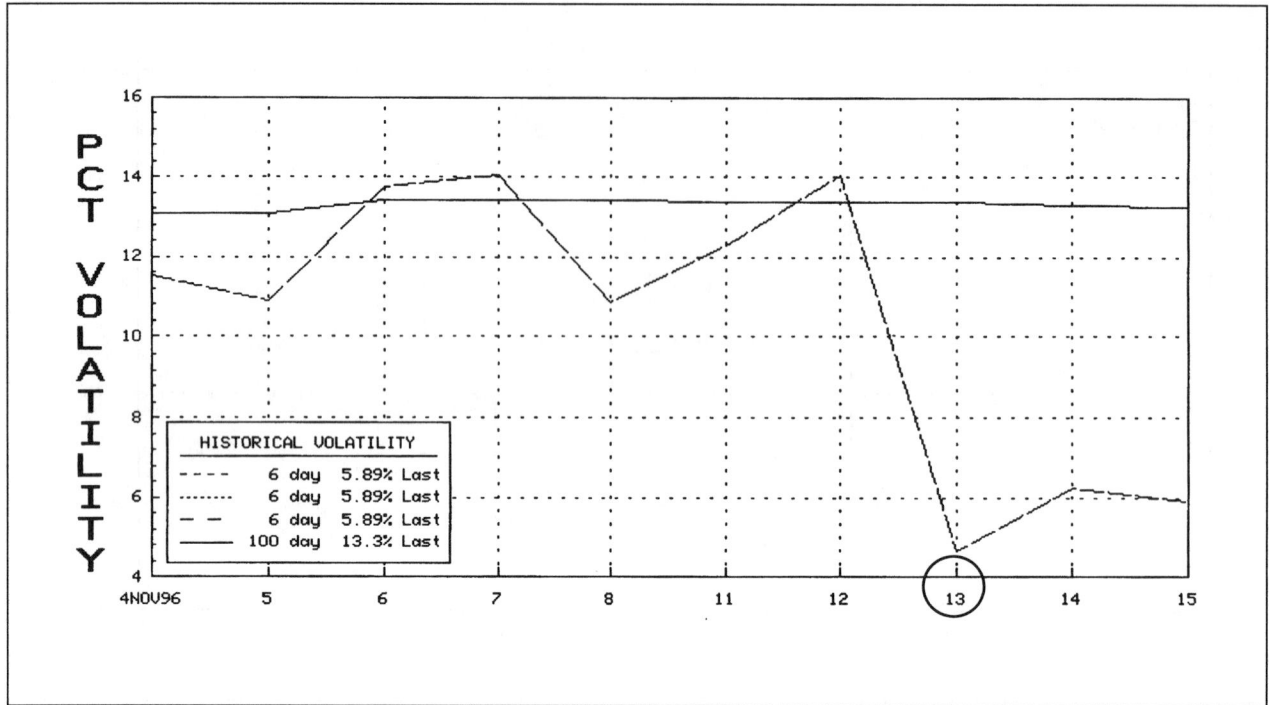

FIGURE 25.4b   December 96 S&P 500 Futures

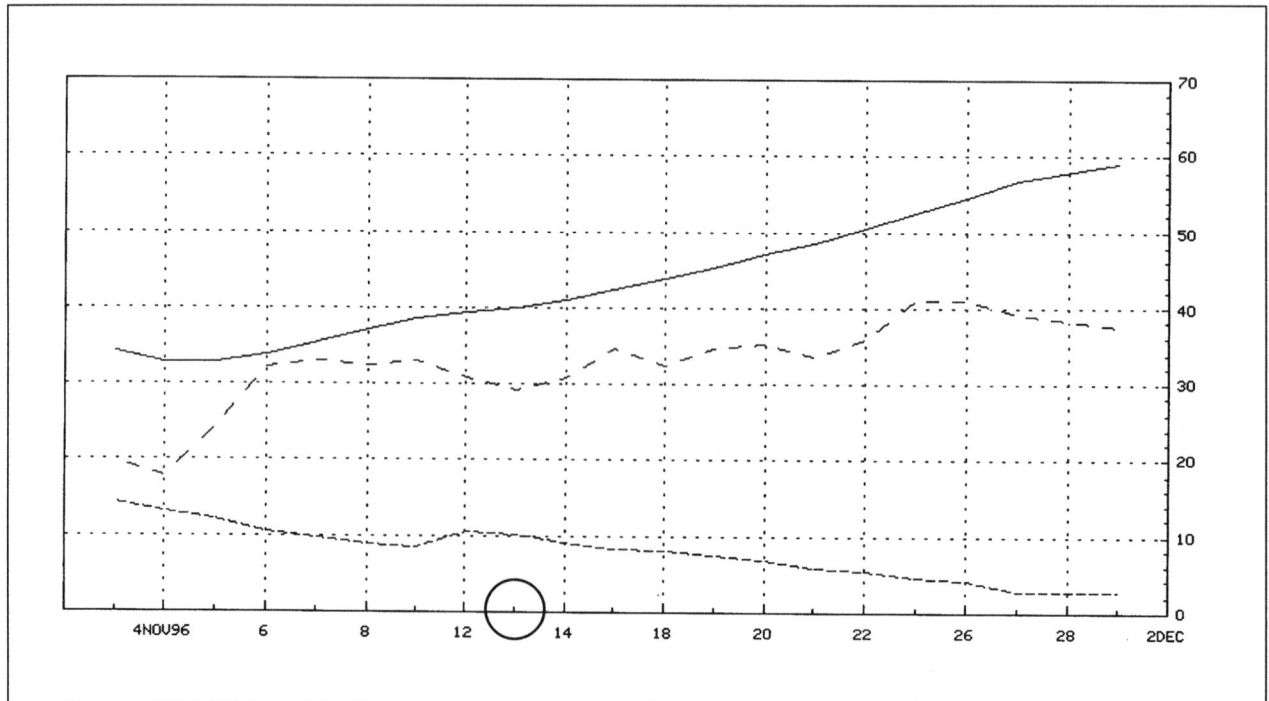

FIGURE 25.3c   December 96 S&P 500 Futures

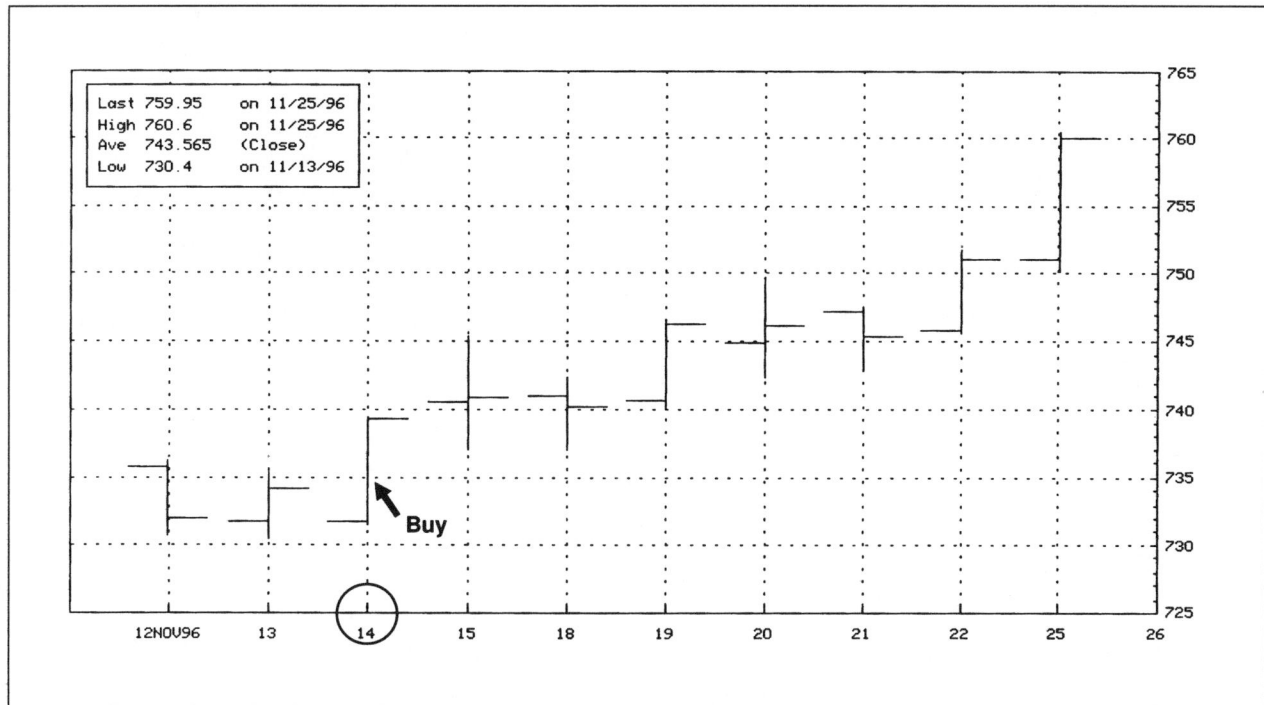

On (Figure 25.4a), November 13, 1996, the six-day H.V. reading is less than 40 percent of the 100-day H.V. The ADX reading (Figure 25.4b) is a powerful 44 and the trend is up. A buy signal (Figure 25.4c) is triggered the next day on November 14 and the futures explode nearly 25 points in eight trading sessions.

SUMMARY

Gipsons are obviously not 100 percent correct, but they do give you an edge in predicting direction during periods of low volatility. What occurs is, a strongly trending market (ADX) rests (low volatility), and when its rest is over, the trend resumes and many times does it in explosive fashion. I mentioned earlier that I created this methodology mostly to use in my options trading, but it assuredly lends itself to traders looking for short-term moves in the futures and equities markets.

CHAPTER 26

MAXIMIZING PROFITS IN SHORT-TERM MARKET DECLINES

▪ ▪

Imagine **this scenario:** It is late Friday afternoon and the stock market has been acting poorly over the past few days. Bigger picture, the market has risen for six straight years without a major correction. With 14 minutes to go in trading, a major negative news event with long-term consequences hits the wires. The market immediately begins to sell off. Your adrenaline is racing because you know that this sell-off will surely follow through on Monday.

Do you have an exact game plan to fully maximize the profit potential of the situation?

Common sense tells you to either buy OEX puts or to sell the S&P futures to capture the profits. This chapter will show you these strategies are potentially wrong (certainly not the best) and will show you which strategies are the best to exploit the situation.

USING OPTIONS

Do *not* buy OEX and SPX puts! *Do* buy puts on the brokerage house index (XBD), the NASDAQ 100 index (NDX), and the insurance index (IUX).

There are a number of reasons for this, but let's look at the most important: implied volatility. During periods of market weakness and periods of uncertainty, the implied volatility of the OEX options (especially the puts) greatly increases. *This means that you are almost certainly buying overvalued options.* These options will become even more overvalued in the scenario I presented because of the thousands of traders who have reached the same conclusions as you. I have witnessed times where the puts options were so overpriced that they actually lost value after the market opened lower the next day. (Traders think, "No market crash—sell the puts.")

Which options should you use to participate in a market sell-off? The following three are, in my opinion, the best.

Strategy #1—Buy Puts on the Brokerage House Index (XBD), the NASDAQ 100 Index (NDX), and the Insurance Index (IUX)

Why these three indices? Three reasons.

1. These three indices will not only participate in any market decline, they will probably exceed the broader market decline.

    Let's look at the three indices individually:

    - On Monday, October 17, 1987, the stock market as a whole lost 22.6 percent. Not only did the brokerage house stocks also decline, they lost an average of a nearly 29 percent for the day. Why? Who are the biggest losers in a bear market? (Enough said).

    - The NASDAQ 100 (NDX) is made up of the 100 largest OTC stocks. This index is more volatile than the S&P 500. Because of this volatility, the index usually drops on a percentage basis more than the other averages.

    - The insurance index is the most conservative of the three indices. This index should especially be used when a stock market sell-off is accompanied by a drop in the bond market. Why? Because insurance companies' profits are tied to the profitability of their stock and bond portfolios. Insurance companies get hurt badly when both stock and bond markets drop. An example of this occurred on March 8, 1996, when bonds collapsed. The stock market dropped just under 3 percent, yet the insurance index lost more than 4 percent of its value.

2.   The options on these three indices are usually priced in-line with the historical volatility readings. Let's look at the pricing of these as of March 29, 1996.

    As you can see from Figures 26.1a, 26.1b, 26.2a, 26.2b, 26.3a, and 26.3b, the historical volatility for the XBD index is 23.1 percent and the implied volatility is approximately 27 percent, the historical volatility for the NDX is 27.6 percent and the implied volatility is approximately 24.5 percent. The historical volatility for the IUX index is 15.4 percent and the implied volatility is approximately 17.9 percent. During market sell-offs, the puts on the OEX are at times as much as 50 percent overpriced, whereas these three indices basically trade in-line. You are therefore not "paying up" as you are on the OEX.

3.   The final reason for trading these indices instead of the OEX, is that the option prices of the indices are not as quickly marked up by traders. Whereas traders stampede into the OEX options and immediately inflate the prices, trading in the three indices is more orderly. Also, because the pricing mechanisms of these indices tend to be done off the cash market, one has more time to get in before a sell-off snowballs.

FIGURE 26.1a Brokerage House Index—Historical Volatility

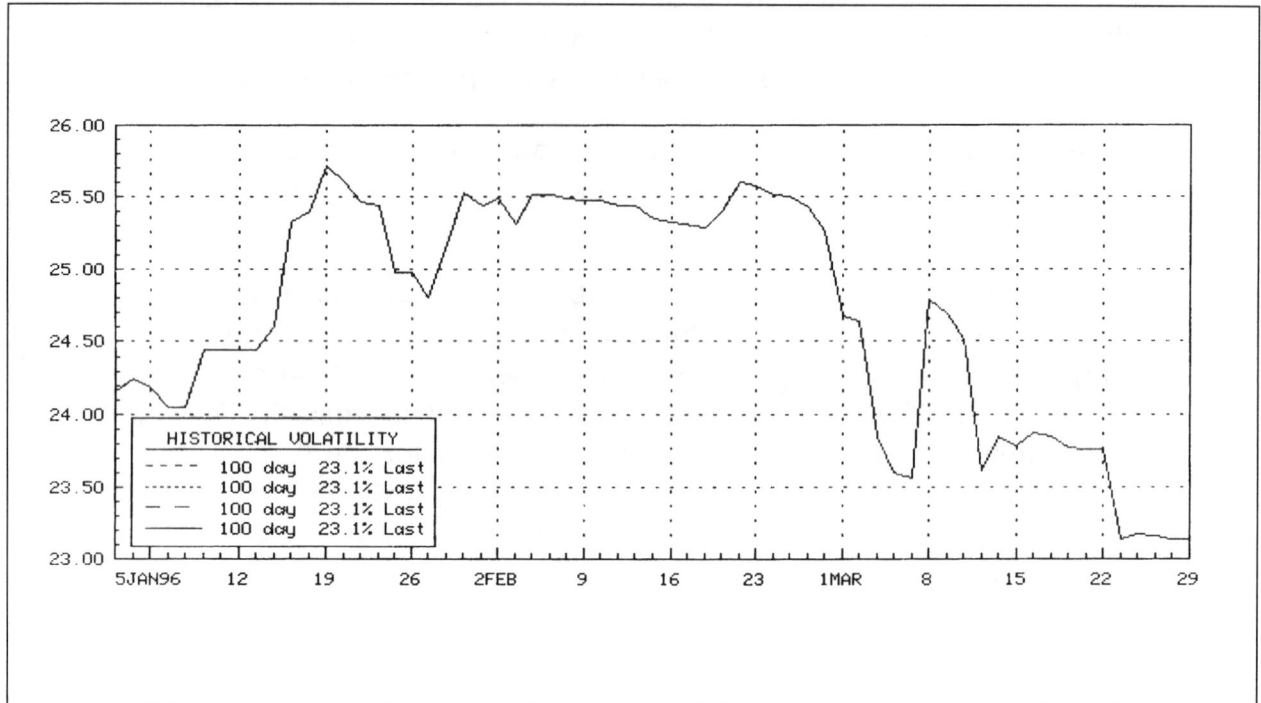

FIGURE 26.1b Brokerage House Index—Implied Volatility

```
XBD Index OHT                                    DG28 Index  O H T
Screen printed.
11:28                              DISPLAY:  C C-chg/%chg, D-delta/volat
Mon 4/1
Assume Index       O P T I O N   H O R I Z O N   A N A L Y S I S
$ 4.6/yr Div.      APR OPTIONS ON AMEX SEC BROKER/DEAL IDX
      X B D                  W O R K S H E E T
```

		T O D A Y					**7 D A Y S L A T E R**			
OPTION		403.17					403.17	u n c h		
PRICING:						Volat=**Same**		Volat=**Same**		
	C A L L S			**P U T S**			**C A L L S**		**P U T S**	
STRIKE	Prc	Del	I.Vol	Prc	Del	I.Vol	Prc Chg %Chg		Prc Chg %Chg	
385				0	n/a	n/a	0	unch n/a%		
390				3^{11}_{16}	.28	25.28	13^{11}_{16} $-^5_{16}$ -2%		2^1_8 -1^7_{16} -38%	
395	n/a	n/a		6^1_{16}	.36	27.17	8^{11}_{16} $-^5_{16}$ -3%		4^1_4 -1^{11}_{16} -30%	
*400	12^1_{16}	.57	27.10	7^{15}_{16}	.43	26.68	9^7_8 -2^3_{16} -18%		6^1_{16} -1^7_8 -24%	
*405	8^3_4	.50	25.12				6^3_4 -2 -23%			
410	6^3_4	.42	25.61				4^{13}_{16} -1^{11}_{16} -29%			
415	0	n/a	n/a	n/a	n/a		0	unch n/a%	11^{11}_{16} unch +0%	
420										

```
          Mon  4/ 1/96( 19days Expr)  5.17%Fin |Mon  4/ 8/96( 12days Expr)  5.17%Fin
```

OPTION	T -"Tickr" volatility	S -"Same" volatility
PRICING:	M - Trade "Match" volatility	1 2 . 5 % (or any other volat.)

FIGURE 26.2a   NASDAQ 100 Index—Historical Volatility

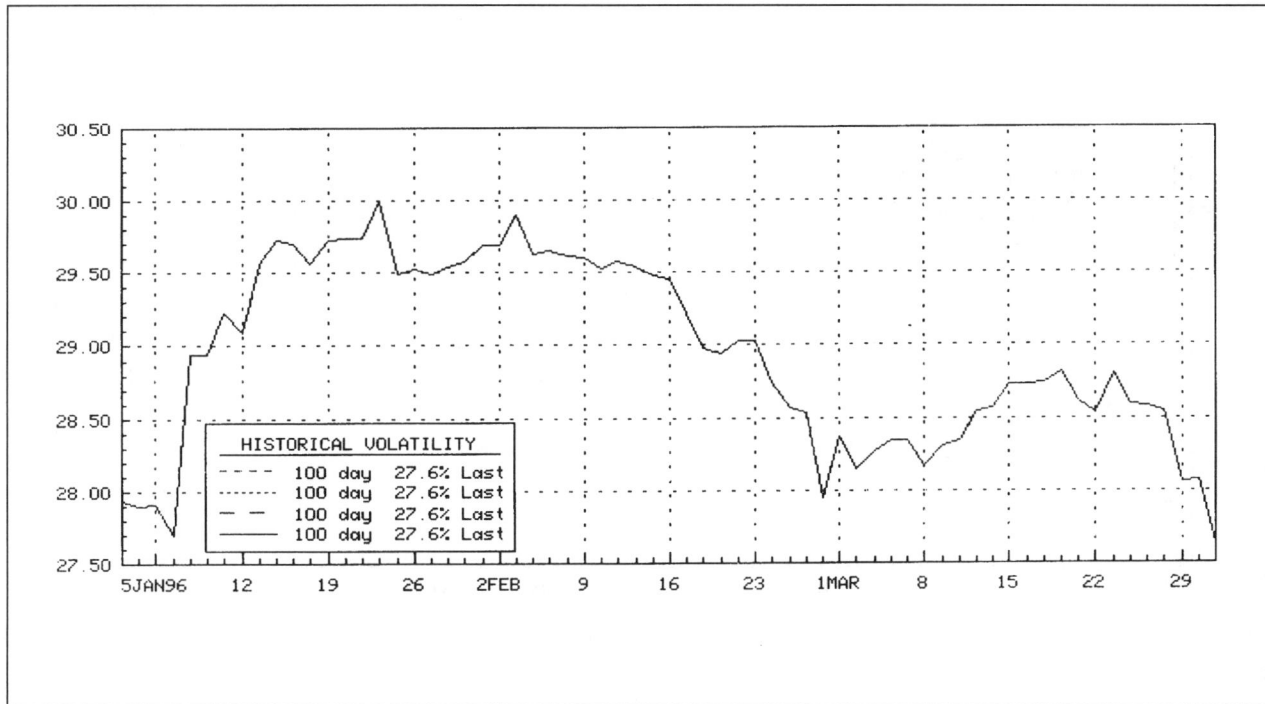

FIGURE 26.2b   NASDAQ 100 Index—Implied Volatility

```
NDX Index OHT                                    DG28 Index  O H T
For specific month: OHT 5 for May, OHT 6 for June, ...
16:56                              DISPLAY:  C C-chg/%chg, D-delta/volat
Mon 4/1
Assume Index        O P T I O N   H O R I Z O N   A N A L Y S I S
5 .6/yr Div.          APR OPTIONS ON NASDAQ 100 STOCK INDX
    N D X             M A R K E T   I S   C L O S E D
```

							7 DAYS LATER				
	TODAY 612.99						612.99 u n c h				
OPTION							Volat=**Same**		Volat=**Same**		
PRICING:	**Tickr**			**Tickr**			C A L L S			P U T S	
	C A L L S			P U T S							
STRIKE	Prc	Del	I.Vol	Prc	Del	I.Vol	Prc	Chg %Chg	Prc	Chg %Chg	
595				7	.29	26.91	21$^1_4$	-2$^1_8$	-9%	4$^5_8$	-2$^3_8$ -34%
600	23$^3_4$	.66	27.88	8$^1_4$	.33	26.09	20$^1_2$	-3$^1_4$	-14%	5$^1_4$	-2$^1_2$ -30%
605	18$^3_4$e	.62	24.22	10$^3_4$	.39	27.22	15$^1_4$	-3	-16%	8	-2$^3_4$ -26%
*610	16$^1_4$	.56	24.87	11$^1_4$	.43	24.17	13$^1_8$	-3$^1_8$	-19%	8$^{13}_{16}$	-2$^7_{16}$ -22%
*615	12$^7_8$	.51	23.41	14$^3_8$	.49	25.43	9$^{15}_{16}$	-2$^{15}_{16}$	-23%	11$^3_4$	-2$^5_8$ -18%
620	12 e	.45	25.92	15$^{11}_{16}$e	.56	23.12	8$^{13}_{16}$	-3$^1_{16}$	-27%	13$^9_{16}$	-2$^1_4$ -14%
625	8	.38	22.21	20$^1_8$e	.60	25.53	5$^3_8$	-2$^5_8$	-33%	17$^{11}_{16}$	-2$^7_{16}$ -12%
630	5$^3_4$	.31	21.02	23$^3_8$e	.65	25.55	3$^9_{16}$	-2$^3_{16}$	-38%	21$^1_{16}$	-2$^1_{16}$ -9%

```
       Mon  4/ 1/96 ( 19days Expr)  5.16%Fin  Mon  4/ 8/96 ( 12days Expr)  5.16%Fin
```

```
OPTION        T -"Tickr" price            S -"Same" volatility
PRICING:      M - Trade "Match" volatility  1 2 . 5 %  (or any other volat.)
```

FIGURE 26.3a Insurance Index—Historical Volatility

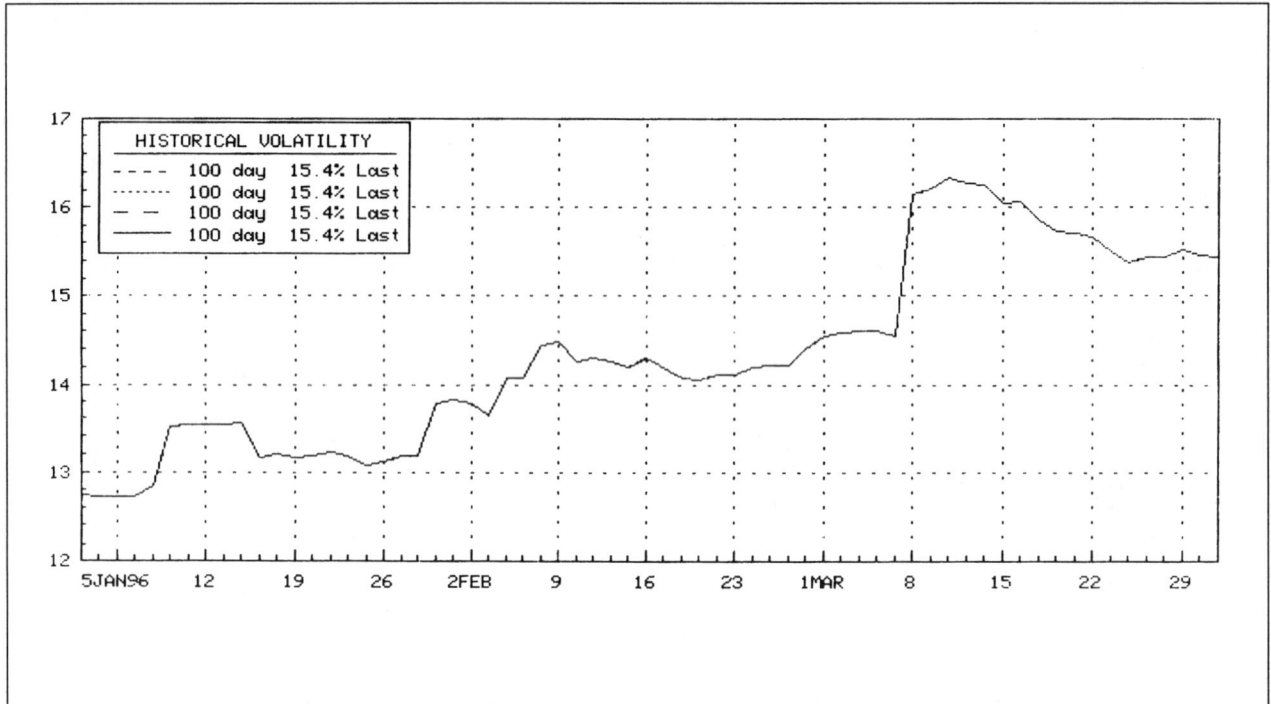

```
HISTORICAL VOLATILITY
---- 100 day  15.4% Last
.... 100 day  15.4% Last
- - 100 day  15.4% Last
—— 100 day  15.4% Last
```

FIGURE 26.3b Insurance Index—Implied Volatility

IUX Index OHT   DG28 **Index O H T**
Screen printed.
11:31   DISPLAY: ₵ C-chg/%chg, D-delta/volat
Mon 4/1
Assume Index
$ 5.5/yr Div.   **O P T I O N   H O R I Z O N   A N A L Y S I S**
                         APR OPTIONS ON S&P INSURANCE INDEX
      I U X   **W O R K S H E E T**

		T O D A Y					**7 D A Y S L A T E R**				
OPTION		**334.97**						**334.97** u n c h			
PRICING:						Volat=**Same**		Volat=**Same**			
	C A L L S			**P U T S**			**C A L L S**		**P U T S**		
STRIKE	Prc	Del	I.Vol	Prc	Del	I.Vol	Prc	Chg %Chg	Prc	Chg %Chg	
315											
320											
325				$1^3{}_4$	.21	18.31			1	$-{}^1{}_4$ -43%	
330				$3^1{}_8$	.33	18.11			$2^3{}_{16}$	$-{}^{15}{}_{16}$ -30%	
✳ 335	$5^3{}_4$	.53	17.89	$5^1{}_8$	.47	17.80	$4^1{}_2$	$-1^1{}_4$ -22%	$4^1{}_8$	-1 -20%	
340	$3^1{}_2$	.38	17.66	$4^3{}_8$	n/a	n/a	$2^3{}_8$	$-1^1{}_8$ -32%	$4^5{}_8$	$+{}^1{}_4$ +6%	
345	$1^3{}_4$	.24	16.62	$9^3{}_8$	n/a	n/a	${}^{15}{}_{16}$	$-1^1{}_{16}$ -46%	$9^5{}_8$	$+{}^1{}_4$ +3%	
350									$14^5{}_8$	$+{}^1{}_4$ +2%	

Mon **4/ 1/96** (**19**days Expr) **5.17%**Fin │Mon **4/ 8/96** (**12**days Expr) **5.17%**Fin

OPTION	**T** -"Tickr" volatility	**S** -"Same" volatility
PRICING:	**M** - Trade "Match" volatility	**1 2 . 5 %** (or any other volat.)

Strategy #2—Sell OEX Calls

Though you will not hit a home run if the market crashes, you will make money with this strategy. More importantly, you may profit even if the market rises. How is this possible? When the market rises, the implied volatility in the options tends to drop, thereby offsetting a portion of the market's increase in price. Remember, they are overvalued derivatives with time decay in your favor (*see* Figure 26.4). Finally, as with all strategies, stops must be used to protect yourself in case you were wrong.

FIGURE 26.4

OEX Index OHT DG28 **Index O H T**

For other months enter a month # such as "CVT 4" for calls in April.

17:07 DISPLAY: **C** C-chg/%chg, D-delta/volat

Mon 4/1

Assume Index
$ 7.7/yr Div.

O E X

O P T I O N H O R I Z O N A N A L Y S I S

APR OPTIONS ON S&P 100 INDEX

W O R K S H E E T

OPTION PRICING: TODAY **630.80** — Calls: **Tickr** — Puts: **Tickr**

2 DAYS LATER **633.00 + 2 . 2 0** — Calls: Volat=**14.71** — Puts: Volat=**15.85**

	TODAY CALLS			TODAY PUTS			2 DAYS LATER CALLS			2 DAYS LATER PUTS		
STRIKE	Prc	Del	I.Vol	Prc	Del	I.Vol	Prc	Chg	%Chg	Prc	Chg	%Chg
615	21 1/4	.73	18.66	4 1/2	.27	19.29	20 7/8	-3/8	-2%	2 3/16	-2 5/16	-51%
620	17 1/2	.68	18.21	5 5/8	.33	18.51	16 15/16	-9/16	-3%	3 5/16	-2 5/16	-41%
625	13 5/8	.61	16.95	7	.39	17.72	13 3/8	-1/4	-2%	4 13/16	-2 3/16	-31%
(1) *630	10 1/8	.54	15.71	8 3/4	.47	16.85	(2) 10 1/4	+1/8	+1%	6 3/4	-2	-23%
635	7 3/8	.46	15.13	10 3/4	.55	15.77	7 5/8	+1/4	+3%	9 1/8	-1 5/8	-15%
640	5	.37	14.41	13 3/4	.63	15.71	5 1/2	+1/2	+10%	12	-1 3/4	-13%
645	3 1/8	.28	13.67	16 3/4	.73	14.74	3 13/16	+11/16	+22%	15 5/16	-1 7/16	-9%
650	1 15/16	.20	13.41	22 1/2	.73	19.03	2 9/16	+5/8	+32%	19 1/16	-3 7/16	-15%

Mon **4/ 1/96** (**19**days Expr) **5.16**%Fin | Wed **4/ 3/96** (**17**days Expr) **5.16**%Fin

OPTION PRICING: **T** -"Tickr" volatility **S** -"Same" volatility
M - Trade "Match" volatility **1 2 . 5 %** (or any other volat.)

1. When the OEX is at 630.80 and the implied volatility is at 15.71, the at-the-money option is priced at 10 1/8.

2. Two days later, even though prices are higher, the drop in implied volatility combined with the time decay, leaves option prices with little gain.

Strategy #3 (Equities)—Stocks to Sell Short

No reason to get cute. Short the stocks of brokerage houses and the stocks of the mutual fund companies. As I mentioned earlier, no industry gets hurt more than the brokerage houses in a bear market. The industry's profits are highly correlated and dependent upon higher stock and bond prices. These are the first stocks to decline in any sell-off.

As I mentioned earlier, if interest rates are rising, also look to short the insurance stocks and possibly the major banks and mortgage companies.

A final note: if you are unable to get an uptick before the market closes to short these stocks, buy deep in the money puts on these companies (to make sure the premium is small).

Strategy #4 (Futures)—Short the S&P 500 Futures

Obviously, the strategy with the largest profit potential is to sell the S&P on the futures market. What concerns me here is the risk and the volatility. Unlike buying the index options, your risk is unlimited if you are wrong. With that said, let's look at a way to minimize the risk.

- Sell the futures "market on close." This will allow you to avoid a market snap-back which may happen in the last few minutes of trading (short covering). Research has shown that sharp afternoon sell-offs have a higher likelihood of follow-through into the next morning.

- Protect yourself on Globex. Should the market rally in the evening, there is less likelihood of a down opening the following morning. Though you may lose some sleep during these occasions, it's better than losing money.

- Finally, one of the surest phenomena I have observed is that Friday afternoon weakness begets Sunday evening weakness. This is a scenario that all futures traders should be aware of.

Strategy #5—Spiders (SPY)

Spiders (Standard & Poor's Depository Receipts) are the safest, most efficient and most liquid vehicle to trade to capitalize on market moves. These American Stock Exchange securities are simply a basket of the Standard & Poor's 500 index divided by 10. For example, if the Standard & Poor's cash index is at 935.00, the spiders will be trading at approximately 93 1/2 (935 ÷ 10). Also, a terrific feature of this derivative is you do not need an uptick to go short, therefore, giving you an instant fill on a market order.

The specialist of the security usually maintains a market of 100,000 shares on each side which means that there is always liquidity. Also, the spread (difference between the bid and ask) tends to rest between 1/16 and 1/8, which is as low as you will see on a listed security. (The daily volume is approximately one-half million shares per day.)

One final thought: Spiders are an inexpensive method to hedge a net long portfolio when you do not have the time, nor the inclination, to liquidate your stocks.

SUMMARY

The profits from declining markets come fast and large. I cannot stress enough the importance of being prepared for these sell-offs. At times they come so quickly that unless you are fully ready, you will miss the move. As I am writing this, we are still in a major uptrend, but the recent increase in volatility may signal more opportunities for traders to profit from market declines. With the strategies in this chapter, you will be better prepared than the average trader who will attempt to participate in these declines by "shooting from the hip."

CHAPTER 27

LARGE-RANGE DAYS

In this chapter we will look at the times markets make large one day moves. I will show you why it is usually wrong to enter these markets immediately following these moves and I will show you why it is an even bigger mistake to buy options immediately following such a move.

Conventional wisdom states that large one day moves immediately continue in the direction of the move. My research indicates otherwise. Markets that have big one day moves attract attention. For example, when the Dow has a large move (100+ points) most news channels carry the story, most newspapers make it the lead business story and every market analyst and guru tells how the move will certainly continue. In looking at these large one-day moves, the reality is that the majority of time these markets do not follow through—they move sideways!

In studying this phenomenon, I looked at a market which closed two standard deviations (*see* box for calculation) from its previous days close (this occurs approximately once out of every twenty trading days). The majority of the time, the market didn't follow through over the next few days. In fact, from a directional viewpoint, you could flip a coin as to whether the move would be up or down the next day. Just as importantly, the market many times closed near the closing price of the large move day, three to four days later.

Here is how to calculate a two standard deviation move in bonds. We will assume bonds are trading at 110 and its 100 day historical volatility is at 10 percent.

10% H.V. / Square Root of 265 trading days = .6250%

.6250% × 110.00 (bond price) = .6875 or 22/32 (one standard deviation)

22/32 × 2 (standard deviations) = 1.375 or 1 12/32

110.00 + 1 12/32 = 111 12/32

110 − 1 12/32 = 108 20/32

Now, let's apply this to the real world. The strong urge (human nature) is to allow ourselves to get caught up in the hype and trade in the direction of the move. Worse, the urge among traders is to do this via options. These options will be overpriced. This is because the implied volatility increases due to the excitement among traders caused by the move. Not only is there a high likelihood that the move won't continue (causing time erosion in the options) but worse, you are buying overvalued options! You have the *worst* of all worlds. In fact, the smarter strategy is to sell the overpriced options via a naked combination. You can sell the calls that are one standard deviation from the large day move's high and the puts that are one standard deviation from the big move's low. If the market moves sideways the premiums on both sides will collapse.

When markets move two standard deviations from their normal volatility, the reversion to the mean principle will kick in and more than likely, the market will take a few days to rest.

A word of warning—in strongly trending markets (ADX greater than 25), this principle does not hold true. Our research has found it works best in non-trending markets.

As an example, the following dates in the bond market had a two standard deviation move from the previous day's close. When you look at these moves, notice how many times the market closed within the large-move day's range three to four days later.

Daily Two Standard Deviation Moves in Bonds Over the Past Two Years—Reflects 100-Day Historical Volatility

Date	Date	Date
1/13/95	7/21/95	3/11/96
1/27/95	8/25/95	3/12/96
2/3/95	9/21/95	3/27/96
3/14/95	9/29/95	3/28/96
3/24/95	10/13/95	4/5/96
5/4/95	12/4/95	4/12/96
5/5/95	12/18/95	5/2/96
5/9/95	12/20/95	5/10/96
5/24/95	1/5/96	6/7/96
6/2/95	1/10/96	7/5/96
6/9/95	1/25/96	8/1/96
6/13/95	2/20/96	9/13/96
6/29/95	2/23/96	10/4/96
7/6/95	3/1/96	10/29/96
7/19/95	3/8/96	

CHAPTER 28

TWO-FOR-ONE MONEY MANAGEMENT

●　●

Here is a specific money management methodology to use which helps maximize profits while keeping risks to a minimum. I believe the "Two-for-One Money Management" strategy gives you more confidence in taking trades as it allows you to enter into potentially explosive setups while reducing the risk inherent in these setups. *Please note that this is not original research.* Variations of this method can be found in other publications. To me it is one of the better money management methods a short-term trader can rely on.

The Two-for-One Money Management strategy allows you to minimize risk while maximizing gains. Many traders I've talked to say they do not have the proper method to allow profits to run. This strategy partially offsets those concerns.

Here's how the strategy works:

1. We will use one "unit" as our position size. For our purposes in this chapter, each unit will be worth 1,000 shares for equities and two contracts for futures.

The general idea is to take off half a unit at a profit target equal to the position's original stop loss. As you will see, by having cashed in half a unit early, there is no loss if the trade turns against you and takes out the original stop. You've created a free trade (minus commissions).

You should note that while this is a "conservative" method of trading, it many times leads to two profits. The first at the "free trade" profit target and the second on the profitable close of the second half of the unit. (You'll see this in example two in the bonds and in others).

2.   Let's assume for equities we have a set-up pattern which triggers a buy signal at 53 and our initial protective stop is at 52 1/4 (risking 3/4 of a point). If our sell stop is not triggered we will take profits on 1/2 of our position (500 shares) at a distance off our entry price that is equal to our original stop, (53 + 3/4 = 53 3/4) and leave the stop on the other half at 52 1/4.

We now have a free shot at being in a position that may continue to run. With strategies such as 1-2-3-4's, historical volatility, etc. many times markets explode from our entry point and with the "Two-for-One" method you have a low-risk strategy to participate in these explosions.

To help clarify this strategy let's look at intraday Turtle Soups (from *Street Smarts*) and daily 1-2-3-4's.

FIGURE 28.1 June S&P's (10 Minutes)

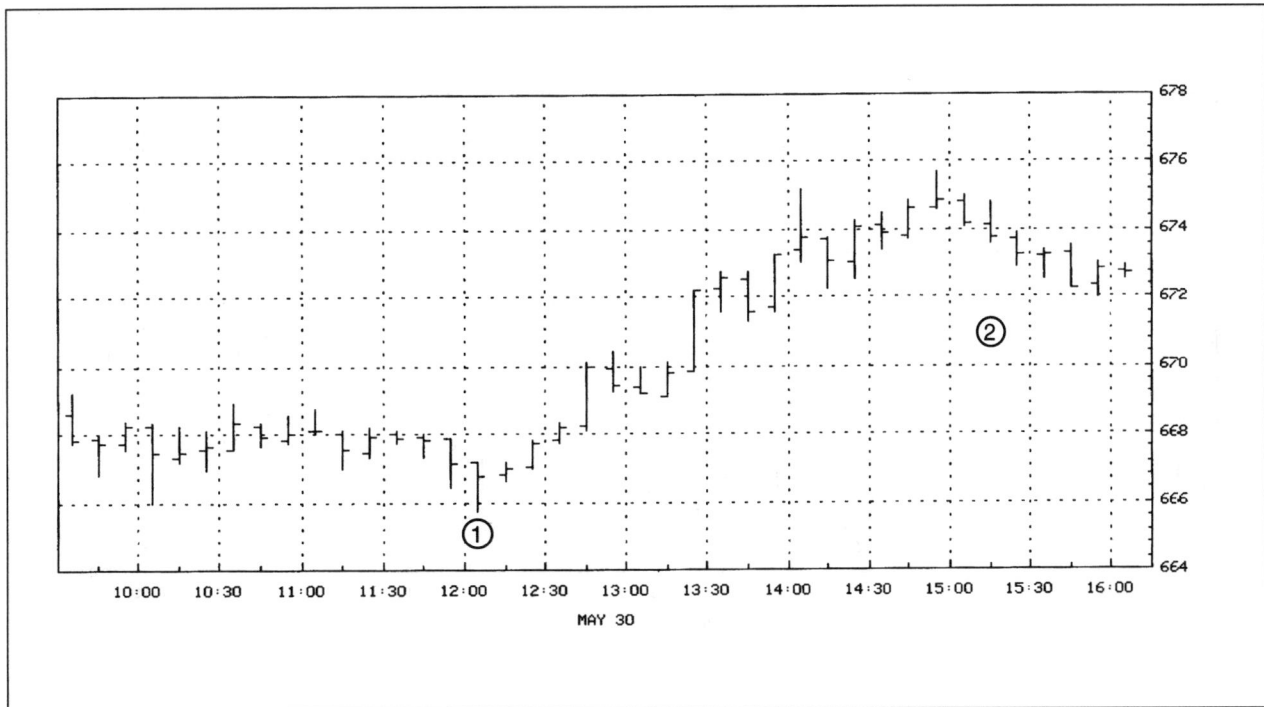

1.   On May 30, 1996, the S&P's make a 20-bar low and reverse trigger-ing a Turtle Soup buy signal at 666.05 for two contracts (one unit). Our stop is at 665.65, one tick under this bar's low. Let's assume the unthinkable and there is no slippage, so our risk is .40. We will sell 1/2 our position (one contract) at 666.45 (666.05 + .40). On being filled we cancel selling two at 665.65 and replace it with selling one at that price.

2.   Our strategy gave us a free shot at picking the low for the day. The market rallies sharply and we have the option of locking into prof-its at higher levels or selling MOC.

In studying and trading this strategy, I have observed that the Turtle Soup setups on average tend to pick the top or bottom of the day ap-proximately one out of every eight days. That is, on one out of every eight days the daily high or low is created via a Turtle Soup setup.

FIGURE 28.2 June Bonds (10 Minutes)

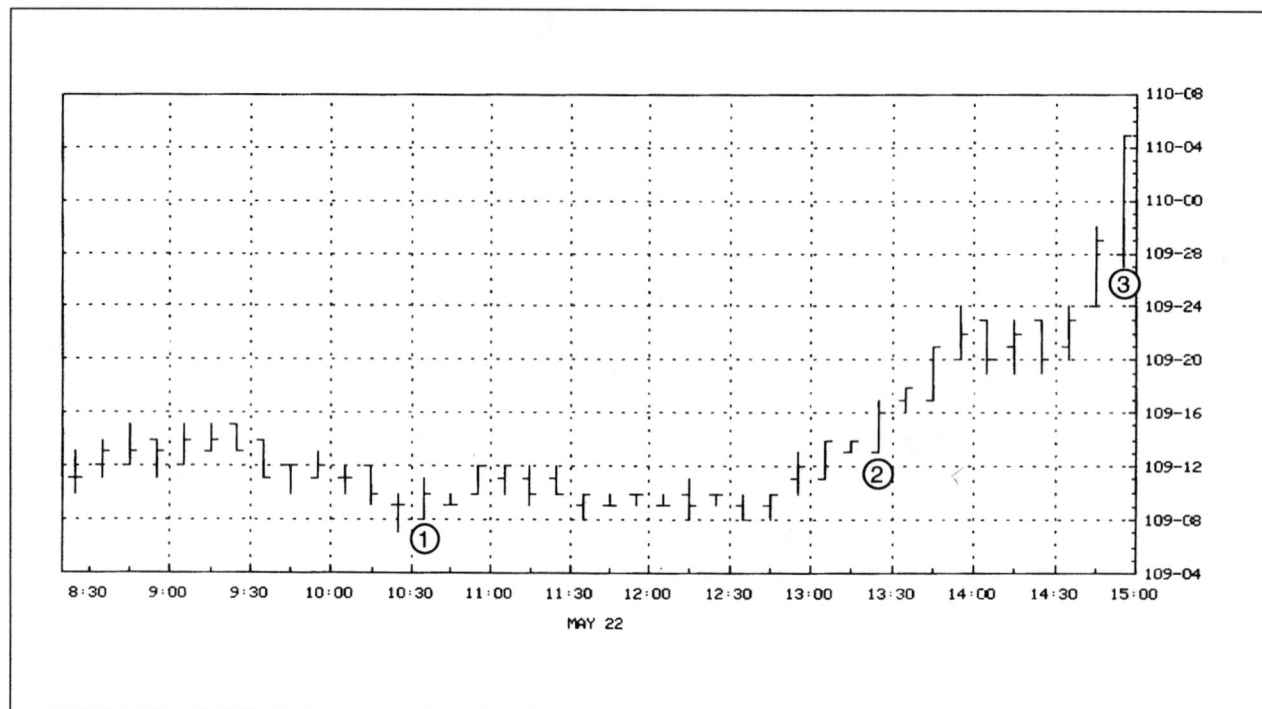

1.   A Turtle Soup Plus One setup. We buy two contracts at 109-11 and our initial stop is a 109-06 risking five ticks.

2.   After trading sideways for two hours, bonds explode to the upside and we sell one contract at 109-16 and cancel and replace our two-lot stop with an order to sell one at 109-06.

3.   The second half of our unit closes at 110-05. We make five ticks on one contract and 26 ticks on the second.

FIGURE 28.3 July Soybeans (10 Minutes)

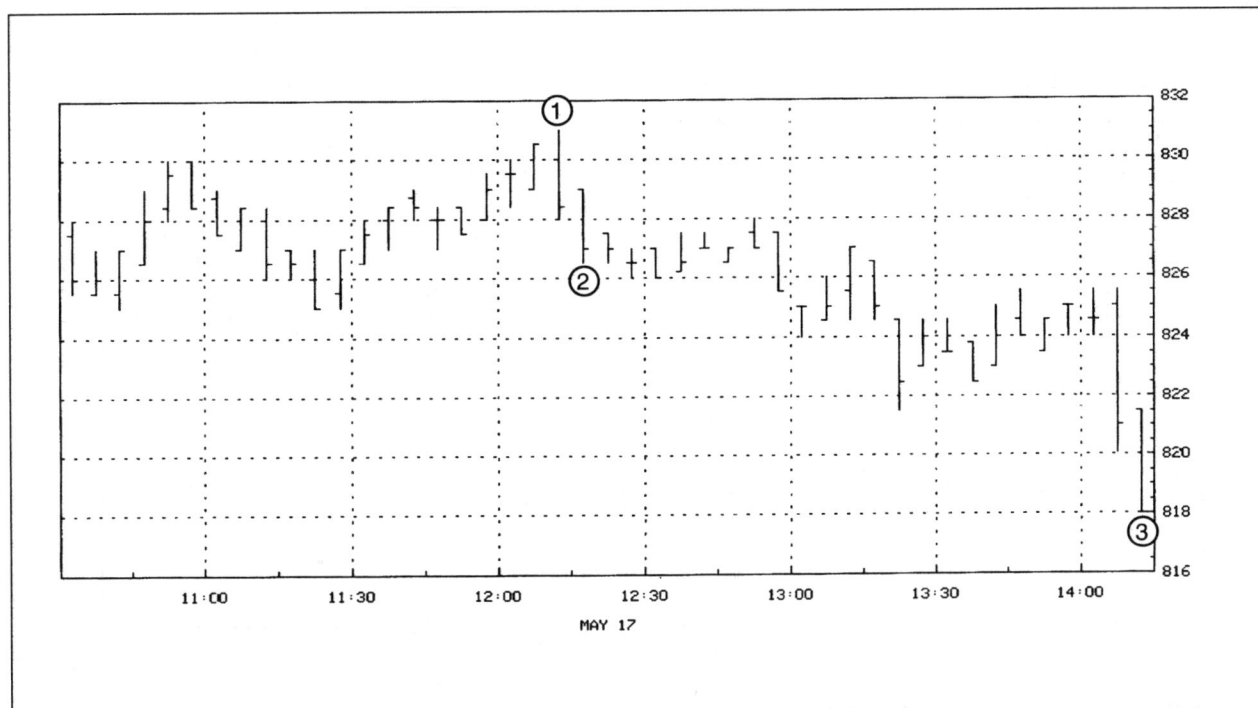

1. A short Turtle Soup Plus One setup on July Beans on May 17. Sell at 829 1/4 and our protective stop is at 831 1/4 (risking two cents).

2. Take profits on half at 827 1/4 and reduce the sell stop size by half.

3. Beans close on their low with a good profit for those trading this methodology MOC.

Please don't think that picking tops and bottoms happens every day. However, setups like the Turtle Soup and Turtle Soup Plus One combined with "Two-for-One" money management do meld into a strategy which allows you to maximize profits at intraday tops and bottoms.

FIGURE 28.4 Proxim Inc. (PROX)

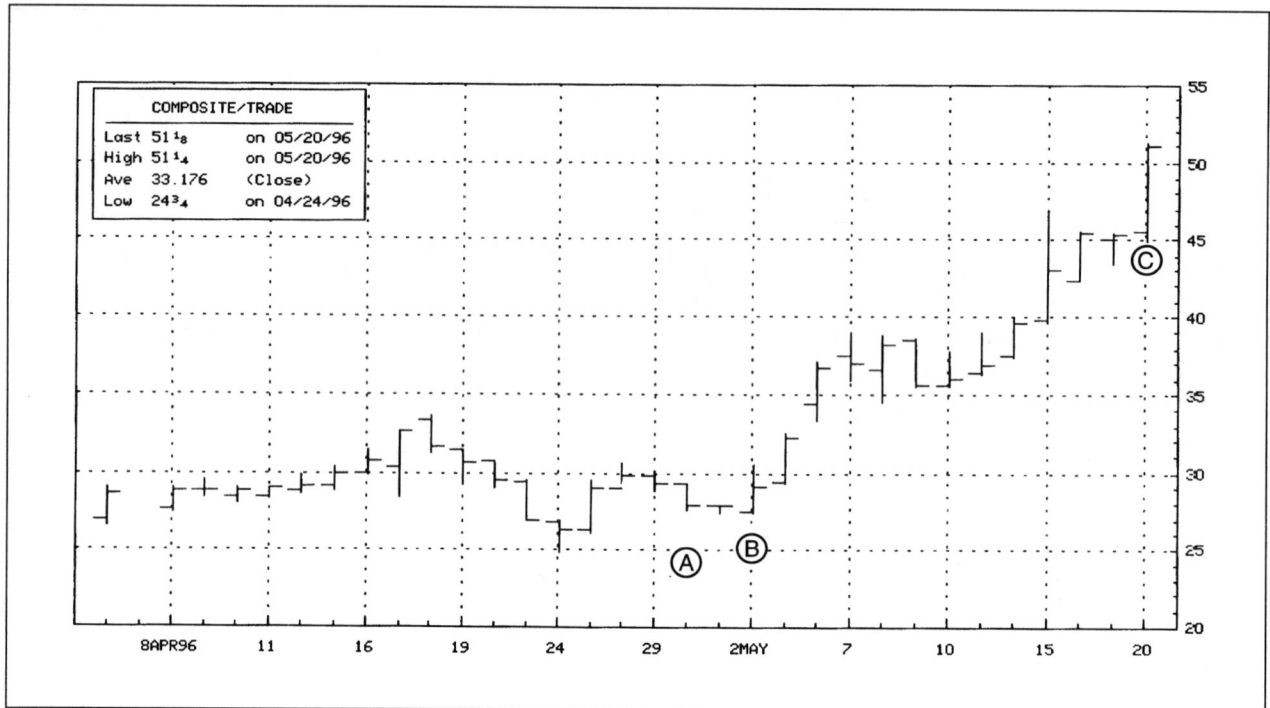

```
         COMPOSITE/TRADE
  Last  51 1/8      on 05/20/96
  High  51 1/4      on 05/20/96
  Ave   33.176      (Close)
  Low   24 3/4      on 04/24/96
```

Here's "Two-for-One" money management in action on 1-2-3-4's.

A. A 1-2-3-4 buy setup (ADX is above 30)

B. On May 2, we buy one unit (1,000 shares) of Proxim at 28. Our sell stop is at 27 3/8, the low of the previous day and our risk is 5/8 of a point. The market immediately trades higher and we sell 1/2 our position at 28 5/8 and reduce our sell stop to 500 shares.

C. As does happen from time to time with this strategy, the stock explodes and moves more than 65 percent higher over the next three weeks. (Note that we have again shown a profit on both halves of the unit).

FIGURE 28.5 Tommy Hilfiger (TOM)

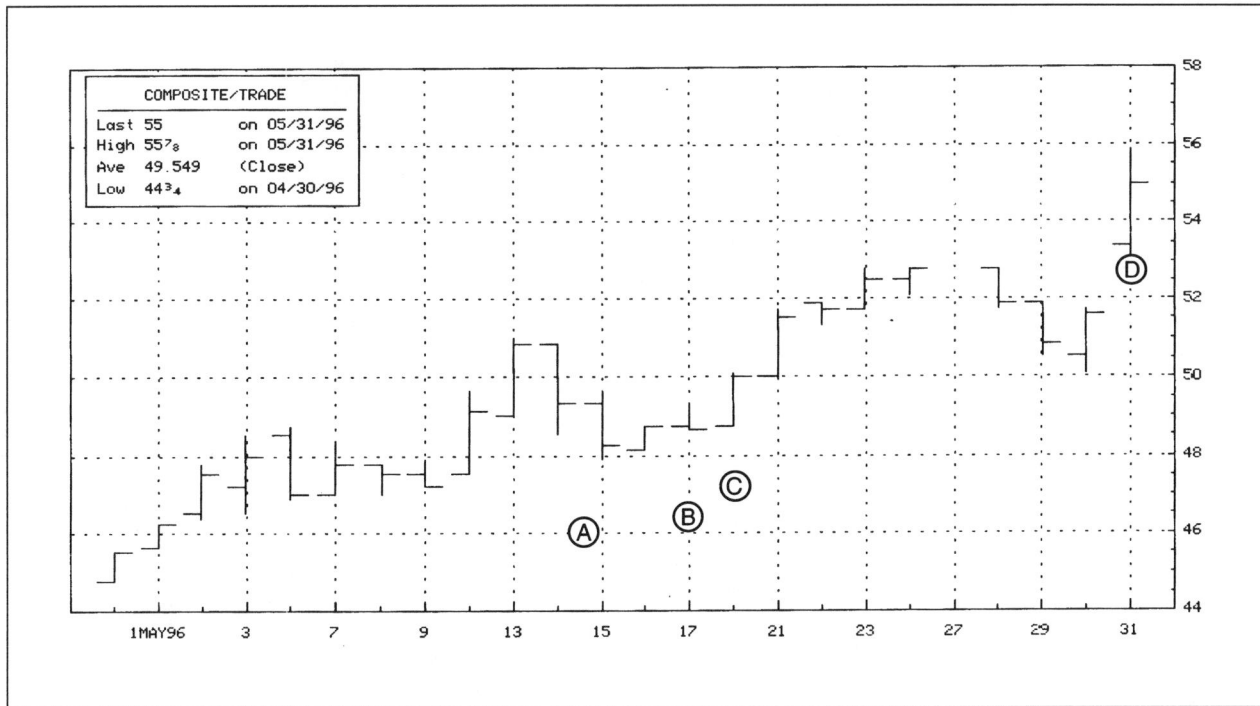

A.   1-2-3-4 setup. ADX @ 37.

B.   Buy one unit @ 48 7/8. Stop @ 47 7/8.

C.   Sell of 500 shares @ 49 7/8.

D.   Six points higher in two weeks.

(1-for-1 reward/risk on 500 shares, 6-for-1 reward/risk on 500 shares)

SUMMARY

As you can see from the examples, this exit strategy does a good job at allowing us to participate in potentially large moves with reduced exposure.

CHAPTER 29

MORE THOUGHTS

. . . .

I had a small handful of friends who trade read the galleys of this book and they came back to me with a series of questions. I hope this section will help answer many of your own questions.

Q: Do you trade every strategy?

A: No, there are obviously too many. A good handful now make up the methodology we use in our money management firm.

Q: Can these strategies be improved upon?

A: Yes, and I have evidence of this. I consider the subscribers to my newsletter the *Professional Traders Journal*, to be among the smartest people who trade. Over the last two years I have received numerous suggestions of enhancements for many of the strategies.

Q: Why don't you publish those enhancements?

A: Unless someone gives me specific permission, I will never reveal their improvements. As with many other traders, I have unfortunately been associated with a few individuals who have revealed my research after I have asked them not to (I was dumb enough to let one person do it to me twice!). Fortunately, these individuals are the exception, not the rule. Therefore, I will always keep private the research that others share with me.

Q: What do you think is the best way to improve one's trading?

A: Obviously, the first and most important thing to do is to implement very disciplined money management. A second way is to act in a manner opposite to human nature.

Let me dwell on this point a bit. I am as guilty as anyone of pouncing on a methodology after it has had two or three successful trades. After these successful trades I immediately ask myself why don't I make my life simple and only trade this strategy? I then load up on the next signal only to watch my net-worth get reduced. Every methodology has a "reversion to the mean" principle built into it. This means, that the best time to trade the methodology is after it has had two or three consecutive losses, not winners! Human nature is to trade a strategy only after it has worked a number of times in a row. This success reinforces in your mind the pleasure of the strategy, not the pain. If a trader waited only for each of these strategies to have two or three consecutive losses and then traded it, his returns would be much higher. Unfortunately, we all do the opposite.

This is further evidenced in the money management world. There is a high-profile hedge fund manager whose overall performance is well above average. The problem is that many people lose money with him. This is because he has large swings in his quarterly and yearly performance. When he has a spectacular quarter (or year) the money pours into him. Then the reversion to the mean principle kicks in and he has horrendous drawdowns and these same investors, who originally believed they were investing with GOD, now hate him and pull their money out, usually at the bottom. His smallest account accepted is one million dollars so we are not dealing with an uneducated group of people. These are successful pension fund managers and businessmen—all affected by the same human nature.

If you can find the courage to trade a methodology only after consecutive losses instead of gains, you will likely improve your performance.

Q: Why publish your research. Why not keep it only for yourself?

A: Obviously, it's an extension of my business. More importantly, it serves no purpose to take the information to my grave. And most importantly, I have yet to see it have a negative effect, in terms of slippage, on my trading.

Q: Why not trade just one strategy?

A: I have thought about that a lot and I have great deal of respect for traders who do it. Unfortunately, I am not wired that way and I need diversity.

Q: What about mechanical exit strategies?

A: Even though I have presented mechanical exit strategies with some methods, I can never use them myself. I am much too hands-on to sit tight as a position is running one way or another. This does not mean this is the way you should trade. This is the way *I* need to trade. I know successful traders who exit mechanically and I know successful traders who exit with discretion. These people are successful not because of their exits, but because they have an edge, and they know what works for them.

Q: Can you recommend other researchers/traders whom you look up to?

A: There are too many to list, but I'll name a few. I relate well to many things written by Gerald Appel. I think most of Larry Williams research is very strong, I have business relationships with Mark Boucher and Jeff Cooper, and I'm biased toward their work. Nelson Freeburg's research is solid, Welles Wilder's techniques such as ADX and RSI are brilliant, Shellie Natenberg's work on option volatility is the best. The list can go on but if you study the concepts of the above group first, you won't go wrong.

Q: Why not a chapter on money management?

A: First, because this is an advanced trading book, I assume everyone understands the importance of stops. Without them you will eventually get blown out. I have attempted to show you where to place your stops in many of the strategies.

Where you decide to place your stops and the position size you decide to take is a personal decision in which many factors come into play. The most important factor is your risk tolerance. If past history is any guide, thousands of traders will read this book. Every single one will have a different level of risk tolerance. I will not impose my risk tolerance levels upon you. You know what is best. I cannot tell you that your position risk should be 1 percent or 5 percent of your portfolio size. I cannot tell you that your account size should be $50,000 or $250,000. I cannot tell you how many shares or contracts to trade per $25,000. You, and only you, know the correct answers.

Let me go one step further. Over the past decade or so, one of the best performing groups of traders in the money management business have been the original Turtles Richard Dennis taught. They employ a breakout method that has stood the test of time. Their method has one major drawback though: it experiences large, and sometimes very large, drawdowns of 20, 30, and 40 percent.

I am convinced the Turtle methodology works. Will I trade it? Never! Why not? I do not have the stomach to live through the drawdowns. Those Turtles who are the most successful have learned to live with the risk levels associated with the drawdowns. Their money management risk tolerance is far different than mine. If I worked for them, I would think they were insane to take such risks. And if they worked for me, they would think I was insane for keeping my stops so tight. Again, only you know what your risk tolerance is and your stop placement, account size, and position size should be reflected upon it.

With that said, let me mention a few additional thoughts on the topic:

1. Every position must have a protective stop in place. This rule must never be broken!

2. If you are selling options, you should have an offsetting long position (creating a spread) to avoid a catastrophe (the bad tail).

3. You must be aware of markets that are related. If you are long bonds and long Euro dollars, you have basically doubled your risk as they move in a high correlation to each other.

4. Volatility changes! As mentioned in an earlier chapter, the Canadian dollar usually trades with a volatility of under 10 percent. If you normally trade 10 contracts in it, you must lower your position size when the volatility drastically rises. Very few people follow this guideline and it is a major reason why catastrophic loses occur.

5. When multiple signals occur, a larger than normal position size should be considered. For example, a Connors VIX Reversal combined with a TRIN Thrust increases the likelihood that the market will follow through for the next few days.

These guidelines are a good place to begin to build your money management strategies. If you desire a more in-depth academic view on the subject, read *The Mathematics of Money Management* by Ralph Vince. It is filled with solid statistical advice.

CHAPTER 30

HOW SUPERIOR INDIVIDUALS BECOME

▪ ▪

I would like to conclude this book with a look at the role that practice, experience, and psychology play in leading one to become a superior trader. Through the use of a study done on elite musicians, chess players, and athletes published in 1993, we will correlate these findings to our own profession.

One of the subjects I have always been fascinated by is how and why individuals achieve greatness in their fields. Why does one individual dominate a sport, an industry, or an art, while the masses fail? Does genetics predetermine greatness or is it some other factor that allows individuals to become leaders in their field?

I recently finished reading a book by Howard Gardner entitled *Extraordinary Minds*. In the bibliography, he refers to a study published in *Psychological Review* in 1993. The study, "The Role of Deliberate Practice in the Acquisition of Expert Performance," looked at whether "great" musicians, chess players, and athletes were genetically predisposed to achieve greatness (physiological) or whether greatness came as a result of external factors such as practice. (Of course, since I am a trader, I ask the question from this perspective—"are great traders born or can they be developed?")

The study's findings overwhelmingly showed that there was absolutely no basis to the argument that genetics is the sole determinant in predicting success. In fact, genetics played at best a very minor role in differentiating between those who were "great" in their field versus those who were merely "good." *The number one factor in determining whether or not one reached the highest levels in their field was the amount of time these individuals spent on "deliberate practice."* Deliberate practice is defined as the amount of time one spends in attempting to *improve* their performance. Simply performing the act is not deliberate practice; deliberately attempting to *push oneself further* is.

Drs. Ericksson, Krampe, and Tesch-Roemer found that those who achieved greatness in their fields spent anywhere from 30 minutes to 2 hours *more* per day on deliberate practice than those who were only "good" in their field. The authors go on to say that 30 to 120 minutes of extra practice does not seem like much until one begins adding up the difference over a period of time. For example, they cite numerous studies that show that *it is virtually impossible to reach the pinnacle in one's field without at least 10 years of concentrated effort.* Therefore, the 30 to 120 minutes each day the "future greats" spend on improving themselves works out to be *many thousands of hours of extra practice* over a 10-year period!

I suspect that had the authors looked at the most successful traders, their findings would be the same. Buying blackbox systems, trading crazy methodologies, or listening to gurus who claim they can tell you where the Dow will be three years from now will never bring you into the ranks of the trading elite. Simply put, 10 years of deliberate practice and hard work is the only sure recipe for success!

CHAPTER 31

FINAL THOUGHTS

■ ■

I am writing these final pages after four friends read, proofed, and critiqued the galleys. These individuals all trade. Two are private traders whose main source of income is derived from the markets, one is a CTA, and the fourth is not only a professional trader, but he also possesses a Ph.D. in mathematical statistics. Each is as different as night and day and I have a great deal of respect for their insights.

Their response to the trading methods was very good. I would expect that, for each is a trading strategies junkie, just as I am. More importantly, these four very different gentlemen saw something that was bigger than the strategies. They each saw my point of first needing to understand market dynamics before creating a trading methodology. They saw things such as the principle of volatility reverting to its mean and when it is extremely low you trade breakout strategies and when it is extremely high, you trade strategies to exploit price implosion. They saw that markets are made up of human beings and human beings are irrational. The Options on Stock Splits strategy exploits this, but bigger picture, these types of irrational occurrences will be with us long after the stock split strategy fades away. Each, in their own way, was fascinated by the Victor Niederhoffer saga, not because they liked to see someone get hurt, but because, like me, they saw a piece of themselves in him. Each realized that without a proper understanding and respect for volatility, it could just as easily have happened to them.

The majority of readers will finish this book and tell themselves they now have 30 plus more strategies to trade the markets. This is fine, and it is the main reason they bought the book. A small handful, though, will see deeper and realize that markets have inherent features. They will go on in the future and trade methodologies that best exploit these features. If you are part of this small group, congratulations. I strongly suspect you will become a far better trader than most.

APPENDIX

※ ※

While the following formula for historical volatility may be of use to a mathematician, you should ideally have a software program calculate this for you.

HISTORICAL VOLATILITY BENCHMARK CALCULATION

Historical volatility (HVG) calculates the volatility of the underlying security log-normally following the assumptions of most standard option pricing models. The N-day price volatility as of a specific date is the unbiased standard deviation of the "N" minus one most recent logarithmic daily returns times the annualization factor, expressed as a percentage. (Logarithmic daily return is the log of one day's price divided by the prior day's price. This is algebraically the same as the difference of the logs of the individual prices.) For example:

	10/8/92	10/7/92	10/6/92	10/5/92
price:	81.76	82.87	83.43	83.35
natural log:	4.403788	4.417273	4.424007	4.423048
difference:	–.01348	–0.00673	.000959	
unbiased std. dev.:	.007227			
times sqrt (260):	.116536			
times 100%:	11.65% (same as HVG)			

TRADE SUMMARIES

Because of the multiple uses of the Connors VIX Reversals, I have included a trade-by-trade breakdown for your reference.

CVR I S&P 500 Index—CME—Daily—01/01/93–10/01/97

Date	Type	Contracts	Price	P/L	Cumulative
06/18/93	Sell	1	536.740		
06/23/93	SExit	1	533.740	$ 1,500.00	$ 1,500.00
07/12/93	Sell	1	539.990		
07/15/93	SExit	1	540.340	$ −175.00	$ 1,325.00
07/16/93	Sell	1	537.540		
07/21/93	SExit	1	538.190	$ −325.00	$ 1,000.00
08/12/93	Buy	1	540.240		
08/17/93	LExit	1	544.690	$ 2,225.00	$ 3,225.00
09/08/93	Buy	1	547.190		
09/13/93	LExit	1	552.590	$ 2700.00	$ 5925.00
10/01/93	Sell	1	552.140		
10/06/93	SExit	1	551.690	$ 225.00	$ 6150.00
11/02/93	Buy	1	558.240		
11/10/93	LExit	1	554.240	$ −2,000.00	$ 4,150.00
11/19/93	Sell	1	551.290		
11/24/93	SExit	1	552.640	$ −675.00	$ 3,475.00
01/19/94	Buy	1	562.840		
01/24/94	LExit	1	561.340	$ −750.00	$ 2,725.00
01/31/94	Sell	1	570.390		
02/03/94	SExit	1	568.890	$ 750.00	$ 3,475.00
02/11/94	Buy	1	558.690		
02/16/94	LExit	1	561.840	$ 1,575.00	$ 5,050.00
03/02/94	Buy	1	553.290		
03/07/94	LExit	1	555.890	$ 1,300.00	$ 6,350.00
03/31/94	Buy	1	534.090		
04/06/94	LExit	1	534.590	$ 250.00	$ 6,600.00

CVR I S&P 500 Index—CME—Daily—01/01/93–10/01/97

Date	Type	Contracts	Price	P/L	Cumulative
05/13/94	Buy	1	531.490		
05/18/94	LExit	1	541.440	$ 4,975.00	$ 11,575.00
06/06/94	Sell	1	546.490		
06/09/94	SExit	1	544.940	$ 775.00	$ 12,350.00
06/15/94	Sell	1	546.940		
06/20/94	SExit	1	541.740	$ 2,600.00	$ 14,950.00
06/20/94	Buy	1	541.740		
06/23/94	LExit	1	535.640	$ –3,050.00	$ 11,900.00
07/18/94	Sell	1	540.490		
07/21/94	SExit	1	538.290	$ 1,100.00	$ 13,000.00
08/05/94	Buy	1	542.390		
08/10/94	LExit	1	546.090	$ 1,850.00	$ 14,850.00
09/21/94	Buy	1	545.940		
09/26/94	LExit	1	545.440	$ -250.00	$ 14,600.00
10/05/94	Buy	1	536.540		
10/10/94	LExit	1	542.940	$ 3,200.00	$ 17,800.00
11/15/94	Buy	1	547.940		
11/18/94	LExit	1	545.490	$ –1,225.00	$ 16,575.00
11/23/94	Buy	1	532.840		
11/29/94	LExit	1	538.640	$ 2,900.00	$ 19,475.00
03/02/95	Buy	1	565.850		
03/07/95	LExit	1	561.450	$ –2,200.00	$ 17,275.00
03/21/95	Sell	1	574.750		
03/24/95	SExit	1	580.800	$ –3,025.00	$ 14,250.00
03/30/95	Buy	1	581.800		
04/04/95	LExit	1	583.200	$ 700.00	$ 14,950.00
04/07/95	Buy	1	584.050		
04/12/95	LExit	1	585.350	$ 650.00	$ 15,600.00
04/17/95	Sell	1	583.800		
04/20/95	SExit	1	582.700	$ 550.00	$ 16,150.00

CVR I S&P 500 Index—CME—Daily—01/01/93–10/01/97

Date	Type	Contracts	Price	P/L	Cumulative
05/19/95	Buy	1	595.750		
05/24/95	LExit	1	604.850	$ 4,550.00	$ 20,700.00
05/30/95	Buy	1	598.900		
06/02/95	LExit	1	607.450	$ 4,275.00	$ 24,975.00
07/06/95	Buy	1	628.750		
07/11/95	LExit	1	628.650	$ −50.00	$ 24,925.00
07/13/95	Buy	1	634.900		
07/18/95	LExit	1	631.800	$ −1,550.00	$ 23,375.00
07/19/95	Buy	1	624.800		
07/24/95	LExit	1	631.300	$ 3,250.00	$ 26,625.00
08/18/95	Sell	1	632.500		
08/23/95	SExit	1	628.700	$ 1,900.00	$ 28,525.00
09/20/95	Buy	1	658.500		
09/25/95	LExit	1	652.350	$ −3,075.00	$ 25,450.00
09/27/95	Buy	1	651.800		
10/02/95	LExit	1	651.400	$ −200.00	$ 25,250.00
10/03/95	Buy	1	652.650		
10/06/95	LExit	1	652.950	$ 150.00	$ 25,400.00
10/10/95	Buy	1	647.600		
10/13/95	LExit	1	654.550	$ 3,475.00	$ 28,875.00
10/20/95	Sell	1	656.000		
10/25/95	SExit	1	650.300	$ 2,850.00	$ 31,725.00
12/05/95	Sell	1	685.500		
12/08/95	SExit	1	685.250	$ 125.00	$ 31,850.00
01/05/96	Buy	1	680.350		
01/10/96	LExit	1	661.800	$ −9,275.00	$ 22,575.00
02/07/96	Buy	1	712.800		
02/12/96	LExit	1	725.300	$ 6,250.00	$ 28,825.00
02/14/96	Buy	1	716.950		
02/20/96	LExit	1	704.550	$ −6,200.00	$ 22,625.00

CVR I S&P 500 Index—CME—Daily—01/01/93–10/01/97

Date	Type	Contracts	Price	P/L		Cumulative	
02/29/96	Buy	1	699.150				
03/05/96	LExit	1	718.550	$	9,700.00	$	32,325.00
04/04/96	Sell	1	714.500				
04/08/96	SExit	1	701.900	$	6,300.00	$	38,625.00
04/08/96	Buy	1	701.900				
04/16/96	LExit	1	702.200	$	150.00	$	38,775.00
04/22/96	Sell	1	706.950				
04/25/96	SExit	1	709.950	$	–1,500.00	$	37,275.00
06/07/96	Buy	1	728.850				
06/12/96	LExit	1	724.750	$	–2,050.00	$	35,225.00
07/16/96	Buy	1	681.250				
07/19/96	LExit	1	691.150	$	4,950.00	$	40,175.00
07/24/96	Buy	1	679.850				
07/29/96	LExit	1	680.150	$	150.00	$	40,325.00
09/03/96	Buy	1	705.050				
09/06/96	LExit	1	707.500	$	1,225.00	$	41,550.00
09/27/96	Buy	1	734.650				
10/02/96	LExit	1	742.600	$	3,975.00	$	45,525.00
10/07/96	Sell	1	751.450				
10/10/96	SExit	1	741.650	$	4,900.00	$	50,425.00
10/17/96	Sell	1	754.250				
10/22/96	SExit	1	752.350	$	950.00	$	51,375.00
10/23/96	Buy	1	754.300				
10/28/96	LExit	1	743.600	$	–5,350.00	$	46,025.00
10/31/96	Buy	1	752.900				
11/05/96	LExit	1	758.650	$	2,875.00	$	48,900.00
11/15/96	Sell	1	784.100				
11/20/96	SExit	1	789.400	$	–2,650.00	$	46,250.00
12/04/96	Buy	1	790.950				
12/09/96	LExit	1	794.750	$	1,900.00	$	48,150.00

CVR I S&P 500 Index—CME—Daily—01/01/93–10/01/97

Date	Type	Contracts	Price	P/L	Cumulative
12/13/96	Buy	1	772.600		
12/18/96	LExit	1	774.350	$ 875.00	$ 49,025.00
01/02/97	Buy	1	780.900		
01/07/97	LExit	1	795.850	$ 7,475.00	$ 56,500.00
01/23/97	Sell	1	816.450		
01/28/97	SExit	1	807.700	$ 4,375.00	$ 60,875.00
02/20/97	Buy	1	840.550		
02/25/97	LExit	1	850.450	$ 4,950.00	$ 65,825.00
02/28/97	Buy	1	826.600		
03/05/97	LExit	1	840.500	$ 6,950.00	$ 72,775.00
03/17/97	Buy	1	833.100		
03/25/97	LExit	1	823.900	$ –4,600.00	$ 68,175.00
03/27/97	Sell	1	804.200		
04/02/97	SExit	1	780.000	$ 12,100.00	$ 80,275.00
04/25/97	Buy	1	797.600		
04/30/97	LExit	1	831.500	$ 16,950.00	$ 97,225.00
05/06/97	Buy	1	863.550		
05/09/97	LExit	1	858.350	$ –2,600.00	$ 94,625.00
05/19/97	Buy	1	864.750		
05/22/97	LExit	1	868.950	$ 2,100.00	$ 96,725.00
06/16/97	Buy	1	924.250		
06/19/97	LExit	1	927.600	$ 1,675.00	$ 98,400.00
08/11/97	Buy	1	962.650		
08/14/97	LExit	1	948.150	$ –7,250.00	$ 91,150.00
08/22/97	Buy	1	946.250		
08/27/97	LExit	1	934.100	$ –6,075.00	$ 85,075.00
09/24/97	Sell	1	964.700		
09/29/97	SExit	1	972.050	$ –3,675.00	$ 81,400.00

- end -

CVR II S&P 500 Index—CME—Daily—01/01/90–10/01/97

Date	Type	Contracts	Price	P/L	Cumulative
03/29/93	Sell	1	542.990		
04/06/93	SExit	1	533.340	$ 4,825.00	$ 4,825.00
04/06/93	Buy	1	533.340		
04/14/93	LExit	1	540.490	$ 3,575.00	$ 8,400.00
04/14/93	Sell	1	540.490		
04/26/93	SExit	1	524.290	$ 8,100.00	$ 16,500.00
04/27/93	Buy	1	529.090		
05/07/93	LExit	1	533.390	$ 2,150.00	$ 18,650.00
05/17/93	Buy	1	531.490		
05/27/93	LExit	1	542.890	$ 5,700.00	$ 24,350.00
06/09/93	Buy	1	537.790		
06/18/93	LExit	1	536.740	$ −525.00	$ 23,825.00
06/18/93	Sell	1	536.740		
06/30/93	SExit	1	541.590	$ −2,425.00	$ 21400.00
07/07/93	Buy	1	534.040		
07/19/93	LExit	1	537.340	$ 1,650.00	$ 23,050.00
07/21/93	Sell	1	538.190		
08/02/93	SExit	1	540.190	$ −1,000.00	$ 22,050.00
08/09/93	Buy	1	541.190		
08/19/93	LExit	1	547.190	$ 3,000.00	$ 25,050.00
08/25/93	Sell	1	551.690		
09/07/93	SExit	1	549.190	$ 1,250.00	$ 26,300.00
09/09/93	Buy	1	548.290		
09/21/93	LExit	1	543.140	$ −2,575.00	$ 23,725.00
09/22/93	Buy	1	547.390		
10/04/93	LExit	1	552.190	$ 2,400.00	$ 26,125.00
10/15/93	Sell	1	560.090		
10/27/93	SExit	1	555.440	$ 2,325.00	$ 28,450.00
11/05/93	Buy	1	549.340		

CVR II S&P 500 Index—CME—Daily—01/01/90–10/01/97

Date	Type	Contracts	Price	P/L	Cumulative
11/17/93	LExit	1	554.140	$ 2,400.00	$ 30,850.00
11/18/93	Buy	1	553.140		
12/01/93	LExit	1	552.740	$ −200.00	$ 30,650.00
12/07/93	Sell	1	556.440		
12/17/93	SExit	1	555.640	$ 400.00	$ 31,050.00
12/27/93	Sell	1	560.340		
01/04/94	SExit	1	556.190	$ 2,075.00	$ 33,125.00
01/04/94	Buy	1	556.190		
01/14/94	LExit	1	563.340	$ 3,575.00	$ 36,700.00
01/18/94	Buy	1	563.090		
01/28/94	LExit	1	567.390	$ 2,150.00	$ 38,850.00
01/31/94	Sell	1	570.390		
02/07/94	SExit	1	560.740	$ 4,825.00	$ 43,675.00
02/07/94	Buy	1	560.740		
02/17/94	LExit	1	559.090	$ −825.00	$ 42,850.00
03/18/94	Sell	1	557.540		
03/30/94	SExit	1	533.490	$ 12,025.00	$ 54,875.00
04/05/94	Buy	1	535.990		
04/15/94	LExit	1	533.090	$ −1,450.00	$ 53,425.00
04/28/94	Sell	1	536.390		
05/10/94	SExit	1	533.090	$ 1,650.00	$ 55,075.00
05/10/94	Buy	1	533.090		
05/19/94	LExit	1	543.690	$ 5,300.00	$ 60,375.00
05/19/94	Sell	1	543.690		
06/01/94	SExit	1	545.040	$ −675.00	$ 59,700.00
06/15/94	Sell	1	546.940		
06/22/94	SExit	1	539.390	$ 3,775.00	$ 63,475.00
06/22/94	Buy	1	539.390		
07/05/94	LExit	1	532.040	$ −3,675.00	$ 59,800.00

CVR II S&P 500 Index—CME—Daily—01/01/90–10/01/97

Date	Type	Contracts	Price	P/L	Cumulative
07/19/94	Sell	1	539.840		
07/29/94	SExit	1	543.890	$ –2,025.00	$ 57,775.00
08/02/94	Sell	1	545.940		
08/12/94	SExit	1	547.640	$ –850.00	$ 56,925.00
08/29/94	Buy	1	559.940		
09/09/94	LExit	1	552.440	$ –3,750.00	$ 53,175.00
09/13/94	Buy	1	551.540		
09/23/94	LExit	1	544.240	$ –3,650.00	$ 49,525.00
09/26/94	Buy	1	545.440		
10/06/94	LExit	1	536.190	$ –4,625.00	$ 44,900.00
10/25/94	Buy	1	544.690		
11/01/94	LExit	1	551.440	$ 3,375.00	$ 48,275.00
11/01/94	Sell	1	551.440		
11/07/94	SExit	1	546.790	$ 2,325.00	$ 50,600.00
11/07/94	Buy	1	546.790		
11/17/94	LExit	1	546.640	$ –75.00	$ 50,525.00
11/23/94	Buy	1	532.840		
12/06/94	LExit	1	536.290	$ 1,725.00	$ 52,250.00
12/06/94	Sell	1	536.290		
12/09/94	SExit	1	530.190	$ 3,050.00	$ 55,300.00
12/09/94	Buy	1	530.190		
12/15/94	LExit	1	537.940	$ 3,875.00	$ 59,175.00
12/15/94	Sell	1	537.940		
01/10/95	SExit	1	543.490	$ –2,775.00	$ 56,400.00
01/17/95	Sell	1	551.290		
02/08/95	SExit	1	561.640	$ –5,175.00	$ 51,225.00
02/28/95	Buy	1	567.950		
03/10/95	LExit	1	570.400	$ 1,225.00	$ 52,450.00
03/21/95	Sell	1	574.750		

CVR II S&P 500 Index—CME—Daily—01/01/90–10/01/97

Date	Type	Contracts	Price	P/L	Cumulative
03/31/95	SExit	1	579.800	$ −2,525.00	$ 49,925.00
04/03/95	Buy	1	580.000		
04/13/95	LExit	1	587.550	$ 3,775.00	$ 53,700.00
04/17/95	Sell	1	583.800		
04/27/95	SExit	1	590.700	$ −3,450.00	$ 50,250.00
05/04/95	Sell	1	598.400		
05/16/95	SExit	1	604.900	$ −3,250.00	$ 47,000.00
06/01/95	Buy	1	609.200		
06/13/95	LExit	1	611.700	$ 1,250.00	$ 48,250.00
06/14/95	Sell	1	611.500		
06/26/95	SExit	1	619.100	$ −3,800.00	$ 44,450.00
07/14/95	Buy	1	633.650		
07/26/95	LExit	1	634.950	$ 650.00	$ 45,100.00
08/09/95	Sell	1	632.800		
08/24/95	SExit	1	630.000	$ 1,400.00	$ 46,500.00
08/24/95	Buy	1	630.000		
09/05/95	LExit	1	640.350	$ 5,175.00	$ 51,675.00
09/05/95	Sell	1	640.350		
09/15/95	SExit	1	655.450	$ −7,550.00	$ 44,125.00
09/20/95	Buy	1	658.500		
10/02/95	LExit	1	651.400	$ −3,550.00	$ 40,575.00
10/03/95	Buy	1	652.650		
10/13/95	LExit	1	654.550	$ 950.00	$ 41,525.00
10/27/95	Buy	1	649.850		
11/06/95	LExit	1	657.650	$ 3,900.00	$ 45,425.00
11/06/95	Sell	1	657.650		
11/16/95	SExit	1	666.250	$ −4,300.00	$ 41,125.00
11/22/95	Sell	1	666.750		
12/15/95	SExit	1	683.800	$ −8,525.00	$ 32,600.00

CVR II S&P 500 Index—CME—Daily—01/01/90–10/01/97

Date	Type	Contracts	Price	P/L		Cumulative	
12/19/95	Buy	1	678.900				
01/02/96	LExit	1	686.150	$	3,625.00	$	36,225.00
01/11/96	Buy	1	666.700				
01/23/96	LExit	1	677.200	$	5,250.00	$	41,475.00
01/30/96	Sell	1	693.000				
02/07/96	SExit	1	712.800	$	–9,900.00	$	31,575.00
02/07/96	Buy	1	712.800				
02/20/96	LExit	1	704.550	$	–4,125.00	$	27,450.00
02/21/96	Buy	1	712.750				
03/04/96	LExit	1	711.800	$	–475.00	$	26,975.00
03/11/96	Buy	1	699.850				
03/21/96	LExit	1	709.550	$	4,850.00	$	31,825.00
04/03/96	Sell	1	714.000				
04/11/96	SExit	1	688.500	$	12,750.00	$	44575.00
04/11/96	Buy	1	688.500				
04/23/96	LExit	1	709.900	$	10,700.00	$	55,275.00
04/24/96	Sell	1	706.600				
05/03/96	SExit	1	698.400	$	4,100.00	$	59,375.00
05/03/96	Buy	1	698.400				
05/15/96	LExit	1	722.250	$	11,925.00	$	71,300.00
06/19/96	Buy	1	717.850				
06/26/96	LExit	1	717.800	$	–25.00	$	71,275.00
06/26/96	Sell	1	717.800				
07/09/96	SExit	1	708.300	$	4,750.00	$	76,025.00
07/09/96	Buy	1	708.300				
07/19/96	LExit	1	691.150	$	–8575.00	$	67450.00
07/24/96	Buy	1	679.850				
08/05/96	LExit	1	710.850	$	15,500.00	$	82,950.00
08/05/96	Sell	1	710.850				

CVR II S&P 500 Index—CME—Daily—01/01/90–10/01/97

Date	Type	Contracts	Price	P/L	Cumulative
08/15/96	SExit	1	712.750	$ −950.00	$ 82,000.00
08/19/96	Sell	1	717.350		
08/29/96	SExit	1	706.250	$ 5,550.00	$ 87,550.00
09/06/96	Buy	1	707.500		
09/18/96	LExit	1	730.450	$ 11,475.00	$ 99,025.00
10/01/96	Buy	1	738.350		
10/11/96	LExit	1	749.150	$ 5,400.00	$ 104,425.00
10/14/96	Sell	1	750.750		
10/24/96	SExit	1	747.000	$ 1,875.00	$ 106,300.00
10/30/96	Buy	1	746.050		
11/07/96	LExit	1	774.200	$ 14,075.00	$ 120,375.00
11/07/96	Sell	1	774.200		
11/19/96	SExit	1	789.550	$ −7,675.00	$ 112,700.00
11/27/96	Buy	1	799.250		
12/10/96	LExit	1	791.300	$ −3,975.00	$ 108,725.00
12/17/96	Buy	1	769.450		
12/30/96	LExit	1	795.300	$ 12,925.00	$ 121,650.00
01/03/97	Buy	1	793.400		
01/15/97	LExit	1	807.850	$ 7,225.00	$ 128,875.00
01/23/97	Sell	1	816.450		
01/29/97	SExit	1	814.500	$ 975.00	$ 129,850.00
01/29/97	Buy	1	814.500		
02/10/97	LExit	1	824.250	$ 4,875.00	$ 134,725.00
02/21/97	Buy	1	840.650		
03/05/97	LExit	1	840.500	$ −75.00	$ 134,650.00
03/27/97	Sell	1	804.200		
04/01/97	SExit	1	793.700	$ 5,250.00	$ 139,900.00
04/01/97	Buy	1	793.700		
04/09/97	LExit	1	794.300	$ 300.00	$ 140,200.00

CVR II S&P 500 Index—CME—Daily—01/01/90–10/01/97

Date	Type	Contracts	Price	P/L	Cumulative
04/09/97	Sell	1	794.300		
04/21/97	SExit	1	792.850	$ 725.00	$ 140,925.00
04/28/97	Buy	1	803.900		
05/05/97	LExit	1	865.300	$ 30,700.00	$ 171,625.00
05/05/97	Sell	1	865.300		
05/15/97	SExit	1	873.450	$ –4,075.00	$ 167,550.00
05/15/97	Buy	1	873.450		
05/28/97	LExit	1	879.300	$ 2,925.00	$ 170,475.00
06/06/97	Buy	1	891.400		
06/30/97	LExit	1	910.350	$ 9,475.00	$ 179,950.00
07/07/97	Sell	1	938.450		
07/17/97	SExit	1	958.050	$ –9,800.00	$ 170,150.00
07/22/97	Buy	1	962.350		
08/01/97	LExit	1	973.100	$ 5,375.00	$ 175,525.00
08/07/97	Sell	1	976.350		
08/14/97	SExit	1	948.150	$ 14,100.00	$ 189,625.00
08/14/97	Buy	1	948.150		
08/26/97	LExit	1	927.100	$ –10,525.00	$ 179,100.00
09/24/97	Sell	1	964.700		- end -

CVR III S&P 500 Index—CME—Daily—01/01/93–10/01/97

Date	Type	Contracts	Price	P/L	Cumulative
04/26/93	Buy	1	524.290		
05/10/93	LExit	1	534.640	$ 5,175.00	$ 5175.00
06/08/93	Buy	1	537.140		
06/11/93	LExit	1	539.640	$ 1,250.00	$ 6,425.00
06/28/93	Sell	1	543.240		
07/01/93	SExit	1	539.890	$ 1,675.00	$ 8,100.00
07/06/93	Buy	1	532.490		
07/08/93	LExit	1	539.040	$ 3,275.00	$ 11375.00
09/21/93	Buy	1	543.140		
09/23/93	LExit	1	548.740	$ 2,800.00	$ 14,175.00
09/27/93	Sell	1	552.640		
10/05/93	SExit	1	551.390	$ 625.00	$ 14,800.00
10/14/93	Sell	1	557.690		
10/19/93	SExit	1	556.090	$ 800.00	$ 15,600.00
11/03/93	Buy	1	551.740		
11/11/93	LExit	1	552.640	$ 450.00	$ 16,050.00
11/17/93	Buy	1	554.140		
11/18/93	LExit	1	553.140	$ −500.00	$ 15,550.00
11/24/93	Sell	1	552.640		
11/30/93	SExit	1	551.690	$ 475.00	$ 16,025.00
12/06/93	Sell	1	556.940		
12/28/93	SExit	1	560.590	$ −1,825.00	$ 14,200.00
12/31/93	Buy	1	555.640		
01/07/94	LExit	1	559.940	$ 2,150.00	$ 16,350.00
01/27/94	Sell	1	566.240		
02/01/94	SExit	1	568.590	$ −1,175.00	$ 15,175.00
02/07/94	Buy	1	560.740		
02/16/94	LExit	1	561.840	$ 550.00	$ 15,725.00
02/24/94	Buy	1	552.190		

CVR III S&P 500 Index—CME—Daily—01/01/93–10/01/97

Date	Type	Contracts	Price	P/L	Cumulative
02/28/94	LExit	1	554.790	$ 1,300.00	$ 17,025.00
03/03/94	Buy	1	551.490		
03/08/94	LExit	1	554.140	$ 1,325.00	$ 18,350.00
03/16/94	Sell	1	557.990		
03/22/94	SExit	1	557.840	$ 75.00	$ 18,425.00
03/29/94	Buy	1	538.990		
04/05/94	LExit	1	535.990	$ –1,500.00	$ 16,925.00
04/14/94	Sell	1	533.290		
04/15/94	SExit	1	533.090	$ 100.00	$ 17,025.00
04/25/94	Sell	1	539.490		
04/28/94	SExit	1	536.390	$ 1,550.00	$ 18,575.00
05/06/94	Buy	1	533.940		
05/12/94	LExit	1	530.440	$ –1,750.00	$ 16,825.00
05/18/94	Sell	1	541.440		
05/31/94	SExit	1	543.640	$ –1,100.00	$ 15,725.00
06/21/94	Buy	1	537.490		
06/29/94	LExit	1	533.790	$ –1,850.00	$ 13,875.00
06/30/94	Buy	1	530.040		
07/05/94	LExit	1	532.040	$ 1,000.00	$ 14,875.00
07/11/94	Sell	1	532.190		
07/12/94	SExit	1	533.740	$ –775.00	$ 14,100.00
07/13/94	Sell	1	534.540		
07/26/94	SExit	1	538.940	$ –2,200.00	$ 11,900.00
09/20/94	Buy	1	546.240		
09/28/94	LExit	1	548.740	$ 1,250.00	$ 13,150.00
10/04/94	Buy	1	537.340		
10/10/94	LExit	1	542.940	$ 2,800.00	$ 15,950.00
10/24/94	Buy	1	544.440		
10/26/94	LExit	1	545.640	$ 600.00	$ 16,550.00

CVR III S&P 500 Index—CME—Daily—01/01/93–10/01/97

Date	Type	Contracts	Price	P/L	Cumulative
10/31/94	Sell	1	554.740		
11/02/94	SExit	1	549.140	$ 2,800.00	$ 19,350.00
11/23/94	Buy	1	532.840		
11/28/94	LExit	1	537.290	$ 2,225.00	$ 21,575.00
12/05/94	Sell	1	536.490		
12/07/94	SExit	1	534.390	$ 1,050.00	$ 22,625.00
12/14/94	Sell	1	537.390		
12/28/94	SExit	1	543.590	$ –3,100.00	$ 19,525.00
12/30/94	Buy	1	540.640		
01/06/95	LExit	1	542.290	$ 825.00	$ 20,350.00
01/13/95	Sell	1	548.340		
01/19/95	SExit	1	547.890	$ 225.00	$ 20,575.00
03/07/95	Buy	1	561.450		
03/10/95	LExit	1	570.400	$ 4,475.00	$ 25,050.00
03/31/95	Buy	1	579.800		
04/10/95	LExit	1	585.100	$ 2,650.00	$ 27,700.00
04/12/95	Sell	1	585.350		
04/17/95	SExit	1	583.800	$ 775.00	$ 28,475.00
05/31/95	Buy	1	608.800		
06/09/95	LExit	1	604.050	$ –2,375.00	$ 26,100.00
06/13/95	Sell	1	611.700		
06/19/95	SExit	1	620.550	$ –4,425.00	$ 21,675.00
09/01/95	Sell	1	635.900		
09/08/95	SExit	1	644.500	$ –4,300.00	$ 17,375.00
10/02/95	Buy	1	651.400		
10/12/95	LExit	1	653.850	$ 1,225.00	$ 18,600.00
10/26/95	Buy	1	645.000		
10/30/95	LExit	1	653.050	$ 4,025.00	$ 22,625.00
11/03/95	Sell	1	658.850		

CVR III S&P 500 Index—CME—Daily—01/01/93–10/01/97

Date	Type	Contracts	Price	P/L	Cumulative
11/10/95	SExit	1	660.800	$ −975.00	$ 21,650.00
11/28/95	Sell	1	674.300		
12/08/95	SExit	1	685.250	$ −5,475.00	$ 16,175.00
12/18/95	Buy	1	672.650		
12/20/95	LExit	1	674.100	$ 725.00	$ 16,900.00
01/09/96	Buy	1	669.550		
01/16/96	LExit	1	671.950	$ 1,200.00	$ 18,100.00
02/06/96	Buy	1	709.250		
02/21/96	LExit	1	712.750	$ 1,750.00	$ 19,850.00
03/08/96	Buy	1	692.900		
03/14/96	LExit	1	702.400	$ 4,750.00	$ 24,600.00
04/02/96	Sell	1	713.500		
04/09/96	SExit	1	699.900	$ 6,800.00	$ 31,400.00
04/10/96	Buy	1	688.150		
04/12/96	LExit	1	695.500	$ 3,675.00	$ 35,075.00
04/19/96	Sell	1	701.950		
05/02/96	SExit	1	700.750	$ 600.00	$ 35,675.00
05/02/96	Buy	1	700.750		
05/08/96	LExit	1	702.400	$ 825.00	$ 36,500.00
06/27/96	Sell	1	722.200		
07/05/96	SExit	1	710.250	$ 5,975.00	$ 42,475.00
07/08/96	Buy	1	705.450		
07/10/96	LExit	1	710.850	$ 2,700.00	$ 45,175.00
07/11/96	Buy	1	697.500		
07/18/96	LExit	1	696.600	$ −450.00	$ 44,725.00
07/22/96	Buy	1	686.700		
07/25/96	LExit	1	684.350	$ −1,175.00	$ 43,550.00
07/26/96	Sell	1	688.500		
07/30/96	SExit	1	686.850	$ 825.00	$ 44,375.00

CVR III S&P 500 Index—CME—Daily—01/01/93–10/01/97

Date	Type	Contracts	Price	P/L		Cumulative	
08/02/96	Sell	1	715.500				
08/13/96	SExit	1	710.950	$	2,275.00	$	46,650.00
08/30/96	Buy	1	700.450				
09/09/96	LExit	1	714.300	$	6,925.00	$	53,575.00
10/24/96	Buy	1	747.000				
11/04/96	LExit	1	754.500	$	3,750.00	$	57,325.00
11/08/96	Sell	1	777.500				
11/19/96	SExit	1	789.550	$	–6,025.00	$	51,300.00
11/26/96	Buy	1	800.650				
12/09/96	LExit	1	794.750	$	–2,950.00	$	48,350.00
12/12/96	Buy	1	770.700				
12/18/96	LExit	1	774.350	$	1,825.00	$	50,175.00
01/22/97	Sell	1	827.800				
01/24/97	SExit	1	805.950	$	10,925.00	$	61,100.00
02/20/97	Buy	1	840.550				
02/24/97	LExit	1	848.800	$	4,125.00	$	65,225.00
03/18/97	Buy	1	823.700				
03/21/97	LExit	1	820.450	$	–1,625.00	$	63,600.00
03/26/97	Sell	1	826.900				
03/27/97	SExit	1	804.200	$	11,350.00	$	74,950.00
04/07/97	Sell	1	796.000				
04/11/97	SExit	1	767.200	$	14,400.00	$	89,350.00
05/02/97	Sell	1	845.250				
05/05/97	SExit	1	865.300	$	–10,025.00	$	79,325.00
07/03/97	Sell	1	947.850				
07/09/97	SExit	1	938.100	$	48,75.00	$	84,200.00
07/18/97	Buy	1	937.100				
07/24/97	LExit	1	965.950	$	14,425.00	$	98,625.00
08/06/97	Sell	1	983.700				

CVR III S&P 500 Index—CME—Daily—01/01/93–10/01/97

Date	Type	Contracts	Price	P/L	Cumulative
08/08/97	SExit	1	956.500	$ 13,600.00	$ 112,225.00
08/13/97	Buy	1	945.900		
08/19/97	LExit	1	951.100	$ 2,600.00	$ 114,825.00
09/22/97	Sell	1	976.500		
09/30/97	SExit	1	964.800	$ 5,850.00	$ 120,675.00
					- end -

Other Publications from
M. GORDON PUBLISHING GROUP

BOOKS

Street Smarts: High Probability Short-Term Trading Strategies—Laurence A. Connors and Linda Bradford Raschke. This 245-page manual is considered by many to be one of the best books written on trading futures. Twenty-five years of combined trading experience is divulged as you will learn 20 of their best strategies. *$175*

Hit and Run Trading: The Short-Term Stock Traders' Bible—Jeff Cooper. This best-selling manual teaches traders how to day-trade and short-term trade stocks. Jeff's strategies identify daily the ideal stocks to trade and point out the exact entry and protective exit point. Most trades risk 1 point or less and last from a few hours to a few days. *$100*

The 5-Day Momentum Method—Jeff Cooper. Strongly trending stocks always pause before they resume their move. *The 5-Day Momentum Method* identifies 3–7 day explosive moves on strongly trending momentum stocks. Highly recommended for traders who are looking for larger than normal short-term gains and who do not want to sit in front of the screen during the day. *The 5-Day Momentum Method* works as well shorting declining stocks as it does buying rising stocks. Also, there is a special sections written for option traders. *$50*

Investments Secrets of a Hedge Fund Manager—Laurence A. Connors and Blake E. Hayward. This top-selling trading book reveals strategies that give you the tools to stand apart from the crowd. Among the strategies you will learn from this book are: **Connors-Hayward Historical Volatility System,** this revolutionary method utilized historical volatility to pinpoint markets that are ready to explode; **News Reversals,** a rule-based strategy to exploit the irrational crowd psychology caused by news events; **NDX-SPX,** an early-warning signal that uses the NASDAQ 100 Index to anticipate moves in the S&P 500; and **Globex,** cutting edge techniques that identify mis-pricings that regularly occur on the Globex markets. *$49.95*

Method in Dealing in Stocks—Joseph H. Kerr, Jr. This gem, originally published in 1931 by Joseph Kerr, has been expanded and updated to reflect today's markets. This book is considered to be the bible of interpreting both daily market action and daily news events. *$35*

TRADING COURSE

Turning the Art of Trading into a Science—Taught by professional money manager Mark Boucher (author of Chapter 24) and Stanford Ph.D. Tom Johnson, you will learn exactly how to combine profitable patterns with timing methods. This course will teach you pattern recognition, market timing, options selection, statistical probabilities, how to identify runaway markets, and many new strategies. 500 pages of instruction and eleven 90-minute cassette tapes. Highly recommended. *$350*

SOFTWARE

Indicators for Omega Trade Station™ and SuperCharts—We have created an add-on module that allows you to identify the setups from *Connors on Advanced Trading Strategies*. This software alerts you to daily and intraday market signals, plots the indicators, and also provides you with a daily printout for each day's entry points. *$175*

Indicators for MetaStock Software Version 6.5—We have also created an add-on module for Meta-Stock users. It includes indicators, systems, expert studies, and commentaries. This software will scan a portfolio for daily signals, plot the indicators, and provide alerts and commentaries on the setups. *$175*

NEWSLETTER

Professional Traders Journal—In an effort to bring a continuous flow of trading ideas to traders, Larry Connors and his staff publish a monthly teaching newsletter entitled, the *Professional Traders Journal*. The Journal reveals trading strategies and concepts for futures traders, equity traders, and option traders. Special emphasis is placed on short-term, low-risk strategies and methods to allow you to profit from specific identifiable periods. Subscription price six months, $175, one year $295

TO ORDER CALL:

1-800-797-2584
or
1-310-317-0361

OR FAX YOUR ORDER TO:

1-310-317-4621

OR MAIL YOUR ORDER TO:

M. Gordon Publishing Group
23805 Stuart Ranch Road, Suite 245
Malibu, California 90265

All orders please add $5.00 for shipping and handling.

California residents include 8.5% sales tax.

www.mgordonpub.com

ABOUT THE AUTHOR

Laurence Connors is President of Connors, Bassett, and Associates, an investment firm, and President of Oceanview Financial Research. Larry is also the co-author of *Investment Secrets of a Hedge Fund Manager* with Blake Hayward, co-author of *Street Smarts* with Linda Raschke, and editor of *The Professional Traders Journal*. He resides in Malibu, California, with his wife Karen and two daughters (and their pet zoo).

PUBLISHED IN 2022 BY AMERICA'S FOOD

ISBN: 9798498214429

All inquiries, requests & correspondence about this book should be directed to the following email address:

americasfoodhub@gmail.com

British Library Cataloguing in Publication Data
A catalogue record for this book is available from the British Library.
Repository XI—Domicile 23, Data Bank 2—Cooking Manuals.

Library of Congress Cataloguing in Publication Data
Eva Garcia-Diaz, 2021—Index 22a, Cookbooks & Household Media.

Front, Interior & Back Design
By Excelsior Designs, 1 Rockwell Ave, New York, NY, 10504.

Printed in the United States of America
By Amazon and its Affiliates.

TITANGATE PRESS
Time is knowledge.

PREFACE

Master your Air Fryer with affordable, quick & easy meals for effortless cooking! In this new edition, you'll learn how to cook 2022's most affordable, quick & easy Air Fryer recipes on a budget. Do you want to cook with your Air Fryer but don't know where to start? Quit worrying! In this cookbook, you'll learn how to not only start, but love, your Air Fryer! You'll cook tons of awesome recipes, with over 1001 amazing meals you can cook in the most affordable, quick & easy way possible. Along the way, you'll cook using only the highest quality super tasty and affordable ingredients, offering plenty of scientifically proven health benefits, such as improving your appetite, cholesterol, blood pressure & reversing diabetes. Rest assured, you, the Air Fryer beginner, will master your Air Fryer in no time! In this cookbook, you'll love cooking…

⇒ **AFFORDABLE INGREDIENTS:** cut expensive and hard to find ingredients.
⇒ **EASY TO FIND INGREDIENTS:** find recipe ingredients easily online and at your local grocery store.
⇒ **QUICK & EASY RECIPES:** cook simple, tasty and wholesome meals.
⇒ **NUTRITIONAL INFORMATION:** keep track of your daily calories.
⇒ **SERVINGS:** cook right-sized food portions.
⇒ **COOKING TIMES:** save time and stress around the kitchen.
⇒ **HIGHLY RATED RECIPES:** enjoy 1001 most popular hand-selected recipes.
⇒ **HOLIDAY SPECIAL RECIPES:** feast on holiday meals all year round!
⇒ **AIR FRYER GUIDE:** learn everything there is to know about your Air Fryer.

Don't miss out on the cooking fun! Pick up your copy today & start cooking amazing Air Fryer recipes that cater for the diverse needs of you & your family, allowing you, the Air Fryer beginner, to save time, money & stress in the kitchen.

My Warmest Regards,

Eva Garcia-Dias

Nutritionist & Diet Coach, MD.
America's Food Hub.

CONTENTS

SIDE DISHES 76

APPETIZERS 103

POULTRY 111

BEEF 134

AIR FRYER GUIDE

IT'S ALL HOT AIR!

T he big day has arrived! You finally have your hands on your shiny new Air Fryer. But you're probably wondering what it is and how to get set up. No worries, this first chapter is designed with beginners in mind. First, let's begin by talking about the Air Fryer in general. Simply put, an Air Fryer is a countertop convection oven that cooks food with hot air. This is great because it means you can cook food affordably, quickly and easily! I personally think the term "air fryer" is misleading because people get confused by the old-fashioned Air Fryer that your grandma might have in her pantry. The big difference, however, between these two types of fryers is that the modern air fryer does not require huge amounts of oil because it cooks food with only hot air—nothing else is required! So, hopefully you have learned that the Air Fryer cooks food by circulating hot air around using a convection mechanism. Enough of the interesting science, for now.

Did you forget to prepare something for dinner? No problem—the Air Fryer can cook such lovely, delicious food in just moments! Such scrumptious food includes sizzling burgers and dry crispy fries–all super affordable, quick & easy too! What's more? When your Air Fryer finishes cooking, the latent heat inside keeps your food warm. I can confidently say that my air fryer has changed the way I cook because I now spend less time in the kitchen and more time doing the things I enjoy, like spending precious time with family and walking my dogs. In fact, even my weekly shop at my local grocery store is super cheap and easy. I like to fill my grocery basket to the brim with all kinds of locally sourced, affordable and easy to find ingredients which I whack into my Air Fryer, allowing me to whip up amazing meals for my family to enjoy. Buying ingredients for all the recipes inside this book is easy and affordable. I can buy them from my local store because they are so easy to find and are very cheap too. Yes, cooking with my Air Fryer means cooking with simple, affordable and yet wholesome, delicious and yummy foods—the best of both worlds! Yum yum!

Every week, I love frying a batch of burgers for a quick 'on-the-go' lunch after I take my grandchildren to school. What's great is the temperature control on my Air Fryer dial because it means I can have it all cooked for when I return home. In fact, I whack all manner of things in the frying basket on a low temperature because my Air Fryer keeps it warm for hours. This appliance has revolutionized how I cook, and I have even retired my once beloved Instant Pot back to the pantry. My Air Fryer allows me to cook delicious food in a matter of minutes thanks to the technological advances given to us by modern science. If my grandma were alive today, she would stare in awe at my Air Fryer because it revolutionizes the cooking process from start to finish. This means you and I can spend more time doing the things we enjoy the most, without having to worry about allocating enough time to prepare our next meal. The Air Fryer takes care of that by offering a very quick and efficient way of cooking food to cater for any budget, even a low one. Don't miss out, get yours today!

YOUR SAFETY COMES FIRST!

You, like most people, are probably wondering why I would want an Air Fryer? I mean, aren't they those machines that explode oil on the countertop? Well, that might have been the case for old-fashioned fryers, but this is not one of those! Rest assured, a modern Air Fryer comes equipped with loads of safety features. For example, it is physically impossible to open the frying basket without pressing the lock button first, either naturally or manually—so burning hazards are minimized! This is great to know if you have small children around the house. Indeed, modern day Air Fryers are quiet, safe and easy to use. In fact, the US government recognizes their safety and so they even have 10 UL Certified proven safety mechanisms to prevent most issues. So, Air Fryers are a very safe appliance to have around your kitchen provided, of course, you use your common sense. Importantly, mop up any water spillages close to your fryer and keep it away from children, pets and

vulnerable people at all times. For your safety, I have compiled a list of steps below that you should follow when using your Air Fryer. We don't want you getting into any nasty accidents in the kitchen!

⇒ **YOUR AIR FRYER GETS HOT!** Do not touch your Air Fryer during and shortly after cooking is over. When cooking time is over, use oven mitts or potholders to touch its surfaces and wait for it to cool down. Be patient and allow time for it to cool to room temperature! Your food will remain hot inside, so don't worry about it getting cold. Be sure to move your head away from the top to avoid getting burned by hot steam when you open it.

⇒ **AVOID ELECTROCUTION!** Avoid immersing the cord, plug or the Air Fryer unit in water or other liquid. If a spillage occurs, quicky mop it up with a dry paper towel. Do not operate your Air Fryer during a natural disaster or power surge to avoid damaging the unit and minimizing your chances of electrocution. If you have young children around the house, warm them not to use your Air Fryer and better still, keep away hidden away inside a cupboard or even in the attic or cellar. The less people that know about your Air Fryer, the better!

⇒ **BE MINDFUL OF OTHERS.** Think about other people around you when using your Fryer. Be especially mindful of people who might be considered more at risk of accidents than yourself, such as those who are disabled or impaired. People with reduced physical, sensory or mental capabilities, or lack of experience and knowledge, should not use your Air Fryer without your supervision. Always keep children away from your Air Fryer, unless under strict supervision or educational reasons.

⇒ **AIR FRYER CONDITION.** Always check to make sure your Air Fryer is in good working order before turning it on. This means checking the surfaces for any visible signs of wear and tear, such as broken or split power cords and cracks in the unit itself. Like anything else, your Air Fryer is not immune to damage and will begin to show signs of aging with continual and frequent use, like if you cook with it daily. So, you should always be prepared to take your Air Fryer for repair, providing you have a returns warranty, and even eventually buying a new one. The great thing is that new and improved Air Fryers are released all the time, so don't worry if you have to part with your old fryer friend one day, as there's plenty more at the store waiting for a good, homely kitchen like yours.

⇒ **THINK ABOUT THE WEATHER.** Living in the USA means we experience so much changing and oftentimes downright hazardous weather. If you live in a part of the country where the weather is a little more dangerous than others, think twice about using your Air Fryer during times of intense weather such as storms. Do not use your Air Fryer outside if there is even the slightest chance of rain, snow or any kind of precipitation. You must keep your Air Fryer dry to stay safe, protect your health and avoid electrocution. When the weather is nice, you can take your Air Fryer to a BBQ and cook up some delicious recipes inside this book. Be watchful of the weather and always carry around your Air Fryer inside a waterproof bag to protect it. Avoid using your Air Fryer outdoors due to adverse weather conditions.

⇒ **THINK ABOUT 'HOW' YOU'RE COOKING.** Are you the type of person who gets so carried away cooking that they oftentimes leave a mess in the kitchen? Don't worry, you're not alone. In fact, most people are like this when cooking, even me! But this doesn't mean you should be careless and place your Air Fryer in places that might be a little more dangerous than others in your kitchen, such as next to a window or on a countertop where a door swings open and close nearby. Place your Air Fryer on a flat, even surface away from nearby interacting objects like windows and doors. Think about the parts attached to your Air Fryer too, such as the power cord. Do not let the cord hang over the edge of a table or countertop, as, from my painful experience, it can be pulled by young children and pets, leading to more dangerous kitchen mis happenings. I like to tape my power cord to the wall using simple masking tape. Safety comes first, not kitchen aesthetics. Sometimes, people like to gift Air Fryer as wedding gifts or hand me down presents. Be sure to always check the condition of your Air Fryer if this applies to you, as sometimes people like to give away faulty items as gifts!

⇒ **TURN IT ON AND OFF PROPERLY.** In a rush? Got to get the kids off to school or make that 9AM meeting at work? Sure, we've all been there, but this doesn't mean you should be sloppy when using your Air Fryer. Bad habits like this lead to accidents and can easily be avoided by being more focused in the kitchen. When you've cooked your food, don't leave the temperature dial on a high temperature. Don't leave the timer on. Turn them both back to 0. This way, when you turn it back on again for the next meal, you won't get a nasty burn. Being disciplined around your Air Fryer is more important than making the tastiest recipe, as you want to make sure you're around to make many more delicious meals! If you haven't used your Air Fryer for a long time, be sure to check there's no dust, insects and strange things on or around it. Give it a wipe down with a dry paper towel before turning it on again.

⇒ **LOCK AND LOAD!** Your Air Fryer is such a well-designed machine that it makes all kind of clicky sounds when you use it. The most important sound is a mechanical sound your Air Fryer makes when you remove and insert the frying basket. Click! This sound is what you want to hear and happens when you have properly inserted the frying basket inside, and the handle is locked securely. Be careful when removing food though, as your Air Fryer gets very hot, even the outside surfaces such as the handle. The main take home message here is to give it a little time to cool down before touching it to avoid being burned.

CONTROL DIALS

Now that you've got to know more about your Air Fryer and how to use it safely, check out this picture below that shows you what a typical Air Fryer looks like and all its different parts. The Air Fryer in this picture is a standard model you might find online or in your department store. It's by no means typical of what your Air Fryer might look like and work like. Instead, it's supposed to give you a general idea of all of the different parts to your Air Fryer, so you learn how to use it safely and properly. Did you know that selecting the wrong temperature setting on your Air Fryer can mean paying a substantial amount more in electricity bills each year? I figured out that by cooking my food 20 degrees lower saved, on average, $50 in my annual electricity bill, money which I can save and buy more delicious ingredients with instead! So, using your Air Fryer properly doesn't just give you a health benefit, it actually saves you money too!

All the parts that make your Air Fryer cook delicious food...

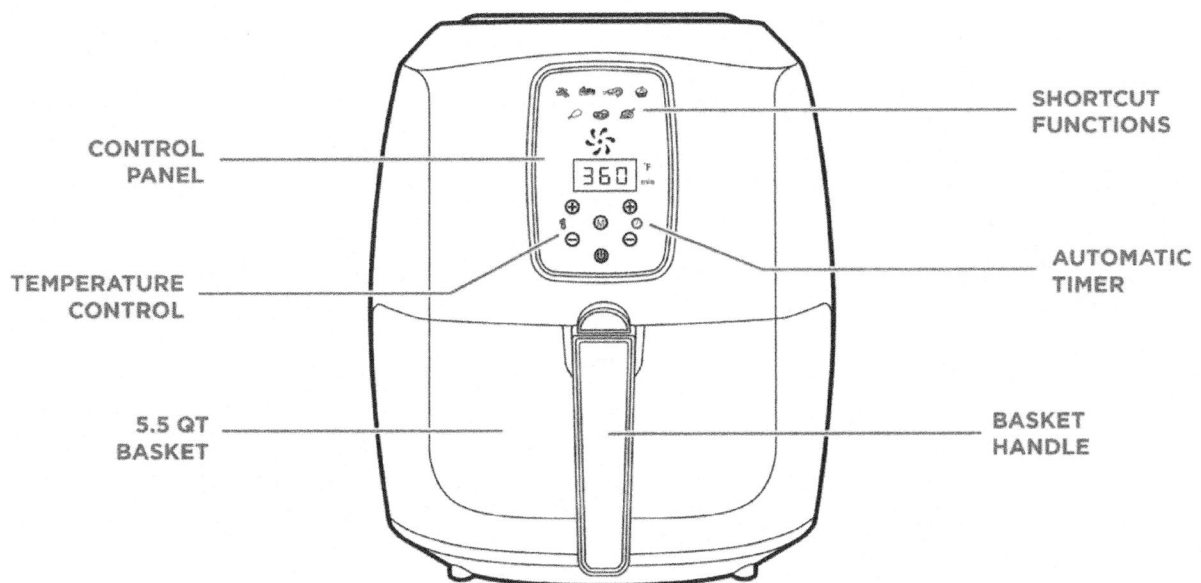

CONTROL PANEL

TEMPERATURE CONTROL

5.5 QT BASKET

SHORTCUT FUNCTIONS

AUTOMATIC TIMER

BASKET HANDLE

CONTROL PANEL. Most modern Air Fryer will come with a user control panel. This is the interface that allows you to communicate with your Air Fryer. Think of it like a mobile phone screen. You use it to select different cooking options and importantly turn your Air Fryer on and off. Some Air Fryers come with settings that allow you to adjust the brightness of the lights on the control panel, which is helpful if you are visually impaired or operate your Fryer in settings where the light isn't optimal such as your garden and garage. The Control Panel shows the HEAT ON light when cooking temperature is reached. It also shows the Red POWER light, which will turn on when you use your Fryer.

⇒ **Shortcut Function**—The shortcut functions are specifically designed for certain kinds of food, like poultry and fish, and you can select these if you think they are a better option than manually setting the frying temperature. Don't get confused by the term 'Air Fryer' as modern machines will do all kinds of things like defrost, bake etc. New cooks should avoid using these options until they have more experience using their Air Fryer and stick to using the temperature control dial instead, while more experienced cooks can use them to produce more optimal results. Consult your Air Fryer manufacturer's manual for more instructions.

⇒ **Automatic Timer**—This setting allows you to select how long your food will cook for and will automatically count down during the cooking period. Typically, one beep sounds when frying time has reached 0 minutes. Most Air Fryers turn OFF automatically, but you should always check and turn both the temperature control dial and the timer dial to 0 (OFF). This setting is useful for properly timing the cooking process to ensure that your food cooks according to the recipe instructions.

⇒ **Basket**—All modern Air Fryer will have a basket. This is where the food goes to cook. The size and shape of baskets vary from fryer to fryer. Most baskets will be of a size sufficient for placing cake pans and tins inside them, which is common for baking cakes and muffins. Consult your recipe instructions for information on whether a recipe includes the use of additional equipment such as this, as not every recipe will only use the frying basket that comes as the default setup for most modern Air Fryers.

⇒ **Handle**—The majority of modern Air Fryers also come equipped with a basket handle. This is a lever that allows you to insert and remove the frying basket in order to place food inside of it properly. You should remove the basket prior to placing food inside your Air Fryer and insert it properly by hearing a mechanical clicking sound prior to the cooking process. Always ensure the handle is 'locked' before cooking.

TEMPERATURE CONTROL DIAL. This is the second most important function. It allows you to set and control the cooking temperature inside the fryer during the cooking process. What shape and form the 'dial' looks like varies from model to model, and sometimes there might not be a dial at all on some models but push buttons and a 'keypad' style interface instead. The shape of the temperature control isn't important. Knowing how to use it correctly and safety is. Most recipes, such as those included inside this book for example, specifically state a cooking temperature, such as 380°F. Frying temperatures can range from 175°F to 400°F. Temperatures can be adjusted at any time before or during the cooking period. More experienced cooks can experiment and vary this temperature to tweak recipes in the search for more optimal results.

AIR FRYER PREP

Now that you've learned how your Air Fryer cooks, it's time to get it prepped and ready for cooking. Check out the list of steps below. You should follow these to avoid damaging your Air Fryer or causing yourself unnecessary injury. This guide assumes you have your Air Fryer boxed up in front on you in a 'just delivered' state, as if you've just had it delivered to your door.

⇒ **ASSESS THE BOX.** How big is it? Is it heavy? Can you lift it on your own? If not, don't try! Take a step back and assess the situation. Does the box come with warning stickers on the side? Fragile? Heavy? Would ripping off the cardboard carelessly damage the Air Fryer inside? These are all thoughts which you need to consider in order to ensure that you get from A, the boxing, to B, the unboxing, successfully. You've just paid a lot of money for this expensive machine and the last

thing you want to do is damage it before you've even had chance to cook your first meal with it. The majority of modern Air Fryer models can be lifted with 1 person of any gender, assuming they're healthy and of an average weight and height for their age and gender. If this is you, carefully grasp your box with both hands and place it gently on a flat and even surface like a kitchen countertop. If you struggle lifting the box on your own, call a friend, neighbor or family member to come and give you a helping hand. Failing that, contact the company or a local tech firm where you bought it and arrange an installation time. They will likely send trained engineers and technicians out to your home to help you unbox your Air Fryer and get it set up and working correctly, as it should.

⇒ **DE-BOX.** Now assuming you're that first group of people who can do this themselves without any assistance, gently pull away the cardboard delivery packaging on the outside to begin the de-boxing process. When done, you should have the manufacturer's box with your Air Fryer inside out in front of you. Now, carefully open the box, grasp the Air Fryer unit with both hands firmly, and lift it vertically out of its box, giving up a few light shakes to wiggle it free from friction and any external polystyrene/foam interior packaging inside. Place the Air Fryer on a flat countertop surface. Remove any plastic protection stickers if applicable. Consult your Air Fryer manufacturer's installation guide for further information.

⇒ **BASKET PREP.** Approach the front of your Air Fryer and firmly grip the frying basket handle to open the frying basket drawer. Remove the frying basket from your Air Fryer and place it on a flat, clean countertop. The purpose of this is to ensure that there isn't any plastic packaging inside the basket. If there is, remove it as per your manufacturer's installation manual. Ensure no packaging of any kind is on, under and around the frying basket drawer as any unremoved packaging will melt during the first cooking attempt and is hazardous. Once removed, wash the frying basket and drawer with a dry or damp kitchen towel. Dry all parts thoroughly with a kitchen towel before switching on the device.

⇒ **WARNING!** DO NOT immerse the main Air Fryer unit in water or liquid of any kind. Lock the frying basket into the drawer before operation—you should hear a seal/click when it is locked securely in place.

YOUR FIRST MEAL

Are you feeling hungry? Well, I am! Now that you've prepped your Air Fryer, it's time to start cooking amazing recipes. The checklist below will guide you to cook your first meal.

1. Place your Air Fryer on a kitchen countertop next to a power outlet.
2. Grip the frying basket handle and remove the frying basket. Carefully place it on a flat countertop.
3. Choose your recipe and toss in your food/ingredients into the frying basket. For proper cooking, do not overfill the basket.
4. Put the frying basket back into your Air Fryer, making sure you hear a nice audible click/lock sound.
5. Plug your Air Fryer into the nearest power outlet.
6. Following your recipe instructions, choose an air frying temperature between 175°F to 400°F.
7. Following your recipe instructions, choose a cooking time using the temperature control dial. Your Air Fryer may illuminate when this cooking temperature is reached. Optional: Halfway through cooking, you might want to open the frying basket and give it a good shake to ensure even, consistent cooking.
8. When cooking is done, you Air Fryer may make a beeping noise. Wait for it to cool down.
9. Using oven mitts, open the drawer and shake the frying basket vigorously to see if your food is cooked properly.
10. If satisfied, remove the frying basket from your Air Fryer and place it on a flat countertop.
11. Using kitchen utensils, scoop/take out the food from the frying basket and place it onto a plate.
12. Unplug your Air Fryer when finished. You can also cover it using a range of jazzy Air Fryer covers available online at Amazon.

HELPFUL HINTS

Are you full up after your delicious first meal? I certainly am! Here you'll find steps which you can follow when cooking your other meals. Pay attention to the 'shake, empty, spray' rule to ensure your recipes come out of your Air Fryer looking the best they can possibly be!

⇒ **A DASH OF OLIVE OIL.** I've discovered through years of cooking that adding a dash of olive oil or vegetable oil works well for air frying because it gives the food a tasty golden-brown appearance. Of course, using oil is entirely optional as your Air Fryer is designed to cook without it. You should follow your recipe instructions for more information on this.

⇒ **DON'T OVERFILL.** Never overfill your frying basket with food because doing so results in poorly and unevenly cooked food. As a rule, I never go over the two thirds level when I'm filling the basket. This varies from fryer to fryer, but the general principle remains the same across most modern models.

⇒ **SHAKE.** For the best cooking results, certain types of foods (i.e., vegetables) will have to be shaken vigorously or turned over halfway through cooking. This is to ensure they are cooked evenly and in the best way possible. Even if the recipe doesn't say to shake halfway through cooking, I always do. This is because shaking the food removes coatings of oil buildup and ensures fresh hot air can circulate over the food to produce a golden-brown texture.

⇒ **EMPTY.** Sometimes during cooking, smoke might occur and set off your fire alarm. This can happen a lot if you're cooking high fat foods like chicken wings, sausages and meats in general. To stop this, I like to empty my frying basket of oil halfway through the cooking period (it is the excess oil that causes the smoke!). This will also ensure that your food comes out with a golden-brown texture too.

⇒ **SPRAY.** Another tip I have is to spray your food with oil and pat it dry before cooking to ensure browning, not burning—works well with fish and chicken recipes. When I first started cooking using my Air Fryer, oftentimes I would burn food and had to literally scrape away the burned coating using a knife. This made a mess and dampened my cooking experience. I figured out, through trial and error, that simply spraying food like fries and other foods with batter and coating with a bit of oil stops the burning altogether and makes my recipes look and taste better too. Many recipes inside this book will include using specific cooking spray to avoid burning and promote browning.

CLEANING

So, you've been cooking with your Air Fryer for some time and have noticed that it needs a clean. To help you out with the cleaning, be sure to follow the tips outlined below

⇒ **CLEAN THE BASKET!** If, like me, you cook with your Air Fryer on a day-to-day basis, you may start to notice that the frying basket gets coated with layers of grease from repeated and frequent use. Not only does this make your Air Fryer look unhygienic and the food it cooks unappetizing, but it also leads to a more serious problem: smoking. Smoking, which is the release of toxic smoke from the frying unit, can occur when bits of burnt food are recooked many times, which happens naturally as a result of all those layers of accumulated grease. It is the grease and the food particles trapped inside which causes the smoking. So, as well as learning how to properly operate your Air Fryer, as discussed earlier on, you should get into the habit of cleaning it properly too. So, you should get into the habit of cleaning your frying basket after every use, otherwise you'll have to keep fanning your smoke alarm every time you use your fryer, which is a noise nuisance to your neighbors! You can use a degreasing agent to remove grease and grime. When not in use, you can cover your Fryer with a jazzy cover to avoid dust accumulation. This brightens up my kitchen and somehow magically makes my food taste that bit nicer!

⇒ **CLEAN WITH CAUTION.** On many Air Fryer models, the pan, basket and the inside of the appliance have a non-stick coating. This means that you should avoid using abrasive materials to clean them, otherwise you'll risk damaging the exterior of your Air Fryer and make it look worn out. You can avoid this by wiping the outside of the appliance with a damp kitchen towel. Be careful not to wet it too much or you'll risk jeopardizing your safety when you turn it on. This is because your Air Fryer operates using electricity and electrocution is always a risk which you should aim to minimize when cooking with it.

TROUBLESHOOTING

Sometimes cooking with your Air Fryer isn't as smooth as you'd like it to be. Not to worry! Thousands of Air Fryer cooks report the same problems they encounter when cooking. These problems are summarized below. This guide should help you fix any problems you may experience using your Air Fryer, and while very helpful, it isn't supposed to be treated as a technical remedy or technical advice. For those more technical faults, I suggest visiting a local repair shop or taking or Fryer back to the store where you purchased it. They will have trained staff who can help fix your Air Fryer so you can get cooking again in no time.

⇒ **AIR FRYER WON'T TURN ON!** This is the most common problem reported by cooks. In most cases, cooks forget to turn on their Air Fryer in one of two places: 1) the unit itself, 2) the power socket on the wall. Ensure that both are turned on to power your Air Fryer. Be sure to check that the plug socket isn't lose or partially plugged into the wall socket and that there isn't a bad electrical connection at the power outlet. If you're still facing the power problem, call out an electrician to take a look. If that doesn't fix the problem, you'll be glad to know that most electrical faults on your Air Fryer are covered by its manufacturer's warranty, so return it to the store so they can help you. The last resort is to buy a new fryer.

⇒ **THE AIR FRYER SMELLS MOLDY!** As discussed in prior sections, if you have a regular habit of using your Air Fryer, food will inevitably begin to accumulate on and around the surfaces, even in places where you least expect, such as the base and bottom. Unless you thoroughly deep clean your Air Fryer after every use, which I recommend, you might start to smell old and previously cooked food even if you're not cooking it, which can be a downer on your appetite. To solve this, I suggest using a toothpick and toothbrush to reach those difficult to clean places and scrub out any food residue that might be the cause of the bad smell. Again, I can't emphasize enough the importance of properly and regularly cleaning your Air Fryer, to protect your physical health by minimizing kitchen bugs like E. coli and ensure each cooking experience turns out the best it can possibly be.

⇒ **MY FOOD IS SOFT, NOT CRISPY.** Two things determine the crispiness of food:

1. Hot air and its ability to circulate properly around your Air Fryer
2. Oil on your food.

If you find that your food is coming out too soft and even soggy, try coating it on oil. The hot air will 'crisp' the oil coating during cooking, meaning your food comes out crispier and tastier than before. If that doesn't work, your fryer might have an air circulation problem. Is old food blocking hot air from circulating? If not, your fryer might be faulty, and you should consult your warranty.

You have reached the end of this guide. Thank you for taking your time to read through it. If you have any further questions or suggestions on how we can help you better, please don't hesitate to contact us via our email address: americasfoodfub@gmail.com. Failing that, you might prefer to do your own research via the internet. Google is a great place to get answers to your questions. Remember, cooking requires passion and patience. If that is you, then you'll master your Air Fryer in no time at all! From all of us here at the Food Hub, have a great day ahead and good luck starting your Air Fryer journey, which I know will be awesome just like your amazing cooking skills!

KITCHEN CONVERSIONS

SPOONS & CUPS

TSP	TBSP	FL OZ	CUP	PINT	QUART	GALLON
3	1	1/2	1/16	1/32	–	–
6	2	1	1/8	1/16	1/32	–
12	4	2	1/4	1/8	1/16	–
18	6	3	3/8	–	–	–
24	8	4	1/2	1/4	1/8	1/32
36	12	6	3/4	–	–	–
48	16	8	1	1/2	1/4	1/16
96	32	16	2	1	1/2	1/8
–	64	32	4	2	1	1/4
–	256	128	16	8	4	1

MILLILITERS

TSP	ML	OZ	ML	CUP	ML
1/2	2.5	2	60	1/4	60
1	5	4	115	1/2	120
		6	150	2/3	160
		8	230	3/4	180
TBSP	ML	10	285	1	240
1	15	12	340		

GRAMS

OZ	G	LB
2	58	–
4	114	–
6	170	–
8	226	1/2
12	340	–
16	454	1

RECIPES

1. ENGLISH EGG BREAKFAST

Prep & Cook Time: 25 minutes | Servings: 2

INGREDIENTS

2 cups of flour
1 cup of pumpkin puree
1 tbsp. of oil
2 tbsp. of vinegar

2 tsp. of baking powder
½ cup of milk
2 eggs
1 tsp. of baking soda

1 tbsp. of sugar
1 tsp. of cinnamon powder

INSTRUCTIONS

1. Set your Air Fryer at 300°F to pre-heat.
2. Crack the eggs into a bowl & beat with a whisk. Combine with the milk, flour, baking powder, sugar, pumpkin purée, cinnamon powder, & baking soda, mixing well & adding more milk if necessary.
3. Grease the baking tray with oil. Add in the mixture & transfer into the Air Fryer. Cook for 10 minutes.

---

2. PANCAKES

Prep & Cook Time: 15 minutes | Servings: 2

INGREDIENTS

2 tbsp. of coconut oil
1 tsp. of maple extract

2 tbsp. of cashew milk
2 eggs

1 oz./110g of flour

INSTRUCTIONS

1. Mix the flour with the rest of the ingredients inside a mixing bowl, except the oil.
2. Add the oil to a skillet. Add a quarter-cup of the batter & fry inside your Air Fryer at 390°F until golden on each side.

---

3. BREAKFAST SANDWICH

Prep & Cook Time: 10 minutes | Servings: 1

INGREDIENTS

2 oz./60g of cheddar cheese
⅙ oz./30g of smoked ham

2 tbsp. of butter
4 eggs

INSTRUCTIONS

1. Fry all of the eggs inside a greased non-stick pan inside your Air Fryer at 390°F & sprinkle the pepper & salt on them.
2. Place an egg down as the sandwich base. Top with the ham & cheese & a drop or two of Tabasco.
3. Place the other egg on top & enjoy!

---

4. BREAKFAST POTATOES

Prep & Cook Time: 25 minutes | Servings: 4

INGREDIENTS

1 ½ lbs. of cubed golden potatoes
4 oz. of Greek yogurt

2 tbsp. of olive oil
1 tbsp. of sweet paprika

1 tbsp. of chopped cilantro
salt & black pepper to taste

INSTRUCTIONS

1. In an air fryer, put the golden potatoes then add the olive oil, salt, black pepper & paprika.
2. At 360°F, stir & cook for 20 minutes.
3. In a bowl, toss the cooked potatoes with Greek yogurt & cilantro.
4. Serve & Enjoy!

---

5. SCRAMBLED EGGS

Prep & Cook Time: 15 minutes | Servings: 4

INGREDIENTS

4 pcs. of eggs, whisked
1 pc. of red onion, chopped

2 tsp. of sweet paprika
a drizzle of olive oil

salt & black pepper to taste

INSTRUCTIONS

1. Mix all ingredients in a bowl.
2. At 240°F, heat up the air fryer with Olive Oil & add the mixed ingredients.
3. Stir & cook for 10 minutes.
4. Serve & enjoy!

---

6. GREEN BEANS OMELETTE

Prep & Cook Time: 15 minutes | Servings: 4

INGREDIENTS

3 oz. of trimmed & halves of green beans
4 pcs. of eggs, whisked

4 pcs. of garlic cloves, minced
1 tsp. of soy sauce

1 tbsp. of olive oil
salt & black pepper to taste

INSTRUCTIONS

1. In a bowl, mix the eggs, minced garlic cloves, soy sauce, salt & black pepper. Whisk well.
2. At 320°F, heat up the air fryer with olive oil.
3. For 3 minutes, stir & sauté the green beans.
4. For 7 – 8 more minutes, spread the egg mixture over the beans.
5. Slice the omelet & serve immediately.

---

7. DELICIOUS HAM ROLLS

Prep & Cook Time: 20 Minutes | Servings: 4

INGREDIENTS

1 sheet of puff pastry
8 slices of ham, chopped

4 handful of grated gruyere cheese
4 tsp. of mustard

INSTRUCTIONS

1. On a working surface, roll out puff pastry.
2. Place the sliced cheese, ham & mustard.
3. Roll tight & slice into medium rounds.
4. Put all rolls in the air fryer at 370°F & cook for 10 minutes.
5. Place the rolls on plates.
6. Serve & enjoy!

---

8. SAUSAGE OMELETTE

Prep & Cook Time: 16 minutes | Servings: 2

INGREDIENTS

1 sausage link, sliced

2 pcs. of eggs, whisked

4 cherry tomatoes, halved

1 tbsp. of olive oil
1 tbsp. of grated cheddar cheese

1 tbsp. of chopped cilantro
salt & black pepper to taste

INSTRUCTIONS
1. Cook the tomatoes & sausage in an air fryer at 360°F for 5 minutes
2. Grease a pan that fits in air fryer with olive oil.
3. Transfer the tomatoes & sausage to the pan.
4. In a bowl, mix the rest of the ingredients & stir.
5. Spread the mixture over the sausage & tomatoes.
6. Place the pan in the air fryer.
7. For 6 more minutes, cook at 360°F.
8. Serve while it's hot!

9. ZUCCHINI & CHICKEN TORTILLAS
Prep & Cook Time: 12 minutes | Servings: 4

INGREDIENTS

6 oz. of cooked & shredded rotisserie chicken
4 pcs. of tortillas
⅓ cup of mayonnaise

1 cup of shredded zucchini
1 cup of grated parmesan cheese
4 tbsp. of melted butter

2 tbsp. of mustard

INSTRUCTIONS
1. Spread the butter on the tortillas.
2. At 400°F, heat up the tortillas in an air fryer for 3 minutes.
3. Mix & stir the chicken, zucchini, mayonnaise & mustard in a bowl.
4. Split the mixture between the tortillas & sprinkle with cheese.
5. Roll & put them in an air fryer's basket.
6. Cook for 4 more minutes at 400°F.
7. Serve & enjoy!

10. HASH BROWNS BREAKFAST
Prep & Cook Time: 30 minutes | Servings: 4

INGREDIENTS

1½ lbs. of hash browns
2 pcs. of eggs
1 pc. of red bell pepper, chopped

1 pc. of red onion, chopped
2 tsp. of vegetable oil
1 tsp. of chopped thyme

salt & black pepper to taste

INSTRUCTIONS
1. Heat up the vegetable oil on the air fryer at 350°F.
2. Cook all ingredients for 25 minutes.
3. Split between plates.
4. Serve and enjoy!

11. ROASTED PEPPERS FRITTATA
Prep & Cook Time: 30 minutes | Servings: 6

INGREDIENTS

6 oz. of chopped jarred roasted red bell peppers
½ cup of grated parmesan cheese
12 pcs. of eggs, whisked

3 pcs. of garlic cloves, minced
2 tbsp. of chopped parsley
2 tbsp. of chopped chives

6 tbsp. of ricotta cheese
a drizzle of olive oil
salt & black pepper to taste

INSTRUCTIONS
1. Mix & whisk well all the ingredients except for the Parmesan cheese & olive oil in a bowl.
2. Heat up & spread the olive oil in air fryer at 300°F.
3. Place & spread the egg mixture.
4. Sprinkle the parmesan on top and cook for 20 minutes.
5. Split between plates & serve.

12. TOMATO & EGGS
Prep & Cook Time: 35 minutes | Servings: 2

INGREDIENTS

½ cup of shredded cheddar cheese
¼ cup of milk

½ cup of chopped tomatoes
2 pcs. of eggs

2 tbsp. of chopped red onion
a pinch of salt & black pepper

INSTRUCTIONS
1. In a bowl, mix & stir well all ingredients except for the cheese.
2. Put the mixture into a pan that fits an air fryer.
3. Sprinkle the cheese on top.
4. Put the pan in the fryer.
5. Cook at 350°F for 30 minutes.
6. Split between plates.
7. Serve & enjoy!

13. BREAKFAST BISCUITS
Prep & Cook Time: 18 minutes | Servings: 12

INGREDIENTS

2 cups of white flour
1 cup of buttermilk

5 tbsp. of butter
¼ tsp. of baking soda

½ tsp. of baking powder
1 tsp. of sugar

INSTRUCTIONS
1. In a mixing bowl, mix the dry ingredients, 4 tbsp. of the butter & the buttermilk, beat until a dough is obtained.
2. Sprinkle the working surface with flour.
3. Roll the dough & cut into 12 pieces using a cookie cutter.
4. Melt the remaining 1 tbsp. of butter & brush the biscuits with it
5. Put the dough in air fryer's cake pan.
6. Cook at 400°F for 8 minutes.
7. Serve & enjoy!

14. FRIED MUSHROOM
Prep & Cook Time: 25 minutes | Servings: 4

INGREDIENTS

7 oz. of torn spinach
8 pcs. of cherry tomatoes, halved
4 slices of bacon, chopped.

4 pcs. of eggs
8 pcs. of white mushrooms, sliced
1 pc. of garlic clove, minced

a drizzle of olive oil
salt & black pepper to taste

INSTRUCTIONS

1. Greased a pan that fits the air fryer with oil.
2. Mix and stir all ingredients except for the spinach.
3. Place the pan in the air fryer and cook at 400°F for 15 minutes.
4. Add the spinach, toss and cook for 5 minutes more.
5. Share between plates & serve.

15. ITALIAN EGGPLANT SANDWICH

Prep & Cook Time: 55 minutes | Servings: 2

INGREDIENTS

1 pc. of eggplant, sliced
½ cup of panko breadcrumbs
4 slices of bread
½ cup of mayonnaise
3/4 cup of tomato paste

½ tsp. of garlic powder
2 tsp. of chopped parsley
½ tsp. of Italian seasoning
1 tbsp. & a drizzle of avocado oil
2 tbsp. of coconut milk

2 tbsp. of chopped fresh basil
2 tbsp. of grated cheddar cheese
2 cups of grated mozzarella cheese
salt & black pepper to taste

INSTRUCTIONS

1. Season the eggplant slices with salt & pepper. Set aside for 30 minutes.
2. Pat & dry them, and brush with mayo and milk.
3. In a bowl, combine and stir parsley, breadcrumbs, Italian seasoning, garlic powder, salt & black pepper.
4. Dip the eggplant slices into the mixture & place them on a lined baking sheet, drizzle with oil.
5. Place the baking sheet in the air fryer's basket and cook at 400°F for 15 minutes, flipping the eggplant slices halfway.
6. Coat the bread slices with the remaining 1 tbsp. of the oil.
7. Arrange 2 of them on a working surface.
8. Add cheddar, mozzarella, baked eggplant slices, tomato paste and basil, top with the other 2 bread slices.
9. Grill sandwiches for 10 minutes.
10. Serve while it's hot!

16. HERBED TOMATOES BREAKFAST

Prep & Cook Time: 25 minutes | Servings: 2

INGREDIENTS

1 lb. of cherry tomatoes, halved
a drizzle of olive oil
1 pc. of cucumber, chopped

1 pc. of spring onion, chopped
1 tsp. of chopped cilantro
1 tsp. of chopped basil

1 tsp. of chopped oregano
1 tsp. of chopped rosemary
salt & black pepper to taste

INSTRUCTIONS

1. Grease the tomatoes with the oil, and season with salt & pepper.
2. Put them in the air fryer's basket.
3. Cook the tomatoes at 320°F for 20 minutes and transfer them to a bowl.
4. Add all remaining ingredients, toss & serve.

17. CHICKEN & SPINACH CASSEROLE

Prep & Cook Time: 30 minutes | Servings: 4

INGREDIENTS

1 lb. of ground chicken meat
12 pcs. of eggs, whisked

1 cup of baby spinach
1 tbsp. of olive oil

½ tsp. of sweet paprika
salt & black pepper to taste

INSTRUCTIONS

1. In a bowl, whisk the eggs with the salt, pepper and paprika.
2. Add the spinach and chicken. Mix well.
3. Heat up the air fryer at 350°F, add the oil & allow it to heat up.
4. Place the chicken and spinach mix, cover and cook for 25 minutes.
5. Share between plates.
6. Serve while it's hot!

18. SMOKED BACON & BREAD

Prep & Cook Time: 40 minutes | Servings: 6

INGREDIENTS

1 lb. of cubed white bread
1 lb. of cooked and chopped smoked bacon
½ lb. of shredded cheddar cheese
½ lb. of shredded Monterey jack cheese

30 oz. of chopped canned tomatoes
¼ cup of avocado oil
1 pc. of red onion, chopped
2 tbsp. of chicken stock
2 tbsp. of chopped chives

8 pcs. of eggs, whisked
salt & black pepper to taste

INSTRUCTIONS

1. Grease the air fryer with oil and heat it up at 350°F.
2. Add all other ingredients except the chives and cook for 30 minutes, shaking halfway.
3. Share between plates.
4. Sprinkled with Chives.
5. Serve & Enjoy!

19. SAUSAGE BAKE

Prep & Cook Time: 25 minutes | Servings: 4

INGREDIENTS

1 lb. of chopped breakfast sausage
4 slices of bacon, cooked & crumbled
a drizzle of olive oil

2 cups of coconut milk
2½ cups of shredded cheddar cheese
3 tbsp. of chopped cilantro

2 pcs. of eggs
salt & black pepper to taste

INSTRUCTIONS

1. Mix and whisk well the eggs with milk, cheese, salt, pepper & cilantro.
2. Put a drizzle of oil to the air fryer and heat it up at 320°F.
3. Add the bacon, sausage and spread the egg mixture.
4. Cook for 20 minutes.
5. Serve hot & enjoy!

20. TOFU & QUINOA BOWLS

Prep & Cook Time: 25 minutes | Servings: 4

INGREDIENTS

1 lb. of torn fresh Romanesco
12 oz. of cubed firm tofu
8 oz. of torn baby spinach

3 pcs. of carrots, chopped
1 pc. of red bell pepper, chopped
¼ cup of soy sauce

2 cups of cooked red quinoa
3 tbsp. of maple syrup
2 tbsp. of olive oil

2 tbsp. of lime juice
INSTRUCTIONS
1. Combine the tofu with the oil, maple syrup, soy sauce and lime juice in the air fryer.
2. At 370°F, cook for 15 minutes, shaking halfway and transfer to a bowl.
3. Toss Romanesco, carrots, spinach, bell peppers and quinoa.
4. Share between bowls.
5. Serve and enjoy.

21. TASTY TUNA SANDWICHES
Prep & Cook Time: 15 Minutes | Servings: 4

INGREDIENTS

16 oz. of drained canned tuna
¼ cup of mayonnaise
2 tbsp. of mustard

1 tbsp. of lemon juice
2 pcs. of green onions, chopped
3 pcs. of English muffins, halved

3 tbsp. of butter
6 provolone cheese

INSTRUCTIONS
1. Combine and stir tuna with mayo, lemon juice, mustard and green onions.
2. Grease muffin halves with the butter
3. Put them in preheated air fryer and bake at 350°F for 4 minutes.
4. Spread tuna mix on muffin halves, top each with provolone cheese.
5. Place sandwiches to air fryer and cook for 4 minutes.
6. Split among plates.
7. Serve immediately.

22. HAM & CHEESE PATTIES
Prep & Cook Time: 20 minutes | Servings: 4

INGREDIENTS

8 slices of ham, chopped
4 handfuls of grated mozzarella cheese

1 puff of pastry sheet
4 tsp. of mustard

INSTRUCTIONS
1. Roll out puff pastry on a working surface and cut it in 12 squares.
2. Split cheese, ham and mustard on half of them.
3. Top with the other halves and close the edges.
4. Put all the patties in air fryer's basket and cook at 370°F for 10 minutes.
5. Split the patties between plates.
6. Serve & enjoy!

23. CHILI & PARSLEY SOUFFLÉ
Prep & Cook Time: 14 minutes | Servings: 3

INGREDIENTS

3 pcs. of eggs
1 pc. of red chili pepper, chopped

2 tbsp. of heavy cream
2 tbsp. of finely chopped parsley

salt & white pepper to taste

INSTRUCTIONS
1. Combine all ingredients in a bowl.
2. Whisk and pour into 3 ramekins.
3. Put ramekins in the air fryer's basket and cook at 400°F for 9 minutes.
4. Serve the soufflés immediately & enjoy!

24. PEPPERS & LETTUCE SALAD
Prep & Cook Time: 15 minutes | Servings: 4

INGREDIENTS

2 oz. of rocket leaves
4 pcs of red bell peppers
1 pc of lettuce head, torn

2 tbsp. of olive oil
1 tbsp. of lime juice
3 tbsp. of heavy cream

salt & black pepper to taste

INSTRUCTIONS
1. Put the bell peppers in air fryer's basket and cook at 400°F for 10 minutes.
2. Remove and peel the peppers.
3. Cut into strips and place in a bowl.
4. Add all remaining ingredients.
5. Toss and serve.

25. BREAKFAST SAUSAGE ROLLS
Prep & Cook Time: 16 minutes | Servings: 4

INGREDIENTS

8 pcs. of crescent roll dough, separated

8 slices of cheddar cheese

8 pcs. small sausages

INSTRUCTIONS
1. Unroll the crescent roll pieces on a working surface.
2. Put one sausage and one slice of cheese on each roll.
3. Wrap the sausage and cheese with each roll and close the edges.
4. Put 4 wraps in air fryer, cook at 380°F for 3 minutes.
5. Transfer to a plate.
6. Do it again with the remaining 4 sausage rolls.
7. Serve and enjoy!

26. PARMESAN MUFFINS
Prep & Cook Time: 20 minutes | Servings: 4

INGREDIENTS

3 oz. of almond milk
4 oz. of white flour
2 oz. of grated parmesan cheese

2 pcs. of eggs
2 tbsp. of olive oil
1 tbsp. of baking powder

a splash of Worcestershire sauce

INSTRUCTIONS
1. Combine and stir well the eggs with 1 tbsp. of the oil, milk, baking powder, flour, Worcestershire sauce & parmesan.
2. Oil a muffin pan that fits the air fryer.
3. Spread the cheesy mixture evenly.
4. Put the pan in the air fryer.
5. Cook at 320°F for 15 minutes.
6. Serve & enjoy!

27. LEEK & POTATO FRITTATA

Prep & Cook Time: 28 Minutes | Servings: 4

INGREDIENTS

2 pcs. of boiled golden potatoes, peeled & chopped
¼ cup of whole milk

5 oz. of crumbled fromage blanc
2 tbsp. of butter
2 pcs. of leeks, sliced

10 pcs. of eggs, whisked
salt & black pepper to the taste

INSTRUCTIONS

1. Heat up a pan that fits the air fryer with the butter over medium heat.
2. Add leeks, stir and cook for 4 minutes.
3. Put and whisk well potatoes, salt, pepper, eggs, cheese & milk. Cook for 1 minute more.
4. Introduce in your air fryer and cook at 350°F, for 13 minutes.
5. Slice frittata.
6. Share among plates and serve.

28. PANCAKES

Prep & Cook Time: 30 minutes | Servings: 4

INGREDIENTS

1¾ cups of white flour
1 cup of peeled, cored & chopped apple
1¼ cups of milk

1 pc. of egg, whisked
2 tbsp. of sugar
2 tsp. of baking powder

¼ tsp. of vanilla extract
2 tsp. of cinnamon powder
cooking spray

INSTRUCTIONS

1. Combined and stir all ingredients, except cooking spray, until a smooth batter is obtain.
2. Grease air fryer's pan with the cooking spray.
3. Spread ¼ of the batter into the pan.
4. Cover and cook at 360°F for 5 minutes, flipping it halfway.
5. Repeat Step 2 – 4 for the remaining batter.
6. Serve while it's hot!

29. FRUITY CASSEROLE

Prep & Cook Time: 30 minutes | Servings: 6

INGREDIENTS

1 pc. of banana, peeled & mashed
2 pcs. of eggs, whisked
2 cups of milk
1 cup of blueberries

2 cups of old-fashioned oats
⅓ cup of sugar
1 tsp. of cinnamon powder
1 tsp. of vanilla extract

1 tsp. of baking powder
2 tbsp. of butter
cooking spray

INSTRUCTIONS

1. Combine and whisk the sugar, baking powder, cinnamon, blueberries, banana, eggs, butter & vanilla.
2. Heat up air fryer at 320°F, and grease with cooking spray.
3. Place the oats, berries and banana mix, cover and cook for 20 minutes.
4. Share into bowls and serve.

30. ARTICHOKE OMELET

Prep & Cook Time: 20 minutes | Servings: 3

INGREDIENTS

3 pcs. of artichoke hearts, canned, drained & chopped.
6 pcs. of eggs, whisked

2 tbsp. of avocado oil
½ tsp. of dried oregano
salt & black pepper to taste

INSTRUCTIONS

1. Combine and stir well all ingredients except the oil.
2. Put the oil to air fryer's pan and heat it up at 320°F.
3. Place the egg mixture, cook for 15 minutes.
4. Share between plates and serve.

31. CHORIZO OMELET

Prep & Cook Time: 12 minutes | Servings: 4

INGREDIENTS

½ lb. of chopped chorizo
½ cup of corn
4 pcs. of eggs, whisked

1 tbsp. of crumbled feta cheese
1 tbsp. of vegetable oil
1 tbsp. of chopped cilantro

salt & black pepper to taste

INSTRUCTIONS

1. Heat up the oil in an air fryer at 350°F.
2. Place the chorizo, stir and cook for 1-2 minutes.
3. Combine and whisk all remaining ingredients in a bowl.
4. Pour over the chorizo. Cook for 5 minutes.
5. Share between plates and serve.

32. CREAMY PEAS OMELET

Prep & Cook Time: 15 minutes | Servings: 8

INGREDIENTS

½ lb. of baby peas
8 pcs. of eggs, whisked

1½ cups of yogurt
½ cup of chopped mint

3 tbsp. of avocado oil
salt & black pepper to taste

INSTRUCTIONS

1. Heat up the oil in a pan that fits your air fryer over medium heat.
2. Place the peas, stir and cook for 3-4 minutes.
3. Combine and whisk the yogurt, salt, pepper, eggs & mint.
4. Pour yogurt mixture over the peas, toss and cook at 350°F for 7 minutes.
5. Cut the omelet and serve right away.

33. APPLE OATMEAL

Prep & Cook Time: 20 minutes | Servings: 6

INGREDIENTS

1¼ cups of steel cut oats
3 cups of almond milk
2 pcs. of apples, cored, peeled & chopped

2 tsp. of vanilla extract
2 tsp. of sugar
½ tsp. of cinnamon powder

¼ tsp. of ground nutmeg
¼ tsp. of ground allspice
¼ tsp. of ginger powder

¼ tsp. of ground cardamom   cooking spray

INSTRUCTIONS
1. Spray air fryer with cooking spray.
2. Put all ingredients and stir.
3. Cover and cook at 360°F for 15 minutes.
5. Place into bowls and serve.

34. POLENTA CAKES
Prep & Cook Time: 35 minutes | Servings: 4

INGREDIENTS

¼ cup of potato starch
1 cup of cornmeal
3 cups of water

a drizzle of vegetable oil
maple syrup for serving
1 tbsp. of melted butter

salt & black pepper to taste

INSTRUCTIONS
1. Pour water in a pot, heat up over medium heat.
2. Add cornmeal, whisk and cook for 10 minutes.
3. Put the butter, whisk well, then take off the heat and allow to cool down.
4. Take spoonful of polenta and shape into balls and flattened them.
5. Coat in potato starch and place on a lined baking sheet that fits the air fryer.
6. Drizzle with oil.
7. Put the baking sheet in the fryer and cook at 380°F for 15 minutes, flipping them halfway.
8. Serve with maple syrup drizzled on top.

35. CARROTS & CAULIFLOWER MIX
Prep & Cook Time: 30 minutes | Servings: 4

INGREDIENTS

1 pc. of steamed cauliflower head, stems removed
& florets separated
2 oz. of milk

2 oz. of grated cheddar cheese
3 pcs. of steamed carrots, chopped
3 pcs. of eggs

2 tsp. of chopped cilantro
salt & black pepper to taste

INSTRUCTIONS
1. Combine the eggs with the milk, parsley, salt and pepper, whisk.
2. Add the cauliflower and the carrots in the air fryer.
3. Pour the egg mixture and spread.
4. Sprinkle the cheese on top.
5. Cook at 350°F for 20 minutes.
6. Share between plates and serve.

36. PESTO TOAST
Prep & Cook Time: 13 minutes | Servings: 3

INGREDIENTS

6 slices of bread
3 pcs. of garlic cloves, minced

1 cup of grated mozzarella cheese
6 tsp. of basil & tomato pesto

5 tbsp. of melted butter

INSTRUCTIONS
1. Arrange bread slices on a working surface.
2. Combine the butter, pesto and garlic.
3. Spread on each bread slices.
4. Put them in the air fryer's basket, sprinkle the cheese on top,
5. Cook at 350°F for 8 minutes.
6. Serve immediately.

37. VANILLA OATMEAL
Prep & Cook Time: 22 minutes | Servings: 4

INGREDIENTS

1 cup of steel cut oats
1 cup of milk

2½ cups of water
2 tsp. of vanilla extract

2 tbsp. of brown sugar

INSTRUCTIONS
1. In a pan, combine all ingredients and stir well.
2. Place the pan in the air fryer and cook at 360°F for 17 minutes.
3. Put into bowls and serve.

38. COD TORTILLA
Prep & Cook Time: 27 minutes | Servings: 4

INGREDIENTS

4 pcs. of skinless & boneless cod fillets
4 pcs. of tortillas
1 pc. of green bell pepper, chopped.

1 pc. of red onion, chopped.
a drizzle of olive oil
1 cup of corn

½ cup of salsa
4 tbsp. of grated parmesan cheese
a handful of baby spinach

INSTRUCTIONS
1. At 350°F, cook the fish fillet in the air fryer for 6 minutes, and transfer to a plate.
2. Heat up a pan with the oil over medium heat.
3. Sauté bell peppers, onions & corn for 5 minutes, and take off the heat.
4. Arrange all the tortillas on a working surface.
5. Divide the cod, salsa, sautéed veggies, spinach & parmesan evenly between the 4 tortillas, then wrap/roll them.
6. Put the tortillas in the air fryer's basket and cook at 350°F for 6 minutes.
7. Share between plates and serve.

39. CREAMY MUSHROOM PIE
Prep & Cook Time: 20 minutes | Servings: 4

INGREDIENTS

6 pcs. of white mushrooms, chopped
3 pcs. of eggs
1 pc. of red onion, chopped
9-inch of Pie dough

¼ cup of grated cheddar cheese
½ cup of heavy cream
2 tbsp. of bacon, cooked and crumbled
1 tbsp. of olive oil

½ tsp. of thyme, dried
salt & black pepper to taste

INSTRUCTIONS
1. Roll the dough on a working surface.
2. Place it on the bottom of a pie pan and grease with oil.
3. Combine all other ingredients except for the cheese, stir well & pour mixture into the pie pan. Sprinkle cheese on top.

4. Place the pan in the air fryer and cook at 400°F for 10 minutes.
5. Slice & serve.

40. CHICKEN BURRITO
Prep & Cook Time: 15 minutes | Servings: 2

INGREDIENTS

4 slices of chicken breast, cooked & shredded
2 pcs. of tortillas
1 pc. of avocado, peeled, pitted & sliced

1 pc. of green bell pepper, sliced
2 pcs. of eggs, whisked
2 tbsp. of mild salsa

2 tbsp. of grated cheddar cheese
salt & black pepper to taste

INSTRUCTIONS

1. In a bowl, beat the eggs with the salt & pepper, and pour them into a pan.
2. Place the pan in the air fryer's basket, cook for 5 minutes at 400°F.
3. Transfer the mix to a plate.
4. Fill the tortillas with eggs, chicken, bell peppers, avocado & cheese, roll the burritos.
5. Line air fryer with tin foil, and place the burritos
6. Cook at 300°F for 3-4 minutes.
7. Serve and enjoy!

41. BLACKBERRIES & CORNFLAKES
Prep & Cook Time: 15 minutes | Servings: 4

INGREDIENTS

3 cups of milk
¼ cup of blackberries
2 pcs. of eggs, whisked

1 tbsp. of sugar
¼ tsp. of ground nutmeg
4 tbsp. of whipped cream cheese

1½ cups of corn flakes

INSTRUCTIONS

1. Combine all ingredients and stir well.
2. Heat up the air fryer at 350°F.
3. Place and spread the corn flakes mixture.
4. Cook for 10 minutes.
5. Share between plates.
6. Serve and enjoy.

42. CHEESY HASH BROWN
Prep & Cook Time: 30 minutes | Servings: 6

INGREDIENTS

1½ lbs. of hash browns
6 slices of bacon, chopped
8 oz. of softened cream cheese
1 pc. of yellow onion, chopped

6 pcs. of eggs
6 pc. of spring onions, chopped
1 cup of shredded cheddar cheese
1 cup of almond milk

a drizzle of olive oil
salt & black pepper to taste

INSTRUCTIONS

1. Heat up the air fryer with the oil at 350°F.
2. Combined all other ingredients except the spring onions, whisk well.
3. Put the mixture to the air fryer, cover and cook for 20 minutes.
4. Share between plates, sprinkle the spring onions on top and serve.

43. POTATO FRITTATA
Prep & Cook Time: 25 minutes | Servings: 6

INGREDIENTS

1 lb. of chopped small potatoes
1 oz. of grated parmesan cheese
½ cup of heavy cream

2 pcs. of red onions, chopped
8 pcs. of eggs, whisked
1 tbsp. of olive oil

salt & black pepper to taste

INSTRUCTIONS

1. Combine all ingredients except the potatoes and oil, mix well.
2. Heat up air fryer's pan with the oil at 320°F.
3. Put the potatoes, stir and cook for 5 minutes.
4. Spread the egg mixture and cook for 15 minutes more.
6. Split the frittata between plates and serve.

44. VANILLA TOAST
Prep & Cook Time: 10 minutes | Servings: 6

INGREDIENTS

12 slices of bread
½ cup of brown sugar

1 stick of butter, softened
2 tsp. of vanilla extract

INSTRUCTIONS

1. Combine butter, sugar and vanilla.
2. Spread the mixture over bread slices.
3. Place them in air fryer and cook at 400°F for 5 minutes.
4. Serve immediately and enjoy!

45. DELICIOUS DOUGHNUTS
Prep & Cook Time: 28 Minutes | Servings: 6

INGREDIENTS

½ cup of sugar
2 ¼ cups of white flour
1 tsp. of cinnamon powder

2 pcs. of egg yolks
⅓ cup of caster sugar
4 tbsp. of softened butter

1 ½ tsp. of baking powder
½ cup of sour cream

INSTRUCTIONS

1. Combine 2 tablespoon butter with simple sugar and egg yolks, whisk well.
2. Add half of the sour cream and stir.
3. In another bowl, combined flour with baking powder, then add to the egg mixture.
4. Beat well until you obtain a dough.
5. Transfer it to a floured working surface, make a doughnut cut.
6. Brush doughnuts with the rest of the butter.
7. Heat up air fryer at 360°F.
8. Put the doughnuts inside and cook them for 8 minutes.
9. In a bowl, mix cinnamon with caster sugar and stir.
10. Arrange doughnuts on plates and dip them in cinnamon mixture.

11. Serve and enjoy!

46. HERBED OMELET

Prep & Cook Time: 20 minutes | Servings: 4

INGREDIENTS

6 pcs. of eggs, whisked
2 tbsp. of grated parmesan cheese
4 tbsp. of heavy cream

1 tbsp. of chopped parsley
1 tbsp. of chopped tarragon
2 tbsp. of chopped chives

salt & black pepper to taste

INSTRUCTIONS

1. Combined all ingredients except for the parmesan, whisk well.
2. Pour mixture into a pan and place it in preheated fryer.
3. Cook at 350°F for 15 minutes.
4. Share the omelet between plates.
5. Serve with the parmesan sprinkled on top.

47. RICE PUDDING

Prep & Cook Time: 25 minutes | Servings: 4

INGREDIENTS

1 cup of brown rice
½ cup of maple syrup

½ cup of chopped almonds
½ cup of shredded coconut

3 cups of almond milk

INSTRUCTIONS

1. Put the rice in a pan.
2. Add all remaining ingredients, toss.
3. Place pan in your air fryer and cook at 360°F for 20 minutes.
4. Share into bowls and serve.

48. CORN PUDDING

Prep & Cook Time: 1 hour 25 minutes | Servings: 6

INGREDIENTS

4 slices of bacon cooked & chopped.
3 pcs. of eggs
3 cups of cubed bread
½ cup of heavy cream
1½ cups of whole milk

1 cup of shredded cheddar cheese
2 cups of corn
½ cup of chopped green bell pepper
1 pc. of yellow onion, chopped
¼ cup of chopped celery

1 tsp. of chopped thyme
2 tsp. of grated garlic
3 tbsp. of grated parmesan cheese
1 tbsp. of olive oil
salt & black pepper

INSTRUCTIONS

1. Heat up the oil in a pan over medium heat.
2. Sauté the corn, celery, onion, bell pepper, salt, pepper, garlic and thyme to the pan for 15 minutes and transfer to a bowl.
3. In the same bowl, add bacon, milk, cream, eggs, salt, pepper, bread & cheddar cheese. Stir well, then pour into a casserole dish that fits your air fryer.
4. Put the dish in the fryer and cook at 350°F for 30 minutes.
5. Sprinkle the pudding with parmesan cheese and cook for 30 minutes more.
6. Share between plates and serve.

49. CHEESE TOAST

Prep & Cook Time: 13 minutes | Servings: 2

INGREDIENTS

4 slices of bread

4 slices of cheddar cheese

4 tsp. of softened butter

INSTRUCTIONS

1. Spread the butter on each slice of bread.
2. Put two slices of cheese in between slices of bread.
3. Cut the sandwiches in half.
4. Arrange them in the air fryer's basket and cook at 370°F for 8 minutes.
5. Serve hot and enjoy!

50. PUMPKIN OATMEAL

Prep & Cook Time: 25 minutes | Servings: 4

INGREDIENTS

½ cup of steel cut oats
1½ cups of milk

½ cup of pumpkin puree
1 tsp. of pumpkin pie spice

3 tbsp. of sugar

INSTRUCTIONS

1. In your air fryer's pan, combine all ingredients.
2. Mix, cover and cook at 360°F for 20 minutes.
3. Share into bowls and serve.

51. EASY ONION FRITTATA

Prep & Cook Time: 30 Minutes | Servings: 6

INGREDIENTS

10 pcs. of eggs, whisked
½ cup of sour cream
2 pc. of yellow onions, chopped

1 tbsp. of olive oil
1 lb. of chopped small potatoes
1 oz. of grated cheddar cheese

salt & black pepper to the taste

INSTRUCTIONS

1. In a large bowl, combine eggs with potatoes, onions, salt, pepper, cheese & sour cream, whisk well.
2. Grease air fryer's pan with the oil.
3. Put the eggs mixture in air fryer and cook for 20 minutes at 320°F.
4. Slice frittata, share among plates.
5. Serve for breakfast

52. BREAKFAST POTATOES

Prep & Cook Time: 45 Minutes | Servings: 2

INGREDIENTS

3 pcs. of potatoes, cubed
2 tbsp. of olive oil
1 tsp. of garlic powder

1 tsp. of sweet paprika
1 tsp. of onion powder
1 pc. of yellow onion, chopped

1 pc. of red bell pepper, chopped
salt & black pepper to the taste

INSTRUCTIONS

1. Grease air fryer's basket with olive oil.
2. Add potatoes, toss and season with salt and pepper.

3. Put onion, bell pepper, garlic powder, paprika and onion powder, toss well.
4. Cover and cook at 370°F, for 30 minutes.
5. Share potatoes mix on plates and serve for breakfast.

---

53. TOFU & BELL PEPPERS
Prep & Cook Time: 15 minutes | Servings: 8

INGREDIENTS
3 oz. of crumbled firm tofu
1 pc. of green onion, chopped
1 pc. of yellow bell pepper, cut into strips

1 pc. of orange bell pepper, cut into strips
1 pc. of green bell pepper, cut into strips
2 tbsp. of chopped parsley

salt & black pepper to taste

INSTRUCTIONS
1. In a pan, put the bell pepper strips and mix.
2. Put all remaining ingredients, toss and place the pan in the air fryer.
3. Cook at 400°F for 10 minutes.
4. Share between plates and serve.

---

54. TUNA SANDWICHES
Prep & Cook Time: 14 minutes | Servings: 3

INGREDIENTS
16 oz. of drained canned tuna
6 slices of bread
6 slices of provolone cheese

2 pcs. of spring onions, chopped
¼ cup of mayonnaise
2 tbsp. of mustard

1 tbsp. of lime juice
3 tbsp. of melted butter

INSTRUCTIONS
1. Combine tuna, mayo, lime juice, mustard and spring onions.
2. Spread the bread slices with the butter.
3. Put them in preheated air fryer and bake them at 350°F for 5 minutes.
4. Spread tuna mix on half of the bread slices and top with the cheese and the other bread slices
5. Put the sandwiches in the air fryer's basket and cook for 4 minutes more.
6. Share between plates and serve.

---

55. CARROT OATMEAL
Prep & Cook Time: 20 minutes | Servings: 4

INGREDIENTS
½ cup of steel cut oats
2 cups of almond milk

1 cup of shredded carrots
2 tsp. of sugar

1 tsp. of ground cardamom
cooking spray

INSTRUCTIONS
1. Spray your air fryer with cooking spray.
2. Place all ingredients, toss and cover.
3. Cook at 365°F for 15 minutes.
4. Share into bowls and serve.

---

56. FISH TACOS BREAKFAST
Prep & Cook Time: 23 Minutes | Servings: 4

INGREDIENTS
4 pcs. of big tortillas
1 pc. of yellow onion, chopped
1 cup of corn
1 pc. of red bell pepper, chopped

½ cup of salsa
4 pcs. of white fish fillets, skinless & boneless
a handful mixed romaine lettuce, spinach &
radicchio

4 tbsp. of grated parmesan

INSTRUCTIONS
1. Put fish fillets in the air fryer and cook at 350°F, for 6 minutes.
2. Heat up a pan over medium high heat.
3. Put bell pepper, onion and corn, stir and cook for 1 - 2 minutes.
4. Arrange tortillas on a working surface. Share fish fillets, spread salsa over them.
5. Share mixed veggies, mixed greens & spread parmesan on each at the end.
6. Roll tacos & place them in preheated air fryer and cook at 350°F, for 6 minutes more.
7. Share fish tacos on plates and serve for breakfast.

---

57. PEAR OATMEAL
Prep & Cook Time: 17 minutes | Servings: 4

INGREDIENTS
1 cup of milk
¼ cups of brown sugar
½ cup of chopped walnuts

2 cups of pear peeled & chopped.
1 cup of old-fashioned oats
½ tsp. of cinnamon powder

1 tbsp. of softened butter

INSTRUCTIONS
1. In a heat-proof bowl, combine all ingredients and stir well.
2. Put in your fryer and cook at 360°F for 12 minutes.
3. Share into bowls and serve.

---

58. STUFFED PEPPERS
Prep & Cook Time: 13 minutes | Servings: 8

INGREDIENTS
3½ oz. of cubed feta cheese

8 pcs. of small bell peppers, tops cut off & seeds
removed

1 tbsp. of avocado oil
salt & black pepper to taste

INSTRUCTIONS
1. Combine cheese, salt, pepper and the oil, toss.
2. Fill the peppers with the cheese.
3. Put the peppers in air fryer's basket and cook at 400°F for 8 minutes.
4. Share the peppers between plates.
5. Serve and enjoy!

---

59. SQUASH BREAKFAST
Prep & Cook Time: 15 minutes | Servings: 4

INGREDIENTS
1 pc. of red bell pepper, roughly chopped
1 cup of sliced white mushrooms

½ cup of crumbled feta cheese
1 pc. of yellow squash, cubed

2 pcs. of green onions, sliced
2 tbsp. of softened butter

INSTRUCTIONS
1. Combine all ingredients except the feta cheese.
2. Transfer the mix to air fryer and cook at 350°F for 10 minutes, shaking the fryer once.
3. Share between plates.
4. Serve with feta cheese sprinkled on top.

60. BEANS OATMEAL
Prep & Cook Time: 20 minutes | Servings: 2

INGREDIENTS
1 cup of steel cut oats
2 pcs. of red bell peppers, chopped

2 tbsp. of drained canned kidney beans
4 tbsp. of heavy cream

¼ tsp. of ground cumin
salt & black pepper to taste

INSTRUCTIONS
1. Heat up your air fryer at 360°F.
2. Put all ingredients, stir.
3. Cover and cook for 15 minutes.
4. Share into bowls.
5. Serve and enjoy!

61. QUICK TURKEY BURRITO
Prep & Cook Time: 20 Minutes | Servings: 2

INGREDIENTS
4 slices of cooked turkey breast
½ pc. of red bell pepper, sliced
1 pc. of small avocado, peeled, pitted & sliced

2 tbsp. of salsa
2 pcs. of eggs
⅛ cup of grated mozzarella cheese

salt & black pepper to the taste
tortillas for serving

INSTRUCTIONS
1. In a bowl, whisk eggs with salt and pepper to the taste.
2. Pour them in a pan and place it in the air fryer's basket.
3. Cook at 400°F, for 5 minutes, take pan out of the fryer and transfer eggs to a plate.
3. Arrange tortillas on a working surface, share eggs on them.
4. Share turkey meat, bell pepper, cheese, salsa and avocado.
5. Lined and roll burritos with some tin foil.
6. Place them in air fryer and heat up at 300°F, for 3 minutes.
7. Share them on plates and serve.

62. STRAWBERRY OATMEAL
Prep & Cook Time: 15 minutes | Servings: 4

INGREDIENTS
1 cup of chopped strawberries
1 cup of almond milk

1 cup of steel cut oats
½ tsp. of vanilla extract

2 tbsp. of sugar
cooking spray

INSTRUCTIONS
1. Spray your air fryer with cooking spray.
2. Place all ingredients, toss and cover.
3. Cook at 365°F for 10 minutes.
4. Serve!

63. KALE SANDWICH
Prep & Cook Time: 11 minutes | Servings: 1

INGREDIENTS
2 cups of torn kale
1 pc. of small shallot, chopped
1 pc. of avocado, sliced

1 pc. of English muffin, halved
1 tsp. of olive oil
2 tbsp. of pumpkin seeds

1½ tbsp. of mayonnaise
a pinch of salt & black pepper

INSTRUCTIONS
1. Heat up your air fryer with the oil at 360°F.
2. Put kale, salt, pepper, pumpkin seeds and shallots, toss.
3. Cover and cook for 6 minutes, shaking halfway.
4. Spread the mayo on the English muffin halves.
5. Place the avocado slice on one half, then add the kale mix.
6. Top with the other muffin half.
7. Serve and enjoy!

64. BISCUITS CASSEROLE DELIGHT
Prep & Cook Time: 25 Minutes | Servings: 8

INGREDIENTS
12 oz. of biscuits, quartered
2 ½ cups of milk

3 tbsp. of flour
½ lb. of chopped sausage

a pinch of salt & black pepper
cooking spray

INSTRUCTIONS
1. Grease your air fryer with cooking spray and heat it over 350°F.
2. Place biscuits on the bottom and mix with sausage.
3. Add flour, milk, salt and pepper, toss a bit and cook for 15 minutes.
4. Share among plates and serve for breakfast.

65. BLACK BEAN BURRITOS
Prep & Cook Time: 19 minutes | Servings: 2

INGREDIENTS
2 cups of drained canned black beans
½ pc. of red bell pepper, sliced
1 pc. of small avocado, peeled, pitted & sliced

⅛ cup of shredded mozzarella cheese
2 pcs. of tortillas
a drizzle of olive oil

2 tbsp. of mild salsa
salt & black pepper to taste

INSTRUCTIONS
1. Grease your air fryer with the oil.
2. Place the beans, bell peppers, salsa, salt and pepper.
3. Cover and cook at 400°F for 6 minutes.
4. Arrange the tortillas on a working surface.
5. Share the bean mixture, avocado and cheese on each, roll the burritos.
6. Place them in air fryer and cook at 300°F for 3 minutes more.
7. Share between plates and serve.

66. SPINACH PIE

Prep & Cook Time: 34 minutes | Servings: 4

INGREDIENTS

3 oz. of crumbled mozzarella cheese
7 oz. of white flour
7 oz. of torn spinach

1 pc. of red onion, chopped
2 pcs. of eggs, whisked
2 tbsp. of olive oil

2 tbsp. of milk
salt & black pepper to taste

INSTRUCTIONS

1. In food processor, combined the flour with 1 tbsp. of the oil, eggs, milk, salt and pepper, pulse, then transfer to a bowl.
2. Knead the mixture a bit, cover and keep in the fridge for 10 minutes.
3. Heat up a pan with the remaining 1 tbsp. of oil over medium heat and add all remaining ingredients.
4. Cook for 4 minutes and remove from heat.
5. Cut the dough into 4 pieces, roll each piece, and place in the bottom of a ramekin.
6. Share the spinach mixture between the ramekins.
7. Put them in your air fryer's basket and cook at 360°F for 15 minutes.
8. Serve and enjoy!

67. TOFU & VEGGIE CASSEROLE

Prep & Cook Time: 35 minutes | Servings: 2

INGREDIENTS

7 oz. of cubed firm tofu
1 pc. of yellow onion, chopped
1 pc. of carrot, chopped
2 stalks of celery, chopped
½ cup of cooked quinoa

½ cup of chopped white mushrooms
½ cup of chopped red bell pepper
1 tsp. of minced garlic
1 tsp. of olive oil
1 tsp. of dried oregano

½ tsp. of ground cumin
1 tbsp. of lemon juice
2 tbsp. of water
2 tbsp. of grated cheddar cheese
salt & black pepper to taste

INSTRUCTIONS

1. Heat up a pan with the oil over medium heat.
2. Sauté the garlic and onion for 3 minutes.
3. Put bell peppers, celery, carrots, salt, pepper, mushrooms, oregano and cumin, stir.
4. Cook for 5-6 minutes more and remove from the heat.
5. In food processor, blend the tofu, cheese, lemon juice, quinoa & water.
6. Pour the tofu mixture over the sautéed veggies and toss.
7. Put everything into air fryer's pan and cook at 350°F for 15 minutes.
8. Share between plates and serve.

68. YAM PUDDING

Prep & Cook Time: 13 minutes | Servings: 4

INGREDIENTS

16 oz. of drained canned candied yams
½ cup of maple syrup
½ cup of coconut sugar

2 pcs. of eggs, whisked
½ tsp. of cinnamon powder
¼ tsp. of ground allspice

2 tbsp. of heavy cream
cooking spray

INSTRUCTIONS

1. Combine yams, cinnamon and all spice, mash with a fork.
2. Grease air fryer with cooking spray and heat it up to 400°F.
3. Spread the yams mixture on the bottom.
4. In another bowl, combine eggs, cream and maple syrup.
5. Put to the air fryer, cover and cook for 8 minutes.
6. Share into bowls and serve.

69. MUSHROOM FRITTERS

Prep & Cook Time: 2 hours 11 minutes | Servings: 8

INGREDIENTS

4 oz. of chopped mushrooms
10 oz. of milk
1 pc. of red onion, chopped

¼ tsp. of ground nutmeg
2 tbsp. of olive oil
1 tbsp. of panko breadcrumbs

salt & black pepper to taste

INSTRUCTIONS

1. Heat up a pan with 1 tbsp. of the oil over medium-high heat.
2. Sauté the onions and mushrooms for 3 minutes
3. Add the milk, salt, pepper and nutmeg, stir.
4. Remove the mixture from heat and set aside for 2 hours.
5. In a bowl, combine the remaining 1 tbsp. of the oil with the panko and stir
6. Take 1 tbsp. of the mushroom mixture, roll in breadcrumbs, flatten with your palms and place it in air fryer's basket.
7. Repeat step 6 with the rest of the mushroom mixture and breadcrumbs and then cook the fritters at 400°F for 8 minutes.
8. Share between plates and serve

70. APPLE BRAN GRANOLA

Prep & Cook Time: 20 minutes | Servings: 4

INGREDIENTS

2 pcs. of green apples, cored, peeled & roughly chopped
¼ cup of apple juice

⅛ cup of maple syrup
½ cup of granola
½ cup of bran flakes

1 tsp. of cinnamon powder
2 tbsp. of butter

INSTRUCTIONS

1. In your air fryer, combine all ingredients.
2. Toss, cover and cook at 365°F for 15 minutes.
3. Share into bowls and serve.

71. CHEESE FRIED BAKE

Prep & Cook Time: 30 Minutes | Servings: 4

INGREDIENTS

4 slices of bacon, cooked & crumbled
1 lb. of breakfast sausage, casings removed & chopped
2 cups of milk

2 ½ cups of shredded cheddar cheese
½ tsp. of onion powder
3 tbsp. of chopped parsley
2 pcs. of eggs

salt & black pepper to the taste
cooking spray

INSTRUCTIONS

1. In a bowl, combine eggs with milk, cheese, onion powder, salt, pepper and parsley.
2. Grease air fryer with cooking spray, heat it up at 320°F and add bacon and sausage.

3. Pour the eggs mix, spread and cook for 20 minutes.
4. Share among plates and serve.

72. BREAKFAST CAULIFLOWER

Prep & Cook Time: 25 minutes | Servings: 4

INGREDIENTS

1 pc. of big cauliflower head, stems discarded,
florets separated & steamed
4 oz. of sour cream

2 tbsp. of olive oil
1 tbsp. of hot paprika
salt & black pepper to taste

INSTRUCTIONS

1. In a pan, combine and stir all ingredients.
2. Place the pan in air fryer and cook at 360°F for 20 minutes.
3. Share into bowls and serve, enjoy!

73. EGGPLANT & ZUCCHINI BREAKFAST

Prep & Cook Time: 55 minutes | Servings: 4

INGREDIENTS

8 oz. of tomatoes, cut into quarters
8 oz. of sliced zucchini
8 oz. of chopped bell peppers

8 oz. of sliced eggplant
2 pcs. of yellow onions, chopped
2 pcs. of garlic cloves, minced

5 tbsp. of olive oil
salt & black pepper to taste

INSTRUCTIONS

1. Heat up a pan with half of the oil over medium heat.
2. Place the eggplant, salt and pepper.
3. Stir, cook for 5 minutes and then transfer to a bowl.
4. Heat up the pan with 1 tbsp. of oil.
5. Add the zucchini and the bell peppers, cook for 4 minutes and then add to the eggplant pieces.
6. Heat up the pan with the remaining oil, sauté onions for 3 minutes.
7. Put the tomatoes, garlic and if desired, more salt and pepper.
8. Transfer the pan to air fryer and cook at 300°F for 30 minutes.
9. Share mixture between plates and serve right away.

74. EGG MUFFINS

Prep & Cook Time: 30 minutes | Servings: 1

INGREDIENTS

1 tbsp. of green pesto
1 oz./75g of shredded cheese

1 oz./150g of cooked bacon
1 scallion, chopped

2 eggs

INSTRUCTIONS

1. Set your Air Fryer to 350°F/175°C.
2. Place liners in a regular cupcake tin. This will help with easy removal & storage.
3. Beat the eggs with pepper, salt, & the pesto. Mix in the cheese.
4. Pour the eggs into the cupcake tin & top with the bacon & scallion.
5. Cook for 15-20 minutes, or until the egg is set.

75. BACON & EGGS

Prep & Cook Time: 5 minutes | Servings: 1

INGREDIENTS

Parsley
Cherry tomatoes

⅓ oz./150g of bacon
2 eggs

INSTRUCTIONS

1. Fry up the bacon in a greased non-stick pan inside your Air Fryer at 390°F for 5 minutes each side.
2. Scramble the eggs in the bacon grease, with some pepper & salt. If you want, scramble in some cherry tomatoes.
3. Sprinkle with some parsley & enjoy.

76. EGGS ON THE GO

Prep & Cook Time: 10 minutes | Servings: 1

INGREDIENTS

1 oz./110g of bacon, cooked
Pepper

Salt
2 eggs

INSTRUCTIONS

1. Set your Air Fryer to 400°F/200°C.
2. Place liners in a regular cupcake tin. This will help with easy removal & storage.
3. Crack an egg into each of the cups & sprinkle some bacon onto each of them. Season with some pepper & salt.
4. Fry for 15 minutes, or until the eggs are set. Plate and serve!

77. CREAM CHEESE PANCAKES

Prep & Cook Time: 10 minutes | Servings: 1

INGREDIENTS

2 oz. of cream cheese
2 eggs

½ tsp. of cinnamon
1 tbsp. of coconut flour

½ tsp. of sugar

INSTRUCTIONS

1. Mix together all the ingredients inside a greased non-stick pan until smooth.
2. Place the pan inside your Air Fryer at 390°F and cook for a few minutes either side.
3. Make them as you would standard pancakes. Cook on one side & then flip to cook the other side!
4. Top with some butter &/or sugar.

78. BREAKFAST MIX

Prep & Cook Time: 15 minutes | Servings: 1

INGREDIENTS

1 tbsp. of coconut flakes
1 tbsp. of hemp seeds

1 tbsp. of flaxseed, ground
2 tbsp. of sesame, ground

2 tbsp. of cocoa, dark

INSTRUCTIONS

1. Grind the flaxseed & the sesame. Only grind the sesame seeds for a very short period.
2. Mix all of ingredients inside a bowl. Place the bowl inside your Air Fryer's frying basket.
3. Cook briefly at 390°F until crispy and golden brown.

4. Keep refrigerated until ready to eat.
5. Serve softened with black coffee or even with still water & add coconut oil if you want to increase the fat content. It also blends well with cream or with mascarpone cheese.

79. BREAKFAST MUFFINS
Prep & Cook Time: 30 minutes | Servings: 1

INGREDIENTS

1 medium egg
¼ cup of heavy cream

1 slice of cooked bacon (cured, pan-fried, cooked)
1 oz. of cheddar cheese

Salt & black pepper (to taste)

INSTRUCTIONS
1. Preheat your Air Fryer to 350°F/175°C.
2. In a bowl, mix the eggs with the cream, salt & pepper.
3. Spread into muffin tins & fill the cups half full.
4. Place 1 slice of bacon into each muffin hole & half ounce of cheese on top of each muffin.
5. Bake for around 15-20 minutes or until slightly browned.
6. Add another ½ oz. of cheese onto each muffin & broil until the cheese is slightly browned. Serve!

80. EGG PORRIDGE
Prep & Cook Time: 15 minutes | Servings: 1

INGREDIENTS

2 organic free-range eggs
⅓ cup of organic heavy cream

½ tbsp. of sugar
2 tbsp. of grass-fed butter ground organic

cinnamon to taste

INSTRUCTIONS
1. Add the eggs, cream, sugar, & to a dish and mix together. Place the dish inside your Air Fryer's frying basket. Cook at 370°F for 5 minutes.
2. Melt the butter in a saucepan over a medium heat. Lower the heat once the butter is melted.
3. Combine together with the egg & cream mixture.
4. While Cooking, mix until it thickens & curdles.
5. When you see the first signs of curdling, remove the saucepan immediately from the heat.
6. Pour the porridge into a bowl. Sprinkle cinnamon on top & serve immediately.

81. EGGS FLORENTINE
Prep & Cook Time: 20 minutes | Servings: 2

INGREDIENTS

1 cup of washed, fresh spinach leaves
2 tbsp. of freshly grated parmesan cheese

Sea salt & pepper
1 tbsp. of white vinegar

2 eggs

INSTRUCTIONS
1. Cook the spinach briefly inside your Air Fryer at 350°F until browned.
2. When done, take out the spinach and sprinkle with parmesan cheese & seasoning.
3. Slice into bite-size pieces & place on a plate.
4. Simmer a pan of water & add the vinegar. Stir quickly with a spoon.
5. Break an egg into the center. Turn off the heat & cover until set.
6. Repeat with the second egg.
7. Place the eggs on top of the spinach & serve.

82. SPANISH OMELET
Prep & Cook Time: 15 minutes | Servings: 2

INGREDIENTS

3 eggs
Cayenne or black pepper

½ cup of finely chopped vegetables

INSTRUCTIONS
1. In a flat greased dish, add the vegetables. Place the dish inside your Air Fryer and cook at 390°F until browned.
2. Take out the dish and put to one side.
3. In another dish, cook the eggs with one tbsp. of water & a pinch of pepper inside your Air Fryer at 390°F.
4. When almost cooked, top with the vegetables & flip to cook briefly.
5. Serve onto plates!

83. CRISTY'S PANCAKES
Prep & Cook Time: 10 minutes | Servings: 1

INGREDIENTS

1 tbsp. of vanilla extract
oz./110g of flour

2 tbsp. of water
1 egg

INSTRUCTIONS
1. Add the ingredients together inside a bowl & mix together.
2. Pour the mixture into a flat dish and place it inside your Air Fryer's frying basket.
3. Cook at 390°F for approximately 2 to 3 minutes on each side (watch carefully as it may burn quickly.)
4. Serve buttered with a handful of mixed berries.

84. BREAKFAST TEA
Prep & Cook Time: 5 minutes | Servings: 1

INGREDIENTS

16 oz. of water
2 tea bags

1 tbsp. of butter
1 tbsp. of coconut oil

½ tsp. of vanilla extract

INSTRUCTIONS
1. Make the tea & put it to one aside.
2. In a bowl, melt the butter.
3. Add the coconut oil & vanilla to the melted butter.
4. Pour the tea into a dish. Place the dish inside your Air Fryer and heat the tea until hot. Pour into mugs and serve hot!

85. SAUSAGE QUICHE
Prep & Cook Time: 35 minutes | Servings: 4

INGREDIENTS

12 large eggs
1 cup of heavy cream

1 tsp. of black pepper
12 oz. of sugar-free breakfast sausage

2 cups of shredded cheddar cheese

INSTRUCTIONS
1. Preheat your Air Fryer to 375°F/190°C.
2. In a large bowl, whisk the eggs, heavy cream, salad & pepper together.
3. Add the breakfast sausage & cheddar cheese.
4. Pour the mixture into a greased casserole dish.
5. Bake for 25 minutes. When done, serve & enjoy!

6. Cut into 12 squares & serve hot.

86. BREAKFAST SAUSAGE CASSEROLE

Prep & Cook Time: 70 minutes | Servings: 4

INGREDIENTS

8 eggs, beaten
1 head of chopped cauliflower

1 lb. of sausage, cooked & crumbled
2 cups of heavy whipping cream

1 cup of sharp cheddar cheese, grated

INSTRUCTIONS

1. Place the sausages onto a greased dish & place the dish inside your Air Fryer at 380°F for 20 minutes (10 each side) until golden brown.
2. When cooked, mix the sausage, heavy whipping cream, chopped cauliflower, cheese & eggs. Mix until well combined.
3. Pour into a greased dish.
4. Cook for 30 minutes at 350°F/175°C inside your Air Fryer.
5. Top with cheese & serve!

87. SCRAMBLED MUG EGGS

Prep & Cook Time: 5 minutes | Servings: 1

INGREDIENTS

1 mug
2 eggs

Salt & pepper
Shredded cheese

Your favorite buffalo wing sauce

INSTRUCTIONS

1. Crack the eggs into a mug & whisk until blended.
2. Put the mug into your Air Fryer & cook at 360°F for 1.5 – 2 minutes, depending on the power of your fryer.
3. Leave for a few minutes & remove from the fryer.
4. Sprinkle with salt & pepper. Add your desired amount of cheese on top.
5. Using a fork, mix everything together.
6. Then add your favorite buffalo or hot sauce & mix again.
7. Serve!

88. BANANA CHIA SEED PUDDING

Prep & Cook Time: 1-2 days | Servings: 1

INGREDIENTS

1 can of full-fat coconut milk
1 medium- or small-sized banana, ripe

½ tsp. of cinnamon
1 tsp. of vanilla extract

¼ cup of chia seeds

INSTRUCTIONS

1. In a bowl, mash the banana until soft.
2. Add the remaining ingredients & mix until incorporated. Cook inside your Air Fryer at 360°F until the bananas are mushy and the cinnamon golden brown.
3. Cover & place in your refrigerator overnight.
4. Serve!

89. STRAWBERRY RHUBARB PARFAIT

Prep & Cook Time: 30 minutes | Servings: 1

INGREDIENTS

1 packet of plain full-fat yogurt (8.5 oz.)
2 tbsp. of toasted flakes

2 tbsp. of toasted coconut flakes
6 tbsp. of strawberry & rhubarb jam

INSTRUCTIONS

1. Add the jam into a dessert bowl (3 tbsp. per serving).
2. Add the crème fraîche & garnish with the toasted & coconut flakes.
3. Place inside your Air fryer and flash fry for a few seconds on a very high heat at 400°F/200°C (maximum possible), until the dessert is crisp on the outside and soft on the inside.
4. Serve!

90. SAUSAGE EGG MUFFINS

Prep & Cook Time: 30 minutes | Servings: 4

INGREDIENTS

6 oz. of Italian sausage
6 eggs

⅛ cup of heavy cream
3 oz. of cheese

INSTRUCTIONS

1. Preheat the Air Fryer to 350°F/175°C.
2. Grease a muffin pan.
3. Slice the sausage links & place them two to a tin.
4. Beat the eggs with the cream & season with salt & pepper.
5. Pour over the sausages in the tin.
6. Sprinkle with cheese & the remaining egg mixture.
7. Cook for 20 minutes or until the eggs are done & serve!

91. SALMON OMELET

Prep & Cook Time: 15 minutes | Servings: 2

INGREDIENTS

3 eggs
1 smoked salmon

3 links of pork sausage
¼ cup of onions

¼ cup of provolone cheese

INSTRUCTIONS

1. Whisk the eggs & pour them into a bowl. Place the bowl inside your Air Fryer's frying basket.
2. Cook briefly at 400°F/200°C for a few minutes each side.
3. Toss in the onions, salmon & cheese before turning the omelet over. Cook for a few more minutes.
4. Sprinkle the omelet with cheese & serve with the sausages on the side.
5. Serve!

92. BLACK'S BANGIN' CASSEROLE

Prep & Cook Time: 40 minutes | Servings: 4

INGREDIENTS

5 eggs
3 tbsp. of chunky tomato sauce

2 tbsp. of heavy cream
2 tbsp. of grated parmesan cheese

INSTRUCTIONS

1. Preheat your Air Fryer to 350°F/175°C.
2. Combine the eggs & cream in a bowl.
3. Mix in the tomato sauce & add the cheese.
4. Spread into a glass baking dish & bake for 25-35 minutes.
5. Top with extra cheese.

6.   Enjoy!

93. HASH BROWN
Prep & Cook Time: 20 minutes | Servings: 2

INGREDIENTS

12 oz. grated fresh cauliflower (about ½ a medium-sized head)

4 slices of bacon, chopped
3 oz. of onion, chopped

1 tbsp. of butter, softened

INSTRUCTIONS
1.   In a skillet, sauté the bacon & onion until brown.
2.   Add in the cauliflower & stir until tender & browned.
3.   Add the butter steadily as it cooks.
4.   Season to taste with salt & pepper.
5.   Enjoy!

94. BACON CUPS
Prep & Cook Time: 40 minutes | Servings: 2

INGREDIENTS

2 eggs
1 sliced tomato

3 slices of bacon
2 slices of ham

2 tsp. of grated parmesan cheese

INSTRUCTIONS
1.   Preheat your Air Fryer to 375°F/190°C.
2.   Cook the bacon for half of the directed time.
3.   Slice the bacon strips in half & line 2 greased muffin tins with 3 half-strips of bacon
4.   Put one slice of ham & half slice of tomato in each muffin tin on top of the bacon
5.   Crack one egg on top of the tomato in each muffin tin & sprinkle each with half a tsp. of grated parmesan cheese.
6.   Bake for 20 minutes.
7.   Remove & let cool.
8.   Serve!

95. SPINACH EGGS AND CHEESE
Prep & Cook Time: 40 minutes | Servings: 2

INGREDIENTS

3 whole eggs
3 oz. of cottage cheese

3-4 oz. of chopped spinach
¼ cup of parmesan cheese

¼ cup of milk

INSTRUCTIONS
1.   Preheat your Air Fryer to 375°F/190°C.
2.   In a large bowl, whisk the eggs, cottage cheese, the parmesan & the milk.
3.   Mix in the spinach.
4.   Transfer to a small, greased, Air Fryer dish.
5.   Sprinkle the cheese on top.
6.   Bake for 25-30 minutes.
7.   Let cool for 5 minutes & serve.

96. FRIED EGGS
Prep & Cook Time: 7 minutes | Servings: 2

INGREDIENTS

2 eggs
3 slices of bacon

INSTRUCTIONS
1.   Heat some oil in a deep Air Fryer at 375°F/190°C.
2.   Fry the bacon.
3.   In a small bowl, add the 2 eggs.
4.   Quickly add the eggs into the center of the Air Fryer.
5.   Using two spatulas, form the egg into a ball while frying.
6.   Fry for 2-3 minutes, until it stops bubbling.
7.   Place on a paper towel & allow to drain.
8.   Enjoy!

97. SCOTCH EGGS
Prep & Cook Time: 40 minutes | Servings: 4

INGREDIENTS

4 large eggs
1 packet of pork sausage (12 oz.)

8 slices of thick-cut bacon
4 toothpicks

INSTRUCTIONS
1.   Hard-boil the eggs, peel the shells & let them cool.
2.   Slice the sausage into four parts & place each part into a large circle.
3.   Put an egg into each circle & wrap it in the sausage.
4.   Place inside your refrigerator for 1 hour.
5.   Make a cross with two pieces of thick-cut bacon.
6.   Place a wrapped egg in the center, fold the bacon over top of the egg & secure with a toothpick.
7.   Cook inside your Air Fryer at 450°F/230°C for 25 minutes.
8.   Enjoy!

98. TOASTIES
Prep & Cook Time: 30 minutes | Servings: 2

INGREDIENTS

¼ cup of milk or cream
2 sausages, boiled
3 eggs

1 slice of bread, sliced lengthwise
4 tbsp. of cheese, grated
Sea salt to taste

Chopped fresh herbs & steamed broccoli [optional]

INSTRUCTIONS
1.   Pre-heat your Air Fryer at 360°F & set the timer for 5 minutes.
2.   In the meantime, scramble the eggs in a bowl & add in the milk.
3.   Grease three muffin cups with a cooking spray. Divide the egg mixture in three & pour equal amounts into each cup.
4.   Slice the sausages & drop them, along with the slices of bread, into the egg mixture. Add the cheese on top & a little salt as desired.
5.   Transfer the cups to the Fryer & cook for 15-20 minutes, depending on how firm you would like them. When ready, remove them from the Air Fryer & serve with fresh herbs & steam broccoli if you prefer.

99. EGG BAKED OMELET

INGREDIENTS

1 tbsp. of ricotta cheese
1 tbsp. of chopped parsley

1 tsp. of olive oil
3 eggs

¼ cup of chopped spinach
Salt & pepper

INSTRUCTIONS

1. Set your Air Fryer at 330°F & allow to warm with the olive oil inside.
2. In a bowl, beat the eggs with a fork & sprinkle some salt & pepper as desired.
3. Add in the ricotta, spinach, & parsley & then transfer to the Air Fryer. Cook for 10 minutes before serving.

100. BREAKFAST OMELET

Prep & Cook Time: 30 minutes | Servings: 2

INGREDIENTS

1 large onion, chopped
2 tbsp. of cheddar cheese, grated
3 eggs

½ tsp. of soy sauce
Salt
Pepper powder

Cooking spray

INSTRUCTIONS

1. In a bowl, mix the salt, pepper powder, soy sauce & eggs with a whisk.
2. Take a small pan small enough to fit inside the Air Fryer & spritz with cooking spray. Spread the chopped onion across the bottom of the pan, then transfer the pan to the Fryer. Cook at 355°F for 6-7 minutes, ensuring the onions turn translucent.
3. Add the egg mixture on top of the onions, coating everything well. Add the cheese on top, then resume cooking for another 5 or 6 minutes.
4. Take care when taking the pan out of the Air Fryer. Enjoy with some toasted bread.

101. RANCH RISOTTO

Prep & Cook Time: 40 minutes | Servings: 2

INGREDIENTS

1 onion, diced
2 cups of chicken stock, boiling
½ cup of parmesan, grated

1 clove of garlic, minced
¾ cup of Arborio rice
1 tbsp. of olive oil

1 tbsp. of butter

INSTRUCTIONS

1. Set the Air Fryer at 390°F for 5 minutes to heat up.
2. With oil, grease a round baking tin, small enough to fit inside the Air Fryer, & stir in the garlic, butter, & onion.
3. Transfer the tin to the Air Fryer & allow to cook for 4 minutes. Add in the rice & cook for a further 4 minutes, giving it a stir three times throughout the cooking time.
4. Turn the Air Fryer down to 320°F & add in the chicken stock, before gently mixing it. Leave to cook for 22 minutes with the Air Fryer uncovered. Before serving, throw in the cheese & give it one more stir. Enjoy!

102. COFFEE DONUTS

Prep & Cook Time: 20 minutes | Servings: 6

INGREDIENTS

1 cup of flour
¼ cup of sugar

½ tsp. of salt
1 tsp. of baking powder

1 tbsp. of sunflower oil
¼ cup of coffee

INSTRUCTIONS

1. In a large bowl, combine the sugar, salt, flour, & baking powder.
2. Add in the coffee & sunflower oil & mix until a dough is formed. Leave the dough to rest in & the refrigerator.
3. Set your Air Fryer at 400°F to heat up.
4. Remove the dough from the refrigerator & divide up, kneading each section into a doughnut.
5. Put the doughnuts inside the Air Fryer, ensuring not to overlap any. Fry for 6 minutes. Do not shake the basket, to make sure the doughnuts hold their shape.

103. TACO WRAPS

Prep & Cook Time: 30 minutes | Servings: 4

INGREDIENTS

1 tbsp. of water
4 pc of commercial vegan nuggets, chopped

1 small yellow onion, diced
1 small red bell pepper, chopped
2 cobs grilled corn kernels

4 large corn tortillas
Mixed greens for garnish

INSTRUCTIONS

1. Pre-heat your Air Fryer at 400°F.
2. Over a medium heat, water-sauté the nuggets with the onions, corn kernels & bell peppers in a skillet, then remove from the heat.
3. Fill the tortillas with the nuggets & vegetables & fold them up. Transfer to the inside of the Air Fryer & cook for 15 minutes. Once crispy, serve immediately, garnished with the mixed greens. Enjoy!

104. BISTRO WEDGES

Prep & Cook Time: 20 minutes | Servings: 4

INGREDIENTS

1 lb. of fingerling potatoes, cut into wedges
1 tsp. of extra virgin olive oil
½ tsp. of garlic powder

Salt & pepper
½ cup of raw cashews
½ tsp. of ground turmeric
½ tsp. of paprika

1 tbsp. of yeast
1 tsp. of fresh lemon juice
2 tbsp. to ¼ cup of water

INSTRUCTIONS

1. Pre-heat your Air Fryer at 400°F.
2. In a bowl, toss together the potato wedges, olive oil, garlic powder, & salt & pepper, making sure to coat the potatoes well.
3. Transfer the potatoes to the basket of your Air Fryer & fry for 10 minutes.
4. In the meantime, prepare the cheese sauce. Pulse the cashews, turmeric, paprika, yeast, lemon juice, & water together in a food processor. Add more water to achieve your desired consistency.
5. When the potatoes are finished cooking, move them to a bowl that is small enough to fit inside the Air Fryer & add the cheese sauce on top. Cook for an additional 3 minutes. Serve when done!

105. SPINACH BALLS

Prep & Cook Time: 20 minutes | Servings: 4

INGREDIENTS

1 carrot, peeled & grated
1 packet of fresh spinach, blanched & chopped
½ onion, chopped

1 egg, beaten
½ tsp. of garlic powder
1 tsp. of garlic, minced
1 tsp. of salt

½ tsp. of black pepper
1 tbsp. of yeast
1 tbsp. of flour
2 slices of bread, toasted

INSTRUCTIONS

1. In a food processor, pulse the toasted bread to form breadcrumbs. Transfer into a shallow dish or bowl.
2. In a bowl, mix together all the other ingredients.
3. Use your hands to shape the mixture into small-sized balls. Roll the balls in the breadcrumbs, ensuring to cover them well.
4. Whack inside the Air Fryer & cook at 390°F for 10 minutes. Serve when done!

106. CHEESE & CHICKEN SANDWICH

Prep & Cook Time: 15 minutes | Servings: 1

INGREDIENTS

⅓ cup of chicken, cooked & shredded
2 mozzarella slices
1 hamburger bun
¼ cup of cabbage, shredded

1 tsp. of mayonnaise
2 tsp. of butter
1 tsp. of olive oil
½ tsp. of balsamic vinegar

¼ tsp. of smoked paprika
¼ tsp. of black pepper
¼ tsp. of garlic powder
Salt

INSTRUCTIONS

1. Pre-heat your Air Fryer at 370°F.
2. Apply some butter to the outside of the hamburger bun with a brush.
3. In a bowl, coat the chicken with the garlic powder, salt, pepper, & paprika.
4. In a separate bowl, stir together the mayonnaise, olive oil, cabbage, & balsamic vinegar to make coleslaw.
5. Slice the bun in two. Start building the sandwich, starting with the chicken, followed by the mozzarella, the coleslaw, & finally the top bun.
6. Transfer the sandwich to the Air Fryer & cook for 5 – 7 minutes.

107. BACON & HORSERADISH CREAM

Prep & Cook Time: 1 hour 40 minutes | Servings: 4

INGREDIENTS

½ lb. of thick cut bacon, diced
2 tbsp. of butter
2 shallots, sliced
½ cup of milk
1 ½ lb. of Brussels sprouts, halved

2 tbsp. of flour
1 cup of heavy cream
2 tbsp. of prepared horseradish
½ tbsp. of fresh thyme leaves
⅛ tsp. of ground nutmeg

1 tbsp. of olive oil
½ tsp. of sea salt
Ground black pepper to taste
½ cup of water

INSTRUCTIONS

1. Pre-heat your Air Fryer at 400°F.
2. Coat the Brussels sprouts with olive oil & sprinkle some salt & pepper on top. Transfer to the Air Fryer & cook for a half hour. At the halfway point, give them a good stir, then take them out of the Air Fryer & set to the side.
3. Put the bacon in the basket of the Air Fryer & pour the water into the drawer underneath to catch the fat. Cook for 10 minutes, stirring 2 or 3 times throughout the cooking time.
4. When 10 minutes are up, add in the shallots. Cook for a further 10 – 15 minutes, making sure the shallots soften up & the bacon turns brown. Add some more pepper & remove. Leave to drain on some paper towels.
5. Melt the butter over the stove or in the microwave, before adding in the flour & mixing with a whisk. Slowly add in the heavy cream & milk & continue to whisk for another 3 – 5 minutes, making sure the mixture thickens.
6. Add the horseradish, thyme, salt, & nutmeg & stirring well once more.
7. Take a 9" x 13" baking dish & grease it with oil. Pre-heat your Air Fryer to 350°F.
8. Put the Brussels sprouts in the baking dish & spread them across the base. Pour over the cream sauce & then top with a layer of bacon & shallots.
9. Cook in the Air Fryer for a half hour & enjoy.

108. VEGETABLE TOAST

Prep & Cook Time: 25 minutes | Servings: 4

INGREDIENTS

4 slices of bread
1 red bell pepper, cut into strips
1 cup of sliced button or cremini

mushrooms
1 small yellow squash, sliced
2 green onions, sliced

1 tbsp. of olive oil
2 tbsp. of softened butter
½ cup of soft goat cheese

INSTRUCTIONS

1. Drizzle the Air Fryer with the olive oil & pre-heat to 350°F.
2. Put the red pepper, green onions, mushrooms, & squash inside the Air Fryer, give them a stir & cook for 7 minutes, shaking the basket once throughout the cooking time. Ensure the vegetables become tender.
3. Remove the vegetables & set them aside.
4. Spread some butter on the slices of bread & transfer to the Air Fryer, butter side-up. Brown for 2 to 4 minutes.
5. Remove the toast from the Air Fryer & top with goat cheese & vegetables. Serve warm.

109. CINNAMON TOASTS

Prep & Cook Time: 15 minutes | Servings: 4

INGREDIENTS

10 slices of bread
1 pack of salted butter

4 tbsp. of sugar
2 tsp. of ground cinnamon

½ tsp. of vanilla extract

INSTRUCTIONS

1. In a bowl, combine the butter, cinnamon, sugar, & vanilla extract. Spread onto the slices of bread.
2. Set your Air Fryer to 380°F. When warmed up, put the bread inside the Air Fryer & cook for 4 – 5 minutes.

110. TOASTED CHEESE

Prep & Cook Time: 20 minutes | Servings: 2

INGREDIENTS

2 slices of bread

4 oz. cheese, grated

Small amount of butter

INSTRUCTIONS

1. Grill the bread in the toaster.
2. Butter the toast & top with the grated cheese.
3. Set your Air Fryer to 350°F to pre-heat.
4. Put the toast slices inside the Air Fryer & cook for 4 - 6 minutes.
5. Serve & enjoy!

111. PEANUT BUTTER BREAD

Prep & Cook Time: 15 minutes | Servings: 3

INGREDIENTS

1 tbsp. of oil
2 tbsp. of peanut butter

4 slices of bread
1 banana, sliced

INSTRUCTIONS

1. Spread the peanut butter on top of each slice of bread, then arrange the banana slices on top. Sandwich two slices together, then the other two.
2. Oil the inside of the Air Fryer & cook the bread for 5 minutes at 300°F.

112. ENGLISH BUILDER'S BREAKFAST

Prep & Cook Time: 35 minutes | Servings: 2

INGREDIENTS

1 cup of potatoes, sliced & diced
2 cups of beans in tomato sauce

2 eggs
1 tbsp. of olive oil

1 sausage
Salt

INSTRUCTIONS

1. Set your Air Fryer at 390°F to pre-heat.
2. Break the eggs onto an Air Fryer-safe dish & sprinkle on some salt.
3. Lay the beans on the dish, next to the eggs.
4. In a bowl small enough to fit inside your Air Fryer, coat the potatoes with the olive oil. Sprinkle on the salt, as desired.
5. Transfer the bowl of potato slices to the Air Fryer & cook for 10 minutes.
6. Swap out the bowl of potatoes for the dish containing the eggs & beans. Leave to cook for another 10 minutes. Cover the potatoes with parchment paper.
7. Slice up the sausage & throw the slices in on top of the beans & eggs. Resume cooking for another 5 minutes. Serve with the potatoes, as well as toast & coffee if desired.

113. AVOCADO EGGS
Prep & Cook Time: 15 minutes | Servings: 4

INGREDIENTS

2 large avocados, sliced
1 cup of breadcrumbs

½ cup of flour
2 eggs, beaten

¼ tsp. of paprika
Salt & pepper

INSTRUCTIONS
1. Pre-heat your Air Fryer at 400°F for 5 minutes.
2. Sprinkle some salt & pepper on the slices of avocado. Optionally, you can enhance the flavor with a half-tsp. of dried oregano.
3. Lightly coat the avocados with flour. Dredge them in the eggs, before covering with breadcrumbs. Transfer to the Air Fryer & cook for 6 minutes.

114. AVOCADO TEMPURA
Prep & Cook Time: 20 minutes | Servings: 4

INGREDIENTS

½ cup of breadcrumbs
½ tsp. of salt

1 avocado, pitted, peeled & sliced
Liquid from 1 can white beans

INSTRUCTIONS
1. Set your Air Fryer to 350°F to pre-heat.
2. Mix the breadcrumbs & salt in a shallow bowl until well-incorporated.
3. Dip the avocado slices in the bean juice, then into the breadcrumbs. Put the avocados in the Air Fryer, taking care not to overlap any slices, & fry for 10 minutes, giving the basket a good shake at the halfway point. Serve when done!

115. POTATO & KALE NUGGETS
Prep & Cook Time: 25 minutes | Servings: 4

INGREDIENTS

1 tsp. of extra virgin olive oil
1 clove of garlic, minced
4 cups of kale, rinsed & chopped

2 cups of potatoes, boiled & mashed
⅛ cup of milk

Salt & pepper
Vegetable oil

INSTRUCTIONS
1. Pre-heat your Air Fryer at 390°F.
2. In a skillet over medium heat, fry the garlic in the olive oil, until it turns golden brown. Cook with the kale for an additional 3 minutes & remove from the heat.
3. Mix the mashed potatoes, kale & garlic in a bowl. Throw in the milk & sprinkle with some salt & pepper as desired.
4. Shape the mixture into nuggets & spritz each one with a little vegetable oil. Put in the basket of your Air Fryer & leave to cook for 15 minutes, shaking the basket halfway through cooking to make sure the nuggets fry evenly.

116. BREAD ROLLS
Prep & Cook Time: 30 minutes | Servings: 5

INGREDIENTS

5 large potatoes, boiled & mashed
Salt & pepper
1 tbsp. of olive oil
½ tsp. of mustard seeds

2 small onions, chopped
½ tsp. of turmeric
2 sprigs of curry leaves
8 slices of bread, brown sides discarded

2 green chilis, seeded & chopped
1 bunch of coriander, chopped

INSTRUCTIONS
1. Pre-heat your Air Fryer at 400°F.
2. Put the mashed potatoes in a bowl & sprinkle on salt & pepper. Set to one side.
3. Fry the mustard seeds in a little olive oil over a medium-low heat, stirring continuously, until they sputter.
4. Add in the onions & cook until they turn translucent. Add the curry leaves & turmeric powder & stir. Cook for a further 2 minutes until fragrant.
5. Remove the pan from the heat & combine the contents with the potatoes. Remove from heat & add to the potatoes. Mix in the green chilies & coriander.
6. Wet the bread slightly & drain of any excess liquid.
7. Spoon a small amount of the potato mixture into the center of the bread & enclose the bread around the filling, sealing it entirely. Continue until the rest of the bread & filling is used up. Brush each bread roll with some oil & transfer to the basket of your Air Fryer.
8. Cook for 15 minutes, gently shaking the Air Fryer basket at the halfway point to ensure each roll is cooked evenly.

117. VEG FRITTATA
Prep & Cook Time: 35 minutes | Servings: 2

INGREDIENTS

¼ cup of milk
1 zucchini
½ bunch of asparagus
½ cup of mushrooms

½ cup of spinach or baby spinach
½ cup of red onion, sliced
4 eggs
½ tbsp. of olive oil

5 tbsp. of feta cheese, crumbled
4 tbsp. of cheddar, grated
¼ bunch of chives, minced
Sea salt & pepper to taste

INSTRUCTIONS
1. In a bowl, mix together the eggs, milk, salt & pepper.
2. Cut up the zucchini, asparagus, mushrooms & red onion into slices. Shred the spinach using your hands.
3. Over a medium heat, stir-fry the vegetables for 5 – 7 minutes with the olive oil in a non-stick pan.
4. Place some parchment paper in the base of a baking tin. Pour in the vegetables, followed by the egg mixture. Top with the feta & grated cheddar.
5. Set the Air Fryer at 320°F & allow to warm for five minutes.
6. Transfer the baking tin to the Air Fryer & allow to cook for 15 minutes. Take care when removing the frittata from the Air Fryer & leave to cool for 5 minutes.
7. Top with the minced chives & serve.

118. MAPLE CINNAMON BUNS
Prep & Cook Time: 1 hour 55 minutes | Servings: 9

INGREDIENTS

¾ cup of milk
4 tbsp. of maple syrup
1 ½ tbsp. of active yeast
1 tbsp. of ground flaxseed

1 tbsp. of coconut oil, melted
1 cup of flour
1 ½ cup of flour
2 tsp. of cinnamon powder

½ cup of pecan nuts, toasted
2 ripe bananas, sliced
4 Medjool dates, pitted
¼ cup of sugar

INSTRUCTIONS
1. Over a low heat, warm the milk until it is tepid. Combine with the yeast & maple syrup, waiting 5 – 10 minutes to allow the yeast to activate.
2. In the meantime, put 3 tbsp. of water & the flaxseed in a bowl & stir together. This is your egg substitute. Let the flaxseed absorb the water for about 2 minutes.
3. Pour the coconut oil into the bowl, then combine the flaxseed mixture with the yeast mixture.
4. In a separate bowl, mix together one tbsp. of the cinnamon powder & the white & flour. Add the yeast-flaxseed mixture & mix to create a dough.
5. Dust a flat surface with flour. On this surface, knead the dough with your hands for a minimum of 10 minutes.

6. Grease a large bowl & transfer the dough inside. Cover with a kitchen towel or saran wrap. Let sit in a warm, dark place for an hour so that the dough may rise.
7. In the meantime, prepare the filling. Mix the banana slices, dates, & pecans together before throwing in a tbsp. of cinnamon powder.
8. Set the Air Fryer to 390°F & allow to warm. On your floured surface, flatten the dough with a rolling pin, making it thin. Spoon the pecan mixture onto the dough & spread out evenly.
9. Roll up the dough & then slice it in nine. Transfer the slices to a dish small enough to fit in the Air Fryer, set the dish inside, & cook for 30 minutes.
10. Top with a thin layer of sugar before serving.

119. TAJ TOFU

Prep & Cook Time: 40 minutes | Servings: 4

INGREDIENTS

1 block of firm tofu, cut into 1-inch thick cubes

2 tbsp. of soy sauce
2 tsp. of sesame seeds, toasted

1 tsp. of rice vinegar
1 tbsp. of corn-starch

INSTRUCTIONS
1. Set your Air Fryer at 400°F to pre-heat.
2. Add the tofu, soy sauce, sesame seeds & rice vinegar in a bowl together & mix well to coat the tofu cubes. Then cover the tofu in cornstarch & put it in the basket of your Air Fryer.
3. Cook for 25 minutes, giving the basket a shake at five-minute intervals to ensure the tofu cooks evenly.

120. RICE PAPER BACON

Prep & Cook Time: 30 minutes | Servings: 4

INGREDIENTS

3 tbsp. of soy sauce or tamari
2 tbsp. of cashew butter

2 tbsp. of liquid smoke
2 tbsp. of water

4 pc. of white rice paper, cut into 1-inch-thick strips

INSTRUCTIONS
1. Pre-heat your Air Fryer at 350°F.
2. Mix together the soy sauce/tamari, liquid smoke, water, & cashew butter in a large bowl.
3. Take the strips of rice paper & soak them for 5 minutes. Arrange in one layer in the bottom of your Air Fryer.
4. Cook for 15 minutes, ensuring they become crispy, before serving with some vegetables.

121. POSH SOUFFLÉ

Prep & Cook Time: 25 minutes | Servings: 4

INGREDIENTS

¼ cup of flour
⅓ cup of butter
1 cup of milk

4 egg yolks
1 tsp. of vanilla extract
6 egg whites

1 oz. of sugar
1 tsp. of cream of tartar

INSTRUCTIONS
1. Set your Air Fryer at 320°F & allow to warm.
2. In a bowl, mix together the butter & flour until a smooth consistency is achieved.
3. Pour the milk into a saucepan over a low-to-medium heat. Add in the & allow to dissolve before raising the heat to boil the milk.
4. Pour in the flour & butter mixture & stir rigorously for 7 minutes to eliminate any lumps. Make sure the mixture thickens. Take off the heat & allow to cool for 15 minutes.
5. Spritz 6 soufflé dishes with oil spray.
6. Place the egg yolks & vanilla extract in a separate bowl & beat them together with a fork. Pour in the milk & combine well to incorporate everything.
7. In a smaller bowl mix together the egg whites & cream of tartar with a fork. Fold into the egg yolks-milk mixture before adding in the flour mixture. Transfer equal amounts to the 6 soufflé dishes.
8. Put the dishes in the Air Fryer & cook for 15 minutes.

122. EGG MUFFIN SANDWICH

Prep & Cook Time: 15 minutes | Servings: 1

INGREDIENTS

1 egg

2 slices of bacon

1 English muffin

INSTRUCTIONS
1. Pre-heat your Air Fryer at 395°F
2. Take a ramekin & spritz it with cooking spray. Break an egg into the ramekin before transferring it to the basket of your Air Fryer, along with the English muffin & bacon slices, keeping each component separate.
3. Allow to cook for 6 minutes. After removing from the Air Fryer, allow to cool for around two minutes. Halve the muffin.
4. Create your sandwich by arranging the egg & bacon slices on the base & topping with the other half of the muffin.

123. PEA DELIGHT

Prep & Cook Time: 25 minutes | Servings: 2 – 4

INGREDIENTS

1 cup of flour
1 tsp. of baking powder
3 eggs

1 cup of coconut milk
1 cup of cream cheese
3 tbsp. of pea protein

½ cup chicken/turkey strips
1 pinch sea salt
1 cup of mozzarella cheese

INSTRUCTIONS
1. Set your Air Fryer at 390°F & allow to warm.
2. In a large bowl, mix all ingredients together using a large wooden spoon.
3. Spoon equal amounts of the mixture into muffin cups & allow to cook for 15 minutes.

124. CHOCO BARS

Prep & Cook Time: 30 minutes | Servings: 8

INGREDIENTS

2 cups of old-fashioned oats
½ cup of quinoa, cooked
½ cup of chia seeds
½ cup almonds, sliced

½ cup of dried cherries, chopped
½ cup of dark chocolate, chopped
¾ cup of butter
⅓ cup of honey

2 tbsp. of coconut oil
¼ tsp. of salt
½ cup of prunes, pureed

INSTRUCTIONS
1. Pre-heat your Air Fryer at 375°F.
2. Put the oats, quinoa, almonds, cherries, chia seeds, & chocolate in a bowl & mix well.
3. Heat the butter, honey, & coconut oil in a saucepan, gently stirring together. Pour this over the oat mixture.
4. Mix in the salt & pureed prunes & combine well.
5. Transfer this to a baking dish small enough to fit inside the Air Fryer & cook for 15 minutes. Remove from the Air Fryer & allow to cool completely. Cut into bars & enjoy.

125. FRENCH TOAST

Prep & Cook Time: 25 minutes | Servings: 2

INGREDIENTS

4 slices of bread of your choosing
2 tbsp. of soft butter

2 eggs, lightly beaten
Salt

Pinch of cinnamon
Pinch of ground nutmeg

Pinch of ground cloves   Non-stick cooking spray   Sugar for serving

INSTRUCTIONS
1. In a shallow bowl, mix together the salt, spices & eggs.
2. Butter each side of the slices of bread & slice into strips. You may also use cookie cutters for this step.
3. Set your Air Fryer to 350°F & allow to warm up briefly.
4. Dredge each strip of bread in the egg & transfer to the Air Fryer. Cook for two minutes, ensuring the toast turns golden brown.
5. At this point, spritz the tops of the bread strips with cooking spray, flip, & cook for another 4 minutes on the other side. Top with a light dusting of sugar before serving.

126. CHEDDAR & BACON QUICHE

Prep & Cook Time: 30 minutes | Servings: 4

INGREDIENTS

3 tbsp. of Greek yogurt
½ cup of grated cheddar cheese
3 oz. of chopped bacon
4 eggs, beaten

¼ tsp. of garlic powder
Pinch of black pepper
1 short crust pastry
¼ tsp. of onion powder

¼ tsp. of sea salt
Pinch of flour for topping

INSTRUCTIONS
1. Pre-heat your Air Fryer at 330°F.
2. Take 8 ramekins & grease with a little oil. Coat with a sprinkling of flour, tapping to remove any excess.
3. Cut the shortcrust pastry in 8 & place each piece at the bottom of each ramekin.
4. Put all of the other ingredients in a bowl & combine well. Spoon equal amounts of the filling into each piece of pastry.
5. Cook the ramekins in the Air Fryer for 20 minutes.

127. CHORIZO RISOTTO

Prep & Cook Time: 1 hour 20 minutes | Servings: 4

INGREDIENTS

¼ cup of milk
½ cup of flour
4 oz. of breadcrumbs

4 oz. of chorizo, finely sliced
1 serving mushroom risotto rice
1 egg

Sea salt to taste

INSTRUCTIONS
1. In a bowl, combine the mushroom risotto rice with the risotto & salt before refrigerating to cool.
2. Set your Air Fryer at 390°F & leave to warm for 5 minutes.
3. Use your hands to form 2 tablespoons of risotto into a rice ball. Repeat until you have used up all the risotto. Roll each ball in the flour.
4. Crack the egg into a bowl & mix with the milk using a whisk. Coat each rice ball in the egg-milk mixture, & then in breadcrumbs.
5. Space the rice balls out in the baking dish of the Air Fryer. Bake for 20 minutes, ensuring they develop a crispy golden-brown crust.
6. Serve warm with a side of fresh vegetables & salad if desired.

128. CHOCO BREAD

Prep & Cook Time: 30 minutes | Servings: 12

INGREDIENTS

1 tbsp. of flax egg [1 tbsp. flax meal + 3 tbsp. of water]
1 cup of zucchini, shredded & squeezed
½ cup of sunflower oil
½ cup of maple syrup

1 tsp. of vanilla extract
1 tsp. of apple cider vinegar
½ cup of milk
1 cup of flour
1 tsp. of baking soda

½ cup of cocoa powder
¼ tsp. of salt
⅓ cup of chocolate chips

INSTRUCTIONS
1. Pre-heat your Air Fryer to 350°F.
2. Take a baking dish small enough to fit inside the Air Fryer & line it with parchment paper.
3. Mix together the flax meal, zucchini, sunflower oil, maple, vanilla, apple cider vinegar & milk in a bowl.
4. Incorporate the flour, cocoa powder, salt & baking soda, stirring all the time to combine everything well.
5. Finally, throw in the chocolate chips.
6. Transfer the batter to the baking dish & cook in the Air Fryer for 15 minutes. Make sure to test with a toothpick before serving by sticking it in the center. The bread is ready when the toothpick comes out clean.

129. RED ROLLS

Prep & Cook Time: 45 minutes | Servings: 6

INGREDIENTS

7 cups of minced meat
1 small onion, diced
1 packet of spring roll sheets

2 oz. of Asian noodles
3 cloves of garlic, crushed
1 cup of mixed vegetables

1 tbsp. of sesame oil
2 tbsp. of water
1 tsp. of soy sauce

INSTRUCTIONS
1. Cook the noodles in hot water until they turn soft. Drain & cut to your desired length.
2. Grease the wok with sesame oil. Put it over a medium-high heat & fry the minced meat, mixed vegetables, garlic, & onion, stirring regularly to ensure the minced meat cooks through. The cooking time will vary depending on the pan you are using – allow 3-5 minutes if using a wok, & 7-10 if using a standard frying pan.
3. Drizzle in the soy sauce & add to the noodles, tossing well to allow the juices to spread & absorb evenly.
4. Spoon the stir-fry diagonally across a spring roll sheet & fold back the top point over the filling. Fold over the sides. Before folding back the bottom point, brush it with cold water, which will act as an adhesive.
5. Repeat until all the filling & sheets are used.
6. Pre-heat your Air Fryer at 360°F.
7. If desired, drizzle a small amount of oil over the top of the spring rolls to enhance the taste & ensure crispiness.
8. Cook the spring rolls in the Air Fryer for 8 minutes, in multiple batches if necessary. Serve & enjoy.

130. CHIA & OAT PORRIDGE

Prep & Cook Time: 15 minutes | Servings: 4

INGREDIENTS

4 cups of milk
2 tbsp. of peanut butter

2 cups of oats
1 cup of chia seeds

4 tbsp. of honey
1 tbsp. of butter, melted

INSTRUCTIONS
1. Pre-heat the Air Fryer to 390°F.
2. Put the peanut butter, honey, butter, & milk in a bowl & mix together using a whisk. Add in the oats & chia seeds & stir.
3. Transfer the mixture to an Air Fryer-proof bowl that is small enough to fit inside the Air Fryer & cook for 5 minutes. Give another stir before serving.

131. AMERICAN DONUTS

Prep & Cook Time: 1 hour 20 minutes | Servings: 6

INGREDIENTS

1 cup of flour
¼ cup of sugar
1 tsp. of baking powder

½ tsp. of salt
¼ tsp. of cinnamon
1 tbsp. of coconut oil, melted

2 tbsp. of liquid from canned chickpeas
¼ cup of milk

INSTRUCTIONS
1. Put the sugar, flour & baking powder in a bowl & combine. Mix in the salt & cinnamon.

2. In a separate bowl, combine the chickpea liquid, milk & coconut oil.
3. Slowly pour the dry ingredients into the wet ingredients & combine well to create a sticky dough.
4. Refrigerate for at least an hour.
5. Pre-heat your Air Fryer at 370°F.
6. Using your hands, shape the dough into several small balls & place each one inside the Air Fryer. Cook for 10 minutes, refraining from shaking the basket as they cook.
7. Lightly dust the balls with sugar & cinnamon & serve with a hot cup of coffee.

132. TOFU SCRAMBLE
Prep & Cook Time: 40 minutes | Servings: 3

INGREDIENTS

2 ½ cups red potato, chopped
1 tbsp. of olive oil
1 block of tofu, chopped finely
1tbsp. of olive oil

2 tbsp. of tamari
1 tsp. of turmeric powder
½ tsp. of onion powder
½ tsp. of garlic powder

½ cup of onion, chopped
4 cups of broccoli florets

INSTRUCTIONS
1. Pre-heat the Air Fryer at 400°F.
2. Toss together the potatoes & olive oil.
3. Cook the potatoes in a baking dish for 15 minutes, shaking once during the cooking time to ensure they fry evenly.
4. Combine the tofu, olive oil, turmeric, onion powder, tamari, & garlic powder together, before stirring in the onions, followed by the broccoli.
5. Top the potatoes with the tofu mixture & allow to cook for an additional 15 minutes. Serve warm.

133. SPINACH QUICHE
Prep & Cook Time: 1 hour 15 minutes | Servings: 4

INGREDIENTS

¾ cup of flour
½ cup of cold coconut oil
2 tbsp. of water
2 tbsp. of olive oil
1 onion, chopped

4 oz. of mushrooms, sliced
1 packet of firm tofu, pressed to remove
excess water, then crumbled
1 lb. of spinach, washed & chopped
½ tbsp. of dried dill

2 tbsp. of yeast
Salt & pepper
Sprig of fresh parsley, chopped

INSTRUCTIONS
1. Pre-heat the Air Fryer at 375°F.
2. Firstly, prepare the pastry. Use a sieve to sift together the salt & flour into a bowl. Combine with the coconut oil to make the flour crumbly. Slowly pour in the water until a stiff dough is formed.
3. Wrap the dough in saran wrap & refrigerate for a half hour.
4. Sauté the onion in a skillet over medium heat for a minute. Add in the tofu & mushroom, followed by the spinach, yeast, & dill.
5. Sprinkle in salt & pepper as desired. Finally add in the parsley. Take the skillet off the heat.
6. Dust a flat surface with flour & roll out the dough until it is thin.
7. Grease a baking dish that is small enough to fit inside the Air Fryer. Place the dough in the tin & pour in the tofu mixture. Transfer the dish to the Air Fryer & cook for 30 minutes, ensuring the pastry crisps up.

134. MONKEY SALAD
Prep & Cook Time: 10 minutes | Servings: 1

INGREDIENTS

2 tbsp. of butter
1 cup of coconut flakes

1 cup of cashews
1 cup of almonds

1 cup of 90% dark chocolate shavings

INSTRUCTIONS
1. Inside your Air Fryer, melt the butter and add the coconut flakes.
2. Flash fry at 400°F/200°C for a few minutes.
3. Add the cashews & almonds & sauté for 3 minutes. Remove from the heat & sprinkle with dark chocolate shavings.
4. Serve!

135. JARLSBERG LUNCH OMELET
Prep & Cook Time: 10 minutes | Servings: 2

INGREDIENTS

4 medium mushrooms, sliced, 2 oz.
1 green onion, sliced

2 eggs, beaten
1 oz. of Jarlsberg or Swiss cheese,

1 oz. of ham, diced

INSTRUCTIONS
1. Add the mushrooms & green onion to a bowl and cook until tender inside your Air Fryer at 400°F/200°C.
2. Add the eggs & mix well.
3. Sprinkle with salt & top with the mushroom mixture, cheese & the ham.
4. When the egg is set, fold the plain side of the omelet on the filled side.
5. Cook for 1-2 more minutes & let it stand until the cheese has melted.
6. Serve!

36. MU SHU LUNCH PORK
Prep & Cook Time: 20 minutes | Servings: 2

INGREDIENTS

4 cups of coleslaw mix, with carrots
1 small onion, sliced thin

1 lb. of cooked pork, cut into ½" cubes
2 tbsp. of hoisin sauce

2 tbsp. of soy sauce

INSTRUCTIONS
1. In a bowl, add the oil. Toss in the cabbage, onions & pork. Mix.
2. Fry the 400°F/200°C inside your Air Fryer for 10 minutes.
3. Top with the hoisin & soy sauce. Fry for 2 more minutes.
4. Cook until browned.
5. Enjoy!

137. FIERY JALAPENO POPPERS
Prep & Cook Time: 40 minutes | Servings: 4

INGREDIENTS

5 oz. of cream cheese
¼ cup of mozzarella cheese

8 medium jalapeno peppers
½ tsp. of Mrs. Dash Table Blend

8 slices of bacon

INSTRUCTIONS
1. Preheat your Air Fryer to 400°F/200°C.
2. Cut the jalapenos in half.
3. Use a spoon to scrape out the insides of the peppers.
4. In a bowl, add together the cream cheese, mozzarella cheese & spices of your choice.
5. Pack the cream cheese mixture into the jalapenos & place the peppers on top.
6. Wrap each pepper in 1 slice of bacon, starting from the bottom & working up.
7. Bake for 30 minutes. Broil for an additional 3 minutes.

8. Serve!

138. BACON & CHICKEN PATTIES
Prep & Cook Time: 15 minutes | Servings: 2

INGREDIENTS

1 ½ oz. of chicken breast
4 slices of bacon

¼ cup of parmesan cheese
1 large egg

3 tbsp. of flour

INSTRUCTIONS
1. Cook the bacon inside your Air Fryer at 400°F/200°C until crispy.
2. Chop the chicken & bacon together in a food processor until fine.
3. Add in the parmesan, egg, flour & mix.
4. Make the patties by hand & fry on a medium heat in a pan with some oil.
5. Once browned, flip over, continue frying.
6. Serve!

139. CHEDDAR BACON BURST
Prep & Cook Time: 90 minutes | Servings: 8

INGREDIENTS

30 slices of bacon
2 ½ cups of cheddar cheese

4-5 cups of raw spinach
1-2 tbsp. of Southwest Seasoning

2 tsp. of Mrs. Dash Table Seasoning

INSTRUCTIONS
1. Preheat your Air Fryer to 375°F/190°C.
2. Weave the bacon into 15 vertical pieces & 12 horizontal pieces. Cut the extra 3 in half to fill in the rest, horizontally.
3. Season the bacon.
4. Add the cheese to the bacon.
5. Add the spinach & press down to compress.
6. Tightly roll up the woven bacon.
7. Line a baking sheet with kitchen foil & add plenty of salt to it.
8. Put the bacon on top of a cooling rack & put that on top of your baking sheet.
9. Bake for 60-70 minutes.
10. Let cool for 10-15 minutes before
11. Slice & enjoy!

140. GRILLED HAM & CHEESE
Prep & Cook Time: 30 minutes | Servings: 2

INGREDIENTS

3 buns
4 slices of medium-cut deli ham

1 tbsp. of salted butter
1 oz. of flour

3 slices of cheddar cheese
3 slices of muenster cheese

INSTRUCTIONS
Bread:
1. Preheat your Air Fryer to 350°F/175°C.
2. Mix the flour, salt & baking powder in a bowl. Put to the side.
3. Add in the butter & coconut oil to a skillet.
4. Melt for 20 seconds & pour into another bowl.
5. In this bowl, mix in the dough.
6. Scramble two eggs. Add to the dough.
7. Add ½ tbsp. of coconut flour to thicken, & place evenly into a cupcake tray. Fill about ¾ inch.
8. Bake for 20 minutes until browned.
9. Allow to cool for 15 minutes & cut each in half for the buns.
Sandwich:
1. Fry the deli meat in a skillet on a high heat.
2. Put the ham & cheese between the buns.
3. Heat the butter on medium high.
4. When brown, turn to low & add the dough to pan.
5. Press down with a weight until you smell burning, then flip to crisp both sides.
6. Enjoy!

141. MELTED PROSCIUTTO SPINACH SALAD
Prep & Cook Time: 5 minutes | Servings: 2

INGREDIENTS

2 cups of baby spinach
⅓ lb. of prosciutto

1 cantaloupe
1 avocado

¼ cup of diced red onion
handful of raw, of walnuts

INSTRUCTIONS
1. Put a cup of spinach on each plate.
2. Top with the diced prosciutto, cubes of balls of melon, slices of avocado, a handful of red onion & a few walnuts.
3. Add some freshly ground pepper, if you like.
4. Flash fry inside your Air Fryer at 400°F/200°C until the salad is crisp.
5. Serve!

142. RICED CAULIFLOWER & CURRY CHICKEN
Prep & Cook Time: 40 minutes | Servings: 6

INGREDIENTS

2 lb. of chicken (4 breasts)
1 packet of curry paste

3 tbsp. of butter
½ cup of heavy cream

1 head cauliflower (around 1 kg)

INSTRUCTIONS
1. Add the curry paste and chicken to a dish. Mix. Place inside your Air Fryer and cook at 400°F/200°C for 25 minutes.
2. Cut a cauliflower head into florets & blend in a food processor to make the riced cauliflower.
3. When the chicken is cooked, uncover, add the cream & cook for an additional 7 minutes.
4. Serve!

143. MASHED GARLIC TURNIPS
Prep & Cook Time: 10 minutes | Servings: 2

INGREDIENTS

3 cups of diced turnip
2 cloves of garlic, minced

¼ cup of heavy cream
3 tbsp. of melted butter

Salt & pepper to season

INSTRUCTIONS
1. Fry the turnips inside your Air Fryer at 400°F/200°C until tender.
2. Drain & mash the turnips.
3. Add the cream, butter, salt, pepper & garlic. Combine well.

4. Serve!

144. LASAGNA SPAGHETTI SQUASH
Prep & Cook Time: 90 minutes | Servings: 6

INGREDIENTS

25 slices of mozzarella cheese
1 jar (40 oz.) of Marinara sauce

30 oz. of whole-milk ricotta cheese
2 large spaghetti squash, cooked (44 oz.)

4 lb. of ground beef

INSTRUCTIONS
1. Preheat your Air Fryer to 375°F/190°C.
2. Slice the spaghetti squash & place it face down inside an Air Fryer proof dish. Fill with water until covered.
3. Bake for 45 minutes until skin is soft.
4. Sear the meat until browned.
5. In a large skillet, heat the browned meat & marinara sauce. Set aside when warm.
6. Scrape the flesh off the cooked squash to resemble strands of spaghetti.
7. Layer the lasagna in a large, greased pan in alternating layers of spaghetti squash, meat sauce, mozzarella, ricotta. Repeat until all increased have been used.
8. Bake for 30 minutes & serve!

145. BLUE CHEESE CHICKEN WEDGES
Prep & Cook Time: 45 minutes | Servings: 4

INGREDIENTS

Blue cheese dressing
2 tbsp. of crumbled blue cheese

4 strips of bacon
2 chicken breasts (boneless)

¾ cup of your favorite buffalo sauce

INSTRUCTIONS
1. Cook the chicken & buffalo sauce inside your Air Fryer at 400°F/200°C for 35 minutes.
2. Add the blue cheese & buffalo pulled chicken. Top with the cooked bacon crumble.
3. Serve & enjoy.

146. 'OH SO GOOD' SALAD
Prep & Cook Time: 10 minutes | Servings: 2

INGREDIENTS

6 brussels sprouts
½ tsp. of apple cider vinegar

1 tsp. of olive/grapeseed oil
1 grind of salt

1 tbsp. of freshly grated parmesan

INSTRUCTIONS
1. Slice the clean brussels sprouts in half.
2. Cut thin slices in the opposite direction.
3. Once sliced, cut the roots off & discard.
4. Toss together with the apple cider, oil & salt.
5. Sprinkle with the parmesan cheese.
6. Flash fry in your Air Fryer at 400°F/200°C for 23 minutes until the cheese is melted and crisp. Take out and let cool. Serve!

147. 'I LOVE BACON'
Prep & Cook Time: 90 minutes | Servings: 4

INGREDIENTS

30 slices of thick-cut bacon
12 oz. of steak

10 oz. of pork sausage
4 oz. of cheddar cheese, shredded

INSTRUCTIONS
1. Lay out 5 x 6 slices of bacon in a woven pattern & bake inside your Air Fryer at 400°F/200°C for 20 minutes until crisp.
2. Combine the steak, bacon & sausage to form a meaty mixture.
3. Lay out the meat in a rectangle of similar size to the bacon strips. Season with salt/pepper.
4. Place the bacon weave on top of the meat mixture.
5. Place the cheese in the center of the bacon.
6. Roll the meat into a tight roll & refrigerate.
7. Make a 7 x 7 bacon weave & roll the bacon weave over the meat, diagonally.
8. Bake at 400°F/200°C for 60 minutes or 165°F/75°C internally.
9. Let rest for 5 minutes before serving.

148. LEMON DILL TROUT
Prep & Cook Time: 15 minutes | Servings: 1

INGREDIENTS

2 lb. of pan-dressed trout (or other small
fish), fresh or frozen

1 ½ tsp. of salt
½ cup of butter or margarine

2 tbsp. of dill weed
3 tbsp. of lemon juice

INSTRUCTIONS
1. Cut the fish lengthwise & season the with pepper.
2. Prepare a skillet by melting the butter & dill weed.
3. Cook inside your air Fryer at 400°F/200°C, flesh side down, for 5 minutes per side.
4. Remove the fish. Add the lemon juice to the butter & dill to create a sauce.
5. Serve the fish with the sauce.

149. 'NO POTATO' SHEPHERD'S PIE
Prep & Cook Time: 70 minutes | Servings: 6

INGREDIENTS

1 lb. of lean ground beef
8 oz. of mushroom sauce mix

¼ cup of ketchup
1 lb. packet of frozen mixed vegetables

1 lb. of bake mix

INSTRUCTIONS
1. Preheat your Air Fryer to 375°F/190°C.
2. Prepare the bake mix according to packet instructions. Layer into the skillet base.
3. Cut the dough into triangles & roll them from base to tip. Set to the side.
4. Brown the ground beef with the salt. Stir in the mushroom sauce, ketchup & mixed vegetables.
5. Bring the mixture to the boil & reduce the heat to medium, cover & simmer until tender.
6. Put the dough triangles on top of the mixture, tips pointing towards the center.
7. Bake for 60 minutes until piping hot & serve!

150. EASY SLIDER
Prep & Cook Time: 70 minutes | Servings: 6

INGREDIENTS

1 lb. of Ground Beef
1 egg

Garlic/salt/pepper/onion powder to taste
Several dashes of Worcestershire sauce

8 oz. of cheddar cheese (½ oz. per patty)

INSTRUCTIONS

1. Mix the beef, eggs & spices together.
2. Divide the meat into 1.5 oz. patties.
3. Add a half-ounce of cheese to each patty & combine two patties to make one burger, like a sandwich.
4. Bake in a preheated 375°F/190°C Air Fryer for 40 minutes. Serve!

151. DIJON HALIBUT STEAK
Prep & Cook Time: 40 minutes | Servings: 1

INGREDIENTS

1 6-oz. fresh or thawed halibut steak
1 tbsp. of butter

1 tbsp. of lemon juice
½ tbsp. of Dijon mustard

1 tsp. of fresh basil

INSTRUCTIONS

1. Heat the butter, basil, lemon juice & mustard in a small saucepan to make a glaze.
2. Brush both sides of the halibut steak with the mixture.
3. Grill the fish in a preheated 375°F/190°C Air Fryer for 30 minutes. Serve!

152. CAST-IRON CHEESY CHICKEN
Prep & Cook Time: 50 minutes | Servings: 4

INGREDIENTS

4 chicken breasts
4 bacon strips

4 oz. of ranch dressing
2 green onions

4 oz. of cheddar cheese

INSTRUCTIONS

1. Pour the oil into a dish. Add the chicken breasts. Bake in a preheated 375°F/190°C Air Fryer for 20 minutes.
2. Fry the bacon in a skillet until brown. Dice the green onions.
3. Take the chicken out of the Air Fryer & top with soy sauce and onions.
4. Toss in the ranch, bacon, green onions & top with cheese.
5. Cook until the cheese is browned, for around 4 minutes.
6. Serve.

153. CAULIFLOWER RICE CHICKEN CURRY
Prep & Cook Time: 50 minutes | Servings: 4

INGREDIENTS

2 lb. of chicken (4 breasts)
1 packet of curry paste

3 tbsp. of butter
½ cup of heavy cream

1 head of cauliflower (around 1 kg/2.2 lb.)

INSTRUCTIONS

1. Melt the butter in a pot. Mix in the curry paste. Add the water and chicken. Mix.
2. Bake in a preheated 375°F/190°C Air Fryer for 40 minutes.
3. Shred the cauliflower florets in a food processor to resemble rice.
4. Once the chicken is cooked, uncover, & incorporate the cauliflower mix.
5. Cook for 5 minutes & serve.

154. BACON CHOPS
Prep & Cook Time: 40 minutes | Servings: 2

INGREDIENTS

2 pork chops (I prefer bone-in, but
boneless chops work great as well)

1 bag of shredded brussels sprouts
4 slices of bacon

Worcestershire sauce
Lemon juice (optional)

INSTRUCTIONS

1. Place the pork chops on a baking sheet with the Worcestershire sauce.
2. Bake in a preheated 375°F/190°C Air Fryer for 30 minutes.
3. Turnover & cook for another 5 minutes. Put to the side when done.
4. Cook the chopped bacon in a large pan until browned. Add the shredded brussels sprouts & cook together.
5. Stir the brussels sprouts with the bacon & grease & cook for 5 minutes until the bacon is crisp.

155. CHICKEN IN A BLANKET
Prep & Cook Time: 60 minutes | Servings:

INGREDIENTS

3 boneless chicken breasts
1 packet of bacon

1 8-oz. of packet cream cheese
3 jalapeno peppers

Salt, pepper, garlic powder or other
seasonings

INSTRUCTIONS

1. Cut the chicken breast in half lengthwise to create two pieces.
2. Cut the jalapenos in half lengthwise & remove the seeds.
3. Dress each breast with a half-inch slice of cream cheese & half a slice of jalapeno. Sprinkle with garlic powder, salt & pepper.
4. Roll the chicken & wrap 2 to 3 pieces of bacon around it—secure with toothpicks.
5. Bake in a preheated 375°F/190°C Air Fryer for 50 minutes.
6. Serve!

156. STUFFED CHICKEN ROLLS
Prep & Cook Time: 45 minutes | Servings: 4

INGREDIENTS

4 boneless, skinless chicken breasts
7 oz. of cream cheese

¼ cup of green onions, chopped
4 slices of bacon, partially cooked

INSTRUCTIONS

1. Partially cook your strips of bacon, about 5 minutes for each side & set aside.
2. Pound the chicken breasts to a quarter-inch thick.
3. Mix the cream cheese & green onions together. Spread 2 tbsp. of the mixture onto each breast. Roll & wrap them with the strip of bacon, then secure with a toothpick.
4. Place the chicken on a baking sheet & bake in a preheated Air Fryer at 375°F/190°C for 30 minutes.
5. Broil for 5 minutes to crisp the bacon.
6. Serve.

157. DUCK FAT RIBEYE
Prep & Cook Time: 20 minutes | Servings: 1

INGREDIENTS

One 16-oz. of ribeye steak (1 - 1 ¼ inch
thick)
1 tbsp. of duck fat (or other high smoke

point oil like peanut oil)
½ tbsp. of butter
½ tsp. of thyme, chopped

Salt & pepper

INSTRUCTIONS

1. Preheat a skillet in your Air Fryer at 400°F/200°C.
2. Season the steaks with the oil, salt & pepper. Remove the skillet from the Air Fryer once pre-heated.

3. Put the skillet on your stove top burner on a medium heat & drizzle in the oil.
4. Sear the steak for 1-4 minutes, depending on if you like it rare, medium or well done.
5. Turn over the steak & place in your Air Fryer for 6 minutes.
6. Take out the steak from your Air Fryer & place it back on the stove top on low heat.
7. Toss in the butter & thyme & cook for 3 minutes, basting as you go along.
8. Rest for 5 minutes & serve.

158. EASY ZOODLES & TURKEY BALLS

Prep & Cook Time: 35 minutes | Servings: 2

INGREDIENTS

1 zucchini, cut into spirals

1 can of vodka pasta sauce

1 packet of meatballs

INSTRUCTIONS
1. Cook the meatballs & sauce on a high heat in your Air Fryer for 25 minutes, shaking occasionally.
2. Wash the zucchini & put through a vegetable spiral maker.
3. Boil the water & blanch the raw zoodles for 60 seconds. Remove & drain.
4. Combine the zoodles & prepared saucy meatballs.
5. Serve!

159. SAUSAGE BALLS

Prep & Cook Time: 25 minutes | Servings: 6

INGREDIENTS

12 oz. of Jimmy Dean's Sausage

6 oz. of shredded cheddar cheese

10 cubes cheddar (optional)

INSTRUCTIONS
1. Mix the shredded cheese & sausage.
2. Divide the mixture into 12 equal parts to be stuffed.
3. Add a cube of cheese to the center of the sausage & roll into balls.
4. Air Fry at 375°F/190°C for 15 minutes until crisp.
5. Serve!

160. BACON SCALLOPS

Prep & Cook Time: 10 minutes | Servings: 6

INGREDIENTS

12 scallops
12 thin bacon slices

12 toothpicks
Salt & pepper

½ tbsp. of oil

INSTRUCTIONS
1. Wrap each scallop with a piece of thinly cut bacon—secure with a toothpick.
2. Air Fry at 375°F/190°C for 15 minutes until crisp.
3. Season to taste.
4. Cook for 3 minutes per side.
5. Serve!

161. BUFFALO CHICKEN SALAD

Prep & Cook Time: 40 minutes | Servings: 1

INGREDIENTS

3 cups of salad of your choice
1 chicken breast

½ cup of shredded cheese of your choice
Buffalo wing sauce of your choice

Ranch or blue cheese dressing

INSTRUCTIONS
1. Preheat your Air Fryer to 400°F/200°C.
2. Douse the chicken breast in the buffalo wing sauce & bake for 25 minutes. In the last 5 minutes, throw the cheese on the wings until it melts.
3. When cooked, remove from the Air Fryer & slice into pieces.
4. Place on a bed of lettuce.
5. Pour the salad dressing of your choice on top.
6. Serve!

162. MEATBALLS

Prep & Cook Time: 30 minutes | Servings: 6

INGREDIENTS

1 lb. of ground beef (or ½ lb. beef, ½ lb. pork)

½ cup of grated parmesan cheese
1 tbsp. of minced garlic (or paste)

½ cup of mozzarella cheese
1 tsp. of freshly ground pepper

INSTRUCTIONS
1. Preheat your Air Fryer to 400°F/200°C.
2. In a bowl, mix all the ingredients together.
3. Roll the meat mixture into 5 generous meatballs.
4. Bake inside your Air Fryer at 170°F/80°C for about 18 minutes.
5. Serve with sauce!

163. FAT BOMBS

Prep & Cook Time: 100 minutes | Servings: 2

INGREDIENTS

1 cup of coconut butter
1 cup of coconut milk (full fat, canned)

1 tsp. of vanilla extract
½ tsp. of nutmeg

½ cup of coconut shreds

INSTRUCTIONS
1. Add all the ingredients except the shredded coconut into your Air Fryer basket.
2. Cook at 400°F/200°C for 10 minutes. Stir & melt until they start melting.
3. Then, take them off of the heat.
4. Put the glass bowl into your refrigerator until the mix can be rolled into doughy balls. Usually this happens after around 30 minutes.
5. Roll the dough into 1-inch balls through the coconut shreds.
6. Place the balls on a plate & refrigerate for one hour.
7. Serve!

164. CABBAGE & BEEF CASSEROLE

Prep & Cook Time: 40 minutes | Servings: 6

INGREDIENTS

½ lb. of ground beef
½ cup of chopped onion

½ bag coleslaw mix
1-½ cups of tomato sauce

1 tbsp. of lemon juice

INSTRUCTIONS
1. In your Air Fryer, cook the ground beef at 400°F/200°C for 30 minutes until browned & to the side.
2. Mix in the onion & cabbage to the skillet & sauté until soft.

3. Add the ground beef back in along with the tomato sauce & lemon juice.
4. Bring the mixture to a boil, then cover & simmer for 30 minutes.
5. Enjoy!

165. ROAST BEEF LETTUCE WRAPS
Prep & Cook Time: 10 minutes | Servings: 4

INGREDIENTS
8 large iceberg lettuce leaves
8 oz. (8 slices) of rare roast beef

½ cup of homemade mayonnaise
8 slices of provolone cheese

1 cup of baby spinach

INSTRUCTIONS
1. Wash the lettuce leaves & sake them dry. Try not to rip them.
2. Place 1 slice of roast beef inside each wrap.
3. Smother 1 tbsp. of mayonnaise on top of each piece of roast beef.
4. Top the mayonnaise with 1 slice of provolone cheese & 1 cup of baby spinach.
5. Roll the lettuce up around the toppings. Crisp inside your Air Fryer at 400°F/200°C for 2 minutes until browned.
6. Serve & enjoy!

166. TURKEY AVOCADO ROLLS
Prep & Cook Time: 10 minutes | Servings: 6

INGREDIENTS
12 slices (12 oz.) of turkey breast
12 slices of Swiss cheese

2 cups of baby spinach
1 large avocado, cut into 12 slices

INSTRUCTIONS
1. Lay out the slices of turkey breast flat & place a slice of Swiss cheese on top of each one.
2. Top each slice with 1 cup baby spinach & 3 slices of avocado.
3. Sprinkle each "sandwich" with lemon pepper.
4. Roll up the sandwiches & secure with toothpicks.
5. Cook for a few minutes inside your Air Fryer on a low heat until crisp.
6. Serve & season immediately or refrigerate until ready to serve.

167. NEARLY PIZZA
Prep & Cook Time: 30 minutes | Servings: 4

INGREDIENTS
4 large portobello mushrooms
4 tsp. of olive oil

1 cup of marinara sauce
1 cup of shredded mozzarella cheese

10 slices of sugar-free pepperoni

INSTRUCTIONS
1. Preheat your Air Fryer to 375°F/190°C.
2. De-steam the 4 mushrooms & brush each cap with the olive oil, one spoon for each cap.
3. Place on a baking sheet & bake stem side down for 8 minutes.
4. Take out of the Air Fryer & fill each cap with 1 cup marinara sauce, 1 cup of mozzarella cheese & 3 slices of pepperoni.
5. Cook for another 10 minutes until browned.
6. Serve hot.

168. TACO STUFFED PEPPERS
Prep & Cook Time: 30 minutes | Servings: 4

INGREDIENTS
1 lb. of ground beef
1 tbsp. of taco seasoning mix

1 can of diced tomatoes & green chilis
4 green bell peppers

1 cup of shredded Monterey jack cheese, divided

INSTRUCTIONS
1. Set a skillet over a high heat & cook the ground beef for seven to ten minutes. Make sure it is cooked through & brown all over. Drain the fat.
2. Stir in the taco seasoning mix, as well as the diced tomatoes & green chilis. Allow the mixture to cook for a further three to five minutes.
3. In the meantime, slice the tops off the green peppers & remove the seeds & membranes.
4. When the meat mixture is fully cooked, spoon equal amounts of it into the peppers & top with the Monterey jack cheese. Then place the peppers into your Air Fryer.
5. Cook at 350°F for fifteen minutes.
6. The peppers are ready when they are soft, & the cheese is bubbling & brown. Serve warm & enjoy!

169. BEEF TENDERLOIN & PEPPERCORN CRUST
Prep & Cook Time: 45 minutes | Servings: 6

INGREDIENTS
2 lb. of beef tenderloin
2 tsp. of roasted garlic, minced

2 tbsp. of salted butter, melted
3 tbsp. of ground 4-peppercorn blender

INSTRUCTIONS
1. Remove any surplus fat from the beef tenderloin.
2. Combine the roasted garlic & melted butter to apply to your tenderloin with a brush.
3. On a plate, spread out the peppercorns & roll the tenderloin in them, making sure they are covering & clinging to the meat.
4. Cook the tenderloin in your Air Fryer for twenty-five minutes at 400°F, turning halfway through cooking.
5. Let the tenderloin rest for ten minutes before slicing & serving.

170. BRATWURSTS
Prep & Cook Time: 18 minutes | Servings: 4

INGREDIENTS
4 x 3-oz. beef bratwursts

INSTRUCTIONS
1. Place the beef bratwursts in the basket of your Air Fryer & cook for fifteen minutes at 375°F, turning once halfway through.
2. Enjoy with toppings & sides of your choice.

171. BACON-WRAPPED HOT DOG
Prep & Cook Time: 25 minutes | Servings: 4

INGREDIENTS
4 slices of sugar-free bacon
4 beef hot dogs

INSTRUCTIONS
1. Take a slice of bacon & wrap it around the hot dog, securing it with a toothpick. Repeat with the other pieces of bacon & hot dogs, placing each wrapped dog in the basket of your Air Fryer.
2. Cook at 370°F for ten minutes, turning halfway through to fry the other side.
3. Once hot & crispy, the hot dogs are ready to serve. Enjoy!

172. HERB SHREDDED BEEF

Prep & Cook Time: 25 minutes | Servings: 6

INGREDIENTS

1 tsp. of dried dill
1 tsp. of dried thyme

1 tsp. of garlic powder
2 lb. of beefsteak

3 tbsp. of butter

INSTRUCTIONS

1. Pre-heat your Air Fryer at 360°F.
2. Combine the dill, thyme, & garlic powder together, & massage into the steak.
3. Cook the steak in the Air Fryer for twenty minutes, then remove, shred, & return to the Air Fryer. Add the butter & cook for a further two minutes at 365°F. Make sure the beef is coated in the butter before serving.

173. HERBED BUTTER RIB EYE STEAK

Prep & Cook Time: 60 minutes | Servings: 4

INGREDIENTS

4 ribeye steaks
Olive oil

¾ tsp. of dry rub
½ cup of butter

1 tsp. of dried basil
3 tbsp. of lemon garlic seasoning

INSTRUCTIONS

1. Massage the olive oil into the steaks & your favorite dry rub. Leave aside to sit for thirty minutes.
2. In a bowl, combine the button, dried basil, & lemon garlic seasoning, then refrigerate.
3. Pre-heat the Air Fryer at 450°F & set a rack inside. Place the steaks on top of the rack & allow to cook for fifteen minutes.
4. Remove the steaks from the Air Fryer when cooked & serve with the herbed butter.

174. FLANK STEAK & AVOCADO BUTTER

Prep & Cook Time: 40 minutes | Servings: 1

INGREDIENTS

1 flank steak
Salt & pepper

2 avocados
2 tbsp. of butter, melted

½ cup of chimichurri sauce

INSTRUCTIONS

1. Rub the flank steak with salt & pepper to taste & leave to sit for twenty minutes.
2. Pre-heat the Air Fryer at 400°F & place a rack inside.
3. Halve the avocados & take out the pits. Spoon the flesh into a bowl & mash with a fork. Mix in the melted butter & chimichurri sauce, making sure everything is well combined.
4. Put the steak in the Air Fryer & cook for six minutes. Flip over & allow to cook for another six minutes.
5. Serve the steak with the avocado butter & enjoy!

175. MOZZARELLA BEEF

Prep & Cook Time: 30 minutes | Servings: 6

INGREDIENTS

12 oz. of beef brisket
2 tsp. of Italian herbs

2 tsp. of butter
1 onion, sliced

7 oz. of mozzarella cheese, sliced

INSTRUCTIONS

1. Pre-heat the Air Fryer at 365°F.
2. Cut up the brisket into four equal slices & season with the Italian herbs.
3. Allow the butter to melt in the Air Fryer. Place the slices of beef inside along with the onion. Put a piece of mozzarella on top of each piece of brisket & cook for twenty-five minutes.
4. Enjoy!

176. ROSEMARY RIB EYE STEAKS

Prep & Cook Time: 40 minutes | Servings: 2

INGREDIENTS

¼ cup of butter
1 clove minced garlic

Salt & pepper
1 ½ tbsp. of balsamic vinegar

¼ cup of rosemary, chopped
2 ribeye steaks

INSTRUCTIONS

1. Melt the butter in a skillet over medium heat. Add the garlic & fry until fragrant.
2. Remove the skillet from the heat & add in the salt, pepper, & vinegar. Allow it to cool.
3. Add the rosemary, then pour the whole mixture into a Ziploc bag.
4. Put the ribeye steaks in the bag & shake well, making sure to coat the meat well. Refrigerate for an hour, then allow to sit for a further twenty minutes.
5. Pre-heat the Air Fryer at 400°F & set the rack inside. Cook the ribeyes for fifteen minutes.
6. Take care when removing the steaks from the Air Fryer & plate up. Enjoy!

177. HERBED BUTTER BEEF LOIN

Prep & Cook Time: 25 minutes | Servings: 4

INGREDIENTS

1 tbsp. of butter, melted
¼ of dried thyme

1 tsp. of garlic salt
¼ tsp. of dried parsley

1 lb. of beef loin

INSTRUCTIONS

1. In a bowl, combine the melted butter, thyme, garlic salt, & parsley.
2. Cut the beef loin into slices & generously apply the seasoned butter using a brush.
3. Pre-heat your Air Fryer at 400°F & place a rack inside.
4. Cook the beef for fifteen minutes.
5. Take care when removing it & serve hot.

178. LAMB RIBS

Prep & Cook Time: 25 minutes | Servings: 4

INGREDIENTS

1 lb. of lamb ribs
2 tbsp. of mustard

1 tsp. of rosemary, chopped
Salt & pepper

¼ cup mint leaves, chopped
1 cup of green yogurt

INSTRUCTIONS

1. Pre-heat the Air Fryer at 350°F.
2. Use a brush to apply the mustard to the lamb ribs, & season with rosemary, as well as salt & pepper as desired.
3. Cook the ribs in the Air Fryer for eighteen minutes.
4. Meanwhile, combine together the mint leaves & yogurt in a bowl.
5. Remove the lamb ribs from the Air Fryer when cooked & serve with the mint yogurt. Enjoy!

179. LAMB SATAY

Prep & Cook Time: 25 minutes | Servings: 2

INGREDIENTS

¼ tsp. of cumin
1 tsp. of ginger

½ tsp. of nutmeg
Salt & pepper

2 boneless lamb steaks
Olive oil cooking spray

INSTRUCTIONS

1. Combine the cumin, ginger, nutmeg, salt & pepper in a bowl.
2. Cube the lamb steaks & massage the spice mixture into each one.
3. Leave to marinate for ten minutes, then transfer onto metal skewers.
4. Pre-heat the Air Fryer at 400°F.
5. Spritz the skewers with the olive oil cooking spray, then cook them in the Air Fryer for eight minutes.
6. Take care when removing them from the Air Fryer & serve with sauce of your choice.

180. ITALIAN LAMB CHOPS

Prep & Cook Time: 20 minutes | Servings: 2

INGREDIENTS

2 lamp chops
2 tsp. of Italian herbs

2 avocados
½ cup of mayonnaise

1 tbsp. of lemon juice

INSTRUCTIONS

1. Season the lamb chops with the Italian herbs, then set aside for five minutes.
2. Pre-heat the Air Fryer at 400°F & place the rack inside.
3. Put the chops on the rack & allow to cook for twelve minutes.
4. In the meantime, halve the avocados & open to remove the pits. Spoon the flesh into a blender.
5. Add in the mayonnaise & lemon juice & pulse until a smooth consistency is achieved.
6. Take care when removing the chops from the Air Fryer, then plate up & serve with the avocado mayo.

181. BREADED PORK CHOPS

Prep & Cook Time: 25 minutes | Servings: 4

INGREDIENTS

1 tsp. of chili powder
½ tsp. of garlic powder

½ oz. of flour, finely ground
4 x 4-oz. of pork chops

1 tbsp. of coconut oil, melted

INSTRUCTIONS

1. Combine the chili powder, garlic powder, & flour.
2. Coat the pork chops with the coconut oil, followed by the flour mixture, taking care to cover them completely. Then place the chops in the basket of the Air Fryer.
3. Cook the chops for fifteen minutes at 400°F, turning halfway through.
4. Once they are browned, check the temperature has reached 145°F before serving with the sides of your choice.

182. JUICY MEXICAN PORK CHOPS

Prep & Cook Time: 25 minutes | Servings: 2

INGREDIENTS

¼ tsp. of dried oregano
1 ½ tsp. of taco seasoning mix

2 x 4-oz. of boneless pork chops
2 tbsp. of butter, divided

INSTRUCTIONS

1. Combine the dried oregano & taco seasoning to rub into the pork chops.
2. In your Air Fryer, cook the chops at 400°F for fifteen minutes, turning them over halfway through to cook on the other side.
3. When the chops are a brown color, check the internal temperature has reached 145°F & remove from the Air Fryer. Serve with a garnish of butter.

183. BABY BACK RIBS

Prep & Cook Time: 45 minutes | Servings: 2

INGREDIENTS

2 tsp. of red pepper flakes
¾ of ground ginger

3 cloves minced garlic
Salt & pepper

2 baby back ribs

INSTRUCTIONS

1. Pre-heat your Air Fryer at 350°F.
2. Combine the red pepper flakes, ginger, garlic, salt & pepper in a bowl, making sure to mix well. Massage the mixture into the baby back ribs.
3. Cook the ribs in the Air Fryer for thirty minutes.
4. Take care when taking the rubs out of the Air Fryer. Place them on a serving dish & enjoy with a barbecue sauce of your choosing.

184. PULLED PORK

Prep & Cook Time: 30 minutes | Servings: 1

INGREDIENTS

1 lb. of pork tenderloin
2 tbsp. of barbecue dry rub

⅓ cup of heavy cream
1 tsp. of butter

INSTRUCTIONS

1. Pre-heat your Air Fryer at 370°F.
2. Massage the dry rub of your choice into the tenderloin, coating it well.
3. Cook the tenderloin in the Air Fryer for twenty minutes. When cooked, shred with two forks.
4. Add the heavy cream & butter into the Air Fryer along with the shredded pork & stir well. Cook for a further four minutes.
5. Allow to cool a little, then serve & enjoy.

185. RIBS

Prep & Cook Time: 60 minutes | Servings: 4

INGREDIENTS

1 lb. of pork ribs
1 tbsp. of barbecue dry rub

1 tsp. of mustard
1 tbsp. of apple cider vinegar

1 tsp. of sesame oil

INSTRUCTIONS

1. Chop up the pork ribs.
2. Combine the dry rub, mustard, apple cider vinegar, & sesame oil, then coat the ribs with this mixture. Refrigerate the ribs for twenty minutes.
3. Preheat the Air Fryer at 360°F.
4. When the ribs are ready, place them in the Air Fryer & cook for 15 minutes. Flip them & cook on the other side for a further fifteen minutes. Then serve & enjoy!

186. PORK CHOPS

Prep & Cook Time: 15 minutes | Servings: 3

INGREDIENTS

3 pork chops
½ tsp. of dried rosemary

1 tsp. of garlic salt
1 tsp. of peppercorns

1 tbsp. of butter

INSTRUCTIONS

1. Pre-heat your Air Fryer to 365°F.
2. Combine the dried rosemary & garlic salt & rub into the pork chops.

3. Place the peppercorns & butter into the Air Fryer & allow the butter to melt.
4. Add in the pork chops & cook for six minutes. Flip them & cook for an additional five minutes before serving.

187. SRIRACHA CAULIFLOWER
Prep & Cook Time: 25 minutes | Servings: 4

INGREDIENTS

¼ cup of vegan butter, melted
¼ cup of sriracha sauce

4 cups of cauliflower florets
1 cup of breadcrumbs

1 tsp. of salt

INSTRUCTIONS
1. Mix together the sriracha & vegan butter in a bowl & pour this mixture over the cauliflower, taking care to cover each floret entirely.
2. In a separate bowl, combine the breadcrumbs & salt.
3. Dip the cauliflower florets in the breadcrumbs, coating each one well. Cook in the Air Fryer for 17 minutes in a 375°F pre-heated Air Fryer.

188. RATATOUILLE
Prep & Cook Time: 30 minutes | Servings: 4

INGREDIENTS

1 sprig of basil
1 sprig of flat-leaf parsley
1 sprig of mint
1 tbsp. of coriander powder
1 tsp. of capers
½ lemon, juiced

Salt & pepper
2 eggplants, sliced crosswise
2 red onions, chopped
4 cloves of garlic, minced
2 red peppers, sliced crosswise
1 fennel bulb., sliced crosswise

3 large zucchinis, sliced crosswise
5 tbsp. of olive oil
4 large tomatoes, chopped
2 tsp. of herbs de Provence

INSTRUCTIONS
1. Blend together the basil, parsley, coriander, mint, lemon juice & capers, with a little salt & pepper. Make sure all ingredients are well-incorporated.
2. Pre-heat the Air Fryer at 400°F.
3. Coat the eggplant, onions, garlic, peppers, fennel, & zucchini with olive oil.
4. Take a baking dish small enough to fit inside the Air Fryer. Transfer the vegetables into the dish & top with the tomatoes & herb puree. Sprinkle on some more salt & pepper if desired, as well as the herbs de Provence.
5. Fry for 25 minutes. Serve!

189. PESTO STUFFED BELLA MUSHROOMS
Prep & Cook Time: 25 minutes | Servings: 6

INGREDIENTS

1 cup of basil
½ cup of cashew nuts, soaked overnight
½ cup of yeast

1 tbsp. of lemon juice
2 cloves of garlic
1 tbsp. of olive oil

Salt
1 lb. of baby Bella mushroom, stems removed

INSTRUCTIONS
1. Pre-heat the Air Fryer at 400°F.
2. Prepare your pesto. In a food processor, blend together the basil, cashew nuts, yeast, lemon juice, garlic & olive oil to combine well. Sprinkle on salt as desired.
3. Turn the mushrooms cap-side down & spread the pesto on the underside of each cap.
4. Transfer to the Air Fryer & cook for 15 minutes. Serve!

190. VEG BURGER
Prep & Cook Time: 25 minutes | Servings: 8

INGREDIENTS

½ lb. of cauliflower, steamed & diced
2 tsp. of coconut oil melted
2 tsp. of garlic, minced
¼ cup of desiccated coconut
½ cup of oats

3 tbsp. of flour
1 flax egg [1 tbsp. flaxseed + 3 tbsp. of water]
1 tsp. of mustard powder
2 tsp. of thyme

2 tsp. of parsley
2 tsp. of chives
Salt & pepper
1 cup of breadcrumbs

INSTRUCTIONS
1. Pre-heat the Air Fryer at 390°F.
2. Drain any excess water out of the cauliflower on a kitchen towel.
3. Combine the cauliflower with all of ingredients bar the breadcrumbs, incorporating everything well.
4. Using your hands, shape 8 equal-sized amounts of the mixture into burger patties. Coat the patties in breadcrumbs before putting them in the basket of the Air Fryer in a single layer.
5. Cook for 10-15 minutes, ensuring the patties crisp up.

191. CHILI POTATO WEDGES
Prep & Cook Time: 50 minutes | Servings: 4

INGREDIENTS

1 lb. of fingerling potatoes, washed & cut into wedges
1 tsp. of olive oil

1 tsp. of salt
1 tsp. of black pepper
1 tsp. of cayenne pepper

1 tsp. of yeast
½ tsp. of garlic powder

INSTRUCTIONS
1. Pre-heat the Air Fryer at 400°F.
2. Coat the potatoes with the rest of the ingredients.
3. Transfer to the basket of your Air Fryer & allow to cook for 16 minutes, shaking the basket at the halfway point.

192. LOBSTER TAILS
Prep & Cook Time: 16minutes | Servings: 4

INGREDIENTS

2 lobster tails, shell cut from the top ½
1 cup of butter, melted

½ tsp. of ground paprika
Salt

White pepper, to taste
1 lemon, juiced

INSTRUCTIONS
1. Whack the lobster tails inside your Air Fryer.
2. Combine the remaining ingredients inside a mixing bowl & pour them over the lobster tails.
3. Switch your Air Fryer to 'broil' mode and cook for 15 minutes at 350°F.
4. Serve warm.

193. CHRISTMAS BRUSSELS SPROUTS
Prep & Cook Time: 20 minutes | Servings: 2

INGREDIENTS

2 cups of Brussels sprouts, halved
1 tbsp. of olive oil

1 tbsp. of balsamic vinegar
1 tbsp. of maple syrup

¼ tsp. of sea salt

INSTRUCTIONS
1. Pre-heat the Air Fryer at 375°F.
2. Evenly coat the Brussels sprouts with the olive oil, balsamic vinegar, maple syrup, & salt.
3. Transfer to the basket of your Air Fryer & cook for 5 minutes. Give the basket a good shake, turn the heat up to 400°F & continue to cook for another 8 minutes.

194. SUMMER ROLLS
Prep & Cook Time: 25 minutes | Servings: 4

INGREDIENTS
1 cup of shiitake mushroom, sliced thinly
1 celery stalk, chopped
1 medium carrot, shredded
½ tsp. of ginger, finely chopped

1 tsp. of sugar
1 tbsp. of soy sauce
1 tsp. of yeast
8 spring roll sheets

1 tsp. of corn starch
2 tbsp. of water

INSTRUCTIONS
1. In a bowl, combine the ginger, soy sauce, yeast, carrots, celery, & sugar.
2. Mix together the cornstarch & water to create an adhesive for your spring rolls.
3. Scoop a teaspoonful of the vegetable mixture into the middle of the spring roll sheets. Brush the edges of the sheets with the cornstarch adhesive & enclose around the filling to make spring rolls.
4. Pre-heat your Air Fryer at 400°F. When warm, place the rolls inside & cook for 15 minutes or until crisp.

95. RICE BOWL
Prep & Cook Time: 55 minutes | Servings: 4

INGREDIENTS
¼ cup of cucumber, sliced
1 tsp. of salt
1 tbsp. of sugar
7 tbsp. of Japanese rice vinegar

3 medium-sized eggplants, sliced
3 tbsp. of white miso paste
1 tbsp. of mirin rice wine
4 cups of sushi rice, cooked

4 spring onions
1 tbsp. of sesame seeds, toasted

INSTRUCTIONS
1. Coat the cucumber slices with the rice wine vinegar, salt, & sugar.
2. Place a dish on top of the bowl to weight it down completely.
3. Pre-heat the Air Fryer at 400°F.
4. In a bowl, mix together the eggplants, mirin rice wine, & miso paste. Allow to marinate for half an hour.
5. Cook the eggplant in the Air Fryer for 10 minutes.
6. Place the eggplant slices in the Air Fryer & cook for 10 minutes.
7. Fill the bottom of a serving bowl with rice & top with the eggplants & pickled cucumbers. Add the spring onions & sesame seeds for garnish.

196. ASIAN TOFU BITES
Prep & Cook Time: 20 minutes | Servings: 4

INGREDIENTS
1 packet of firm tofu, cubed & pressed to remove excess water
1 tbsp. of soy sauce
1 tbsp. of ketchup

1 tbsp. of maple syrup
½ tsp. of vinegar
1 tsp. of liquid smoke
1 tsp. of hot sauce

2 tbsp. of sesame seeds
1 tsp. of garlic powder
Salt & pepper

INSTRUCTIONS
1. Pre-heat the Air Fryer at 375°F.
2. Take a baking dish small enough to fit inside the Air Fryer & spritz it with cooking spray.
3. Combine all the ingredients to coat the tofu completely & allow the marinade to absorb for half an hour.
4. Transfer the tofu to the baking dish, then cook for 15 minutes. Flip the tofu over & cook for another 15 minutes on the other side.

197. CHICKPEAS
Prep & Cook Time: 20 minutes | Servings: 4

INGREDIENTS
One 15-oz. of can chickpeas, drained but not rinsed

2 tbsp. of olive oil
1 tsp. of salt

2 tbsp. of lemon juice

INSTRUCTIONS
1. Pre-heat the Air Fryer at 400°F.
2. Add all the ingredients together in a bowl & mix. Transfer this mixture to the basket of the Air Fryer.
3. Cook for 15 minutes, ensuring the chickpeas become nice & crispy.

198. CAULIFLOWER CHEESE TATER TOTS
Prep & Cook Time: 25 minutes | Servings: 12

INGREDIENTS
1 lb. of cauliflower, steamed & chopped
½ cup of yeast
1 tbsp. of oats
1 flax egg [1 tbsp. desiccated coconut + 3 tbsp. flaxseed meal

3 tbsp. of water
1 onion, chopped
1 tsp. of garlic, minced
1 tsp. of parsley, chopped
1 tsp. of oregano, chopped

1 tsp. of chives, chopped
Salt & pepper
½ cup of breadcrumbs

INSTRUCTIONS
1. Pre-heat the Air Fryer at 390°F.
2. Drain any excess water out of the cauliflower by wringing it with a paper towel.
3. In a bowl, combine the cauliflower with the remaining ingredients, save the breadcrumbs. Using your hands, shape the mixture into several small balls.
4. Coat the balls in the breadcrumbs & transfer to the basket of your Air Fryer. Allow to cook for 6 minutes, after which you should raise the temperature to 400°F & then leave to cook for an additional 10 minutes.

199. SWEET ONIONS & POTATOES
Prep & Cook Time: 30 minutes | Servings: 6

INGREDIENTS
2 sweet potatoes, peeled & cut into chunks
2 sweet onions, cut into chunks

3 tbsp. of olive oil
1 tsp. of dried thyme
Salt & pepper

¼ cup almonds, sliced & toasted

INSTRUCTIONS
1. Pre-heat the Air Fryer at 425°F.
2. In a bowl, combine all of the ingredients, except for the sliced almonds.
3. Transfer the vegetables & dressing to a ramekin & cook in the Air Fryer for 20 minutes.
4. When ready to serve, add the almonds on top.

200. MUSHROOM PIZZA SQUARES

Prep & Cook Time: 20 minutes | Servings: 10

INGREDIENTS

1 vegan pizza dough
1 cup of oyster mushrooms, chopped

1 shallot, chopped
¼ red bell pepper, chopped

2 tbsp. of parsley
Salt & pepper

INSTRUCTIONS

1. Pre-heat the Air Fryer at 400°F.
2. Cut the vegan pizza dough into squares.
3. In a bowl, combine the oyster mushrooms, shallot, bell pepper & parsley. Sprinkle some salt & pepper as desired.
4. Spread this mixture on top of the pizza squares.
5. Cook in the Air Fryer for 10 minutes.

201. TOFU & SWEET POTATOES

Prep & Cook Time: 50 minutes | Servings: 8

INGREDIENTS

8 sweet potatoes, scrubbed
2 tbsp. of olive oil
1 large onion, chopped

2 green chilies, deseeded & chopped
½ lb. of tofu, crumbled
2 tbsp. of Cajun seasoning

cup of tomatoes
1 can of kidney beans, drained & rinsed
Salt & pepper

INSTRUCTIONS

1. Pre-heat the Air Fryer at 400°F.
2. With a knife, pierce the skin of the sweet potatoes in numerous places & cook in the Air Fryer for half an hour, making sure they become soft. Remove from the Air Fryer, halve each potato, & set to one side.
3. Over a medium heat, fry the onions & chilis in a little oil for 2 minutes until fragrant.
4. Add in the tofu & Cajun seasoning & allow to cook for a further 3 minutes before incorporating the kidney beans & tomatoes. Sprinkle some salt & pepper as desire.
5. Top each sweet potato half with a spoonful of the tofu mixture & serve.

202. RISOTTO

Prep & Cook Time: 40 minutes | Servings: 2

INGREDIENTS

1 onion, diced
2 cups of chicken stock, boiling
½ cup of parmesan cheese or cheddar

cheese, grated
1 clove of garlic, minced
¾ cup of arborio rice

1 tbsp. of olive oil
1 tbsp. of butter

INSTRUCTIONS

1. Turn the Air Fryer to 390°F & set for 5 minutes to warm.
2. Grease a round baking tin with oil & stir in the butter, garlic, & onion.
3. Put the tin in the Air Fryer & allow to cook for 4 minutes.
4. Pour in the rice & cook for a further 4 minutes, stirring three times throughout the cooking time.
5. Turn the temperature down to 320°F.
6. Add the chicken stock & give the dish a gentle stir. Cook for 22 minutes, leaving the Air Fryer uncovered.
7. Pour in the cheese, stir once more & serve.

203. CHICKPEA & AVOCADO MASH

Prep & Cook Time: 30 minutes | Servings: 4

INGREDIENTS

1 medium-sized head of cauliflower, cut into florets
1 can of chickpeas, drained & rinsed

1 tbsp. of extra-virgin olive oil
2 tbsp. of lemon juice
Salt & pepper

4 flatbreads, toasted
2 ripe avocados, mashed

INSTRUCTIONS

1. Pre-heat the Air Fryer at 425°F.
2. In a bowl, mix together the chickpeas, cauliflower, lemon juice & olive oil. Sprinkle salt & pepper as desired.
3. Put inside the Air Fryer basket & cook for 25 minutes.
4. Spread on top of the flatbread along with the mashed avocado. Sprinkle on more pepper & salt as desired & enjoy with hot sauce.

204. FRIED POTATOES

Prep & Cook Time: 55 minutes | Servings: 1

INGREDIENTS

1 medium russet potato, scrubbed & peeled
1 tsp. of olive oil

¼ tsp. of onion powder
⅛ tsp. of salt
A dollop of vegan butter

A dollop of vegan cream cheese
1 tbsp. of Kalamata olives
1 tbsp. of chives, chopped

INSTRUCTIONS

1. Pre-heat the Air Fryer at 400°F.
2. In a bowl, coat the potatoes with the onion powder, salt, olive oil, & vegan butter.
3. Transfer to the Air Fryer & allow to cook for 40 minutes, turning the potatoes over at the halfway point.
4. Take care when removing the potatoes from the Air Fryer & enjoy with the vegan cream cheese, Kalamata olives & chives on top, plus any other vegan sides you desire.

205. FRENCH GREEN BEANS

Prep & Cook Time: 20 minutes | Servings: 4

INGREDIENTS

1 ½ lb. of French green beans, stems removed & blanched
1 tbsp. of salt

½ lb. of shallots, peeled & cut into quarters
½ tsp. of ground white pepper

2 tbsp. of olive oil
¼ cup of almonds, toasted

INSTRUCTIONS

1. Pre-heat the Air Fryer at 400°F.
2. Coat the vegetables with the rest of the ingredients in a bowl.
3. Transfer to the basket of your Air Fryer & cook for 10 minutes, making sure the green beans achieve a light brown color.

206. BLACK BEAN CHILI

Prep & Cook Time: 25 minutes | Servings: 6

INGREDIENTS

1 tbsp. of olive oil
1 medium onion, diced
3 cloves of garlic, minced
1 cup of vegetable broth

3 cans of black beans, drained & rinsed
2 cans of diced tomatoes
2 chipotle peppers, chopped
2 tsp. of cumin

2 tsp. of chili powder
1 tsp. of dried oregano
½ tsp. of salt

INSTRUCTIONS

1. Over a medium heat, fry the garlic & onions in a little oil for 3 minutes.
2. Add in the remaining ingredients, stirring constantly & scraping the bottom to prevent sticking.
3. Pre-heat your Air Fryer at 400°F.

4. Take a heat-resistant dish small enough to fit inside the Air Fryer & place the mixture inside. Put a sheet of aluminum foil on top.
5. Transfer to the Air Fryer & cook for 20 minutes.
6. When ready, plate up & serve with diced avocado, chopped cilantro, & chopped tomatoes.

207. CAULIFLOWER

Prep & Cook Time: 20 minutes | Servings: 4

INGREDIENTS

1 head of cauliflower, cut into florets
1 tbsp. of extra-virgin olive oil
2 scallions, chopped

5 cloves of garlic, sliced
1 ½ tbsp. of tamari
1 tbsp. of rice vinegar

½ tsp. of sugar
1 tbsp. of sriracha

INSTRUCTIONS

1. Pre-heat the Air Fryer to 400°F.
2. Put the cauliflower florets in the Air Fryer & drizzle some oil over them before cooking for 10 minutes.
3. Turn the cauliflower over, throw in the onions & garlic, & stir. Cook for another 10 minutes.
4. Mix together the rest of the ingredients in a bowl.
5. Remove the cooked cauliflower from the Air Fryer & coat it in the sauce.
6. Return to the Air Fryer & allow to cook for another 5 minutes. Enjoy with a side of rice.

208. TOFU BITES

Prep & Cook Time: 65 minutes | Servings: 3

INGREDIENTS

2 tbsp. of sesame oil
¼ cup of maple syrup
3 tbsp. of peanut butter
¼ cup of soy sauce
3 tbsp. of chili garlic sauce

2 tbsp. of rice wine vinegar
2 cloves of garlic, minced
1-inch of fresh ginger, peeled & grated
1 tsp. of red pepper flakes
1 block of extra firm tofu, pressed to

remove excess water & cubed
Toasted peanuts, chopped
1 tsp. of sesame seeds
1 sprig of cilantro, chopped

INSTRUCTIONS

1. Whisk together the first 9 ingredients in a large bowl to well combine.
2. Transfer to an airtight bag along with the cubed tofu. Allow to marinate for a minimum of a half hour.
3. Pre-heat the Air Fryer to 425°F.
4. Put the tofu cubes in the Air Fryer, keep any excess marinade for the sauce. Cook for 15 minutes.
5. In the meantime, heat the marinade over a medium heat to reduce by half.
6. Plate up the cooked tofu with some cooked rice & serve with the sauce. Complete the dish with the sesame seeds, cilantro & peanuts.

209. FAUX RICE

Prep & Cook Time: 60 minutes | Servings: 8

INGREDIENTS

1 medium-to-large head of cauliflower
½ lemon, juiced
2 garlic cloves, minced
2 cans of mushrooms, 8 oz. each

1 can of water chestnuts, 8 oz.
¾ cup of peas
½ cup of egg substitute or 1 egg, beaten
4 tbsp. of soy sauce

1 tbsp. of peanut oil
1 tbsp. of sesame oil
1 tbsp. of ginger, fresh & minced
Cooking spray

INSTRUCTIONS

1. Mix together the peanut oil, soy sauce, sesame oil, minced ginger, lemon juice, & minced garlic to combine well.
2. Peel & wash the cauliflower head before cutting it into small florets.
3. In a food processor, pulse the florets in small batches to break them down to resemble rice grains.
4. Pour into your Air Fryer basket.
5. Drain the can of water chestnuts & roughly chop them. Pour into the basket.
6. Cook at 350°F for 20 minutes.
7. In the meantime, drain the mushrooms. When the 20 minutes are up, add the mushrooms & the peas to the Air Fryer & continue to cook for another 15 minutes.
8. Lightly spritz a frying pan with cooking spray. Prepare an omelet with the egg substitute or the beaten egg, ensuring it is firm. Lay on a cutting board & slice it up.
9. When the cauliflower is ready, throw in the omelet & cook for an additional 5 minutes. Serve hot.

210. POTATO CROQUETTES

Prep & Cook Time: 25 minutes | Servings: 10

INGREDIENTS

¼ cup of yeast
2 cups of boiled potatoes, mashed
1 flax egg [1 tbsp. flaxseed meal + 3 tbsp.

of water]
1 tbsp. of flour
2 tbsp. of chives, chopped

Salt & pepper
2 tbsp. of vegetable oil
¼ cup of breadcrumbs

INSTRUCTIONS

1. Pre-heat the Air Fryer to 400°F.
2. In a bowl, combine together the yeast, potatoes, flax eggs, flour, & chives. Sprinkle with salt & pepper as desired.
3. In separate bowl mix together the vegetable oil & breadcrumbs to achieve a crumbly consistency.
4. Use your hands to shape the potato mixture into small balls & dip each one into the breadcrumb mixture.
5. Place the croquettes inside the Air Fryer & cook for 15 minutes, ensuring the croquettes turn golden brown.

211. SWEET & SOUR TOFU

Prep & Cook Time: 55 minutes | Servings: 2

INGREDIENTS

2 tsp. of apple cider vinegar
1 tbsp. of sugar
1 tbsp. of soy sauce
3 tsp. of lime juice

1 tsp. of ground ginger
1 tsp. of garlic powder
½ block firm tofu, pressed to remove
excess liquid & cut into cubes

1 tsp. of cornstarch
2 green onions, chopped
Toasted sesame seeds for garnish

INSTRUCTIONS

1. In a bowl, thoroughly combine the apple cider vinegar, sugar, soy sauce, lime juice, ground ginger, & garlic powder.
2. Cover the tofu with this mixture & leave to marinate for at least 30 minutes.
3. Transfer the tofu to the Air Fryer, keeping any excess marinade for the sauce. Cook at 400°F for 20 minutes or until crispy.
4. In the meantime, thicken the sauce with the cornstarch over a medium-low heat.
5. Serve the cooked tofu with the sauce, green onions, sesame seeds, & some rice.

212. VEGETABLE SALAD

Prep & Cook Time: 20 minutes | Servings: 4

INGREDIENTS

6 plum tomatoes, halved
2 large red onions, sliced
4 long red pepper, sliced
2 yellow peppers, sliced

6 cloves of garlic, crushed
1 tbsp. of extra-virgin olive oil
1 tsp. of paprika
½ lemon, juiced

Salt & pepper
1 tbsp. of baby capers

INSTRUCTIONS

1. Pre-heat the Air Fryer at 420°F.
2. Put the tomatoes, onions, peppers, & garlic in a large bowl & cover with the extra virgin olive oil, paprika, & lemon juice. Sprinkle with salt & pepper as desired.

3. Line the inside of your Air Fryer with aluminum foil. Place the vegetables inside & allow to cook for 10 minutes, ensuring the edges turn brown.
4. Serve in a salad bowl with the baby capers. Make sure all the ingredients are well combined.

213. MEDITERRANEAN VEGETABLES

Prep & Cook Time: 30 minutes | Servings: 4

INGREDIENTS

1 cup cherry tomatoes, halved
1 large zucchini, sliced
1 green pepper, sliced
1 parsnip, sliced

1 carrot, sliced
1 tsp. of mixed herbs
1 tsp. of mustard
1 tsp. of garlic puree

6 tbsp. of olive oil
Salt & pepper

INSTRUCTIONS

1. Pre-heat the Air Fryer at 400°F.
2. Combine all the ingredients in a bowl, making sure to coat the vegetables well.
3. Transfer to the Air Fryer & cook for 6 minutes, ensuring the vegetables are tender & browned.

214. SWEET POTATOES

Prep & Cook Time: 55 minutes | Servings: 4

INGREDIENTS

2 potatoes, peeled & cubed
4 carrots, cut into chunks
1 head of broccoli, cut into florets

4 zucchinis, sliced thickly
Salt & pepper
¼ cup of olive oil

1 tbsp. of dry onion powder

INSTRUCTIONS

1. Pre-heat the Air Fryer to 400°F.
2. In a baking dish small enough to fit inside the Air Fryer, add all the ingredients & combine well.
3. Cook for 45 minutes in the Air Fryer, ensuring the vegetables are soft & the sides have browned before serving.

215. SAGE CHICKEN ESCALLOPS

Prep & Cook Time: 45 minutes | Servings: 4

INGREDIENTS

4 skinless chicken breasts
2 eggs, beaten
½ cup of flour

6 sage leaves
¼ cup of breadcrumbs
¼ cup of parmesan cheese

Cooking spray

INSTRUCTIONS

1. Cut the chicken breasts into thin, flat slices.
2. In a bowl, combine the parmesan with the sage.
3. Add in the flour & eggs & sprinkle with salt & pepper as desired. Mix well.
4. Dip chicken in the flour-egg mixture.
5. Coat the chicken in the breadcrumbs.
6. Spritz the inside of the Air Fryer with cooking spray & set it to 390°F, allowing it to warm.
7. Cook the chicken for 20 minutes.
8. When golden, serve with fried rice.

216. FRIED PICKLES

Prep & Cook Time: 30 minutes | Servings: 4

INGREDIENTS

14 dill pickles, sliced
¼ cup of flour
⅛ tsp. of baking powder

Salt
2 tbsp. of cornstarch + 3 tbsp. of water
6 tbsp. of breadcrumbs

½ tsp. of paprika
Cooking spray

INSTRUCTIONS

1. Pre-heat your Air Fryer at 400°F.
2. Drain any excess moisture out of the dill pickles on a paper towel.
3. In a bowl, combine the flour, baking powder & salt.
4. Throw in the cornstarch & water mixture & combine well with a whisk.
5. Put the panko breadcrumbs in a shallow dish along with the paprika. Mix thoroughly.
6. Dip the pickles in the flour batter, before coating in the breadcrumbs. Spritz all the pickles with the cooking spray.
7. Transfer to the Air Fryer & cook for 15 minutes, until a golden-brown color is achieved.

217. CAULIFLOWER BITES

Prep & Cook Time: 30 minutes | Servings: 4

INGREDIENTS

1 cup of flour
⅓ cup of desiccated coconut
Salt & pepper
1 flax egg [1 tbsp. flaxseed meal + 3 tbsp.

of water]
1 small cauliflower, cut into florets
1 tsp. of mixed spice
½ tsp. of mustard powder

2 tbsp. of maple syrup
1 clove of garlic, minced
2 tbsp. of soy sauce

INSTRUCTIONS

1. Pre-heat the Air Fryer to 400°F.
2. In a bowl, mix together the oats, flour, & desiccated coconut, sprinkling with some salt & pepper as desired.
3. In a separate bowl, season the flax egg with a pinch of salt.
4. Coat the cauliflower with mixed spice & mustard powder.
5. Dip the florets into the flax egg, then into the flour mixture. Cook for 15 minutes in the Air Fryer.
6. In the meantime, place a saucepan over medium heat & add in the maple syrup, garlic, & soy sauce. Boil first, before reducing the heat to allow the sauce to thicken.
7. Remove the florets from the Air Fryer & transfer to the saucepan. Coat the florets in the sauce before returning to the Air Fryer & allowing to cook for an additional 5 minutes.

218. CHICKEN & VEGGIES

Prep & Cook Time: 30 minutes | Servings: 4

INGREDIENTS

8 chicken thighs
5 oz. of mushrooms, sliced
1 red onion, diced
Fresh black pepper, to taste
10 medium asparagus

½ cup of carrots, diced
¼ cup of balsamic vinegar
2 red bell peppers, diced
½ tsp. of sugar
2 tbsp. of extra-virgin olive oil

1 ½ tbsp. of fresh rosemary
2 cloves of garlic, chopped
½ tbsp. of dried oregano
1 tsp. of salt
2 fresh sages, chopped

INSTRUCTIONS

1. Pre-heat the Air Fryer to 400°F.
2. Grease the inside of a baking tray with the oil.
3. Season the chicken with salt & pepper.
4. Put all of the vegetables in a large bowl & throw in the oregano, garlic, sugar, mushrooms, vinegar, & sage. Combine everything well before transferring to the baking tray.
5. Put the chicken thighs in the baking tray. Cook in the Air Fryer for about 20 minutes.
6. Serve hot.

219. FALAFEL

Prep & Cook Time: 30 minutes | Servings: 8

INGREDIENTS

1 tsp. of cumin seeds
½ tsp. of coriander seeds
2 cups of chickpeas from can, drained
½ tsp. of red pepper flakes

3 cloves of garlic
¼ cup of parsley, chopped
¼ cup of coriander, chopped
½ onion, diced

1 tbsp. of lemon juice
3 tbsp. of flour
½ tsp. of salt cooking spray

INSTRUCTIONS

1. Fry the cumin & coriander seeds over medium heat until fragrant.
2. Grind using a mortar & pestle.
3. Put all of ingredients, except for the cooking spray, in a food processor & blend until a fine consistency is achieved.
4. Use your hands to mold the mixture into falafels & spritz with the cooking spray.
5. Preheat your Air Fryer at 400°F.
6. Transfer the falafels to the Air Fryer in one single layer.
7. Cook for 15 minutes, serving when they turn golden brown.

220. EASY ASPARAGUS

Prep & Cook Time: 10 minutes | Servings: 4

INGREDIENTS

1 lb. of fresh asparagus spears, trimmed

1 tbsp. of olive oil

Salt & pepper

INSTRUCTIONS

1. Pre-heat the Air Fryer at 375°F.
2. Combine all of the ingredients & transfer to the Air Fryer.
3. Cook for 5 minutes until soft.

221. CAULIFLOWER STEAK

Prep & Cook Time: 30 minutes | Servings: 2

INGREDIENTS

1 cauliflower, sliced into two
1 tbsp. of olive oil

2 tbsp. of onion, chopped
¼ tsp. of vegetable stock powder

¼ cup of milk
Salt & pepper

INSTRUCTIONS

1. Place the cauliflower in a bowl of salted water & allow to absorb for at least 2 hours.
2. Pre-heat the Air Fryer to 400°F.
3. Rinse off the cauliflower, put inside the Air Fryer & cook for 15 minutes.
4. In the meantime, fry the onions over medium heat, stirring constantly, until they turn translucent. Pour in the vegetable stock powder & milk. Bring to a boil & then lower the heat.
5. Let the sauce reduce & add in salt & pepper.
6. Plate up the cauliflower steak & top with the sauce.

222. ROCKET SALAD

Prep & Cook Time: 35 minutes | Servings: 4

INGREDIENTS

8 fresh figs, halved
1 ½ cups of chickpeas, cooked
1 tsp. of cumin seeds, crushed

4 tbsp. of balsamic vinegar
2 tbsp. of extra-virgin olive oil
Salt & pepper

3 cups of arugula rocket, washed & dried

INSTRUCTIONS

1. Pre-heat the Air Fryer to 375°F.
2. Cover the Air Fryer basket with aluminum foil & grease lightly with oil. Put the figs in the Air Fryer & allow to cook for 10 minutes.
3. In a bowl, combine the chickpeas & cumin seeds.
4. Remove the cooked figs from the Air Fryer & replace with chickpeas. Cook for 10 minutes. Leave to cool.
5. In the meantime, prepare the dressing. Mix together the balsamic vinegar, olive oil, salt & pepper.
6. In a salad bowl combine the arugula rocket with the cooled figs & chickpeas.
7. Toss with the sauce & serve right away.

223. VEGAN RAVIOLI

Prep & Cook Time: 15 minutes | Servings: 4

INGREDIENTS

½ cup of breadcrumbs
2 tsp. of yeast
1 tsp. of dried basil

1 tsp. of dried oregano
1 tsp. of garlic powder
Salt & pepper

¼ cup of aquafaba
8 oz. of vegan ravioli
Cooking spray

INSTRUCTIONS

1. Cover the Air Fryer basket with aluminum foil & coat with a light brushing of oil.
2. Pre-heat the Air Fryer to 400°F. Combine together the panko breadcrumbs, yeast, basil, oregano, & garlic powder. Sprinkle on salt & pepper to taste.
3. Put the aquafaba in a separate bowl. Dip the ravioli in the aquafaba before coating it in the panko mixture. Spritz with cooking spray & transfer to the Air Fryer.
4. Cook for 6 minutes ensuring to shake the Air Fryer basket halfway.

224. THANKSGIVING SPROUTS

Prep & Cook Time: 20 minutes | Servings: 6

INGREDIENTS

1 ½ lb. of Brussels sprouts, cleaned & trimmed
3 tbsp. of olive oil

1 tsp. of salt
1 tsp. of black pepper

INSTRUCTIONS

1. Pre-heat the Air Fryer to 375°F. Cover the basket with aluminum foil & coat with a light brushing of oil.
2. In a mixing bowl, combine all ingredients, coating the sprouts well.
3. Put in the Air Fryer basket & cook for 10 minutes. Shake the Air Fryer basket throughout the duration to ensure even cooking.

225. ROASTED GARLIC, BROCCOLI & LEMON

Prep & Cook Time: 25 minutes | Servings: 6

INGREDIENTS

2 heads of broccoli, cut into florets
2 tsp. of extra virgin olive oil

1 tsp. of salt
½ tsp. of black pepper

1 clove of garlic, minced
½ tsp. of lemon juice

INSTRUCTIONS

1. Cover the Air Fryer basket with aluminum foil & coat with a light brushing of oil.
2. Pre-heat the Air Fryer to 375°F.
3. In a bowl, combine all ingredients save for the lemon juice & transfer to the Air Fryer basket. Allow to cook for 15 minutes.
4. Serve with the lemon juice.

226. PEPPERONI PIZZA

Prep & Cook Time: 15 minutes | Servings: 3

INGREDIENTS

3 portobello mushroom caps, scooped
3 tbsp. of olive oil
3 tbsp. of tomato sauce

3 tbsp. of mozzarella, shredded
12 slices of pepperoni
Salt

1 pinch of dried Italian seasoning

INSTRUCTIONS

1. Pre-heat the Air Fryer to 330°F.
2. Season both sides of the portobello mushrooms with a drizzle of olive oil, then sprinkle salt & the Italian seasonings on the insides.
3. With a knife, spread the tomato sauce evenly over the mushroom, before adding the mozzarella on top.
4. Put the portobello in the cooking basket & place in the Air Fryer.
5. Cook for 1 minute, before taking the cooking basket out of the Air Fryer & putting the pepperoni slices on top.
6. Cook for another 3 to 5 minutes. Garnish with freshly grated parmesan cheese & crushed red pepper flakes & serve.

227. BABY CORN PAKODAS

Prep & Cook Time: 20 minutes | Servings: 5

INGREDIENTS

1 cup of flour
¼ tsp. of baking soda
¼ tsp. of salt

½ tsp. of curry powder
½ tsp. of red chili powder
¼ tsp. of turmeric powder

¼ cup of water
10 pc. of baby corn, blanched

INSTRUCTIONS

1. Pre-heat the Air Fryer to 425°F.
2. Cover the Air Fryer basket with aluminum foil & coat with a light brushing of oil.
3. In a bowl, combine all ingredients save for the corn. Stir with a whisk until well combined.
4. Coat the corn in the batter & put inside the Air Fryer.
5. Cook for 8 minutes until a golden-brown color is achieved.

228. CHICKEN-MUSHROOM CASSEROLE

Prep & Cook Time: 30 minutes | Servings: 4

INGREDIENTS

4 chicken breasts
½ cup of shredded cheese
Salt

1 cup of coconut milk
1 cup of mushrooms
1 broccoli, cut into florets

1 tbsp. of curry powder

INSTRUCTIONS

1. Pre-heat your Air Fryer to 350°F. Spritz a casserole dish with some cooking spray.
2. Cube the chicken breasts & combine with curry powder & coconut milk in a bowl. Season with salt.
3. Add in the broccoli & mushroom & mix well.
4. Pour the mixture into the casserole dish. Top with the cheese.
5. Transfer to your Air Fryer & cook for about 20 minutes.
6. Serve warm.

229. PITA BREAD PIZZA

Prep & Cook Time: 15 minutes | Servings: 1

INGREDIENTS

1 pita bread
1 tbsp. of pizza sauce
6 pepperoni slices

¼ cup of grated mozzarella cheese
1 tsp. of olive oil
¼ tsp. of garlic powder

¼ tsp. of dried oregano

INSTRUCTIONS

1. Pre-heat your Air Fryer to 350°F.
2. Spread the pizza sauce on top of the pita bread. Place the pepperoni slices over the sauce, followed by the mozzarella cheese.
3. Season with garlic powder & oregano.
4. Put the pita pizza inside the Air Fryer & place a trivet on top.
5. Cook for 6 minutes & enjoy.

230. PAPRIKA TOFU

Prep & Cook Time: 25 minutes | Servings: 4

INGREDIENTS

2 block extra firm tofu, pressed to remove
excess water & cubed

¼ cup of cornstarch
1 tbsp. of smoked paprika

Salt & pepper

INSTRUCTIONS

1. Cover the Air Fryer basket with aluminum foil & coat with a light brushing of oil.
2. Pre-heat the Air Fryer to 370°F.
3. Combine all ingredients in a bowl, coating the tofu well.
4. Put in the Air Fryer basket & allow to cook for 12 minutes. Serve!

231. MAC & CHEESE

Prep & Cook Time: 15 minutes | Servings: 2

INGREDIENTS

1 cup of cooked macaroni
½ cup of warm milk

1 tbsp. of parmesan cheese
1 cup of grated cheddar cheese

Salt & pepper, to taste

INSTRUCTIONS

1. Pre-heat the Air Fryer to 350°F.
2. In a baking dish, mix together all of the ingredients, except for Parmesan.
3. Put the dish inside the Air Fryer & allow to cook for 10 minutes.
4. Add the Parmesan cheese on top & serve.

232. PASTA SALAD

Prep & Cook Time: 2 hours 25 minutes | Servings: 8

INGREDIENTS

4 tomatoes, medium & cut in eighths
3 eggplants, small
3 zucchinis, medium sized
2 bell peppers, any color

4 cups of large pasta, uncooked in any
1 cup of cherry tomatoes, sliced
½ cup of Italian dressing, fat-free
8 tbsp. of parmesan, grated

2 tbsp. of extra virgin olive oil
2 tsp. of pink Himalayan salt
1 tsp. of basil, dried
High quality cooking spray

INSTRUCTIONS

1. Wash & dry the eggplant. Cut off the stem & throw it away. Do not peel the eggplant. Cut it into half-inch-thick round slices.
2. Coat the eggplant slices with 1 tbsp. of extra virgin olive oil, & transfer to the Air Fryer basket.
3. Cook the eggplant for 40 minutes at 350°F. Once it is tender & cooked through, remove from the Air Fryer & set to one side.

4. Wash & dry the zucchini. Cut off the stem & throw it away. Do not peel the zucchini. Cut the zucchini into half-inch-thick round slices.
5. Combine with the olive oil to coat & put it in the Air Fryer basket.
6. Cook the zucchini for about 25 minutes at 350°F. Once it is tender & cooked through, remove from the Air Fryer & set to one side.
7. Wash the tomatoes & cut them into eight equal slices. Transfer them to the Air Fryer basket & spritz lightly with high quality cooking spray. Cook the tomatoes for 30 minutes at 350°F. Once they have shrunk & are beginning to turn brown, set them to one side.
8. Cook the pasta & drain it. Rinse with cold water & set it aside to cool.
9. Wash, dry & halve the bell peppers. Remove the stems & seeds.
10. Wash & halve the cherry tomatoes.
11. In a large bowl, mix together the bell peppers & cherry tomatoes. Stir in the roasted vegetables, cooked pasta, pink Himalayan salt, dressing, chopped basil leaves, & grated parmesan, ensuring to incorporate everything well.
12. Let the salad cool & marinate in the refrigerator.
13. Serve the salad cold or at room temperature.

233. PROSCIUTTO & POTATO SALAD

Prep & Cook Time: 15 minutes | Servings: 8

INGREDIENTS

4 lb. of potatoes, boiled & cubed
15 slices of prosciutto, diced
15 oz. of sour cream

2 cups of shredded cheddar cheese
2 tbsp. of mayonnaise
1 tsp. of salt

1 tsp. of black pepper
1 tsp. of dried basil

INSTRUCTIONS

1. Pre-heat the Air Fryer to 350°F.
2. Place the potatoes, prosciutto, & cheddar in a baking dish. Put it in the Air Fryer & allow to cook for 7 minutes.
3. In a separate bowl, mix together the sour cream, mayonnaise, salt, pepper, & basil using a whisk.
4. Coat the salad with the dressing & serve.

234. CHICKEN QUESADILLAS

Prep & Cook Time: 20 minutes | Servings: 4

INGREDIENTS

2 soft taco shells
1 lb. of boneless chicken breasts
1 large green pepper, sliced

1 medium-sized onion, sliced
½ cup of Cheddar cheese, shredded
½ cup of salsa sauce

2 tbsp. of olive oil
Salt & pepper, to taste

INSTRUCTIONS

1. Pre-heat the Air Fryer to 370°F & drizzle the basket with 1 tbsp. of olive oil.
2. Lay one taco shell into the bottom of the Air Fryer & spread some salsa inside the taco. Slice the chicken breast into strips & put the strips into taco shell.
3. Top the chicken with the onions & peppers.
4. Season with salt & pepper. Add the shredded cheese & top with the second taco shell.
5. Drizzle with another tbsp. of olive oil. Put the rack over the taco to keep it in place.
6. Cook for 4 – 6 minutes, until it turns lightly brown & is cooked through. Serve either hot or cold.

235. MOZZARELLA BRUSCHETTA

Prep & Cook Time: 10 minutes | Servings: 1

INGREDIENTS

6 small loaf slices
½ cup of tomatoes, finely chopped

3 oz. of mozzarella cheese, grated
1 tbsp. of fresh basil, chopped

1 tbsp. of olive oil

INSTRUCTIONS

1. Pre-heat the Air Fryer to 350°F. Place the bread inside & cook for about 3 minutes.
2. Add the tomato, mozzarella, prosciutto, & a drizzle of olive oil on top.
3. Cook the bruschetta for an additional minute before serving.

236. SAUSAGE-CHICKEN CASSEROLE

Prep & Cook Time: 30 minutes | Servings: 8

INGREDIENTS

2 cloves of minced garlic
10 eggs
1 cup of broccoli, chopped

½ tbsp. of salt
1 cup of cheddar, shredded & divided
¼ tbsp. of pepper

¾ cup of whipping cream
1 x 12-oz. packet of cooked chicken sausage

INSTRUCTIONS

1. Pre-heat the Air Fryer to 400°F.
2. In a large bowl, beat the eggs with a whisk. Pour in the whipping cream & cheese. Combine well.
3. In a separate bowl, mix together the garlic, broccoli, salt, pepper & cooked sausage.
4. Place the chicken sausage mix in a casserole dish. Top with the cheese mixture.
5. Transfer to the Air Fryer & cook for about 20 minutes.

237. CASHEW & CHICKEN MANCHURIAN

Prep & Cook Time: 30 minutes | Servings: 6

INGREDIENTS

1 cup chicken boneless
1 spring onions, chopped
1 onion, chopped
3 green chilis
6 cashew nuts

1 tsp. ginger, chopped
½ tsp. of garlic, chopped
1 Egg
2 tbsp. of flour
1 tbsp. of cornstarch

1 tsp. of soy sauce
2 tsp. of chili paste
1 tsp. of pepper
Pinch of MSG
1 tbsp. of oil

INSTRUCTIONS

1. Pre-heat your Air Fryer at 360°F
2. Toss together the chicken, egg, salt & pepper to coat well.
3. Combine the cornstarch & flour & use this to cover the chicken.
4. Cook in the Air Fryer for 10 minutes.
5. In the meantime, toast the nuts in a frying pan. Add in the onions & cook until they turn translucent. Combine with the remaining ingredients to create the sauce.
6. Finally, add in the chicken. When piping hot, garnish with the spring onions & serve.

238. CHEESE & BACON ROLLS

Prep & Cook Time: 25 minutes | Servings: 4

INGREDIENTS

8 oz. of refrigerated crescent roll dough [usually 1 can]

6 oz. of sharp cheddar cheese, grated
1 lb. of bacon, cooked & chopped

INSTRUCTIONS

1. Roll out the crescent dough flat & slice it into 1" x 1 ½" pieces.
2. In a bowl, mix together the cheese & bacon. Take about ¼ cup of this mixture & spread it across one slice of dough. Repeat with the rest of the mixture & dough.
3. Set your Air Fryer to 330°F & allow to warm.
4. Place the rolls on the Air Fry tray & transfer to the Air Fryer. Alternatively, you can put them in the food basket.

5. Bake for roughly 6 – 8 minutes until a golden-brown color is achieved. Watch them carefully to prevent burning, as they may cook very quickly.

239. KIDNEY BEANS OATMEAL

Prep & Cook Time: 25 minutes | Servings: 2 – 4

INGREDIENTS

2 large bell peppers, halved lengthwise, deseeded
2 tbsp. of cooked kidney beans
2 tbsp. of cooked chickpeas

2 cups of oatmeal, cooked
1 tsp. of ground cumin
½ tsp. of paprika
½ tsp. of salt or to taste

¼ tsp. of black pepper powder
¼ cup yogurt

INSTRUCTIONS

1. Pre-heat the Air Fryer at 355°F.
2. Put the bell peppers, cut-side-down, in the Air Fryer. Allow to cook for 2 – 3 minutes.
3. Take the peppers out of the Air Fryer & let cool.
4. In a bowl, combine together the rest of the ingredients.
5. Divide the mixture evenly & use each portion to stuff a pepper.
6. Return to the Air Fryer & continue to air fry for 4 minutes. Serve hot.

240. CHICKEN FILLETS & BRIE

Prep & Cook Time: 40 minutes | Servings: 4

INGREDIENTS

4 slices of turkey, cured
2 large chicken fillets

4 slices of brie cheese
1 tbsp. of chives, chopped

Salt & pepper

INSTRUCTIONS

1. Pre-heat Air Fryer to 360°F. Slice each chicken fillet in half & sprinkle on salt & pepper. Coat with the brie & chives.
2. Wrap the turkey around the chicken & secure with toothpick.
3. Cook for 15 minutes until a brown color is achieved.

241. CHEESE & MACARONI BALLS

Prep & Cook Time: 25 minutes | Servings: 2

INGREDIENTS

2 cups of leftover macaroni
1 cup of cheddar cheese, shredded
3 large eggs

1 cup of milk
½ cup of flour
1 cup of breadcrumbs

½ tsp. of salt
¼ tsp. of black pepper

INSTRUCTIONS

1. In a bowl, combine the leftover macaroni & shredded cheese.
2. Pour the flour in a separate bowl. Put the breadcrumbs in a third bowl. Finally, in a fourth bowl, mix together the eggs & milk with a whisk.
3. With an ice-cream scoop, create balls from the macaroni mixture. Coat them the flour, then in the egg mixture, & lastly in the breadcrumbs.
4. Pre-heat the Air Fryer to 365°F & cook the balls for about 10 minutes, giving them an occasional stir. Ensure they crisp up nicely.
5. Serve with the sauce of your choice.

242. CHEESE PIZZA

Prep & Cook Time: 15 minutes | Servings: 4

INGREDIENTS

1 pc. of bread
½ lb. of mozzarella cheese

1 tbsp. of olive oil
2 tbsp. of ketchup

⅓ cup of sausage
1 tsp. of garlic powder

INSTRUCTIONS

1. Using a tbsp., spread the ketchup over the pita bread.
2. Top with the sausage & cheese. Season with the garlic powder & 1 tbsp. of olive oil.
3. Pre-heat the Air Fryer to 340°F.
4. Put the pizza in the Air Fryer basket & cook for 6 minutes. Enjoy!

243. PORTABELLA PIZZA

Prep & Cook Time: 15 minutes | Servings: 3

INGREDIENTS

3 tbsp. of olive oil
3 portobello mushroom caps, cleaned & scooped

3 tbsp. of mozzarella, shredded
3 tbsp. of tomato sauce
Salt

12 slices of pepperoni
Pinch of dried Italian seasonings

INSTRUCTIONS

1. Pre-heat the Air Fryer to 330°F.
2. Coat both sides of the mushroom cap with a drizzle of oil, before seasoning the inside with the Italian seasonings & salt. Evenly spread the tomato sauce over the mushroom & add the cheese on top.
3. Put the mushroom into the cooking basket of the Air Fryer. Place the slices of pepperoni on top of the portobello pizza after a minute of cooking & continue to cook for another 3-5 minutes. Serve!

244. AMERICAN HOT DOGS

Prep & Cook Time: 20 minutes | Servings: 4

INGREDIENTS

3 Brazilian sausages, cut into 3 equals pieces

9 bacon fillets, raw
Black pepper to taste

Salt

INSTRUCTIONS

1. Pre-heat the Air Fryer for 5 minutes at 355°F.
2. Take a slice of bacon & wrap it around each piece of sausage. Sprinkle with some salt & pepper as desired, as well as a half-tsp. of Italian herbs if you like.
3. Fry the sausages for 15 minutes & serve warm.

245. GARLIC BACON

Prep & Cook Time: 40 minutes | Servings: 4

INGREDIENTS

4 potatoes, peeled & cut into bite-size chunks
6 cloves garlic, unpeeled

4 strips of bacon, chopped
1 tbsp. of fresh rosemary, finely chopped

INSTRUCTIONS

1. In a large bowl, thoroughly combine the potatoes, garlic, bacon, & rosemary. Place the ingredients in a baking dish.
2. Set your Air Fryer to 350°F & briefly allow to warm.
3. Cook the potatoes for 25-30 minutes until a golden-brown color is achieved.

246. MEXICAN PIZZA

INGREDIENTS
¾ cup refried beans
1 cup salsa
12 frozen beef meatballs, pre-cooked

2 jalapeno peppers, sliced
6 slices of bread
1 cup of pepper Jack cheese, shredded

1 cup of Colby cheese, shredded

INSTRUCTIONS
1. Pre-heat the Air Fryer for 4 minutes at 370°F.
2. In a bowl, mix together the salsa, meatball, jalapeno pepper & beans.
3. Place a spoonful of this mixture on top of each pita bread, along with a topping of pepper Jack & Colby cheese.
4. Bake in the Air Fryer for 10 minutes. Serve hot.

247. PESTO GNOCCHI
Prep & Cook Time: 30 minutes | Servings: 4

INGREDIENTS
1 packet [16-oz.] of shelf-stable gnocchi
1 medium-sized onion, chopped
3 cloves of garlic, minced

1 jar [8 oz.] of pesto
⅓ cup of parmesan cheese, grated
1 tbsp. of extra virgin olive oil

Salt & black pepper to taste

INSTRUCTIONS
1. Pre-heat the Air Fryer to 340°F.
2. In a large bowl combine the onion, garlic, & gnocchi, & drizzle with the olive oil. Mix thoroughly.
3. Transfer the mixture to the Air Fryer & cook for 15 – 20 minutes, stirring occasionally, making sure the gnocchi become lightly brown & crispy.
4. Add in the pesto & Parmesan cheese & give everything a good stir before serving straightaway.

248. CHEESEBURGER SLIDERS
Prep & Cook Time: 20 minutes | Servings: 3

INGREDIENTS
1 lb. of ground beef
6 slices of cheddar cheese

6 dinner rolls
Salt & pepper

INSTRUCTIONS
1. Pre-heat the Air Fryer to 390°F.
2. With your hands, shape the ground beef into 6 x 2.5-oz. patties. Sprinkle on some salt & pepper to taste.
3. Place the burgers in the cooking basket & cook for 10 minutes. Take care when removing them from the Air Fryer.
4. Top the patties with the cheese. Put them back in the Air Fryer & allow to cook for another minute before serving.

249. TENDER PORK & BELL PEPPERS
Prep & Cook Time: 32 minutes | Servings: 2

INGREDIENTS
7 oz. of pork tenderloin, cut into strips
1 pc. of green bell pepper, cut into strips
1 pc. of yellow bell pepper, cut in strips

1 pc. of sweet onion, chopped
1 pc. of red bell pepper, cut into strips
1 tbsp. of olive oil

salt & black pepper to taste

INSTRUCTIONS
1. Combine all of the ingredients into a pan and toss well.
2. Transfer the pan in the fryer and cook at 390°F for 22 minutes.
3. Distribute the mixture between plates and serve.

250. PORK & BELL PEPPER
Prep & Cook Time: 25 minutes | Servings: 4

INGREDIENTS
1 lb. of pork, cut into strips
½ cup of beef stock
4 pcs. of shallots, chopped

2 pcs. of red bell peppers, cut in strips
4 pcs. of garlic cloves, minced
2 tbsp. of olive oil

a pinch of salt & black pepper
2 tbsp. of fish sauce

INSTRUCTIONS
1. In a pan, combine all ingredients and toss well.
2. Transfer the pan in the fryer and cook at 400°F for 20 minutes, shaking the fryer halfway.
3. Distribute everything between plates and serve.

251. BEEF & MUSHROOM
Prep & Cook Time: 22 minutes | Servings: 2

INGREDIENTS
8 oz. of white mushrooms, sliced
1 pc. of yellow onion, chopped

2 cuts of beef steaks, cut to strips
2 tbsp. of dark soy sauce

1 tsp. of olive oil
salt & black pepper to taste

INSTRUCTIONS
1. Mix all ingredients in a baking dish and toss well.
2. Transfer the baking dish in the fryer and cook at 390°F for 17 minutes.
3. Distribute everything between plates and serve.

252. SMOKED PORK ROAST
Prep & Cook Time: 60 minutes | Servings: 4

INGREDIENTS
2 lbs. of pork loin roast
2 tbsp. of chopped oregano
3 tbsp. of smoked paprika

1 tbsp. of olive oil
1 tsp. of liquid smoke
1 tbsp. of brown sugar

salt & black pepper to taste

INSTRUCTIONS
1. Combine all ingredients except for the Roast.
2. Coat the Roast with the mixture.
3. Place the roast to air fryer and cook at 370°F for 55 minutes.
4. Cut the roast and distribute it between plates.
5. Serve and enjoy!

253. RUBBED STEAKS
Prep & Cook Time: 20 minutes | Servings: 4

INGREDIENTS
¼ cup of ancho chili powder
4 cuts of flank steaks
2 tsp. of grated ginger

1 tbsp. of dried oregano
1 tbsp. of dry mustard
2 tbsp. of sweet paprika

1 tbsp. of ground coriander
cooking spray
salt & black pepper to taste

INSTRUCTIONS
1. Combine all spices in a bowl. Coat the steak with the mixture.
3. In air fryer's basket, grease with cooking spray.
4. Transfer the streak to the fryer and cook at 370°F for 7 minutes on each side.

5. Serve the steaks with a side salad and enjoy!

254. COCONUT PORK
Prep & Cook Time: 20 minutes | Servings: 4

INGREDIENTS

7 oz. of coconut milk
14 oz. of pork chops, cut into strips
2 garlic cloves, minced

1 pc. of shallot, chopped
1 tsp. of grated ginger
2 tsp. of chili paste

2 tbsp. of olive oil
3 tbsp. of soy sauce
salt & black pepper to taste

INSTRUCTIONS

1. Combine all ingredients except for the coconut milk in a baking dish.
2. Transfer the pan in the fryer and cook at 400°F for 12 minutes, shaking the fryer halfway.
3. Pour the coconut milk, toss and cook for 3-4 minutes more.
4. Distribute everything into bowls and serve.

255. TARRAGON PORK LOIN
Prep & Cook Time: 65 minutes | Servings: 6

INGREDIENTS

3 lbs. of pork loin roast, trimmed
¼ cup of olive oil

3 pcs. of garlic cloves, minced
2 tbsp. of chopped tarragon

2 tsp. of sweet paprika
salt & black pepper to taste

INSTRUCTIONS

1. Combine all ingredients except for the roast.
2. Coat the roast with the mixture. Rub well.
3. Place the coated roast to air fryer and cook at 390°F for 55 minutes.
4. Cut the roast and distribute it between plates.
5. Serve and enjoy

256. FRENCH BEEF
Prep & Cook Time: 20 minutes | Servings: 2

INGREDIENTS

7 oz. of beef fillets, cut into strips
1 pc. of green bell pepper, cut in strips
1 pc. of red onion, sliced

2 tsp. of provencal herbs
½ tbsp. of mustard
1 tbsp. of olive oil

salt & black pepper to taste

INSTRUCTIONS

1. Combine all ingredients in a pan.
2. Transfer the pan in the fryer and cook at 400°F for 15 minutes.
3. Distribute the mixture between bowls and serve.

257. DELICIOUS RACK OF LAMB
Prep & Cook Time: 30 minutes | Servings: 4

INGREDIENTS

28 oz. of rack of lamb
1 pc. of egg, whisked
2 pcs. of garlic cloves, minced

2 tbsp. of macadamia nuts, toasted & crushed
1 tbsp. of vegetable oil
1 tbsp. of chopped oregano

salt & black pepper to taste

INSTRUCTIONS

1. In a bowl, coat the lamb with the salt, pepper, garlic and the oil.
2. In another bowl, combine the macadamia nuts with the oregano, salt and pepper.
3. Place the egg in a third bowl.
4. Coat the lamb with the egg, then with the macadamia nuts mix.
5. Transfer the lamb in air fryer's basket and cook at 380°F for 10 minutes on each side.
6. Distribute between plates and serve with a side salad.

258. OREGANO PORK CHOPS
Prep & Cook Time: 20 minutes | Servings: 4

INGREDIENTS

4 cuts of pork chops
4 pcs. of garlic cloves, minced

2 tbsp. olive oil
2 tbsp. chopped oregano

salt & black pepper to taste

INSTRUCTIONS

1. In a bowl, combine all ingredients.
2. Place the chops to air fryer's basket and cook at 400°F for 15 minutes.
3. Serve with a side salad and enjoy!

259. LAMB CHOPS & DILL
Prep & Cook Time: 30 minutes | Servings: 6

INGREDIENTS

1 lb. of lamb chops
2 pcs. of yellow onions, chopped
3 cups of chicken stock

1½ cups of heavy cream
1 pc. of garlic clove, minced
1 tbsp. of olive oil

2 tbsp. of sweet paprika
2 tbsp. of chopped dill
salt & black pepper to taste

INSTRUCTIONS

1. Season the lamb with the salt, pepper, garlic and paprika, rub the chops thoroughly.
2. Put the lamb chops in air fryer and cook at 380°F for 10 minutes.
3. Place the lamb to a baking dish and add the onions, stock, cream and dill, toss.
4. Transfer the pan in the fryer and cook everything for 7-8 minutes more.
5. Distribute everything between plates and serve hot.

260. BEEF & SAUCE
Prep & Cook Time: 50 minutes | Servings: 6

INGREDIENTS

3 lbs. of beef roast
1¾ cups of beef stock
3/4 cup of red wine

3 pcs. of garlic cloves, minced
2 tbsp. of melted butter
1 tbsp. of mustard

salt & black pepper to taste

INSTRUCTIONS

1. In a bowl, coat the beef with the butter, mustard, garlic, salt and pepper.
2. Transfer the beef roast in air fryer's basket and cook at 400°F for 15 minutes.
3. Heat up a pan over medium-high heat and add the stock and the wine.
4. Put the beef roast and place the pan in the fryer, cook at 380°F for 25 minutes more.
5. Distribute into bowls and serve.

261. MUSTARD PORK CHOPS
Prep & Cook Time: 25 minutes | Servings: 6

INGREDIENTS

2 cuts of pork chops

2 pcs. of garlic cloves, minced

¼ cup of olive oil

1 tsp. of sweet paprika   1 tbsp. of mustard   salt & black pepper to taste

INSTRUCTIONS
1. Combine all ingredients except for the pork chops.
2. Coat the pork chops with the mixture and place it to air fryer's basket.
3. Cook at 400°F for 15 minutes. Distribute the chops between plates and serve.

262. PORK & BROCCOLI
Prep & Cook Time: 20 minutes | Servings: 4

INGREDIENTS
1 lb. of pork stew meat, cut into strips   ⅓ cup of oyster sauce
1 lb. of broccoli florets   1 tsp. of soy sauce
1 pc. of garlic clove, minced   2 tsp. of olive oil

INSTRUCTIONS
1. Combine the pork with all other ingredients in a bowl and toss well.
2. Place the mixture into air fryer and cook at 390°F for 15 minutes.
3. Distribute into bowls and serve.

263. FENNEL PORK
Prep & Cook Time: 20 minutes | Servings: 4

INGREDIENTS
2 cuts of pork chops   1 tbsp. of chopped rosemary   salt & black pepper to taste
1 tsp. of roasted fennel seeds   3 tbsp. of olive oil

INSTRUCTIONS
1. Combine all ingredients except for the pork chops.
2. Coat the pork chops with the mixture.
3. Put the chops to air fryer and cook at 400°F for 15 minutes.
4. Distribute the chops between plates and serve.

264. PORK CHOPS & SPINACH
Prep & Cook Time: 20 minutes | Servings: 4

INGREDIENTS
2 cuts of pork chops   2 cups of baby spinach   salt & black pepper to taste
¼ cup of beef stock   3 tbsp. spinach pesto

INSTRUCTIONS
1. In a bowl, combine the pork chops, salt, pepper and spinach pesto.
2. Transfer the pork chops in the air fryer and cook at 400°F for 4 minutes on each side.
3. Place the chops to a pan, pour the stock and add the baby spinach.
4. Transfer the pan in the fryer and cook at 400°F for 7 minutes more.
5. Distribute everything between plates and serve.

265. PORK & SPROUTS
Prep & Cook Time: 35 minutes | Servings: 4

INGREDIENTS
1½ lbs. of brussels sprouts, trimmed   2 tbsp. of olive oil   1 pc. of garlic clove, minced
1 lb. of pork tenderloin, cubed   2 tbsp. of chopped rosemary   salt & black pepper to taste
½ cup of sour cream   salt & black pepper to taste

INSTRUCTIONS
1. In a pan, combine pork with oil, rosemary, salt, pepper, garlic, salt and pepper.
2. Transfer the pan in the fryer and cook at 400°F for 17 minutes.
3. Put the sprouts and the sour cream, toss.
4. Transfer the pan in the fryer and cook for 8 more minutes.
5. Distribute everything into bowls and serve.

266. PORK & CHIVES
Prep & Cook Time: 32 minutes | Servings: 6

INGREDIENTS
1 lb. of pork tenderloin, cubed   2 pcs. of garlic cloves, minced   salt & black pepper to taste
¼ cup of chopped tarragon   2 tbsp. of mustard
1 cup of mayonnaise   2 tbsp. of chopped chives

INSTRUCTIONS
1. In a pan, combine all ingredients except the mayonnaise.
2. Transfer the pan in the fryer and cook at 400°F for 15 minutes.
3. Add mayonnaise and toss.
4. Place the pan in the fryer for 7 more minutes.
5. Distribute into bowls and serve.

267. GROUND BEEF
Prep & Cook Time: 25 minutes | Servings: 4

INGREDIENTS
1 lb. of ground beef   1 pc. of green bell pepper, chopped   ½ tsp. of cumin
¼ cup of tomato salsa   1 pc. of yellow onion, chopped   salt & black pepper to taste
2 pcs. of garlic cloves, minced   1 tbsp. of olive oil

INSTRUCTIONS
1. Heat up the oil in a pan over medium heat.
2. Sauté onion, garlic, bell peppers and cumin for 3 minutes.
3. Put the meat inside your Air Fryer's basket and cook for 3 minutes more and turn off the heat.
4. Pour the salsa, toss and place the pan in the fryer.
5. Cook at 380°F for 14 minutes more.
6. Distribute everything into bowls and serve.

268. BEEF ROAST & GRAPES
Prep & Cook Time: 50 minutes | Servings: 4

INGREDIENTS
1 lb. of beef roast meat, cubed   1½ cups of chicken stock   1 tsp. of chopped thyme
½ lb. of red grapes   ½ cup of dry white wine   3 tbsp. of olive oil
½ pc. of red onion, chopped   2 pcs. of garlic cloves, minced   salt & black pepper to taste

INSTRUCTIONS
1. Heat up the oil in a pan over medium-high heat.
2. Put the beef, salt and pepper, toss and brown for 5 minutes.
3. Pour the stock, wine, garlic, thyme and onions, cook for 5 minutes more.
4. Place the pan to the air fryer and cook at 390°F for 25 minutes.
5. Put the grapes, toss gently and cook everything for 5-6 minutes more.

6. Distribute between plates and serve right away.

---

269. PORK STEAKS

Prep & Cook Time: 20 minutes | Servings: 4

INGREDIENTS

4 cuts of pork steaks
1 tbsp. of sweet paprika

1 tbsp. of melted butter

salt & black pepper to taste

INSTRUCTIONS

1. Coat the pork steaks with the salt, pepper, butter and paprika.
2. Put the steaks to air fryer's basket and cook at 390°F for 7 minutes on each side.
3. Distribute the steaks between plates and serve.

---

270. SAGE PORK

Prep & Cook Time: 60 minutes | Servings: 6

INGREDIENTS

2½ lbs. of pork loin, boneless & cubed
3/4 cup of beef stock
½ tbsp. of smoked paprika

½ tbsp. of garlic powder
2 tbsp. of olive oil
1 tsp. of dried basil

3 tsp. of dried sage
1 tsp. of dried oregano
salt & black pepper to taste

INSTRUCTIONS

1. In a pan, heat up the oil over medium heat.
2. Put the pork, toss and brown for 5 minutes.
3. Put the remaining ingredients except for the beef stock, toss and cook for 2 more minutes.
4. Pour the stock and toss.
5. Transfer the pan in the fryer and cook at 360°F for 40 minutes.
6. Distribute everything between plates and serve.

---

271. PORK CHOPS

Prep & Cook Time: 20 minutes | Servings: 4

INGREDIENTS

4 cuts of medium pork chops
1 tbsp. of olive oil
1 tbsp. of ground cumin

1 tbsp. of dried rosemary
2 tbsp. of sweet paprika
2 tbsp. of onion powder

2 tbsp. of garlic powder
2 tbsp. of dried oregano
salt & black pepper to taste

INSTRUCTIONS

1. In a bowl, combine all of the ingredients and coat the pork chops well.
2. Transfer the pork chops in air fryer's basket.
3. Cook at 400°F for 15 minutes, flipping them halfway.
4. Distribute between plates.
5. Serve and enjoy!

---

272. JALAPENO BEEF

Prep & Cook Time: 45 minutes | Servings: 6

INGREDIENTS

1½ lbs. of ground beef
16 oz. of drained canned white beans
20 oz. of chopped canned tomatoes
1 pc. of red onion, chopped

6 pcs. of garlic cloves, chopped
7 pcs. of jalapeno peppers, diced
1 cup of beef stock
3 tbsp. of chili powder

2 tbsp. of olive oil
salt & black pepper to taste

INSTRUCTIONS

1. Heat up the oil in a pan over medium heat.
2. Put the beef and the onions, stir and cook for 2 minutes.
3. Put all remaining ingredients and stir, cook for 3 minutes more.
4. Transfer the pan in the air fryer and cook at 380°F for 35 minutes.
5. Distribute everything into bowls and serve.

---

273. BEEF ROAST

Prep & Cook Time: 65 minutes | Servings: 4

INGREDIENTS

2 lbs. of beef roast
3 tbsp. of minced garlic

3 tbsp. of olive oil
1 tbsp. of smoked paprika

salt & black pepper to taste

INSTRUCTIONS

1. In a bowl, mix all the ingredients and rub the roast well.
2. Transfer the roast in air fryer and cook at 390°F for 55 minutes.
3. Cut the roast and distribute it between plates.
4. Serve with a side salad.

---

274. BEEF &CELERY

Prep & Cook Time: 65 minutes | Servings: 6

INGREDIENTS

1 lb. of chopped yellow onion
3 lbs. of beef roast
16 oz. of chopped canned tomatoes

1 lb. of chopped celery
3 cups of beef stock
2 tbsp. of olive oil

salt & black pepper to taste

INSTRUCTIONS

1. Combine all ingredients in baking dish.
2. Transfer the baking dish in the fryer and cook at 390°F for 55 minutes.
3. Cut the roast and then distribute it with the celery mix between plates.
4. Serve and enjoy!

---

275. GARLICKY LOIN ROAST

Prep & Cook Time: 60 minutes | Servings: 4

INGREDIENTS

1 lb. of pork loin roast
3 pcs. of garlic cloves, minced

1 tbsp. of chopped rosemary
2 tbsp. of panko breadcrumbs

1 tbsp. of olive oil
salt & black pepper to taste

INSTRUCTIONS

1. Combine all ingredients except the roast into a bowl.
2. Coat the roast with the mixture.
3. Transfer the roast in the air fryer and cook at 360°F for 55 minutes.
4. Cut the roast and distribute it between plates.
5. Serve with a side salad.

---

276. PORK & CAULIFLOWER

Prep & Cook Time: 28 minutes | Servings: 4

INGREDIENTS

1 lb. of pork stew meat, cubed
1 pc. of cauliflower head, florets separated
⅓ cup of balsamic vinegar

1 pc. of garlic clove, minced
2 tbsp. of olive oil
1 tsp. of soy sauce

1 tsp. of sugar

INSTRUCTIONS
1. Combine all the ingredients in a pan and mix well.
2. Transfer the pan into the fryer and cook at 390°F for 22 minutes.
3. Distribute into bowls.
4. Serve and enjoy!

277. CHINESE STYLE BEEF
Prep & Cook Time: 25 minutes | Servings: 4

INGREDIENTS

1 lb. of beef stew meat, cut into strips
¼ cup of toasted sesame seeds

1 cup of chopped green onion
1 cup of soy sauce

5 pcs. of garlic cloves, minced
black pepper to taste

INSTRUCTIONS
1. In a pan, combine all ingredients.
2. Transfer the pan in the fryer and cook at 390°F for 20 minutes.
3. Distribute everything into bowls and serve.

278. PORK & PEANUTS
Prep & Cook Time: 20 minutes | Servings: 4

INGREDIENTS

14 oz. cubed pork chops
3 oz. chopped peanuts
7 oz. coconut milk

2 pcs. of garlic cloves, minced
1 pc. of shallot, chopped
2 tsp. chili paste

1 tsp. ground coriander
2 tbsp. olive oil
salt & black pepper to taste

INSTRUCTIONS
1. Combine all of the ingredients into a pan.
2. Transfer the pan in the fryer and cook at 400°F for 15 minutes.
3. Distribute into bowls and serve.

279. LAMB & BEANS
Prep & Cook Time: 35 minutes | Servings: 4

INGREDIENTS

3 oz. of drained canned kidney beans
8 oz. of cubed lamb loin
1 pc. of garlic clove, minced

1 pc. of yellow onion, sliced
1 pc. of carrot, chopped
½ tbsp. of olive oil

1 tbsp. of grated ginger
3 tbsp. of soy sauce
salt & black pepper to taste

INSTRUCTIONS
1. In baking dish, combine all of the ingredients.
2. Transfer the dish in the fryer and cook at 390°F for 30 minutes.
3. Distribute everything into bowls and serve.

280. PORK CHOPS & MUSHROOMS MIX
Prep & Cook Time: 50 Minutes | Servings: 3

INGREDIENTS

3 cuts of pork chops, boneless
8 oz. of sliced mushrooms
1 tsp. of garlic powder

1 pc. of yellow onion, chopped
1 tsp. of nutmeg
1 tbsp. of balsamic vinegar

1 cup of mayonnaise
½ cup of olive oil

INSTRUCTIONS
1. Heat up a pan with the oil over medium heat.
2. Put mushrooms and onions inside your Air Fryer's basket and cook for 4 minutes.
3. Put pork chops, nutmeg and garlic powder and brown on both sides.
4. Transfer pan your air fryer at 330°F and cook for 30 minutes.
5. Pour vinegar and mayo, stir.
6. Distribute everything on plates and serve.

281. BEEF & PEAS
Prep & Cook Time: 25 minutes | Servings: 2

INGREDIENTS

2 cuts of beef steaks, cut into strips
14 oz. of snow peas

2 tbsp. of soy sauce
1 tbsp. of olive oil

salt & black pepper to taste

INSTRUCTIONS
1. In a pan, combine all ingredients.
2. Transfer the pan in the fryer and cook at 390°F for 25 minutes.
3. Distribute everything between plates and serve!

282. LAMB MEATBALLS
Prep & Cook Time: 22 minutes | Servings: 8

INGREDIENTS

4 oz. of minced lamb meat
1 pc. of egg, whisked

1 tbsp. of chopped oregano
½ tbsp. of lemon zest

cooking spray
salt & black pepper to taste

INSTRUCTIONS
1. In a bowl, mix all of the ingredients except the cooking spray.
2. Mould medium-sized meatballs out of this mixture.
3. Transfer the meatballs in your air fryer's basket, grease them with cooking spray.
4. Cook at 400°F for 12 minutes.
5. Distribute between plates and serve.

283. BEEF, ARUGULA & LEEKS
Prep & Cook Time: 22 minutes | Servings: 4

INGREDIENTS

1 lb. of ground beef
5 oz. of baby arugula

3 pcs. of leeks, roughly chopped
1 tbsp. of olive oil

2 tbsp. of tomato paste
salt & black pepper to taste

INSTRUCTIONS
1. In a pan, combine the beef with the leeks, salt, pepper, oil and the tomato paste, toss well.
2. Transfer the pan in the fryer and cook at 380°F for 12 minutes.
3. Put the arugula and toss.
4. Distribute into bowls and serve.

284. PORK MEATLOAF
Prep & Cook Time: 25 minutes | Servings: 4

INGREDIENTS

1 lb. of ground pork meat
1 oz. of chopped chorizo
1 pc. of egg, whisked

1 pc. of yellow onion, chopped
3 tbsp. of breadcrumbs
1 tbsp. of chopped thyme

cooking spray
salt & black pepper to taste

INSTRUCTIONS

1. Combine all of the ingredients (except the cooking spray) in a bowl.
2. Place the mixture to a loaf pan, greased with cooking spray.
3. Transfer the pan in the fryer and cook at 390°F for 20 minutes.
4. Cut and serve.

285. PAPRIKA BEEF

Prep & Cook Time: 30 minutes | Servings: 4

INGREDIENTS

1½ lbs. of beef fillet
1 pc. of red onion, roughly chopped
½ cup of beef stock

3 tsp. of sweet paprika
2 tbsp. of olive oil
1 tbsp. of tomato paste

1 tbsp. of Worcestershire sauce
salt & black pepper to taste

INSTRUCTIONS

1. In a bowl, combine all remaining ingredients, toss well.
2. Place the mixture to a pan and cook at 400°F for 26 minutes, shaking the air fryer halfway.
3. Distribute everything between plates and serve.

286. LAMB RIBS

Prep & Cook Time: 20 minutes | Servings: 4

INGREDIENTS

4 lamb ribs
1 cup of veggie stock
4 pcs. of garlic cloves, minced

¼ tsp. smoked paprika
½ tsp. chili powder
2 tbsp. extra virgin olive oil

salt & black pepper to taste

INSTRUCTIONS

1. In a bowl, mix all of the ingredients except the ribs.
2. Place the ribs and coat them thoroughly with the mixture.
3. Put the ribs to air fryer's basket and cook at 390°F for 7 minutes on each side.
4. Serve with a side salad.

287. BEEF & PLUMS

Prep & Cook Time: 50 minutes | Servings: 6

INGREDIENTS

1½ lbs. beef stew meat, cubed
9 oz. of plums, pitted & halved
8 oz. of beef stock
2 pcs. of yellow onions, chopped

2 pcs. of garlic cloves, minced
3 tbsp. of honey
2 tbsp. of olive oil
1 tsp. of ginger powder

1 tsp. of cinnamon powder
1 tsp. of turmeric powder
salt & black pepper to taste

INSTRUCTIONS

1. In a pan, heat up the oil over medium heat.
2. Put the beef, stir and brown for 2 minutes.
3. Pour the honey, onions, garlic, salt, pepper, turmeric, ginger and cinnamon, toss and cook for 2-3 minutes more
4. Put the plums and the stock, toss again.
5. Transfer the pan in the fryer and cook at 380°F for 30 minutes.
6. Distribute everything into bowls and serve.

288. DELICIOUS SAUSAGE

Prep & Cook Time: 25 minutes | Servings: 4

INGREDIENTS

6 pcs. of pork sausage links, halved
1 pc. of red onion, sliced
2 pcs. of garlic cloves, minced

1 tbsp. of sweet paprika
1 tbsp. of olive oil
1 tbsp. of chopped rosemary

salt & black pepper to taste

INSTRUCTIONS

1. In a pan, combine all of the ingredients and toss.
2. Transfer the pan in the fryer and cook at 360°F for 20 minutes.
3. Distribute between plates and serve

289. MARINATED LAMB & VEGGIES

Prep & Cook Time: 40 Minutes | Servings: 4

INGREDIENTS

1 pc. of carrot, chopped
1 pc. of onion, sliced

8 oz. of lamb loin, sliced
½ tbsp. of olive oil

3 oz. of bean sprouts

FOR THE MARINADE:

1 pc. of garlic clove, minced
½ of apple, grated
1 tbsp. of grated ginger

1 pc. of small yellow onion, grated
2 tbsp. of orange juice
5 tbsp. of soy sauce

1 tbsp. of sugar
salt & black pepper to the taste

INSTRUCTIONS

1. In a bowl, combine 1 grated onion with the apple, garlic, 1 tablespoon ginger, soy sauce, orange juice, sugar and black pepper, whisk well, add lamb and set aside for 10 minutes.
2. Heat up a pan with the olive oil over medium high heat.
3. Put 1 sliced onion, carrot and bean sprouts, stir and cook for 3 minutes.
4. Put the lamb and the marinade.
5. Place pan to your preheated air fryer and cook at 360°F, for 25 minutes.
6. Distribute everything into bowls and serve.

290. CREAMY BEEF

Prep & Cook Time: 55 minutes | Serving: 4

INGREDIENTS

1½ lbs. of cubed beef
4 oz. of brown mushrooms, sliced
8 oz. of sour cream

1 pc. of red onion, chopped
2 pcs. of garlic cloves, minced
2½ tbsp. of vegetable oil

1½ tbsp. of white flour
1 tbsp. of chopped cilantro
salt & black pepper to taste

INSTRUCTION

1. In a bowl, combine the beef with the salt, pepper and flour, toss.
2. Heat up the oil in a pan over medium-high heat.
3. Put the beef, onions and garlic, stir and cook for 5 minutes.
4. Put the mushrooms and toss.
5. Transfer the pan in the fryer and cook at 380°F for 35 minutes.
6. Pour the sour cream and cilantro and toss, cook for 5 minutes more.
7. Distribute everything between plates and serve.

291. CINNAMON BEEF

Prep & Cook Time: 60 minutes | Servings: 6

INGREDIENTS

2 lbs. of beef roast
2 pcs. of yellow onions, thinly sliced
2 pcs. of garlic cloves, minced

1 cup of beef stock
juice of 1 lemon
1 tbsp. of chopped cilantro

1½ tbsp. of cinnamon powder
salt & black pepper to taste

INSTRUCTIONS

1. In a baking dish, combine the roast with all other ingredients.
2. Transfer the dish in your fryer and cook at 390°F for 55 minutes, flipping the roast halfway.
3. Carve the roast and distribute between plates
4. Serve with the cooking juices drizzled on top, enjoy!

292. BEEF KABOBS RECIPE

Prep & Cook Time: 20 Minutes | Servings: 4

INGREDIENTS

2 pcs. of red bell peppers, chopped
2 lbs. of sirloin steak, cut into medium pieces
1 pc. of red onion, chopped
1 pc. of zucchini, sliced

juice form 1 lime
2 tbsp. of chili powder
2 tbsp. of hot sauce
½ tbsp. of ground cumin

¼ cup of olive oil
¼ cup of salsa
salt & black pepper to the taste

INSTRUCTIONS

1. In a bowl, combine salsa with lime juice, oil, hot sauce, chili powder, cumin, salt and black pepper and whisk well.
2. Split meat bell peppers, zucchini and onion on skewers, brush kabobs with the salsa mix you made earlier, put them in your preheated air fryer and cook them for 10 minutes at 370°F, flipping kabobs halfway.
3. Distribute among plates and serve with a side salad.

293. CRISPY LAMB RECIPE

Prep & Cook Time: 40 Minutes | Servings: 2

INGREDIENTS

1 tbsp. of breadcrumbs
1 tbsp. of olive oil
1 pc. of egg,

1 tbsp. of chopped rosemary
1 pc. of garlic clove, minced
28 oz. of rack of lamb

2 tbsp. of macadamia nuts, toasted & crushed
salt & black pepper to the taste

INSTRUCTIONS

1. In a bowl, combine oil with garlic and stir well.
2. Coat lamb with salt, pepper and brush with the oil.
3. In another bowl, combine nuts with breadcrumbs and rosemary.
4. Put the egg in a separate bowl and whisk well.
5. Dip lamb in egg, then in macadamia mix.
6. Place them in your air fryer's basket, cook at 360°F and cook for 25 minutes, increase heat to 400°F and cook for 5 minutes more.
7. Distribute among plates and serve right away.

294. HOT PORK DELIGHT

Prep & Cook Time: 28 minutes | Servings: 4

INGREDIENTS

1 lb. of pork tenderloin, cubed
1 pc. of red onion, chopped
1 pc. garlic clove, minced

½ tsp. of hot chili powder
1 tsp. of cinnamon powder
2 tbsp. of olive oil

3 tbsp. of chopped parsley
salt & black pepper to taste

INSTRUCTIONS

1. In a bowl, mix the chili, cinnamon, garlic, salt, pepper and the oil.
2. Coat the pork with the mixture.
3. Place the meat to your air fryer and cook at 280°F for 12 minutes.
4. Put the onions and cook for 5 minutes more.
5. Distribute everything between plates.
6. Serve with the parsley sprinkled on top.

295. BASIL BEEF ROAST

Prep & Cook Time: 60 minutes | Servings: 6

INGREDIENTS

1½ lbs. of beef roast
2 pcs. of garlic cloves, minced

2 pcs. of carrots, sliced
1 cup of beef stock

1 tbsp. of dried basil
salt & black pepper to taste

INSTRUCTIONS

1. In a pan, mix all ingredients well.
2. Transfer the pan in the fryer and cook at 390°F for 55 minutes.
3. Cut the roast and distribute it with the carrots between plates.
4. Serve with cooking juices drizzled on top.

296. BEEF & CHIVES MARINADE

Prep & Cook Time: 60 minutes | Servings: 6

INGREDIENTS

2 lbs. of beef roast
3 pcs. of garlic cloves, minced

1 cup of balsamic vinegar
2 tbsp. of olive oil

2 tbsp. of minced chives
salt & black pepper to taste

INSTRUCTIONS

1. In a bowl, combine the oil, vinegar and spices (all ingredients except for the roast)
2. Coat the roast with the mixture.
3. Place the roast to your air fryer's basket and cook at 390°F for 55 minutes, flipping the roast halfway.
4. Carve and serve right away.

297. CUMIN BEEF

Prep & Cook Time: 40 minutes | Servings: 4

INGREDIENTS

1 lb. of ground beef
4 oz. of drained canned kidney beans
8 oz. of chopped canned tomatoes

1 pc. of yellow onion, chopped
2 pcs. of garlic cloves, minced
2 tbsp. of olive oil

2 tsp. of ground cumin
salt & black pepper to taste

INSTRUCTIONS

1. Heat up the oil in a pan over medium heat.
2. Put the onion and the beef, stir and cook for 2-3 minutes.
3. Put the garlic, salt, pepper, beans, tomatoes and the cumin, cook for another 2 minutes.
4. Place the pan to your air fryer and cook at 380°F for 30 minutes.
5. Distribute everything into bowls and serve.

298. MARINATED BEEF

Prep & Cook Time: 30 minutes | Servings: 4

INGREDIENTS

3 lbs. chuck roast, cut into thin strips
½ cup soy sauce
½ cup black soy sauce

5 pcs. of garlic cloves, minced
3 pcs. of red peppers, dried & crushed
1 tbsp. olive oil

2 tbsp. fish sauce

INSTRUCTIONS

1. In a bowl, mix the beef with all ingredients, set aside in the fridge for 10 minutes.
2. Place the beef to air fryer's basket and cook at 380°F for 20 minutes.
3. Serve with a side salad.

299. LAMB & CARROTS

Prep & Cook Time: 40 minutes | Servings: 6

INGREDIENTS

1½ lbs. of ground lamb
4 pcs. of garlic cloves, minced
4 pcs. of carrots, grated

1 cup of beef stock
1 pc. of yellow onion, chopped
½ tbsp. of olive oil

1 tbsp. of red wine
½ tsp. of smoked paprika
salt & black pepper to taste

INSTRUCTIONS

1. Heat up a pan that with the oil over medium heat, add the lamb, brown for 1-2 minutes.
2. Put all remaining ingredients and toss well, cook for 2 more minutes.
3. Place the pan to your air fryer and cook at 380°F for 25 minutes.
4. Distribute the mix into bowls and serve.

300. BEEF CURRY

Prep & Cook Time: 40 minutes | Servings: 4

INGREDIENTS

2 lbs. of cubed beef
10 oz. of coconut milk
2 pcs. of yellow onions, chopped

2 pcs. of garlic cloves, minced
3 pcs. of potatoes, diced
1 pc. of tomato, cubed

2 tbsp. of olive oil
2½ tbsp. of curry powder
salt & black pepper to taste

INSTRUCTIONS

1. In a pan, heat up the oil over medium heat.
2. Put the meat and brown it for 2-3 minutes.
3. Put the potatoes, tomato, curry powder, onions, garlic, salt and pepper, toss and cook for 2 more minutes.
4. Place the pan to your air fryer and cook at 380°F for 25 minutes.
5. Pour the coconut milk, toss and cook for 5 minutes more.
6. Distribute everything into bowls, serve and enjoy.

301. PORK CHOPS & GREEN BEANS

Prep & Cook Time: 25 Minutes | Servings: 4

INGREDIENTS

4 cuts of pork chops, bone in
3 pcs. of garlic cloves, minced
2 tbsp. of chopped parsley

1 tbsp. of chopped sage
2 tbsp. of olive oil
16 oz. of green beans

salt & black pepper to the taste

INSTRUCTIONS

1. In a pan, combine pork chops with olive oil, sage, salt, pepper, green beans, garlic and parsley.
2. Transfer in your air fryer and cook at 360°F, for 15 minutes.
2. Distribute everything on plates and serve

302. LAMB ROAST & POTATOES RECIPE

Prep & Cook Time: 55 Minutes | Servings: 6

INGREDIENTS

4 lbs. of lamb roast
6 pcs. of potatoes, halved
½ cup of lamb stock

4 pcs. of bay leaves
3 pcs. of garlic cloves, minced
1 spring rosemary

salt & black pepper to the taste

INSTRUCTIONS

1. Place potatoes in a dish, add lamb, garlic, rosemary spring, salt, pepper, bay leaves and stock.
2. Transfer in air fryer and cook at 360°F, for 45 minutes.
3. Cut lamb and distribute among plates.
4.Sserve with potatoes and cooking juices.

303. MILKY LAMB

Prep & Cook Time: 20 minutes | Servings: 4

INGREDIENTS

1 lb. of lamb chops
1 cup of coconut milk
1 pc. of garlic clove, minced

2 tbsp. of olive oil
1 tbsp. of chopped rosemary
1 tbsp. of melted butter

salt & black pepper to taste

INSTRUCTIONS

1. In a pan, coat the lamb chops with salt and pepper.
2. Put the oil, rosemary, garlic, butter and milk to the pan, toss well.
3. Transfer the pan in the fryer and cook at 400°F for 15 minutes.
4. Distribute the mix between plates and serve.

304. PORK CURRY

Prep & Cook Time: 35 minutes | Servings: 4

INGREDIENTS

1 lb. of pork stew meat, cubed
2 oz. of coconut cream
1 pc. of yellow onion, chopped

3 tbsp. of pure cream
3 tbsp. of curry powder
1 tbsp. of chopped cilantro

2 tbsp. of olive oil
salt & black pepper to taste

INSTRUCTIONS

1. In a bowl, combine the pork with the curry powder, salt and pepper.
2. Heat up a pan with the oil over medium-high heat, add the pork, toss and brown for 3 minutes.
3. Pour the coconut cream, pure cream and onions, toss.
4. Transfer the pan in the fryer and cook at 380°F for 25 minutes.
5. Put the cilantro and toss.
6. Distribute everything into bowls and serve.

305. HAM & VEGGIE AIR FRIED MIX

Prep & Cook Time: 30 Minutes | Servings: 6

INGREDIENTS

¼ cup of butter

3 cups of milk

½ tsp. of dried thyme

2 cups of chopped ham　　　　　6 oz. of sweet peas　　　　　1 cup of baby carrots
¼ cup of flour　　　　　4 oz. of mushrooms, halved
INSTRUCTIONS
1. Heat up a large pan with the butter over medium heat, melt it, add flour and whisk well.
2. Pour milk and turn off heat.
3. Put thyme, ham, peas, mushrooms and baby carrots.
4. Place it in your air fryer and cook at 360°F, for 20 minutes.
5. Distribute everything on plates and serve.

306. MUSTARD PORK CHOPS
Prep & Cook Time: 20 minutes | Servings: 6

INGREDIENTS
2 lbs. pork chops　　　　　4 tbsp. mustard　　　　　salt & black pepper to taste
3 pcs. of garlic cloves, minced　　　　　2 tbsp. chopped chives
INSTRUCTIONS
1. In a bowl, Combine the pork chops with the other ingredients and coat the chops well.
2. Transfer the pork chops in air fryer's basket and cook at 400°F for 7 minutes on each side.
3. Serve right away.

307. SIMPLE BRAISED PORK RECIPE
Prep & Cook Time: 1 hour 20 Minutes | Servings: 4

INGREDIENTS
2 lbs. of pork loin roast, boneless & cubed　　　2 pcs. of garlic cloves, minced　　　1 bay leaf
2 cups of chicken stock　　　　　1 tsp. of chopped thyme　　　　　½ pc. yellow onion, chopped
4 tbsp. of melted butter　　　　　1 pc. of thyme spring　　　　　2 tbsp. of white flour
½ cup of dry white wine　　　　　½ lb. of red grapes　　　　　salt & black pepper to the taste
INSTRUCTIONS
1. Season pork cubes with salt and pepper, coat with 2 tablespoon melted butter, put in your air fryer and cook at 370°F, for 8 minutes.
2. In the meantime, heat up a pan with 2 tablespoon of butter over medium high heat, sauté garlic and onion for 2 minutes.
3. Pour wine, stock, salt, pepper, thyme, flour and bay leaf.
4. Bring to a simmer and turn off heat.
5. Put pork cubes and grapes, toss.
6. Transfer in your air fryer and cook at 360°F, for 30 minutes more.
7. Distribute everything on plates and serve.

308. BBQ LAMB CHOPS
Prep & Cook Time: 20 minutes | Servings: 4

INGREDIENTS
14 oz. of chopped canned tomatoes　　　2 tbsp. of olive oil　　　2 tbsp. of tomato sauce
4 cuts of lamb chops　　　　　2 pcs. of garlic cloves, crushed　　　salt & black pepper to taste
3 oz. of red wine　　　　　2 tbsp. of BBQ sauce
2 tbsp. of flour　　　　　2 tbsp. of cilantro, chopped.
INSTRUCTIONS
1. In a bowl, combine the lamb chops with salt, pepper and the flour, coat the lamb chops well.
2. Heat up a pan with the oil over medium heat, add the lamb, toss and brown for 2-3 minutes.
3. Put the garlic, wine, tomato sauce, barbeque sauce and tomatoes, toss again.
4. Transfer the pan in the fryer and cook at 400°F for 12 minutes.
5. Distribute between plates and serve.

309. FRYER LAMB SHANKS RECIPE
Prep & Cook Time: 55 Minutes | Servings: 4

INGREDIENTS
4 cuts of lamb shanks　　　　　2 tbsp. of white flour　　　　　4 bay leaves
1 pc. of yellow onion, chopped　　　1 tbsp. of olive oil　　　salt & pepper to the taste
2 ½ cups of chicken stock　　　　　2 tsp. of honey
4 tsp. of crushed coriander seeds　　　5 oz. of dry sherry
INSTRUCTIONS
1. Season lamb shanks with salt and pepper, coat with half of the oil.
2. Transfer in your air fryer and cook at 360°F, for 10 minutes.
3. Heat up a pan with the rest of the oil over medium high heat.
4. Put onion and coriander, stir and cook for 5 minutes.
5. Put flour, sherry, stock, honey and bay leaves, salt and pepper, let it simmer, add lamb.
6. Transfer everything in your air fryer and cook at 360°F, for 30 minutes.
7. Distribute everything on plates and serve.

310. FRENCH STYLE LAMB
Prep & Cook Time: 30 minutes | Servings: 4

INGREDIENTS
1½ lbs. of lamb chops　　　　　4 pcs. of tomatoes, chopped　　　½ tsp. of dried mint
½ lbs. of sliced mushrooms　　　2 tbsp. of tomato paste　　　a handful of chopped cilantro
1 pc. of small yellow onion, chopped　　　1 tsp. of olive oil　　　salt & black pepper to taste
6 pcs. of garlic cloves, minced　　　1 tsp. of dried oregano
INSTRUCTIONS
1. Heat up a pan with the oil over medium heat.
2. Put the lamb chops, salt, pepper, oregano and mint, toss and brown for 2-3 minutes.
3. Put the mushrooms, onions, garlic, tomatoes and tomato paste, toss and cook for 2 more minutes.
4. Transfer the pan in the fryer and cook at 400°F for 12 minutes more.
5. Put the cilantro and toss.
6. Distribute everything between plates and serve.

311. GREAT PORK CHOPS
Prep & Cook Time: 25 minutes | Servings: 2

INGREDIENTS
4 cuts of pork chops　　　　　2 pcs. of garlic cloves, minced　　　2 tbsp. of tomato paste
4 oz. of red wine　　　　　2 tbsp. of olive oil　　　　　1 tsp. of dried oregano
1 pc. of yellow onion, minced　　　2 tbsp. of white flour　　　salt & black pepper to taste
INSTRUCTIONS
1. In a bowl, combine the pork chops with the flour, salt and pepper, coat the chops well.
2. Heat up the oil in a pan over medium heat.
3. Put the pork chops and brown for 2-3 minutes.
4. Put the onions, garlic, oregano and wine, stir and cook for 2 more minutes.
5. Pour tomato paste, toss and transfer the pan into the fryer.
6. Cook at 380°F for 14 minutes and distribute between plates.

7. Serve with a side salad and enjoy!

312. PORK & SHALLOTS
Prep & Cook Time: 45 minutes | Servings: 4

INGREDIENTS

1½ lbs. of cubed pork stew meat
3 oz. of sliced white mushrooms
16 oz. of chopped shallots
2 oz. of white wine

2 oz. of cubed canned tomatoes
2 pcs. of garlic cloves, minced
½ cup of beef stock
2 tbsp. of chopped chives

2 tbsp. of olive oil
1 tbsp. of chopped cilantro
salt & black pepper to taste

INSTRUCTIONS

1. Heat up a pan with the oil over medium heat.
2. Put the meat, stir and brown for 2 minutes.
3. Put the shallots, garlic, chives, salt, pepper and mushrooms, toss and cook for 2 minutes more.
4. Put the mushrooms, tomatoes, wine and stock, stir well.
5. Simmer for about 1 minute.
6. Place the pan to an air fryer, cook at 380°F for 30 minutes.
7. Put the cilantro and toss.
8. Distribute everything into bowls and serve.

313. BEEF CASSEROLE
Prep & Cook Time: 45 minutes | Servings: 4

INGREDIENTS

1 lb. of ground beef, browned
13 oz. of shredded mozzarella cheese
16 oz. of tomato puree

17 oz. of cooked small pasta
1 pc. of yellow onion, chopped
1 pc. of carrot, chopped

1 stalk of celery, chopped
cooking spray
salt & black pepper to taste

INSTRUCTIONS

1. Grease a baking dish with cooking spray and spread the pasta on the bottom.
2. Layer beef, tomato puree, celery, onion and carrots.
3. Season with salt and pepper and sprinkle the mozzarella on top.
4. Transfer the dish in the air fryer and cook at 380°F for 35 minutes.
5. Distribute between plates and serve.

314. BEEF CASSEROLE RECIPE
Prep & Cook Time: 65 Minutes | Servings: 12

INGREDIENTS

28 oz. of chopped canned tomatoes
1 tbsp. of olive oil
2 lbs. of ground beef
16 oz. of tomato sauce

2 tsp. of mustard
2 tbsp. of chopped parsley
2 cups of chopped eggplant
2 tsp. of gluten free Worcestershire sauce

2 cups of grated mozzarella
1 tsp. of dried oregano
salt & black pepper to taste

INSTRUCTIONS

1. In a bowl, combine eggplant with salt, pepper and oil and toss to coat
2. In another bowl, combine beef with salt, pepper, mustard and Worcestershire sauce
3. Spread mixture on the bottom of a pan.
4. Put eggplant mix, tomatoes, tomato sauce, parsley, oregano and sprinkle mozzarella at the end.
5. Transfer in air fryer and cook at 360°F, for 35 minutes.
6. Distribute among plates and serve hot.

315. PORK & CABBAGE
Prep & Cook Time: 45 minutes | Servings: 6

INGREDIENTS

2½ lbs. of pork stew meat, cubed
3 pcs. of garlic cloves, chopped
4 pcs. of carrots, chopped.

1 pc. of red cabbage head, shredded
2 pcs. of bay leaves
½ cup of tomato sauce

2 tsp. of olive oil
salt & black pepper to taste

INSTRUCTIONS

1. Heat up a pan with the oil over medium-high heat, add the meat and brown it for 5 minutes.
2. Put all remaining ingredients and toss.
3. Transfer the pan in the fryer and cook at 380°F for 30 minutes.
4. Distribute the mix between plates and serve.

316. BEEF & TOFU
Prep & Cook Time: 40 minutes | Servings: 6

INGREDIENTS

2 lbs. beef steak, cut into thin strips &browned
12 oz. extra firm tofu, cubed
1 pc. of chili pepper, sliced

1 pc. of scallion, chopped
1 pc. of yellow onion, thinly sliced
1 cup of beef stock

salt & black pepper to taste

INSTRUCTIONS

1. Combine all of the ingredients in a pan.
2. Transfer the pan in the fryer and cook at 380°F for 30 minutes.
3. Distribute between plates and serve.

317. PORK & CELERY
Prep & Cook Time: 40 minutes | Servings: 4

INGREDIENTS

1½ lbs. of cubed pork stew meat
1 pc. of yellow onion, chopped
2 cups of beef stock
¼ cup of tomato sauce

2 pcs. of garlic cloves, minced
3 stalks of celery, chopped
½ bunch of parsley, chopped
2 tbsp. of olive oil

2 tbsp. of red wine
salt & black pepper to taste

INSTRUCTIONS

1. In a pan, heat up the oil over medium heat.
2. Put the pork and brown for 2-3 minutes.
3. Put the onions, garlic, wine, salt, pepper, tomato sauce and celery, cook for 2 minutes more.
4. Transfer the pan in the fryer and cook at 380°F for 30 minutes.
5. Distribute between plates and serve with the parsley sprinkled on top.

318. GREEK STYLE LAMB CHOPS
Prep & Cook Time: 24 minutes | Servings: 4

INGREDIENTS

4 cuts of lamb chops

1 cup of green olives, pitted & sliced

3 pcs. of garlic cloves, minced

½ cup of veggie stock
1 tbsp. of white flour

2 tbsp. of olive oil
1 tsp. of dried marjoram

1 tsp. of dried thyme
salt & black pepper to taste

INSTRUCTIONS
1. Combine all ingredients except the olives in a bowl. Set aside in the fridge for 10 minutes.
2. Place the lamb chops to air fryer's basket and cook at 390°F for 7 minutes on each side.
3. Distribute the lamb chops between plates, sprinkle the olives on top and serve.

---

319. BEEF FILLETS WITH GARLIC MAYO RECIPE

Prep & Cook Time: 50 Minutes | Servings: 8

INGREDIENTS
3 lbs. of beef fillet
1 cup of mayonnaise
2 tbsp. of mustard
¼ cup of chopped tarragon

⅓ cup of sour cream
2 tbsp. of chopped chives
2 tbsp. of mustard
2 pcs. of garlic cloves, minced

salt & black pepper to the taste

INSTRUCTIONS
1. Season beef with salt and pepper to the taste.
2. Transfer in air fryer and cook at 370°F for 20 minutes.
3. Place to a plate and set aside for a few minutes.
4. In a bowl, combine garlic with sour cream, chives, mayo, some salt and pepper. Set aside.
5. In another bowl, combine mustard with Dijon mustard and tarragon, add beef, toss, return to your air fryer and cook at 350°F, for 20 minutes more.
6. Distribute beef on plates, spread garlic mayo on top and serve.

---

320. COD FILLETS & KALE SALAD

Prep & Cook Time: 20 minutes | Servings: 2

INGREDIENTS
2 pcs. of black cod fillets, boneless
1 pc. of fennel bulb, thinly sliced
3 cups of shredded kale leaves

½ cup of pecans
1 cup of halved grapes
2 tbsp. of olive oil + 1 tsp.

2 tsp. of balsamic vinegar
salt & black pepper to taste

INSTRUCTIONS
1. Place the fish in the air fryer's basket, add salt and pepper.
2. Drizzle 1 tsp. of the olive oil over the fish, cook at 400°F for 10 minutes.
3. Distribute fish between plates.
4. In a bowl, combine the remaining ingredients.
5. Distribute the salad next to the fish.
6. Serve and enjoy.

---

321. CHICKEN PIZZA ROLLS

Prep & Cook Time: 40 minutes | Servings: 4

INGREDIENTS
2 pcs. of chicken breasts, skinless, boneless & sliced
14 oz. of pizza dough

1½ cups of grated parmesan cheese
½ cup of tomato sauce
1 pc. of yellow onion, sliced

2 tsp. of olive oil
1 tbsp. of Worcestershire sauce
salt & black pepper to taste

INSTRUCTIONS
1. Preheat the air fryer at 400°F.
2. Put the onion and half of olive oil.
3. Fry for 8 minutes, shaking the fryer halfway.
4. Put the chicken, Worcestershire sauce, salt and pepper, and fry for 8 minutes more.
5. Transfer to the bowl.
6. Roll the pizza dough on a working surface, and shape into a rectangle.
7. Layer with cheese, chicken and onion mix, and tomato sauce.
8. Roll the dough and brush it with the remaining oil.
9. Put it in the air fryer's basket, cook at 370°F for 14 minutes, flipping the roll halfway.
10. Slice your roll and serve.

---

322. DIJON HOT DOGS

Prep & Cook Time: 13 minutes | Servings: 2

INGREDIENTS
2 pcs. of hot dog buns
2 pcs. of hot dogs

2 tbsp. of grated parmesan cheese
1 tbsp. of Dijon mustard

INSTRUCTIONS
1. Place hot dogs in preheated air fryer and cook them at 390°F for 5 minutes.
2. Put the hot dogs into the buns, spread mustard all over, and sprinkle with the parmesan.
3. Air fry the hot dogs at 390°F for 3 minutes more.
4. Serve and enjoy!

---

323. VEGGIE PUDDING

Prep & Cook Time: 40 minutes | Servings: 6

INGREDIENTS
2 cups of corn
½ cup of heavy cream
3 cups of cubed bread
1½ cups of milk
¼ cup of chopped celery

1 tbsp. of softened butter
2 pcs. of red bell peppers, chopped
1 pc. of yellow onion, chopped
4 tbsp. of grated cheddar cheese
1 tsp. of chopped thyme

2 tsp. of minced garlic
3 pcs. of eggs, whisked
salt & black pepper to taste

INSTRUCTIONS
1. Use the butter to grease a baking dish.
2. Place all other ingredients except the cheddar cheese, toss.
3. Sprinkle the cheese all over, place the dish in the fryer and cook at 360°F for 30 minutes.
4. Distribute between plates.
5. Serve and enjoy.

---

324. COD MEATBALLS

Prep & Cook Time: 22 minutes | Servings: 4

INGREDIENTS
1 lb. of cod, skinless & chopped
1 pc. of yellow onion, chopped
1 pc. of egg
3 tbsp. of minced fresh cilantro

¼ cup of panko breadcrumbs
2 pcs. of garlic cloves, minced
½ tsp. of sweet paprika
½ tsp. of ground oregano

a drizzle of olive oil
salt & black pepper to taste

INSTRUCTIONS
1. In food processor, combine all ingredients except the oil.
2. Blend and then shape medium-sized meatballs out of the mixture.
3. Put the meatballs in the air fryer's basket, grease them with oil and cook at 320°F for 12 minutes, shaking halfway.
4. Distribute the meatballs between plates and, if desired, serve with a side salad.

325. VEGGIE STEW

Prep & Cook Time: 30 minutes | Servings: 6

INGREDIENTS

7 oz. of tomato paste
2 pcs. of tomatoes, roughly chopped
2 pcs. of green bell peppers, cut into strips
2 pcs. of garlic cloves, minced
2 pcs. of yellow onions, roughly chopped

4 pcs. of zucchinis, halved lengthwise & sliced
1 pc. of eggplant, cubed
1 tsp. of dried oregano
1 tsp. of sugar
1 tsp. of dried basil

2 tbsp. of olive oil
2 tbsp. of chopped cilantro
salt & black pepper to taste

INSTRUCTIONS

1. In a pan, mix all ingredients except the cilantro, toss well.
2. Put the pan in the air fryer and cook the stew at 360°F for 20 minutes.
3. Distribute the stew into bowls, sprinkle the cilantro on top, and serve.

326. CHICKEN CASSEROLE

Prep & Cook Time: 40 minutes | Servings: 6

INGREDIENTS

2 cups of chicken meat, cooked & cubed
6 oz. of grated Monterey jack cheese
12 oz. of softened cream cheese
4 pcs. of scallions, chopped

1 cup of yogurt
¼ cup of chopped cilantro
½ cup of chutney
½ cup of sliced almonds

2 tbsp. of melted butter
2 tsp. of curry powder
salt & black pepper to taste

INSTRUCTIONS

1. In a baking dish, combine all ingredients except the Monterey jack cheese.
2. Sprinkle the Monterey jack cheese all over chicken mixture.
3. Place the dish in air fryer and cook at 350°F for 25 minutes.
4. Distribute between plates and serve.

327. CHICKEN & CAULIFLOWER BAKE

Prep & Cook Time: 30 minutes | Servings: 4

INGREDIENTS

2 pcs. of chicken breasts, skinless, boneless &
cubed
1 cup of tomato sauce

1 cup of cauliflower florets
1 tbsp. of olive oil
1 tsp. of sweet paprika

salt & black pepper to taste

INSTRUCTIONS

1. In a baking dish, combine all ingredients.
2. Put the dish in the fryer and bake at 370°F for 25 minutes.
3. Distribute between plates and serve.

328. COD & WARM TOMATO

Prep & Cook Time: 22 minutes | Servings: 2

INGREDIENTS

2 pcs. of boneless cod fillets
8 pcs. of cherry tomatoes, halved
¼ cup of dry vermouth

1 pc. of fennel bulb, sliced
4 tbsp. of softened butter
2 tbsp. of chopped dill

salt & black pepper to taste

INSTRUCTIONS

1. Split the butter onto two parchment paper pieces.
2. In bowl, combine the fennel, tomatoes, dill, salt, pepper, and vermouth.
3. Distribute the mixture between the two parchment papers.
4. Top this mixture with cod fillets and fold the packets.
5. Put the packets in the preheated air fryer and cook at 400°F for 12 minutes.
6. Unwrap the packets, place on plates.
7. Serve and enjoy!

329. LENTILS CAKES

Prep & Cook Time: 20 minutes | Servings: 2

INGREDIENTS

1 pc. of hot chili pepper, chopped.
1 cup of drained canned yellow lentils
1 tsp. of grated ginger
½ tsp. of turmeric powder
1 tsp. of garam masala

1 tsp. of baking powder
2 tsp. of olive oil
4 pcs. of garlic cloves, minced
⅓ cup of water
½ cup of chopped cilantro

3/4 cup of chopped yellow onion
1½ cups of chopped baby spinach
salt & black pepper to taste

INSTRUCTIONS

1. In a blender, mix all ingredients.
2. From the mixture, shape 2 medium cakes.
3. Put the lentils cakes in the preheated air fryer at 400°F and cook for 10 minutes.
4. Put lentils cakes on plates.
5. Serve and enjoy.

330. LAMB RECIPE

Prep & Cook Time: 40 minutes | Servings: 4

INGREDIENTS

1½ lbs. of rack of lamb
1 pc. of egg, whisked
1 pc. of garlic clove, minced

2 tbsp. of macadamia nuts
1 tbsp. of breadcrumbs
1 tbsp. of olive oil

1 tbsp. of chopped rosemary
salt & black pepper to taste

INSTRUCTIONS

1. In a bowl, whisk oil and garlic.
2. Coat the rack of lamb with the mixture and season with salt & pepper.
3. In a bowl, whisk the egg with salt and pepper.
4. In another bowl, combine the breadcrumbs and rosemary.
5. Coat the lamb with the egg mixture, then with the breadcrumbs.
6. Put it in air fryer's basket and cook at 400°F for 30 minutes.
7. Serve right away and enjoy!

331. JAPANESE PORK

Prep & Cook Time: 25 minutes | Servings: 2

INGREDIENTS

¼ lb. of cubed pork tenderloin
2 slices of ginger, minced
3 pcs. of garlic cloves, minced
⅛ cup of sake

⅛ cup of water
¼ cup of soy sauce
¼ cup of mirin
½ tsp. of olive oil

2 tbsp. of sugar
1 tbsp. of cornstarch mixed with 2 tbsp. water

INSTRUCTIONS

1. In a pan, combined all ingredients and toss.
2. Put the pan in the fryer and cook at 370°F for 15 minutes.
3. Distribute into bowls and serve.

332. SHRIMP PASTA

Prep & Cook Time: 25 minutes | Servings: 4

INGREDIENTS
5 oz. of cooked spaghetti
8 oz. of shrimp, peeled & deveined
5 pcs. of garlic cloves, minced

1 tbsp. of melted butter
2 tbsp. of olive oil
1 tsp. of chili powder

salt & black pepper to taste

INSTRUCTIONS
1. In air fryer, spread 1 tbsp. of the oil, along with the butter.
2. Preheat the air fryer at 350°F.
3. Put the shrimp and cook for 10 minutes.
4. Place the remaining ingredients and cook for 5 minutes more.
5. Distribute between plates.
6. Serve and enjoy!

333. CHICKEN & MUSHROOM PIE

Prep & Cook Time: 20 minutes | Servings: 4

INGREDIENTS
1 large chicken breast, boneless, skinless & cubed
1 pc. of yellow onion, chopped
6 pcs. of white mushrooms, chopped
1 pc. of carrot, chopped

1 tsp. of soy sauce
2 puff pastry sheets
1 tsp. of Italian seasoning
½ tsp. of garlic powder
1 tsp. of Worcestershire sauce

1 tbsp. of milk
2 tbsp. of olive oil
1 tbsp. of white flour
salt & black pepper to taste

INSTRUCTIONS
1. Heat up a pan with half of the oil over medium-high heat.
2. Put the carrots and onions, stir and cook for 2 minutes.
3. Place the remaining ingredients. Stir well and remove from the heat.
4. In a pan, fill the chicken mix in between puff pastry sheets.
5. Coat the pastry with the rest of the oil and place the pan in the fryer.
6. Cook at 360°F for 8 minutes. Slice, serve and enjoy.

334. CHICKEN & BEANS CASSEROLE

Prep & Cook Time: 30 minutes | Servings: 6

INGREDIENTS
6 pcs. of kale leaves, chopped.
24 oz. of drained and rinsed canned black beans
3 cups of chicken breast, skinless, boneless, cooked & shredded

½ cup of chopped cilantro
½ cup of chopped green onions
2 cups of salsa
3 cups of shredded mozzarella cheese

a drizzle of olive oil
2 tsp. of chili powder
2 tsp. of ground cumin
1 tbsp. garlic powder

INSTRUCTIONS
1. Grease a baking dish with olive oil.
2. Put all other ingredients except the cheese to the baking dish.
3. Sprinkle the cheese all over.
4. Put the dish in the air fryer and cook at 350°F for 20 minutes.
5. Distribute between plates, serve and enjoy!

335. TURKEY LUNCH

Prep & Cook Time: 1 hour 10 minutes | Servings: 6

INGREDIENTS
1 whole turkey breast
¼ cup of maple syrup
2 tsp. of olive oil

½ tsp. of sweet paprika
1 tsp. of dried thyme
1 tbsp. of melted butter

2 tbsp. of mustard
salt & black pepper to taste

INSTRUCTIONS
1. Coat the turkey breast with the oil and season with salt, pepper, paprika and thyme.
2. Put the turkey in the air fryer and cook at 350°F for 25 minutes.
3. Flip the turkey breast and cook for 12 minutes more. Repeat for another 12 minutes.
4. In a bowl, whisk the butter, mustard and maple syrup.
5. Coat the turkey breast with the maple syrup mixture and cook for another 5 minutes.
6. Transfer the meat to a cutting board, slice and, if desired, serve with a side salad.

336. BOURBON LUNCH BURGER

Prep & Cook Time: 40 minutes | Servings: 2

INGREDIENTS
1 lb. of lean ground beef
3 strips of maple bacon, halved
2 slices of Colby jack cheese
2 tbsp. of brown sugar
1 tbsp. of bourbon

1 tbsp. of chopped onion
2 tbsp. of barbecue sauce
a pinch of salt & black pepper
2 Kaiser rolls
FOR THE SAUCE:

2 tbsp. of mayonnaise
¼ tsp. of sweet paprika
2 tbsp. of barbecue sauce
a pinch of salt & black pepper

INSTRUCTIONS
1. In a bowl, combine brown sugar with bourbon.
2. Put the bacon strips in the air fryer's basket.
3. Coat them with the bourbon mix and cook at 390°F for 4 minutes on each side.
4. In the meantime, mix beef with 2 tbsp. of barbecue sauce, salt, pepper and onions.
5. Shape the mixture into patties.
6. Put the patties in air fryer's basket and cook at 370°F for 20 minutes. Flip them halfway.
7. Top each patty with a Colby jack cheese slice and leave in the fryer for 1-2 minutes more.
8. In a bowl, combine all sauce ingredients.
9. Spread the sauce on the inside of the Kaiser rolls.
10. Place the patties on the rolls, top with the bourbon bacon.
11. Serve and enjoy!

337. GREEK SANDWICHES

Prep & Cook Time: 11 minutes | Servings: 4

INGREDIENTS
8 slices of bacon, cooked & cut into thirds
1¼ cups of torn lettuce
2 pcs. of tomatoes, sliced

2 pcs. of red bell peppers, sliced
3 pcs. of pita pockets, halved
⅓ cup of barbecue sauce

2 tbsp. of honey

INSTRUCTIONS
1. In a bowl, combine barbecue sauce with honey.
2. Coat the bacon and bell peppers with the mixture.

3. Put the bacon and bell peppers in the air fryer and cook at 350°F for 6 minutes, shaking once.
4. Stuff pita pockets with the bacon and bell peppers mixture, then add tomatoes and lettuce.
5. Brush with the rest of the barbecue sauce and honey.
5. Serve and enjoy!

338. BEEF & POTATO STEW
Prep & Cook Time: 35 minutes | Servings: 4

INGREDIENTS

2 lbs. of cubed beef stew meat
1 qt. of beef stock
1 pc. of carrot, sliced

4 pcs. of gold potatoes, cubed
a handful of chopped cilantro
½ tsp. of smoked paprika

4 tbsp. of Worcestershire sauce
salt & black pepper to taste

INSTRUCTIONS

1. In a pan, combine all the ingredients except the cilantro.
2. Put in your air fryer and cook at 375°F for 25 minutes.
3. Distribute into bowls, sprinkle the cilantro on top.
4. Serve right away.

339. PORK BITES
Prep & Cook Time: 17 minutes | Servings: 4

INGREDIENTS

2 lbs. of cubed pork stew meat
1 cup of cornstarch
2 pcs. of eggs

1 tsp. of sesame oil
¼ tsp. of Chinese five spice
3 tbsp. of olive oil

salt & black pepper to taste

INSTRUCTIONS

1. In a bowl, mix the Chinese spice, salt, pepper and cornstarch.
2. In another bowl, whisk the eggs and sesame oil.
3. Coat the pork cubes in the cornstarch mix, then in the egg mixture.
4. Put the pork cubes in the air fryer.
5. Drizzle all over with the olive oil and cook at 360°F for 12 minutes.
6. Distribute into bowls and, if desired, serve with a side salad.

340. CHEESE RAVIOLI
Prep & Cook Time: 10 minutes | Servings: 6

INGREDIENTS

15 oz. of cheese ravioli
10 oz. of marinara sauce

2 cups of breadcrumbs
¼ cup of crated cheddar cheese

1 cup of buttermilk
1 tsp. of melted butter

INSTRUCTIONS

1. Pour buttermilk in one bowl and the breadcrumbs in another.
2. Coat each ravioli in buttermilk, then in breadcrumbs.
3. Place the ravioli in the air fryer's basket.
4. Garnish with the melted butter and cook at 400°F for 5 minutes.
5. Distribute the ravioli between plates, sprinkle cheddar cheese on top.
6. Serve and enjoy!

341. CHICKEN, KALE & MUSHROOM
Prep & Cook Time: 25 minutes | Servings: 6

INGREDIENTS

1 bunch of kale, torn
1 cup of chicken breast, skinless, boneless,
cooked & shredded

1½ cups of roughly sliced shiitake mushrooms
¼ cup of tomato sauce
2 tbsp. of chicken stock

salt & black pepper to taste

INSTRUCTIONS

1. In a pan, combine all ingredients and toss.
2. Put the pan in the fryer and cook at 350°F for 20 minutes.
3. Distribute between plates and serve.

342. BEEF MEATBALL SANDWICHES
Prep & Cook Time: 32 minutes | Servings: 4

INGREDIENTS

3 pcs. of baguettes, sliced halfway
14 oz. of minced beef
7 oz. of tomato sauce
1 pc. of yellow onion, chopped

1 pc. of egg, whisked
1 tsp. of chopped fresh basil
1 tbsp. of chopped oregano
1 tbsp. of olive oil

1 tbsp. of breadcrumbs
2 tbsp. of grated parmesan cheese
salt & black pepper to taste

INSTRUCTIONS

1. In a bowl, combine all ingredients except the tomato sauce, oil and baguettes.
2. Shape the mixture into medium-sized meatballs.
3. Heat up the air fryer with the oil at 375°F.
4. Put the meatballs and cook for 12 minutes. Flip halfway.
5. Put the tomato sauce and cook for 10 minutes more.
6. Distribute the meatballs and sauce in between two baguette halves.
7. Serve and enjoy!

343. BEEF & CABBAGE BOWLS
Prep & Cook Time: 20 minutes | Servings: 4

INGREDIENTS

½ lb. of sirloin steak, cut into strips
1 pc. of yellow bell pepper, chopped
2 pcs. of green onions, chopped

2 pcs. of garlic cloves, minced
2 cups of shredded green cabbage
1 tbsp. of olive oil

1 tsp. of soy sauce
salt & black pepper to taste

INSTRUCTIONS

1. In a pan, combine and toss cabbage, salt, pepper and oil.
2. Place the pan in the air fryer and cook at 370°F for 4 minutes.
3. Put the remaining ingredients, cover and cook for another 6 minutes.
4. Distribute into bowls and serve.

344. CHICKEN WINGS
Prep & Cook Time: 50 minutes | Servings: 4

INGREDIENTS

3 lbs. of chicken wings
3/4 cup of potato starch

½ cup of melted butter
1 tbsp. of old bay seasoning

1 tsp. of lemon juice

INSTRUCTIONS

1. In a bowl, coat chicken wings with starch and Old Bay seasoning.

2. Put the pieces in the air fryer's basket, cook at 360°F for 35 minutes, shaking the fryer from time to time.
3. Increase temperature to 400°F and cook chicken wings for 10 minutes more.
4. Distribute the wings between plates.
5. Drizzled all over with mixture of melted butter and lemon juice.
6. Serve and enjoy!

345. OKRA LUNCH SALAD
Prep & Cook Time: 20 minutes | Servings: 4

INGREDIENTS

15 oz. of okra, sliced
12 oz. of chopped canned tomatoes
1 pc. of red bell pepper, chopped
1 pc. of red onion, chopped

2 pcs. of garlic cloves, minced
2 cups of corn
1 tsp. of sweet paprika
1 tsp. of dried thyme

1 tsp. of dried oregano
1 tsp. of dried rosemary
salt & black pepper to taste

INSTRUCTIONS
1. Put all ingredients in a pan, toss well.
2. Put the pan in the fryer and cook at 370°F for 15 minutes.
3. Distribute the salad into bowls and serve cold.

346. BEEF MEATBALLS & SAUCE
Prep & Cook Time: 25 minutes | Servings: 4

INGREDIENTS

1 lb. of lean ground beef
16 oz. of tomato sauce
¼ cup of panko breadcrumbs

1 pc. of red onion, chopped
2 pcs. of garlic cloves, minced
1 pc. of egg yolk

1 tbsp. of olive oil
salt & black pepper to taste

INSTRUCTIONS
1. In a bowl, combine all ingredients except for the tomato sauce and olive oil.
2. Shape mixture into medium-sized meatballs.
3. Coat the meatballs with oil.
4. Put them in the air fryer and cook at 400°F for 10 minutes.
5. Heat up a pan over medium heat, add tomato sauce and heat it up for 2 minutes.
6. Put the meatballs, toss a bit and cook for 3 minutes more.
7. Distribute the meatballs between plates and serve.

347. COD CURRY
Prep & Cook Time: 25 minutes | Servings: 4

INGREDIENTS

4 pcs. of cod fillets, skinless, boneless & cubed
1½ cups of hot milk

2 tbsp. of chopped cilantro
2 tsp. of grated ginger

2 tsp. of curry paste
salt & black pepper to taste

INSTRUCTIONS
1. In a bowl, combine and whisk milk, curry paste, ginger, salt and pepper.
2. Place the fish in a pan, then pour the milk and curry mixture, toss gently.
3. Put the pan in the fryer and cook at 400°F for 15 minutes, shaking halfway.
4. Distribute the curry into bowls, sprinkle the cilantro on top.
5. Serve and enjoy!

348. SEA BASS STEW
Prep & Cook Time: 30 minutes | Servings: 4

INGREDIENTS

1½ lbs. of sea bass fillets, skinless, boneless & cubed
4 pcs. of shrimps
14 oz. of white wine

3 oz. of water
5 oz. of white rice
2 oz. of peas
1 pc. of red bell pepper, chopped

1 tbsp. of olive oil
salt & black pepper to taste

INSTRUCTIONS
1. In air fryer's pan, combine all ingredients and toss.
2. Put the pan in the air fryer and cook at 400°F for 20 minutes, stirring halfway.
3. Distribute into bowls.
4. Serve and enjoy!

349. CREAMY POTATO
Prep & Cook Time: 27 minutes | Servings: 4

INGREDIENTS

4 pcs. of gold potatoes, cut into medium wedges
¼ cup of sour cream
1 tsp. of olive oil

1½ tsp. of sweet paprika
½ tsp. of Cajun seasoning
2 pcs. of eggs

1 tsp. of garlic powder
salt & black pepper to taste

INSTRUCTIONS
1. In a bowl, combine eggs with sour cream, paprika, garlic powder, Cajun seasoning, salt and pepper, whisk well.
2. Grease a pan with oil.
3. Arrange the potatoes on the bottom of the pan and spread the sour cream mixture all over.
4. Put the pan in the fryer and cook at 370°F for 17 minutes.
5. Distribute between plates and serve.

350. GREEK QUINOA SALAD
Prep & Cook Time: 25 minutes | Servings: 6

INGREDIENTS

2 oz. of crumbled feta cheese
1 cup of halved cherry tomatoes
2 pcs. of green onions, chopped
½ cup of kalamata olives, pitted & chopped

1½ cups of cooked quinoa
1 tbsp. of olive oil
1 tbsp. of balsamic vinegar
a handful of chopped basil leaves

a handful of chopped parsley leaves
salt & black pepper to taste

INSTRUCTIONS
1. In a pan, put and toss all the ingredients except the feta cheese.
2. Sprinkle the cheese on top.
3. Put the pan in the air fryer and cook at 370°F for 15 minutes.
4. Distribute into bowls and serve.

351. HONEY CHICKEN THIGHS
Prep & Cook Time: 35 minutes | Servings: 4

INGREDIENTS

1½ lbs. of chicken thighs, skinless & boneless
3/4 cup of honey

½ cup of chicken stock
½ tsp. of dried basil

2 tsp. of sweet paprika
salt & black pepper to taste

INSTRUCTIONS
1. In a bowl, combine and whisk well all the ingredients except the chicken thighs.
2. Coat the chicken thighs with the mixture.

3. Place the chicken in the air fryer's basket and cook at 380°F for 25 minutes.
4. Distribute between plates.
5. Serve and enjoy.

352. COCONUT ZUCCHINI
Prep & Cook Time: 21 minutes | Servings: 8

INGREDIENTS

8 pcs. of zucchinis, cut in medium wedges
2 pcs. of yellow onions, chopped
1 cup of coconut cream
1 cup of veggie stock

2 tbsp. of olive oil
1 tbsp. of soy sauce
¼ tsp. of dried thyme
¼ tsp. of dried rosemary

½ tsp. of chopped basil
salt & black pepper to taste

INSTRUCTIONS

1. Grease a pan with olive oil. Put all other ingredients to the pan and toss.
2. Put the pan in the fryer and cook at 360°F for 16 minutes.
3. Distribute the mixture between plates.
4. Serve and enjoy.

353. TOMATO & OKRA STEW
Prep & Cook Time: 25 minutes | Servings: 5

INGREDIENTS

20 oz. of roughly cubed canned tomatoes
3 pcs. of celery ribs, chopped
1 pc. of yellow onion, chopped

1 cup of sliced okra
1 pc. of red bell pepper, chopped
2 pcs. of garlic cloves, minced

½ cup of veggie stock
½ tsp. of sweet paprika
salt & black pepper to taste

INSTRUCTIONS

1. In air fryer, combine all ingredients, cover and cook at 360°F for 20 minutes.
2. Distribute into bowls.
3. Serve and enjoy!

354. ASIAN CHICKEN
Prep & Cook Time: 40 Minutes | Servings: 4

INGREDIENTS

2 pcs. of chicken breasts, skinless, boneless &
sliced
14 oz. of pizza dough

1 ½ cups of grated cheddar cheese
½ cup of jarred cheese sauce
1 tsp. of olive oil

1 pc. of yellow onion, sliced
1 tbsp. of Worcestershire sauce
salt & black pepper to the taste

INSTRUCTIONS

1. Preheat air fryer at 400°F. Put half of the oil and onions, fry them for 8 minutes, stirring once.
2. Place and toss chicken pieces, Worcestershire sauce, salt and pepper, air fry for 8 minutes more, stirring once.
3. Set aside everything into a bowl.
4. Roll pizza dough on a working surface and shape a rectangle.
5. Layer half of the cheese all over.
6. Put chicken and onion mix and top with cheese sauce.
7. Roll the dough and shape into a "U".
8. Put the roll in the air fryer's basket.
9. Coat with the rest of the oil and cook at 370°F for 12 minutes, flipping the roll halfway.
10. Cut the roll when it's warm and serve for lunch.

355. TURKISH STYLE KOFTAS
Prep & Cook Time: 25 Minutes | Servings: 2

INGREDIENTS

2 tbsp. of crumbled feta cheese
½ lb. of lean beef, minced
1 tbsp. of ground cumin

1 tbsp. of chopped mint
1 pc. of leek, chopped
1 tbsp. of chopped parsley

1 tsp. of minced garlic
salt & black pepper to the taste

INSTRUCTIONS

1. In a bowl, combine beef with leek, cheese, cumin, mint, parsley, garlic, salt and pepper, stir.
2. Shape koftas and place on sticks.
3. Put koftas to the preheated air fryer at 360°F and cook for 15 minutes.
4. Serve with a side salad for lunch.

356. QUINOA & SPINACH PESTO
Prep & Cook Time: 20 minutes | Servings: 4

INGREDIENTS

1 cup of cooked quinoa
3/4 cup of jarred spinach pesto

1 pc. of green apple, chopped
¼ cup of chopped celery

3 tbsp. of chicken stock
salt & black pepper to taste

INSTRUCTIONS

1. Combine all the ingredients in a pan, toss.
2. Put the pan in the fryer and cook at 370°F for 15 minutes.
3. Distribute into bowls and serve right away.

357. BROCCOLI MIX
Prep & Cook Time: 25 minutes | Servings: 4

INGREDIENTS

2 pcs. of broccoli heads, florets separated
½ cup of bacon, cooked & crumbled
3 pcs. of garlic cloves, minced

2 tsp. of sweet paprika
juice of half lemon
1 tbsp. of olive oil

1 tbsp. of sesame seeds
salt & black pepper to taste

INSTRUCTIONS

1. In air fryer's pan, combine all ingredients except the bacon, toss.
2. Cover and cook at 360°F for 15 minutes.
3. Put the bacon and cook for 5 more minutes.
4. Distribute between plates and serve.

358. CHICKPEAS STEW
Prep & Cook Time: 20 minutes | Servings: 4

INGREDIENTS

15 oz. of drained canned chickpeas
28 oz. of chopped canned tomatoes
1 pc. of red onion, chopped

2 pcs. of garlic cloves, minced
2 tsp. of sweet paprika
1 tbsp. of olive oil

salt & black pepper to taste

INSTRUCTIONS

1. In a pan, combine all ingredients.
2. Place the pan in the air fryer and cook at 370°F for 15 minutes.
3. Distribute the stew into bowls and serve.

359. FRESH STYLE CHICKEN

Prep & Cook Time: 32 Minutes | Servings: 4

INGREDIENTS

2 pcs. of chicken breasts, skinless, boneless & cubed
8 pcs. of button mushrooms, sliced

1 pc. of red bell pepper, chopped
1 tbsp. of olive oil
6 slices of bread

½ tsp. of dried thyme
10 oz. of alfredo sauce
2 tbsp. of softened butter

INSTRUCTIONS

1. In your air fryer, combined chicken with mushrooms, bell pepper and oil.
2. Cook at 350°F for 15 minutes.
3. Transfer chicken mix into a bowl.
4. Put and toss thyme and alfredo sauce.
5. Place back the mixture to air fryer and cook at 350°F for 4 minutes more.
6. Spread butter on bread slices, add it to the fryer, butter side up and cook for 4 minutes more.
7. Arrange toasted bread slices on a platter.
8. Top each with chicken mix and serve for lunch.

360. POTATOES & CALAMARI STEW

Prep & Cook Time: 26 minutes | Servings: 4

INGREDIENTS

10 oz. of calamari, cut into strips
1 cup of red wine
1 cup of water
½ bunch of cilantro, chopped
2 pcs. of garlic cloves, minced

1 pc. of yellow onion, chopped
4 pcs. of potatoes, cut into quarters
2 tbsp. of olive oil
2 tsp. of pepper sauce
1 tbsp. of hot sauce

1 tbsp. of sweet paprika
1 tbsp. of tomato sauce
salt & black pepper to taste

INSTRUCTIONS

1. In a pan, toss all the ingredients.
2. Place the pan in the fryer and cook at 400°F for 16 minutes.
3. Distribute the stew between bowls and serve.

361. BEEF MEATBALLS

Prep & Cook Time: 25 Minutes | Servings: 4

INGREDIENTS

½ lb. of chopped Italian sausage
½ cup of cheddar cheese
½ lb. of ground beef

½ tsp. of garlic powder
½ tsp. of onion powder
mashed potatoes for serving

salt & black pepper to the taste

INSTRUCTIONS

1. In a bowl, combine beef with sausage, garlic powder, onion powder, salt, pepper and cheese.
2. Make 16 meatballs.
3. Put meatballs in air fryer and cook them at 370°F for 15 minutes.
4. Serve meatballs with some mashed potatoes on the side.

362. GREEN BEANS LUNCH STEW

Prep & Cook Time: 20 minutes | Servings: 4

INGREDIENTS

1 lb. of green beans, halved
1 pc. of yellow onion, chopped
4 pcs. of carrots, sliced

4 pcs. of garlic cloves, minced
1 tbsp. of chopped thyme
3 tbsp. of tomato paste

salt & black pepper to taste

INSTRUCTIONS

1. In a pan, combine all the ingredients.
2. Put the pan in the air fryer and cook at 365°F for 15 minutes.
3. Distribute the stew into bowls and serve.

363. TASTY TURKEY BURGERS

Prep & Cook Time: 18 Minutes | Servings: 4

INGREDIENTS

1 lb. of ground turkey meat
1 pc. of shallot, minced
1 tsp. of ground cumin
1 tsp. of sweet paprika

a drizzle of olive oil
1 pc. of small jalapeno pepper, minced
2 tsp. of lime juice
zest from 1 lime

salt & black pepper to the taste
guacamole for serving

INSTRUCTIONS

1. In a bowl, combine turkey meat with salt, pepper, cumin, paprika, shallot, jalapeno, lime juice and zest.
2. Shape into patties, drizzle the oil over them.
3. Introduce in preheated air fryer and cook them at 370°F for 8 minutes on each side.
4. Distribute among plates.
5. Serve with guacamole on top.

364. DILL & SCALLOPS

Prep & Cook Time: 15 Minutes | Servings: 4

INGREDIENTS

1 lb. of sea scallops, debearded
1 tbsp. of lemon juice

1 tsp. of chopped dill
2 tsp. of olive oil

salt & black pepper to the taste

INSTRUCTIONS

1. In air fryer, combine scallops with dill, oil, salt, pepper and lemon juice.
2. Cover and cook at 360°F for 5 minutes. Discard unopened ones.
3. Distribute scallops and dill sauce on plates.
4. Serve for lunch.

365. CORN STEW

Prep & Cook Time: 20 minutes | Servings: 4

INGREDIENTS

2 pcs. of leeks, chopped
4 cups of corn
¼ cup of chicken stock
4 sprigs of tarragon, chopped

2 pcs. of tomatoes, cubed
2 pcs. of garlic cloves, minced
1 tbsp. of chopped chives
2 tbsp. of melted butter

1 tsp. of olive oil
salt & black pepper to taste

INSTUCTIONS

1. In a pan, grease with oil and toss all the ingredients.
2. Put the pan in the fryer and cook at 370°F for 15 minutes.
3. Distribute the stew between bowls and serve.

366. CHEESE & MACARONI

Prep & Cook Time: 40 Minutes | Servings: 3

INGREDIENTS

1 ½ cups of favorite macaroni
1 cup of chicken stock
3/4 cup of shredded cheddar cheese

½ cup of heavy cream
½ cup of shredded mozzarella cheese
¼ cup of shredded parmesan

salt & black pepper to the taste
cooking spray

INSTRUCTIONS

1. Spray a pan with cooking spray, combine all ingredients.
2. Put the pan in your air fryer's basket and cook for 30 minutes.
3. Distribute among plates.
4. Serve for lunch.

367. LENTILS LUNCH CURRY

Prep & Cook Time: 20 minutes | Servings: 6

INGREDIENTS

10 oz. of baby spinach
15 oz. of canned tomatoes, drained & chopped
2 cups of drained canned lentils
1 pc. of red onion, chopped
1 tbsp. of lemon juice

2 tbsp. of curry paste
2 tbsp. of chopped cilantro
1 tbsp. of minced garlic
1 tsp. of grated ginger
½ tsp. of ground cumin

2 tsp. of sugar
½ tsp. of ground coriander
salt & black pepper to taste

INSTRUCTIONS

1. In a pan, combine all the ingredients except cilantro and lemon juice.
2. Put the pan in the air fryer and cook at 370°F for 15 minutes.
3. Put the cilantro and the lemon juice, and toss.
4. Distribute into bowls.
5. Serve and enjoy.

368. BUTTERNUT SQUASH STEW

Prep & Cook Time: 25 minutes | Servings: 5

INGREDIENTS

1½ lbs. of butternut squash, cubed
15 oz. of chopped canned tomatoes
½ cup of chopped green onions
1 cup of cooked quinoa
1½ cups of heavy cream

1 cup of chicken meat, already cooked & shredded
½ cup of chopped carrots
½ cup of chopped celery
1 pc. of garlic clove, minced

½ tsp. of Italian seasoning
⅛ tsp. of dried red pepper flakes
3 tbsp. of melted butter
salt & black pepper to taste

INSTRUCTIONS

1. Toss all the ingredients in a pan that fits your air fryer.
2. Place the pan into the fryer and cook at 400°F for 15 minutes.
3. Distribute the stew between bowls. Serve and enjoy.

369. SALSA CHICKEN

Prep & Cook Time: 27 minutes | Servings: 4

INGREDIENTS

4 pcs. of chicken breasts, skinless, boneless & cubed
16 oz. of jarred chunky salsa
20 oz. of canned tomatoes, peeled & chopped

12 oz. of drained canned black beans
1 pc. of onion, chopped
3 pcs. of garlic cloves, minced
1 tsp. of garlic powder

2 tbsp. of dried parsley
2 tbsp. of olive oil
1 tbsp. of chili powder
salt & black pepper to taste

INSTRUCTIONS

1. Toss all ingredients into a pan that fits your air fryer.
2. Place the pan in the fryer and cook at 380°F for 17 minutes.
3. Distribute into bowls.
4. Serve and enjoy!

370. BLACK BEANS LUNCH MIX

Prep & Cook Time: 35 minutes | Servings: 6

INGREDIENTS

30 oz. of drained canned black beans
1 pc. of yellow onion, chopped
1 pc. of jalapeno, chopped
1 pc. of red bell pepper, chopped
2 pcs. of garlic cloves, minced

3 cups of cooked brown rice
1 cup of veggie stock
1 tbsp. of olive oil
1 tsp. of grated ginger
½ tsp. of ground cumin

½ tsp. of dried oregano
½ tsp. of ground allspice
salt & black pepper to taste

INSTRUCTIONS

1. In a pan, toss all ingredients except rice.
2. Put the pan in air fryer and cook at 360°F for 25 minutes. Add rice and toss again.
3. Distribute into bowls. Serve and enjoy!

371. EGGPLANT STEW

Prep & Cook Time: 20 minutes | Servings: 4

INGREDIENTS

25 oz. of canned tomatoes, chopped
3 pcs. of eggplants, cubed
2 pcs. of red bell peppers, cubed

1 pc. of red onion, chopped
2 tsp. of ground cumin
1 tsp. of sweet paprika

1 tbsp. of chopped cilantro
juice of ½ lime
salt & black pepper to taste

INSTRUCTIONS

1. In a pan, combine all ingredients except the lime juice and cilantro.
2. Put the pan in the fryer and cook at 370°F for 15 minutes.
3. Squeeze lime juice and cilantro.
4. Distribute the stew between bowls.
5. Serve and enjoy!

372. BEANS & QUINOA STEW

Prep & Cook Time: 25 minutes | Servings: 4

INGREDIENTS

30 oz. of drained canned black beans
30 oz. of chopped canned tomatoes
1 cup of quinoa
2 pcs. of sweet potatoes, cubed

1 pc. of yellow onion, chopped
1 pc. of green bell pepper, chopped
2 tsp. of ground cumin
¼ tsp. of sweet paprika

1 tbsp. of chili powder
2 tbsp. of cocoa powder
salt & black pepper to taste

INSTRUCTIONS

1. Put all ingredients in a pan that fits your air fryer and stir well.
2. Place the pan in the air fryer and cook at 400°F for 15 minutes.
3. Distribute into bowls.
4. Serve right away.

373. QUINOA & SPINACH SALAD

Prep & Cook Time: 25 minutes | Servings:

INGREDIENTS
1½ cups of cooked quinoa
2 pcs. of tomatoes, chopped
1 pc. of red bell pepper, chopped
3 stalks of celery, chopped.

½ cup of chicken stock
½ cup of black olives, pitted & chopped
½ cup of crumbled feta cheese
⅓ cup of basil pesto

¼ cup of sliced almonds
4 cups of torn spinach
salt & black pepper to taste

INSTRUCTIONS
1. In a pan, mix all ingredients except the almond and cheese.
2. Sprinkle the almonds and the cheese on top.
3. Put the pan in the air fryer and cook at 380°F for 15 minutes.
4. Distribute between plates and serve.

374. CHICKEN & CABBAGE CURRY
Prep & Cook Time: 40 minutes | Servings: 3

INGREDIENTS
1½ lbs. of boneless chicken thighs
10 oz. of coconut milk
1 pc. of green cabbage, shredded
2 pcs. of chili peppers, chopped

1 pc. of yellow onion, chopped
½ cup of white wine
4 pcs. of garlic cloves, minced
1 tbsp. of olive oil

3 tbsp. of curry paste
1 tbsp. of soy sauce
salt & black pepper to taste

INSTRUCTIONS
1. Grease a baking dish with olive oil, toss all ingredients.
2. Put the baking dish in the fryer and cook at 380°F for 30 minutes.
3. Distribute between bowls.
4. Serve and enjoy.

375. ITALIAN CHICKEN MIX
Prep & Cook Time: 30 minutes | Servings: 4

INGREDIENTS
28 oz. of canned tomatoes, chopped
8 pcs. of chicken drumsticks, bone-in
1 cup of chicken stock

1 pc. of yellow onion, chopped
½ cup of black olives, pitted & sliced
1 tsp. of garlic powder

1 tsp. of dried oregano
salt & black pepper to taste

INSTRUCTIONS
1. In a baking dish, toss all the ingredients.
2. Place the dish in your air fryer and cook at 380°F for 20 minutes.
3. Distribute the mixture into bowls.
4. Serve and enjoy!

376. GREEN BEANS CASSEROLE
Prep & Cook Time: 25 minutes | Servings: 4

INGREDIENTS
3 cups of green beans, trimmed &halved
2 pcs. of red chilies, chopped
½ tsp. of black mustard seeds
½ cup of chopped yellow onion
2 pcs. of tomatoes, chopped

3 pcs. of garlic cloves, minced
2 tsp. of tamarind paste
¼ tsp. of fenugreek seeds
½ tsp. of turmeric powder
1 tsp. of olive oil

2 tsp. of coriander powder
1 tbsp. of chopped cilantro
salt & black pepper to taste

INSTRUCTIONS
1. Grease a heat-proof dish with olive oil, toss all the ingredients.
2. Put the dish in the fryer and cook at 370°F for 20 minutes.
3. Distribute between plates.
4. Serve and enjoy!

377. BABY CARROTS MIX
Prep & Cook Time: 20 minutes | Servings: 4

INGREDIENTS
4 oz. of chicken stock
16 oz. of baby carrots

2 tbsp. of melted butter
2 tbsp. of chopped dill

salt & black pepper to taste

INSTRUCTIONS
1. In a pan, combine all the ingredients and toss.
2. Put the pan in the fryer and cook at 380°F for 15 minutes.
3. Distribute between bowls.
4. Serve and enjoy.

378. LOW-CARB PIZZA CRUST
Prep & Cook Time: 20 minutes | Servings: 4

INGREDIENTS
1 tbsp. of full-fat cream cheese
½ cup of whole milk

mozzarella cheese, grated
2 tbsp. of flour

1 egg white

INSTRUCTIONS
1. In a microwave-safe bowl, combine the cream cheese, mozzarella, & flour & heat in the microwave for half a minute. Mix well to create a smooth consistency. Add in the egg white & stir to form a soft ball of dough.
2. With slightly wet hands, press the dough into a pizza crust about six inches in diameter.
3. Place a sheet of parchment paper in the bottom of your Air Fryer & lay the crust on top. Cook for ten minutes at 350°F, turning the crust over halfway through the cooking time.
4. Top the pizza base with the toppings of your choice & enjoy!

379. BACON-WRAPPED ONION RINGS
Prep & Cook Time: 15 minutes | Servings: 8

INGREDIENTS
1 large onion, peeled

8 slices of sugar-free bacon

1 tbsp. of sriracha

INSTRUCTIONS
1. Chop up the onion into slices a quarter-inch thick. Gently pull apart the rings. Take a slice of bacon & wrap it around an onion ring. Repeat with the rest of the ingredients. Place each onion ring in your Air Fryer.
2. Cut the onion rings at 350°F for ten minutes, turning them halfway through to ensure the bacon crisps up.
3. Serve hot with the sriracha.

380. SMOKED BBQ TOAST
Prep & Cook Time: 10 minutes | Servings: 1

INGREDIENTS
2 tsp. of coconut oil, melted

¼ tsp. of smoked paprika

1 tsp. of chili powder

¼ tsp. cumin

2 slices of bread

INSTRUCTIONS
1. Mix the melted coconut oil with the paprika, chili powder, & cumin. Place the bread slices in a large bowl & pour the coconut oil over them, tossing them to cover them evenly.
2. Place the slices in the basket of your Air Fryer & spread them out across the base.
3. Cook for six minutes at 320°F, giving the basket an occasional shake to make sure everything is cooked evenly.
4. Leave to cool & serve.

381. ROASTED EGGPLANT
Prep & Cook Time: 20 minutes | Servings: 1

INGREDIENTS

1 large eggplant
2 tbsp. of olive oil

¼ tsp. of salt
½ tsp. of garlic powder

INSTRUCTIONS
1. Prepare the eggplant by slicing off the top & bottom & cutting it into slices around a quarter-inch thick.
2. Apply olive oil to the slices with a brush, coating both sides. Season each side with sprinklings of salt & garlic powder.
3. Place the slices in the Air Fryer & cook for fifteen minutes at 390°F.
4. Serve right away.

382. LOW-CARB PITA CHIPS
Prep & Cook Time: 15 minutes | Servings: 1

INGREDIENTS

1 cup of mozzarella cheese, shredded
1 egg

¼ cup of blanched finely ground   flour
½ oz. of flour

INSTRUCTIONS
1. Melt the mozzarella in the microwave. Add the egg & flour, combine together to form a smooth paste. Microwave the cheese again if it begins to set.
2. Put the dough between two sheets of parchment paper & use a rolling pin to flatten it out into a rectangle. The thickness is up to you. With a sharp knife, cut into the dough to form triangles. It may be necessary to complete this step in multiple batches.
3. Place the chips in the Air Fryer & cook for five minutes at 350°F. Turn them over & cook on the other side for another five minutes, or until the chips are golden & firm.
4. Allow the chips to cool & harden further. They can be stored in an airtight container.

383. FLATBREAD
Prep & Cook Time: 20 minutes | Servings: 1

INGREDIENTS

1 cup of mozzarella cheese, shredded

¼ cup of blanched finely ground   flour

1 oz. of full-fat cream cheese, softened

INSTRUCTIONS
1. Microwave the mozzarella for half a minute until melted. Combine with the flour to achieve a smooth consistency, before adding the cream cheese. Keep mixing to create a dough, microwaving the mixture again if the cheese begins to harden.
2. Divide the dough into two equal pieces. Between two sheets of parchment paper, roll out the dough until it is about a quarter-inch thick. Cover the bottom of your Air Fryer with another sheet of parchment.
3. Transfer the dough into the Air Fryer & cook at 320°F for seven minutes. You may need to complete this step in two batches. Make sure to turn the flatbread halfway through cooking. Take care when removing it from the Air Fryer & serve warm.

384. BUFFALO CAULIFLOWER
Prep & Cook Time: 10 minutes | Servings: 1

INGREDIENTS

½ packet of dry ranch seasoning
2 tbsp. of salted butter, melted

cauliflower florets
¼ cup of buffalo sauce

INSTRUCTIONS
1. In a bowl, combine the dry ranch seasoning & butter. Toss with the cauliflower florets to coat & transfer them to the Air Fryer.
2. Cook at 400°F for five minutes, shaking the basket occasionally to ensure the florets cook evenly.
3. Remove the cauliflower from the Air Fryer, pour the buffalo sauce over it, & enjoy.

385. BRUSSELS SPROUT CHIPS
Prep & Cook Time: 15 minutes | Servings: 1

INGREDIENTS

1 lb. of Brussels sprouts

1 tbsp. of coconut oil, melted

1 tbsp. of butter, melted

INSTRUCTIONS
1. Prepare the Brussels sprouts by halving them, discarding any loose leaves.
2. Combine with the melted coconut oil & transfer to your Air Fryer.
3. Cook at 400°F for ten minutes, giving the basket a good shake throughout the cooking time to brown them up if desired.
4. The sprouts are ready when they are partially caramelized. Remove them from the Air Fryer & serve with a topping of melted butter before serving.

386. CAULIFLOWER TOTS
Prep & Cook Time: 20 minutes | Servings: 8

INGREDIENTS

1 large head of cauliflower
½ cup of parmesan cheese, grated

1 cup of mozzarella cheese, shredded
1 tsp. of seasoned salt

1 egg

INSTRUCTIONS
1. Place a steamer basket over a pot of boiling water, ensuring the water is not high enough to enter the basket.
2. Cut up the cauliflower into florets & transfer to the steamer basket. Cover the pot with a lid & leave to steam for seven minutes, making sure the cauliflower softens.
3. Place the florets on a cheesecloth & leave to cool. Remove as much moisture as possible. This is crucial as it ensures the cauliflower will harden.
4. In a bowl, break up the cauliflower with a fork.
5. Stir in the parmesan, mozzarella, seasoned salt, & egg, incorporating the cauliflower well with all of the other ingredients. Make sure the mixture is firm enough to be moldable.
6. Using your hand, mold about two tbsp. of the mixture into tots & repeat until you have used up all of the mixture. Put each tot into your Air Fryer basket. They may need to be cooked in multiple batches.
7. Cook at 320°F for twelve minutes, turning them halfway through. Ensure they are brown in color before serving.

387. HERBED GARLIC RADISHES
Prep & Cook Time: 15 minutes | Servings: 2

INGREDIENTS

1 lb. of radishes
2 tbsp. of butter, melted

¼ tsp. of dried oregano
½ tsp. of dried parsley

½ tsp. of garlic powder

INSTRUCTIONS
1. Prepare the radishes by cutting off their tops & bottoms & quartering them.
2. In a bowl, combine the butter, dried oregano, dried parsley, & garlic powder. Toss with the radishes to coat.

3. Transfer the radishes to your Air Fryer & cook at 350°F for ten minutes, shaking the basket at the halfway point to ensure the radishes cook evenly through. The radishes are ready when they begin to turn brown.

388. JICAMA FRIES

Prep & Cook Time: 25 minutes | Servings: 1

INGREDIENTS

1 small jicama, peeled
¼ tsp. of onion powder
¾ tsp. of chili powder
¼ tsp. of garlic powder
¼ tsp. of ground black pepper

INSTRUCTIONS

1. To make the fries, cut the jicama into matchsticks of your desired thickness.
2. In a bowl, toss them with the onion powder, chili powder, garlic powder, & black pepper to coat. Transfer the fries into the basket of your Air Fryer.
3. Cook at 350°F for twenty minutes, giving the basket an occasional shake throughout the cooking process. The fries are ready when they are hot & golden in color. Enjoy!

389. ZESTY SALMON JERKY

Prep & Cook Time: 6 hours | Servings: 2

INGREDIENTS

1 lb. of boneless skinless salmon
½ tsp. of liquid smoke
½ tsp. of ground ginger
¼ cup of soy sauce
¼ tsp. of red pepper flakes

INSTRUCTIONS

1. Cut the salmon into strips about four inches long & a quarter-inch thick.
2. Put the salmon in an airtight container or bag along with the liquid smoke, ginger, soy sauce, & red pepper flakes, combining everything to coat the salmon completely. Leave the salmon in the refrigerator for at least two hours.
3. Transfer the salmon slices in the Air Fryer, taking care not to overlap any pieces. This step may need to be completed in multiple batches.
4. Cook at 140°F for four hours.
5. Take care when removing the salmon from the Air Fryer & leave it to cool. This jerky makes a good snack & can be stored in an airtight container.

390. ZUCCHINI BITES

Prep & Cook Time: 15 minutes | Servings: 4

INGREDIENTS

4 zucchinis
1 egg
½ cup of parmesan cheese, grated
1 tbsp. of Italian herbs
1 cup of coconut, grated

INSTRUCTIONS

1. Thinly grate the zucchini & dry with a cheesecloth, ensuring to remove all of the moisture.
2. In a bowl, combine the zucchini with the egg, parmesan, Italian herbs, & grated coconut, mixing well to incorporate everything. Using your hands, mold the mixture into balls.
3. Pre-heat the Air Fryer at 400°F & place a rack inside. Lay the zucchini balls on the rack & cook for ten minutes. Serve hot.

391. POP CORN BROCCOLI

Prep & Cook Time: 10 minutes | Servings: 1

INGREDIENTS

4 egg yolks
¼ cup of butter, melted
2 cups of coconut flower
Salt & pepper
2 cups of broccoli florets

INSTRUCTIONS

1. In a bowl, whisk the egg yolks & melted butter together. Throw in the coconut flour, salt & pepper, then stir again to combine well.
2. Pre-heat the Air Fryer at 400°F.
3. Dip each broccoli floret into the mixture & place in the Air Fryer. Cook for six minutes, in multiple batches if necessary. Take care when removing them from the Air Fryer & enjoy!

392. ROSEMARY GREEN BEANS

Prep & Cook Time: 10 minutes | Servings: 1

INGREDIENTS

1 tbsp. of butter, melted
2 tbsp. of rosemary
½ tsp. of salt
3 cloves garlic, minced
¾ cup of green beans, chopped

INSTRUCTIONS

1. Pre-heat your Air Fryer at 390°F.
2. Combine the melted butter with the rosemary, salt, & minced garlic. Toss in the green beans, making sure to coat them well.
3. Cook in the Air Fryer for five minutes.

393. CARROT CROQUETTES

Prep & Cook Time: 10 minutes | Servings: 4

INGREDIENTS

2 medium-sized carrots, trimmed & grated
2 medium-sized celery stalks, trimmed & grated
½ cup of leek, finely chopped
1 tbsp. of garlic paste
¼ tsp. of freshly cracked black pepper
1 tsp. of sea salt
1 tbsp. of fresh dill, finely chopped
1 egg, lightly whisked
¼ cup of flour
¼ tsp. of baking powder
½ cup of breadcrumbs [seasoned or regular]
Chive mayo to serve

INSTRUCTIONS

1. Drain any excess liquid from the carrots & celery by placing them on a paper towel.
2. Stir together the vegetables with all of the other ingredients, save for the breadcrumbs & chive mayo.
3. Use your hands to mold 1 tbsp. of the vegetable mixture into a ball & repeat until all of the mixture has been used up. Press down on each ball with your hand or a palette knife. Cover completely with breadcrumbs. Spritz the croquettes with a non-stick cooking spray.
4. Arrange the croquettes in a single layer in your Air Fryer & fry for 6 minutes at 360°F.
5. Serve warm with the chive mayo on the side.

394. PEPPERED PUFF PASTRY

Prep & Cook Time: 25 minutes | Servings: 4

INGREDIENTS

1 ½ tbsp. of sesame oil
1 cup of white mushrooms, sliced
2 cloves garlic, minced
1 bell pepper, seeded & chopped
¼ tsp. of sea salt
¼ tsp. of dried rosemary
½ tsp. of ground black pepper
11 oz. of puff pastry sheets
½ cup of crème fraiche
1 egg, well whisked
½ cup of parmesan cheese, preferably freshly grated

INSTRUCTIONS

1. Pre-heat your Air Fryer to 400°F.
2. In a skillet, heat the sesame oil over a moderate heat & fry the mushrooms, garlic, & pepper until soft & fragrant.
3. Sprinkle on the salt, rosemary, & pepper.
4. In the meantime, unroll the puff pastry & slice it into 4-inch squares.
5. Spread the crème fraiche across each square.
6. Spoon equal amounts of the vegetables into the puff pastry squares. Enclose each square around the filling in a triangle shape, pressing the edges with your fingertips.
7. Brush each triangle with some whisked egg & cover with grated Parmesan.

8. Cook for 22-25 minutes.

395. SAUTÉED GREEN BEANS
Prep & Cook Time: 12 minutes | Servings: 4

INGREDIENTS

¾ lb. of green beans, cleaned
1 tbsp. of balsamic vinegar

¼ tsp. of salt
½ tsp. of mixed peppercorns, freshly cracked

1 tbsp. of butter
Sesame seeds to serve

INSTRUCTIONS
1. Pre-heat your Air Fryer at 390°F.
2. Combine the green beans with the rest of the ingredients, except for the sesame seeds. Transfer to the Air Fryer & cook for 10 minutes.
3. In the meantime, heat the sesame seeds in a small skillet to toast all over, stirring constantly to prevent burning.
4. Serve the green beans accompanied by the toasted sesame seeds.

396. HORSERADISH MAYO & GORGONZOLA MUSHROOMS
Prep & Cook Time: 15 minutes | Servings: 5

INGREDIENTS

½ cup of breadcrumbs
2 cloves garlic, pressed
2 tbsp. of fresh coriander, chopped
⅓ tsp. of salt

½ tsp. of crushed red pepper flakes
1 ½ tbsp. of olive oil
20 medium-sized mushrooms
½ cup of Gorgonzola cheese, grated

¼ cup of low-fat mayonnaise
1 tsp. of prepared horseradish
1 tbsp. of fresh parsley, finely chopped

INSTRUCTIONS
1. Combine the breadcrumbs together with the garlic, coriander, salt, red pepper, & the olive oil.
2. Take equal-sized amounts of the bread crumb mixture & use them to stuff the mushroom caps. Add the grated Gorgonzola on top of each.
3. Put the mushrooms in the Air Fryer grill pan & transfer to the Air Fryer.
4. Grill them at 380°F for 8-12 minutes, ensuring the stuffing is warm throughout.
5. In the meantime, prepare the horseradish mayo. Mix together the mayonnaise, horseradish & parsley.
6. When the mushrooms are ready, serve with the mayo.

397. SCALLION & RICOTTA POTATOES
Prep & Cook Time: 15 minutes | Servings: 4

INGREDIENTS

4 baking potatoes
2 tbsp. of olive oil
½ cup of Ricotta cheese
2 tbsp. of scallions, chopped

1 tbsp. of fresh parsley, chopped
1 heaped tbsp. of coriander, minced
2 oz. of Cheddar cheese, grated
1 tsp. of celery seeds

½ tsp. of salt
½ tsp. of garlic pepper

INSTRUCTIONS
1. Pierce the skin of the potatoes with a knife.
2. Cook in the Air Fryer basket for roughly 13 minutes at 350°F. If they are not cooked through by this time, leave for 2 – 3 minutes longer.
3. In the meantime, make the stuffing by combining all the other ingredients.
4. Cut halfway into the cooked potatoes to open them.
5. Spoon equal amounts of the stuffing into each potato & serve hot.

398. CRUMBED BEANS
Prep & Cook Time: 10 minutes | Servings: 4

INGREDIENTS

½ cup of flour
1 tsp. of smoky chipotle powder
½ tsp. of ground black pepper

1 tsp. of sea salt flakes
2 eggs, beaten
½ cup of crushed saltines

10 oz. of wax beans

INSTRUCTIONS
1. Combine the flour, chipotle powder, black pepper, & salt in a bowl. Put the eggs in a second bowl. Place the crushed saltines in a third bowl.
2. Wash the beans with cold water & discard any tough strings.
3. Coat the beans with the flour mixture, before dipping them into the beaten egg. Lastly cover them with the crushed saltines.
4. Spritz the beans with a cooking spray.
5. Air-fry at 360°F for 4 minutes. Give the cooking basket a good shake & continue to cook for 3 minutes. Serve hot.

399. COLBY POTATO PATTIES
Prep & Cook Time: 15 minutes | Servings: 8

INGREDIENTS

2 lb. of white potatoes, peeled & grated
½ cup of scallions, finely chopped
½ tsp. of freshly ground black pepper, or more to taste

1tbsp. of sea salt
½ tsp. of hot paprika
2 cups of Colby cheese, shredded
¼ cup of canola oil

1 cup crushed crackers

INSTRUCTIONS
1. Boil the potatoes until soft. Dry them off & peel them before mashing thoroughly, leaving no lumps.
2. Combine the mashed potatoes with scallions, pepper, salt, paprika, & cheese.
3. Mold the mixture into balls with your hands & press with your palm to flatten them into patties.
4. In a shallow dish, combine the canola oil & crushed crackers. Coat the patties in the crumb mixture.
5. Cook the patties inside your Air Fryer at 360°F for about 10 minutes, in multiple batches if necessary.
6. Serve with tabasco mayo or the sauce of your choice.

400. TURKEY GARLIC POTATOES
Prep & Cook Time: 45 minutes | Servings: 2

INGREDIENTS

3 unsmoked turkey strips
6 small potatoes

1 tsp. of garlic, minced
2 tsp. of olive oil

Salt
Pepper

INSTRUCTIONS
1. Peel the potatoes & cube them finely.
2. Coat in 1 tsp. of oil & cook in the Air Fryer for 10 minutes at 350°F.
3. In a separate bowl, slice the turkey finely & combine with the garlic, oil, salt & pepper. Pour the potatoes into the bowl & mix well.
4. Lay the mixture on some silver aluminum foil, transfer to the Air Fryer & cook for about 10 minutes.
5. Serve with raita.

401. CROUTONS
Prep & Cook Time: 25 minutes | Servings: 4

INGREDIENTS

2 slices of bread
1 tbsp. of olive oil

INSTRUCTIONS
1. Cut the slices of bread into medium-size chunks.
2. Coat the inside of the Air Fryer with the oil. Set it to 390°F & allow it to heat up.
3. Place the chunks inside & shallow fry for at least 8 minutes.
4. Serve with hot soup.

402. GARLIC STUFFED MUSHROOMS
Prep & Cook Time: 25 minutes | Servings: 4

INGREDIENTS

6 small mushrooms
1 oz. of onion, peeled & diced
1 tbsp. of breadcrumbs

1 tbsp. of olive oil
1 tsp. of garlic, pureed
1 tsp. of parsley

Salt & pepper

INSTRUCTIONS
1. Combine the breadcrumbs, oil, onion, parsley, salt, pepper & garlic in a bowl. Cut out the mushrooms' stalks & stuff each cap with the crumb mixture.
2. Cook in the Air Fryer for 10 minutes at 350°F.
3. Serve with a side of mayo dip.

403. ZUCCHINI SWEET POTATOES
Prep & Cook Time: 20 minutes | Servings: 4

INGREDIENTS

2 large-sized sweet potatoes, peeled & quartered
1 medium-sized zucchini, sliced
1 Serrano pepper, deveined & thinly sliced
1 bell pepper, deveined & thinly sliced

1 – 2 carrots, cut into matchsticks
¼ cup olive oil
1 ½ tbsp. of maple syrup
½ tsp. of porcini powder
¼ tsp. of mustard powder
½ tsp. of fennel seeds

1 tbsp. of garlic powder
½ tsp. of fine sea salt
¼ tsp. of ground black pepper
Tomato ketchup to serve

INSTRUCTIONS
1. Put the sweet potatoes, zucchini, peppers, & the carrot into the basket of your Air Fryer. Coat with a drizzling of olive oil.
2. Pre-heat the Air Fryer at 350°F.
3. Cook the vegetables for 15 minutes.
4. In the meantime, prepare the sauce by vigorously combining the other ingredients, save for the tomato ketchup, with a whisk.
5. Lightly grease a baking dish small enough to fit inside your Air Fryer.
6. Move the cooked vegetables to the baking dish, pour over the sauce & make sure to coat the vegetables well.
7. Raise the temperature to 390°F & cook the vegetables for an additional 5 minutes.
8. Serve warm with a side of ketchup.

404. CHEESE LINGS
Prep & Cook Time: 25 minutes | Servings: 6

INGREDIENTS

1 cup of flour
small cubes cheese, grated

¼ tsp. of chili powder
1 tsp. of butter

Salt
1 tsp. of baking powder

INSTRUCTIONS
1. Combine all the ingredients to form a dough, along with a small amount water as necessary.
2. Divide the dough into equal portions & roll each one into a ball.
3. Pre-heat Air Fryer at 360°F.
4. Transfer the balls to the Air Fryer & air fry for 5 minutes, stirring periodically.

405. POTATO SIDE DISH
Prep & Cook Time: 30 minutes | Servings: 2

INGREDIENTS

2 medium potatoes
1 tsp. of butter

3 tbsp. of sour cream
1 tsp. of chives

1 ½ tbsp. of cheese, grated
Salt & pepper

INSTRUCTIONS
1. Pierce the potatoes with a fork & boil them in water until they are cooked.
2. Transfer to the Air Fryer & cook for 15 minutes at 350°F.
3. In the meantime, combine the sour cream, cheese & chives in a bowl. Cut the potatoes halfway to open them up & fill with the butter & toppings.
4. Serve with salad.

406. ROASTED POTATOES & CHEESE
Prep & Cook Time: 55 minutes | Servings: 4

INGREDIENTS

4 medium potatoes
1 asparagus bunch

⅓ cup of cottage cheese
⅓ cup of low-fat crème fraiche

1 tbsp. of wholegrain mustard

INSTRUCTIONS
1. Pour some oil into your Air Fryer & pre-heat to 390°F.
2. Cook potatoes for 20 minutes.
3. Boil the asparagus in salted water for 3 minutes.
4. Remove the potatoes & mash them with rest of ingredients. Sprinkle on salt & pepper.
5. Serve with rice.

407. VEGETABLE & CHEESE OMELET
Prep & Cook Time: 15 minutes | Servings: 2

INGREDIENTS

3 tbsp. of milk
4 eggs, whisked
1 tsp. of melted butter

Salt & ground black pepper, to taste
1 red bell pepper, deveined & chopped
1 green bell pepper, deveined & chopped

1 white onion, finely chopped
½ cup of baby spinach leaves, roughly chopped
½ cup of Halloumi cheese, shaved

INSTRUCTIONS
1. Grease the Air Fryer baking pan with some canola oil.
2. Place all of the ingredients in the baking pan & stir well.
3. Transfer to the Air Fryer & cook at 350°F for 13 minutes.
4. Serve warm.

408. SCRAMBLED EGGS
Prep & Cook Time: 15 minutes | Servings: 2

INGREDIENTS

2 tbsp. of olive oil, melted
4 eggs, whisked

5 oz. of fresh spinach, chopped
1 medium-sized tomato, chopped

1 tsp. of fresh lemon juice
½ tsp. of coarse salt

½ tsp. of ground black pepper

½ cup of fresh basil, roughly chopped

INSTRUCTIONS
1. Grease the Air Fryer baking pan with the oil, tilting it to spread the oil around. Pre-heat the Air Fryer at 280°F.
2. Mix the remaining ingredients, apart from the basil leaves, whisking well until everything is completely combined.
3. Cook in the Air Fryer for 8 - 12 minutes.
4. Top with fresh basil leaves before serving with a little sour cream if desired.

409. SWEET CORN FRITTERS

Prep & Cook Time: 20 minutes | Servings: 4

INGREDIENTS

1 medium-sized carrot, grated
1 yellow onion, finely chopped
4 oz. canned sweet corn kernels, drained
1 tsp. of sea salt flakes

1 heaping tbsp. of fresh cilantro, chopped
1 medium-sized egg, whisked
2 tbsp. of plain milk
1 cup of Parmesan cheese, grated

¼ cup of flour
⅓ tsp. of baking powder
⅓ tsp. of sugar

INSTRUCTIONS
1. Place the grated carrot in a colander & press down to squeeze out any excess moisture. Dry it with a paper towel.
2. Combine the carrots with the remaining ingredients.
3. Mold 1 tbsp. of the mixture into a ball & press it down with your hand or a spoon to flatten it. Repeat until the rest of the mixture is used up.
4. Spritz the balls with cooking spray.
5. Arrange in the basket of your Air Fryer, taking care not to overlap any balls. Cook at 350°F for 8 to 11 minutes or until they're firm.
6. Serve warm.

410. ROSEMARY CORNBREAD

Prep & Cook Time: 1 hr. | Servings: 6

INGREDIENTS

1 cup of cornmeal
1 ½ cups of flour
½ tsp. of baking soda
½ tsp. of baking powder

¼ tsp. of salt
1 tsp. of dried rosemary
¼ tsp. of garlic powder
2 tbsp. of sugar

2 eggs
¼ cup of melted butter
1 cup of buttermilk
½ cup of corn kernels

INSTRUCTIONS
1. In a bowl, combine all the dry ingredients. In a separate bowl, mix together all the wet ingredients. Combine the two.
2. Fold in the corn kernels & stir vigorously.
3. Pour the batter into a lightly greased round loaf pan that is lightly greased.
4. Cook inside your Air Fryer for 1 hour at 380°F.

411. VEGGIE ROLLS

Prep & Cook Time: 30 minutes | Servings: 6

INGREDIENTS

2 potatoes, mashed
¼ cup of peas
¼ cup of carrots, mashed
1 small cabbage, sliced
¼ beans
2 tbsp. of sweetcorn

1 small onion, chopped
1 tsp. of capsicum
1 tsp. of coriander
2 tbsp. of butter
Ginger
Garlic to taste

½ tsp. of masala powder
½ tsp. of chili powder
½ cup of breadcrumbs
1 packet of spring roll sheets
½ cup of cornstarch slurry

INSTRUCTIONS
1. Boil all the vegetables in water over a low heat. Rinse & allow to dry.
2. Unroll the spring roll sheets & spoon equal amounts of vegetable onto the center of each one. Fold into spring rolls & coat each one with the slurry & breadcrumbs.
3. Pre-heat the Air Fryer to 390°F. Cook the rolls for 10 minutes.
4. Serve with a side of boiled rice.

412. GRILLED CHEESE

Prep & Cook Time: 25 minutes | Servings: 2

INGREDIENTS

4 slices of bread

½ cup of sharp cheddar cheese

¼ cup of butter, melted

INSTRUCTIONS
1. Pre-heat the Air Fryer at 360°F.
2. Put cheese & butter in separate bowls.
3. Apply the butter to each side of the bread slices with a brush.
4. Spread the cheese across two of the slices of bread & make two sandwiches. Transfer to the Air Fryer.
5. Cook for 5 – 7 minutes or until a golden-brown color is achieved & the cheese is melted.

413. POTATO GRATIN

Prep & Cook Time: 55 minutes | Servings: 6

INGREDIENTS

½ cup of milk
7 medium russet potatoes, peeled

1 tsp. of black pepper
½ cup of cream

½ cup of semi-mature cheese, grated
½ tsp. of nutmeg

INSTRUCTIONS
1. Pre-heat the Air Fryer to 390°F.
2. Cut the potatoes into wafer-thin slices.
3. In a bowl, combine the milk & cream & sprinkle with salt, pepper, & nutmeg as desired.
4. Use the milk mixture to coat the slices of potatoes. Place in an 8" heat-resistant baking dish. Top the potatoes with the rest of the cream mixture.
5. Put the baking dish into the basket of the Air Fryer & cook for 25 minutes.
6. Pour the cheese over the potatoes.
7. Cook for an additional 10 minutes, ensuring the top is nicely browned before serving.

414. ROASTED VEGETABLES

Prep & Cook Time: 30 minutes | Servings: 6

INGREDIENTS

1 ⅓ cup of small parsnips
1 ⅓ cup of celery [3 – 4 stalks]
2 red onions

1 ⅓ cup of small butternut squash
1 tbsp. of fresh thyme needles
1 tbsp. of olive oil

Salt & pepper

INSTRUCTIONS
1. Pre-heat the Air Fryer to 390°F.
2. Peel the parsnips & onions & cut them into 2-cm cubes. Slice the onions into wedges.
3. Do not peel the butternut squash. Cut it in half, de-seed it, & cube.
4. Combine the cut vegetables with the thyme, olive oil, salt & pepper.
5. Put the vegetables in the basket & transfer the basket to the Air Fryer.
6. Cook for 20 minutes, stirring once throughout the cooking time, until the vegetables are nicely browned & cooked through.

415. SWEET POTATO CURRY FRIES

Prep & Cook Time: 55 minutes | Servings: 4

INGREDIENTS

2.2 lb. of sweet potatoes
1 tsp. of curry powder

2 tbsp. of olive oil
Salt

INSTRUCTIONS

1. Pre-heat Air Fryer to 390°F.
2. Wash the sweet potatoes before slicing them into matchsticks.
3. Drizzle the oil in the pan, place the fries inside & bake for 25 minutes.
4. Sprinkle with curry & salt before serving with ketchup if desired.

416. MIXED PEPPERS DISH

Prep & Cook Time: 25 minutes | Servings: 4

INGREDIENTS

4 pcs. of red bell peppers, cut into medium strips
4 pcs. of green bell peppers, cut in medium strips

1 pc. of red onion, chopped
1 tbsp. of smoked paprika

1 tbsp. of olive oil
salt & black pepper to taste

INSTRUCTIONS

1. In air fryer, combine all ingredients, toss and cook at 360°F for 20 minutes.
2. Distribute the peppers between plates and serve as a side dish.

417. FRIED BEANS

Prep & Cook Time: 25 minutes | Servings: 4

INGREDIENTS

1 cup of drained canned garbanzo beans
4 cups of water
1 cup of drained canned cranberry beans
1½ cups of blanched green beans

1 pc. of garlic clove, minced
2 stalks of celery, chopped
1 bunch of cilantro, chopped
1 pc. of small red onion, chopped

5 tbsp. of apple cider vinegar
4 tbsp. of olive oil
1 tbsp. of sugar

INSTRUCTIONS

1. In a pan, combine all ingredients except the cilantro, stir well.
2. Transfer the pan in the air fryer and cook at 380°F for 15 minutes.
3. Add the cilantro, stir.
4. Distribute between plates and serve as a side dish.

418. YELLOW SQUASH & ZUCCHINI

Prep & Cook Time: 45 minutes | Servings: 4

INGREDIENTS

1 lb. of sliced zucchinis
1 pc. of yellow squash, halved, deseeded & cut in chunks

1 tbsp. of chopped cilantro
5 tsp. of olive oil
salt & white pepper to taste

INSTRUCTIONS

1. In a bowl, combine all the ingredients, toss well and transfer them to your air fryer's basket.
2. Cook for 35 minutes at 400°F.
3. Distribute everything between plates and serve as a side dish.

419. ITALIAN MUSHROOM

Prep & Cook Time: 20 minutes | Servings: 4

INGREDIENTS

1 lb. of button mushrooms, halved
3 tbsp. of melted butter

2 tbsp. of grated parmesan cheese
1 tsp. of Italian seasoning

a pinch of salt & black pepper

INSTRUCTIONS

1. In a pan, combine all the ingredients and toss.
2. Transfer the pan in the air fryer and cook at 360°F for 15 minutes.
3. Distribute the mix between plates and serve.

420. ZUCCHINI FRIES

Prep & Cook Time: 22 minutes | Servings: 4

INGREDIENTS

2 pcs. of small zucchinis, cut into fries
1 Cup of Breadcrumbs

2 Pcs. of Eggs, Whisked
½ cup of white flour

2 tsp. of olive oil
salt & black pepper to taste

INSTRUCTIONS

1. In a bowl, combine flour, salt and pepper, stir.
2. In another bowl, place the breadcrumbs.
3. Whisk the eggs in a separate bowl.
4. Coat the zucchini fries in the flour, then in the eggs and then in the breadcrumbs.
5. Use oil to grease air fryer and heat to 400°F.
6. Dip the zucchini fries and cook for 12 minutes.
7. Serve as a side dish.

421. CREAMY RISOTTO

Prep & Cook Time: 30 minutes | Servings: 4

INGREDIENTS

8 oz. of sliced mushrooms
4 oz. of heavy cream
2 cups of risotto rice

4 cups of chicken stock, heated up
2 pcs. of garlic cloves, minced
1 pc. of yellow onion, chopped

1 tbsp. of olive oil
1 tbsp. of cilantro, chopped
2 tbsp. of grated parmesan cheese

INSTRUCTIONS

1. In a pan, put all ingredients except for the cilantro.
2. Transfer the pan in the fryer and cook at 360°F for 20 minutes.
3. Put the cilantro, stir.
4. Distribute between plates and serve.

422. SWEET POTATO SIDE SALAD

Prep & Cook Time: 25 minutes | Servings: 2

INGREDIENTS

2 pcs. of sweet potatoes, peeled & cut into wedges
2 tbsp. of avocado oil
½ tsp. of curry powder

½ tsp. of ground cumin
¼ tsp. of ground coriander
4 tbsp. of mayonnaise
a pinch of cinnamon powder

a pinch of ginger powder
salt & black pepper to taste

INSTRUCTIONS
1. In air fryer's basket, combine sweet potato wedges with salt, pepper, coriander, curry powder and the oil, toss well.
2. Cook at 370°F for 20 minutes, flipping them once.
3. Put the potatoes to a bowl, then add the mayonnaise, cumin, ginger and the cinnamon.
4. Toss and serve as a side salad.

423. MOROCCAN EGGPLANT DISH
Prep & Cook Time: 25 minutes | Servings: 6

INGREDIENTS
1½ lbs. of cubed eggplant
1 tsp. of onion powder

1 tsp. of sumac
1 tbsp. of olive oil

2 tsp. of za'atar
juice of 1 lime

INSTRUCTIONS
1. Combine all ingredients in an air fryer.
2. Cook at 370°F for 20 minutes.
3. Distribute between plates and serve as a side dish.

424. GARLIC POTATOES
Prep & Cook Time: 45 minutes | Servings: 4

INGREDIENTS
4 pcs. of large potatoes, pricked with a fork
2 tbsp. of olive oil

1 tbsp. of minced garlic
salt & black pepper to taste

INSTRUCTIONS
1. In a bowl, combine all ingredients, make sure the potatoes are coated.
2. Place the potatoes in air fryer's basket and cook at 400°F for 40 minutes.
3. Peel potatoes (if desired), cut up.
4. Distribute between plates and serve as a side dish.

425. FRIED BEETS
Prep & Cook Time: 40 minutes | Servings: 6

INGREDIENTS
3 lbs. of small beets, trimmed & halved

1 tbsp. of olive oil

4 tbsp. of maple syrup

INSTRUCTIONS
1. Heat up air fryer with oil at 360°F.
2. Add the beets and maple syrup, toss and cook for 35 minutes.
3. Distribute the beets between plates and serve as a side dish.

426. GREEN BEANS & SHALLOTS
Prep & Cook Time: 30 minutes | Servings: 4

INGREDIENTS
1½ lbs. of trimmed green beans
½ lb. of chopped shallots

¼ cup of chopped walnuts
2 tbsp. of olive oil

INSTRUCTIONS
1. Combine all ingredients and toss in an air fryer.
2. Cook at 350°F for 25 minutes.
3. Distribute between plates and serve as a side dish.

427. MAPLE PARSNIPS
Prep & Cook Time: 45 minutes | Servings: 6

INGREDIENTS
2 lbs. of parsnips, roughly cubed
1 tbsp. of chopped cilantro

1 tbsp. of olive oil
2 tbsp. of maple syrup

INSTRUCTIONS
1. Preheat air fryer with olive oil at 360°F.
2. Put all ingredients, toss and cook for 40 minutes.
3. Distribute between plates and serve as a side dish.

428. BRUSSELS SPROUTS SIDE DISH
Prep & Cook Time: 35 minutes | Servings: 5

INGREDIENTS
3 lbs. of brussels sprouts, halved
1 lb. of chopped bacon
1 cup of milk
2 cups of heavy cream

3 pcs. of shallots, chopped
1 tsp. of olive oil
¼ tsp. of ground nutmeg
4 tbsp. of melted butter

3 tbsp. of prepared horseradish
salt & black pepper to taste

INSTRUCTIONS
1. Preheat the air fryer at 370°F.
2. Put oil, bacon, salt, pepper and Brussels sprouts, toss.
3. Add butter, shallots, heavy cream, milk, nutmeg and horseradish, toss again and cook for 25 minutes.
4. Distribute between plates and serve as a side dish.

429. FRIED CAULIFLOWER
Prep & Cook Time: 25 minutes | Servings: 4

INGREDIENTS
1 pc. of cauliflower head, florets separated
3 pcs. of garlic cloves, minced

1 tbsp. of olive oil
1 tbsp. of black sesame seeds

juice of 1 lime

INSTRUCTIONS
1. Heat up air fryer with olive oil at 350°F.
2. Put the cauliflower, garlic and lime juice, toss and then cook for 20 minutes.
3. Distribute between plates, sprinkle the sesame seeds on top.
4. Serve as a side dish.

430. MAYO BRUSSELS SPROUTS
Prep & Cook Time: 20 minutes | Servings: 4

INGREDIENTS
1 lb. of brussels sprouts, trimmed & halved
½ cup of mayonnaise

6 tsp. of olive oil
2 tbsp. of minced garlic

salt & black pepper to taste

INSTRUCTIONS
1. In air fryer, combine sprouts, salt, pepper and oil, toss well.
2. Cook sprouts at 390°F for 15 minutes.
3. Put them to a bowl, add mayo and garlic, toss.

4. Distribute between plates and serve as a side dish.

431. ENDIVES & RICE
Prep & Cook Time: 25 minutes | Servings: 4

INGREDIENTS
2 pcs. of scallions, chopped
½ cup of white rice
1 cup of veggie stock

4 pcs. of endives, trimmed & shredded
3 pcs. of garlic cloves, minced
1 tbsp. of olive oil

1 tsp. of chili sauce

INSTRUCTIONS
1. Grease a pan with olive oil. Combine all ingredients.
2. Transfer the pan in the air fryer and cook at 365°F for 20 minutes.
3. Distribute everything between plates and serve as a side dish.

432. PARSLEY QUINOA
Prep & Cook Time: 23 minutes | Servings: 4

INGREDIENTS
2 cups of quinoa
3 cups of veggie stock
2 pcs. of garlic cloves, minced

2 tbsp. of olive oil
2 tsp. of turmeric powder
a handful of chopped parsley

salt & black pepper to taste

INSTRUCTIONS
1. Heat the oil up in a pan over medium heat.
2. Put garlic, stir and cook for 2 minutes.
3. Put the quinoa, salt, pepper, turmeric and the stock, cover and cook at 360°F for 16 minutes.
4. Put the parsley, stir.
5. Distribute between plates and serve as a side dish.

433. MUSHROOM MIX
Prep & Cook Time: 20 minutes | Servings: 6

INGREDIENTS
15 oz. of mushrooms, roughly sliced
6 oz. of canned tomatoes, chopped

1 pc. of red onion, chopped
½ tsp. of ground nutmeg

2 tbsp. of olive oil
salt & black pepper to taste

INSTRUCTIONS
1. Combine all ingredients in a pan.
2. Transfer the pan in the fryer and cook at 380°F for 15 minutes.
3. Distribute the mix between plates and serve as a side dish.

434. PINEAPPLE RICE
Prep & Cook Time: 25 minutes | Servings: 6

INGREDIENTS
2 cups of rice
4 Cups of Chicken Stock, Heated Up

1 Pineapple, Peeled & Chopped
2 tsp. of olive oil

salt & black pepper to taste

INSTRUCTIONS
1. Combine all ingredients in a pan.
2. Transfer the pan into preheated air fryer and cook at 370°F for 20 minutes.
3. Distribute between plates and serve as a side dish.

435. CREAMY TOMATOES
Prep & Cook Time: 11 minutes | Servings: 4

INGREDIENTS
1 lb. of cherry tomatoes, halved
1 cup of heavy cream

½ tbsp. of creole seasoning
a drizzle of olive oil

salt & black pepper to taste

INSTRUCTIONS
1. Mix all the ingredients in a pan and toss well.
2. Transfer the pan in the fryer and cook at 400°F for 6 minutes.
3. Distribute between plates and serve.

436. SIMPLE EGGPLANT
Prep & Cook Time: 20 minutes | Servings: 4

INGREDIENTS
8 pcs. of baby eggplants, cubed
1 pc. of yellow onion, chopped
1 bunch of coriander, chopped

1 pc. of green bell pepper, chopped
1 tbsp. of tomato sauce
½ tsp. of garlic powder

1 tbsp. olive oil
Salt & Black Pepper to taste

INSTRUCTIONS
1. In a pan, mix all the ingredients and toss well.
2. Transfer the pan in the fryer and cook at 370°F for 10 minutes.
3. Distribute between plates and serve as a side dish.

437. FRENCH CARROTS
Prep & Cook Time: 25 minutes | Servings: 4

INGREDIENTS
1 lb. of trimmed baby carrots
2 tbsp. of lime juice

2 tsp. of olive oil
1 tsp. of herbs de provence

INSTRUCTIONS
1. In a bowl, combine all ingredients well and transfer to air fryer's basket.
2. Cook at 320°F for 20 minutes.
3. Distribute between plates and serve as a side dish.

438. CREAMY POTATOES
Prep & Cook Time: 25 minutes | Servings: 4

INGREDIENTS
2 pcs. of gold potatoes, cut into medium pieces
3 tbsp. of sour cream

1 tbsp. of olive oil
salt & black pepper to taste

INSTRUCTIONS
1. In a baking dish, combine all the ingredients and toss well.
2. Transfer the dish in the air fryer and cook at 370°F for 20 minutes.
3. Distribute between plates and serve as a side dish.

439. CAULIFLOWER & MUSHROOM RISOTTO
Prep & Cook Time: 50 minutes | Servings: 6

INGREDIENTS

1 pc. of cauliflower head, riced
10 oz. of drained water chestnuts
15 oz. of chopped mushrooms

3 pcs. of garlic cloves, minced
1 pc. of egg, whisked
2 tbsp. of olive oil

4 tbsp. of soy sauce
1 tbsp. of grated ginger
juice of 1 lime

INSTRUCTIONS

1. Mix all ingredients except for the egg in an air fryer.
2. Stir, cover and cook at 350°F for 20 minutes.
3. Put the egg, toss and cook at 360°F for 20 minutes more.
4. Distribute between plates and serve.

440. MINT & CHERRIES RICE

Prep & Cook Time: 32 minutes | Servings: 6

INGREDIENTS

10 pcs. of mint leaves, chopped
¼ cup of chopped green onions
2 cups of cherries, pitted & halved

3 cups of hot water
1 cup of white rice
1 tsp. of lemon juice

1 tbsp. of apple cider vinegar
1 tsp. of olive oil
salt & black pepper to taste

INSTRUCTIONS

1. In a pan, combine all ingredients and mix well.
2. Transfer the pan in the fryer and cook at 370°F for 22 minutes.
3. Distribute between plates and serve as a side dish.

441. PUMPKIN RICE

Prep & Cook Time: 30 minutes | Servings: 4

INGREDIENTS

12 oz. of risotto rice
6 oz. of pumpkin puree
4 oz. of heavy cream
1 pc. of small yellow onion, chopped

4 cups of chicken stock
2 pcs. of garlic cloves, minced
½ tsp. of ground nutmeg
½ tsp. of grated ginger

½ tsp. of cinnamon powder
½ tsp. of allspice
2 tbsp. of olive oil

INSTRUCTIONS

1. In a pan, heat up the oil over medium heat.
2. Sauté the onion and the garlic for 2 minutes.
3. Put nutmeg, ginger, cinnamon and allspice, cook for 1 more minute.
4. Put the rice, stock, pumpkin puree and the cream, stir
5. Transfer the pan in the fryer and cook at 360°F for 20 minutes.
6. Distribute between plates and serve as a side dish.

442. CHEESY MUSHROOM SALAD

Prep & Cook Time: 20 minutes | Servings: 3

INGREDIENTS

10 pcs. of large mushrooms, halved
1 tbsp. of grated cheddar cheese

1 tbsp. of grated mozzarella cheese
1 tbsp. of dried mixed herbs

2 tsp. of parsley flakes
a drizzle of olive oil

INSTRUCTIONS

1. Grease the pan with olive oil. Combine all ingredients and toss well.
2. Transfer the pan in the fryer and cook at 380°F for 15 minutes.
3. Distribute between plates and serve as a side dish.

443. BLACK BEANS

Prep & Cook Time: 20 minutes | Servings: 6

INGREDIENTS

1 cup of drained canned black beans
1 pc. of spring onion, chopped

2 pcs. of garlic cloves, minced
1 cup of water

½ tsp. of cumin seeds
salt & black pepper to taste

INSTRUCTIONS

1. In a pan, mix well all ingredients.
2. Transfer the pan in the fryer and cook at 370°F for 15 minutes.
3. Distribute between plates and serve as a side dish.

444. WILD RICE

Prep & Cook Time: 35 minutes | Servings: 8

INGREDIENTS

1 pc. of shallot, chopped
1½ cups of wild rice
4 cups of chicken stock

½ cup of hazelnuts, toasted & chopped
1 tsp. of minced garlic
1 tsp. of olive oil

1 tbsp. of chopped parsley
salt & black pepper to taste

INSTRUCTIONS

1. Heat up the oil in a pan over medium heat.
2. Sauté the garlic and the shallots for 2-3 minutes.
3. Put the rice, stock, salt and pepper and stir completely.
4. Transfer the pan in the air fryer and cook at 380°F for 25 minutes.
5. Put the parsley and the hazelnuts, stir.
6. Distribute between plates and serve as a side dish.

445. CRAB LEGS

Prep & Cook Time: 20 minutes | Servings: 3

INGREDIENTS

3 lb. of crab legs
¼ cup of salted butter, melted & divided

½ lemon, juiced

¼ tsp. of garlic powder

INSTRUCTIONS

1. In a bowl, toss the crab legs & two tbsp. of the melted butter together. Place the crab legs in the basket of the Air Fryer.
2. Cook at 400°F for fifteen minutes, giving the basket a good shake halfway through.
3. Combine the remaining butter with the lemon juice & garlic powder.
4. Crack open the cooked crab legs & remove the meat. Serve with the butter dip on the side & enjoy!

446. CRUSTY PESTO SALMON

Prep & Cook Time: 15 minutes | Servings: 2

INGREDIENTS

¼ cup of spinach, roughly chopped
¼ cup of pesto

2 x 4-oz. of salmon fillets
2 tbsp. of butter, melted

INSTRUCTIONS

1. Mix the spinach & pesto together.
2. Place the salmon fillets in a round baking dish, roughly six inches in diameter.
3. Brush the fillets with butter, followed by the pesto mixture, ensuring to coat both the top & bottom. Put the baking dish inside the Air Fryer.

4.   Cook for twelve minutes at 390°F.
5.   The salmon is ready when it flakes easily when prodded with a fork. Serve warm.

447. BUTTERY COD
Prep & Cook Time: 12 minutes | Servings: 2

INGREDIENTS

2 x 4-oz. of cod fillets
2 tbsp. of salted butter, melted

1 tsp. of Old Bay seasoning
½ medium lemon, sliced

INSTRUCTIONS
1.   Place the cod fillets in a baking dish.
2.   Brush with melted butter, season with Old Bay, & top with some lemon slices.
3.   Wrap the fish in aluminum foil & put into your Air Fryer.
4.   Cook for eight minutes at 350°F.
5.   The cod is ready when it flakes easily. Serve hot.

448. SESAME TUNA STEAK
Prep & Cook Time: 12 minutes | Servings: 2

INGREDIENTS

1 tbsp. of coconut oil, melted
2 x 6-oz. of tuna steaks

½ tsp. of garlic powder
2 tsp. of black sesame seeds

2 tsp. of white sesame seeds

INSTRUCTIONS
1.   Apply the coconut oil to the tuna steaks with a brunch, then season with garlic powder.
2.   Combine the black & white sesame seeds. Embed them in the tuna steaks, covering the fish all over. Place the tuna into your Air Fryer.
3.   Cook for eight minutes at 400°F, turning the fish halfway through.
4.   The tuna steaks are ready when they have reached a temperature of 145°F. Serve straightaway.

449. LEMON GARLIC SHRIMP
Prep & Cook Time: 15 minutes | Servings: 2

INGREDIENTS

1 medium lemon
½ lb. of medium shrimp, deveined

½ tsp. of Old Bay seasoning
2 tbsp. of butter, melted

½ tsp. of minced garlic

INSTRUCTIONS
1.   Grate the rind of the lemon into a bowl. Cut the lemon in half & juice it over the same bowl. Toss in the shrimp, Old Bay, & butter, mixing everything to make sure the shrimp is completely covered.
2.   Transfer to a round baking dish roughly six inches wide, then place this dish in your Air Fryer.
3.   Cook at 400°F for six minutes. The shrimp is cooked when it turns a bright pink color.
4.   Serve hot, drizzling any leftover sauce over the shrimp.

450. FOIL PACKET SALMON
Prep & Cook Time: 15 minutes | Servings: 2

INGREDIENTS

2 x 4-oz. skinless salmon fillets
2 tbsp. of butter, melted

½ tsp. of garlic powder
1 medium lemon

½ tsp. of dried dill

INSTRUCTIONS
1.   Take a sheet of aluminum foil & cut into two squares measuring roughly 5" x 5". Lay each of the salmon fillets at the center of each piece. Brush both fillets with a tbsp. of bullet & season with a quarter tsp. of garlic powder.
2.   Halve the lemon & grate the skin of one half over the fish. Cut four half-slices of lemon, using two to top each fillet. Season each fillet with a quarter tsp. of dill.
3.   Fold the tops & sides of the aluminum foil over the fish to create a kind of packet. Place each one in the Air Fryer.
4.   Cook for twelve minutes at 400°F.
5.   The salmon is ready when it flakes easily. Serve hot.

451. FOIL PACKET LOBSTER TAIL
Prep & Cook Time: 15 minutes | Servings: 2

INGREDIENTS

2 x 6-oz. lobster tail halves
2 tbsp. of salted butter, melted

½ medium lemon, juiced
½ tsp. of Old Bay seasoning

1 tsp. of dried parsley

INSTRUCTIONS
1.   Lay each lobster on a sheet of aluminum foil. Pour a light drizzle of melted butter & lemon juice over each one, & season with Old Bay.
2.   Fold down the sides & ends of the foil to seal the lobster. Place each one in the Air Fryer.
3.   Cook at 375°F for twelve minutes.
4.   Just before serving, top the lobster with dried parsley.

452. AVOCADO SHRIMP
Prep & Cook Time: 20 minutes | Servings: 2

INGREDIENTS

½ cup of onion, chopped
2 lb. of shrimp

1 tbsp. of seasoned salt
1 avocado

½ cup of pecans, chopped

INSTRUCTIONS
1.   Pre-heat the Air Fryer at 400°F.
2.   Put the chopped onion in the basket of the Air Fryer & spritz with some cooking spray. Leave to cook for five minutes.
3.   Add the shrimp & set the timer for a further five minutes. Sprinkle with some seasoned salt, then allow to cook for an additional five minutes.
4.   During these last five minutes, halve your avocado & remove the pit. Cube each half, then scoop out the flesh.
5.   Take care when removing the shrimp from the Air Fryer. Place it on a dish & top with the avocado & the chopped pecans.

453. LEMON BUTTER SCALLOPS
Prep & Cook Time: 30 minutes | Servings: 1

INGREDIENTS

1 lemon
1 lb. of scallops

½ cup of butter
¼ cup of parsley, chopped

INSTRUCTIONS
1.   Juice the lemon into a Ziploc bag.
2.   Wash your scallops, dry them, & season to taste. Put them in the bag with the lemon juice. Refrigerate for an hour.
3.   Remove the bag from the refrigerator & leave for about twenty minutes until it returns to room temperature. Transfer the scallops into a foil pan that is small enough to be placed inside the Air Fryer.
4.   Pre-heat the Air Fryer at 400°F & put the rack inside.
5.   Place the foil pan on the rack & cook for five minutes.
6.   In the meantime, melt the butter in a saucepan over a medium heat. Zest the lemon over the saucepan, then add in the chopped parsley. Mix well.
7.   Take care when removing the pan from the Air Fryer. Transfer the contents to a plate & drizzle with the lemon-butter mixture. Serve hot.

454. CHEESY LEMON HALIBUT

Prep & Cook Time: 20 minutes | Servings: 2

INGREDIENTS

1 lb. of halibut fillet
½ cup of butter

2 ½ tbsp. of mayonnaise
2 ½ tbsp. of lemon juice

¾ cup of parmesan cheese, grated

INSTRUCTIONS

1. Pre-heat your Air Fryer at 375°F.
2. Spritz the halibut fillets with cooking spray & season as desired.
3. Put the halibut in the Air Fryer & cook for twelve minutes.
4. In the meantime, combine the butter, mayonnaise, & lemon juice in a bowl with a hand mixer. Ensure a creamy texture is achieved.
5. Stir in the grated parmesan.
6. When the halibut is ready, open the drawer & spread the butter over the fish with a butter knife. Allow to cook for a further two minutes, then serve hot.

455. SPICY MACKEREL

Prep & Cook Time: 20 minutes | Servings: 2

INGREDIENTS

2 mackerel fillets
2 tbsp. of red chili flakes

2 tsp. of garlic, minced
1 tsp. of lemon juice

INSTRUCTIONS

1. Season the mackerel fillets with the red pepper flakes, minced garlic, & a drizzle of lemon juice. Allow to sit for five minutes.
2. Preheat your Air Fryer at 350°F.
3. Cook the mackerel for five minutes, before opening the drawer, flipping the fillets, & allowing to cook on the other side for another five minutes.
4. Plate the fillets, making sure to spoon any remaining juice over them before serving.

456. THYME SCALLOPS

Prep & Cook Time: 12 minutes | Servings: 1

INGREDIENTS

1 lb. of scallops
Salt & pepper

½ tbsp. of butter
½ cup thyme, chopped

INSTRUCTIONS

1. Wash the scallops & dry them completely. Season with pepper & salt, then set aside while you prepare the pan.
2. Grease a foil pan in several spots with the butter & cover the bottom with the thyme. Place the scallops on top.
3. Pre-heat the Air Fryer at 400°F & set the rack inside.
4. Place the foil pan on the rack & allow to cook for seven minutes.
5. Take care when removing the pan from the Air Fryer & transfer the scallops to a serving dish. Spoon any remaining butter in the pan over the fish & enjoy.

457. CRISPY CALAMARI

Prep & Cook Time: 15 minutes | Servings: 4

INGREDIENTS

1 lb. of fresh squid
Salt & pepper

2 cups of flour
1 cup of water

2 cloves garlic, minced
½ cup of mayonnaise

INSTRUCTIONS

1. Remove the skin from the squid & discard any ink. Slice the squid into rings & season with some salt & pepper.
2. Put the flour & water in separate bowls. Dip the squid firstly in the flour, then into the water, then into the flour again, ensuring that it is entirely covered with flour.
3. Pre-heat the Air Fryer at 400°F. Put the squid inside & cook for six minutes.
4. In the meantime, prepare the aioli by combining the garlic with the mayonnaise in a bowl.
5. Once the squid is ready, plate up & serve with the aioli.

458. FILIPINO BISTEK

Prep & Cook Time: 10 minutes + marinating time | Servings: 4

INGREDIENTS

2 milkfish bellies, sliced into four portions
¾ tsp. of salt
¼ tsp. of ground black pepper
¼ tsp. of cumin powder

2 tbsp. of calamansi juice
2 lemongrasses, cut crosswise into small pieces
½ cup of tamari sauce
2 tbsp. of fish sauce [Patis]

2 tbsp. of sugar
1 tsp. of garlic powder
½ cup of chicken broth
2 tbsp. of olive oil

INSTRUCTIONS

1. Dry the fish using some paper towels.
2. Put the fish in a large bowl & coat with the rest of the ingredients. Allow to marinate for 3 hours in the refrigerator.
3. Cook the fish steaks on an Air Fryer grill basket at 340°F for 5 minutes.
4. Turn the steaks over & allow to grill for an additional 4 minutes. Cook until medium brown.
5. Serve with steamed white rice.

459. SALTINE FISH FILLETS

Prep & Cook Time: 15 minutes | Servings: 4

INGREDIENTS

1 cup of crushed saltines
¼ cup of extra-virgin olive oil
1 tsp. of garlic powder

½ tsp. of shallot powder
1 egg, well whisked
4 white fish fillets

Salt & ground black pepper to taste
Fresh Italian parsley to serve

INSTRUCTIONS

1. In a shallow bowl, combine the crushed saltines & olive oil.
2. In a separate bowl, mix together the garlic powder, shallot powder, & the beaten egg.
3. Sprinkle a good amount of salt & pepper over the fish, before dipping each fillet into the egg mixture.
4. Coat the fillets with the crumb mixture.
5. Air fry the fish at 370°F for 10 - 12 minutes.
6. Serve with fresh parsley.

460. COD NUGGETS

Prep & Cook Time: 25 minutes | Servings: 4

INGREDIENTS

1 lb. of cod fillet, cut into chunks
1 tbsp. of olive oil

1 cup of cracker crumbs
1 tbsp. of egg & water

½ cup of flour
Salt & pepper

INSTRUCTIONS

1. Place the cracker crumbs & oil in food processor & pulse together. Sprinkle the cod pieces with salt & pepper.
2. Roll the cod pieces in the flour before dredging them in egg & coating them in the cracker crumbs.
3. Pre-heat the Air Fryer to 350°F.
4. Put the fish in the basket & air fry to 350°F for 15 minutes or until a light golden-brown color is achieved.

5. Serve hot.

461. SWEET POTATOES & SALMON

Prep & Cook Time: 45 minutes | Servings: 4

INGREDIENTS

For the Salmon Fillets:
4 x 6-oz. of skin-on salmon fillets
1 tbsp. of extra-virgin olive oil
1 tsp. of celery salt
¼ tsp. of ground black pepper, or more to taste

2 tbsp. of capers
Pinch of dry mustard
Pinch of ground mace
1 tsp. of smoked cayenne pepper

For the Potatoes:
4 sweet potatoes, peeled & cut into wedges
1 tbsp. of sesame oil
Kosher salt & pepper, to taste

INSTRUCTIONS
1. Coat all sides of the salmon filets with a brushing of oil. Cover with all the seasonings for the fillets.
2. Air fry at 360°F for 5 minutes, flip them over, & proceed to cook for 5 more minutes.
3. In the meantime, coat the sweet potatoes with the sesame oil, salt, & pepper.
4. Cook the potatoes at 380°F for 15 minutes.
5. Turn the potatoes over & cook for another 15 - 20 minutes.
6. Serve the potatoes & salmon together.

462. GRILLED SHRIMP

Prep & Cook Time: 35 minutes | Servings: 4

INGREDIENTS

18 shrimps, shelled & deveined
2 tbsp. of freshly squeezed lemon juice
½ tsp. of hot paprika
½ tsp. of salt

1 tsp. of lemon-pepper seasoning
2 tbsp. of extra-virgin olive oil
2 garlic cloves, peeled & minced
1 tsp. of onion powder

¼ tsp. of cumin powder
½ cup of fresh parsley, coarsely chopped

INSTRUCTIONS
1. Put all the ingredients in a bowl, making sure to coat the shrimp well. Refrigerate for 30 minutes.
2. Pre-heat the Air Fryer at 400°F
3. Air-fry the shrimp for 5 minutes, ensuring that the shrimps turn pink.
4. Serve with pasta or rice.

463. HOMEMADE COD FILLETS

Prep & Cook Time: 15 minutes | Servings: 4

INGREDIENTS

4 cod fillets
¼ tsp. of fine sea salt
¼ tsp. of ground black pepper, or more to taste

1 tsp. of cayenne pepper
½ cup of non-dairy milk
½ cup of fresh Italian parsley, coarsely chopped

1 tsp. of dried basil
½ tsp. of dried oregano
1 Italian pepper, chopped
4 garlic cloves, minced

INSTRUCTIONS
1. Lightly grease a baking dish with some vegetable oil.
2. Coat the cod fillets with salt, pepper, & cayenne pepper.
3. Blend the rest of the ingredients in a food processor. Cover the fish fillets in this mixture.
4. Transfer the fillets to the Air Fryer & cook at 380°F for 10 to 12 minutes, ensure the cod is flaky before serving.

464. CHRISTMAS FLOUNDER

Prep & Cook Time: 15 minutes + marinating time | Servings: 4

INGREDIENTS

4 flounder fillets
Sea salt & freshly cracked mixed peppercorns, to taste
1 ½ tbsp. of dark sesame oil

2 tbsp. of sake
¼ cup of soy sauce
1 tbsp. of grated lemon rind
2 garlic cloves, minced

1 tsp. of sugar
Fresh chopped chives, to serve

INSTRUCTIONS
1. Put all of the ingredients, except for the chives, in a large bowl. Coat the fillets well with the seasoning.
2. Refrigerate for 2 hours to let it marinate.
3. Place the fish fillets in the Air Fryer cooking basket & cook at 360°F for 10 to 12 minutes, turning once during the cooking time.
4. Simmer the rest of the marinade over a medium-to-low heat, stirring constantly, allowing it to thicken.
5. Plate up the flounder & add the glaze on top. Serve with fresh chives.

465. COCONUT PRAWNS

Prep & Cook Time: 10 minutes | Servings: 4

INGREDIENTS

12 prawns, cleaned & deveined
Salt & ground black pepper, to taste
½ tsp. of cumin powder
1 tsp. of fresh lemon juice

1 medium egg, whisked
⅓ cup of beer
½ cup of flour
1 tsp. of baking powder

1 tbsp. of curry powder
½ tsp. of grated fresh ginger
1 cup of flaked coconut

INSTRUCTIONS
1. Coat the prawns in the salt, pepper, cumin powder, & lemon juice.
2. In a bowl, combine together the whisked egg, beer, a quarter-cup of the flour, baking powder, curry, & ginger.
3. In a second bowl, put the remaining quarter-cup of flour, & in a third bowl, the flaked coconut.
4. Dredge the prawns in the flour, before coating them in the beer mixture. Finally, coat your prawns in the flaked coconut.
5. Air-fry at 360°F for 5 minutes. Flip them & allow to cook on the other side for another 2 to 3 minutes before serving.

466. CAJUN SHRIMP

Prep & Cook Time: 25 minutes | Servings: 4

INGREDIENTS

¼ tsp. of cayenne pepper
¼ tsp. of smoked paprika

½ tsp. of old bay seasoning
1 tbsp. of olive oil

Salt
1 ¼ lb. of tiger shrimp

INSTRUCTIONS
1. Pre-heat your Air Fryer to 390°F.
2. In a large bowl, combine together all the ingredients, ensuring to coat the shrimps well.
3. Transfer to the Air Fryer & cook for 5 minutes.
4. Serve over boiled rice.

467. CATFISH

Prep & Cook Time: 30 minutes | Servings: 4

INGREDIENTS

2 catfish fillets [catfish]

1 medium egg, beaten

1 cup of breadcrumbs

1 cup of tortilla chips
1 lemon, juiced & peeled

1 tsp. of parsley
Salt & pepper

INSTRUCTIONS
1. Slice up the catfish fillets neatly & drizzle lightly with the lemon juice.
2. In a separate bowl, combine the breadcrumbs with the lemon rind, parsley, tortillas, salt & pepper. Pour into your food processor & pulse.
3. Put the fillets in a tray & spread it evenly across the base. Pour the mixture over the fish to cover well.
4. Transfer to your Air Fryer & cook at 350°F for 15 minutes. Serve with chips & a refreshing drink.

468. FISH FILLETS
Prep & Cook Time: 25 minutes | Servings: 4

INGREDIENTS

4 fish fillets
1 egg, beaten

1 cup of breadcrumbs
4 tbsp. of olive oil

Salt & pepper

INSTRUCTIONS
1. Pre-heat the Air Fryer at 350°F.
2. In a shallow dish, combine together the breadcrumbs, oil, pepper, & salt.
3. Pour the beaten egg into a second dish.
4. Dredge each fish fillet in the egg before rolling them in the breadcrumbs. Place in the Air Fryer basket.
5. Allow to cook in the Air Fryer for 12 minutes.

469. BEAN BURRITOS
Prep & Cook Time: 15 minutes | Servings: 4

INGREDIENTS

4 tortillas
1 can of beans
1 cup of cheddar cheese, grated

¼ tsp. of paprika
¼ tsp. of chili powder
¼ tsp. of garlic powder

Salt & pepper

INSTRUCTIONS
1. Pre-heat the Air Fryer to 350°F.
2. In a bowl, mix together the paprika, chili powder, garlic powder, salt & pepper.
3. Fill each tortilla with an equal portion of beans before adding the spice mixture & the cheddar cheese. Roll the tortilla wraps into burritos.
4. Cover the base of a baking dish with parchment paper.
5. Transfer the burritos to the baking dish.
6. Put in the Air Fryer & cook for roughly 5 minutes. Serve hot.

470. FISHMAN CAKES
Prep & Cook Time: 35 minutes | Servings: 4

INGREDIENTS

2 cups of white fish
1 cup of potatoes, mashed
1 tsp. of mix herbs
1 tsp. of mix spice

1 tsp. of coriander
1 tsp. of Worcestershire sauce
2 tsp. of chili powder
1 tsp. of milk

1 tsp. of butter
1 small onion, diced
¼ cup of breadcrumbs
Salt & pepper

INSTRUCTIONS
1. Place all of the ingredients in a bowl & combine.
2. Using your hands, mold equal portions of the mixture into small patties & refrigerate for 2 hours.
3. Put the fish cakes in the Air Fryer basket & cook at 400°F for 15 minutes. Serve hot.

471. SUNDAY'S SALMON
Prep & Cook Time: 20 minutes | Servings: 3

INGREDIENTS

½ lb. of salmon fillet, chopped
2 egg whites
2 tbsp. of chives, chopped
2 tbsp. of garlic, minced

½ cup of onion, chopped
⅔ cup of carrots, grated
⅔ cup of potato, grated
½ cup of breadcrumbs

¼ cup of flour
Pepper & salt

INSTRUCTIONS
1. In a shallow dish, combine the breadcrumbs with the pepper & salt.
2. Pour the flour into another dish.
3. In a third dish, add the egg whites.
4. Put all of the other ingredients in a large mixing bowl & stir together to combine.
5. Using your hands, shape equal amounts of the mixture into small balls. Roll each ball in the flour before dredging it in the egg & lastly covering it with breadcrumbs. Transfer all the coated croquettes to the Air Fryer basket & air fry at 320°F for 6 minutes.
6. Increase the heat to 350°F & allow to cook for another 4 minutes.
7. Serve hot.

472. WHITEFISH CAKES
Prep & Cook Time: 1 hr. 20 minutes | Servings: 4

INGREDIENTS

1 ½ cups of whitefish fillets, minced
1 ½ cups of green beans, finely chopped
½ cup of scallions, chopped
1 chili pepper, deveined & minced
1 tbsp. of red curry paste

1 tsp. of sugar
1 tbsp. of fish sauce
2 tbsp. of apple cider vinegar
1 tsp. of water
Sea salt flakes, to taste

½ tsp. of cracked black peppercorns
1 ½ tsp. of butter, at room temperature
1 lemon

INSTRUCTIONS
1. Place all of the ingredients a bowl, following the order in which they are listed.
2. Combine well with a spatula or your hands.
3. Mold the mixture into several small cakes & refrigerate for 1 hour.
4. Put a piece of aluminum foil in the cooking basket & lay the cakes on top.
5. Cook inside your Air Fryer at 390°F for 10 minutes. Turn each fish cake over before air-frying for another 5 minutes.
6. Serve the fish cakes with a side of cucumber relish.

473. MARINATED SARDINES
Prep & Cook Time: 1 hr. 15 minutes | Servings: 4

INGREDIENTS

¾ lb. of sardines, cleaned & rinsed
Salt & ground black pepper, to taste
For the Potatoes:
8 medium Russet potatoes, peeled & quartered

1 tsp. of smoked cayenne pepper
1 tbsp. of lemon juice

½ stick of melted butter
Salt & pepper, to taste

1 tbsp. of soy sauce
2 tbsp. of olive oil

1 tsp. of granulated garlic

INSTRUCTIONS
1. Dry the sardines with a paper towel.
2. Cover the sardines in the salt, black pepper, cayenne pepper, lemon juice, soy sauce, & olive oil, & leave to marinate for half an hour.
3. Air-fry the sardines at 350°F for roughly 5 minutes.
4. Raise the heat to 385°F & cook for an additional 7 - 8 minutes. Remove the sardines & plate up.
5. Wipe the cooking basket clean & pour in the potatoes, butter, salt, pepper, & garlic.
6. Roast at 390°F for 30 minutes. Serve the vegetables & the sardines together.

474. HALIBUT STEAKS
Prep & Cook Time: 15 minutes | Servings: 4

INGREDIENTS

1 lb. of halibut steaks
Salt & pepper
1 tsp. of dried basil
2 tbsp. of honey

¼ cup of vegetable oil
2 ½ tbsp. of Worcester sauce
1 tbsp. of freshly squeezed lemon juice
2 tbsp. of vermouth

1 tbsp. of fresh parsley leaves, coarsely chopped

INSTRUCTIONS
1. Put all of the ingredients in a large bowl. Combine & cover the fish completely with the seasoning.
2. Transfer to your Air Fryer & cook at 390°F for 5 minutes.
3. Turn the fish over & allow to cook for a further 5 minutes.
4. Ensure the fish is cooked through, leaving it in the Air Fryer for a few more minutes if necessary.
5. Serve with a side of potato salad.

475. FISHERMAN'S FISH FINGERS
Prep & Cook Time: 40 minutes | Servings: 4

INGREDIENTS

¾ lb. of fish, cut into fingers
1 cup of breadcrumbs
2 tsp. of mixed herbs
¼ tsp. of baking soda
2 eggs, beaten

3 tsp. of flour
2 tbsp. of Maida
1 tsp. of garlic ginger puree
½ tsp. of black pepper
2 tsp. of garlic powder

½ tsp. of red chili flakes
½ tsp. of turmeric powder
2 tbsp. of lemon juice
½ tsp. of salt

INSTRUCTIONS
1. Put the fish, garlic ginger puree, garlic powder, red chili flakes, turmeric powder, lemon juice, 1 tsp. of the mixed herbs, & salt in a bowl & combine well.
2. In a separate bowl, combine the flour, Maida, & baking soda.
3. In a third bowl pour in the beaten eggs.
4. In a fourth bowl, stir together the breadcrumbs, black pepper, & another tsp. of mixed herbs.
5. Pre-heat the Air Fryer to 350°F.
6. Coat the fish fingers in the flour. Dredge in the egg, then roll in the breadcrumb mixture.
7. Put the fish fingers in the Air Fryer's basket & allow to cook for 10 minutes, ensuring they crisp up nicely.

476. FISH TACO
Prep & Cook Time: 30 minutes | Servings: 4

INGREDIENTS

12 oz. of cod filet
1 cup of breadcrumbs
4 – 6 flour tortillas
1 cup of tempura butter

½ cup of salsa
½ cup of guacamole
2 tbsp. of freshly chopped cilantro
½ tsp. of salt

¼ tsp. of black pepper
Lemon wedges for garnish

INSTRUCTIONS
1. Slice the cod filets lengthwise & sprinkle salt & pepper on all sides.
2. Put the tempura butter in a bowl & coat each cod piece in it. Dip the fillets into the breadcrumbs.
3. Pre-heat the Air Fryer to 340°F.
4. Fry the cod sticks for about 10 – 13 minutes in the Air Fryer. Flip each one once while cooking.
5. In the meantime, coat one side of each tortilla with an even spreading of guacamole.
6. Put a cod stick in each tortilla & add the chopped cilantro & salsa on top. Lightly drizzle over the lemon juice. Fold into tacos.

477. CRISPY FISH FILLET
Prep & Cook Time: 15 minutes | Servings: 4

INGREDIENTS

2 fish fillets, each sliced into 4 pieces
1 tbsp. of lemon juice
1 tsp. of chili powder

4 tbsp. of mayonnaise
3 tbsp. of cornmeal
¼ tsp. of black pepper

4 tbsp. of flour
¼ tsp. of salt

INSTRUCTIONS
1. Pre-heat the Air Fryer at 400°F.
2. Combine together the flour, pepper, cornmeal, salt, & chili powder.
3. In a shallow bowl, stir together the lemon juice & mayonnaise.
4. Coat the fillets in the mayonnaise mixture, before covering with the flour mixture, ensuring they crisp up nicely. Serve hot.
5. Put the coated fish into the Air Fryer's basket & cook for 5 minutes, ensuring they crisp up nicely. Serve hot.

478. CRISPY SHRIMP
Prep & Cook Time: 20 minutes | Servings: 8

INGREDIENTS

2 lb. of shrimp, peeled & deveined
4 egg whites
2 tbsp. of olive oil

1 cup of flour
½ tsp. of cayenne pepper
1 cup of breadcrumbs

Salt & pepper

INSTRUCTIONS
1. Combine together the flour, pepper, & salt in a shallow bowl.
2. In a separate bowl mix the egg whites using a whisk.
3. In a third bowl, combine the breadcrumbs, cayenne pepper, & salt.
4. Pre-heat your Air Fryer to 400°F.
5. Cover the shrimp with the flour mixture before dipping it in the egg white & lastly rolling in the breadcrumbs.
6. Put the coated shrimp in the Air Fryer's basket & top with a light drizzle of olive oil. Air fry the shrimp at 400°F for 8 minutes, in multiple batches if necessary.

479. FISH STICKS
Prep & Cook Time: 20 minutes | Servings: 4

INGREDIENTS

1 lb. of tilapia fillets, cut into strips
1 large egg, beaten

2 tsp. of Old Bay seasoning
1 tbsp. of olive oil

1 cup of breadcrumbs

INSTRUCTIONS
1. Pre-heat the Air Fryer at 400°F.
2. In a shallow dish, combine together the breadcrumbs, Old Bay, & oil. Put the egg in a small bowl.

3. Dredge the fish sticks in the egg. Cover them with breadcrumbs & put them in the Air Fryer's basket.
4. Cook the fish for 10 minutes or until they turn golden brown.
5. Serve hot.

480. CRAB HERB CROQUETTES

Prep & Cook Time: 30 minutes | Servings: 6

INGREDIENTS

1 lb. of crab meat
1 cup of breadcrumbs
2 egg whites
½ tsp. of parsley
¼ tsp. of chives

¼ tsp. of tarragon
2 tbsp. of celery, chopped
¼ cup of red pepper, chopped
1 tsp. of olive oil
½ tsp. of lime juice

4 tbsp. of sour cream
4 tbsp. of mayonnaise
¼ cup of onion, chopped
¼ tsp. of salt

INSTRUCTIONS
1. Put the breadcrumbs & salt in a bowl.
2. Pour the egg whites in a separate bowl.
3. Place the rest of the ingredients in a third bowl & combine thoroughly.
4. Using your hands, shape equal amounts of the mixture into small balls & dredge each ball in the egg white before coating with the breadcrumbs.
5. Put the croquettes in the Air Fryer basket & cook at 400°F for 18 minutes. Serve hot.

481. BROILED TILAPIA

Prep & Cook Time: 10 minutes | Servings: 4

INGREDIENTS

1 lb. of tilapia fillets

½ tsp. of lemon pepper

Salt

INSTRUCTIONS
1. Spritz the Air Fryer basket with some cooking spray.
2. Put the tilapia fillets in basket & sprinkle on the lemon pepper & salt.
3. Cook at 400°F for 7 minutes.
4. Serve with a side of vegetables.

482. SALMON PATTIES

Prep & Cook Time: 20 minutes | Servings: 4

INGREDIENTS

1 egg
14 oz. of canned salmon, drained
4 tbsp. of flour

4 tbsp. of cup cornmeal
4 tbsp. of onion, minced
½ tsp. of garlic powder

2 tbsp. of mayonnaise
Salt & pepper

INSTRUCTIONS
1. Flake apart the salmon with a fork.
2. Put the flakes in a bowl & combine with the garlic powder, mayonnaise, flour, cornmeal, egg, onion, pepper, & salt.
3. Use your hands to shape equal portions of the mixture into small patties & put each one in the Air Fryer basket.
4. Air fry the salmon patties at 350°F for 15 minutes. Serve hot.

483. LEMON FISH

Prep & Cook Time: 25 minutes | Servings: 2

INGREDIENTS

2 tsp. of green chili sauce
2 tsp. of oil
2 egg whites
Salt

1 tsp. of red chili sauce
2 – 3 lettuce leaves
4 tsp. of flour
2 lemons

¼ cup of sugar
4 fish fillets

INSTRUCTIONS
1. Slice up one of the lemons & set aside.
2. Boil a half-cup of water in a saucepan. Stir in the sugar, ensuring it dissolves completely.
3. Put 1 cup of the flour, salt, green chili sauce, 2 teaspoons of oil & the egg white in a bowl & combine well.
4. Add 3 tbsp. of water & mix with a whisk until a smooth, thick consistency is achieved. Evenly spread the refined flour across a plate.
5. Dredge the fish fillets in the batter & cover with the refined flour.
6. Coat the Air Fryer's basket with a brushing of oil. Put the fish fillets in the basket & cook at 180°F for 10 – 15 minutes.
7. Add salt to the saucepan & combine well. Pour in the corn flour slurry & mix once more.
8. Add in the red chili sauce & stir.
9. Add the lemon slices. Squeeze the juice of the other lemon into the saucepan. Continue to cook, ensuring the sauce thickens well, stirring all the time.
10. Take the fish out of the Air Fryer, coat with a light brushing of oil & return to the Air Fryer basket.
11. Allow to cook for 5 additional minutes.
12. Shred up the lettuce leaves with your hands & arrange them on a serving platter.
13. Serve the fish over the lettuce & with the lemon sauce drizzled on top.

484. JUMBO SHRIMP

Prep & Cook Time: 10 minutes | Servings: 4

INGREDIENTS

12 jumbo shrimps
½ tsp. of garlic salt
¼ tsp. of freshly cracked mixed
peppercorns

For the Sauce:
1 tsp. of Dijon mustard
4 tbsp. of mayonnaise
1 tsp. of lemon zest

1 tsp. of chipotle powder
½ tsp. of cumin powder

INSTRUCTIONS
1. Sprinkle the garlic salt over the shrimp & coat with the cracked peppercorns.
2. Fry the shrimp in your Air Fryer at 395°F for 5 minutes.
3. Turn the shrimp over & allow to cook for a further 2 minutes.
4. In the meantime, mix together all ingredients for the sauce with a whisk.
5. Serve over the shrimp.

485. COD

Prep & Cook Time: 20 minutes | Servings: 5

INGREDIENTS

1 lb. of cod
3 tbsp. of milk
1 cup of oatmeal

2 cups of breadcrumbs
2 large eggs, beaten
½ tsp. of pepper

¼ tsp. of salt

INSTRUCTIONS
1. Combine together the milk & eggs in a bowl.
2. In a shallow dish, stir together breadcrumbs, pepper, & salt.
3. Pour the oatmeal into a second shallow dish.
4. Coat the cod sticks with the meal before dipping each one in the egg & rolling in breadcrumbs.
5. Put the fish sticks in the Air Fryer basket. Cook at 350°F for 12 minutes, shaking the basket halfway through cooking.

486. CHEESE TILAPIA

Prep & Cook Time: 20 minutes | Servings: 4

INGREDIENTS

1 lb. of tilapia fillets
¾ cup of parmesan cheese, grated

1 tbsp. of parsley, chopped
2 tsp. of paprika

1 tbsp. of olive oil
Salt & pepper

INSTRUCTIONS

1. Pre-heat the Air Fryer to 400°F.
2. In a shallow dish, combine together the paprika, grated cheese, pepper, salt & parsley.
3. Pour a light drizzle of olive oil over the tilapia fillets. Cover the fillets with the paprika & cheese mixture.
4. Lay the fillets on a sheet of aluminum foil & transfer to the Air Fryer basket. Fry for 10 minutes. Serve hot.

487. CHEESE CRUST SALMON

Prep & Cook Time: 20 minutes | Servings: 5

INGREDIENTS

2 lb. of salmon fillet
2 garlic cloves, minced

¼ cup of fresh parsley, chopped
½ cup of parmesan cheese, grated

Salt & pepper

INSTRUCTIONS

1. Pre-heat the Air Fryer to 350°F.
2. Lay the salmon, skin-side-down, on a sheet of aluminum foil. Place another sheet of foil on top.
3. Transfer the salmon to the Air Fryer & cook for 10 minutes.
4. Remove the salmon from the Air Fryer. Take off the top layer of foil & add the minced garlic, parmesan cheese, pepper, salt & parsley on top of the fish.
5. Return the salmon to the Air Fryer & resume cooking for another minute.

488. PARMESAN CRUSTED TILAPIA

Prep & Cook Time: 15 minutes | Servings: 4

INGREDIENTS

¾ cup of grated parmesan cheese
4 tilapia fillets

1 tbsp. of olive oil
1 tbsp. of chopped parsley

2 tsp. of paprika
Pinch of garlic powder

INSTRUCTIONS

1. Pre-heat your Air Fryer at 350°F.
2. Coat each of the tilapia fillets with a light brushing of olive oil.
3. Combine all of the other ingredients together in a bowl.
4. Cover the fillets with the parmesan mixture.
5. Line the base of a baking dish with a sheet of parchment paper & place the fillets in the dish.
6. Transfer to the Air Fryer & cook for 5 minutes. Serve hot.

489. SALMON CROQUETTES

Prep & Cook Time: 15 minutes | Servings: 4

INGREDIENTS

1 lb. of can red salmon, mashed
⅓ cup of olive oil

2 eggs, beaten
1 cup of breadcrumbs

½ bunch of parsley, chopped

INSTRUCTIONS

1. Pre-heat the Air Fryer to 400°F.
2. In a mixing bowl, combine together the drained salmon, eggs, & parsley.
3. In a shallow dish, stir together the breadcrumbs & oil to combine well.
4. Mold equal-sized amounts of the mixture into small balls & coat each one with breadcrumbs.
5. Put the croquettes in the Air Fryer's basket & air fry for 7 minutes.

490. CREAMY SALMON

Prep & Cook Time: 20 minutes | Servings: 2

INGREDIENTS

¾ lb. of salmon, cut into 6 pieces
¼ cup of yogurt

1 tbsp. of olive oil
1 tbsp. of dill, chopped

3 tbsp. of sour cream
Salt

INSTRUCTIONS

1. Sprinkle some salt on the salmon.
2. Put the salmon slices in the Air Fryer basket & add in a drizzle of olive oil.
3. Air fry the salmon at 285°F for 10 minutes.
4. In the meantime, combine together the cream, dill, yogurt, & salt.
5. Plate up the salmon & pour the creamy sauce over it. Serve hot.

491. FRIED CAJUN SHRIMP

Prep & Cook Time: 10 minutes | Servings: 4

INGREDIENTS

1 ¼ lb. of shrimp, peeled & deveined
½ tsp. of old bay seasoning

¼ tsp. of cayenne pepper
1 tbsp. of olive oil

½ tsp. of paprika
¼ tsp. of salt

INSTRUCTIONS

1. Pre-heat the Air Fryer to 400°F.
2. Place all of the ingredients in a bowl & mix well to coat the shrimp evenly.
3. Put the seasoned shrimp in the Air Fryer's basket & air fry for 5 minutes. Serve hot.

492. GRILLED SALMON FILLETS

Prep & Cook Time: 20 minutes | Servings: 2

INGREDIENTS

2 salmon fillets
⅓ cup of water
⅓ cup of light soy sauce

⅓ cup of sugar
2 tbsp. of olive oil
Black pepper & salt to taste

Garlic powder [optional]

INSTRUCTIONS

1. Sprinkle some salt & pepper on top of the salmon fillets. Season with some garlic powder if desired.
2. In a medium bowl, mix together the remaining ingredients with a whisk & use this mixture to coat the salmon fillets. Leave to marinate for 2 hours.
3. Pre-heat the Air Fryer at 355°F.
4. Remove any excess liquid from the salmon fillets & transfer to the Air Fryer. Cook for 8 minutes before serving warm.

493. PRAWNS

Prep & Cook Time: 30 minutes | Servings: 4

INGREDIENTS

1 lb. of prawns, peeled
1 lb. of bacon slices
INSTRUCTIONS
1   Pre-heat the Air Fryer to 400°F.
2   Wrap the bacon slices around the prawns & put them in Air Fryer's basket.
3   Air fry for 5 minutes & serve hot.

494. CHUNKY FISH

Prep & Cook Time: 10 minutes + chilling time | Servings: 4

INGREDIENTS

2 cans of canned fish
2 celery stalks, trimmed & finely chopped
1 egg, whisked

1 cup of breadcrumbs
1 tsp. of whole-grain mustard
½ tsp. of sea salt

¼ tsp. of freshly cracked black peppercorns
1 tsp. of paprika

INSTRUCTIONS
1   Combine all of the ingredients in the order in which they appear. Mold the mixture into four equal-sized cakes. Leave to chill in the refrigerator for 50 minutes.
2   Put on an Air Fryer grill pan. Spritz all sides of each cake with cooking spray.
3   Grill at 360°F for 5 minutes. Turn the cakes over & resume cooking for an additional 3 minutes.
4   Serve with mashed potatoes if desired.

495. GLAZED HALIBUT STEAK

Prep & Cook Time: 70 minutes | Servings: 3

INGREDIENTS

1 lb. of halibut steak
⅔ cup of low-sodium soy sauce
½ cup of mirin

2 tbsp. of lime juice
¼ cup of sugar
¼ tsp. of crushed red pepper flakes

¼ cup of orange juice
1 garlic clove, smashed
¼ tsp. of ginger, ground

INSTRUCTIONS
1   Make the teriyaki glaze by mixing together all of the ingredients except for the halibut in a saucepan.
2   Bring it to a boil & lower the heat, stirring constantly until the mixture reduces by half. Remove from the heat & leave to cool.
3   Pour half of the cooled glaze into a Ziploc bag. Add in the halibut, making sure to coat it well in the sauce. Place in the refrigerator for 30 minutes.
4   Pre-heat the Air Fryer to 390°F.
5   Put the marinated halibut in the Air Fryer & allow to cook for 10 – 12 minutes.
6   Use any the remaining glaze to lightly brush the halibut steak with.
7   Serve with white rice or shredded vegetables.

496. BREADCRUMBED FISH

Prep & Cook Time: 25 minutes | Servings: 2 – 4

INGREDIENTS

4 tbsp. of vegetable oil
5 oz. of breadcrumbs

1 egg
4 medium fish fillets

INSTRUCTIONS
1   Pre-heat your Air Fryer to 350°F.
2   In a bowl, combine the breadcrumbs & oil.
3   In a separate bowl, stir the egg with a whisk. Dredge each fish fillet in the egg before coating it in the crumbs mixture. Put them in Air Fryer basket.
4   Cook for 12 minutes & serve hot.

497. CAJUN LEMON SALMON

Prep & Cook Time: 15 minutes | Servings: 1

INGREDIENTS

1 salmon fillet
1 tsp. of Cajun seasoning

½ lemon, juiced
¼ tsp. of sugar

2 lemon wedges, for serving

INSTRUCTIONS
1   Pre-heat the Air Fryer to 350°F.
2   Combine the lemon juice & sugar.
3   Cover the salmon with the sugar mixture.
4   Coat the salmon with the Cajun seasoning.
5   Line the base of your Air Fryer with a sheet of parchment paper.
6   Transfer the salmon to the Air Fryer & allow to cook for 7 minutes.

498. BREADED SALMON

Prep & Cook Time: 25 minutes | Servings: 4

INGREDIENTS

2 cups of breadcrumbs
4 fillets of salmon

1 cup of Swiss cheese, shredded
2 eggs, beaten

INSTRUCTIONS
1   Pre-heat your Air Fryer to 390°F.
2   Dredge the salmon fillets into the eggs. Add the Swiss cheese on top of each fillet.
3   Coat all sides of the fish with breadcrumbs. Put in an oven safe dish, transfer to the Air Fryer, & cook for 20 minutes.

499. ASIAN STYLE FISH

Prep & Cook Time: 35 minutes | Servings: 2

INGREDIENTS

1 medium sea bass, halibut [11 – 12 oz.]
1 tomato, cut into quarters
1 lime, cut thinly
1 stalk of green onion, chopped

3 slices of ginger, julienned
2 garlic cloves, minced
1 chili, sliced
2 tbsp. cooking wine

1 tbsp. of olive oil
Steamed rice [optional]

INSTRUCTIONS
1   Fry the ginger & garlic in the oil until they turn golden brown.
2   Pre-heat the Air Fryer to 360°F.
3   Wash & dry the fish. Halve it, ensuring each half is small enough to fit inside the Air Fryer.
4   Put the fish in the basket of the Air Fryer. Pour in a drizzle of the cooking wine.
5   Place the tomato & lime slices on top of the fish slices.
6   Add the garlic ginger oil mixture on top, followed by the green onion & chili slices.
7   Top with a sheet of aluminum foil. Cook for 15 minutes, or longer if necessary.
8   Serve hot with a side of steamed rice if desired.

500. SEAFOOD FRITTERS

INGREDIENTS

2 cups of clam meat
1 cup of shredded carrot
½ cup of shredded zucchini

1 cup of flour, combined with ¾ cup of water to make a batter
2 tbsp. of olive oil

¼ tsp. of pepper

INSTRUCTIONS

1   Pre-heat your Air Fryer to 390°F.
2   Combine the clam meat with the olive oil, shredded carrot, pepper & zucchini.
3   Using your hands, shape equal portions of the mixture into balls & roll each ball in the chickpea mixture.
4   Put the balls in the Air Fryer & cook for 30 minutes, ensuring they turn nice & crispy before serving.

501. CALAMARI

Prep & Cook Time: 25 minutes | Servings: 2

INGREDIENTS

1 cup of club soda
½ lb. of calamari tubes [or tentacles], about ¼ inch wide, rinsed & dried

½ cup of honey
1 – 2 tbsp. of sriracha
1 cup of flour

Sea salt to taste
Red pepper & black pepper to taste
Red pepper flakes to taste

INSTRUCTIONS

1   In a bowl, cover the calamari rings with club soda & mix well. Leave to sit for 10 minutes.
2   In another bowl, combine the flour, salt, red & black pepper.
3   In a third bowl mix together the honey, pepper flakes, & Sriracha to create the sauce.
4   Remove any excess liquid from the calamari & coat each one with the flour mixture.
5   Spritz the Air Fryer basket with the cooking spray.
6   Arrange the calamari in the basket, well-spaced out & in a single layer.
7   Cook at 380°F for 11 minutes, shaking the basket at least two times during the cooking time.
8   Take the calamari out of the Air Fryer, coat it with half of the sauce & return to the Air Fryer. Cook for an additional 2 minutes.
9   Plate up the calamari & pour the rest of the sauce over it.

502. SALMON & DILL SAUCE

Prep & Cook Time: 45 minutes | Servings: 4

INGREDIENTS

For the Salmon:
1 ½ lb. of salmon
1 tsp. of olive oil

For the Dill Sauce:
½ cup of non-fat Greek yogurt
½ cup of sour cream

Salt
2 tbsp. of dill, finely chopped

INSTRUCTIONS

1   Pre-heat the Air Fryer to 270°F.
2   Slice the salmon into four 6-oz. pieces & pour a light drizzling of olive oil over each slice. Sprinkle on the salt.
3   Put the salmon in the cooking basket & allow to cook for 20 - 23 minutes.
4   Prepare the dill sauce by mixing together the yogurt, sour cream, chopped dill & salt.
5   Pour the sauce over the salmon & top with another sprinkling of chopped dill before serving.

503. BLACK COD

Prep & Cook Time: 30 minutes | Servings: 2

INGREDIENTS

2 [6- to 8-oz.] fillets of black cod
Salt
Freshly ground black pepper
Olive oil

1 cup of grapes, halved
1 small bulb. fennel, sliced ¼-inch thick
½ cup of pecans
3 cups of shredded kale

2 tsp. of white balsamic vinegar
2 tbsp. of extra-virgin olive oil

INSTRUCTIONS

1   Pre-heat the Air Fryer to 400°F.
2   Sprinkle the cod fillets with salt & pepper & drizzle some olive oil over the fish.
3   Put the fish skin-side-down in the Air Fryer basket. Air fry for 10 minutes. Transfer the fillets to a side plate & loosely cover with aluminum foil.
4   Coat the grapes, fennel & pecans with a drizzle of olive oil & sprinkle on some salt & pepper.
5   Place the grapes, fennel & pecans in the Air Fryer's basket & cook for 5 minutes at 400°F. Shake the basket occasionally throughout the cooking time.
6   Put the grapes, fennel & pecans in a bowl & add the kale.
7   Pour over the balsamic vinegar & olive oil & sprinkle with salt & pepper as desired. Serve with the fish & enjoy.

504. TILAPIA FILLETS

Prep & Cook Time: 25 minutes | Servings: 3

INGREDIENTS

1 lb. of tilapia fillets, sliced
4 wheat buns
2 egg yolks

1 tbsp. of fish sauce
2 tbsp. of mayonnaise
3 sweet pickle relish

1 tbsp. of hot sauce
1 tbsp. of nectar

INSTRUCTIONS

1   In a bowl, mix together the egg yolks & fish sauce.
2   Throw in the mayonnaise, sweet pickle relish, hot sauce & nectar.
3   Transfer the mixture to a round baking tray.
4   Put it in the Air Fryer & line the sides with the tilapia fillets. Cook for 15 minutes at 300°F.
5   Remove & serve on hamburger buns if desired.

505. SALMON MIXED EGGS

Prep & Cook Time: 25 minutes | Servings: 2

INGREDIENTS

1 lb. of salmon, cooked
2 eggs

1 onion, chopped
1 cup of celery, chopped

1 tbsp. of oil
Salt & pepper

INSTRUCTIONS

1   In a bowl, mix the eggs with a whisk. Stir in the celery, onion, salt & pepper.
2   Grease a round baking tray with the oil. Transfer the egg mixture to the tray. Cook in the Air Fryer on 300°F for 10 minutes.
3   Serve with cooked salmon.

506. CAJUN SALMON

Prep & Cook Time: 20 minutes | Servings: 1

INGREDIENTS

1 salmon fillet
Cajun seasoning

Light sprinkle of sugar
¼ lemon, juiced, to serve

INSTRUCTIONS

1   Pre-heat Air Fryer to 355°F.
2   Lightly cover all sides of the salmon with Cajun seasoning. Sprinkle conservatively with sugar.

3   For a salmon fillet about three-quarters of an inch thick, cook in the Air Fryer for 7 minutes, skin-side-up on the grill pan.
4   Serve with the lemon juice.

507. FISH FINGERS
Prep & Cook Time: 40 minutes | Servings: 2

INGREDIENTS

2 eggs
10 oz. of cod cut into fingers
½ tsp. of Turmeric Powder
½ Lemon, juiced
1 + 1 tsp. of mixed dried herbs
1 + 1 tsp. of Garlic Powder, separately

½ tsp. of Red Chili Flakes
1 cup of breadcrumbs
2 tbsp. of Maida
3 tsp. of flour
¼ tsp. of baking soda
1 tsp. of ginger garlic paste

½ tsp. of black pepper
½ tsp. of sea salt
1 – 2 tbsp. of olive oil
Ketchup or tartar sauce [optional]

INSTRUCTIONS

1   Put the fish fingers in a bowl. Cover with 1 tsp. of mixed herbs, 1 tsp. of garlic powder, salt, red chili flakes, turmeric powder, black pepper, ginger garlic paste, & lemon juice. Leave to absorb for at least 10 minutes.
2   In a separate bowl, mix together the flour & baking soda. Crack the eggs in the mixture & stir again.
3   Throw in the marinated fish & set aside again for at least 10 minutes.
4   Combine the breadcrumbs & the remaining tsp. of mixed herbs & tsp. of garlic powder.
5   Roll the fish sticks with the bread crumb & herb mixture.
6   Pre-heat the Air Fryer at 360°F.
7   Line the basket of the Air Fryer with a sheet of aluminum foil. Place the fish fingers inside the Air Fryer & pour over a drizzle of the olive oil.
8   Cook for 10 minutes, ensuring the fish is brown & crispy before serving. Enjoy with ketchup or tartar sauce if desired

508. MEDITERRANEAN SALAD
Prep & Cook Time: 15 minutes | Servings: 2

INGREDIENTS

1 cup of cooked quinoa
1 red bell pepper, chopped
2 prosciutto slices, chopped

¼ cup of chopped kalamata olives
½ cup of crumbled feta cheese
1 tsp. of olive oil

1 tsp. of dried oregano
6 cherry tomatoes, halved
Salt & pepper, to taste

INSTRUCTIONS

1   Pre-heat your Air Fryer to 350°F.
2   Drizzle the inside of the Air Fryer with the olive oil. Place the red bell pepper inside & allow to cook for roughly 2 minutes. Put the prosciutto slices in the Air Fryer & cook for an additional 3 minutes.
3   Put the ham & pepper in an oven-proof bowl & remove any excess grease. Combine with the remaining ingredients, save for the tomatoes.
4   Finally, stir in the cherry tomato halves.

509. SHRIMP & VEGGIES
Prep & Cook Time: 30 minutes | Servings: 4

INGREDIENTS

1 lb. of shrimp, peeled & deveined
½ cup of chopped red onion
1 cup of chopped red bell pepper

1 cup of chopped celery
1 tbsp. of melted butter
1 tsp. of sweet paprika

1 tsp. of Worcestershire sauce
salt & black pepper to taste

INSTRUCTIONS

1. Combine all the ingredients into a bowl.
2. Place everything to air fryer and cook 320°F for 20 minutes, shaking halfway.
3. Distribute between plates and serve.

510. SALMON FILLETS
Prep & Cook Time: 18 minutes | Servings: 4

INGREDIENTS

4 pcs. of salmon fillets, boneless
1 tsp. of ground cumin
1 tsp. of sweet paprika

½ tsp. of chili powder
1 tbsp. of olive oil
1 tsp. of garlic powder

juice of 1 lime
salt & black pepper to taste

INSTRUCTIONS

1. In a bowl, combine and coat the salmon with the other ingredients.
2. Place the coated salmon to air fryer.
3. Cook at 350°F for 6 minutes on each side.
4. Distribute the fish between plates.
5. Serve right away with a side salad.

511. SAFFRON SHRIMP MIX
Prep & Cook Time: 18 minutes | Servings: 4

INGREDIENTS

20 pcs. shrimp, peeled and deveined
¼ cup of chopped parsley
4 pcs. of garlic cloves, minced

2 tbsp. of melted butter
½ tsp. of saffron powder
juice of 1 lemon

salt & black pepper to taste

INSTRUCTIONS

1. Combine all ingredients in a pan.
2. Transfer the pan in the fryer and cook at 380°F for 8 minutes.
3. Distribute between plates and serve hot

512. TROUT MIX
Prep & Cook Time: 23 minutes | Servings: 2

INGREDIENTS

2 trout fillets, boneless
1 pc. of red chili pepper, chopped

1 tbsp. of minced garlic
1 tbsp. of lemon juice

1 tbsp. of olive oil
salt and black pepper to taste

INSTRUCTIONS

1. In air fryer, coat the trout with all other ingredients.
2. Cook at 360°F for 13 minutes.
3. Distribute between plates and

513. ROSEMARY SHRIMP KABOBS
Prep & Cook Time: 13 minutes | Servings: 2

INGREDIENTS

8 pcs. of shrimps, peeled and deveined
8 pcs. of red bell pepper, sliced

4 pcs. of garlic cloves, minced
1 tbsp. chopped rosemary

1 tbsp. of olive oil
salt and black pepper to taste

INSTRUCTIONS

1. In a bowl, combine all ingredients.
2. Thread 2 shrimp and 2 bell pepper slices on a skewer, repeat twice. Make two of this.
4. Add the kabobs in air fryer's basket and cook at 360°F for 7 minutes.

5. Serve at once with a side salad.

514. CHILI SALMON FILLETS
Prep & Cook Time: 14 minutes | Servings: 2

INGREDIENTS
2 salmon fillets, boneless
3 pcs. red chili peppers, chopped
2 tbsp. of lemon juice
2 tbsp. of minced garlic
2 tbsp. of olive oil
salt & black pepper to taste

INSTRUCTIONS
1. In a bowl, mix all ingredients except for the fish.
2. Coat the fish with the mixture.
3. Place everything to air fryer and cook at 365°F for 8 minutes, flipping the fish halfway.
4. Distribute between plates and serve right away.

515. ROASTED COD & PARSLEY
Prep & Cook Time: 20 minutes | Servings: 4

INGREDIENTS
4 pcs. medium cod fillets, boneless
1 pc. of shallot, chopped
¼ cup of melted butter
2 pcs. of garlic cloves, minced
3 tbsp. of chopped parsley
2 tbsp. of lemon juice
salt & black pepper to taste

INSTRUCTIONS
1. In a bowl, combine all ingredients except the fish.
2. Coat the cod fillets with the mixture.
3. Transfer them in air fryer and cook at 390°F for 10 minutes.
4. Distribute the fish between plates and serve.

516. BALSAMIC COD FILLETS
Prep & Cook Time: 18 minutes | Servings: 2

INGREDIENTS
2 pcs. of cod fillets, boneless
3 pcs. of shallots, chopped
⅓ cup of water
⅓ cup of balsamic vinegar
½ tsp. of garlic powder
2 tbsp. of olive oil
2 tbsp. of lemon juice
salt and black pepper to taste

INSTRUCTIONS
1. In a bowl, coat the cod with all other ingredients (except for the shallots).
2. Put the coated fish to fryer's basket and cook at 360°F for 12 minutes, flipping them halfway.
3. Distribute the fish between plates.
4. Sprinkle the shallots on top and serve.

517. WHITE FISH & PEAS
Prep & Cook Time: 22 minutes | Servings: 4

INGREDIENTS
4 pcs. white fish fillets, boneless
2 cups of peas, cooked & drained
2 pcs. of garlic cloves, minced
½ tsp. of dried basil
½ tsp. of sweet paprika
2 tbsp. of chopped cilantro
4 tbsp. of veggie stock
salt & pepper to taste

INSTRUCTIONS
1. In a bowl, coat the fish with all other ingredients (except the peas).
2. Put the coated fish to air fryer and cook at 360°F for 12 minutes.
3. Add the peas and distribute between plates.
4. Serve and enjoy!

518. COD FILLETS
Prep & Cook Time: 25 minutes | Servings: 4

INGREDIENTS
4 pcs. of cod fillets, boneless
4 slices of ginger
3 pcs. of spring onions, chopped
1 cup of water
3 tbsp. of olive oil + a drizzle
2 tbsp. of chopped coriander
4 tbsp. of light soy sauce
1 tbsp. of sugar
salt & black pepper to taste

INSTRUCTIONS
1. Coat the fish with salt and pepper, then drizzle some oil over it.
2. Place the fish in your air fryer and cook at 360°F for 12 minutes.
3. Pour water in a pot and heat up over medium heat, add soy sauce and sugar, let it simmer and remove from the heat.
4. Heat up a pan with the olive oil over medium heat, add ginger and green onions, cook for 2-3 minutes and remove from the heat.
5. Distribute the fish between plates and top with ginger, coriander and green onions.
6. Drizzle the soy sauce mixture all over.
7. Serve and enjoy!

519. COCONUT COD FILLETS
Prep & Cook Time: 15 minutes | Servings: 4

INGREDIENTS
4 pcs. of medium cod fillets, boneless
½ cup of chopped parsley
2 pcs. of garlic cloves, chopped
½ pcs. of jalapeno, chopped
½ cup of coconut milk
a drizzle of olive oil
1 tsp. of grated ginger
salt & black pepper to taste

INSTRUCTIONS
1. In a blender, combine all ingredients except the fish.
2. In a baking dish, put the fish and pour with the coconut mixture.
3. Transfer the dish in air fryer and cook at 380°F for 10 minutes.
4. Distribute between plates and serve hot.

520. COD & LIME SAUCE
Prep & Cook Time: 18 minutes | Servings: 4

INGREDIENTS
4 pcs. of cod fillets, boneless
2 tsp. of lime juice
3 tsp. of lime zest
6 tbsp. of butter
2 tbsp. of olive oil
3 tbsp. of chopped chives
salt & black pepper to taste

INSTRUCTIONS
1. Coat the fish with the salt, pepper and oil, put the coated fish in an air fryer.
2. Cook at 360°F for 10 minutes, flipping once.
3. Heat up a pan with butter over medium heat, add remaining ingredients. cook for 1-2 minutes.
4. Distribute the fish between plates, drizzle the lime sauce all over.
5. Serve instantly.

521. CHILI TOMATO SHRIMP

Prep & Cook Time: 20 minutes | Servings: 4

INGREDIENTS

1 lb. of shrimp, peeled & deveined
1 cup of tomato juice
1 pc. of yellow onion, chopped

½ tsp. of sugar
2 tsp. of vinegar
1 tsp. of chili powder

2 tbsp. of olive oil
salt and black pepper to taste

INSTRUCTIONS

1. In a pan, combine all ingredients.
2. Transfer the pan in the fryer and cook at 370°F for 10 minutes.
3. Distribute into bowls and serve.

---

522. SALMON & FENNEL

Prep & Cook Time: 30 minutes | Servings: 4

INGREDIENTS

2 pcs. of red onions, chopped
2 pcs. of small fennel bulbs, trimmed & sliced

¼ cup of almonds, toasted & sliced
4 pcs. of salmon fillets, boneless

2 tbsp. of olive oil
5 tsp. of toasted fennel seeds

INSTRUCTIONS

1. Season the fish with salt and pepper and grease it with 1 tbsp. of the oil.
2. Put the fish in air fryer's basket and cook at 350°F for 5-6 minutes on each side. Set aside.
3. Heat up a pan with the remaining oil over medium-high heat, sauté the onions for 2 minutes.
4. Add the remaining ingredients and cook for 2- 3 minutes more.
5. Distribute the fish between plates and spread the mixture over the fish.
6. Serve right away and enjoy!

---

523. COCONUT SHRIMP

Prep & Cook Time: 15 minutes | Servings: 4

INGREDIENTS

12 Large Shrimp, Deveined & Peeled
1 Cup of Coconut Cream

1 Tbsp. of Chopped Parsley
1 tbsp. of corn starch

salt & black pepper to taste

INSTRUCTIONS

1. In a pan, combine all ingredients.
2. Transfer the pan in the fryer and cook at 360°F for 10 minutes.
3. Serve hot and enjoy!

---

524. SHRIMP & MUSHROOMS

Prep & Cook Time: 15 minutes | Servings: 2

INGREDIENTS

1 lb. of shrimp, peeled & deveined
8 oz. of mushrooms, roughly sliced
½ cup of beef stock
¼ cup of heavy cream

2 pcs. of garlic cloves, minced
a drizzle of olive oil
1 tbsp. of chopped parsley, chopped
1 tbsp. of butter

1 tbsp. of chopped chives
a pinch of red pepper flakes
salt & black pepper to taste

INSTRUCTIONS

1. Season the shrimp with salt and pepper and coat with the oil.
2. Transfer the shrimp in air fryer, cook at 360°F for 7 minutes. Set aside.
3. Heat up a pan with the butter over medium heat, add the mushrooms, cook for 3-4 minutes.
4. Put all remaining ingredients, stir and cook for a few minutes more.
5. Serve the shrimp with a drizzle of butter/garlic mixture.

---

525. SALMON & ORANGE VINAIGRETTE

Prep & Cook Time: 15 minutes | Servings: 2

INGREDIENTS

2 cuts of salmon fillets, boneless
2 tsp. of honey
2 tbsp. of mustard

2 tbsp. of olive oil
2 tbsp. of chopped parsley
1 tbsp. of chopped dill

a pinch of salt & black pepper
zest of ½ orange
juice of ½ orange

INSTRUCTIONS

1. In a bowl, combine all ingredients except for the fish and oranges.
2. Put the salmon to the mixture, toss and transfer the fish to air fryer.
3. Cook at 350°F for 10 minutes, flipping halfway.
4. Distribute the fish between plates and drizzle the orange vinaigrette all over.
5. Serve and enjoy.

---

526. HERBED TUNA

Prep & Cook Time: 18 minutes | Servings: 4

INGREDIENTS

½ cup of chopped cilantro
⅓ cup of olive oil
1 pc. of jalapeno pepper, chopped
4 cuts of sushi tuna steaks
3 pcs. of garlic cloves, minced

1 pc. of small red onion, chopped
3 tbsp. of balsamic vinegar
2 tbsp. of chopped parsley
2 tbsp. of chopped basil
1 tsp. of red pepper flakes

1 tsp. of chopped thyme
salt & black pepper to taste

INSTRUCTIONS

1. In a pan, coat the fish with all other ingredients.
2. Put the coated fish to air fryer and cook at 360°F for 4 minutes on each side.
3. Distribute the fish between plates and serve.

---

527. SALMON FILLETS & BELL PEPPERS

Prep & Cook Time: 20 minutes | Servings: 6

INGREDIENTS

6 cuts of medium salmon fillets, skinless & boneless
3 pcs. of red bell peppers, cut into medium pieces

1 cup of pitted green olives
½ tsp. of smoked paprika
3 tbsp. of olive oil

2 tbsp. of chopped cilantro
salt & black pepper to taste

INSTRUCTIONS

1. In a baking dish, combine all the ingredients and toss gently.
2. Transfer the baking dish in air fryer and cook at 360°F for 15 minutes.
3. Distribute the fillets between plates and serve.

---

528. SALMON & ORANGE MARMALADE RECIPE

Prep & Cook Time: 25 Minutes | Servings: 4

INGREDIENTS

1 lb. of wild salmon, skinless, boneless & cubed
2 pcs. of lemons, sliced

¼ cup of balsamic vinegar
¼ cup of orange juice

⅓ cup of orange marmalade
a pinch of salt & black pepper

INSTRUCTIONS
1. Heat up a pot with the vinegar over medium heat.
2. Pour marmalade and orange juice, let it simmer. Cook for 1 minute and turn off heat.
3. Thread salmon cubes and lemon slices on skewers.
4. Season salmon with salt and black pepper, and coat with half of the mix.
5. Put salmon in air fryer's basket and cook at 360°F, for 3 minutes on each side.
6. Coat skewers with the rest of the vinegar mix.
7. Distribute among plates.
8. Serve right away with a side salad.

529. SALMON & BALSAMIC ORANGE SAUCE
Prep & Cook Time: 20 minutes | Servings: 4

INGREDIENTS
4 cuts of salmon fillets, boneless & cubed
¼ cup of balsamic vinegar

¼ cup of orange juice
2 pcs. of lemons, sliced

a pinch of salt & black pepper

INSTRUCTIONS
1. In a pan, combine all ingredients except the fish.
2. Heat the mixture up over medium-high heat for 5 minutes and add salmon.
3. Toss gently and place the pan in the air fryer and cook at 360°F for 10 minutes.
4. Distribute between plates and serve right away with a side salad.

530. EASY SHRIMP
Prep & Cook Time: 20 minutes | Servings: 4

INGREDIENTS
1 lb. of shrimp, peeled & deveined
1 cup of chicken stock

2 tbsp. of olive oil
1 tbsp. of chopped red onion

INSTRUCTIONS
1. In a pan, combine all the ingredients.
2. Transfer the pan in the fryer and cook at 380°F for 10 minutes.
3. Distribute into bowls and serve

531. MAPLE SALMON
Prep & Cook Time: 15 minutes | Servings: 2

INGREDIENTS
2 cuts of salmon fillets, boneless
1 tbsp. of olive oil

1 tbsp. of maple syrup
2 tbsp. of mustard

salt & black pepper to taste

INSTRUCTIONS
1. In a bowl, combine the mustard with the oil and the maple syrup, coat salmon with this mix.
2. Transfer the salmon in air fryer and cook it at 370°F for 5 minutes on each side.
3. Serve at once with a side salad.

532. SALMON & CARROTS
Prep & Cook Time: 25 minutes | Servings: 2

INGREDIENTS
2 cuts of salmon fillets, boneless
¼ cup of veggie stock

1 cup of baby carrots
3 pcs. of garlic cloves, minced

1 tbsp. of olive oil
salt & black pepper to taste

INSTRUCTIONS
1. Combine all ingredients in an air fryer.
2. Cook at 370°F for 20 minutes.
3. Distribute everything between plates and serve.

533. PISTACHIO CRUSTED COD
Prep & Cook Time: 20 minutes | Servings: 4

INGREDIENTS
4 cuts of cod fillets, boneless
¼ cup of lime juice
1 cup of Chopped pistachios

2 tbsp. of honey
1 tbsp. of mustard
1 tsp. of chopped parsley

salt & black
pepper to taste

INSTRUCTIONS
1. Combine all the ingredients except the fish into a bowl.
2. Coat the fish with the mix, put in your air fryer, and cook at 350°F for 10 minutes.
3. Distribute the fish between plates and serve at once with a side salad.

534. COD FILLETS WITH LEEKS
Prep & Cook Time: 25 minutes | Servings: 2

INGREDIENTS
2 cuts of black cod fillets, boneless
2 pcs. of leeks, sliced

½ cup of pecans, chopped
1 tbsp. of olive oil

salt & black pepper to taste

INSTRUCTIONS
1. In a bowl, coat the cod with oil, salt, pepper and leeks.
2. Place the cod to an air fryer and cook at 360°F for 15 minutes.
3. Distribute the fish and leeks between plates, sprinkle the pecans on top.
4. Serve at once.

535. SALMON & CAPERS
Prep & Cook Time: 18 minutes | Servings: 4

INGREDIENTS
4 cuts of salmon fillets, boneless
juice of 1 lemon

2 tsp. of olive oil
1 tbsp. of drained capers

1 tbsp. of chopped dill
salt & black pepper to taste

INSTRUCTIONS
1. In air fryer, combine capers, dill, salt, pepper and oil,
2. Coat the fish gently with this mixture.
3. Cook at 360°F for 6 minutes on each side.
4. Distribute the fish between plates and drizzle the lemon juice all over.
5. Serve and enjoy!

536. SALMON FILLETS & PINEAPPLE MIX
Prep & Cook Time: 15 minutes | Servings: 2

INGREDIENTS
20 oz. canned pineapple pieces
a drizzle of olive oil

2 cuts of medium salmon fillets, boneless
½ tsp. grated ginger

2 tsp. garlic powder
1 tbsp. balsamic vinegar

salt and black pepper to taste
INSTRUCTIONS
1. Grease a pan with the oil and put the fish.
2. Put the remaining ingredients and transfer the pan in the air fryer.
3. Cook at 350°f for 10 minutes.
4. Distribute between plates and serve.

537. BUTTER SHRIMP
Prep & Cook Time: 15 minutes | Servings: 2

INGREDIENTS

8 pcs. of large shrimp
4 pcs. of garlic cloves, minced

1 tbsp. of chopped rosemary
2 tbsp. of melted butter

salt & black pepper to taste

INSTRUCTIONS
1. Combine all ingredients.
2. Place the shrimp to air fryer and cook at 360°F for 10 minutes.
3. Distribute into bowls.
4. Serve and enjoy!

538. TIGER SHRIMP
Prep & Cook Time: 15 minutes | Servings: 2

INGREDIENTS

20 pcs. of tiger shrimp, peeled & deveined
½ tsp. of Italian seasoning

1 tbsp. of extra virgin olive oil
¼ tsp. of smoked paprika

salt & black pepper to taste

INSTRUCTIONS
1. Combine all ingredients to a bowl and toss.
2. Transfer the shrimp in the air fryer's basket and cook at 380°F for 10 minutes.
3. Distribute into bowls and serve.

539. BABY SHRIMP
Prep & Cook Time: 22 minutes | Servings: 4

INGREDIENTS

1 lb. of baby shrimp, peeled & deveined
1 cup of mayonnaise
½ cup of chopped yellow onion

1 cup of chopped green bell pepper
1 cup of chopped red bell pepper
1 tbsp. of olive oil

1 tsp. of sweet paprika
salt & black pepper to taste

INSTRUCTIONS
1. In a pan, combine all the ingredients except the mayo, toss well.
2. Transfer the pan in the fryer and cook at 380°F for 12 minutes.

540. HOT SHRIMP
Prep & Cook Time: 2 hour 10 minutes | Servings: 4

INGREDIENTS

1 lb. of large shrimp, peeled & deveined
½ tsp. of garlic powder
½ tsp. of sweet paprika
1 tsp. of tabasco sauce

1 tsp. of red pepper flakes
1 tsp. of dried basil
2 tbsp. of water
2 tbsp. of olive oil

1 tbsp. of chopped parsley
salt & black pepper to taste

INSTRUCTIONS
1. In a bowl, coat shrimp with all ingredients except parsley, set aside in the fridge for 2 hours.
2. Put the shrimp to air fryer's basket and cook at 370°F for 10 minutes.
3. Distribute into bowls, sprinkle with parsley.
4. Serve with a side salad.

541. SEA BASS PAELLA
Prep & Cook Time: 35 minutes | Servings: 4

INGREDIENTS

1 lb. of sea bass fillets, cubed
1 pc. of ed bell pepper, deseeded & chopped.
14 oz. of dry white wine
3½ oz. of chicken stock

6 pcs. of scallops
8 pcs. of shrimp, peeled & deveined
5 oz. of wild rice
2 oz. of peas

a drizzle of olive oil
salt & black pepper to taste

INSTRUCTIONS
1. In a baking dish, combine all the ingredients and toss.
2. Transfer the dish in your air fryer and cook at 380°F and cook for 25 minutes, stirring halfway.
3. Distribute between plates and serve.

542. HALIBUT & SUN-DRIED TOMATOES
Prep & Cook Time: 20 Minutes | Servings: 2

INGREDIENTS

2 pcs. of medium halibut fillets
2 pcs. of garlic cloves, minced
9 pcs. of black olives, pitted & sliced
4 pcs. of rosemary springs, chopped

½ tsp. of crushed red pepper flakes
2 tsp. of olive oil
6 pcs. of sun-dried tomatoes, chopped
2 pcs. of small red onions, sliced

1 pc. of fennel bulb, sliced
salt & black pepper to the taste

INSTRUCTIONS
1. In a baking dish, season fish with salt, pepper, coat with garlic and oil.
2. Put the remaining ingredients and place to air fryer, cook at 380°F for 10 minutes.
3. Distribute fish and veggies on plates and serve.

543. CILANTRO TROUT FILLETS
Prep & Cook Time: 18 minutes | Servings: 4

INGREDIENTS

4 pcs. of trout fillets, boneless
1 cup of black olives, pitted & chopped

4 pcs. of garlic cloves, minced
1 tbsp. of olive oil

3 tbsp. of chopped cilantro

INSTRUCTIONS
1. In air fryer, combine all ingredients.
2. Cook at 360°F for 6 minutes on each side.
3. Distribute everything between plates and serve.

544. SALMON STEAKS
Prep & Cook Time: 20 minutes | Servings: 6

INGREDIENTS

6 cuts of salmon steaks
2 pcs. of garlic cloves, minced

1 cup of clam juice
⅓ cup of chopped dill

2 tbsp. of olive oil
2 tbsp. of chopped parsley

2 tbsp. of lemon juice

1 tsp. of sherry

salt & white pepper to taste

INSTRUCTIONS
1. In a pan, combine the salmon with all other ingredients.
2. Transfer the pan in the fryer and cook at 370°F for 15 minutes.
3. Distribute everything between plates and serve.

545. SALMON & JASMINE RICE
Prep & Cook Time: 35 minutes | Servings: 2

INGREDIENTS
2 cuts of wild salmon fillets, boneless
½ cup of jasmine rice

1 cup of chicken stock
1 tbsp. of melted butter

¼ tsp. of saffron
salt & black pepper to taste

INSTRUCTIONS
1. Combine all ingredients except fish into a pan.
2. Transfer the pan in the air fryer and cook at 360°F for 15 minutes.
3. Put the fish, cover and cook at 360°F for 12 minutes more.
4. Distribute everything between plates and serve right away.

546. SPICY COD
Prep & Cook Time: 15 minutes | Servings: 4

INGREDIENTS
4 cuts of cod fillets, boneless
1 pc. of lemon, sliced

2 tbsp. of assorted chili peppers
juice of 1 lemon

INSTRUCTIONS
1. In air fryer, combine the cod with the chili pepper, lemon juice, salt and pepper
2. layer the lemon slices on top and cook at 360°F for 10 minutes.
3. Distribute the fillets between plates and serve.

547. PARMESAN CLAMS
Prep & Cook Time: 22 minutes | Servings: 4

INGREDIENTS
24 pcs. of clams, shucked
¼ cup of chopped parsley
1 cup of breadcrumbs

¼ cup of grated parmesan cheese
3 minced garlic cloves
4 tbsp. of softened butter

1 tsp. of dried oregano

INSTRUCTIONS
1. In a bowl, mix the breadcrumbs, parmesan, oregano, parsley, butter and garlic.
2. Put the mixture into the exposed clams.
3. Transfer the clams in air fryer and cook at 380°F for 12 minutes.
4. Serve and enjoy!

548. MUSSELS BOWLS
Prep & Cook Time: 18 minutes | Servings: 4

INGREDIENTS
2 lbs. of scrubbed mussels
8 oz. of chopped spicy sausage

12 oz. of black beer
1 pc. of yellow onion, chopped

1 tbsp. of olive oil
1 tbsp. of paprika

INSTRUCTIONS
1. In a pan, mix all ingredients.
2. Transfer the pan in the air fryer and cook at 400°F for 12 minutes.
3. Distribute the mussels into bowls.
4. Serve and enjoy!

549. SHRIMP & CORN
Prep & Cook Time: 20 minutes | Servings: 4

INGREDIENTS
1½ lbs. of shrimp, peeled & deveined
2 cups of corn
¼ cup of chicken stock

2 pcs. of sweet onions, cut into wedges
8 pcs. of garlic cloves, crushed
a drizzle of olive oil

1 tbsp. of old bay seasoning
1 tsp. of crushed red pepper flakes
salt & black pepper to taste

INSTRUCTIONS
1. Grease a pan with oil, put all other ingredients and toss well.
2. Transfer the pan in the fryer and cook at 390°F for 10 minutes.
3. Distribute everything into bowls and serve.

550. SNAPPER FILLETS
Prep & Cook Time: 20 minutes | Servings: 4

INGREDIENTS
4 cuts of medium snapper fillets, boneless
8 pcs. of garlic cloves, minced
⅓ cup of olive oil

juice of 2 limes
1 tbsp. of lemon zest
1½ tbsp. of green olives, pitted & sliced

salt & black pepper to taste

INSTRUCTIONS
1. Combine all ingredients except the fish to a baking dish.
2. Put the fish and toss gently, then place in the fryer and cook at 360°F for 15 minutes.
3. Distribute everything between plates and serve.

551. TROUT BITES
Prep & Cook Time: 18 minutes | Servings: 4

INGREDIENTS
1 lb. of trout fillets, boneless & cut into cubes
1 pc. of sweet onion, chopped
⅓ cup of sake
⅓ cup of mirin
¼ cup of miso

2 stalks of celery, sliced
1 pc. of garlic clove, crushed
1 pc. of shallot, sliced
1 in. of ginger piece, chopped
1 tsp. of mustard

1 tsp. of sugar
1 tbsp. of rice vinegar

NSTRUCTIONS
1. In a pan, combine all ingredients.
2. Transfer the pan in the fryer and cook at 370°F for 12 minutes.
3. Distribute into bowls and serve.

552. CLAMS & POTATOES
Prep & Cook Time: 20 minutes | Servings: 4

INGREDIENTS
1 lb. of baby red potatoes, scrubbed
10 oz. of beer

2 pcs. of chorizo links, sliced
1 pc. of yellow onion, chopped

15 pcs. of small clams, shucked
2 tbsp. of chopped cilantro

1 tsp. of olive oil
INSTRUCTIONS
1. In a pan, combine all of the ingredients and toss.
2. Transfer the pan in the fryer and cook at 390°F for 15 minutes.
3. Distribute into bowls and serve.

553. BAKED COD
Prep & Cook Time: 18 minutes | Servings: 4

INGREDIENTS
4 cuts of cod fillets, boneless
3/4 tsp. of sweet paprika
½ tsp. of dried oregano
½ tsp. of dried thyme

½ tsp. of dried basil
a drizzle of olive oil
juice of 1 lemon
2 tbsp. of chopped parsley

2 tbsp. of melted butter
salt & black pepper to taste

INSTRUCTIONS
1. Combine all ingredients to a bowl and toss gently.
2. Place the fish to your air fryer and cook at 380°F for 6 minutes on each side.
3. Serve right away.

554. PEA PODS & SHRIMP MIX
Prep & Cook Time: 18 minutes | Servings: 4

INGREDIENTS
1 lb. of shrimp, peeled & deveined
½ lb. of pea pods

3/4 cup of pineapple juice
2 tbsp. of soy sauce

3 tbsp. of sugar
3 tbsp. of balsamic vinegar

INSTRUCTIONS
1. In a pan, combine all the ingredients.
2. Transfer the pan in the fryer and cook at 380°F for 8 minutes.
3. Distribute into bowls and serve.

555. EASY TROUT
Prep & Cook Time: 25 minutes | Servings: 4

INGREDIENTS
4 whole trout
3 oz. of breadcrumbs
1 pc. of egg, whisked

1 tbsp. of butter
1 tbsp. of chopped chives
1 tbsp. of olive oil

juice of 1 lemon
salt & black pepper to taste

INSTRUCTIONS
1. In a bowl, mix the breadcrumbs, lemon juice, salt, pepper, egg and chives.
2. Cover the trout with breadcrumb mix.
3. Heat up air fryer with the oil and the butter at 370°F.
4. Put the trout and cook for 10 minutes on each side.
5. Distribute between plates and serve with a side salad.

556. SIMPLE LIME SALMON
Prep & Cook Time: 17 minutes | Servings: 5

INGREDIENTS
½ cup of butter
½ cup of olive oil
3 pcs. of garlic cloves, minced

2 pcs. of shallots, chopped
2 pcs. of salmon fillets, boneless
1 pc. of lime, sliced

6 pcs. of green onions, chopped
juice of 1 lime
salt & black pepper to taste

INSTRUCTIONS
1. In a bowl, combine the salmon with all other ingredients.
2. Place the fish to air fryer, layer with lime slices and cook at 380°F for 6 minutes on each side.
3. Serve with a side salad.

557. MUSSELS & SHRIMP
Prep & Cook Time: 25 minutes | Servings: 6

INGREDIENTS
1½ lbs. of large shrimp, peeled & deveined
20 oz. of chopped canned tomatoes
8 oz. of clam juice
12 mussels

2 tbsp. of melted butter
2 pcs. of yellow onions, chopped
3 pcs. of garlic cloves, minced
½ cup of chopped parsley

½ tsp. of dried marjoram
1 tbsp. of dried basil
salt & black pepper to taste

INSTRUCTIONS
1. Combine all the ingredients in a pan.
2. Transfer the pan into the fryer and cook at 380°F for 15 minutes.
3. Distribute into bowls and serve right away.

558. FRIED SALMON
Prep & Cook Time: 22 minutes | Servings: 4

INGREDIENTS
4 cuts of salmon fillets, boneless
1 pc. of white onion, chopped
3 pcs. of tomatoes, sliced

4 pcs. of thyme sprigs, chopped
4 pcs. of cilantro sprigs, chopped
1 pc. of lemon, sliced

3 tbsp. of olive oil
salt & black pepper to taste

INSTRUCTIONS
1. In air fryer, combine salmon all other ingredients.
2. Layer with lemon slices and cook at 360°F for 12 minutes.
3. Distribute everything between plates and serve.

559. SALMON THYME & PARSLEY
Prep & Cook Time: 25 Minutes | Servings: 4

INGREDIENTS
4 cuts of salmon fillets, boneless
1 pc. of yellow onion, chopped
3 pcs. of tomatoes, sliced

4 pcs. of thyme springs
4 pcs. of parsley springs
3 tbsp. of extra virgin olive oil

juice from 1 lemon
salt & black pepper to the taste

INSTRUCTIONS
1. In a pan, drizzle a tablespoon of oil.
2. Layer with tomatoes, salt and pepper, drizzle a tablespoon of oil on top.
3. Put the fish, season with salt and pepper, drizzle the rest of the oil.
4. Put the remaining ingredients and transfer in air fryer's basket.
5. Cook at 360°F, for 12 minutes shaking once.
6. Distribute everything on plates and serve right away.

560. TARRAGON SHRIMP

INGREDIENTS

1 lb. of shrimp, peeled & deveined
2 pcs. of garlic cloves, minced
1 pc. of yellow onion, chopped

½ cup of chicken stock
3/4 cup of grated parmesan cheese
¼ cup of chopped tarragon

2 tbsp. of olive oil
2 tbsp. of dry white wine
salt & black pepper to taste

INSTRUCTIONS

1. In a pan, combine all ingredients except the parmesan cheese.
2. Transfer the pan in the air fryer and cook at 380°F for 12 minutes.
3. Put the parmesan and toss.
4. Distribute everything between plates and serve.

561. SHRIMP & TOMATOES

Prep & Cook Time: 25 minutes | Servings: 4

INGREDIENTS

2 lbs. of shrimp, peeled & deveined
1 lb. of tomatoes, peeled & chopped
4 pcs. of onions, chopped

¼ cup of veggie stock
4 tbsp. of olive oil
1 tsp. of ground coriander

juice of 1 lemon
salt & black pepper to taste

INSTRUCTIONS

1. In a pan, combine all the ingredients well.
2. Transfer the pan in the fryer and cook at 360°F for 15 minutes.
3. Distribute into bowls.
4. Serve and enjoy!

562. SHRIMP & SPAGHETTI

Prep & Cook Time: 20 minutes | Servings: 4

INGREDIENTS

1 lb. of shrimp, cooked, peeled & deveined
10 oz. of chopped canned tomatoes
12 oz. of cooked spaghetti

1pc. of garlic clove, minced
1 cup of grated parmesan cheese
2 tbsp. of olive oil

¼ tsp. of dried oregano
1 tbsp. of finely chopped parsley

INSTRUCTIONS

1. In a pan, combine shrimp with oil, garlic, tomatoes, oregano and parsley, toss well.
2. Transfer the pan in the fryer and cook at 380°F for 10 minutes.
3. Put the spaghetti and parmesan, toss well.
4. Distribute between plates.
5. Serve and enjoy!

563. SALMON & BLACKBERRY SAUCE

Prep & Cook Time: 18 minutes | Servings: 2

INGREDIENTS

2 cuts of salmon fillets, boneless
½ cup of blackberries

1 tbsp. of olive oil
1 tbsp. of honey

juice of ½ lemon
salt & black pepper to taste

INSTRUCTIONS

1. In a blender, mix all ingredients except for the salmon.
2. Pour the mixture over the salmon and transfer the fish in air fryer's basket.
3. Cook at 380°F for 12 minutes, flipping the fish halfway.
4. Serve hot and enjoy!

564. TROUT & ALMOND BUTTER SAUCE

Prep & Cook Time: 25 minutes | Servings: 5

INGREDIENTS

4 cuts of trout fillets, boneless
cooking spray
salt & black pepper to taste
For the sauce:

1 cup of almond butter
¼ cup of lemon juice
¼ cup of water
4 tsp. of soy sauce

1 tsp. of almond oil

INSTRUCTIONS

1. Put the fish fillets in air fryer, season with salt and pepper and grease with the cooking spray.
2. Cook at 380°F for 5 minutes on each side. Set aside.
3. Heat up a pan with the almond butter over medium heat, add the remaining ingredients.
4. Whisk the sauce well and cook for 2-3 minutes.
5. Drizzle the almond butter sauce over the fish.
6. Serve and enjoy!

565. AWESOME SHRIMP MIX

Prep & Cook Time: 20 minutes | Servings: 4

INGREDIENTS

18 oz. of shrimp, peeled & deveined
2 pcs. green chilies, minced
2 pcs. onions, chopped

4 oz. of beaten curd
1 in. of ginger, chopped
½ tbsp. of mustard seeds

1 tbsp. of olive oil
1 tsp. of turmeric powder
salt & black pepper to taste

INSTRUCTIONS

1. In a pan, combine all the ingredients.
2. Transfer the pan in the fryer and cook at 380°F for 10 minutes.
3. Distribute into bowls and serve.

566. PEAS & COD FILLETS

Prep & Cook Time: 20 Minutes | Servings: 4

INGREDIENTS

4 cuts of cod fillets, boneless
2 cups of peas
4 tbsp. of wine

2 pcs. of garlic cloves, minced
½ tsp. of dried oregano
½ tsp. of sweet paprika

2 tbsp. of chopped parsley

INSTRUCTIONS

1. In food processor, blend garlic, parsley, salt, pepper, oregano, paprika and wine.
2. Coat the fish with half of the mixture, place in air fryer and cook at 360°F, for 10 minutes.
3. In the meantime, add peas in a pot, pour water and put salt.
4. Let it boil over medium high heat, cook for 10 minutes.
5. Drain and distribute among plates.
6. Distribute the fish on plates, pour the rest of the herb dressing all over.
7. Serve and enjoy!

567. HAWAIIAN SALMON RECIPE

Prep & Cook Time: 20 Minutes | Servings: 2

INGREDIENTS

20 oz. of canned pineapple pieces & juice
2 tsp. of garlic powder
1 tsp. of onion powder

1 tbsp. of balsamic vinegar
2 cuts of medium salmon fillets, boneless
½ tsp. of grated ginger

salt & black pepper to the taste

INSTRUCTIONS
1. Coat salmon with garlic powder, onion powder, salt and black pepper, rub well.
2. Transfer to a baking dish, add ginger and pineapple chunks, toss really gently.
3. Drizzle the vinegar all over and transfer in air fryer. Cook at 350°F, for 10 minutes.
4. Distribute everything on plates and serve.

568. SHRIMP, CRAB & SAUSAGE
Prep & Cook Time: 30 minutes | Servings: 6

INGREDIENTS
½ lb. of crab meat
24 shrimp, peeled & deveined
1 lb. of sausage, sliced
4 pcs. of garlic cloves, chopped
6 pcs. of plum tomatoes, chopped
1 cup of chicken stock

1 cup of chopped yellow onions
½ cup of chopped celery
1 cup of chopped green bell pepper
2 tbsp. of olive oil
1 tsp. of celery seeds
1 tsp. of sweet paprika

½ tsp. of onion powder
½ tsp. of garlic powder
1 tsp. of dried thyme
salt & black pepper to taste

INSTRUCTIONS
1. Heat up a pan with the oil over medium heat.
2. Put the onions and celery, stir and cook for 1-2 minutes.
3. Put the bell peppers, garlic, tomatoes, onion powder, garlic powder, thyme, celery seeds and paprika, stir and cook for another 2 minutes
4. Add the sausage, stock, shrimp, crab, salt and pepper.
5. Transfer the pan into the fryer and cook at 380°F for 15 minutes.
6. Distribute into bowls and serve.

569. SHRIMP & CHESTNUT
Prep & Cook Time: 25 minutes | Servings: 4

INGREDIENTS
½ lb. of shrimp, peeled & deveined
½ lb. of shiitake mushrooms, sliced
3 pcs. of scallions, chopped

1 pc. of garlic clove, minced
8 oz. of water chestnuts, chopped
2 tbsp. of olive oil

1 tsp. of minced ginger
salt & black pepper to taste

INSTRUCTIONS
1. In air fryer, combine all the ingredients.
2. Cook at 380°F for 15 minutes.
3. Serve hot and enjoy!

570. FLOUNDER FILLETS
Prep & Cook Time: 18 minutes | Servings: 4

INGREDIENTS
2 lbs. of flounder fillets
4 tbsp. of melted butter

juice of 1 lime
salt & black pepper to taste

INSTRUCTIONS
1. Place the flounder fillets in air fryer. Pour the melted butter, salt, pepper and lime juice.
2. Cook at 390°F for 6 minutes on each side.
3. Distribute between plates.
4. Serve with a side salad and enjoy.

571. SHRIMP & ZUCCHINI
Prep & Cook Time: 18 minutes | Servings: 4

INGREDIENTS
1 lb. of shrimp, peeled & deveined
1 pc. of garlic clove, minced
½ cup of chopped parsley

¼ cup of tomato sauce
2 pcs. of red onions, cut into chunks
3 pcs. of zucchinis, cut in medium chunks

2 tbsp. of olive oil
1 tbsp. of lemon juice
salt & black pepper to taste

INSTRUCTIONS
1. In a baking dish, combine all the ingredients except the parsley, toss well.
2. Transfer the baking dish into the fryer and cook at 400°F for 8 minutes.
3. Put the parsley and stir.
4. Distribute everything between plates and serve.

572. TROUT FILLET & ORANGE SAUCE
Prep & Cook Time: 20 Minutes | Servings: 4

INGREDIENTS
4 cuts of trout fillets, skinless & boneless
1 tbsp. of olive oil

1 tbsp. of minced ginger
4 pcs. of spring onions, chopped

salt & black pepper to the taste
juice & zest from 1 orange

INSTRUCTIONS
1. In a pan, coat trout fillets with salt, pepper and olive oil.
2. Put ginger, green onions, orange zest and juice, toss well.
3. Transfer in your air fryer and cook at 360°F for 10 minutes.
4. Distribute fish and sauce on plates.
5. Serve at once.

573. SALMON WITH MASH & CAPERS
Prep & Cook Time: 30 Minutes | Servings: 4

INGREDIENTS
4 cuts salmon fillets, skinless & boneless
1 tbsp. of drained capers
juice from 1 lemon
2 tsp. of olive oil

salt & black pepper to the taste
FOR THE POTATO MASH:
1 lb. of potatoes, chopped
2 tbsp. of olive oil

½ cup of milk
1 tbsp. of dried dill

INSTRUCTIONS
1. Place potatoes in a pot, pour water and add some salt.
2. Let it boil over medium high heat and cook for 15 minutes, drain.
3. In a bowl, mash the potatoes. Add two tablespoons of oil, dill, salt, pepper and milk. Set aside.
4. Coat salmon with salt and pepper, and drizzle two teaspoons of oil.
5. Place to an air fryer's basket, put capers on top and cook at 360°F and cook for 8 minutes.
6. Distribute the salmon and capers on plates
7. Put mashed potatoes on the side, drizzle lemon juice all over.
8. Serve and enjoy.

574. CURLY'S CAULIFLOWER
Prep & Cook Time: 30 minutes | Servings: 4

INGREDIENTS

4 cups of bite-sized cauliflower florets
1 cup of breadcrumbs, mixed with 1 tsp. of salt

¼ cup of melted butter [vegan/other]
¼ cup of buffalo sauce [vegan/other]

Mayo [vegan/other] or creamy dressing for dipping

INSTRUCTIONS

1   In a bowl, combine the butter & buffalo sauce to create a creamy paste.
2   Completely cover each floret with the sauce.
3   Coat the florets with the bread crumb mixture. Cook the florets in the Air Fryer for approximately 15 minutes at 350°F, shaking the basket occasionally.
4   Serve with a raw vegetable salad, mayo or creamy dressing.

575. FRIED MUSHROOMS

Prep & Cook Time: 40 minutes | Servings: 4

INGREDIENTS

2 lb. of button mushrooms
3 tbsp. of white or French vermouth [optional]

1 tbsp. of coconut oil
2 tsp. of herbs of your choice

½ tsp. of garlic powder

INSTRUCTIONS

1   Wash & dry the mushrooms. Slice them into quarters.
2   Pre-heat your Air Fryer at 320°F & add the coconut oil, garlic powder, & herbs to the basket.
3   Briefly cook the ingredients for 2 minutes & give them a stir. Put the mushrooms in the Air Fryer & cook for 25 minutes, stirring occasionally throughout.
4   Pour in the white vermouth & mix. Cook for an additional 5 minutes.
5   Serve hot.

576. CHEESY GARLIC BREAD

Prep & Cook Time: 20 minutes | Servings: 2

INGREDIENTS

1 baguette
4 tsp. of butter, melted

3 chopped garlic cloves
5 tsp. of sundried tomato pesto

1 cup of mozzarella cheese, grated

INSTRUCTIONS

1   Cut your baguette into 5 thick round slices.
2   Add the garlic cloves to the melted butter & brush onto each slice of bread.
3   Spread a tsp. of sun-dried tomato pesto onto each slice.
4   Top each slice with the grated mozzarella.
5   Transfer the bread slices to the Air Fryer & cook them at 180°F for 6 – 8 minutes.
6   Top with some freshly chopped basil leaves, chili flakes & oregano if desired.

577. STUFFED MUSHROOMS

Prep & Cook Time: 25 minutes | Servings: 4

INGREDIENTS

6 small mushrooms
1 tbsp. of onion, peeled & diced
1 tbsp. of breadcrumbs

1 tbsp. of olive oil
1 tsp. of garlic, pureed
1 tsp. of parsley

Salt & pepper

INSTRUCTIONS

1   Combine the breadcrumbs, oil, onion, parsley, salt, pepper & garlic in a bowl.
2   Scoop the stalks out of the mushrooms & spoon equal portions of the crumb mixture in the caps. Transfer to the Air Fryer & cook for 10 minutes at 350°F.
3   Serve with mayo dip if desired.

578. GRILLED TOMATOES

Prep & Cook Time: 25 minutes | Servings: 2

INGREDIENTS

2 tomatoes, medium to large
Herbs of your choice, to taste

Pepper
Cooking spray

INSTRUCTIONS

1   Wash & dry the tomatoes, before chopping them in half.
2   Lightly spritz them all over with cooking spray.
3   Season each half with herbs (oregano, basil, parsley, rosemary, thyme, sage, etc.) as desired & black pepper.
4   Put the halves in the tray of your Air Fryer. Cook for 20 minutes at 320°F, or longer if necessary. Larger tomatoes will take longer to cook.

579. CARROTS & RHUBARB

Prep & Cook Time: 35 minutes | Servings: 4

INGREDIENTS

1 lb. of heritage carrots
1 lb. of rhubarb

1 medium orange
½ cup of walnuts, halved

2 tsp. of walnut oil
½ tsp. of sugar

INSTRUCTIONS

1   Rinse the carrots to wash. Dry & chop them into 1-inch pieces.
2   Transfer them to the Air Fryer basket & drizzle over the walnut oil.
3   Cook at 320°F for about 20 minutes.
4   In the meantime, wash the rhubarb & chop it into ½-inch pieces.
5   Coarsely dice the walnuts.
6   Wash the orange & grate its skin into a small bowl. Peel the rest of the orange & cut it up into wedges.
7   Place the rhubarb, walnuts & sugar in the Air Fryer & allow to cook for an additional 5 minutes.
8   Add in 2 tbsp. of the orange zest, along with the orange wedges. Serve immediately.

580. BROCCOLI

Prep & Cook Time: 30 minutes | Servings: 4

INGREDIENTS

1 large head of broccoli
½ lemon, juiced

3 cloves garlic, minced
1 tbsp. of coconut oil

1 tbsp. of white sesame seeds
2 tsp. of Maggi sauce or other seasonings to taste

INSTRUCTIONS

1   Wash & dry the broccoli. Chop it up into small florets.
2   Place the minced garlic in your Air Fryer basket, along with the coconut oil, lemon juice & Maggi sauce.
3   Heat for 2 minutes at 320°F & give it a stir. Put the garlic & broccoli in the basket & cook for another 13 minutes.
4   Top the broccoli with the white sesame seeds & resume cooking for 5 more minutes, ensuring the seeds become nice & toasty.

581. MAPLE GLAZED BEETS

Prep & Cook Time: 60 minutes | Servings: 8

INGREDIENTS

3 ½ lb. of beetroots

4 tbsp. of maple syrup

1 tbsp. of coconut oil

INSTRUCTIONS
1. Wash & peel the beets. Cut them up into 1-inch pieces.
2. Put the coconut oil in the Air Fryer & melt for 1 minute at 320°F.
3. Place the beet cubes to the Air Fryer Basket & allow to cook for 40 minutes. Coat the beetroots in two tbsp. of the maple syrup & cook for another 10 minutes, ensuring the beets become soft.
4. Toss the cooked beets with the remaining two tbsp. of maple syrup & serve right away.

582. ENDIVE MARINATED IN CURRIED YOGURT
Prep & Cook Time: 20 minutes | Servings: 6

INGREDIENTS
6 heads of endive
½ cup plain & fat-free yogurt
3 tbsp. of lemon juice

1 tsp. of garlic powder [or 2 minced cloves of garlic]
½ tsp. of curry powder

Salt & ground black pepper to taste

INSTRUCTIONS
1. Wash the endives & slice them in half lengthwise.
2. In a bowl, mix together the yogurt, lemon juice, garlic powder [or minced garlic], curry powder, salt & pepper. If you would like you marinade to be thinner, add some more lemon juice.
3. Brush the endive halves with the marinade, coating them completely. Allow to sit for a minimum of a half-hour & a maximum of one day.
4. Pre-heat Air Fryer to 320°F. Allow the endives to cook for 10 minutes & serve hot.

583. TASTY TOFU
Prep & Cook Time: 35 minutes | Servings: 4

INGREDIENTS
1x 12 oz. of packet low-fat & firm tofu
2 tbsp. of low-sodium soy sauce
2 tbsp. of fish sauce

1 tbsp. of coriander paste
1 tsp. of sesame oil
1 tsp. of duck fat or coconut oil

1 tsp. of Maggi sauce

INSTRUCTIONS
1. Remove the liquid from the packet of tofu & chop the tofu into 1-inch cubes. Line a plate with paper towels & spread the tofu out on top in one layer. Place another paper towel on top, followed by another plate, weighting it down with a heavier object if necessary. This is to dry the tofu out completely. Leave for a minimum of 30 minutes or a maximum of 24 hours, replacing the paper towels once or twice throughout the duration.
2. In a medium bowl, mix together the sesame oil, Maggi sauce, coriander paste, fish sauce, & soy sauce. Stir to combine fully.
3. Coat the tofu cubes with this mixture & allow to marinate for at least a half-hour, tossing the cubes a few times throughout to ensure even coating. Add another few drops of fish sauce or soy sauce to thin out the marinade if necessary.
4. Melt the duck fat/coconut oil in your Air Fryer at 350°F for about 2 minutes. Place the tofu cubes in the basket & cook for about 20 minutes or longer to achieve a crispier texture. Flip the tofu over or shake the basket every 10 minutes.
5. Serve hot with the dipping sauce of your choosing.

584. ROASTED PEPPERS
Prep & Cook Time: 40 minutes | Servings: 4

INGREDIENTS
12 medium bell peppers
1 sweet onion, small

1 tbsp. of Maggi sauce
1 tbsp. of extra virgin olive oil

INSTRUCTIONS
1. Warm up the olive oil & Maggi sauce in Air Fryer at 320°F.
2. Peel the onion, slice it into 1-inch pieces, & add it to the Air Fryer.
3. Wash & de-stem the peppers. Slice them into 1-inch pieces & remove all the seeds, with water if necessary [ensuring to dry the peppers afterwards].
4. Place the peppers in the Air Fryer.
5. Cook for about 25 minutes, or longer if desired. Serve hot.

585. ROASTED PARSNIP
Prep & Cook Time: 55 minutes | Servings: 5

INGREDIENTS
2 lb. of parsnips [about 6 large parsnips]
2 tbsp. of maple syrup

1 tbsp. of coconut oil
1 tbsp. of parsley, dried flakes

INSTRUCTIONS
1. Melt the duck fat or coconut oil in your Air Fryer for 2 minutes at 320°F.
2. Rinse the parsnips to clean them & dry them. Chop into 1-inch cubes. Transfer to the Air Fryer.
3. Cook the parsnip cubes in the fat/oil for 35 minutes, tossing them regularly.
4. Season the parsnips with parsley & maple syrup & allow to cook for another 5 minutes or longer to achieve a soft texture throughout. Serve straightaway.

586. CHEESE BOATS
Prep & Cook Time: 30 minutes | Servings: 2

INGREDIENTS
1 cup of ground chicken
1 zucchini
1 ½ cups of crushed tomatoes

½ tsp. of salt
¼ tsp. of pepper
½ tsp. of garlic powder

2 tbsp. of butter or olive oil
½ cup of cheese, grated
¼ tsp. of dried oregano

INSTRUCTIONS
1. Peel & halve the zucchini. Use a spoon to scoop out the flesh.
2. In a bowl, combine the ground chicken, tomato, garlic powder, butter, cheese, oregano, salt, & pepper. Fill in the hollowed-out zucchini with this mixture.
3. Transfer to the Air Fryer & bake for about 10 minutes at 400°F. Serve warm.

587. EGGPLANT
Prep & Cook Time: 45 minutes | Servings: 6

INGREDIENTS
3 eggplants, medium
½ lemon, juiced
1 tbsp. of duck fat, or coconut oil
1 tbsp. of Maggi sauce

3 tsp. of za'atar
1 tsp. of sumac
1 tsp. of garlic powder
1 tsp. of onion powder

1 tsp. of extra virgin olive oil
2 bay leaves

INSTRUCTIONS
1. Wash, dry & destem the eggplants. Chop them into 1-inch cubes.
2. In the Air Fryer basket, combine duck fat [or coconut oil], maggi sauce, za'atar, onion powder, garlic powder, sumac & bay leaves.
3. Melt the ingredients for 2 minutes at 320°F, stirring well.
4. Place the eggplant in the Air Fryer basket & allow to cook for 25 minutes.
5. In a large bowl, mix together the lemon juice & extra virgin olive oil. Add the cooked eggplant & stir to coat evenly.
6. Serve immediately with grated parmesan or fresh chopped basil if desired.

588. SWEET POTATO FRIES
Prep & Cook Time: 35 minutes | Servings: 5

INGREDIENTS

2 large, sweet potatoes
1 tbsp. of extra virgin olive oil

INSTRUCTIONS

1   Wash the sweet potatoes. Dry & peel them before chopping them into shoestring fries. In a bowl, toss the fries with the olive oil to coat well.
2   Set your Air Fryer to 320°F & briefly allow to warm. Put the sweet potatoes in the Air Fryer basket & fry for 15 minutes, stirring them at the halfway point.
3   Once done, toss again to make sure no fries are sticking to each other.
4   Turn the heat to 350°F & cook for a further 10 minutes, again giving them a good stir halfway through the cooking time.
5   Serve your fries straightaway.

589. CHICKEN, MUSHROOM & SPINACH PIZZA

Prep & Cook Time: 25 minutes | Servings: 4

INGREDIENTS

10 ½ oz. of minced chicken
1 tsp. of garlic powder

1 tsp. of black pepper
2 tbsp. of tomato basil sauce

5 button mushrooms, sliced thinly
Handful of spinach

INSTRUCTIONS

1   Pre-heat your Air Fryer at 450°F.
2   Add parchment paper onto your baking tray.
3   In a large bowl add the chicken with the black pepper & garlic powder.
4   Add one spoonful of the chicken mix onto your baking tray.
5   Flatten them into 7-inch rounds.
6   Bake in the Air Fryer for about 10 minutes.
7   Take out off the Air Fryer & add the tomato basil sauce onto each round.
8   Add the mushroom on top. Bake again for 5 minutes.
9   Serve immediately.

590. TURKEY SAUSAGE PATTIES

Prep & Cook Time: 20 minutes | Servings: 6

INGREDIENTS

1 lb. of lean ground turkey
1 tsp. of olive oil
1 tbsp. of chopped chives
1 small onion, diced

1 large garlic clove, chopped
¾ tsp. of paprika
Kosher salt & pepper to taste
Pinch of raw sugar

1 tbsp. of vinegar
1 tsp. of fennel seed
Pinch of nutmeg

INSTRUCTIONS

1   Pre-heat the Air Fryer to 375°F.
2   Add a half-tsp. of the oil to the Air Fryer, along with the onion & garlic. Air fry for 30 seconds before adding in the fennel. Place everything on a plate.
3   In a bowl, combine the ground turkey with the sugar, paprika, nutmeg, vinegar, chives & the onion mixture. Divide into equal portions & shape each one into a patty.
4   Add another tsp. of oil to the Air Fryer. Put the patties in the Air Fryer & cook for roughly 3 minutes.
5   Serve with salad or on hamburger buns.

591. BACON FRIES

Prep & Cook Time: 60 minutes | Servings: 2 – 4

INGREDIENTS

2 large russet potatoes, peeled & cut into ½ inch
    sticks
5 slices of bacon, diced
2 tbsp. of vegetable oil

2 ½ cups of cheddar cheese, shredded
3 oz. of cream cheese, melted
Salt & freshly ground black pepper
¼ cup of chopped scallions

Ranch dressing

INSTRUCTIONS

1   Boil a large pot of salted water.
2   Briefly cook the potato sticks in the boiling water for 4 minutes.
3   Drain the potatoes & run some cold water over them in order to wash off the starch. Pat them dry with a kitchen towel.
4   Pre-heat the Air Fryer to 400°F.
5   Put the chopped bacon in the Air Fryer & air-fry for 4 minutes. Shake the basket at the halfway point.
6   Place the bacon on paper towels to drain any excess fat & remove the grease from the Air Fryer drawer.
7   Coat the dried potatoes with oil & put them in the Air Fryer basket. Air-fry at 360°F for 25 minutes, giving the basket the occasional shake throughout the cooking time & sprinkling the fries with salt & freshly ground black pepper at the halfway point.
8   Take a casserole dish or baking pan that is small enough to fit inside your Air Fryer & place the fries inside.
9   Mix together the 2 cups of the Cheddar cheese & the melted cream cheese.
10 Pour the cheese mixture over the fries & top them with the rest of the Cheddar cheese & the cooked bacon crumbles.
11 Take absolute care when placing the baking pan inside the cooker. Use a foil sling [a sheet of aluminum foil folded into a strip about 2 inches wide by 24 inches long].
12 Cook the fries at 340°F for 5 minutes, ensuring the cheese melts.
13 Garnish the fries with the chopped scallions & serve straight from in the baking dish with some ranch dressing.

592. TOASTED PUMPKIN SEEDS

Prep & Cook Time: 25 minutes | Servings: 4

INGREDIENTS

1 ½ cups of pumpkin seeds [cut a whole pumpkin
    & scrape out the insides]

1 tsp. of smoked paprika
1 ½ tsp. of salt

Olive oil

INSTRUCTIONS

1   Run the pumpkin seeds under some cold water.
2   Over a medium heat, boil two quarts of salted water in a pot.
3   Add in the pumpkin seeds & cook in the water for 8 to 10 minutes.
4   Dump the contents of the pot into a sieve to drain the seeds. Place them on paper towels & allow them to dry for at least 20 minutes.
5   Pre-heat your Air Fryer to 350°F.
6   In a medium bowl coat the pumpkin seeds with olive oil, smoked paprika & salt.
7   Put them in the Air Fryer's basket & air fry for at least 30 minutes until slightly browned & crispy. Shake the basket a few times during the cooking time.
8   Allow the seeds to cool. Serve with a salad or keep in an airtight container for snacking.

593. BANANA PEPPERS

Prep & Cook Time: 20 minutes | Servings: 8

INGREDIENTS:

1 cup of full-fat cream cheese
cooking spray

16 avocado slices
16 slices of salami

salt & pepper
16 banana peppers

INSTRUCTIONS

1   Pre-heat the Air Fryer to 400°F.
2   Spritz a baking tray with cooking spray.
3   Remove the stems from the banana peppers with a knife.
4   Cut a slit into one side of each banana pepper.
5   Season the cream cheese with the salt & pepper & combine well.
6   Fill each pepper with one spoonful of the cream cheese, followed by one slice of avocado.

7   Wrap the banana peppers in the slices of salami & secure with a toothpick.
8   Place the banana peppers in the baking tray & transfer it to the Air Fryer. Bake for roughly 8 - 10 minutes.

594. BARBECUE SAUCE
Prep & Cook Time: 20 minutes | Servings: 6

INGREDIENTS
For the Sauce:
1 tbsp. of yellow mustard
1 tbsp. of apple cider vinegar
1 tbsp. of olive oil
¼ cup of unsulfured blackstrap molasses
¼ cup of ketchup

2 tbsp. of sugar
1 garlic clove, minced
Salt & ground black pepper, to taste
⅛ tsp. of ground allspice
¼ cup of water

For the Wings
2 lb. of chicken wings
¼ tsp. of celery salt
¼ cup of habanero hot sauce
Chopped fresh parsley, or garnish

INSTRUCTIONS:
1   Put all the ingredients for the sauce in a pan over a medium-to-high heat & bring the mixture to a boil.
2   Lower the heat & allow to simmer & thicken.
3   In the meantime, pre-heat your Air Fryer to 400°F.
4   Place the chicken wings in the Air Fryer & cook for 6 minutes.
5   Turn the wings & cook for another 6 minutes on the other side. Sprinkle some celery salt over them.
6   Serve the chicken wings with the prepared sauce, along with habanero sauce or any other accompaniment of your choice.

595. COCONUT SHRIMP
Prep & Cook Time: 20 minutes | Servings: 16

INGREDIENTS
½ tsp. of salt
1 lb. of large shrimp [about 16 to 20 peeled/de-veined]
½ cup of flour

2 egg whites
½ cup of breadcrumbs
½ cup of coconut, shredded
Zest of 1 lime

¼ tsp. of cayenne pepper
Spray can of vegetable or canola oil
Sweet chili sauce or duck sauce, to serve

INSTRUCTIONS
1   In a shallow dish, beat the eggs with a whisk.
2   Combine the breadcrumbs, coconut, lime zest, salt & cayenne pepper in a separate dish.
3   Pre-heat the Air Fryer to 400°F.
4   Coat the shrimp in the flour. Dip the shrimp into the egg mixture, & then into the breadcrumb coconut mixture, ensuring to coat the shrimp all over.
5   Place the shrimp on a plate & spritz with oil. Move the shrimp to the basket of your Air Fryer, taking care not to overlap the fish.
6   Air fry the shrimp for 5 - 6 minutes, ensuring that each shrimp is cooked through & firm before serving.

596. TORTILLA CHIPS
Prep & Cook Time: 5 minutes | Servings: 2

INGREDIENTS
8 corn tortillas

Salt

1 tbsp. of olive oil

INSTRUCTIONS
1   Pre-heat your Air Fryer to 390°F.
2   Slice the corn tortillas into triangles. Coat with a light brushing of olive oil.
3   Put the tortilla pieces in the wire basket & air fry for 3 minutes. You may need to do this in multiple batches.
4   Season with salt before serving.

597. NAAN BREAD DIPPERS
Prep & Cook Time: 50 minutes | Servings: 10

INGREDIENTS
4 naan breads, cut into 2-inch strips
3 tbsp. of butter, melted
12 oz. of light cream cheese, softened
1 cup of plain yogurt
2 tsp. of curry powder

2 cups of cooked chicken, shredded
4 scallions, minced
⅓ cup of golden raisins
6 oz. of cheese, grated [about 2 cups]
¼ cup of fresh cilantro, chopped

Salt & freshly ground black pepper
½ cup of sliced almonds
½ cup Major Grey's Chutney

INSTRUCTIONS
1   Pre-heat Air Fryer to 400°F.
2   Slice up the naan in thirds lengthwise before cutting crosswise into 2-inch strips. In a bowl, toss the strips with the melted butter.
3   Move the naan strips to Air Fryer basket. Toast for 5 minutes, shaking the basket halfway through. You will have to do this in two batches.
4   Mix together the softened cream cheese & yogurt with a hand mixer or in a food processor. Add in the curry powder & combine evenly.
5   Fold in the shredded chicken, scallions, golden raisins, Monterey Jack cheese & chopped cilantro.
6   Sprinkle with salt & freshly ground black pepper as desired.
7   Pour the mixture into a 1-quart baking dish & spread out evenly. Arrange the sliced almonds on top. Air-fry at 300°F for 25 minutes.
8   Put a dollop of Major Grey's chutney in the center of the dip & scatter the scallions on top.
9   Serve the naan dippers with the hot dip.

598. SNACK MIX
Prep & Cook Time: 30 minutes | Servings: 10

INGREDIENTS
½ cup of honey
3 tbsp. of butter, melted
1 tsp. of salt

2 cups of sesame sticks
2 cups of pepitas [pumpkin seeds]
2 cups of granola

1 cup of cashews
2 cups of crispy corn puff cereal
2 cups of mini pretzel crisps

INSTRUCTIONS
1   In a bowl, combine the honey, butter, & salt.
2   In another bowl, mix together the sesame sticks, pepitas, granola, cashews, corn puff cereal, & pretzel crisps.
3   Combine the contents of the two bowls.
4   Pre-heat your Air Fryer to 370°F.
5   Put the mixture in the Air Fryer basket & air-fry for 10 - 12 minutes to toast the snack mixture, shaking the basket frequently. You will have to do this in two batches.
6   Place the snack mix on a cookie sheet & allow it to cool fully.
7   Store in an airtight container for up to one week. Makes a great holiday gift!

599. FETA TRIANGLES
Prep & Cook Time: 55 minutes | Servings: 5

INGREDIENTS
1 egg yolk, beaten
4 oz. of feta cheese

2 tbsp. of flat-leafed parsley, chopped
1 scallion, finely chopped

2 sheets of frozen filo pastry, defrosted
2 tbsp. of olive oil ground black pepper to taste

INSTRUCTIONS
1   In a bowl, combine the beaten egg yolk with the feta, parsley & scallion. Sprinkle on some pepper to taste.
2   Slice each sheet of filo dough into three strips.
3   Place a teaspoonful of the feta mixture on each strip of pastry.

4   Pinch the tip of the pastry & fold it up to enclose the filling & create a triangle. Continue folding the strip in zigzags until the filling is wrapped in a triangle. Repeat with all of the strips of pastry.
5   Pre-heat the Air Fryer to 390°F.
6   Coat the pastry with a light coating of oil & arrange in the cooking basket.
7   Place the basket in the Air Fryer & cook for 3 minutes.
8   Lower the heat to 360°F & cook for a further 2 minutes or until a golden-brown color is achieved

600. SAGE & ONION STUFFING

Prep & Cook Time: 35 minutes | Servings: 6

INGREDIENTS

2 lb. of sausage meat
½ onion
½ tsp. of garlic puree

1 tsp. of sage
3 tbsp. of breadcrumbs
Salt

Black pepper

INSTRUCTIONS

1   Combine all of the ingredients in a large bowl.
2   Take equal portions of the mixture, mold them into medium sized balls & put them in the Air Fryer.
3   Cook at 355°F for 15 minutes.

601. PUPPY POPPERS

Prep & Cook Time: 25 minutes | Servings: 50 treats

INGREDIENTS

½ cup of unsweetened applesauce
1 cup of peanut butter

2 cups of oats
1 cup of flour

1 tsp. of baking powder

INSTRUCTIONS

1   Combine the applesauce & peanut butter in a bowl to create a smooth consistency.
2   Pour in the oats, flour & baking powder. Continue mixing to form a soft dough.
3   Shape a half-tsp. of dough into a ball & continue with the rest of the dough.
4   Pre-heat the Air Fryer to 350°F.
5   Grease the bottom of the basket with oil.
6   Place the poppers in the Air Fryer & cook for 8 minutes, flipping the balls at the halfway point. You may need to cook the poppers in batches.
7   Let the poppers cool & serve immediately or keep in an airtight container for up to 2 weeks.

602. MASALA CASHEW

Prep & Cook Time: 20 minutes | Servings: 3

INGREDIENTS

½ lb. of cashew nuts
½ tsp. of garam masala powder
1 tsp. of coriander powder

1 tsp. of butter
1 tsp. of red chili powder
½ tsp. of black pepper

2 tsp. of dry mango powder
1 tsp. of sea salt

INSTRUCTIONS

1   Put all the ingredients in a large bowl & toss together well.
2   Arrange the cashew nuts in the basket of your Air Fryer.
3   Cook at 250°F for 15 minutes until the nuts are brown & crispy.
4   Let the nuts cool before serving or transferring to an airtight container to be stored for up to 2 weeks.

603. BACON WRAPPED SHRIMP

Prep & Cook Time: 50 minutes | Servings: 4

INGREDIENTS

1 ¼ lb. of tiger shrimp, deveined [16 pieces]

1 lb. of bacon, thinly sliced, room temperature

INSTRUCTIONS

1   Wrap each bacon slice around a piece of shrimp, from the head to the tail. Refrigerate for 20 minutes.
2   Pre-heat the Air Fryer to 390°F.
3   Place the shrimp in the Air Fryer's basket & cook for 5 – 7 minutes.
4   Allow to dry on a paper towel before serving.

604. TOMATO & AVOCADO EGG ROLLS

Prep & Cook Time: 20 minutes | Servings: 5

INGREDIENTS

10 egg roll wrappers
3 avocados, peeled & pitted

1 tomato, diced
Salt & pepper, to taste

INSTRUCTIONS

1   Pre-heat your Air Fryer to 350°F.
2   Put the tomato & avocados in a bowl. Sprinkle on some salt & pepper & mash together with a fork until a smooth consistency is achieved.
3   Spoon equal amounts of the mixture onto the wrappers. Roll the wrappers around the filling, enclosing them entirely.
4   Transfer the rolls to a lined baking dish & cook for 5 minutes.

605. MEATBALLS IN TOMATO SAUCE

Prep & Cook Time: 35 minutes | Servings: 4

INGREDIENTS

1 small onion, finely chopped
¾ lb. [12 oz.] of ground beef
1 tbsp. of chopped fresh parsley

½ tbsp. of chopped fresh thyme leaves
1 egg
3 tbsp. of breadcrumbs

Salt & pepper
10 oz. of favorite tomato sauce if desired

INSTRUCTIONS

1   Put all the ingredients in a bowl & combine well. Use your hands to mold the mixture into 10 - 12 balls.
2   Pre-heat the Air Fryer to 390°F.
3   Put the meatballs in the Air Fryer basket & place the basket in the Air Fryer.
4   Cook the meatballs for 8 minutes.
5   Put the meatballs in an oven dish, pour in the tomato sauce & set the dish in the basket of the Air Fryer.
6   Reduce the temperature to 330°F & warm the meatballs for 5 minutes.

606. AMAZING BLOOMING ONION

Prep & Cook Time: 40 minutes | Servings: 4

INGREDIENTS

4 medium/small onions

1 tbsp. of olive oil

4 dollops of butter

INSTRUCTIONS

1   Peel the onion. Cut off the top & bottom.
2   To make it bloom, cut as deeply as possible without slicing through it completely. 4 cuts [i.e. 8 segments] should do it.
3   Place the onions in a bowl of salted water & allow to absorb for 4 hours to help eliminate the sharp taste & induce the blooming process.

4   Pre-heat your Air Fryer to 355°F.
5   Transfer the onions to the Air Fryer. Pour over a light drizzle of olive oil & place a dollop of butter on top of each onion.
6   Cook or roast for 30 minutes. Remove the outer layer before serving if it is too brown.

---

607. CRAB CROQUETTES

Prep & Cook Time: 5 minutes | Servings: 6

INGREDIENTS

For the Filling:
1 lb. of lump crab meat
2 egg whites, beaten
1 tbsp. of olive oil
¼ cup of red onion, finely chopped
¼ red bell pepper, finely chopped
2 tbsp. of celery, finely chopped

¼ tsp. of tarragon, finely chopped
¼ tsp. of chives, finely chopped
½ tsp. of parsley, finely chopped
½ tsp. of cayenne pepper
¼ cup of mayonnaise
¼ cup of sour cream

For the Breading
3 eggs, beaten
1 cup of flour
1 cup of breadcrumbs
1 tsp. of olive oil
½ tsp. of salt

INSTRUCTIONS

1   Sauté the olive oil, onions, peppers, & celery over a medium heat, allowing to sweat until the vegetables turn translucent. This should take about 4 – 5 minutes.
2   Take off the heat & allow to cool.
3   In a food processor, pulse the breadcrumbs, olive oil & salt to form a fine crumb.
4   Place the eggs, panko mixture & flour in three separate bowls.
5   Combine the crabmeat, egg whites, mayonnaise, sour cream, spices & vegetables in a large bowl.
6   Pre-heat the Air Fryer to 390°F.
7   Take equal amounts of the crab mixture & shape into golf balls. Coat the balls in the flour, before dipping them in the eggs & finally in the panko, making sure the breadcrumbs stick well.
8   Put croquettes in the Air Fryer basket in a single layer & well-spaced.
9   Cook the croquettes for 8 – 10 minutes or until a golden-brown color is achieved.

---

608. PUMPKIN SEEDS

Prep & Cook Time: 55 minutes | Servings: 1 ½ cups

INGREDIENTS

1 ½ cups of pumpkin seeds from a large whole
    pumpkin

olive oil
1 ½ tsp. of salt

1 tsp. of smoked paprika

INSTRUCTIONS

1   Boil two quarts of well-salted water in a pot. Cook the pumpkin seeds in the boiling water for 10 minutes.
2   Dump the content of the pot into a sieve & dry the seeds on paper towels for at least 20 minutes.
3   Pre-heat the Air Fryer to 350°F.
4   Cover the seeds with olive oil, salt & smoked paprika, before placing them in the Air Fryer basket.
5   Air fry for 35 minutes. Give the basket a good shake several times throughout the cooking process to ensure the pumpkin seeds are crispy & lightly browned.
6   Let the seeds cool before serving. Alternatively, you can keep them in an air-tight container or bag for snacking or for use as a yogurt topping.

---

609. COCKTAIL FLANKS

Prep & Cook Time: 45 minutes | Servings: 4

INGREDIENTS

1x 12-oz. of packet cocktail franks
1x 8-oz. of can crescent rolls

INSTRUCTIONS

1   Drain the cocktail franks & dry with paper towels.
2   Unroll the crescent rolls & slice the dough into rectangular strips, roughly 1" by 1.5".
3   Wrap the franks in the strips with the ends poking out. Leave in the freezer for 5 minutes.
4   Pre-heat the Air Fryer to 330°F.
5   Take the franks out of the freezer & put them in the cooking basket. Cook for 6 – 8 minutes.
6   Reduce the heat to 390°F & cook for another 3 minutes or until a golden-brown color is achieved.

---

610. GARLIC MUSHROOMS

Prep & Cook Time: 30 minutes | Servings: 4

INGREDIENTS

16 small button mushrooms
For the Stuffing:
1 ½ slices of bread
1 garlic clove, crushed

1 tbsp. of flat-leafed parsley, chopped
Ground black pepper to taste

1 ½ tbsp. of olive oil

INSTRUCTIONS

1   Pre-heat the Air Fryer to 390°F.
2   Blend together the bread slices, garlic, parsley & pepper until a fine crumb is formed.
3   Mix in the olive oil.
4   Remove the mushroom stalks & spoon even amounts of the filling into the caps. Press the crumbs in well to make sure none fall out
5   Put the mushroom caps in the cooking basket & place it in the Air Fryer.
6   Cook the mushrooms for 7 – 8 minutes or until they turn golden & crispy.

---

611. EGGPLANT CHIPS

Prep & Cook Time: 45 minutes | Servings: 4

INGREDIENTS

2 eggplants, peeled & thinly sliced
Salt
½ cup of tapioca starch
¼ cup of canola oil

½ cup of water
1 tsp. of garlic powder
½ tsp. of dried dill weed

½ tsp. of ground black pepper, to taste

INSTRUCTIONS

1   Season the eggplant slices with salt & leave for half an hour.
2   Run them under cold water to rinse off any excess salt.
3   In a bowl, coat the eggplant slices with all of the other ingredients.
4   Cook inside your Air Fryer 390°F for 13 minutes. You may need to do this in batches.
5   Serve with the dipping sauce of your choice.

---

612. SAGE POTATOES

Prep & Cook Time: 45 minutes | Servings: 8

INGREDIENTS

1 ½ lb. of fingerling potatoes, halved
2 tbsp. of melted butter
¼ cup of fresh sage leaves, chopped

2 sprigs of thyme, chopped
1 tsp. of lemon zest, finely grated
¼ tsp. of ground pepper

1 tbsp. of sea salt flakes
½ tsp. of grated ginger

INSTRUCTIONS

1. Place the potatoes in a bowl of cold water & allow to absorb for about half an hour.
2. Dry them with a clean kitchen towel.
3. Transfer to the Air Fryer & roast at 400°F for 15 minutes.
4. Serve with tomato ketchup & mayonnaise if desired.

613. DIJON & QUINOA COCKTAIL MEATBALLS

Prep & Cook Time: 20 minutes | Servings: 6

INGREDIENTS

½ lb. of ground pork
½ lb. of ground beef
1 cup of quinoa, cooked
1 egg, beaten
2 scallions, finely chopped

½ tsp. of onion powder
1 ½ tbsp. of Dijon mustard
¾ cup of ketchup
1 tsp. of ancho chili powder
1 tbsp. of sesame oil

2 tbsp. of tamari sauce
¼ cup of balsamic vinegar
2 tbsp. of sugar

INSTRUCTIONS

1. In a bowl, stir together all the ingredients & combine well.
2. Use your hands to shape equal amounts of the mixture into small meatballs.
3. Place the meatballs in the Air Fryer & cook at 370°F for 10 minutes. Give the basket a good shake & allow to cook for another 5 minutes.

614. RICOTTA BALLS

Prep & Cook Time: 25 minutes | Servings: 2 – 4

INGREDIENTS

2 cups of ricotta, grated
2 eggs, separated
2 tbsp. of chives, finely chopped
2 tbsp. of fresh basil, finely chopped

4 tbsp. of flour
¼ tsp. of salt to taste
¼ tsp. of pepper powder to taste
1 tsp. orange zest, grated

For the Coating:
¼ cup of breadcrumbs
1 tbsp. of vegetable oil

INSTRUCTIONS

1. Pre-heat your Air Fryer at 390°F.
2. In a bowl, combine the yolks, flour, salt, pepper, chives & orange zest. Throw in the ricotta & incorporate with your hands.
3. Mold equal amounts of the mixture into balls.
4. Mix the oil with the breadcrumbs until a crumbly consistency is achieved.
5. Coat the balls in the breadcrumbs & transfer each one to the Air Fryer's basket.
6. Put the basket in the Air Fryer. Air fry for 8 minutes or until a golden-brown color is achieved.
7. Serve with a sauce of your choosing, such as ketchup.

615. SPICED NUTS

Prep & Cook Time: 40 minutes | Servings: 3 cups

INGREDIENTS

1 egg white, lightly beaten
¼ cup of sugar
1 tsp. of salt
½ tsp. of ground cinnamon

¼ tsp. of ground cloves
¼ tsp. of ground allspice
Pinch of ground cayenne pepper
1 cup of pecan halves

1 cup of cashews
1 cup of almonds

INSTRUCTIONS

1. In a bowl, combine the egg white with the sugar & spices.
2. Pre-heat the Air Fryer to 300°F.
3. Coat the inside of the Air Fryer's basket with vegetable oil.
4. Cover the nuts with the spiced egg white. Place half of them in the Air Fryer.
5. Air fry for 25 minutes, giving the nuts a few good stirs throughout the cooking time, until they are crunchy & toasted.
6. Repeat with the other half of the nuts.
7. Serve immediately or store in an airtight container for up to two weeks.

616. SHRIMP BITES

Prep & Cook Time: 45 minutes | Servings: 10

INGREDIENTS

1 ¼ lb. shrimp, peeled & deveined
1 tsp. of paprika
½ tsp. of ground black pepper

½ tsp. of red pepper flakes, crushed
1 tbsp. of salt
1 tsp. of chili powder

1 tbsp. of shallot powder
¼ tsp. of cumin powder
1 ¼ lb. of thin bacon slices

INSTRUCTIONS

1. Coat the shrimps with all of the seasonings.
2. Wrap a slice of bacon around each shrimp & hold it in place with a toothpick. Refrigerate for half an hour.
3. Transfer to the Air Fryer & fry at 360°F for 7 - 8 minutes.

617. CAJUN SPICED SNACK

Prep & Cook Time: 30 minutes | Servings: 5

INGREDIENTS

2 tbsp. of Cajun or Creole seasoning
½ cup of butter, melted
2 cups of peanuts
2 cups of mini wheat thin crackers
2 cups of mini pretzels

2 tsp. of salt
1 tsp. of cayenne pepper
4 cups of plain popcorn
1 tsp. of paprika
1 tsp. of garlic

½ tsp. of thyme
½ tsp. of oregano
1 tsp. of black pepper
½ tsp. of onion powder

INSTRUCTIONS

1. Pre-heat the Air Fryer to 370°F.
2. In a bowl, combine the Cajun spice with the melted butter.
3. In a separate bowl, stir together the peanuts, crackers, popcorn & pretzels. Coat the snacks with the butter mixture.
4. Place in the Air Fryer & fry for 8 - 10 minutes, shaking the basket frequently during the cooking time. You will have to complete this step in two batches.
5. Put the snack mix on a cookie sheet & leave to cool.
6. The snacks can be kept in an airtight container for up to one week.

618. CHEESY BROCCOLI BALLS

Prep & Cook Time: 20 minutes | Servings: 6

INGREDIENTS

2 eggs, well whisked
2 cups of Colby cheese, shredded
1 cup of flour

Seasoned salt, to taste
¼ tsp. of ground black pepper, or more if preferred

1 head of broccoli, chopped into florets
1 cup of crushed saltines

INSTRUCTIONS

1. Mix together the eggs, cheese, flour, salt, pepper, & broccoli until a dough-like paste is formed.
2. Refrigerate for 1 hour. Divide the mixture evenly & mold each portion into small balls. Coat the balls in the crushed saltines & spritz them all over with cooking spray.
3. Cook inside your Air Fryer at 360°F for 10 minutes. At this point, you should check how far along in the cooking process they are & allow to cook for a further 8 - 10 minutes as needed.

4.   Serve with the dipping sauce of your choice.

619. GOULASH

Prep & Cook Time: 20 minutes | Servings: 2

INGREDIENTS

2 chopped bell peppers
2 diced tomatoes

1 lb. of ground chicken
½ cup of chicken broth

Salt & pepper

INSTRUCTIONS
1.   Pre-heat your Air Fryer at 365°F & spray with cooking spray.
2.   Cook the bell pepper for five minutes.
3.   Add in the diced tomatoes & ground chicken. Combine well, then allow to cook for a further six minutes.
4.   Pour in chicken broth, & season to taste with salt & pepper. Cook for another six minutes before serving.

620. GARLICKY MEATBALLS

Prep & Cook Time: 20 minutes | Servings: 2

INGREDIENTS

½ lb. of boneless chicken thighs
1 tsp. of minced garlic

1 ¼ cup of roasted pecans
½ cup of mushrooms

1 tsp. of extra virgin olive oil

INSTRUCTIONS
1.   Preheat your Air Fryer to 375°F.
2.   Cube the chicken thighs.
3.   Place them in the food processor along with the garlic, pecans, & other seasonings as desired. Pulse until a smooth consistency is achieved.
4.   Chop the mushrooms finely. Add to the chicken mixture & combine.
5.   Using your hands, shape the mixture into balls & brush them with olive oil.
6.   Put the balls into the Air Fryer & cook for eighteen minutes. Serve hot.

621. CILANTRO DRUMSTICKS

Prep & Cook Time: 30 minutes | Servings: 4

INGREDIENTS:

8 chicken drumsticks

½ cup of chimichurri sauce

¼ cup of lemon juice

INSTRUCTIONS
1.   Coat the chicken drumsticks with chimichurri sauce & refrigerate in an airtight container for no less than an hour, ideally overnight.
2.   When it's time to cook, pre-heat your Air Fryer to 400°F.
3.   Remove the chicken from refrigerator & allow return to room temperature for roughly twenty minutes.
4.   Cook for eighteen minutes in the Air Fryer. Drizzle with lemon juice to taste & enjoy.

622. POPPIN' POP CORN CHICKEN

Prep & Cook Time: 20 minutes | Servings: 1

INGREDIENTS

1 lb. of skinless, boneless chicken breast
1 tsp. of chili flakes

1 tsp. of garlic powder
½ cup of flour

1 tbsp. of olive oil cooking spray

INSTRUCTIONS
1.   Pre-heat your Air Fryer at 365°F. Spray with olive oil.
2.   Cut the chicken breasts into cubes & place in a bowl. Toss with the chili flakes, garlic powder, & additional seasonings to taste & make sure to coat entirely.
3.   Add the coconut flour & toss once more.
4.   Cook the chicken in the Air Fryer for ten minutes. Turnover & cook for a further five minutes before serving.

623. CRISPY CHICKEN

Prep & Cook Time: 10 minutes | Servings: 2

INGREDIENTS

1 lb. of chicken skin
1 tsp. of butter

½ tsp. of chili flakes
1 tsp. of dill

INSTRUCTIONS
1.   Pre-heat the Air Fryer at 360°F.
2.   Cut the chicken skin into slices.
3.   Heat the butter until melted & pour it over the chicken skin. Toss with chili flakes, dill, & any additional seasonings to taste, making sure to coat well.
4.   Cook the skins in the Air Fryer for three minutes. Turn them over & cook on the other side for another three minutes.
5.   Serve immediately or save them for later – they can be eaten hot or at room temperature.

624. SOUTHERN FRIED CHICKEN

Prep & Cook Time: 30 minutes | Servings: 2

INGREDIENTS

2 x 6-oz. of boneless skinless chicken breasts

2 tbsp. of hot sauce
½ tsp. of onion powder

1 tbsp. of chili powder
½ oz. of flour

INSTRUCTIONS
1.   Cut the chicken breasts in half lengthwise & rub in the hot sauce. Combine the onion powder with the chili powder, then rub into the chicken. Leave to marinate for at least a half hour.
2.   Use the flour to coat the chicken breasts, covering them thoroughly. Place the chicken in your Air Fryer.
3.   Set the Air Fryer at 350°F & cook the chicken for 13 minutes. Flip the chicken & cook the other side for another 13 minutes or until golden.
4.   Test the chicken with a meat thermometer. When fully cooked, it should reach 165°F. Serve hot, with the sides of your choice.

625. JALAPENO CHICKEN BREASTS

Prep & Cook Time: 25 minutes | Servings: 2

INGREDIENTS

2 oz. of full-fat cream cheese, softened
4 slices of sugar-free bacon, cooked & crumbled

¼ cup of pickled jalapenos, sliced
½ cup of sharp cheddar cheese,

shredded & divided
2 x 6-oz. of boneless skinless chicken breasts

INSTRUCTIONS
1.   In a bowl, mix the cream cheese, bacon, jalapeno slices, & half of the cheddar cheese until well-combined.
2.   Cut parallel slits in the chicken breasts of about ¾ the length – make sure not to cut all the way down. You should be able to make between six & eight slices, depending on the size of the chicken breast.
3.   Insert evenly sized dollops of the cheese mixture into the slits of the chicken breasts. Top the chicken with sprinkles of the rest of the cheddar cheese. Place the chicken in the basket of your Air Fryer.
4.   Set the Air Fryer to 350°F & cook the chicken breasts for twenty minutes.
5.   Test with a meat thermometer. The chicken should be at 165°F when fully cooked. Serve hot & enjoy!

626. FAJITA STYLE CHICKEN BREAST

Prep & Cook Time: 35 minutes | Servings: 2

INGREDIENTS

2 x 6-oz. of boneless skinless chicken breasts

1 green bell pepper, sliced
¼ medium white onion, sliced

1 tbsp. of coconut oil, melted
3 tsp. of taco seasoning mix

INSTRUCTIONS
1. Cut each chicken breast in half & place each one between two sheets of cooking parchment. Using a mallet, pound the chicken to flatten to a quarter-inch thick.
2. Place the chicken on a flat surface, with the short end facing you. Place four slices of pepper & three slices of onion at the end of each piece of chicken. Roll up the chicken tightly, making sure not to let any veggies fall out. Secure with some toothpicks or with butcher's string.
3. Coat the chicken with coconut oil & then with taco seasoning. Place into your Air Fryer.
4. Turn the Air Fryer to 350°F & cook the chicken for twenty-five minutes.
5. Serve the rolls immediately with your favorite dips & sides.

627. LEMON PEPPER CHICKEN LEGS
Prep & Cook Time: 30 minutes | Servings: 4

INGREDIENTS

½ tsp. of garlic powder
2 tsp. of baking powder

8 chicken legs
4 tbsp. of salted butter, melted

1 tbsp. of lemon pepper seasoning

INSTRUCTIONS
1. In a small bowl combine the garlic powder & baking powder, then use this mixture to coat the chicken legs. Lay the chicken in the basket of your Air Fryer.
2. Cook the chicken legs at 375°F for twenty-five minutes. Halfway through, turn them over & allow to cook on the other side.
3. When the chicken has turned golden brown, test with a thermometer to ensure it has reached an ideal temperature of 165°F. Remove from the Air Fryer.
4. Mix together the melted butter & lemon pepper seasoning & toss with the chicken legs until the chicken is coated all over. Serve hot.

628. GREEK CHICKEN MEATBALLS
Prep & Cook Time: 15 minutes | Servings: 1

INGREDIENTS

½ oz. of flour
1 lb. of ground chicken

1 tsp. of Greek seasoning
⅓ cup feta, crumbled

⅓ cup of frozen spinach, thawed

INSTRUCTIONS
1. Place all the ingredients in a large bowl & combine using your hands. Take equal-sized portions of this mixture & roll each into a 2-inch ball. Place the balls in your Air Fryer.
2. Cook the meatballs at 350°F for twelve minutes, in several batches if necessary.
3. Once they are golden, ensure they have reached an ideal temperature of 165°F & remove from the Air Fryer. Keep each batch warm while you move on to the next one. Serve with Tzatziki if desired.

629. CRUSTED CHICKEN
Ingredients: Prep & Cook Time: 30 minutes | Servings: 2

INGREDIENTS

¼ cup of slivered almonds
2x 6-oz. of boneless skinless chicken

breasts
2 tbsp. of full-fat mayonnaise

1 tbsp. of Dijon mustard

INSTRUCTIONS
1. Pulse the almonds in a food processor until they are finely chopped. Spread the almonds on a plate & set aside.
2. Cut each chicken breast in half lengthwise.
3. Mix the mayonnaise & mustard together & then spread evenly on top of the chicken slices.
4. Place the chicken into the plate of chopped almonds to coat completely, laying each coated slice into the basket of your Air Fryer.
5. Cook for 25 minutes at 350°F until golden. Test the temperature, making sure the chicken has reached 165°F. Serve hot.

630. BUFFALO CHICKEN TENDERS
Ingredients: Prep & Cook Time: 20 minutes | Servings: 4

INGREDIENTS

1 egg
1 cup of mozzarella cheese, shredded

¼ cup of buffalo sauce
1 cup of cooked chicken, shredded

¼ cup of feta cheese

INSTRUCTIONS
1. Combine all ingredients (except for the feta). Line the basket of your Air Fryer with a suitably sized piece of parchment paper. Lay the mixture into the Air Fryer & press it into a circle about half an inch thick. Crumble the feta cheese over it.
2. Cook for eight minutes at 400°F. Turn the Air Fryer off & allow the chicken to rest inside before removing with care.
3. Cut the mixture into slices & serve hot.

631. BUFFALO CHICKEN STRIPS
Ingredients: Prep & Cook Time: 30 minutes | Servings: 1

INGREDIENTS

¼ cup of hot sauce
1 lb. of boneless skinless chicken tenders

1 tsp. of garlic powder
½ oz. of flour

1 tsp. of chili powder

INSTRUCTIONS
1. Toss the hot sauce & chicken tenders together in a bowl, ensuring the chicken is completely coated.
2. In another bowl, combine the garlic powder, flour, & chili powder. Use this mixture to coat the tenders, covering them well. Place the chicken into your Air Fryer, taking care not to layer pieces on top of one another.
3. Cook the chicken at 375°F for twenty minutes until cooked all the way through & golden. Serve warm with your favorite dips & sides.

632. CHICKEN & PEPPERONI PIZZA
Ingredients: Prep & Cook Time: 20 minutes | Servings: 6

INGREDIENTS:

2 cups of cooked chicken, cubed
20 slices of pepperoni

1 cup of sugar-free pizza sauce
1 cup of mozzarella cheese, shredded

¼ cup of parmesan cheese, grated

INSTRUCTIONS
1. Place the chicken into the base of a four-cup baking dish & add the pepperoni & pizza sauce on top. Mix well so as to completely coat the meat with the sauce.
2. Add the parmesan & mozzarella on top of the chicken, then place the baking dish into your Air Fryer.
3. Cook for 15 minutes at 375°F.
4. When everything is bubbling & melted, remove from the Air Fryer. Serve hot.

633. ITALIAN CHICKEN THIGHS
Ingredients: Prep & Cook Time: 30 minutes | Servings: 4

INGREDIENTS

4 skin-on bone-in chicken thighs
2 tbsp. of butter, melted

3 tsp. of Italian herbs
½ tsp. of garlic powder

¼ tsp. of onion powder

INSTRUCTIONS
1. Using a brush, coat the chicken thighs with the melted butter. Combine the herbs with the garlic powder & onion powder, then massage into the chicken thighs. Place the thighs in the Air Fryer.

2. Cook at 380°F for 20 minutes, turning the chicken halfway through to cook on the other side.
3. When the thighs have achieved a golden color, test the temperature with a meat thermometer. Once they have reached 165°F, remove from the Air Fryer & serve.

634. TERIYAKI CHICKEN WINGS
Ingredients: Prep & Cook Time: 45 minutes | Servings: 4

INGREDIENTS:
¼ tsp. of ground ginger
2 tsp. of minced garlic

½ cup of sugar-free teriyaki sauce
2 lb. of chicken wings

2 tsp. of baking powder

INSTRUCTIONS
1. In a small bowl, combine together the ginger, garlic, & teriyaki sauce. Place the chicken wings in a separate, larger bowl & pour the mixture over them. Toss to coat until the chicken is well covered.
2. Refrigerate for at least an hour.
3. Remove the marinated wings from the refrigerator & add the baking powder, tossing again to coat. Then place the chicken in the basket of your Air Fryer.
4. Cook for 25 minutes at 400°F, giving the basket a shake intermittently throughout the cooking time.
5. When the wings are 165°F & golden in color, remove from the Air Fryer & serve immediately.

635. CHICKEN PIZZA CRUSTS
Ingredients: Prep & Cook Time: 35 minutes | Servings: 1

INGREDIENTS:
½ cup of mozzarella, shredded

¼ cup of parmesan cheese, grated

1 lb. of ground chicken

INSTRUCTIONS
1. In a large bowl, combine all the ingredients & then spread the mixture out, dividing it into four parts of equal size.
2. Cut a sheet of parchment paper into four circles, roughly six inches in diameter, & put some of the chicken mixture onto the center of each piece, flattening the mixture to fill out the circle.
3. Depending on the size of your Air Fryer, cook either one or two circles at a time at 375°F for 25 minutes. Halfway through, turn the crust over to cook on the other side. Keep each batch warm while you move onto the next one.
4. Once all the crusts are cooked, top with cheese & the toppings of your choice. If desired, cook the topped crusts for an additional five minutes.
5. Serve hot or freeze & save for later!

636. CRISPY CHICKEN THIGHS
Ingredients: Prep & Cook Time: 35 minutes | Servings: 1

INGREDIENTS:
1 lb. of chicken thighs
Salt & pepper

2 cups of roasted pecans
1 cup of water

1 cup of flour

INSTRUCTIONS
1. Pre-heat your Air Fryer to 400°F.
2. Season the chicken with salt & pepper, then set aside.
3. Pulse the roasted pecans in a food processor until a flour-like consistency is achieved.
4. Fill a dish with the water, another with the flour, & a third with the pecans.
5. Coat the thighs with the flour. Mix the remaining flour with the processed pecans.
6. Dredge the thighs in the water & then press into the -pecan mix, ensuring the chicken is completely covered.
7. Cook the chicken in the Air Fryer for twenty-two minutes, with an extra five minutes added if you would like the chicken a darker-brown color. Check the temperature has reached 165°F before serving.

637. STRAWBERRY TURKEY
Ingredients: Prep & Cook Time: 50 minutes | Servings: 2

INGREDIENTS:
2 lb. of turkey breast
1 tbsp. of olive oil

Salt & pepper
1 cup of fresh strawberries

INSTRUCTIONS
1. Pre-heat your Air Fryer to 375°F.
2. Massage the turkey breast with olive oil, before seasoning with a generous amount of salt & pepper.
3. Cook the turkey in the Air Fryer for fifteen minutes. Flip the turkey & cook for a further fifteen minutes.
4. During these last fifteen minutes, blend the strawberries in a food processor until a smooth consistency has been achieved.
5. Heap the strawberries over the turkey, then cook for a final seven minutes & enjoy.

638. CHIMICHURRI TURKEY
Ingredients: Prep & Cook Time: 70 minutes | Servings: 1

INGREDIENTS:
1 lb. of turkey breast
½ cup of chimichurri sauce

½ cup of butter
¼ cup of parmesan cheese, grated

¼ tsp. of garlic powder

INSTRUCTIONS
1. Massage the chimichurri sauce into the turkey breast, then refrigerate in an airtight container for at least a half hour.
2. In the meantime, prepare the herbed butter. Mix together the butter, parmesan, & garlic powder, using a hand mixer if desired (this will make it extra creamy)
3. Preheat your Air Fryer at 350°F & place a rack inside. Remove the turkey from the refrigerator & allow to return to room temperature for roughly twenty minutes while the Air Fryer warms.
4. Place the turkey in the Air Fryer & allow to cook for twenty minutes. Flip & cook on the other side for a further twenty minutes.
5. Take care when removing the turkey from the Air Fryer. Place it on a serving dish & enjoy with the herbed butter.

639. BETTY'S BAKED CHICKEN
Ingredients: Prep & Cook Time: 70 minutes | Servings: 1

INGREDIENTS:
½ cup of butter
1 tsp. of pepper

3 tbsp. of garlic, minced
1 whole chicken

INSTRUCTIONS
1. Pre-heat your Air Fryer at 350°F.
2. Allow the butter to soften at room temperature, then mix well in a small bowl with the pepper & garlic.
3. Massage the butter into the chicken. Any remaining butter can go inside the chicken.
4. Cook the chicken in the Air Fryer for half an hour. Flip, then cook on the other side for another thirty minutes.
5. Test the temperature of the chicken by sticking a meat thermometer into the fat of the thigh to make sure it has reached 165°F. Take care when removing the chicken from the Air Fryer. Let sit for ten minutes before you carve it & serve.

640. CHICKEN BREASTS & SPICED TOMATOES
Ingredients: Prep & Cook Time: 40 minutes | Servings: 1

INGREDIENTS
1 lb. of boneless chicken breast
Salt & pepper

1 cup of butter
1 cup of tomatoes, diced

1 ½ tsp. of paprika
1 tsp. of pumpkin pie spices

INSTRUCTIONS

1. Preheat your Air Fryer at 375°F.
2. Cut the chicken into relatively thick slices & put them in the Air Fryer. Sprinkle with salt & pepper to taste. Cook for fifteen minutes.
3. In the meantime, melt the butter in a saucepan over medium heat, before adding the tomatoes, paprika, & pumpkin pie spices. Leave simmering while the chicken finishes cooking.
4. When the chicken is cooked through, place it on a dish & pour the tomato mixture over. Serve hot.

641. FENNEL CHICKEN

Ingredients: Prep & Cook Time: 40 minutes | Servings: 4

INGREDIENTS

1 ½ cup of coconut milk
2 tbsp. of garam masala

1 ½ lb. of chicken thighs
¾ tbsp. of coconut oil, melted

INSTRUCTIONS

1. Combine the coconut oil & garam masala together in a bowl. Pour the mixture over the chicken thighs & leave to marinate for a half hour.
2. Pre-heat your Air Fryer at 375°F.
3. Cook the chicken into the Air Fryer for fifteen minutes.
4. Add in the coconut milk, giving it a good stir, then cook for an additional ten minutes.
5. Remove the chicken & place on a serving dish. Make sure to pour all of the coconut "gravy" over it & serve immediately.

642. ROASTED CHICKEN

Ingredients: Prep & Cook Time: 90 minutes | Servings: 6

INGREDIENTS

6 lb. of whole chicken
1 tsp. of olive oil

1 tbsp. of minced garlic
1 white onion, peeled & halved

3 tbsp. of butter

INSTRUCTIONS

1. Pre-heat the Air Fryer at 360°F.
2. Massage the chicken with the olive oil & the minced garlic.
3. Place the peeled & halved onion, as well as the butter, inside of the chicken.
4. Cook the chicken in the Air Fryer for seventy-five minutes.
5. Take care when removing the chicken from the Air Fryer, then carve & serve.

643. CHICKEN & HONEY SAUCE

Prep & Cook Time: 20 minutes | Servings: 4

INGREDIENTS

4 chicken sausages
2 tbsp. of honey

¼ cup of mayonnaise
2 tbsp. of Dijon mustard

1 tbsp. of balsamic vinegar
½ tsp. of dried rosemary

INSTRUCTIONS

1. Pre-heat your Air Fryer at 350°F.
2. Place the sausages on the grill pan of your Air Fryer & grill for about 13 minutes, flipping them halfway through the cooking time.
3. In the meantime, make the sauce by whisking together the rest of the ingredients.
4. Pour the sauce over the warm sausages before serving.

644. PENNE CHICKEN SAUSAGE MEATBALLS

Prep & Cook Time: 20 minutes | Servings: 4

INGREDIENTS

1 cup of chicken meat, ground
1 sweet red pepper, minced
¼ cup of green onions, chopped
1 green garlic, minced

4 tbsp. of breadcrumbs
½ tsp. of cumin powder
1 tbsp. of fresh coriander, minced
½ tsp. of sea salt

¼ tsp. of mixed peppercorns, ground
1 packet of penne pasta, cooked

INSTRUCTIONS

1. Pre-heat the Air Fryer at 350°F.
2. Put the chicken, red pepper, green onions, & garlic into a mixing bowl & stir together to combine.
3. Throw in the seasoned breadcrumbs & all of the seasonings. Combine again.
4. Use your hands to mold equal amounts of the mixture into small balls, each one roughly the size of a golf ball.
5. Put them in the Air Fryer & cook for 15 minutes. Shake once or twice throughout the cooking time for even results.
6. Serve with cooked penne pasta.

645. TARRAGON CHICKEN

Prep & Cook Time: 40 minutes | Servings: 4

INGREDIENTS

2 cups of roasted vegetable broth
2 chicken breasts, cut into halves
¾ tsp. of fine sea salt
¼ tsp. of mixed peppercorns, freshly cracked

1 tsp. of cumin powder
1 ½ tsp. of sesame oil
1 ½ tbsp. of Worcester sauce
½ cup of spring onions, chopped

1 Serrano pepper, deveined & chopped
1 bell pepper, deveined & chopped
1 tbsp. of tamari sauce
½ chopped fresh tarragon

INSTRUCTIONS

1. Cook the vegetable broth & chicken breasts in a large saucepan for 10 minutes.
2. Lower the heat & simmer for another 10 minutes.
3. Let the chicken cool briefly. Then tear the chicken into shreds with a stand mixer or two forks.
4. Coat the shredded chicken with the salt, cracked peppercorns, cumin, sesame oil & the Worcester sauce.
5. Transfer to the Air Fryer & air fry at 380°F for 18 minutes, or longer as needed.
6. In the meantime, cook the remaining ingredients over medium heat in a skillet, until the vegetables are tender & fragrant.
7. Take the skillet off the heat. Stir in the shredded chicken, incorporating all the ingredients well.
8. Serve immediately.

646. PIZZA STUFFED CHICKEN

Prep & Cook Time: 20 minutes | Servings: 4

INGREDIENTS

4 small boneless, skinless chicken breasts
¼ cup of pizza sauce
½ cup of Colby cheese, shredded

16 slices of pepperoni
Salt & pepper, to taste
1 ½ tbsp. of olive oil

1 ½ tbsp. of dried oregano

INSTRUCTIONS

1. Pre-heat your Air Fryer at 370°F.
2. Flatten the chicken breasts with a rolling pin.
3. Top the chicken with equal amounts of each ingredients & roll the fillets around the stuffing. Secure with a small skewer or two toothpicks.
4. Roast in the Air Fryer on the grill pan for 13 - 15 minutes.

647. SPECIAL MAPLE-GLAZED CHICKEN

Prep & Cook Time: 20 minutes | Servings: 4

INGREDIENTS

2 ½ tbsp. of maple syrup
1 tbsp. of tamari soy sauce
1 tbsp. of oyster sauce

1 tsp. of fresh lemon juice
1 tsp. of minced fresh ginger
1 tsp. of garlic puree

Seasoned salt & freshly ground pepper,
to taste
2 boneless, skinless chicken breasts

INSTRUCTIONS

1. In a bowl, combine the maple syrup, tamari sauce, oyster sauce, lemon juice, fresh ginger & garlic puree. This is your marinade.
2. Sprinkle the chicken breasts with salt & pepper.
3. Coat the chicken breasts with the marinade. Place some foil over the bowl & refrigerate for 3 hours, or overnight if possible.
4. Remove the chicken from the marinade. Place it in the Air Fryer & fry for 15 minutes at 365°F, flipping each one once or twice throughout.
5. In the meantime, add the remaining marinade to a pan over medium heat. Allow the marinade to simmer for 3 - 5 minutes until it has reduced by half.
6. Pour over the cooked chicken & serve.

648. TURKEY QUINOA SKEWERS

Prep & Cook Time: 15 minutes | Servings: 8

INGREDIENTS

1 cup of red quinoa, cooked
1 ½ cups of water
14 oz. of ground turkey
2 small eggs, beaten

1 tsp. of ground ginger
2 ½ tbsp. of vegetable oil
1 cup of chopped fresh parsley
2 tbsp. of seasoned breadcrumbs

¾ tsp. of salt
1 heaped tsp. of fresh rosemary, finely
chopped
½ tsp. of ground allspice

INSTRUCTIONS

1. In a bowl, combine all of the ingredients together using your hands, kneading the mixture well.
2. Mold equal amounts of the mixture into small balls.
3. Pre-heat your Air Fryer to 380°F.
4. Place the balls in the Air Fryer basket & fry for 8 - 10 minutes.
5. Skewer them & serve with the dipping sauce of your choice.

649. POTATO CAKES & CAJUN CHICKEN WINGS

Prep & Cook Time: 40 minutes | Servings: 4

INGREDIENTS

4 large-sized chicken wings
1 tsp. of Cajun seasoning
1 tsp. of maple syrup
¾ tsp. of sea salt flakes
¼ tsp. of red pepper flakes, crushed
1 tsp. of onion powder
1 tsp. porcini powder

½ tsp. celery seeds
1 small-seized head of cabbage,
shredded
1 cup of mashed potatoes
1 small-sized brown onion, coarsely
grated
1 tsp. of garlic puree

1 medium whole egg, well whisked
½ tsp. of salt
½ tsp. of ground black pepper
1 ½ tbsp. of flour
¾ tsp. of baking powder
1 tbsp. of cilantro
1 tbsp. of sesame oil

INSTRUCTIONS

1. Pre-heat your Air Fryer to 390°F.
2. Pat the chicken wings dry. Place them in the Air Fryer & cook for 25 - 30 minutes, ensuring they are cooked through.
3. Make the rub by combining the Cajun seasoning, maple syrup, sea salt flakes, red pepper, onion powder, porcini powder, & celery seeds.
4. Mix together the shredded cabbage, potato, onion, garlic puree, egg, table salt, black pepper, flour, baking powder & cilantro.
5. Separate the cabbage mixture into 4 portions & use your hands to mold each one into a cabbage-potato cake.
6. Douse each cake with the sesame oil.
7. Bake the cabbage-potato cakes in the Air Fryer for 10 minutes, turning them once through the cooking time. You will need to do this in multiple batches.
8. Serve the cakes & the chicken wings together.

650. PROVENÇAL CHICKEN

Prep & Cook Time: 25 minutes | Servings: 4

INGREDIENTS

4 medium-sized skin-on chicken drumsticks
1 ½ tsp. of herbs de Provence
Salt & pepper

1 tbsp. of rice vinegar
2 tbsp. of olive oil
2 garlic cloves, crushed

12 oz. of crushed canned tomatoes
1 small-size leek, thinly sliced
2 slices smoked bacon, chopped

INSTRUCTIONS

1. Season the chicken drumsticks with herbs de Provence, salt & pepper. Pour over a light drizzling of the rice vinegar & olive oil.
2. Cook in the baking pan at 360°F for 8 - 10 minutes.
3. Pause the Air Fryer. Add in the rest of the ingredients, give them a stir, & resume cooking for 15 more minutes, checking them occasionally to ensure they don't overcook.
4. Serve with rice & lemon wedges.

651. GOURMET CHICKEN OMELET

Prep & Cook Time: 15 minutes | Servings: 2

INGREDIENTS

4 eggs, whisked
4 oz. of ground chicken
½ cup of scallions, finely chopped

2 cloves garlic, finely minced
½ tsp. of salt
½ tsp. of ground black pepper

½ tsp. of paprika
1 tsp. of dried thyme
Dash of hot sauce

INSTRUCTIONS

1. Mix together all the ingredients in a bowl, ensuring to incorporate everything well.
2. Lightly grease two oven-safe ramekins with vegetable oil. Divide the mixture between them.
3. Transfer them to the Air Fryer, & air fry at 350°F for 13 minutes.
4. Ensure they are cooked through & serve immediately.

652. PEPPERY TURKEY SANDWICHES

Prep & Cook Time: 25 minutes | Servings: 4

INGREDIENTS

1 cup of leftover turkey, cut into chunks
2 bell peppers, deveined & chopped
1 Serrano pepper, deveined & chopped
1 leek, sliced

½ cup of sour cream
1 tsp. of hot paprika
¾ tsp. of salt
½ tsp. of ground black pepper

1 tbsp. of fresh cilantro, chopped
Dash of Tabasco sauce
4 hamburger buns

INSTRUCTIONS

1. Combine all of the ingredients except for the hamburger buns, ensuring to coat the turkey well.
2. Place in an Air Fryer baking pan & roast for 20 minutes at 385°F.
3. Top the hamburger buns with the turkey & serve with mustard or sour cream as desired.

653. CHICKEN WINGS & PIRI PIRI SAUCE

Prep & Cook Time: 1 hr. 30 minutes | Servings: 6

INGREDIENTS

12 chicken wings
1 ½ oz. of butter, melted
1 tsp. of onion powder
½ tsp. of cumin powder

1 tsp. of garlic paste
For the Sauce:
2 oz. of Piri peppers, chopped
1 tbsp. of pimiento, deveined & minced

1 garlic clove, chopped
2 tbsp. of fresh lemon juice
⅓ tsp. of sea salt
½ tsp. of tarragon

¾ tsp. of sugar
INSTRUCTIONS
1. Place the chicken wings in a steamer basket over a saucepan of boiling water. Lower the temperature & steam the chicken for 10 minutes over a medium heat.
2. Coat the wings with the butter, onion powder, cumin powder, & garlic paste.
3. Allow the chicken wings to cool slightly. Place them in the refrigerator for 45 - 50 minutes.
4. Pre-heat your Air Fryer at 330°F.
5. Roast the chicken wings in the Air Fryer for 25 - 30 minutes, turning them once halfway through the cooking time.
6. In the meantime, make the Piri sauce. Blend together all of the sauce ingredients in a food processor.
7. Coat the chicken wings in the sauce before serving.

654. MARROD'S MEATBALLS
Prep & Cook Time: 15 minutes | Servings: 6

INGREDIENTS

1 lb. of ground turkey
1 tbsp. of fresh mint leaves, chopped
1 tsp. of onion powder

1 ½ tsp. of garlic paste
1 tsp. of crushed red pepper flakes
¼ cup of melted butter

¾ tsp. of fine sea salt
¼ cup of grated Pecorino Romano

INSTRUCTIONS
1. In a bowl, combine all of the ingredients well. Using an ice cream scoop, mold the meat into balls.
2. Air fry the meatballs at 380°F for about 7 minutes, in batches if necessary. Shake the basket frequently throughout the cooking time for even results.
3. Serve with basil leaves & tomato sauce if desired.

655. TURMERIC & MUSTARD CHICKEN THIGHS
Prep & Cook Time: 20 minutes | Servings: 6

INGREDIENTS

1 large egg, well whisked
2 tbsp. of whole-grain Dijon mustard
¼ cup of mayonnaise
¼ cup of chili sauce

½ tsp. of sugar
1 tsp. of fine sea salt
½ tsp. of ground black pepper, or more to taste
½ tsp. of turmeric powder

10 chicken thighs
2 cups of crushed saltines

INSTRUCTIONS
1. In a large bowl, combine the egg, mustard, mayonnaise, chili sauce, sugar, salt, pepper, & turmeric, incorporating everything well.
2. Coat the chicken thighs with the mixture. Place a layer of aluminum foil over the bowl, transfer it to the refrigerator & allow the chicken to marinate for at least 5 hours or overnight.
3. Pre-heat the Air Fryer to 360°F.
4. Separate the chicken from the marinade.
5. Put the crushed saltines into a shallow dish & use them to coat the chicken.
6. Place the chicken in the Air Fryer & cook for 15 minutes, ensuring the thighs are cooked through.
7. Serve with the rest of the marinade as a sauce.

656. ROASTED TURKEY THIGHS
Prep & Cook Time: 1 hr. 15 minute | Servings: 4

INGREDIENTS

1 red onion, cut into wedges
1 carrot, trimmed & sliced
1 celery stalk, trimmed & sliced
1 cup of Brussels sprouts, halved
1 cup of roasted vegetable broth

1 tbsp. of apple cider vinegar
1 tsp. of maple syrup
2 turkey thighs
½ tsp. of mixed peppercorns
1 tsp. of fine sea salt

1 tsp. of cayenne pepper
1 tsp. of onion powder
½ tsp. of garlic powder
⅓ tsp. of mustard seeds

INSTRUCTIONS
1. Put the vegetables into a baking dish small enough to fit inside your Air Fryer & add in the roasted vegetable broth.
2. In a large bowl, pour in the rest of the ingredients, & set aside for 30 minutes.
3. Place them on the top of the vegetables.
4. Roast at 330°F for 40 - 45 minutes.

657. VEGETABLES & ITALIAN TURKEY SAUSAGE
Prep & Cook Time: 40 minutes | Servings: 4

INGREDIENTS

1 onion, cut into wedges
2 carrots, trimmed & sliced
1 parsnip, trimmed & sliced
2 potatoes, peeled & diced

1 tsp. of dried thyme
½ tsp. of dried marjoram
1 tsp. of dried basil
½ tsp. of celery seeds

Sea salt & ground black pepper to taste
1 tbsp. of melted butter
¾ lb. of sweet Italian turkey sausage

INSTRUCTIONS
1. Cover the vegetables with all of the seasonings & the melted butter.
2. Place the vegetables in the Air Fryer basket.
3. Add the sausage on top.
4. Roast at 360°F for 33 - 37 minutes, ensuring the sausages are no longer pink, giving the basket a good shake halfway through the cooking time. You may need to cook everything in batches.

658. RICOTTA WRAPS & SPRING CHICKEN
Prep & Cook Time: 20 minutes | Servings: 12

INGREDIENTS

2 large-sized chicken breasts, cooked & shredded
⅓ tsp. of sea salt
¼ tsp. of ground black pepper, or more to taste
2 spring onions, chopped

¼ cup of soy sauce
1 tbsp. of molasses
1 tbsp. of rice vinegar
10 oz. of Ricotta cheese

1 tsp. of grated fresh ginger
50 wonton wrappers

INSTRUCTIONS
1. In a bowl, combine all of the ingredients, minus the wonton wrappers.
2. Unroll the wrappers & spritz with cooking spray.
3. Fill each of the wonton wrappers with equal amounts of the mixture.
4. Dampen the edges with a little water as an adhesive & roll up the wrappers, fully enclosing the filling.
5. Cook the rolls in the Air Fryer for 5 minutes at 375°F. You will need to do this step in batches.
6. Serve with your preferred sauce.

659. CAJUN-MUSTARD TURKEY FINGERS
Prep & Cook Time: 20 minutes | Servings: 4

INGREDIENTS

½ cup of cornmeal mix
½ cup of flour
1 ½ tbsp. of Cajun seasoning
1 ½ tbsp. of whole-grain mustard

1 ½ cups of buttermilk
1 tsp. of soy sauce
¾ lb. of turkey tenderloins, cut into finger-sized strips

Salt & ground black pepper to taste

INSTRUCTIONS
1. In a bowl, combine the cornmeal, flour, & Cajun seasoning.
2. In a separate bowl, combine the whole-grain mustard, buttermilk & soy sauce.
3. Sprinkle some salt & pepper on the turkey fingers.
4. Dredge each finger in the buttermilk mixture, before coating them completely with the cornmeal mixture.
5. Place the prepared turkey fingers in the Air Fryer baking pan & cook for 15 minutes at 360°F.
6. Serve immediately, with ketchup if desired.

660. HONEY GLAZED TURKEY BREAST
Prep & Cook Time: 55 minutes | Servings: 6

INGREDIENTS

2 tsp. of butter, softened
1 tsp. of dried sage
2 sprigs rosemary, chopped
1 tsp. of salt

¼ tsp. of freshly ground black pepper, or more if desired
1 whole turkey breast
2 tbsp. of turkey broth

¼ cup of honey
2 tbsp. of whole-grain mustard
1 tbsp. of butter

INSTRUCTIONS
1. Pre-heat your Air Fryer to 360°F.
2. Mix together the 2 tbsp. of butter, sage, rosemary, salt, & pepper.
3. Rub the turkey breast with this mixture.
4. Place the turkey in your Air Fryer's cooking basket & roast for 20 minutes. Turn the turkey breast over & allow to cook for another 15 - 16 minutes.
5. Finally turn it once more & roast for another 12 minutes.
6. In the meantime, mix together the remaining ingredients in a saucepan using a whisk.
7. Coat the turkey breast with the glaze.
8. Place the turkey back in the Air Fryer & cook for an additional 5 minutes. Remove it from the Air Fryer, let it rest, & carve before serving.

661. CHICKEN CURRY
Prep & Cook Time: 60 minutes | Servings: 2

INGREDIENTS

2 chicken thighs
1 small zucchini
2 cloves garlic
6 dried apricots
1 tsp. of curry powder

3 ½ oz. of long turnip
6 basil leaves
1 tbsp. of whole pistachios
1 tbsp. of raisin soup

1 tbsp. of olive oil
Salt
Pepper

INSTRUCTIONS
1. Pre-heat Air Fryer at 320°F.
2. Cut the chicken into 2 thin slices & chop up the vegetables into bite-sized pieces.
3. In a dish, combine all of the ingredients, incorporating everything well.
4. Place in the Air Fryer & cook for a minimum of 30 minutes.
5. Serve with rice if desired.

662. MARJORAM CHICKEN
Prep & Cook Time: 1 hr. | Servings: 2

INGREDIENTS

2 skinless, small chicken breasts
2 tbsp. of butter

1 tsp. of sea salt
½ tsp. of red pepper flakes, crushed

2 tsp. of marjoram
¼ tsp. of lemon pepper

INSTRUCTIONS
1. In a bowl, coat the chicken breasts with all of the other ingredients. Set aside to marinate for 30 – 60 minutes.
2. Pre-heat your Air Fryer to 390°F.
3. Cook for 20 minutes, turning halfway through cooking time.
4. Check for doneness using an instant-read thermometer. Serve over jasmine rice.

663. HOISIN GLAZED TURKEY DRUMSTICKS
Prep & Cook Time: 40 minutes + marinating time | Servings: 4

INGREDIENTS

2 turkey drumsticks
2 tbsp. of balsamic vinegar
2 tbsp. of dry white wine
1 tbsp. of extra-virgin olive oil
1 sprig of rosemary, chopped

Salt & ground black pepper, to taste
2 ½ tbsp. of butter, melted

For the Hoisin Glaze:

2 tbsp. of hoisin sauce
1 tbsp. of honey
1 tbsp. of honey mustard

INSTRUCTIONS
1. In a bowl, coat the turkey drumsticks with the vinegar, wine, olive oil, & rosemary. Allow to marinate for 3 hours.
2. Pre-heat the Air Fryer to 350°F.
3. Sprinkle the turkey drumsticks with salt & black pepper. Cover the surface of each drumstick with the butter.
4. Place the turkey in the Air Fryer & cook at 350°F for 30 - 35 minutes, flipping it occasionally through the cooking time. You may have to do this in batches.
5. In the meantime, make the Hoisin glaze by combining all the glaze ingredients.
6. Pour the glaze over the turkey, & roast for another 5 minutes.
7. Allow the drumsticks to rest for about 10 minutes before carving.

664. TURKEY SLIDERS & CHIVE MAYONNAISE
Prep & Cook Time: 20 minutes | Servings: 6

INGREDIENTS

For the Turkey Sliders:
¾ lb. of turkey mince
¼ cup of pickled jalapeno, chopped
1 tbsp. of oyster sauce
1 – 2 cloves garlic, minced

1 tbsp. of chopped fresh cilantro
2 tbsp. of chopped scallions
Sea salt & ground black pepper to taste

For the Chive Mayo:
1 cup of mayonnaise
1 tbsp. of chives
1 tsp. of salt
Zest of 1 lime

INSTRUCTIONS:
1. In a bowl, combine together all of the ingredients for the turkey sliders. Use your hands to shape 6 equal amounts of the mixture into slider patties.
2. Transfer the patties to the Air Fryer & fry them at 365°F for 15 minutes.
3. In the meantime, prepare the Chive Mayo by combining the rest of the ingredients.
4. Make sandwiches by placing each patty between two burger buns & serve with the mayo.

665. THAI TURKEY WINGS
Prep & Cook Time: 40 minutes | Servings: 4

INGREDIENTS

¾ lb. of turkey wings, cut into pieces
1 tsp. of ginger powder
1 tsp. of garlic powder
¾ tsp. of paprika

2 tbsp. of soy sauce
1 handful of minced lemongrass
Sea salt flakes & ground black pepper to taste
2 tbsp. of rice wine vinegar

¼ cup of peanut butter
1 tbsp. of sesame oil
½ cup of Thai sweet chili sauce

INSTRUCTIONS
1. Boil the turkey wings in a saucepan full of water for 20 minutes.
2. Put the turkey wings in a large bowl & cover them with the remaining ingredients, minus the Thai sweet chili sauce.
3. Transfer to the Air Fryer & fry for 20 minutes at 350°F, turning once halfway through the cooking time. Ensure they are cooked through before serving with the Thai sweet chili sauce, as well as some lemon wedges if desired.

666. STUFFED TURKEY ROULADE
Prep & Cook Time: 50 minutes | Servings: 4

INGREDIENTS
1 turkey fillet
Salt & garlic pepper to taste
⅓ tsp. of onion powder
½ tsp. of dried basil

⅓ tsp. of ground red chipotle pepper
1 ½ tbsp. of mustard seeds
½ tsp. of fennel seeds
2 tbsp. of melted butter

3 tbsp. of coriander, finely chopped
½ cup of scallions, finely chopped
2 cloves of garlic, finely minced

INSTRUCTIONS
1. Flatten out the turkey fillets with a mallet, until they are about a half-inch thick.
2. Season each one with salt, garlic pepper, & onion powder.
3. In a small bowl, mix together the basil, chipotle pepper, mustard seeds, fennel seeds & butter.
4. Use a pallet knife to spread the mixture over the fillets, leaving the edges uncovered.
5. Add the coriander, scallions & garlic on top.
6. Roll up the fillets into a log & wrap a piece of twine around them to hold them in place.
7. Place them in the Air Fryer cooking basket.
8. Roast at 350°F for about 50 minutes, flipping it at the halfway point. Cook for longer if necessary. Serve warm.

667. MAC'S CHICKEN NUGGETS
Prep & Cook Time: 40 minutes | Servings: 4

INGREDIENTS
2 slices of breadcrumbs
9 oz. of chicken breast, chopped
1 tsp. of garlic, minced

1 tsp. of tomato ketchup
2 medium egg
1 tbsp. of olive oil

1 tsp. of paprika
1 tsp. of parsley
Salt & pepper

INSTRUCTIONS
1. Combine the breadcrumbs, paprika, salt, pepper & oil into a thick batter.
2. Coat the chopped chicken with the parsley, one egg & ketchup.
3. Shape the mixture into several nuggets & dredge each one in the other egg. Roll the nuggets into the breadcrumbs.
4. Cook at 390°F for 10 minutes in the Air Fryer.
5. Serve the nuggets with a side of mayo dip if desired.

668. COLBY'S TURKEY MEATLOAF
Prep & Cook Time: 50 minutes | Servings: 6

INGREDIENTS
1 lb. of turkey mince
½ cup scallions, finely chopped
2 garlic cloves, finely minced
1 tsp. of dried thyme
½ tsp. of dried basil

¾ cup of Colby cheese, shredded
¾ cup of crushed saltines
1 tbsp. of tamari sauce
Salt & black pepper, to taste
¼ cup of red pepper sauce

1 tsp. of sugar
¾ tbsp. of olive oil
1 medium egg, well beaten

INSTRUCTIONS
1. Over a medium heat, fry up the turkey mince, scallions, garlic, thyme, & basil until soft & fragrant.
2. Pre-heat the Air Fryer to 360°F.
3. Combine the mixture with the cheese, saltines & tamari sauce, before shaping it into a loaf.
4. Stir together the remaining items & top the meatloaf with them.
5. Place in the Air Fryer baking pan & allow to cook for 45 - 47 minutes.

669. CHICKEN DRUMSTICKS
Prep & Cook Time: 35 minutes | Servings: 4

INGREDIENTS
8 chicken drumsticks
1 tsp. of cayenne pepper
2 tbsp. of mustard powder
2 tbsp. of oregano

2 tbsp. of thyme
3 tbsp. of coconut milk
1 large egg, lightly beaten
⅓ cup of cauliflower

⅓ cup of oats
Salt & pepper

INSTRUCTIONS
1. Pre-heat the Air Fryer to 350°F.
2. Sprinkle salt & pepper over the chicken drumsticks & massage the coconut milk into them.
3. Put all the ingredients except the egg into the food processor & pulse to create a bread crumb-like mixture.
4. Transfer to a bowl.
5. In a separate bowl, put the beaten egg. Coat each chicken drumstick in the bread crumb mixture before dredging it in the egg. Roll it in the breadcrumbs once more.
6. Put the coated chicken drumsticks in Air Fryer basket & cook for 20 minutes. Serve hot.

670. BACON-WRAPPED CHICKEN
Prep & Cook Time: 20 minutes | Servings: 6

INGREDIENTS
1 chicken breast, cut into 6 pieces

6 rashers of back bacon

1 tbsp. of soft cheese

INSTRUCTIONS
1. Put the bacon rashers on a flat surface & cover one side with the soft cheese.
2. Lay the chicken pieces on each bacon rasher. Wrap the bacon around the chicken & use a toothpick stick to hold each one in place. Put them in Air Fryer basket.
3. Air fry at 350°F for 15 minutes. Serve!

671. FAMILY FARM'S CHICKEN WINGS
Prep & Cook Time: 20 minutes | Servings: 6

INGREDIENTS
6 chicken wings
1 tbsp. of honey

2 cloves garlic, chopped
1 tsp. of red chili flakes

2 tbsp. of Worcestershire sauce
Salt & pepper

INSTRUCTIONS
1. Place all the ingredients, except for the chicken wings, in a bowl & combine well.
2. Coat the chicken with the mixture & refrigerate for 1 hour.
3. Put the marinated chicken wings in the Air Fryer basket & spritz with cooking spray.
4. Air fry the chicken wings at 320°F for 8 minutes. Raise the temperature to 350°F & cook for an additional 4 minutes. Serve hot.

672. CHICKEN SURPRISE
Prep & Cook Time: 30 minutes | Servings: 2

INGREDIENTS

2 chicken breasts, boneless & skinless
2 large eggs
½ cup of skimmed milk
6 tbsp. of soy sauce

1 cup of flour
1 tsp. of smoked paprika
1 tsp. of salt
¼ tsp. of black pepper

½ tsp. of garlic powder
1 tbsp. of olive oil
4 hamburger buns

INSTRUCTIONS

1. Slice the chicken breast into 2 – 3 pieces.
2. Place in a large bowl & drizzle with the soy sauce. Sprinkle on the smoked paprika, black pepper, salt, & garlic powder & mix well.
3. Allow to marinate for 30 – 40 minutes.
4. In the meantime, combine the eggs with the milk in a bowl. Put the flour in a separate bowl.
5. Dip the marinated chicken into the egg mixture before coating it with the flour. Cover each piece of chicken evenly.
6. Pre-heat the Air Fryer to 380°F.
7. Drizzle on the olive oil & put chicken pieces in the Air Fryer.
8. Cook for 10 – 12 minutes. Flip the chicken once throughout the cooking process.
9. Toast the hamburger buns & put each slice of chicken between two buns to make a sandwich. Serve with ketchup or any other sauce of your choice.

673. LEMON & GARLIC CHICKEN
Prep & Cook Time: 25 minutes | Servings: 1

INGREDIENTS

1 chicken breast
1 tsp. of garlic, minced

1 tbsp. of chicken seasoning
1 lemon juice

Handful of black peppercorns
Salt & pepper

INSTRUCTIONS

1. Pre-heat the Air Fryer to 350°F.
2. Sprinkle the chicken with pepper & salt. Massage the chicken seasoning into the chicken breast, coating it well, & lay the seasoned chicken on a sheet of aluminum foil.
3. Top the chicken with the garlic, lemon juice, & black peppercorns. Wrap the foil to seal the chicken tightly.
4. Cook the chicken in the Air Fryer basket for 15 minutes.

674. CAJUN SEASONED CHICKEN
Prep & Cook Time: 15 minutes | Servings: 2

INGREDIENTS

2 boneless chicken breasts
3 tbsp. of Cajun spice

INSTRUCTIONS

1. Coat both sides of the chicken breasts with Cajun spice. Put the seasoned chicken in Air Fryer basket.
2. Air fry at 350°F for 10 minutes, ensuring they are cooked through before slicing up & serving.

675. CHICKEN FILLETS
Prep & Cook Time: 30 minutes | Servings: 3

INGREDIENTS

8 pieces of chicken fillets
1 egg
1 oz. of salted butter, melted

1 cup of breadcrumbs
1 tsp. of garlic powder
½ cup of parmesan cheese

1 tsp. of Italian herbs

INSTRUCTIONS

1. Cover the chicken pieces in the whisked egg, melted butter, garlic powder, & Italian herbs. Allow to marinate for about 10 minutes.
2. In a bowl, mix together the Panko breadcrumbs & parmesan. Use this mixture to coat the marinated chicken.
3. Put the aluminum foil in your Air Fryer basket.
4. Set the Air Fryer to 390°F & briefly allow to warm. Line the basket with aluminum foil.
5. Place 4 pieces of the chicken in the basket. Cook for 6 minutes until golden brown. Don't turn the chicken over.
6. Repeat with the rest of the chicken pieces.
7. Serve the chicken fillets hot.

676. CHICKEN NUGGETS
Prep & Cook Time: 30 minutes | Servings: 4

INGREDIENTS

½ lb. of chicken breast, cut into pieces
1 tsp. of parsley
1 tsp. of paprika

1 tbsp. of olive oil
2 eggs, beaten
1 tsp. of tomato ketchup

1 tsp. of garlic, minced
½ cup of breadcrumbs
Salt & pepper

INSTRUCTIONS

1. In a bowl, combine the breadcrumbs, olive oil, paprika, pepper, & salt.
2. Place the chicken, ketchup, one egg, garlic, & parsley in a food processor & pulse together.
3. Put the other egg in a bowl.
4. Shape equal amounts of the pureed chicken into nuggets. Dredge each one in the egg before coating it in breadcrumbs.
5. Put the coated chicken nuggets in the Air Fryer basket & cook at 390°F for 10 minutes.
6. Serve the nuggets hot.

677. CRACKED CHICKEN TENDERS
Prep & Cook Time: 30 minutes | Servings: 4

INGREDIENTS

2 lb. of skinless chicken tenders
3 large eggs
6 tbsp. of skimmed milk

½ cup of flour
1 cup of breadcrumbs
¼ tsp. of black pepper

1 tsp. of salt
2 tbsp. of olive oil

INSTRUCTIONS

1. In a large bowl, combine the breadcrumbs & olive oil.
2. In a separate bowl, stir together the eggs & milk using a whisk. Sprinkle in the salt & black pepper.
3. Put the flour in a third bowl.
4. Slice up the chicken tenders into 1-inch strips. Coat each piece of chicken in the flour, before dipping it into the egg mixture, followed by the breadcrumbs.
5. Pre-heat the Air Fryer to 380°F.
6. Cook the coated chicken tenders for about 13 – 15 minutes, shaking the basket a few times to ensure they turn crispy. Serve hot, with mashed potatoes & a dipping sauce if desired.

678. RANDY'S ROASTED CHICKEN
Prep & Cook Time: 55 minutes | Servings: 4

INGREDIENTS

5 – 7 lb. of whole chicken with skin
1 tsp. of garlic powder
1 tsp. of onion powder

½ tsp. of dried thyme
½ tsp. of dried basil
½ tsp. of dried rosemary

½ tsp. of black pepper
2 tsp. of salt
2 tbsp. of extra virgin olive oil

INSTRUCTIONS

1. Massage the salt, pepper, herbs, & olive oil into the chicken. Allow to marinade for a minimum of 20 – 30 minutes.
2. In the meantime, pre-heat the Air Fryer to 340 F.

3. Place the chicken in the Air Fryer & cook for 18 – 20 minutes.
4. Flip the chicken over & cook for an additional 20 minutes.
5. Leave the chicken to rest for about 10 minutes before carving & serving.

679. HERBED CHICKEN

Prep & Cook Time: 40 minutes | Servings: 6

INGREDIENTS

4 lb. of chicken wings
6 tbsp. of red wine vinegar
6 tbsp. lime juice
1 tsp. of fresh ginger, minced
1 tbsp. of sugar

1 tsp. of thyme, chopped
½ tsp. of white pepper
¼ tsp. of ground cinnamon
1 habanero pepper, chopped
6 garlic cloves, chopped

2 tbsp. of soy sauce
2 ½ tbsp. of olive oil
¼ tsp. of salt

INSTRUCTIONS

1. Place all of the ingredients in a bowl & combine well, ensuring to coat the chicken entirely.
2. Put the chicken in the refrigerator to marinate for 1 hour.
3. Pre-heat the Air Fryer to 390°F.
4. Put half of the marinated chicken in the Air Fryer basket & cook for 15 minutes, shaking the basket once throughout the cooking process.
5. Repeat with the other half of the chicken.
6. Serve hot.

680. ROSEMARY CHICKEN

Prep & Cook Time: 30 minutes | Servings: 2

INGREDIENTS

¾ lb. of chicken
½ tbsp. of olive oil
1 tbsp. of soy sauce

1 tsp. of fresh ginger, minced
1 tbsp. of oyster sauce
3 tbsp. of sugar

1 tbsp. of fresh rosemary, chopped
½ fresh lemon, cut into wedges

INSTRUCTIONS

1. In a bowl, combine the chicken, oil, soy sauce, & ginger, coating the chicken well.
2. Refrigerate for 30 minutes.
3. Pre-heat the Air Fryer to 390°F for 3 minutes.
4. Place the chicken in the baking pan, transfer to the Air Fryer & cook for 6 minutes.
5. In the meantime, put the rosemary, sugar, & oyster sauce in a bowl & mix together.
6. Add the rosemary mixture in the Air Fryer over the chicken & top the chicken with the lemon wedges.
7. Resume cooking for another 13 minutes, turning the chicken halfway through.

681. CHICKEN STRIPS

Prep & Cook Time: 25 minutes | Servings: 2

INGREDIENTS

1 chicken breast, cut into strips
1 egg, beaten
¼ cup of flour

¾ cup of breadcrumbs
1 tsp. of mix spice
1 tbsp. of plain oats

1 tbsp. of desiccated coconut
Salt & pepper

INSTRUCTIONS

1. In a bowl, mix together the breadcrumbs, mix spice, oats, coconut, pepper, & salt.
2. Put the beaten egg in a separate bowl. Pour the flour into a shallow dish.
3. Roll the chicken strips in the flour. Dredge each one in the egg & coat with the bread crumb mixture. Put the coated chicken strips in the Air Fryer basket & air fry at 350°F for 8 minutes.
4. Reduce the heat to 320°F & cook for another 4 minutes. Serve hot.

682. GRANDMA'S CHICKEN

Prep & Cook Time: 20 minutes | Servings: 4

INGREDIENTS

12 oz. of chicken breast, diced
6 oz. of general Tso sauce

½ tsp. of white pepper
¼ cup of milk

1 cup of cornstarch

INSTRUCTIONS

1. Place the chicken & milk in a bowl.
2. Separate the milk from the chicken & coat the chicken with cornstarch.
3. Put the chicken in the Air Fryer basket & air fry at 350°F for 12 minutes.
4. Plate up the chicken & season with the white pepper.
5. Pour the Tso sauce over the chicken before serving.

683. WORCESTERSHIRE CHICKEN WINGS

Prep & Cook Time: 40 minutes | Servings: 6

INGREDIENTS

6 chicken wings
1 ½ tbsp. of Worcestershire sauce
1 tbsp. of sugar
Juice & zest of 1 orange

½ tsp. of thyme, dried
½ tsp. of sage
1 tsp. of mint
1 tsp. of basil

½ tsp. of oregano
1 tsp. of parsley
1 tsp. of rosemary
Salt & pepper

INSTRUCTIONS

1. Combine all of the ingredients in a bowl, coating the chicken wings well with the other ingredients.
2. Refrigerate the marinated chicken for 30 minutes.
3. Pre-heat the Air Fryer to 350°F.
4. Wrap the marinated chicken in a sheet of aluminum foil, ensuring to seal with the juices. Put the wrapped chicken in Air Fryer basket & cook at 350°F for 20 minutes.
5. Unfold the foil, remove the orange zest & air fry the chicken wings at 350°F for a further 15 minutes. Serve hot.

684. LIME & HONEY CHICKEN WINGS

Prep & Cook Time: 7 hours | Servings: 2

INGREDIENTS

16 winglets
½ tsp. of sea salt
2 tbsp. of light soya sauce

¼ tsp. of white pepper powder
½ crush of black pepper
2 tbsp. of honey

2 tbsp. of lime juice

INSTRUCTIONS

1. Place all of the ingredients in a glass dish. Coat the winglets well & allow to marinate in the refrigerator for a minimum of 6 hours.
2. Allow to return to room temperature for 30 minutes.
3. Put the wings in the Air Fryer & air fry at 355°F for 6 minutes. Turn each wing over before cooking for another 6 minutes.
4. Allow the chicken to cool before serving with a wedge of lemon.

685. CHICKEN KEBABS

Prep & Cook Time: 30 minutes | Servings: 3

INGREDIENTS

1 lb. of chicken breasts, diced
5 tbsp. of honey
½ cup of soy sauce
6 large mushrooms, cut in halves

3 medium bell peppers, cut
1 small zucchini, cut into rings
2 medium tomatoes, cut into rings
Salt & pepper

¼ cup of sesame seeds
1 tbsp. of olive oil

INSTRUCTIONS
1. Cube the chicken breasts & place them in a large bowl.
2. Season with some salt & pepper. Drizzle over one tbsp. of olive oil & mix well.
3. Pour in the honey & soy sauce & add in the sesame seeds.
4. Leave to marinate for 15 – 30 minutes.
5. Slice up the vegetables.
6. Thread the chicken & vegetables on wooden skewers, in alternating patterns.
7. Pre-heat the Air Fryer to 340°F
8. Put the chicken kebabs into the Air Fryer basket.
9. Cook for about 15 minutes, flipping once during cooking. Serve once crispy & brown.

686. CHICKEN TENDERLOINS
Prep & Cook Time: 25 minutes | Servings: 4

INGREDIENTS

8 chicken tenderloins
1 egg, beaten

2 tbsp. of olive oil
1 cup of breadcrumbs

Salt & pepper

INSTRUCTIONS
1. Pre-heat the Air Fryer to 350°F.
2. Combine the breadcrumbs, olive oil, pepper, & salt in a shallow dish.
3. Put the beaten egg in separate dish.
4. Dip the chicken tenderloins into the egg before rolling them in the breadcrumbs.
5. Transfer to the Air Fryer basket. Air fry the chicken for 12 minutes.

687. BUFFALO WINGS
Prep & Cook Time: 35 min. + [2 - 12 hours marinate] | Servings: 4

INGREDIENTS

2 lb. of chicken wings, no wing tips
¼ cup + ¼ cup hot sauce, separately

3 + 3 tbsp. of melted butter, separately
Sea salt to taste

Blue cheese, optional
Celery sticks, optional

INSTRUCTIONS
1. Prepare the chicken wings by separating the drumettes from the wingettes & put them into a bowl.
2. In a separate bowl, thoroughly combine 3 tbsp. of melted butter & ¼ cup of hot sauce.
3. Use this mixture to coat the chicken & marinate for 2 hours or overnight if possible.
4. Briefly pre-heat the Air Fryer to 400°F.
5. Divide the chicken into 2 batches. Put the first batch in the Air Fryer & cook for about 12 minutes. Give the basket a good shake at the halfway point. Repeat with the second batch.
6. Combine the cooked batches & return them to the Air Fryer, cooking for an additional 2 minutes.
7. In the meantime, make the sauce by stirring together the remaining 3 tbsp. of butter & ¼ cup of hot sauce.
8. Coat the cooked wings in the sauce before serving with a side of celery sticks & blue cheese if desired.

688. MOROCCAN CHICKEN
Prep & Cook Time: 25 minutes | Servings: 2

INGREDIENTS

½ lb. of shredded chicken
1 cup broth
1 carrot

1 broccoli, chopped
Pinch of cinnamon
Pinch of cumin

Pinch of red pepper
Pinch of sea salt

INSTRUCTIONS
1. In a bowl, cover the shredded chicken with cumin, red pepper, sea salt & cinnamon.
2. Chop up the carrots into small pieces. Put the carrot & broccoli into the bowl with the chicken.
3. Add the broth & stir everything well. Set aside for about 30 minutes.
4. Transfer to the Air Fryer. Cook for about 15 minutes at 390°F. Serve hot.

689. CHINESE CHICKEN WINGS
Prep & Cook Time: 45 minutes | Servings: 4

INGREDIENTS

8 chicken wings
2 tbsp. of five spice

2 tbsp. of soy sauce
1 tbsp. of mixed spices

Salt & pepper

INSTRUCTIONS
1. In a bowl, mix together all of the ingredients.
2. Cover the base of the Air Fryer with an aluminum foil & pre-heat the Air Fryer to 360°F.
3. Add in some oil & pour in the mixture. Cook for 15 minutes.
4. Turn up the heat to 390°F, turn the chicken wings & cook for another 5 minutes. Serve with mayo dip if desired.

690. CHICKEN & POTATOES
Prep & Cook Time: 45 minutes | Servings: 6

INGREDIENTS

1 lb. of potatoes
2 lb. of chicken

2 tbsp. of olive oil
Salt & pepper

INSTRUCTIONS
1. Pre-heat the Air Fryer to 350°F.
2. Place the chicken in Air Fryer basket along with the potatoes. Sprinkle on the pepper & salt.
3. Add a drizzling of the olive oil, making sure to cover the chicken & potatoes well.
4. Cook for 40 minutes.

691. CHICKEN TENDERS
Prep & Cook Time: 30 minutes | Servings: 4

INGREDIENTS

1 lb. of chicken tenders
1 tsp. ginger, minced
4 garlic cloves, minced

2 tbsp. of sesame oil
6 tbsp. of pineapple juice
2 tbsp. of soy sauce

½ tsp. of pepper

INSTRUCTIONS
1. Put all of the ingredients, except for the chicken, in a bowl & combine well.
2. Thread the chicken onto skewers & coat with the seasonings. Allow to marinate for 2 hours.
3. Pre-heat the Air Fryer to 350°F.
4. Put the marinated chicken in Air Fryer basket & cook for 18 minutes. Serve hot.

692. LIME DIJON CHICKEN

Prep & Cook Time: 20 minutes | Servings: 6

INGREDIENTS

8 chicken drumsticks
1 lime juice
1 lime zest

Kosher salt to taste
1 tbsp. of light mayonnaise
¾ tsp. of black pepper

1 clove garlic, crushed
3 tbsp. of Dijon mustard
1 tsp. of dried parsley

INSTRUCTIONS

1. Pre-heat the Air Fryer to 375°F.
2. Remove the chicken skin & sprinkle the chicken with the salt.
3. In a bowl, mix the Dijon mustard with the lime juice, before stirring in the lime zest, pepper, parsley & garlic.
4. Cover the chicken with the lime mixture. Allow it to marinate for roughly 10 - 15 minutes.
5. Drizzle some oil in the bottom of your Air Fryer. Transfer the chicken drumsticks inside & cook for 5 minutes.
6. Give the basket a shake & fry for an additional 5 minutes.
7. Serve immediately, with a side of mayo.

693. FRIED CHICKEN THIGHS

Prep & Cook Time: 35 minutes | Servings: 4

INGREDIENTS

4 chicken thighs
1 ½ tbsp. Cajun seasoning

1 egg, beaten
½ cup of flour

1 tsp. of seasoning salt

INSTRUCTIONS

1. Pre-heat the Air Fryer to 350°F.
2. In a bowl combine the flour, Cajun seasoning, & seasoning salt.
3. Place the beaten egg in another bowl.
4. Coat the chicken with the flour before dredging it in the egg. Roll once more in the flour.
5. Put the chicken in the Air Fryer & cook for 25 minutes. Serve hot.

694. FRIED WINGS

Prep & Cook Time: 35 minutes | Servings: 6

INGREDIENTS

4 Lb. of chicken wings
1 tbsp. of sugar
1 tbsp. of Worcestershire sauce
½ cup of butter, melted

½ cup of hot sauce
½ tsp. of salt

INSTRUCTIONS

1. In a bowl, combine the sugar, Worcestershire sauce, butter, salt, & hot sauce.
2. Place the chicken wings in the Air Fryer basket & air fry at 380°F for 25 minutes, giving the basket a good shake halfway through the cooking time.
3. Raise the temperature to 400°F & continue to cook for another 5 minutes.
4. Place the air fried chicken wings in the bowl with the sugar mixture & toss to coat. Serve right away.

695. TERIYAKI CHICKEN

Prep & Cook Time: 30 minutes | Servings: 2

INGREDIENTS

2 boneless chicken drumsticks
1 tsp. of ginger, grated

1 tbsp. of cooking wine
3 tbsp. of teriyaki sauce

INSTRUCTIONS

1. Combine all of the ingredients in a bowl. Refrigerate for half an hour.
2. Place the chicken in the Air Fryer baking pan & fry at 350°F for 8 minutes. Turn the chicken over & raise the temperature to 380°F. Allow to cook for another 6 minutes. Serve hot.

696. ASIAN STYLE CHICKEN

Prep & Cook Time: 25 minutes | Servings: 3

INGREDIENTS

1 lb. of skinless & chicken breasts
3 garlic cloves, minced
1 tbsp. of grated ginger

¼ tsp. of ground black pepper
½ cup of soy sauce
½ cup of pineapple juice

1 tbsp. of olive oil
2 tbsp. of sesame seeds

INSTRUCTIONS

1. Mix together all of the ingredients except for the chicken in a large bowl.
2. Slice up the chicken breasts & coat in the mixture. Allow to marinade for at least 30 – 40 minutes.
3. Transfer the marinated chicken to the Air Fryer & cook at 380°F for about 10 – 15 minutes.
4. Top with sesame seeds before serving.

697. WHOLE CHICKEN

Prep & Cook Time: 30 minutes | Servings: 2

INGREDIENTS

1 whole chicken
1 lemon, juiced

1 tsp. of lemon zest
1 tbsp. of soy sauce

1 ½ tbsp. of honey

INSTRUCTIONS

1. Place all of the ingredients in a bowl & combine well. Refrigerate for 1 hour.
2. Put the marinated chicken in the Air Fryer baking pan. Air fry at 320°F for 18 minutes.
3. Raise the heat to 350°F & cook for another 10 minutes or until chicken has turned light brown.

698. HONEY & GARLIC CHICKEN WINGS

Prep & Cook Time: 25 minutes | Servings: 4

INGREDIENTS

16 chicken wings
½ tsp. of salt

¾ cup of potato starch
¼ cup of butter, melted

4 cloves garlic, minced
¼ cup of honey

INSTRUCTIONS

1. Pre-heat your Air Fryer to 370°F.
2. Put the chicken wings in a bowl & cover them well with the potato starch.
3. Spritz a baking dish with cooking spray.
4. Transfer the wings to the dish, place inside the Air Fryer & cook for 5 minutes.
5. In the meantime, mix together the rest of the ingredients with a whisk.
6. Top the chicken with this mixture & allow to cook for another 10 minutes before serving.

699. BUFFALO CHICKEN WINGS

Prep & Cook Time: 37 minutes | Servings: 3

INGREDIENTS

2 lb. of chicken wings
1 tsp. of salt

¼ tsp. of black pepper
1 cup buffalo sauce

INSTRUCTIONS

1. Wash the chicken wings & pat them dry with clean kitchen towels.
2. Place the chicken wings in a large bowl & sprinkle on salt & pepper.
3. Pre-heat the Air Fryer to 380°F.
4. Place the wings in the Air Fryer & cook for 15 minutes, giving them an occasional stir throughout.
5. Place the wings in a bowl. Pour over the buffalo sauce & toss well to coat.
6. Put the chicken back in the Air Fryer & cook for a final 5 – 6 minutes.

700. CHICKEN MEATBALLS

Prep & Cook Time: 20 minutes | Servings: 10

INGREDIENTS

2 chicken breasts
1 tbsp. of mustard powder
1 tbsp. of cumin
1 tbsp. of basil

1 tbsp. of thyme
1 tsp. of chili powder
3 tbsp. of soy sauce
2 tbsp. of honey

1 onion, diced
Salt & pepper

INSTRUCTIONS

1. Blend the chicken in your food processor to make a mince. Place the rest of the ingredients in the processor & pulse to combine well.
2. Shape the mixture into several small meatballs & place each one in the basket of the Air Fryer.
3. Air fry at 350°F for 15 minutes. Serve hot.

701. CHICKEN LEGS

Prep & Cook Time: 35 minutes | Servings: 4

INGREDIENTS

3 chicken legs, bone-in, with ski
3 chicken thighs, bone-in, with skin
2 cups of flour
1 cup of buttermilk

1 tsp. of salt
1 tsp. of ground black pepper
1 tsp. of garlic powder
1 tsp. of onion powder

1 tsp. of ground cumin
2 tbsp. of extra virgin olive oil

INSTRUCTIONS

1. Wash the chicken, dry it, & place it in a large bowl.
2. Pour the buttermilk over the chicken & refrigerate for 2 hours.
3. In a separate bowl, combine the flour with all of the seasonings.
4. Dip the chicken into the flour mixture. Dredge it the buttermilk before rolling it in the flour again.
5. Pre-heat the Air Fryer to 360°F
6. Put the chicken legs & thighs in the Air Fryer basket. Drizzle on the olive oil & cook for roughly 20 minutes, flipping each piece of chicken a few times throughout the cooking time, until cooked through & crisped up.

702. BEASTLY BBQ DRUMSTICKS

Prep & Cook Time: 45 minutes | Servings: 4

INGREDIENTS

4 chicken drumsticks
½ tbsp. of mustard
1 clove garlic, crushed

1 tsp. of chili powder
2 tsp. of sugar
1 tbsp. of olive oil

Freshly ground black pepper

INSTRUCTIONS

1. Pre-heat the Air Fryer to 390°F.
2. Mix together the garlic, sugar, mustard, a pinch of salt, freshly ground pepper, chili powder & oil.
3. Massage this mixture into the drumsticks & leave to marinate for a minimum of 20 minutes.
4. Put the drumsticks in the Air Fryer basket & cook for 10 minutes.
5. Bring the temperature down to 300°F & continue to cook the drumsticks for a further 10 minutes. When cooked through, serve with bread & corn salad.

703. TURKEY LOAF

Prep & Cook Time: 50 minutes | Servings: 4

INGREDIENTS

⅔ cup of finely chopped walnuts
1 egg
1 tbsp. of organic tomato paste
1 ½ lb. of turkey breast, diced
1 tbsp. of Dijon mustard

½ tsp. of dried savory or dill
1 tbsp. of onion flakes
½ tsp. of ground allspice
1 small garlic clove, minced
½ tsp. of sea salt

¼ tsp. of black pepper
1 tbsp. of soy sauce
2 tbsp. of grated parmesan cheese

INSTRUCTIONS

1. Pre-heat Air Fryer to 375°F.
2. Coat the inside of a baking dish with a little oil.
3. Mix together the egg, dill, tomato paste, soy sauce, mustard, salt, dill, garlic, pepper & allspice using a whisk. Stir in the diced turkey, followed by the walnuts, cheese & onion flakes.
4. Transfer the mixture to the greased baking dish & bake in the Air Fryer for 40 minutes.
5. Serve hot.

704. CHARCOAL CHICKEN

Prep & Cook Time: 20 minutes | Servings: 2

INGREDIENTS

2 medium skinless, boneless chicken breasts
½ tsp. of salt

3 tbsp. of Cajun spice
1 tbsp. of olive oil

INSTRUCTIONS

1. Massage the salt & Cajun spice into the chicken breasts. Drizzle with olive oil.
2. Pre-heat the Air Fryer to 370°F.
3. Place the chicken in the Air Fryer & cook for 7 minutes.
4. Flip both chicken breasts over & cook for an additional 3 – 4 minutes.
5. Slice up before serving.

705. BATTERED CHICKEN THIGHS

Prep & Cook Time: 4 hours 45 minutes | Servings: 4

INGREDIENTS

2 cups of buttermilk
3 tsp. of salt
1 tsp. of cayenne pepper

1 tbsp. of paprika
1 ½ lb. of chicken thighs
2 tsp. of black pepper

2 cups of flour
1 tbsp. of garlic powder
1 tbsp. of baking powder

INSTRUCTIONS

1. Put the chicken thighs in a large bowl.
2. In a separate bowl, combine the buttermilk, salt, cayenne, & black pepper.

3. Coat the thighs with the buttermilk mixture. Place a sheet of aluminum foil over the bowl & set in the refrigerator for 4 hours.
4. Pre-heat your Air Fryer to 400°F.
5. Combine together the flour, baking powder, & paprika in a shallow bowl. Cover a baking dish with a layer of parchment paper.
6. Coat the chicken thighs in the flour mixture & bake in the Air Fryer for 10 minutes. Turn the thighs over & air fry for another 8 minutes. You will have to do this in two batches.

706. CHICKEN BITES
Prep & Cook Time: 30 minutes | Servings: 4

INGREDIENTS

1 lb. of skinless, boneless chicken breasts
¼ cup of blue cheese salad dressing
¼ cup of blue cheese, crumbled

½ cup of sour cream
1 cup of breadcrumbs
1 tbsp. of olive oil

½ tsp. of salt
¼ tsp. of black pepper

INSTRUCTIONS

1. In a large bowl, combine the salad dressing, sour cream, & blue cheese.
2. In a separate bowl, combine the breadcrumbs, olive oil, salt & pepper.
3. Chop the chicken breast into 1 - 2-inch pieces & coat in the breadcrumbs.
4. Pre-heat the Air Fryer to 380°F.
5. Place the chicken bites in your Air Fryer's basket.
6. Cook for 12 – 15 minutes. When cooked through & crispy, serve with the sauce of your choice.

707. COCONUT CHICKEN
Prep & Cook Time: 45 minutes | Servings: 2 – 4

INGREDIENTS

3 pcs of whole chicken leg [skinless or with skin, it's up to you]
1.8 oz. pure coconut paste [alternatively,

1.8 oz. of coconut milk]
4 – 5 tsp. of ground turmeric
1.8 oz. of old ginger

1.8 oz. of galangal [a.k.a. lengkuas]
¾ tbsp. of salt

INSTRUCTIONS

1. Mix together all of the ingredients, except for the chicken.
2. Slice a few slits into the chicken leg, mainly around the thick parts. This will help the chicken absorb the marinade.
3. Coat the chicken in the mixture & set aside to absorb.
4. Pre-heat the Air Fryer at 375°F.
5. Air fry the chicken for 20 – 25 minutes, turning it once halfway through, until golden brown.

708. SIMPLE TURKEY BREASTS
Prep & Cook Time: 35 minutes | Servings: 5

INGREDIENTS

6 – 7 lb. of skinless, boneless turkey breast

2 tsp. of salt
1 tsp. of black pepper

½ tsp. of dried cumin
2 tbsp. of olive oil

INSTRUCTIONS

1. Massage all of the other ingredients into the turkey breast.
2. Pre-heat the Air Fryer to 340°F,
3. Cook the turkey breast for 15 minutes. Turn it over & cook for an additional 10 – 15 minutes, until cooked through & crispy.
4. Slice & serve the turkey with rice or fresh vegetables.

709. CHICKEN WRAPPED IN BACON
Prep & Cook Time: 25 minutes | Servings: 6

INGREDIENTS

6 rashers of unsmoked back bacon

1 small chicken breast

1 tbsp. of garlic soft cheese

INSTRUCTIONS

1. Cut the chicken breast into six bite-sized pieces.
2. Spread the soft cheese across one side of each slice of bacon.
3. Put the chicken on top of the cheese & wrap the bacon around it, holding it in place with a toothpick.
4. Transfer the wrapped chicken pieces to the Air Fryer & cook for 15 minutes at 350°F.

710. CHICKEN, RICE & VEGETABLES
Prep & Cook Time: 30 minutes | Servings: 4

INGREDIENTS

1 lb. of skinless, boneless chicken breasts
½ lb. of button mushrooms, sliced
1 medium onion, chopped

1 packet [10 oz.] of Alfredo sauce
2 cups of cooked rice
½ tsp. of dried thyme

1 tbsp. of olive oil
Salt & black pepper to taste

INSTRUCTIONS

1. Slice up the chicken breasts into 1-inch cubes.
2. In a large bowl, combine all of the ingredients. Sprinkle on salt & dried thyme & mix again.
3. Pre-heat the Air Fryer to 370°F & drizzle the basket with the olive oil.
4. Place the chicken & vegetables in the Air Fryer & cook for 10 – 12 minutes. Stir the contents now & again.
5. Pour in the Alfredo sauce & allow to cook for an additional 3 – 4 minutes.
6. Serve with rice if desired.

711. BREADCRUMB TURKEY BREASTS
Prep & Cook Time: 25 minutes | Servings: 6

INGREDIENTS

6 turkey breasts
1 stick butter, melted

1 tsp. of salt
2 cups of breadcrumbs

½ tsp. of cayenne pepper
½ tsp. of black pepper

INSTRUCTIONS

1. Put the breadcrumbs, half a tsp. of the salt, a quarter tsp. of the pepper, & the cayenne pepper in a large bowl. Combine well.
2. In a separate bowl, sprinkle the melted butter with the rest of the salt & pepper.
3. Coat the turkey breasts with the butter using a brush. Roll the turkey in the breadcrumbs & transfer to a lined baking dish. Place in the Air Fryer.
4. Air fry at 390°F for 15 minutes.

712. CHICKEN ESCALLOPS
Prep & Cook Time: 45 minutes | Servings: 4

INGREDIENTS

4 skinless chicken breasts
6 sage leaves
¼ cup of breadcrumbs

2 eggs, beaten
½ cup of flour
¼ cup of parmesan cheese

cooking spray

INSTRUCTIONS

1. Cut the chicken breasts into thin slices.
2. In a bowl, combine the sage & parmesan. Add in the flour, beaten eggs, salt & pepper & mix well.
3. Cover the chicken in the mixture before rolling it in the breadcrumbs.

4. Grease the pan with the cooking spray.
5. Pre-heat your Air Fryer to 390°F & cook the chicken for 20 minutes, until it turns golden. Serve with rice.

713. TURKEY & MAPLE MUSTARD

Prep & Cook Time: 70 minutes | Servings: 6

INGREDIENTS

5 lb. of whole turkey breast
1 tbsp. of olive oil
1 tsp. of dried thyme
½ tsp. of smoked paprika

½ tsp. of dried sage
1 tsp. of sea salt
½ tsp. of black pepper
1 tbsp. of butter, melted

2 tbsp. of Dijon mustard
¼ cup of maple syrup

INSTRUCTIONS

1. Pre-heat the Air Fryer to 350°F.
2. Brush the turkey breast with the olive oil.
3. Mix together the thyme, paprika, sage, salt, & pepper. Coat the turkey breast all over with this mixture.
4. Put the turkey breast in the Air Fryer basket & allow to cook for 25 minutes.
5. Flip it over & cook on the other side for a further 12 minutes.
6. Turn it once again & cook for another 12 minutes.
7. Check the temperature with a meat thermometer & ensure it has reached 165°F before removing it from the Air Fryer.
8. In the meantime, combine the maple syrup, mustard, & melted butter in a saucepan over a medium heat. Stir continuously until a smooth consistency is achieved.
9. Pour the sauce over the cooked turkey in the Air Fryer.
10. Cook for a final 5 minutes, ensuring the turkey turns brown & crispy.
11. Allow the turkey to rest, under a layer of aluminum foil, before carving up & serving.

714. CHICKEN WINGS

Prep & Cook Time: 55 minutes | Servings: 4

INGREDIENTS

3 lb. of bone-in chicken wings
¾ cup of flour

1 tbsp. of old bay seasoning
4 tbsp. of butter

couple fresh lemons

INSTRUCTIONS

1. In a bowl, combine the all-purpose flour & Old Bay seasoning.
2. Toss the chicken wings with the mixture to coat each one well.
3. Pre-heat the Air Fryer to 375°F.
4. Give the wings a shake to shed any excess flour & place each one in the Air Fryer. You may have to do this in multiple batches, so as to not overlap any.
5. Cook for 30 – 40 minutes, shaking the basket frequently, until the wings are cooked through & crispy.
6. In the meantime, melt the butter in a frying pan over a low heat. Squeeze one or two lemons & add the juice to the pan. Mix well.
7. Serve the wings topped with the sauce.

715. MOZZARELLA TURKEY ROLLS

Prep & Cook Time: 20 minutes | Servings: 4

INGREDIENTS

4 slices of turkey breast
1 cup of sliced fresh mozzarella

1 tomato, sliced
½ cup of fresh basil

4 chive shoots

INSTRUCTIONS

1. Pre-heat your Air Fryer to 390°F.
2. Lay the slices of mozzarella, tomato & basil on top of each turkey slice.
3. Roll the turkey up, enclosing the filling well, & secure by tying a chive shoot around each one.
4. Put in the Air Fryer & cook for 10 minutes. Serve with a salad if desired.

716. SAGE & ONION TURKEY BALLS

Prep & Cook Time: 40 minutes | Servings: 2

INGREDIENTS

3.5 oz. of turkey mince
½ small onion, diced
1 medium egg

1 tsp. of sage
½ tsp. of garlic, pureed
3 tbsp. of breadcrumbs

salt
pepper

INSTRUCTIONS

1. Put all of the ingredients in a bowl & mix together well.
2. Take equal portions of the mixture & mold each one into a small ball. Transfer to the Air Fryer & cook for 15 minutes at 350°F.
3. Serve with tartar sauce & mashed potatoes.

717. SALSA VERDE CHICKEN BREAST

Prep & Cook Time: 30 minutes | Servings: 4

INGREDIENTS

16 oz. of salsa verde
1 lb. of chicken breast, boneless & skinless
1½ cups of grated cheddar cheese

¼ cup of chopped parsley
1 tsp. of sweet paprika
1 tbsp. of avocado oil

salt & black pepper to taste

INSTRUCTIONS

1. In a baking dish, toss well all ingredients except the cheese.
2. Place the baking dish into the fryer and cook at 380°F for 17 minutes.
3. Sprinkle with cheese and cook for 3-4 minutes more.
4. Distribute between plates and serve.

718. CHICKEN BREASTS & VEGGIES

Prep & Cook Time: 30 minutes | Servings: 4

INGREDIENTS

2 lbs. of chicken breasts, skinless & boneless
12 pcs. of brown mushrooms, halved
1 pc. of red onion, chopped

1 pc. of red bell pepper, chopped
1 pc. of green bell pepper, roughly chopped
2 pcs. of garlic cloves, minced

2 tbsp. of olive oil
2 tbsp. of shredded cheddar cheese
salt & black pepper to taste

INSTRUCTIONS

1. Season the chicken breasts with salt and pepper, rub with garlic and 1 tbsp. of the oil.
2. Put the chicken breasts in preheated air fryer's basket.
3. Cook at 390°F for 6 minutes on each side and split between plates.
3. Heat up a pan with the remaining oil over medium heat, saute the onions for 2 minutes.
4. Add mushrooms and bell peppers, and cook for 5-6 minutes more.
5. Distribute the mixture next to the chicken, sprinkle the cheese all over and serve.

719. TURKEY & PARSLEY PESTO

Prep & Cook Time: 1 hour 5 minutes | Servings: 4

INGREDIENTS

2 cuts of turkey breasts, boneless, skinless & halved
1 cup of chopped parsley

½ cup of olive oil
¼ cup of red wine
4 pcs. of garlic cloves

a drizzle of maple syrup
a pinch of salt & black pepper

INSTRUCTIONS
1. In a blender, combine parsley, garlic, salt, pepper, oil, wine and maple syrup, pulse to make a parsley pesto, and transfer to a bowl.
2. Put the turkey breasts to the bowl and toss well.
3. Set aside the bowl in the fridge for 30 minutes.
4. Drain the turkey breasts (keeping the parsley pesto).
5. Place in your air fryer's basket and cook at 380°F for 35 minutes, flipping the meat halfway.
6. Distribute the turkey between plates, drizzle the parsley pesto, all over and serve.

720. CHINESE STYLE CHICKEN THIGHS
Prep & Cook Time: 40 minutes | Servings: 4

INGREDIENTS
4 cuts of chicken thighs
1 bunch of spring onions, chopped
14 oz. of water
2 pcs. of green chilies, chopped

1 tbsp. of fish sauce
1 tbsp. of soy sauce
1 tbsp. of rice wine
1 tbsp. of olive oil

1 tbsp. of grated ginger
1 tsp. of sesame oil

INSTRUCTIONS
1. Heat up a pan with the olive and sesame oil over medium heat.
2. Put the chilies, onions, ginger, fish sauce, soy sauce, rice wine and the water.
3. Bring to a simmer, cook for 3-4 minutes and turn off the heat.
4. Put the chicken thighs and mix everything.
5. Put the pan into the air fryer and cook at 370°F for 25 minutes.
6. Distribute between plates and serve.

721. AWESOME OREGANO CHICKEN THIGHS
Prep & Cook Time: 35 minutes | Servings: 4

INGREDIENTS
8 cuts of chicken thighs
2 pcs. of garlic cloves, minced
1 pc. of red onion, chopped

4 tsp. of chopped oregano
½ tsp. of sweet paprika
2 tbsp. of olive oil

salt & black pepper to taste

INSTRUCTIONS
1. In a baking dish, Combine and mix well all ingredients.
2. Transfer the dish to your air fryer and cook at 400°F for 30 minutes, shaking halfway.
3. Distribute between plates and serve.

722. CHICKEN & GREEN COCONUT SAUCE
Prep & Cook Time: 26 minutes | Servings: 4

INGREDIENTS
10 pcs. of green onions, roughly chopped
10 cuts of chicken drumsticks
1 cup of coconut milk
¼ cup of chopped parsley

4 pcs. of garlic cloves, minced
2 tbsp. of oyster sauce
3 tbsp. of soy sauce
1 tbsp. of lemon juice

1 tbsp. of grated ginger
1 tsp. of Chinese five spice
1 tsp. of olive oil
salt & black pepper to taste

INSTRUCTIONS
1. In a blender, combine all ingredients except for the chicken, pulse well.
2. In a baking dish, coat the chicken with the mixture.
3. Place the baking dish in the air fryer and cook at 370°F for 16 minutes, shaking the fryer once.
4. Distribute between plates, sprinkle the parsley on top, drizzle the lemon juice all over.
5. Serve and enjoy!

723. TURMERIC CHICKEN LEGS
Prep & Cook Time: 25 minutes | Servings: 4

INGREDIENTS
4 cuts of chicken legs
2 tbsp. of grated ginger

4 tbsp. of heavy cream
5 tsp. of turmeric powder

salt & black pepper to taste

INSTRUCTIONS
1. Combine all ingredients in a bowl.
2. Put the chicken to the air fryer and cook at 380°F for 20 minutes.
3. Distribute between plates and serve.

724. TOMATO CHICKEN
Prep & Cook Time: 30 minutes | Servings: 6

INGREDIENTS
14 oz. of tomato sauce
6 oz. of grated mozzarella cheese

4 cuts od medium chicken breasts, skinless & boneless
1 tbsp. of olive oil

1 tsp. of dried oregano
1 tsp. of garlic powder
salt & black pepper to taste

INSTRUCTIONS
1. Place the chicken in air fryer, season with salt, pepper, garlic powder and oregano.
2. Cook the chicken at 360°F for 5 minutes.
3. Transfer the chicken to a pan greased with oil.
4. Pour the tomato sauce and sprinkle mozzarella on top.
5. Put the pan in the fryer and cook at 350°F for 15 minutes more.
6. Distribute between plates and serve.

725. FRIED CHICKEN WINGS
Prep & Cook Time: 55 minutes | Servings: 4

INGREDIENTS
16 cuts of chicken wings
¼ cup of butter

¼ cup of clover honey
4 tbsp. of minced garlic

salt & black pepper to taste

INSTRUCTIONS
1. Place the chicken wings in air fryer's basket and season with salt and pepper.
2. Cook at 380°F for 25 minutes, then at 400°F for 5 minutes, and put it in a bowl.
3. Melt the butter in a pan over medium-high heat, sauté the garlic for 5 minutes.
4. Put salt, pepper, the air fried chicken and honey, stir and simmer for 10 minutes more over medium heat.
5. Distribute the chicken wings and the sauce between plates.
6. Serve and enjoy.

726. CINNAMON CHICKEN
Prep & Cook Time: 45 minutes | Servings: 8

INGREDIENTS

1 cup of chicken stock
1 whole chicken, cut into pieces
1½ tsp. of cinnamon powder

2 tsp. of garlic powder
1 tbsp. of olive oil
1½ tbsp. of lemon zest

1 tbsp. of coriander powder
salt & black pepper to taste

INSTRUCTIONS
1. Combine all of the ingredients in a bowl.
2. Place the chicken to air fryer's basket and cook at 370°F for 35 minutes, shaking the fryer from time to time.
3. Distribute chicken between plates and serve with a side salad.

727. CHICKEN THIGHS AND RICE
Prep & Cook Time: 35 minutes | Servings: 4

INGREDIENTS

2 lbs. of chicken thighs, boneless & skinless
1 cup of white rice
¼ cup of red wine vinegar
2 cups of chicken stock

3 pcs. of carrots, chopped
4 pcs. of garlic cloves, minced
4 tbsp. of olive oil
1 tbsp. of garlic powder

1 tbsp. of Italian seasoning
1 tsp. of turmeric powder
salt & black pepper to taste

INSTRUCTIONS
1. In a pan, combine all of the ingredients and toss.
2. Put the pan in the fryer and cook at 370°F for 30 minutes.
3. Distribute between plates and serve.

728. GLAZED CHICKEN & APPLES
Prep & Cook Time: 30 minutes | Servings: 4

INGREDIENTS

6 cuts of chicken thighs, skin-on
3 pcs. of apples, cored & sliced
2/3 cup of apple cider

2 tbsp. of olive oil
1 tbsp. of chopped rosemary
2 tbsp. of honey

1 tbsp. of mustard
salt & black pepper to taste

INSTRUCTIONS
1. Heat up a pan with 1 tbsp. of the oil over medium heat.
2. Pour the cider, honey and mustard, whisk.
3. Bring to a simmer and take off the heat.
4. Put the chicken, apples, salt, pepper and rosemary, toss.
5. Put the pan in air fryer and cook at 390°F for 17 minutes.
6. Distribute between plates and serve.

729. HERBED CHICKEN
Prep & Cook Time: 35 minutes | Servings: 8

INGREDIENTS

8 cuts of chicken thighs
3 pcs. of garlic cloves, minced
1 cup of chicken stock
¼ cup of grated cheddar cheese

¼ cup of heavy cream
3 tbsp. of melted butter
1 tbsp. of mustard
½ tsp. of dried basil

½ tsp. of dried thyme
½ tsp. of dried oregano
salt & black pepper to taste

INSTRUCTIONS
1. In a baking dish, combine all ingredients except the cheddar cheese, mix well.
2. Place the dish to air fryer and cook at 370°F for 25 minutes.
3. Sprinkle cheese on top and cook for 5 more minutes.
4. Distribute everything between plates and serve.

730. CHICKEN WINGS & ENDIVES
Prep & Cook Time: 40 minutes | Servings: 4

INGREDIENTS

8 cuts of chicken wings, halved
6 pcs. of endives, shaved
¼ cup of white wine

2 pcs. of garlic cloves, minced
1 tbsp. of chopped rosemary
1 tbsp. of olive oil

1 tsp. of ground cumin
salt & black pepper to taste

INSTRUCTIONS
1. Season chicken wings with the salt, pepper, cumin and rosemary.
2. Put the wings in your air fryer's basket and cook at 360°F for 10 minutes on each side.
3. Distribute between plates.
4. Heat up a pan with oil over medium heat.
5. Add garlic, endives, salt, pepper and the wine, bring to a simmer.
6. Cook for 8 minutes, spread over the chicken and serve.

731. CHICKEN & YOGURT
Prep & Cook Time: 1 hour 15 minutes | Servings: 4

INGREDIENTS

17 oz. of chicken meat, boneless & cubed
14 oz. of yogurt
3½ oz. of cherry tomatoes, halved
1 pc. of red bell pepper, deseeded & cubed
1 pc. of yellow bell pepper, deseeded & cubed

3 pcs. of mint leaves, torn
1 pc. of green bell pepper, deseeded & cubed
1 tbsp. of grated ginger
2 tbsp. of red chili powder
2 tbsp. of coriander powder

2 tsp. of olive oil
1 tsp. of turmeric powder
2 tbsp. of cumin powder
salt & black pepper to taste

INSTRUCTIONS
1. In a bowl, combine all ingredients, toss well and set aside in the fridge for 1 hour.
2. Place the whole mix to a pan and cook at 400°F for 15 minutes, shaking the pan halfway.
3. Distribute everything between plates and serve.

732. EASY CHICKEN THIGHS
Prep & Cook Time: 21 minutes | Servings: 6

INGREDIENTS

8 cuts of chicken thighs
1 tbsp. of grated ginger
1 tbsp. of turmeric powder

1 tbsp. of ground coriander
1 tbsp. of sweet paprika
1 tbsp. of lime juice

2 tbsp. of olive oil
salt & black pepper to taste

INSTRUCTIONS
1. Combine all the ingredients in a bowl and toss well.
2. Place the chicken thighs to air fryer's basket and cook at 370°F for 8 minutes on each side.
3. Distribute between plates and serve with a side salad.

733. LEMON & GARLIC CHICKEN
Prep & Cook Time: 25 minutes | Servings: 4

INGREDIENTS

4 cuts of chicken breasts, skinless & boneless
4 pcs. of garlic heads, peeled, cloves separated & cut into quarters

2 tbsp. of lemon juice
½ tsp. of lemon pepper
1½ tbsp. of avocado oil

salt & black pepper to taste

INSTRUCTIONS
1. In a bowl, combine all of the ingredients and toss well.
2. Place the chicken mixture to air fryer and cook at 360°F for 15 minutes.
3. Distribute between plates and serve with a side salad.

734. JAPANESE STYLE CHICKEN THIGHS
Prep & Cook Time: 40 minutes | Servings: 5

INGREDIENTS
2 lbs. of chicken thighs
5 pcs. of spring onions, chopped
2 tbsp. of olive oil

1 tbsp. of soy sauce
1 tbsp. of sherry wine
½ tsp. of white vinegar

¼ tsp. of sugar
salt & black pepper to taste

INSTRUCTIONS
1. Season the chicken with salt and pepper, rub with 1 tbsp. of the oil.
2. Place it in the air fryer's basket and cook at 360°F for 10 minutes on each side.
3. Distribute between plates.
4. Heat up a pan with the remaining oil over medium-high heat.
5. Add the spring onions, sherry wine, vinegar, soy sauce and sugar, whisk.
6. Cook for 10 minutes, drizzle over the chicken and serve.

735. CHICKEN & PEAR SAUCE
Prep & Cook Time: 30 minutes | Servings: 6

INGREDIENTS
6 cuts of chicken breasts, skinless & boneless
3 cups of ketchup
1 cup of pear jelly

¼ cup of honey
½ tsp. of smoked paprika
1 tsp. of chili powder

1 tsp. of garlic powder
1 tsp. of mustard powder
salt & black pepper to taste

INSTRUCTIONS
1. Season the chicken with salt and pepper, place it in preheated air fryer and cook at 350°F for 10 minutes.
2. Heat up a pan with the ketchup over medium heat, add the remaining ingredients except for the chicken, whisk and cook for 5-6 minutes. Put the chicken and cook for 4 minutes more.
3. Distribute everything between plates and serve.

736. CHICKEN & DATES
Prep & Cook Time: 35 minutes | Servings: 6

INGREDIENTS
1 whole chicken, cut into medium pieces
4 pcs. of dates, chopped
3/4 cup of water

⅓ cup of honey
¼ cup of olive oil
salt & black pepper to taste

INSTRUCTIONS
1. Pour the water in a pot, bring to a simmer over medium heat.
2. Pour honey, whisk and take off the heat.
3. Coat the chicken with the oil, season with salt and pepper and place in air fryer's basket.
4. Put the dates and cook at 350°F for 10 minutes.
5. Coat the chicken with some of the honey mix, cook for 6 minutes more, flip again.
6. Coat one more time with the honey mix and cook for 7 minutes more.
7. Distribute the chicken and dates between plates and serve.

737. SOY SAUCE CHICKEN
Prep & Cook Time: 50 minutes | Servings: 6

INGREDIENTS
1 whole chicken, cut into pieces
1 pc. of chili pepper, minced

1 tbsp. of grated ginger
1 tsp. of sesame oil

2 tsp. of soy sauce
salt & black pepper to taste

INSTRUCTIONS
1. In a bowl, coat the chicken with all the other ingredients and rub well.
2. Place the chicken pieces to air fryer's basket.
3. Cook at 400°F for 30 minutes, and at 380°F for 10 minutes more.
4. Distribute everything between plates and serve.

738. LEMON CHICKEN & ASPARAGUS
Prep & Cook Time: 20 minutes | Servings: 4

INGREDIENTS
½ lb. of asparagus, trimmed & halved
1 lb. of chicken thighs
1 pc. of zucchini, roughly cubed

1 pc. of lemon, sliced
3 pcs. of garlic cloves, minced
juice of 1 lemon

2 tbsp. of olive oil
1 tsp. of dried oregano
salt & black pepper to taste

INSTRUCTIONS
1. In a pan, combine all of the ingredients.
2. Put the pan in air fryer and cook at 380°F for 15 minutes.
3. Distribute between plates and serve.

739. CHICKEN & VEGGIES
Prep & Cook Time: 35 minutes | Servings: 4

INGREDIENTS
4 cuts of chicken breasts, boneless & skinless
3 pcs. of garlic cloves, minced
1 stalk of celery, chopped
1 pc. of red onion, chopped

1 pc. of carrot, chopped
1 cup of chicken stock
2 tbsp. of olive oil
1 tsp. of dried sage

½ tsp. of dried rosemary
salt & black pepper to taste

INSTRUCTIONS
1. In a pan, combine all ingredients and toss well.
2. Place the pan in the fryer and cook at 360°F for 25 minutes.
3. Distribute everything between plates.
4. Serve and enjoy!

740. CHICKEN THIGHS
Prep & Cook Time: 30 minutes | Servings: 4

INGREDIENTS
5 cuts of chicken thighs
2 pcs. of garlic cloves, minced
¼ cup of grated cheddar cheese
½ cup of heavy cream

3/4 cup of chicken stock
½ cup of chopped tomatoes
2 tbsp. of chopped basil
1 tbsp. of olive oil

1 tbsp. of rosemary
1 tsp. of chili powder
salt & black pepper to taste

INSTRUCTIONS
1. Season the chicken with salt and pepper and coat it with ½ tbsp. of the oil.
2. Place the chicken in air fryer's basket and cook at 350°F for 4 minutes.

3. Heat up a pan with the remaining oil over medium heat.
4. Combine rosemary, garlic, chili powder, tomatoes, cream, stock, cheese, salt and pepper.
5. Bring the mixture to a simmer, turn off the heat and add the chicken thighs, toss.
6. Put the pan in the air fryer and cook at 340°F for 12 minutes.
7. Distribute between plates, sprinkle the basil on top.
8. Serve and enjoy.

741. FRIED WHOLE CHICKEN

Prep & Cook Time: 30 minutes | Servings: 8

INGREDIENTS

1 whole chicken, cut into medium pieces
1 cup of chicken stock

2 pcs. of carrots, chopped
3 tbsp. of white wine

1 tbsp. of grated ginger
salt & black pepper to taste

INSTRUCTIONS

1. In a pan, combine all of the ingredients
2. Place the pan in the air fryer and cook at 370°F for 20 minutes.
3. Distribute between plates and serve.

742. CHICKEN & LEEKS

Prep & Cook Time: 40 minutes | Servings: 4

INGREDIENTS

4 cuts of chicken thighs, bone-in
3 pcs. of leeks, sliced
3 pcs. of carrots, cut into thin sticks

1 cup of chicken stock
2 tbsp. of chopped chives
1 tbsp. of Olive Oil

Salt & Black Pepper to taste

INSTRUCTIONS

1. Heat up a pan over medium heat, add stock, leeks and carrots.
2. Cover and simmer for 20 minutes.
3. Coat the chicken with olive oil, season with salt and pepper.
4. Place it in air fryer and cook at 350°F for 4 minutes.
5. Put the chicken to the leek's mix, place the pan in air fryer and cook for 6 minutes more.
6. Distribute between plates.
7. Serve and enjoy!

743. ROSEMARY CHICKEN BREASTS

Prep & Cook Time: 35 minutes | Servings: 4

INGREDIENTS

2 cuts of chicken breasts, skinless, boneless & halved
1 pc. of yellow onion, sliced
1 cup of chicken stock

4 pcs. of garlic cloves, chopped
1 tsp. of dried rosemary
1 tbsp. of chopped fresh rosemary
2 tbsp. of corn starch mixed with 2½ tbsp. of water

2 tbsp. of butter
1 tbsp. of soy sauce
salt & black pepper to taste

INSTRUCTIONS

1. Heat up the butter in a pan over medium heat.
2. Put all ingredients except for corn starch mix and chicken, let it simmer for 2-3 minutes.
3. Put the corn starch mixture, whisk, cook for 2 minutes more and turn off the heat.
4. Place the chicken, toss gently and put the pan in the fryer, cook at 370°F for 20 minutes.
5. Distribute between plates and serve hot.

744. CHICKEN BREASTS DELIGHT

Prep & Cook Time: 30 minutes | Servings: 6

INGREDIENTS

3½ lbs. of chicken breasts
1¼ cups of yellow onion, chopped
1 cup of chicken stock
1 tsp. of red pepper flakes

2 tsp. of sweet paprika
1 tbsp. of lime juice
1 tbsp. of olive oil

2 tbsp. of chopped green onions
salt & black pepper to taste

INSTRUCTIONS

1. Heat up a pan with oil over medium heat.
2. Put all spices and lime juice, cook for 8 minutes.
3. Place chicken and pour the stock, let it simmer for 1 more minute.
4. Put the pan to air fryer and cook at 370°F for 12 minutes.
5. Distribute between plates and serve.

745. HONEY DUCK BREASTS

Prep & Cook Time: 30 minutes | Servings: 6

INGREDIENTS

6 cuts of duck breasts, boneless
20 oz. of chicken stock
1 tsp. of olive oil

1 tbsp. of grated ginger
4 tbsp. of hoisin sauce
4 tbsp. of soy sauce

2 tbsp. of honey
salt & black pepper to taste

INSTRUCTIONS

1. Combine all of the ingredients in a bowl. Set aside in the fridge for 10 minutes.
2. Place the duck breasts to air fryer's basket and cook at 400°F for 10 minutes on each side.
3. Distribute between plates and serve with a side salad.

746. TURKEY WINGS ORANGE SAUCE

Prep & Cook Time: 45 minutes | Servings: 4

INGREDIENTS

2 cuts of turkey wings
1½ cups of cranberries
1 cup of orange juice

1 pc. of yellow onion, sliced
1 bunch of thyme, roughly chopped
2 tbsp. of butter

salt & black pepper to taste

INSTRUCTIONS

1. Put the butter in a pan and heat up over medium-high heat.
2. Put the cranberries, salt, pepper, onions and orange juice, whisk and cook for 3 minutes.
3. Place the turkey wings, toss and cook for 3-4 minutes more.
4. Put the pan to air fryer and cook at 380°F for 25 minutes.
5. Put the thyme, toss and distribute everything between plates.
6. Serve and enjoy!

747. CHICKEN & PANCETTA

Prep & Cook Time: 35 minutes | Servings: 4

INGREDIENTS

2 cuts of chicken breasts, skinless, boneless, cubed
4 oz. of chopped smoked pancetta

½ bunch of thyme, chopped
½ bunch of rosemary, chopped
½ pc. of fennel bulb, cut into matchsticks

4 pcs. of carrots, cut into thin matchsticks
½ cup of chicken stock
2 pcs. of scallions, chopped

juice of 1 lemon   a drizzle of olive oil   salt & black pepper to taste

INSTRUCTIONS
1. Heat up the oil in a pan over medium heat.
2. Put and toss all ingredients except for the chicken and lemon, cook for 5 minutes.
3. Add the lemon juice and chicken, cook for 5 more minutes.
4. Transfer the pan in the fryer and cook at 380°F for 15 minutes.
5. Distribute everything between plates and serve.

748. TURKEY BREAST
Prep & Cook Time: 60 minutes | Servings: 4

INGREDIENTS
2 cuts of turkey breasts, skinless, boneless & halved
1 tbsp. of lemon juice

2 tbsp. of olive oil
1 tsp. of garlic powder
1 tsp. of onion powder

½ tsp. of dried thyme
1 tsp. of dried rosemary
salt & black pepper to taste

INSTRUCTIONS
1. In a bowl, coat the turkey with all of the ingredients.
2. Place to air fryer's basket and cook at 370°F for 25 minutes on each side.
3. Serve hot with a side salad.

749. TURKEY WITH FIG SAUCE
Prep & Cook Time: 40 minutes | Servings: 4

INGREDIENTS
2 cuts of turkey breasts, halved
1 pc. of shallot, chopped
1 cup of chicken stock
½ cup of red wine

1 tbsp. of olive oil
½ tsp. of garlic powder
¼ tsp. of sweet paprika
3 tbsp. of butter

1 tbsp. of white flour
4 tbsp. of chopped figs
salt & black pepper to taste

INSTRUCTIONS
1. Heat up a pan with olive oil and 1½ tbsp. of the butter over medium- high heat.
2. Put the shallots, stir and cook for 2 minutes.
3. Put garlic powder, paprika, stock, wine and figs, stir and cook for 7-8 minutes.
4. Add the flour, stir well and cook the sauce for 1-2 minutes more, turn off heat.
5. Season the turkey with salt and pepper and drizzle the remaining butter.
6. Put the turkey in air fryer's basket and cook at 380°F for 15 minutes, flipping them halfway.
7. Distribute between plates, drizzle the sauce all over and serve.

750. TARRAGON CHICKEN BREASTS
Prep & Cook Time: 25 minutes | Servings: 2

INGREDIENTS
2 cuts of chicken breasts, skinless & boneless
2 pcs. of garlic cloves, minced
8 sprigs of tarragon, chopped

1 cup of white wine
¼ cup of soy sauce
1 tbsp. of melted butter

salt & black pepper to taste

INSTRUCTIONS
1. In a bowl, combine chicken with the wine, soy sauce, garlic, tarragon, salt, pepper and the butter, toss well and set aside for 10 minutes.
2. Place the marinated chicken to a baking dish and cook at 370°F for 15 minutes, shaking the fryer halfway.
3. Distribute everything between plates and serve.

751. BLUE CHEESE CHICKEN
Prep & Cook Time: 30 minutes | Servings: 4

INGREDIENTS
1 lb. of chicken breasts, skinless, boneless & cut into thin strips

½ cup of buffalo sauce
¼ cup of crumbled blue cheese

½ cup of chicken stock
1 pc. of small yellow onion, sliced

INSTRUCTIONS
1. In a pan, combine the chicken with the onions, buffalo sauce and stock.
2. Toss everything and place the pan in the fryer, cook at 370°F for 20 minutes.
3. Sprinkle the cheese on top.
4. Distribute everything between plates and serve.

752. TOMATO DUCK BREAST
Prep & Cook Time: 25 minutes | Servings: 2

INGREDIENTS
1 cut of smoked duck breast
1 tsp. of honey

½ tsp. of apple vinegar
1 tbsp. of tomato paste

INSTRUCTIONS
1. In a bowl, coat the duck with the other ingredients.
2. Place it to air fryer and cook at 370°F for 10 minutes on each side.
3. Divide the meat into halves.
4. Distribute between plates and serve.

753. TURKEY MEATBALLS
Prep & Cook Time: 25 minutes | Servings: 8

INGREDIENTS
1 lb. of ground turkey meat
¼ cup of chopped parsley
¼ cup of milk
½ cup of panko breadcrumbs
¼ cup of grated parmesan cheese

1 pc. of yellow onion, minced
4 pcs. of garlic cloves, minced
2 tsp. of soy sauce
1 tsp. of fish sauce
1 tsp. of dried oregano

1 pc. of egg, whisked
cooking spray
salt & black pepper to taste

INSTRUCTIONS
1. In a bowl, combine all of the ingredients except the cooking spray, stir well and shape into medium-sized meatballs.
2. Put the meatballs in air fryer's basket, grease them with cooking spray.
3. Cook at 380°F for 15 minutes.
4. Serve the meatballs with a side salad.

754. DUCK & SAUCE
Prep & Cook Time: 30 minutes | Servings: 4

INGREDIENTS
2 cuts of duck breasts, skin scored
8 oz. of white wine
1 tbsp. of minced garlic

2 tbsp. of heavy ream
1 tbsp. of sugar
1 tbsp. of olive oil

2 tbsp. of cranberries
salt & black pepper to taste

INSTRUCTIONS
1. Season the duck breasts with salt and pepper and put in preheated air fryer.

2. Cook at 350°F for 10 minutes on each side and distribute between plates.
3. Heat up a pan with the oil over medium heat.
4. Combine the remaining ingredients.
5. Cook for 3-4 minutes.
6. Drizzle over the duck and serve.

755. CHICKEN & PEPPERCORNS
Prep & Cook Time: 25 minutes | Servings: 4

INGREDIENTS

8 cuts of chicken thighs, boneless
4 pcs. of garlic cloves, minced

½ cup of soy sauce
½ cup of balsamic vinegar

1 tsp. of black peppercorns
salt & black pepper to taste

INSTRUCTIONS
1. In a pan, combine chicken with all other ingredients and toss.
2. Put the pan in the fryer and cook at 380°F for 20 minutes.
3. Distribute everything between plates and serve.

756. TURKEY & SPRING ONIONS
Prep & Cook Time: 40 minutes | Servings: 2

INGREDIENTS

2 cuts of small turkey breasts, boneless & skinless
1 bunch of spring onions, chopped
2 pcs. of red chilies, chopped

1 cup of chicken stock
1 tbsp. of olive oil
1 tbsp. of Chinese rice wine

1 tbsp. of oyster sauce
1 tbsp. of soy sauce

INSTRUCTIONS
1. Put oil to a pan and place it over medium heat
2. Put all ingredients except for the turkey, whisk and let it simmer for 3-4 minutes.
3. Put the turkey, toss and place the pan in the air fryer and cook at 380°F for 30 minutes.
4. Distribute everything between plates and serve.

757. DUCK BREAST & POTATOES
Prep & Cook Time: 40 minutes | Servings: 2

INGREDIENTS

1 cut of duck breast, halved & scored
1 oz. of red wine

2 pcs. of gold potatoes, cubed
2 tbsp. of melted butter

salt & black pepper to taste

INSTRUCTIONS
1. Season the duck with salt and pepper, place it in a pan and heat up over medium-high heat.
2. Cook for 4 minutes on each side.
3. Transfer to air fryer's basket and cook at 360°F for 8 minutes.
4. Put the butter in a pan and heat it up over medium heat, add the potatoes, salt, pepper and wine, and cook for 8 minutes.
5. Add the duck, toss and cook everything for 3-4 minutes more.
6. Distribute all between plates and serve.

758. PARMESAN CHICKEN
Prep & Cook Time: 40 minutes | Servings: 4

INGREDIENTS

4 cuts of chicken breasts, boneless & skinless
½ cup of grated parmesan cheese

1 cup of crushed corn flakes
¼ cup of melted butter

1 tbsp. of olive oil
salt & black pepper to taste

INSTRUCTIONS
1. In a bowl, combine all the ingredients and toss.
2. Transfer the chicken in air fryer's basket and cook at 360°F for 15 minutes on each side.
3. Distribute between plates and serve.

759. CHICKEN & BEER
Prep & Cook Time: 40 minutes | Servings: 4

INGREDIENTS

15 oz. of beer
1 pc. of yellow onion, minced
1 pc. of chili pepper, chopped

4 cuts of chicken drumsticks
1 tbsp. of balsamic vinegar
2 tbsp. of olive oil

salt & black pepper to taste

INSTRUCTIONS
1. Add oil in a pan and heat up over medium heat.
2. Sauté onion and the chili pepper for 2 minutes.
3. Pour the vinegar, beer, salt and pepper, cook for 3 more minutes.
4. Place the chicken, toss and put the pan in the fryer.
5. Cook at 370°F for 20 minutes.
6. Distribute everything between plates and serve.

760. CHICKEN CURRY
Prep & Cook Time: 40 minutes | Servings: 4

INGREDIENTS

15 oz. chicken breast, skinless, boneless, cubed
6 pcs. of potatoes, peeled & cubed
5 oz. heavy cream

½ bunch of coriander, chopped
1 tbsp. olive oil
1 pc. of yellow onion, sliced

1 tsp. of curry powder
salt & black pepper to taste

INSTRUCTIONS
1. Heat up oil in a pan over medium heat.
2. Fry the chicken until brown for 2 minutes.
3. Put the onions, curry powder, salt and pepper, toss and cook for 3 minutes.
4. Put potatoes and cream, toss well.
5. Transfer the pan in the air fryer and cook at 370°F for 20 minutes.
6. Put the coriander and stir. Distribute the curry into bowls and serve.

761. MARINARA CHICKEN
Prep & Cook Time: 35 minutes | Servings: 6

INGREDIENTS

2 lbs. of chicken breasts, skinless, boneless & cubed
1 cup of green bell pepper, chopped

3/4 cup of marinara sauce
3/4 cup of diced yellow onion
½ cup of grated cheddar cheese

1 tbsp. of olive oil
salt & black pepper to taste

INSTRUCTIONS
1. Heat up a pan with the oil over medium heat.
2. Put the chicken, toss and brown for 3 minutes.
3. Put salt, pepper, onions, bell peppers and the marinara sauce, cook for 3 minutes more.
4. Transfer the pan in the air fryer and cook at 370°F for 15 minutes.
5. Sprinkle cheese on top.
6. Distribute the mixture between plates and serve.

762. SESAME CHICKEN

Prep & Cook Time: 30 minutes | Servings: 4

INGREDIENTS

2 lbs. chicken breasts, skinless, boneless & cubed
½ cup of soy sauce
½ cup of honey
½ cup yellow onion, chopped

2 pcs. of garlic cloves, minced
1 tbsp. of olive oil
2 tsp. of sesame oil
¼ tsp. of red pepper flakes

1 tbsp. of sesame seeds, toasted
salt & black pepper to taste

INSTRUCTIONS

1. Heat up oil in a pan over medium heat.
2. Put the chicken, toss and brown for 3 minutes.
3. Put onions, garlic, salt and pepper, stir and cook for 2 minutes more.
4. Pour soy sauce, sesame oil, honey and pepper flakes, toss well.
5. Transfer the pan in the fryer and cook at 380°F for 15 minutes.
6. Top with sesame seeds and toss.
7. Distribute between plates and serve.

763. MEXICAN STYLE TURKEY

Prep & Cook Time: 25 minutes | Servings: 6

INGREDIENTS

1 lb. of ground turkey meat
10 oz. of tomato sauce
4 oz. of sliced mushrooms
1 cup of grated cheddar cheese

1 pc. of yellow onion, chopped
2 tbsp. of olive oil
1 tbsp. of dried oregano
1 tsp. of minced garlic

1 tsp. of dried basil
salt & black pepper to taste

INSTRUCTIONS

1. Heat up oil in a pan over medium heat.
2. Put the turkey, oregano, garlic, basil and onions, toss and cook for 2- 3 minutes.
3. Put the mushrooms and tomato sauce, toss and cook for 2 minutes more.
4. Transfer the pan in the fryer and cook at 370°F for 16 minutes.
5. Sprinkle cheese all over.
6. Distribute the mix between plates and serve.

764. CAJUN CHICKEN & OKRA

Prep & Cook Time: 40 minutes | Servings: 4

INGREDIENTS

1 lb. of chicken thighs, halved
½ lb. of okra
1 pc. of red bell pepper, chopped

1 pc. of yellow onion, chopped
4 pcs. of garlic cloves, minced
1 cup of chicken stock

1 tbsp. of cajun spice
1 tbsp. of olive oil
salt & black pepper to taste

INSTRUCTIONS

1. Put oil to a pan and heat up over medium heat.
2. Place the chicken and brown for 2-3 minutes.
3. Put all remaining ingredients, toss and cook for 3-4 minutes more.
4. Transfer the pan into the air fryer and cook at 380°F for 22 minutes.
5. Distribute everything between plates and serve.

765. ASIAN STYLE CHICKEN

Prep & Cook Time: 40 minutes | Servings: 6

INGREDIENTS

1 lb. of chopped spinach
1½ lbs. of chicken drumsticks
15 oz. of crushed canned tomatoes
¼ cup of lemon juice
½ cup of chopped cilantro

½ cup of chicken stock
½ cup of heavy cream
4 pcs. of garlic cloves, minced
1 pc. of yellow onion, chopped
2 tbsp. of butter

1 tbsp. of grated ginger
1½ tsp. of paprika
1½ tsp. of ground coriander
1 tsp. of turmeric powder
salt & black pepper to taste

INSTRUCTIONS

1. Put the butter in a pan and heat over medium heat.
2. Put onions and garlic, stir and cook for 3 minutes.
3. Add ginger, paprika, coriander, turmeric, salt, pepper and the chicken, toss and cook for 4 minutes more.
4. Put the tomatoes and the stock, stir.
5. Transfer the pan in the fryer and cook at 370°F for 15 minutes.
6. Place the spinach, lemon juice, cilantro and the cream, stir and cook for 5- 6 minutes more.
7. Distribute everything into bowls and serve.

766. SPICED CHICKEN

Prep & Cook Time: 35 minutes | Servings: 6

INGREDIENTS

6 cuts of chicken thighs, boneless
2 pcs. of yellow onions, chopped
5 pcs. of garlic cloves, chopped
¼ cup of white wine
1 cup of chicken stock

½ cup of chopped cilantro
¼ cup of dried cranberries
2 tbsp. of olive oil
½ tsp. of ground coriander
½ tsp. of ground cumin

½ tsp. of ginger powder
½ tsp. of ground turmeric
½ tsp. of ground cinnamon
1 tsp. of sweet paprika
juice of 1 lemon

INSTRUCTIONS

1. Heat up oil in a pan over medium heat.
2. Put all other ingredients except the chicken, lemon juice and cilantro, cook for 5 minutes.
3. Place the chicken and toss.
4. Transfer the pan in the fryer and cook at 380°F for 20 minutes.
5. Put lemon juice and cilantro, and toss.
6. Distribute between plates, serve and enjoy!

767. LEMONGRASS CHICKEN

Prep & Cook Time: 40 minutes | Servings: 5

INGREDIENTS

10 cuts of chicken drumsticks
1 cup of coconut milk
1 bunch of lemongrass, trimmed
¼ cup of parsley, chopped

1 pc. of yellow onion, chopped
1 tbsp. of ginger, chopped
4 pcs. of garlic cloves, minced
2 tbsp. of fish sauce

3 tbsp. of soy sauce
1 tsp. of butter
1 tbsp. of lemon juice
salt & black pepper to taste

INSTRUCTIONS

1. In a blender, mix lemongrass, ginger, garlic, soy sauce, fish sauce and coconut milk.
2. Put butter in a pan and heat it up over medium heat, add onions, and cook for 2-3 minutes.
3. Place the chicken, salt, pepper and the lemongrass mix, toss well.
4. Transfer the pan in the fryer and cook at 380°F for 25 minutes.
5. Put lemon juice and parsley, toss.
6. Distribute everything between plates and serve.

768. CHICKEN & BABY CARROTS

Prep & Cook Time: 35 minutes | Servings: 6

INGREDIENTS

6 cuts of chicken thighs
½ lb. of baby carrots, halved
15 oz. of chopped canned tomatoes
1 cup of chicken stock

½ cup of white wine
1 pc. of yellow onion, chopped
1 tsp. of olive oil
½ tsp. of dried thyme

2 tbsp. of tomato paste
salt & black pepper to taste

INSTRUCTIONS

1. Put oil into a pan and heat up over medium heat.
2. Place the chicken thighs and brown them for 1-2 minutes on each side.
3. Put all the remaining ingredients, toss and cook for 4-5 minutes more.
4. Transfer the pan in the air fryer and cook at 380°F for 22 minutes.
5. Distribute the chicken and carrots mix between plates and serve.

769. CHICKEN & CHICKPEAS

Prep & Cook Time: 35 minutes | Servings: 4

INGREDIENTS

2 lbs. of chicken thighs, boneless
8 oz. of drained canned chickpeas
5 oz. of bacon, cooked & crumbled
1 cup of chopped yellow onion

2 pcs. of carrots, chopped
1 cup of chicken stock
1 tsp. of balsamic vinegar
2 tbsp. of olive oil

1 tbsp. of chopped parsley
salt & black pepper to taste

INSTRUCTIONS

1. Heat up a pan with the oil over medium heat.
2. Put the onions, carrots, salt and pepper, stir and sauté for 3-4 minutes.
3. Place the chicken, stock, vinegar and chickpeas, then toss.
4. Transfer the pan in the fryer and cook at 380°F for 20 minutes.
5. Put the bacon and the parsley and toss again.
6. Distribute everything between plates and serve.

770. TURKEY CHILI

Prep & Cook Time: 35 minutes | Servings: 4

INGREDIENTS

1 lb. of turkey meat, cubed & browned
15 oz. of drained canned lentils
12 oz. of veggie stock

1 pc. of yellow onion, chopped
1 pc. of green bell pepper, chopped
3 pcs. of garlic cloves, chopped

2½ tbsp. of chili powder
1½ tsp. of ground cumin
salt & black pepper to taste

INSTRUCTIONS

1. Combine all ingredients to a pan.
2. Transfer the pan in the fryer and cook at 380°F for 25 minutes.
3. Distribute into bowls and serve hot.

771. CHICKEN & SQUASH

Prep & Cook Time: 35 minutes | Servings: 4

INGREDIENTS

14 oz. of coconut milk
6 cups of cubed squash
8 cuts of chicken drumsticks
½ cup of chopped cilantro

½ cup of chopped basil
2 pcs. of red chilies, minced
3 pcs. of garlic cloves, minced
2 tbsp. of olive oil

2 tbsp. of green curry paste
¼ tsp. of ground coriander
a pinch of ground cumin
salt & black pepper to taste

INSTRUCTIONS

1. Heat up a pan with the oil over medium heat.
2. Stir the garlic, chilies, curry paste, cumin, coriander, salt and pepper cook for 3-4 minutes.
3. Put the chicken pieces and the coconut milk, stir.
4. Transfer the pan in the fryer and cook at 380°F for 15 minutes.
5. Put the squash, cilantro and basil, toss and cook for 5-6 minutes more.
6. Distribute into bowls and serve. Enjoy!

772. BALSAMIC CHICKEN

Prep & Cook Time: 30 minutes | Servings: 4

INGREDIENTS

4 cuts of chicken breasts, skinless & boneless
1 pc. of yellow onion, minced
¼ cup of balsamic vinegar

12 oz. of canned tomatoes, chopped
¼ cup of grated cheddar cheese
¼ tsp. of garlic powder

salt & black pepper to taste

INSTRUCTIONS

1. In a baking dish, combine all ingredients except for the cheese.
2. Sprinkle cheese on top and transfer the pan in the air fryer, cook at 400°F for 20 minutes.
3. Distribute between plates and serve.

773. CHICKEN & POTATOES

Prep & Cook Time: 25 minutes | Servings: 4

INGREDIENTS

1 lb. of chicken thighs, boneless
½ cup of chicken stock

4 pcs. of gold potatoes, cut into medium chunks
1 pc. of yellow onion, thinly sliced

salt & black pepper to taste

INSTRUCTIONS

1. In a pan, combine chicken with salt, pepper, onions and stock.
2. Transfer the pan in the fryer and cook at 380°F for 10 minutes.
3. Add potatoes and cook at 400°F for 10 minutes more.
4. Distribute between plates and serve.

774. MARJORAM CHICKEN

Prep & Cook Time: 40 minutes | Servings: 6

INGREDIENTS

2 lbs. of chicken thighs
¼ cup of white wine
¼ cup of chicken stock

1 tbsp. of olive oil
½ tsp. of sweet paprika
1 tsp. of dried marjoram

salt & black pepper to taste

INSTRUCTIONS

1. Heat up a pan with the oil over medium heat.
2. Put the chicken pieces and brown them for 5 minutes.
3. Place all remaining ingredients and toss well.
4. Transfer the pan in the fryer and cook at 390°F for 25 minutes.
5. Distribute between plates and serve.

775. CHICKEN & BEANS CHILI

Prep & Cook Time: 40 minutes | Servings: 4

INGREDIENTS

1 lb. of ground chicken meat
4 oz. of chopped canned green chilies
15 oz. of chopped canned tomatoes
1½ cups of drained canned kidney beans

1 pc. of yellow onion, minced
2 pcs. of carrots, chopped
2 pcs. of garlic cloves, minced
1 tbsp. of olive oil

1 tsp. of brown sugar
a handful of chopped cilantro
salt & black pepper to taste

INSTRUCTIONS

1. Heat up the oil in a pan over medium heat. Add onion and garlic, cook for 2-3 minutes.
2. Put the chicken, salt, pepper, carrots, chilies, sugar and the tomatoes.
3. Let it simmer and cook for 2-3 minutes more.
4. Put the beans, toss and transfer the pan in the air fryer.
5. Cook at 370°F for 25 minutes.
6. Distribute into bowls, sprinkle the cilantro on top and serve.

776. WARMS WINGS

Prep & Cook Time: 28 minutes | Servings: 6

INGREDIENTS

12 cuts of chicken wings, halves
¼ cup of tomato sauce

¼ cup of honey
4 tbsp. of hot sauce

1 tbsp. of chopped cilantro
salt & black pepper to taste

INSTRUCTIONS

1. In a bowl, combine all ingredients except for the cilantro.
2. Place the chicken wings to air fryer's basket and cook at 400°F for 17 minutes.
3. Distribute between plates, sprinkle the cilantro on top and serve.

777. MARINATED FLANK STEAK

Prep & Cook Time: 15 minutes | Servings: 4

INGREDIENTS

¾ lb. of flank steak
1 ½ tbsp. of sake

1 tbsp. of brown miso paste
1 tsp. of honey

2 cloves garlic, pressed
1 tbsp. of olive oil

INSTRUCTIONS

1. Put all of the ingredients in a Ziploc bag. Shake to cover the steak well with the seasonings & refrigerate for at least 1 hour.
2. Coat all sides of the steak with cooking spray.
3. Put the steak in the Air Fryer baking pan.
4. Cook at 400°F for 12 minutes, turning the steak twice during the cooking time, then serve immediately.

778. FRIED STEAK

Prep & Cook Time: 15 minutes | Servings: 1

INGREDIENTS

3 cm-thick of beef steak
salt & pepper

INSTRUCTIONS

1. Pre-heat the Air Fryer 400°F for 5 minutes.
2. Place the beef steak in the baking tray & sprinkle on pepper & salt.
3. Spritz the steak with cooking spray.
4. Allow to cook for 3 minutes. Turn the steak over & cook on the other side for 3 more minutes. Serve hot.

779. HOMEMADE MEATBALLS

Prep & Cook Time: 20 minutes | Servings: 4

INGREDIENTS

1 lb. of ground beef
1 tsp. of red Thai curry paste

½ lime, rind & juice
1 tsp. of Chinese spice

2 tsp. of lemongrass, finely chopped
1 tbsp. of sesame oil

INSTRUCTIONS

1. Mix all of the ingredients in a bowl, combining well.
2. Take 24 equal amounts of the mixture & shape each one into a meatball. Put them in the Air Fryer cooking basket.
3. Cook at 380°F for 10 minutes.
4. Turn them over & cook for a further 5 minutes on the other side, ensuring they are well-cooked before serving with your favorite dipping sauce.

780. CRUMBED FILET MIGNON

Prep & Cook Time: 20 minutes | Servings: 4

INGREDIENTS

½ lb. of filet mignon
Sea salt & ground black pepper, to taste
½ tsp. of cayenne pepper

1 tsp. of dried basil
1 tsp. of dried rosemary
1 tsp. of dried thyme

1 tbsp. of sesame oil
1 small-sized egg, well-whisked
½ cup of breadcrumbs

INSTRUCTIONS

1. Cover the filet mignon with the salt, black pepper, cayenne pepper, basil, rosemary, & thyme. Coat with a light brushing of sesame oil.
2. Put the egg in a shallow plate.
3. Pour the breadcrumbs in another plate.
4. Dip the filet mignon into the egg. Roll it into the crumbs.
5. Transfer the steak to the Air Fryer & cook for 10 to 13 minutes at 360°F or until it turns golden.
6. Serve with a salad.

781. GRILLED BEEF RIBS

Prep & Cook Time: 20 minutes + marinating time | Servings: 4

INGREDIENTS

1 lb. of meaty beef ribs
3 tbsp. of apple cider vinegar
1 cup of coriander, finely chopped
1 heaped tbsp. of fresh basil leaves

2 garlic cloves, finely chopped
1 chipotle powder
1 tsp. of fennel seeds
1 tsp. of hot paprika

Kosher salt & black pepper, to taste
½ cup of vegetable oil

INSTRUCTIONS

1. Wash & dry the ribs.
2. Coat the ribs with the rest of the ingredients & refrigerate for a minimum of 3 hours.
3. Separate the ribs from the marinade & put them on an Air Fryer grill pan.
4. Cook at 360°F for 8 minutes, or longer as needed.
5. Pour the remaining marinade over the ribs before serving immediately.

782. LONDON BROIL

INGREDIENTS

2 lb. of London broil
3 large garlic cloves, minced
3 tbsp. of balsamic vinegar

3 tbsp. of whole-grain mustard
2 tbsp. of olive oil
Sea salt & ground black pepper, to taste

½ tsp. of dried hot red pepper flakes

INSTRUCTIONS

1. Wash & dry the London broil. Score its sides with a knife.
2. Mix together the rest of the ingredients. Rub this mixture into the broil, coating it well. Allow to marinate for a minimum of 3 hours.
3. Cook the meat at 400°F for 15 minutes.
4. Turn it over & cook for an additional 10 - 12 minutes before serving.

783. SMOKED BEEF ROAST

Prep & Cook Time: 45 minutes | Servings: 8

INGREDIENTS

2 lb. of roast beef, at room temperature
2 tbsp. of extra-virgin olive oil
1 tsp. of sea salt flakes

1 tsp. of black pepper, preferably freshly ground
1 tsp. of smoked paprika

Few dashes of liquid smoke
2 jalapeño peppers, thinly sliced

INSTRUCTIONS

1. Pre-heat the Air Fryer to 330°F.
2. With kitchen towels, pat the beef dry.
3. Massage the extra-virgin olive oil & seasonings into the meat. Cover with liquid smoke.
4. Place the beef in the Air Fryer & roast for 30 minutes. Flip the roast over & allow to cook for another 15 minutes.
5. When cooked through, serve topped with sliced jalapeños.

784. VEGETABLES & BEEF CUBES

Prep & Cook Time: 20 minutes + marinating time | Servings: 4

INGREDIENTS

1 lb. of top round steak, cut into cubes
2 tbsp. of olive oil
1 tbsp. of apple cider vinegar
1 tsp. of fine sea salt
½ tsp. of ground black pepper

1 tsp. of shallot powder
¾ tsp. of smoked cayenne pepper
½ tsp. of garlic powder
¼ tsp. of ground cumin
¼ lb. of broccoli, cut into florets

¼ lb. of mushrooms, sliced
1 tsp. of dried basil
1 tsp. of celery seeds

INSTRUCTIONS

1. Massage the olive oil, vinegar, salt, black pepper, shallot powder, cayenne pepper, garlic powder, & cumin into the cubed steak, ensuring to coat each piece evenly.
2. Allow to marinate for a minimum of 3 hours.
3. Put the beef cubes in the Air Fryer cooking basket & allow to cook at 365°F for 12 minutes.
4. When the steak is cooked through, place it in a bowl.
5. Wipe the grease from the cooking basket & pour in the vegetables. Season them with basil & celery seeds.
6. Cook at 400°F for 5 to 6 minutes. When the vegetables are hot, serve them with the steak.

785. BEEF & KALE OMELET

Prep & Cook Time: 20 minutes | Servings: 4

INGREDIENTS

Cooking spray
½ lb. of leftover beef, coarsely chopped
2 garlic cloves, pressed
1 cup of kale, torn into pieces & wilted

1 tomato, chopped
¼ tsp. of sugar
4 eggs, beaten
4 tbsp. of heavy cream

½ tsp. of turmeric powder
Salt & ground black pepper to taste
⅛ tsp. of ground allspice

INSTRUCTIONS

1. Grease four ramekins with cooking spray.
2. Place equal amounts of each of the ingredients into each ramekin & mix well.
3. Air fry at 360°F for 16 minutes, or longer if necessary. Serve immediately.

786. CHEESEBURGERS

Prep & Cook Time: 15 minutes | Servings: 4

INGREDIENTS

¾ lb. of ground chuck
1 envelope onion soup mix
Kosher salt

Black pepper, to taste
1 tsp. of paprika
4 slices of Monterey-Jack cheese

4 ciabatta rolls
Mustard & pickled salad, to serve

INSTRUCTIONS

1. In a bowl, stir together the ground chuck, onion soup mix, salt, black pepper, & paprika to combine well.
2. Pre-heat your Air Fryer at 385°F.
3. Take four equal portions of the mixture & mold each one into a patty. Transfer to the Air Fryer & air fry for 10 minutes.
4. Put the slices of cheese on the top of the burgers.
5. Cook for another minute before serving on ciabatta rolls along with mustard & the pickled salad of your choosing.

787. SIMPLE BEEF

Prep & Cook Time: 25 minutes | Servings: 1

INGREDIENTS

1 thin beef schnitzel
1 egg, beaten

½ cup of breadcrumbs
2 tbsp. of olive oil

Salt & pepper

INSTRUCTIONS

1. Pre-heat the Air Fryer to 350°F.
2. In a shallow dish, combine the breadcrumbs, oil, pepper, & salt.
3. In a second shallow dish, place the beaten egg.
4. Dredge the schnitzel in the egg before rolling it in the breadcrumbs.
5. Put the coated schnitzel in the Air Fryer basket & air fry for 12 minutes.

788. MEATLOAF

Prep & Cook Time: 30 minutes | Servings: 4

INGREDIENTS

1 lb. of ground beef
1 egg, beaten
1 mushroom, sliced

1 tbsp. of thyme
1 small onion, chopped
3 tbsp. of breadcrumbs

Pepper

INSTRUCTIONS

1. Pre-heat the Air Fryer at 400°F.
2. Place all the ingredients into a large bowl & combine entirely.
3. Transfer the meatloaf mixture into the loaf pan & move it to the Air Fryer basket.
4. Cook for 25 minutes. Slice up before serving.

789. BEEF BURGERS

Prep & Cook Time: 65 minutes | Servings: 4

INGREDIENTS

10.5 oz. of beef, minced
1 onion, diced
1 tsp. of garlic, minced or pureed
1 tsp. of tomato, pureed

1 tsp. of mustard
1 tsp. of basil
1 tsp. of mixed herbs
Salt

Pepper
1 oz. of cheddar cheese
4 buns
Salad leaves

INSTRUCTIONS

1. Drizzle the Air Fryer with one tsp. of olive oil & allow it to warm up.
2. Place the diced onion in the Air Fryer & fry until they turn golden brown.
3. Mix in all of the seasoning & cook for 25 minutes at 390°F.
4. Lay 2 – 3 onion rings & pureed tomato on two of the buns. Place one slice of cheese & the layer of beef on top. Top with salad leaves & any other condiments you desire before closing off the sandwich with the other buns.
5. Serve with ketchup, cold drink & French fries.

790. BRUSSELS SPROUTS & TENDER BEEF CHUCK

Prep & Cook Time: 25 minutes + marinating time | Servings: 4

INGREDIENTS

1 lb. of beef chuck shoulder steak
2 tbsp. of vegetable oil
1 tbsp. of red wine vinegar
1 tsp. of fine sea salt

½ tsp. of ground black pepper
1 tsp. of smoked paprika
1 tsp. of onion powder
½ tsp. of garlic powder

½ lb. of Brussels sprouts, halved
½ tsp. of fennel seeds
1 tsp. of dried basil
1 tsp. of dried sage

INSTRUCTIONS

1. Massage the beef with the vegetable oil, wine vinegar, salt, black pepper, paprika, onion powder, & garlic powder, coating it well.
2. Allow to marinate for a minimum of 3 hours.
3. Air fry at 390°F for 10 minutes.
4. Put the prepared Brussels sprouts in the Air Fryer along with the fennel seeds, basil, & sage.
5. Lower the heat to 380°F & cook everything for another 5 minutes.
6. Pause the machine & give the contents a good stir. Cook for an additional 10 minutes.
7. Take out the beef & allow the vegetables too cook for a few more minutes if necessary or desired.
8. Serve everything together with the sauce of your choice.

791. SWEDISH MEATBALLS

Prep & Cook Time: 25 minutes | Servings: 8

INGREDIENTS

1 lb. ground beef
2 bread slices, crumbled
1 small onion, minced

½ tsp. of garlic salt
1 cup of tomato sauce
2 cups of pasta sauce

1 egg, beaten
2 carrots, shredded
Salt & pepper

INSTRUCTIONS

1. Pre-heat Air Fryer to 400°F.
2. In a bowl, combine the ground beef, egg, carrots, crumbled bread, onion, garlic salt, pepper & salt.
3. Divide the mixture into equal amounts & shape each one into a small meatball.
4. Put them in the Air Fryer basket & cook for 7 minutes.
5. Transfer the meatballs to an oven-safe dish & top with the tomato sauce.
6. Set the dish into the Air Fryer basket & allow to cook at 320°F for 5 more minutes. Serve hot.

792. GERMAN SCHNITZEL

Prep & Cook Time: 15 minutes | Servings: 4

INGREDIENTS

4 thin beef schnitzel
1 tbsp. of sesame seeds
2 tbsp. of paprika

3 tbsp. of olive oil
4 tbsp. of flour
2 eggs, beaten

1 cup of breadcrumbs
Salt & pepper

INSTRUCTIONS

1. Pre-heat the Air Fryer at 350°F.
2. Sprinkle the pepper & salt on the schnitzel.
3. In a shallow dish, combine the paprika, flour, & salt
4. In a second shallow dish, mix the breadcrumbs with the sesame seeds.
5. Place the beaten eggs in a bowl.
6. Coat the schnitzel in the flour mixture. Dip it into the egg before rolling it in the breadcrumbs.
7. Put the coated schnitzel in the Air Fryer basket & allow to cook for 12 minutes before serving hot.

793. STEAK TOTAL

Prep & Cook Time: 30 minutes | Servings: 4

INGREDIENTS

2 lb. of rib eye steak

1 tbsp. of olive oil

1 tbsp. of steak rub

INSTRUCTIONS

1. Set the Air Fryer to 400°F & allow to warm for 4 minutes.
2. Massage the olive oil & steak rub into both sides of the steak.
3. Put the steak in the Air Fryer's basket & cook for 14 minutes. Turn the steak over & cook on the other side for another 7 minutes.
4. Serve hot.

794. BETTY'S BEEF ROAST

Prep & Cook Time: 65 minutes | Servings: 6

INGREDIENTS

2 lb. of beef
1 tbsp. of olive oil
1 tsp. of dried rosemary

1 tsp. of dried thyme
½ tsp. of black pepper
½ tsp. of oregano

½ tsp. of garlic powder
1 tsp. of salt
1 tsp. of onion powder

INSTRUCTIONS

1. Preheat the Air Fryer to 330°F.
2. In a small bowl, mix together all of the spices.
3. Coat the beef with a brushing of olive oil.
4. Massage the spice mixture into the beef.
5. Transfer the meat to the Air Fryer & cook for 30 minutes. Turn it over & cook on the other side for another 25 minutes.

795. BEEF MEATLOAF

Prep & Cook Time: 30 minutes | Servings: 4

INGREDIENTS

¾ lb. of ground chuck

¼ lb. of ground pork sausage

1 cup of shallots, finely chopped

2 eggs, well beaten
3 tbsp. of plain milk
1 tbsp. of oyster sauce
1 tsp. of porcini mushrooms

½ tsp. of cumin powder
1 tsp. of garlic paste
1 tbsp. of fresh parsley
Seasoned salt & crushed red pepper

flakes to taste
1 cup of crushed saltines

INSTRUCTIONS
1. Mix together all of the ingredients in a large bowl, combining everything well.
2. Transfer to the Air Fryer baking dish & cook at 360°F for 25 minutes.
3. Serve hot.

796. STUFFED BELL PEPPER

Prep & Cook Time: 25 minutes | Servings: 4

INGREDIENTS

4 bell peppers, cut top of bell pepper
16 oz. of ground beef
⅔ cup of cheese, shredded
½ cup of rice, cooked

1 tsp. of basil, dried
½ tsp. of chili powder
1 tsp. of black pepper
1 tsp. of garlic salt

2 tsp. of Worcestershire sauce
8 oz. of tomato sauce
2 garlic cloves, minced
1 small onion, chopped

INSTRUCTIONS
1. Grease a frying pan with cooking spray & fry the onion & garlic over a medium heat.
2. Stir in the beef, basil, chili powder, black pepper, & garlic salt, combining everything well. Allow to cook until the beef is nicely browned, before taking the pan off the heat.
3. Add in half of the cheese, the rice, Worcestershire sauce, & tomato sauce & stir to combine.
4. Spoon equal amounts of the beef mixture into the four bell peppers, filling them entirely.
5. Pre-heat the Air Fryer at 400°F.
6. Spritz the Air Fryer basket with cooking spray.
7. Put the stuffed bell peppers in the basket & allow to cook for 11 minutes.
8. Add the remaining cheese on top of each bell pepper with remaining cheese & cook for a further 2 minutes. When the cheese is melted & the bell peppers are piping hot, serve immediately.

797. ASIAN BEEF BURGERS

Prep & Cook Time: 20 minutes | Servings: 4

INGREDIENTS

¾ lb. of lean ground beef
1 tbsp. of soy sauce
1 tsp. of Dijon mustard
Few dashes of liquid smoke

1 tsp. of shallot powder
1 clove of garlic, minced
½ tsp. of cumin powder
¼ cup of scallions, minced

⅓ tsp. of sea salt flakes
⅓ tsp. of peppercorns
1 tsp. of celery seeds
1 tsp. of parsley flakes

INSTRUCTIONS
1. Mix together all of the ingredients in a bowl using your hands, combining everything well.
2. Take four equal amounts of the mixture & mold each one into a patty.
3. Use the back of a spoon to create a shallow dip in the center of each patty. This will prevent them from puffing up during the cooking process.
4. Lightly coat all sides of the patties with cooking spray.
5. Place each one in the Air Fryer & cook for roughly 12 minutes at 360°F.
6. Test with a meat thermometer – the patties are ready once they have reached 160°F. Serve them on top of butter rolls with any sauces & toppings you desire.

798. BURGER PATTIES

Prep & Cook Time: 15 minutes | Servings: 6

INGREDIENTS

1 lb. of ground beef

6 cheddar cheese slices

Salt & pepper

INSTRUCTIONS
1. Pre-heat the Air Fryer to 350°F.
2. Sprinkle the salt & pepper on the ground beef.
3. Shape six equal portions of the ground beef into patties & put each one in the Air Fryer basket.
4. Air fry the patties for 10 minutes.
5. Top the patties with the cheese slices & air fry for one more minute.
6. Serve the patties on top of dinner rolls.

799. BEEF ROLLS

Prep & Cook Time: 30 minutes | Servings: 2

INGREDIENTS

2 lb. of beef flank steak
3 tsp. of pesto
1 tsp. of black pepper

6 slices of provolone cheese
3 oz. of roasted red bell peppers
¾ cup of baby spinach

1 tsp. of sea salt

INSTRUCTIONS
1. Spoon equal amounts of the pesto onto each flank steak & spread it across evenly.
2. Place the cheese, roasted red peppers & spinach on top of the meat, about three-quarters of the way down.
3. Roll the steak up, holding it in place with toothpicks. Sprinkle on the sea salt & pepper.
4. Place inside the Air Fryer & cook for 14 minutes at 400°F, turning halfway through the cooking time.
5. Allow the beef to rest for 10 minutes before slicing up & serving.

800. SPRING ROLLS

Prep & Cook Time: 35 minutes | Servings: 20

INGREDIENTS

⅓ cup of noodles
1 cup beef minced
2 tbsp. of cold water

1 packet spring roll sheets
1 tsp. of soy sauce
1 cup of fresh mix vegetables

3 garlic cloves, minced
1 small onion, diced
1 tbsp. of sesame oil

INSTRUCTIONS
1. Cook the noodle in hot water to soften them up, drain them & snip them to make them shorter.
2. In a frying pan over medium heat, cook the minced beef, soy sauce, mixed vegetables, garlic, & onion in a little oil until the beef minced is cooked through. Take the pan off the heat & throw in the noodles. Mix well to incorporate everything.
3. Unroll a spring roll sheet & lay it flat. Scatter the filling diagonally across it & roll it up, brushing the edges lightly with water to act as an adhesive. Repeat until you have used up all of the sheets & the filling.
4. Pre-heat the Air Fryer to 350°F.
5. Coat each spring roll with a light brushing of oil & transfer to the Air Fryer.
6. Cook for 8 minutes & serve hot.

801. CHEESY SCHNITZEL

Prep & Cook Time: 30 minutes | Servings: 1

INGREDIENTS

1 thin beef schnitzel
1 egg, beaten
½ cup of breadcrumbs

2 tbsp. of olive oil
3 tbsp. pasta sauce
¼ cup of parmesan cheese, grated

Salt & pepper

INSTRUCTIONS

1. Pre-heat the Air Fryer to 350°F.
2. In a shallow dish, combine the breadcrumbs, olive oil, pepper, & salt. In another shallow dish, put the beaten egg.
3. Cover the schnitzel in the egg before press it into the breadcrumb mixture & placing it in the Air Fryer basket. Cook for 15 minutes.
4. Pour the pasta sauce over the schnitzel & top with the grated cheese. Cook for an additional 5 minutes until the cheese melts. Serve hot.

802. BEEF SCHNITZEL

Prep & Cook Time: 30 minutes | Servings: 1

INGREDIENTS

1 egg
1 thin beef schnitzel

3 tbsp. of breadcrumbs
2 tbsp. of olive oil

1 parsley, roughly chopped
½ lemon, cut in wedges

INSTRUCTIONS:
1. Pre-heat your Air Fryer to the 360°F.
2. In a bowl combine the breadcrumbs & olive oil to form a loose, crumbly mixture.
3. Beat the egg with a whisk.
4. Coat the schnitzel first in the egg & then in the breadcrumbs, ensuring to cover it fully.
5. Place the schnitzel in the Air Fryer & cook for 12 – 14 minutes. Garnish the schnitzel with the lemon wedges & parsley before serving.

803. MIGHTY MEATBALLS

Prep & Cook Time: 20 minutes | Servings: 4

INGREDIENTS

1 egg
½ lb. of beef minced
½ cup of breadcrumbs

1 tbsp. of parsley, chopped
2 tbsp. of raisins
1 cup of onion, chopped & fried

½ tbsp. of pepper
½ tsp. of salt

INSTRUCTIONS
1. Place all of the ingredients in a bowl & combine well.
2. Use your hands to shape equal amounts of the mixture into small balls. Place each one in the Air Fryer basket.
3. Air fry the meatballs at 350°F for 15 minutes. Serve with the sauce of your choice.

804. BJORN'S BEEF STEAK

Prep & Cook Time: 15 minutes | Servings: 1

INGREDIENTS

1 steak, 1-inch thick
1 tbsp. of olive oil

Black pepper to taste
Sea salt to taste

INSTRUCTIONS
1. Place the baking tray inside the Air Fryer & pre-heat for about 5 minutes at 390°F.
2. Brush or spray both sides of the steak with the oil.
3. Season both sides with salt & pepper.
4. Take care when placing the steak in the baking tray & allow to cook for 3 minutes. Flip the meat over & cook for an additional 3 minutes.
5. Take it out of the Air Fryer & allow to sit for roughly 3 minutes before serving.

805. BEEF & BROCCOLI

Prep & Cook Time: 25 minutes | Servings: 4

INGREDIENTS

1 lb. of broccoli, cut into florets
¾ lb. of round steak, cut into strips
1 garlic clove, minced
1 tsp. of ginger, minced

1 tbsp. of olive oil
1 tsp. of cornstarch
1 tsp. of sugar
1 tsp. of soy sauce

⅓ cup of sherry wine
2 tsp. of sesame oil
⅓ cup oyster sauce

INSTRUCTIONS
1. In a bowl, combine the sugar, soy sauce, sherry wine, cornstarch, sesame oil, & oyster sauce.
2. Place the steak strips in the bowl, coat each one with the mixture & allow to marinate for 45 minutes.
3. Put the broccoli in the Air Fryer & lay the steak on top.
4. Top with the olive oil, garlic & ginger.
5. Cook at 350°F for 12 minutes. Serve hot with rice if desired.

806. BEEF & MUSHROOMS

Prep & Cook Time: 3 hours 15 minutes | Servings: 1

INGREDIENTS

6 oz. of beef
¼ onion, diced

½ cup of mushroom slices
2 tbsp. of favorite marinade

INSTRUCTIONS
1. Slice or cube the beef & put it in a bowl.
2. Cover the meat with the marinade, place a layer of aluminum foil or saran wrap over the bowl, & place the bowl in the refrigerator for 3 hours.
3. Put the meat in a baking dish along with the onion & mushrooms
4. Air Fry at 350°F for 10 minutes. Serve hot.

807. MAX'S MEATLOAF

Prep & Cook Time: 35 minutes | Servings: 4

INGREDIENTS

1 large onion, peeled & diced
2 kg. of minced beef
1 tsp. of Worcester sauce

3 tbsp. of tomato ketchup
1 tbsp. of basil
1 tbsp. of oregano

1 tbsp. of mixed herbs
1 tbsp. of breadcrumbs
Salt & pepper

INSTRUCTIONS
1. In a large bowl, combine the mince with the herbs, Worcester sauce, onion & tomato ketchup, incorporating every component well.
2. Pour in the breadcrumbs & give it another stir.
3. Transfer the mixture to a small dish & cook for 25 minutes in the Air Fryer at 350°F.

808. PARMESAN ARTICHOKES

Prep & Cook Time: 35 minutes | Servings: 4

INGREDIENTS

2 medium artichokes, trimmed &
quartered, with the centers removed

2 tbsp. of coconut oil, melted
1 egg, beaten

½ cup of parmesan cheese, grated
¼ cup blanched, finely ground flour

INSTRUCTIONS
1. Place the artichokes in a bowl with the coconut oil & toss to coat, then dip the artichokes into a bowl of beaten egg.
2. In a separate bowl, mix together the parmesan cheese & the flour. Combine with the pieces of artichoke, making sure to coat each piece well. Transfer the artichoke to the Air Fryer.
3. Cook at 400°F for ten minutes, shaking occasionally throughout the cooking time. Serve hot.

809. CHEESE PIZZA WITH BROCCOLI CRUST

Prep & Cook Time: 30 minutes | Servings: 1

INGREDIENTS

3 cups of broccoli rice, steamed
½ cup of parmesan cheese, grated

1 egg
3 tbsp. of Alfredo sauce

½ cup of parmesan cheese, grated

INSTRUCTIONS

1. Drain the broccoli rice & combine with the parmesan cheese & egg in a bowl, mixing well.
2. Cut a piece of parchment paper roughly the size of the base of the Air Fryer's basket. Spoon four equal-sized amounts of the broccoli mixture onto the paper & press each portion into the shape of a pizza crust. You may have to complete this part in two batches. Transfer the parchment to the Air Fryer.
3. Cook at 370°F for five minutes. When the crust is firm, flip it over & cook for an additional two minutes.
4. Add the Alfredo sauce & mozzarella cheese on top of the crusts & cook for an additional seven minutes. The crusts are ready when the sauce & cheese have melted. Serve hot.

810. STUFFED EGGPLANT

Prep & Cook Time: 35 minutes | Servings: 2

INGREDIENTS

large eggplant
¼ medium yellow onion, diced

2 tbsp. of red bell pepper, diced
1 cup of spinach

¼ cup of artichoke hearts, chopped

INSTRUCTIONS

1. Cut the eggplant lengthwise into slices & spoon out the flesh, leaving a shell about a half-inch thick. Chop it up & set aside.
2. Set a skillet over a medium heat & spritz with cooking spray. Cook the onions for about three to five minutes to soften. Then add the pepper, spinach, artichokes, & the flesh of eggplant. Fry for a further five minutes, then remove from the heat.
3. Scoop this mixture in equal parts into the eggplant shells & place each one in the Air Fryer.
4. Cook for twenty minutes at 320°F until the eggplant shells are soft. Serve warm.

811. BROCCOLI SALAD

Prep & Cook Time: 15 minutes | Servings: 2

INGREDIENTS

3 cups fresh broccoli florets
2 tbsp. of coconut oil, melted

¼ cup of sliced spinach
½ medium lemon, juiced

INSTRUCTIONS

1. Take a six-inch baking dish & fill with the broccoli florets. Pour the melted coconut oil over the broccoli & add in the sliced spinach. Toss together. Put the dish in the Air Fryer.
2. Cook at 380°F for seven minutes, stirring at the halfway point.
3. Place the broccoli in a bowl & drizzle the lemon juice over it.

812. ROASTED CAULIFLOWER

Prep & Cook Time: 20 minutes | Servings: 2

INGREDIENTS

1 medium head of cauliflower
2 tbsp. of salted butter, melted

1 medium lemon
1 tsp. of dried parsley

½ tsp. of garlic powder

INSTRUCTIONS

1. Having removed the leaves from the cauliflower head, brush it with the melted butter. Grate the rind of the lemon over it & then drizzle some juice. Finally add the parsley & garlic powder on top.
2. Transfer the cauliflower to the basket of the Air Fryer.
3. Cook for fifteen minutes at 350°F, checking regularly to ensure it doesn't overcook. The cauliflower is ready when it is hot & fork tender.
4. Take care when removing it from the Air Fryer, cut up & serve.

813. MUSHROOM LOAF

Prep & Cook Time: 20 minutes | Servings: 2

INGREDIENTS

2 cups of mushrooms, chopped
½ cups of cheddar cheese, shredded

¾ cup of flour
2 tbsp. of butter, melted

2 eggs

INSTRUCTIONS

1. In a food processor, pulse together the mushrooms, cheese, flour, melted butter, & eggs, along with some salt & pepper if desired, until a uniform consistency is achieved.
2. Transfer into a silicone loaf pan, spreading & levelling with a palette knife.
3. Pre-heat the Air Fryer at 375°F & put the rack inside.
4. Set the loaf pan on the rack & cook for fifteen minutes.
5. Take care when removing the pan from the Air Fryer & leave it to cool. Then slice & serve.

814. GREEN BEAN CASSEROLE

Prep & Cook Time: 10 minutes | Servings: 2

INGREDIENTS

1 tbsp. of butter, melted
1 cup of green beans

6 oz. of cheddar cheese, shredded
7 oz. of parmesan cheese, shredded

¼ cup of heavy cream

INSTRUCTIONS

1. Pre-heat your Air Fryer at 400°F.
2. Take a baking dish small enough to fit inside the Air Fryer & cover the bottom with melted butter. Throw in the green beans, cheddar cheese, & any seasoning as desired, then give it a stir. Add the parmesan on top & finally the heavy cream.
3. Cook in the Air Fryer for six minutes. Allow to cool before serving.

815. CABBAGE STEAKS

Prep & Cook Time: 5 minutes | Servings: 2

INGREDIENTS

Small head of cabbage
1 tsp. of butter, butter

1 tsp. of paprika
1 tsp. of olive oil

INSTRUCTIONS

1. Halve the cabbage.
2. In a bowl, mix together the melted butter, paprika, & olive oil. Massage into the cabbage slices, making sure to coat it well. Season as desired with salt & pepper or any other seasonings of your choosing.
3. Pre-heat the Air Fryer at 400°F & set the rack inside.
4. Put the cabbage in the Air Fryer & cook for three minutes. Flip it & cook on the other side for another two minutes. Enjoy!

816. ZUCCHINI GRATIN

Prep & Cook Time: 15 minutes | Servings: 2

INGREDIENTS

| 5 oz. of parmesan cheese, shredded | 1 tbsp. of dried parsley | 1 tsp. of butter, melted |
| 1 tbsp. of coconut flour | 2 zucchinis | |

INSTRUCTIONS
1. Mix the parmesan & coconut flour together in a bowl, seasoning with parsley to taste.
2. Cut the zucchini in half lengthwise & chop the halves into four slices.
3. Pre-heat the Air Fryer at 400°F.
4. Pour the melted butter over the zucchini & then dip the zucchini into the parmesan-flour mixture, coating it all over. Cook the zucchini in the Air Fryer for thirteen minutes.

817. CHEESY KALE
Prep & Cook Time: 15 minutes | Servings: 2

INGREDIENTS
| 1 lb. of kale | 1 onion, diced | 1 cup of heavy cream |
| 8 oz. of parmesan cheese, shredded | 1 tsp. of butter | |

INSTRUCTIONS
1. Dice up the kale, discarding any hard stems. In a baking dish small enough to fit inside the Air Fryer, combine the kale with the parmesan, onion, butter & cream.
2. Pre-heat the Air Fryer at 250°F.
3. Set the baking dish in the Air Fryer & cook for twelve minutes. Make sure to give it a good stir before serving.

818. SPAGHETTI SQUASH
Prep & Cook Time: 45 minutes | Servings: 2

INGREDIENTS
| spaghetti squash | Salt & pepper | 1 tsp. of butter |
| 1 tsp. of olive oil | 4 tbsp. of heavy cream | |

INSTRUCTIONS
1. Pre-heat your Air Fryer at 360°F.
2. Cut & de-seed the spaghetti squash. Brush with the olive oil & season with salt & pepper to taste.
3. Put the squash inside the Air Fryer, placing it cut-side-down. Cook for thirty minutes. Halfway through cooking, fluff the spaghetti inside the squash with a fork.
4. When the squash is ready, fluff the spaghetti some more, then pour some heavy cream & butter over it & give it a good stir. Serve with the tomato sauce of your choice.

819. CHIPOTLE JICAMA HASH
Prep & Cook Time: 15 minutes | Servings: 2

INGREDIENTS
| 4 slices of bacon, chopped | 4 oz. of purple onion, chopped | seeded & chopped |
| 12 oz. of jicama, peeled & diced | 1 oz. of green bell pepper (or poblano), | 4 tbsp. of chipotle mayonnaise |

INSTRUCTIONS
1. Inside your Air Fryer, fry the bacon at 400°F for 10 minutes.
2. Remove & place on a towel to drain the grease.
3. Use the remaining grease to fry the onions & jicama until brown.
4. When ready, add the bell pepper & cook the hash until tender.
5. Transfer the hash onto two plates & serve each plate with 4 tbsp. of Chipotle mayonnaise.

820. FRIED QUESO BLANCO
Prep & Cook Time: 170 minutes | Servings: 4

INGREDIENTS
| 5 oz. of queso blanco | 3 oz. of cheese | 1 pinch of red pepper flakes |
| 1 ½ tbsp. of olive oil | 2 oz. of olives | |

INSTRUCTIONS
1. Cube some cheese & freeze it for 1-2 hours.
2. Pour the oil inside a dish and place the dish inside your Air Fryer.
3. Add the cheese cubes. Close the lid.
4. Cook at 400°F for 20 minutes, flipping regularly.
5. While flipping, fold the cheese into itself to form crispy layers.
6. Use a spatula to roll it into a block.
7. Remove the dish from the Air Fryer, allow it to cool, cut it into small cubes, & serve.

821. SPINACH WITH BACON & SHALLOTS
Prep & Cook Time: 30 minutes | Servings: 4

INGREDIENTS
| 16 oz. of raw spinach | ½ cup of chopped shallot | 2 tbsp. of butter |
| ½ cup of chopped white onion | ½ lb. of raw bacon slices | |

INSTRUCTIONS
1. Slice the bacon strips into small narrow pieces.
2. Inside your Air Fryer, heat the butter & add the chopped onion, shallots & bacon.
3. Cook at 350°F for 15-20 minutes or until the onions start to caramelize & the bacon is cooked.
4. Add the spinach & sauté on a medium heat. Stir frequently to ensure the leaves touch the skillet while cooking.
5. Serve!

822. BACON-WRAPPED SAUSAGE SKEWERS
Prep & Cook Time: 8 minutes | Servings: 2

INGREDIENTS
| 5 Italian chicken sausages | 10 slices of bacon | |

INSTRUCTIONS
1. Preheat your Air Fryer to 370°F/190°C.
2. Cut the sausage into four pieces.
3. Slice the bacon in half.
4. Wrap the bacon over the sausage.
5. Skewer the sausage.
6. Fry for 4-5 minutes until browned.

823. ROASTED BRUSSELS SPROUTS & BACON
Prep & Cook Time: 45 minutes | Servings: 2

INGREDIENTS
| 24 oz. of brussels sprouts | ¼ cup of bacon grease | Pepper |
| ¼ cup of fish sauce | 6 strips of bacon | |

INSTRUCTIONS
1. De-stem & quarter the brussels sprouts.
2. Mix them with the bacon grease & fish sauce.
3. Slice the bacon into small strips & cook.

4. Add the bacon & pepper to the sprouts.
5. Spread onto a greased pan & cook inside your Air Fryer at 450°F/230°C for 35 minutes.
6. Stir every 5 minute or so.
7. Broil for a few more minutes & serve.

824. HOT HAM & CHEESE ROLLS
Prep & Cook Time: 5 minutes | Servings: 4

INGREDIENTS

16 slices of ham

1 packet of chive & onion cream cheese (8 oz.)

16 slices thin Swiss cheese

INSTRUCTIONS
1. Place the ham slices inside your Air Fryer. Flash fry at 400°F for 3 minutes.
2. Remove and dry the slices with a paper towel.
3. Thinly spread 2 teaspoons of Swiss cheese over each slice of ham.
4. On the clean section of ham, add a half inch slice of cheese.
5. On the cheese side, fold the ham over the cheese & roll it up. Serve!

825. HILLBILLY CHEESE SURPRISE
Prep & Cook Time: 40 minutes | Servings: 6

INGREDIENTS

4 cups of broccoli florets
¼ cup of ranch dressing

½ cup of sharp cheddar cheese, shredded

¼ cup of heavy whipping cream
Kosher salt & pepper to taste

INSTRUCTIONS
1. Preheat your Air Fryer to 375°F/190°C.
2. In a bowl, combine all of the ingredients until the broccoli is well-covered.
3. In a casserole dish, spread out the broccoli mixture.
4. Bake for 30 minutes.
5. Take out of your Air Fryer & mix.
6. If the florets are not tender, bake for another 5 minutes until tender.
7. Serve.

826. PARMESAN & GARLIC CAULIFLOWER
Prep & Cook Time: 40 minutes | Servings: 4

INGREDIENTS

¾ cup of cauliflower florets
2 tbsp. of butter

1 clove garlic, sliced thinly
2 tbsp. of shredded parmesan

Salt

INSTRUCTIONS
1. Preheat your Air Fryer to 350°F/175°C.
2. On a low heat, melt the butter with the garlic for 5-10 minutes.
3. Strain the garlic in a sieve.
4. Add the cauliflower, parmesan & salt.
5. Bake for 20 minutes or until golden.

827. JALAPEÑO GUACAMOLE
Prep & Cook Time: 30 minutes | Servings: 4

INGREDIENTS

2 avocados, ripe
¼ red onion

1 jalapeño
1 tbsp. of fresh lime juice

Sea salt

INSTRUCTIONS
1. Spoon the avocado innings into your Air Fryer. Cook at 350°F/175°C for 5 minutes.
2. Dice the jalapeño & onion.
3. Mash the avocado to the desired consistency.
4. Add in the onion, jalapeño & lime juice.
5. Sprinkle with salt

828. GREEN BEANS & SPINACH
Prep & Cook Time: 15 minutes | Servings: 4

INGREDIENTS

1 lb. of fresh green beans, trimmed
2 tbsp. of butter

¼ cup of sliced spinach
2 tsp. of lemon pepper

INSTRUCTIONS
1. Cook the green beans in your Air Fryer at 350°F/175°C for 8 minutes, until tender, then drain.
2. On a medium heat, melt the butter in a skillet.
3. Sauté the spinach until browned.
4. Sprinkle with salt & pepper.
5. Mix in the green beans.

829. SUGAR SNAP BACON
Prep & Cook Time: 25 minutes | Servings: 4

INGREDIENTS

3 cups of sugar snap peas
½ tbsp. of lemon juice

2 tbsp. of bacon fat
2 tsp. of garlic

½ tsp. of red pepper flakes

INSTRUCTIONS
1. Inside your Air Fryer, cook the bacon fat at 400°F for 15 minutes, until it begins to smoke.
2. Add the garlic & cook for 2 minutes.
3. Add the sugar peas & lemon juice.
4. Cook for 2-3 minutes.
5. Remove & sprinkle with red pepper flakes & lemon zest. Serve!
6. Serve!

830. FLAX CHEESE CHIPS
Prep & Cook Time: 20 minutes | Servings: 2

INGREDIENTS

1 ½ cup of cheddar cheese

4 tbsp. of ground flaxseed meal

Seasonings of your choice

INSTRUCTIONS
1. Preheat your Air Fryer to 425°F/220°C.
2. Spoon 2 tbsp. of cheddar cheese into a mound, onto a non-stick pad.
3. Spread out a pinch of flax seed on each chip.
4. Season & bake for 10-15 minutes.

831. COUNTRY STYLE CHARD

Prep & Cook Time: 30 minutes | Servings: 2

INGREDIENTS

4 slices of bacon, chopped
2 tbsp. of butter

2 tbsp. of fresh lemon juice
½ tsp. of garlic paste

1 bunch of Swiss chard, stems removed,
leaves cut into 1-inch pieces

INSTRUCTIONS

1. Cook the bacon inside your Air Fryer at 400°F for 20 minutes, until the fat begins to brown.
2. Melt the butter in the skillet & add the lemon juice & garlic paste.
3. Add the chard leaves & cook until they begin to wilt.
4. Cover & turn up the heat to high.
5. Cook for 3 minutes.
6. Plate the bacon and add the chard. Sprinkle with salt & serve.

832. BAKED TORTILLAS

Prep & Cook Time: 30 minutes | Servings: 4

INGREDIENTS

1 large head of cauliflower divided into
florets.
4 large eggs

2 garlic cloves (minced)
1 ½ tsp. of herbs (whatever your favorite
is - basil, oregano, thyme)

½ tsp. of salt

INSTRUCTIONS

1. Preheat your Air Fryer to 375°F/190°C.
2. Put parchment paper on two baking sheets.
3. In a food processor, break down the cauliflower into rice.
4. Add ¼ cup of water & the riced cauliflower to a saucepan.
5. Cook on a medium high heat until tender for 10 minutes. Drain.
6. Dry with a clean kitchen towel.
7. Mix the cauliflower, eggs, garlic, herbs & salt.
8. Make 4 thin circles on the parchment paper.
9. Bake for 20 minutes, until dry.

833. HOMEMADE MAYONNAISE

Prep & Cook Time: 30 minutes | Servings: 4

INGREDIENTS

1 large egg
Juice from 1 lemon.

1 tsp. of dry mustard
½ tsp. of black pepper

1 cup avocado oil

INSTRUCTIONS

1. Combine the egg & lemon juice inside a dish and let sit for 10 minutes.
2. Add the dry mustard, pepper, & avocado oil.
3. Place the dish inside your Air Fryer and flash fry at 400°F for 2 minutes.
4. Remove and whisk the warm sauce for 30 seconds.
5. Transfer to a sealed container & store in your refrigerator overnight. Serve!

834. HOLLANDAISE SAUCE

Prep & Cook Time: 3 minutes | Servings: 8

INGREDIENTS

8 large egg yolks
½ tsp. of salt

2 tbsp. of fresh lemon juice
1 cup of butter

INSTRUCTIONS

1. Combine the egg yolks, salt, & lemon juice inside a dish until smooth.
2. Place the dish inside your Air Fryer and cook at 400°F for 2 minutes.
3. Serve!

835. GRANNY'S GREEN BEANS

Prep & Cook Time: 10 minutes | Servings: 4

INGREDIENTS

1 lb. of green beans, trimmed
1 cup of butter

2 cloves garlic, minced
1 cup of toasted pine nuts

INSTRUCTIONS

1. Add the green beans to a dish and place it inside your Air Fryer & bake until tender at 350°F for 5 minutes.
2. Heat the butter in a large skillet over a high heat. Add the garlic & pine nuts & sauté for 2 minutes or until the pine nuts are lightly browned.
3. Transfer the green beans to the skillet & turn until coated.
4. Serve!

836. MINI PEPPER POPPERS

Prep & Cook Time: 10 minutes | Servings: 4

INGREDIENTS

8 mini sweet peppers
¼ cup of pepper jack cheese, shredded

4 slices of sugar-free bacon, cooked &
crumbled

4 oz. of full-fat cream cheese, softened

INSTRUCTIONS

1. Prepare the peppers by cutting off the tops & halving them lengthwise. Then take out the membrane & the seeds.
2. In a small bowl, combine the pepper jack cheese, bacon, & cream cheese, making sure to incorporate everything well
3. Spoon equal-sized portions of the cheese-bacon mixture into each of the pepper halves.
4. Place the peppers inside your Air Fryer & cook for eight minutes at 400°F. Take care when removing them from the Air Fryer & enjoy warm.

837. BACON-WRAPPED JALAPENO POPPER

Prep & Cook Time: 20 minutes | Servings: 4

INGREDIENTS

6 jalapenos
⅓ cup medium cheddar cheese

¼ tsp. of garlic powder
3 oz. of full-fat cream cheese

12 slices of sugar-free bacon

INSTRUCTIONS

1. Prepare the jalapenos by slicing off the tops & halving each one lengthwise. Take care when removing the seeds & membranes, wearing gloves if necessary.
2. In a microwavable bowl, combine the cheddar cheese, garlic powder, & cream cheese. Microwave for half a minute & mix again, before spooning equal parts of this mixture into each of the jalapeno halves.
3. Take a slice of bacon & wrap it around one of the jalapeno halves, covering it entirely. Place it in the basket of your Air Fryer. Repeat with the rest of the bacon & jalapenos.
4. Cook at 400°F for twelve minutes, flipping the peppers halfway through in order to ensure the bacon gets crispy. Make sure not to let any of the contents spill out of the jalapeno halves when turning them.
5. Eat the peppers hot or at room temperature.

838. CHEESY BACON BREAD

Prep & Cook Time: 25 minutes | Servings: 2

INGREDIENTS

4 slices of sugar-free bacon, cooked & chopped

2 eggs
¼ cup of pickled jalapenos, chopped

¼ cup of parmesan cheese, grated
2 cups of mozzarella cheese, shredded

INSTRUCTIONS

1. Add all of the ingredients together in a bowl & mix together.
2. Cut out a piece of parchment paper that will fit the base of your Air Fryer's basket. Place it inside the Air Fryer
3. With slightly wet hands, roll the mixture into a circle. You may have to form two circles to cook in separate batches, depending on the size of your Air Fryer.
4. Place the circle on top of the parchment paper inside your Air Fryer. Cook at 320°F for ten minutes.
5. Turn the bread over & cook for another five minutes.
6. The bread is ready when it is golden & cooked all the way through. Slice & serve warm.

839. MOZZARELLA STICKS

Prep & Cook Time: 60 minutes | Servings: 4

INGREDIENTS

6 x 1-oz. of mozzarella string cheese sticks

1 tsp. of dried parsley
½ oz. of flour

½ cup of parmesan cheese, grated
2 eggs

INSTRUCTIONS

1. Halve the mozzarella sticks & freeze for forty-five minutes. Optionally you can leave them longer & place in a Ziploc bag to prevent them from becoming freezer burned.
2. In a small bowl, combine the dried parsley, flour & parmesan cheese.
3. In a separate bowl, beat the eggs with a fork.
4. Take a frozen mozzarella stick & dip it into the eggs, then into the flour mixture, making sure to coat it all over. Proceed with the rest of the cheese sticks, placing each coated stick in the basket of your Air Fryer.
5. Cook at 400°F for ten minutes, until they are golden brown.
6. Serve hot, with some homemade marinara sauce if desired.

840. BEEF JERKY

Prep & Cook Time: 250 minutes | Servings: 4

INGREDIENTS

¼ tsp. of garlic powder
¼ tsp. of onion powder

¼ cup of soy sauce
2 tsp. of Worcestershire sauce

1 lb. of flat iron steak, thinly sliced

INSTRUCTIONS

1. In a bowl, combine the garlic powder, onion powder, soy sauce, & Worcestershire sauce. Marinade the beef slices with the mixture in an airtight bag, shaking it well to ensure the beef is well-coated. Leave to marinate for at least two hours
2. Place the meat in the basket of your Air Fryer, making sure it is evenly spaced. Cook the beef slices in more than one batch if necessary.
3. Cook for four hours at 160°F.
4. Allow to cool before serving. You can keep the jerky in an airtight container for up to a week if you can resist it that long.

841. BACON-WRAPPED BRIE

Prep & Cook Time: 15 minutes | Servings: 1

INGREDIENTS

4 slices of sugar-free bacon

8 oz. of brie cheese

INSTRUCTIONS

1. On a cutting board, lay out the slices of bacon across each other in a star shape (two Xs overlaid). Then place the entire round of brie in the center of this star.
2. Lift each slice of bacon to wrap it over the brie & use toothpicks to hold everything in place. Cut up a piece of parchment paper to fit in your Air Fryer's basket & place it inside, followed by the wrapped brie, setting it in the center of the sheet of parchment.
3. Cook at 400°F for seven minutes. Turn the brie over & cook for a further three minutes.
4. It is ready once the bacon is crisp, & cheese is melted on the inside.
5. Slice up the brie & enjoy hot.

842. CRUST-LESS MEATY PIZZA

Prep & Cook Time: 15 minutes | Servings: 1

INGREDIENTS

½ cup of mozzarella cheese, shredded
2 slices of sugar-free bacon, cooked & crumbled

¼ cup ground sausage, cooked
7 slices of pepperoni

1 tbsp. of parmesan cheese, grated

INSTRUCTIONS

1. Spread the mozzarella across the bottom of a six-inch cake pan. Throw on the bacon, sausage, & pepperoni, then add a sprinkle of the parmesan cheese on top. Place the pan inside your Air Fryer.
2. Cook at 400°F for five minutes. The cheese is ready once brown in color & bubbly. Take care when removing the pan from the Air Fryer & serve.

843. RADISH CHIPS

Prep & Cook Time: 15 minutes | Servings: 1

INGREDIENTS

2 cups of water
1 lb. of radishes

½ tsp. of garlic powder
¼ tsp. of onion powder

2 tbsp. of coconut oil, melted

INSTRUCTIONS

1. Boil the water over the stove.
2. In the meantime, prepare the radish chips. Slice off the tops & bottoms &, using a mandolin, shave into thin slices of equal size. Alternatively, this step can be completed using your food processor if it has a slicing blade.
3. Put the radish chips in the pot of boiling water & allow to cook for five minutes, ensuring they become translucent. Take care when removing from the water & place them on a paper towel to dry.
4. Add the radish chips, garlic powder, onion powder, & melted coconut oil into a bowl & toss to coat. Transfer the chips to your Air Fryer.
5. Cook at 320°F for five minutes, occasionally giving the basket a good shake to ensure even cooking. The chips are done when cooked through & crispy. Serve immediately.

844. PARMESAN ZUCCHINI CHIPS

Prep & Cook Time: 10 minutes | Servings: 1

INGREDIENTS

2 medium zucchinis
1 oz. of flour

½ cup of parmesan cheese, grated
1 egg

INSTRUCTIONS

1. Cut the zucchini into slices about a quarter-inch thick. Lay on a paper towel to dry.
2. In a bowl, combine the flour & the grated parmesan.
3. In a separate bowl, beat the egg with a fork.
4. Take a zucchini slice & dip it into the egg, then into the parmesan mixture, making sure to coat it evenly. Repeat with the rest of the slices. Lay them in the basket of your Air Fryer, taking care not to overlap. This step may need to be completed in more than one batch.
5. Cook at 320°F for five minutes. Turn the chips over & allow to cook for another five minutes.
6. Allow to cool to achieve a crispier texture or serve warm. Enjoy!

845. BUFFALO CAULIFLOWER

Prep & Cook Time: 10 minutes | Servings: 1

INGREDIENTS

½ packet of dry ranch seasoning
2 tbsp. of salted butter, melted

Cauliflower florets
¼ cup of buffalo sauce

INSTRUCTIONS

1. In a bowl, combine the dry ranch seasoning & butter. Toss with the cauliflower florets to coat & transfer them to the Air Fryer.
2. Cook at 400°F for five minutes, shaking the basket occasionally to ensure the florets cook evenly.
3. Remove the cauliflower from the Air Fryer, pour the buffalo sauce over it, & enjoy.

846. ZESTY CILANTRO ROASTED CAULIFLOWER

Prep & Cook Time: 10 minutes | Servings: 2

INGREDIENTS

2 cups of cauliflower florets, chopped
2 tbsp. of coconut oil, melted

2 ½ tsp. of taco seasoning mix
1 medium lime

2 tbsp. of cilantro, chopped

INSTRUCTIONS

1. Mix the cauliflower with the melted coconut oil & the taco seasoning, ensuring to coat the florets all over.
2. Air bake at 350°F for seven minutes, shaking the basket a few times through the cooking time. Then transfer the cauliflower to a bowl.
3. Squeeze the lime juice over the cauliflower & season with the cilantro. Toss once more to coat & enjoy.

847. FRIED GREEN TOMATOES

Prep & Cook Time: 10 minutes | Servings: 2

INGREDIENTS

2 medium green tomatoes
1 egg

¼ cup of blanched finely ground flour
⅓ cup of parmesan cheese, grated

INSTRUCTIONS

1. Slice the tomatoes about a half-inch thick.
2. Crack the egg into a bowl & beat it with a whisk. In a separate bowl, mix together the flour & parmesan cheese.
3. Dredge the tomato slices in egg, then dip them into the flour-cheese mixture to coat. Place each slice into the Air Fryer basket. They may need to be cooked in multiple batches.
4. Cook at 400°F for seven minutes, turning them halfway through the cooking time, & then serve warm.

848. AVOCADO STICKS

Prep & Cook Time: 10 minutes | Servings: 2

INGREDIENTS

2 avocados
4 egg yolks

1 ½ tbsp. of water
Salt & pepper

1 cup of flour
1 cup herbed butter

INSTRUCTIONS

1. Halve the avocados, twist to open, & take out the pits. Cut each half into three equal slices.
2. In a bowl, combine the egg yolks & water. Season with salt & pepper to taste & whisk together.
3. Pour the flour into a shallow bowl.
4. Coat each slice of avocado in the flour, then in the egg, before dipping it in the flour again. Ensure the flour coats the avocado well & firmly.
5. Pre-heat the Air Fryer at 400°F. When it is warm, put the avocados inside & cook for eight minutes.
6. Take care when removing the avocados from the Air Fryer & enjoy with a side of the herbed butter.

849. CHEESY CAULIFLOWER BITES

Prep & Cook Time: 20 minutes | Servings: 3

INGREDIENTS

2 cup of cauliflower florets
¾ cup of cheddar cheese, shredded

½ cup of onion, chopped
1 tsp. of seasoning salt

2 tbsp. of butter, melted
2 cloves garlic, minced

INSTRUCTIONS

1. Pulse the cauliflower florets in the food processor until they become crumbly. Use a cheesecloth to remove all the moisture from the cauliflower.
2. In a bowl, combine the cauliflower with the cheese, onion, seasoning salt, & melted butter. With your hands, roll the mixture into balls.
3. Pre-heat the Air Fryer at 400°F.
4. Fry the balls for fourteen minutes, leaving them in the Air Fryer for an additional two minutes if you like them browner. Serve hot.

850. BRUSSELS SPROUTS WITH CHEESE SAUCE

Prep & Cook Time: 10 minutes | Servings: 2

INGREDIENTS

¾ cups of Brussels sprouts
1 tbsp. of extra virgin olive oil

¼ tsp. of salt
¼ cup of mozzarella cheese, shredded

INSTRUCTIONS

1. Halve the Brussels sprouts & drizzle with the olive oil. Season with salt & toss to coat.
2. Pre-heat your Air Fryer at 375°F. When warm, transfer the Brussels sprouts inside & add the shredded mozzarella on top.
3. Cook for five minutes, serving when the cheese is melted.

851. VEGETABLE MIX

Prep & Cook Time: 45 minutes | Servings: 4

INGREDIENTS

3.5 oz. of radish
½ tsp. of parsley
3.5 oz. of celeriac
1 yellow carrot

1 orange carrot
1 red onion
3.5 oz. of pumpkin
3.5 oz. of parsnips

Salt
Epaulette pepper to taste
1 tbsp. of olive oil
4 cloves garlic, unpeeled

INSTRUCTIONS

1. Peel & slice up all the vegetables into 2- to 3-cm pieces.
2. Pre-heat your Air Fryer to 390°F.
3. Pour in the oil & allow it to warm before placing the vegetables in the Air Fryer, followed by the garlic, salt & pepper.
4. Roast for 18 – 20 minutes.
5. Top with parsley & serve hot with rice if desired.

852. POTATO CHIPS

Prep & Cook Time: 45 minutes | Servings: 4

INGREDIENTS

2 large potatoes, peel & sliced
1 tbsp. of rosemary

3.5 oz. of sour cream
¼ tsp. of salt

INSTRUCTIONS

1. Place the potato slices in water & allow to absorb for 30 minutes.
2. Drain the potato slices & transfer to a large bowl. Toss with the rosemary, sour cream, & salt.
3. Pre-heat the Air Fryer to 320°F
4. Put the coated potato slices in the Air Fryer's basket & cook for 35 minutes. Serve hot.

853. BRUSSELS SPROUTS

Prep & Cook Time: 15 minutes | Servings: 2

INGREDIENTS

2 cups of Brussels sprouts, sliced in half
1 tbsp. of balsamic vinegar

1 tbsp. of olive oil
¼ tsp. of salt

INSTRUCTIONS

1. Toss all of the ingredients together in a bowl, coating the Brussels sprouts well.
2. Place the sprouts in the Air Fryer basket & air fry at 400°F for 10 minutes, shaking the basket at the halfway point.

854. GARLIC POTATOES

Prep & Cook Time: 40 minutes | Servings: 4

INGREDIENTS

1 lb. of russet baking potatoes
1 tbsp. of garlic powder

1 tbsp. of freshly chopped parsley
½ tsp. of salt

¼ tsp. of black pepper
1 – 2 tbsp. of olive oil

INSTRUCTIONS

1. Wash the potatoes & pat them dry with clean paper towels.
2. Pierce each potato several times with a fork.
3. Place the potatoes in a large bowl & season with the garlic powder, salt & pepper.
4. Pour over the olive oil & mix well.
5. Pre-heat the Air Fryer to 360°F.
6. Place the potatoes in the Air Fryer & cook for about 30 minutes, shaking the basket a few times throughout the cooking time.
7. Garnish the potatoes with the chopped parsley & serve with butter, sour cream or another dipping sauce if desired.

855. ZUCCHINI ROLLS

Prep & Cook Time: 15 minutes | Servings: 2 – 4

INGREDIENTS

3 zucchinis, sliced thinly lengthwise with a mandolin or very sharp knife

1 tbsp. of olive oil
1 cup goat cheese

¼ tsp. of black pepper

INSTRUCTIONS

1. Preheat your Air Fryer to 390°F.
2. Coat each zucchini strip with a light brushing of olive oil.
3. Combine the sea salt, black pepper & goat cheese.
4. Scoop a small, equal amount of the goat cheese onto the center of each strip of zucchini. Roll up the strips & secure with a toothpick.
5. Transfer to the Air Fryer & cook for 5 minutes until the cheese is warm & the zucchini slightly crispy. If desired, add some tomato sauce on top.

856. ASPARAGUS

Prep & Cook Time: 15 minutes | Servings: 4

INGREDIENTS

10 asparagus spears, woody end cut off
1 clove garlic, minced

4 tbsp. of olive oil
Pepper

Salt

INSTRUCTIONS

1. Set the Air Fryer to 400°F & allow to heat for 5 minutes.
2. In a bowl, combine the garlic & oil.
3. Cover the asparagus with this mixture & put it in the Air Fryer basket. Sprinkle over some pepper & salt.
4. Cook for 10 minutes & serve hot.

857. ZUCCHINI CHIPS

Prep & Cook Time: 30 minutes | Servings: 2

INGREDIENTS

3 medium zucchinis, sliced
1 tsp. of parsley, chopped

3 tbsp. of parmesan cheese, grated
Pepper

Salt

INSTRUCTIONS

1. Pre-heat the Air Fryer to 425°F.
2. Put the sliced zucchini on a sheet of baking paper & spritz with cooking spray.
3. Combine the cheese, pepper, parsley, & salt. Use this mixture to sprinkle over the zucchini.
4. Transfer to the Air Fryer & cook for 25 minutes, ensuring the zucchini slices have crisped up nicely before serving.

858. SWEET POTATO WEDGES

Prep & Cook Time: 25 minutes | Servings: 2

INGREDIENTS

2 large, sweet potatoes, cut into wedges
1 tbsp. of olive oil
1 tsp. of chili powder

1 tsp. of mustard powder
1 tsp. of cumin
1 tbsp. Mexican seasoning

Pepper
Salt

INSTRUCTIONS

1. Pre-heat the Air Fryer at 350°F.
2. Place all of the ingredients into a bowl & combine well to coat the sweet potatoes entirely.
3. Place the wedges in the Air Fryer basket & air fry for 20 minutes, shaking the basket at 5-minute intervals.

859. POTATO WEDGES

Prep & Cook Time: 30 minutes | Servings: 4

INGREDIENTS

4 medium potatoes, cut into wedges
1 tbsp. of Cajun spice

1 tbsp. of olive oil
Pepper

Salt

INSTRUCTIONS

1. Place the potato wedges in the Air Fryer basket & pour in the olive oil.
2. Cook wedges at 370°F for 25 minutes, shaking the basket twice throughout the cooking time.
3. Put the cooked wedges in a bowl & coat them with the Cajun spice, pepper, & salt. Serve warm.

860. BANANA CHIPS

Prep & Cook Time: 20 minutes | Servings: 3

INGREDIENTS

2 large raw bananas, peel & sliced   1 tsp. of olive oil   1 tsp. of salt
½ tsp. of red chili powder   ¼ tsp. of turmeric powder

INSTRUCTIONS
1. Put some water in a bowl along with the turmeric powder & salt.
2. Place the sliced bananas in the bowl & allow to soak for 10 minutes.
3. Dump the contents into a sieve to strain the banana slices before drying them with a paper towel.
4. Pre-heat the Air Fryer to 350°F.
5. Put the banana slices in a bowl & coat them with the olive oil, chili powder & salt.
6. Transfer the chips to the Air Fryer basket & air fry for 15 minutes.

861. HONEY CARROTS
Prep & Cook Time: 20 minutes | Servings: 4

INGREDIENTS
1 tbsp. of honey   1 tbsp. of olive oil   Ground black pepper to taste
3 cups baby carrots or carrots, sliced   Sea salt to taste

INSTRUCTIONS
1. In a bowl, combine the carrots, honey, & olive oil, coating the carrots completely. Sprinkle on some salt & ground black pepper.
2. Transfer the carrots to the Air Fryer & cook at 390°F for 12 minutes. Serve immediately.

862. POTATO TOTES
Prep & Cook Time: 20 minutes | Servings: 2

INGREDIENTS
1 large potato, diced   1 tsp. of olive oil   Salt
1 tsp. of onion, minced   Pepper

INSTRUCTIONS
1. Boil the potatoes in a saucepan of water over a medium-high heat.
2. Strain the potatoes, transfer them to bowl, & mash them thoroughly.
3. Combine with the olive oil, onion, pepper & salt in mashed potato.
4. Shape equal amounts of the mixture into small tots & place each one in the Air Fryer basket. Cook at 380°F for 8 minutes.
5. Give the basket a good shake & cook for an additional 5 minutes before serving.

863. ZUCCHINI
Prep & Cook Time: 30 minutes | Servings: 6

INGREDIENTS
6 medium zucchinis, cut into sticks   ½ tsp. of garlic powder   Salt
4 tbsp. of parmesan cheese, grated   1 cup of breadcrumbs
4 egg whites, beaten   Pepper

INSTRUCTIONS
1. Pre-heat the Air Fryer to 400°F.
2. In a bowl, mix the beaten egg whites with some salt & pepper.
3. In a separate bowl, combine the breadcrumbs, garlic powder, & parmesan cheese.
4. Dredge each zucchini stick in the egg whites before rolling in the breadcrumbs.
5. Place the coated zucchini in the Air Fryer basket & allow to cook for 20 minutes.

864. CARROTS & CUMIN
Prep & Cook Time: 25 minutes | Servings: 4

INGREDIENTS
2 cups carrots, peeled & chopped   1 tbsp. of olive oil
1 tsp. of cumin seeds   ¼ cup of coriander

INSTRUCTIONS
1. Cover the carrots with the cumin & oil.
2. Transfer to the Air Fryer & cook at 390°F for 12 minutes.
3. Season with the coriander before serving.

865. CHEESE STICKS
Prep & Cook Time: 15 minutes | Servings: 4

INGREDIENTS
1 lb. of mozzarella cheese   1 cup of breadcrumbs   1 cup of flour
2 eggs, beaten   1 tsp. of onion powder   ½ tsp. of salt
1 tsp. of cayenne pepper   1 tsp. of garlic powder

INSTRUCTIONS
1. Slice the mozzarella cheese into 3- x ½-inch sticks.
2. Put the beaten eggs in a bowl.
3. Pour the flour into a shallow dish.
4. In a second bowl combine the breadcrumbs, cayenne pepper, onion powder, garlic powder, & salt.
5. Dredge the mozzarella strips in the beaten egg before coating it in the flour. Dip it in the egg again. Lastly, press it into the breadcrumbs.
6. Refrigerate for 20 minutes.
7. Pre-heat the Air Fryer to 400°F.
8. Spritz the Air Fryer basket with cooking spray.
9. Put the coated cheese sticks in the Air Fryer basket & cook for 5 minutes. Serve immediately.

866. ONION RINGS
Prep & Cook Time: 25 minutes | Servings: 2

INGREDIENTS
1 large onion, cut into slices   1 cup of milk   1 tsp. of salt
1 egg, beaten   1 tsp. of baking powder
¾ cup of breadcrumbs   1 ¼ cup of flour

INSTRUCTIONS
1. Pre-heat the Air Fryer for 5 minutes.
2. In a small bowl, combine the baking powder, flour, & salt
3. In a second bowl, stir together the milk & egg using a whisk.
4. Put the breadcrumbs in a shallow dish.
5. Coat each slice of onion with the flour, then dredge it in the egg mixture. Lastly, press it into the breadcrumbs.
6. Transfer the coated onion rings to the Air Fryer basket & cook at
7. 350°F for 10 minutes.

867. VEGAN VEGGIE DISH
Prep & Cook Time: 30 minutes | Servings: 4

INGREDIENTS

1 large zucchini, sliced
3 – 4 cherry tomatoes on the vine
1 medium carrot, peeled & cubed
1 large parsnip, peeled & cubed

1 green pepper, sliced
1 tsp. of mustard
1 tsp. of mixed herbs
2 cloves garlic, crushed

2 tbsp. of honey
3+3 tbsp. of olive oil, separately
Sea salt to taste
Black pepper to taste

INSTRUCTIONS
1. Place the slices of zucchini, green pepper, parsnip, carrot & cherry tomatoes inside the Air Fryer.
2. Pour 3 tbsp. of oil over the vegetables & cook at 360°F for 15 minutes.
3. In the meantime, make the marinade by mixing together all of the other ingredients in the Air Fryer baking dish.
4. Transfer the cooked vegetables to the baking dish & coat it completely with the marinade. Season with pepper & salt as desired.
5. Return to the Air Fryer & cook at 390°F for 5 minutes. Serve hot.

868. TOFU
Prep & Cook Time: 20 minutes | Servings: 4

INGREDIENTS

15 oz. extra firm tofu, drained & cut into
cubes
1 tsp. chili flakes

¾ cup cornstarch
¼ cup cornmeal
Pepper

Salt

INSTRUCTIONS
1. In a bowl, combine the cornmeal, cornstarch, chili flakes, pepper, & salt.
2. Coat the tofu cubes completely with the mixture.
3. Pre-heat your Air Fryer at 350°F.
4. Spritz the basket with cooking spray.
5. Transfer the coated tofu to the basket & air fry for 8 minutes, shaking the basket at the 4-minute mark.

869. FRIDAY'S FRIES
Prep & Cook Time: 25 minutes | Servings: 2

INGREDIENTS

1 large eggplant, cut into 3-inch slices
¼ cup of water

1 tbsp. of olive oil
¼ cup of cornstarch

¼ tsp. of salt

INSTRUCTIONS
1. Pre-heat the Air Fryer to 400°F.
2. In a bowl, combine the water, olive oil, cornstarch, & salt.
3. Coat the sliced eggplant with the mixture.
4. Put the coated eggplant slices in the Air Fryer basket & cook for 20 minutes.

870. SWEET POTATO BITES
Prep & Cook Time: 30 minutes | Servings: 2

INGREDIENTS

2 sweet potatoes, diced into 1-inch cubes
1 tsp. of red chili flakes

2 tsp. of cinnamon
2 tbsp. of olive oil

2 tbsp. of honey
½ cup of fresh parsley, chopped

INSTRUCTIONS
1. Pre-heat the Air Fryer at 350°F.
2. Place all of the ingredients in a bowl & stir well to coat the sweet potato cubes entirely.
3. Put the sweet potato mixture into the Air Fryer basket & cook for 15 minutes.

871. KALE CHIPS
Prep & Cook Time: 15 minutes | Servings: 2

INGREDIENTS

1 head of kale

1 tbsp. of olive oil

1 tsp. of soy sauce

INSTRUCTIONS
1. De-stem the head of kale & shred each leaf into a 1 ½" piece. Wash & dry well.
2. Toss the kale with the olive oil & soy sauce to coat it completely.
3. Transfer to the Air Fryer & cook at 390°F for 2 to 3 minutes, giving the leaves a good toss at the halfway mark.

872. STUFFED TOMATOES
Prep & Cook Time: 30 minutes | Servings: 4

INGREDIENTS

4 large tomatoes, without tops
1 clove garlic, crushed
1 onion, cubed
1 cup frozen peas

2 cups of cooked rice, cold
1 tbsp. of soy sauce
1 carrot, cubed
1 tbsp. of olive oil

Parsley to taste, roughly chopped
Cooking spray

INSTRUCTIONS
1. Fry up the rice in a pan with the olive oil over a low heat.
2. Add in the cubed onion, carrots, crushed garlic, & frozen peas & allow to cook for 2 minutes, stirring occasionally.
3. Pour in the soy sauce & toss to coat. Remove the pan from the heat.
4. Pre-heat the Air Fryer to 360°F.
5. Stuff each tomato with the rice & vegetables
6. Put the tomatoes in the Air Fryer & cook for 20 minutes.
7. Garnish the cooked tomatoes with the chopped parsley & serve.

873. MIXED NUTS
Prep & Cook Time: 15 minutes | Servings: 8

INGREDIENTS

2 cups of mixed nuts
1 tsp. of chipotle chili powder

1 tsp. of ground cumin
1 tbsp. of butter, melted

1 tsp. of pepper
1 tsp. of salt

INSTRUCTIONS
1. In a bowl, combine all of the ingredients, coating the nuts well.
2. Set your Air Fryer to 350°F & allow to heat for 5 minutes.
3. Place the mixed nuts in the Air Fryer basket & roast for 4 minutes, shaking the basket halfway through the cooking time.

874. CHEESY POTATOES
Prep & Cook Time: 20 minutes | Servings: 4

INGREDIENTS

11 oz. of potatoes, diced & boiled
1 egg yolk
2 tbsp. of flour

3 tbsp. of parmesan cheese
3 tbsp. of breadcrumbs
Pepper

Nutmeg to taste
Salt

INSTRUCTIONS

1. Pre-heat Air Fryer at 390°F.
2. Mash up the potatoes & combine with all of the ingredients, minus the breadcrumbs.
3. Shape equal amounts of the mixture into medium-sized balls & roll each one in the breadcrumbs.
4. Place the potato balls in the Air Fryer & cook for 4 minutes.

875. BAKED POTATOES
Prep & Cook Time: 45 minutes | Servings: 3

INGREDIENTS

3 Idaho or russet baking potatoes, washed
2 cloves garlic, crushed

1 tbsp. of olive oil
1 tbsp. of sea salt

Parsley, roughly chopped
Sour cream to taste

INSTRUCTIONS
1. Pierce each potato several times with a fork.
2. Sprinkle the potatoes with salt & coat with the garlic puree & olive oil.
3. Place the potatoes in the Air Fryer basket & cook at 390°F for 35 - 40 minutes until soft. Serve with parsley & sour cream, or whatever toppings you desire.

876. BABY CORN
Prep & Cook Time: 20 minutes | Servings: 4

INGREDIENTS

8 oz. of baby corns, boiled
1 cup of flour
1 tsp. of garlic powder

½ tsp. of carom seeds
¼ tsp. of chili powder
Pinch of baking soda

Salt

INSTRUCTIONS
1. In a bowl, combine the flour, chili powder, garlic powder, cooking soda, salt & carom seed. Add in a little water to create a batter-like consistency.
2. Coat each baby corn in the batter.
3. Pre-heat the Air Fryer at 350°F.
4. Cover the Air Fryer basket with aluminum foil before laying the coated baby corns on top of the foil.
5. Cook for 10 minutes.

877. FRENCH FRIES
Prep & Cook Time: 25 minutes | Servings: 4

INGREDIENTS

1 lb. of russet potatoes
1 tsp. of salt

½ tsp. of black pepper
1 tbsp. of olive oil

INSTRUCTIONS
1. In a pot filled with water, blanch the potatoes until softened.
2. Remove from the heat & allow to cool. Slice the potatoes into matchstick shapes.
3. Place them in a large bowl & coat with the olive oil, salt & pepper.
4. Pre-heat the Air Fryer to 390°F.
5. Cook the French fries for about 15 minutes, giving the basket a shake now & again throughout the cooking time. Serve with freshly chopped herbs if desired.

878. ROASTED CORN
Prep & Cook Time: 15 minutes | Servings: 8

INGREDIENTS

4 fresh ears of corn

2 to 3 tsp. of vegetable oil

Salt & pepper

INSTRUCTIONS
1. Remove the husks from the corn, before washing & drying the corn. Slice up the corn to fit your Air Fryer basket if necessary.
2. Pour a drizzling of vegetable oil over the corn, coating it well. Sprinkle on salt & pepper.
3. Place in the Air Fryer & cook at 400°F for about 10 minutes.

879. ROASTED CARROTS
Prep & Cook Time: 20 minutes | Servings: 2

INGREDIENTS

1 tbsp. of olive oil
3 cups of baby carrots or carrots

1 tbsp. of honey
Salt & pepper

INSTRUCTIONS
1. In a bowl, coat the carrots with the honey & olive oil before sprinkling on some salt & pepper.
2. Place into the Air Fryer & cook at 390°F for 12 minutes. Serve hot.

880. FRIED KALE CHIPS
Prep & Cook Time: 10 minutes | Servings: 2

INGREDIENTS

1 head of kale, torn into 1 ½-inch pieces

1 tbsp. of olive oil

1 tsp. of soy sauce

INSTRUCTIONS
1. Wash & dry the kale pieces.
2. Transfer the kale to a bowl & coat with the soy sauce & oil.
3. Place it in the Air Fryer & cook at 400°F for 3 minutes, tossing it halfway through the cooking process.

881. ORANGE CAULIFLOWER
Prep & Cook Time: 30 minutes | Servings: 2

INGREDIENTS

½ lemon, juiced
1 head of cauliflower

½ tbsp. of olive oil
1 tsp. of curry powder

Sea salt to taste
Ground black pepper to taste

INSTRUCTIONS
1. Wash the cauliflower. Cut out the leaves & core.
2. Chop the cauliflower into equally sized florets.
3. Coat the inside of the Air Fryer with the oil & allow it to warm up for about 2 minutes at 390°F.
4. In a bowl, mix together the fresh lemon juice & curry powder. Add in the cauliflower florets. Sprinkle in the pepper & salt & mix again, coating the florets well.
5. Transfer to the Air Fryer, cook for 20 minutes, & serve warm.

882. LEMON GREEN BEANS
Prep & Cook Time: 20 minutes | Servings: 4

INGREDIENTS

1 lemon, juiced
1 lb. of green beans, washed

¼ tsp. of extra virgin olive oil
Sea salt to taste

Black pepper to taste

INSTRUCTIONS
1. Pre-heat the Air Fryer to 400°F.

2. Put the green beans in your Air Fryer basket & drizzle the lemon juice over them.
3. Sprinkle on the pepper & salt. Pour in the oil & toss to coat the green beans well.
4. Cook for 10 – 12 minutes & serve warm.

883. BROCCOLI FLORETS
Prep & Cook Time: 20 minutes | Servings: 4

INGREDIENTS

1 lb. of broccoli, cut into florets
1 tbsp. of lemon juice

1 tbsp. of olive oil
1 tbsp. of sesame seeds

3 garlic cloves, minced

INSTRUCTIONS

1. In a bowl, combine all of the ingredients, coating the broccoli well.
2. Transfer to the Air Fryer basket & air fry at 400°F for 13 minutes.

884. AVOCADO FRIES
Prep & Cook Time: 20 minutes | Servings: 4

INGREDIENTS

½ cup of panko
½ tsp. of salt

1 whole avocado
1 oz. of aquafaba

INSTRUCTIONS

1. In a shallow bowl, stir together the panko & salt.
2. In a separate shallow bowl, add the aquafaba.
3. Dip the avocado slices into the aquafaba, before coating each one in the panko.
4. Place the slices in your Air Fryer basket, taking care not to overlap any. Air fry for 10 minutes at 390°F.

885. ORIENTAL SPINACH SAMOSA
Prep & Cook Time: 45 minutes | Servings: 2

INGREDIENTS

¾ cup of boiled & blended spinach puree
¼ cup of green peas
½ tsp. of sesame seeds
Ajwain, salt, chaat masala, chili powder to

taste
2 tsp. of olive oil
1 tsp. of chopped fresh coriander leaves
1 tsp. of garam masala

¼ cup of boiled & cut potatoes
½ 1 cup of flour
½ tsp. of cooking soda

INSTRUCTIONS

1. In a bowl, combine the Ajwain, flour, cooking soda & salt to form a dough-like consistency. Pour in one tsp. of the oil & the spinach puree. Continue to mix the dough, ensuring it is smooth.
2. Refrigerate for 20 minutes. Add another tsp. of oil to a saucepan & sauté the potatoes & peas for 5 minutes.
3. Stir in the sesame seeds, coriander, & any other spices you desire.
4. Use your hands to shape equal sized amounts of the dough into small balls. Mold these balls into cone-shapes.
5. Fill each cone with the potatoes & peas mixture & seal.
6. Pre-heat your Air Fryer to 390°F.
7. Put the samosas in the basket & cook for 10 minutes.
8. Serve the samosas with the sauce of your choice.

886. TOMATOES & HERBS
Prep & Cook Time: 30 minutes | Servings: 2

INGREDIENTS

2 large tomatoes, washed & cut into halves
Herbs, such as oregano, basil, thyme,

rosemary, sage to taste
Cooking spray
Pepper

Parmesan, grated [optional]
Parsley, minced [optional]

INSTRUCTIONS

1. Spritz both sides of each tomato half with a small amount of cooking spray.
2. Coat the tomatoes with a light sprinkling of pepper & the herbs of your choice.
3. Place the tomatoes in your Air Fryer basket, cut-side-up. Cook at 320°F for 20 minutes, or longer if necessary.
4. Serve hot, at room temperature, or chilled as a refreshing summer snack. Optionally, you can garnish them with grated Parmesan & minced parsley before serving.

887. VEGETABLE FRITTERS
Prep & Cook Time: 15 minutes | Servings: 4

INGREDIENTS

1 cup of bell peppers, deveined & chopped
1 tsp. of sea salt flakes
1 tsp. of cumin

¼ tsp. of paprika
½ cup of shallots, chopped
2 cloves of garlic, minced
1 ½ tbsp. of fresh chopped cilantro

1 egg, whisked
¾ cup of cheddar cheese, grated
¼ cup of cooked quinoa
¼ cup of flour

INSTRUCTIONS

1. In a bowl, combine all of the ingredients well.
2. Divide the mixture into equal portions & shape each one into a ball. Use your palm to flatten each ball very slightly to form patties.
3. Lightly coat the patties with a cooking spray.
4. Put the patties in your Air Fryer cooking basket, taking care not to overlap them.
5. Cook at 340°F for 10 minutes, turning them over halfway through.

888. CHEESECAKE CUPS
Prep & Cook Time: 25 minutes | Servings: 4

INGREDIENTS

8 oz. of cream cheese, softened
2 oz. of heavy cream

1 tsp. of sugar
1 tsp. of vanilla flavoring

INSTRUCTIONS

1. Combine all the ingredients.
2. Whip until a pudding consistency is achieved.
3. Divide in cups.
4. Cook inside your Air Fryer at 325°F/160°C for 20 minutes until warm.
5. Refrigerate and serve!

889. STRAWBERRY SHAKE
Prep & Cook Time: 5 minutes | Servings: 1

INGREDIENTS

¾ cup of coconut milk (from the carton)
¼ cup of heavy cream

7 ice cubes
2 tbsp. of sugar-free strawberry Torani syrup

¼ tsp. Xanthan Gum

INSTRUCTIONS

1. Combine all the ingredients into blender.
2. Blend for 1-2 minutes.

3. Cook inside your Air Fryer at 325°F/160°C for 2 minutes until warm.
4. Serve!

890. RASPBERRY PUDDING SURPRISE

Prep & Cook Time: 40 minutes | Servings: 1

INGREDIENTS

3 tbsp. of chia seeds
½ cup of milk

1 scoop of chocolate protein powder
¼ cup of raspberries, fresh or frozen

1 tsp. of honey

INSTRUCTIONS
1. Combine the milk, protein powder & chia seeds together.
2. Let rest for 5 minutes before stirring.
3. Cook inside your Air Fryer at 325°F/160°C for 25 minutes until warm.
4. Top with raspberries.
5. Serve!

891. VANILLA BEAN DREAM

Prep & Cook Time: 35 minutes | Servings: 1

INGREDIENTS

½ cup of extra virgin coconut oil, softened
½ cup of coconut butter, softened

Juice of 1 lemon
Seeds from ½ a vanilla bean

INSTRUCTIONS
1. Whisk the ingredients in an easy-to-pour cup.
2. Pour into a lined cupcake or loaf pan.
3. Cook inside your Air Fryer at 325°F/160°C for 30 minutes until warm.
4. Serve!

892. WHITE CHOCOLATE BERRY CHEESECAKE

Prep & Cook Time: 5-10 minutes | Servings: 4

INGREDIENTS

8 oz. of cream cheese, softened
2 oz. of heavy cream

½ tsp. of sugar
1 tsp. of raspberries

1 tbsp. of white chocolate syrup

INSTRUCTIONS
1. Whip together the ingredients to a thick consistency inside a greased pan. Place the pan inside your Air Fryer at 325°F/160°C for 5 minutes.
2. Divide in cups.
3. Refrigerate.
4. Serve!

893. COCONUT PILLOW

Prep & Cook Time: 1-2 days | Servings: 4

INGREDIENTS

1 can of coconut milk

Berries of choice

Dark chocolate

INSTRUCTIONS
1. Refrigerate the coconut milk for 24 hours.
2. Remove it from your refrigerator & whip for 2-3 minutes.
3. Fold in the berries.
4. Cook inside your Air Fryer at 325°F/160°C for 5 minutes until warm.
5. Season with the chocolate shavings.
6. Serve!

894. COFFEE SURPRISE

Prep & Cook Time: 8 minutes | Servings: 1

INGREDIENTS

2 heaped tbsp. of flaxseed, ground
100ml of cooking cream 35% fat

½ tsp. of cocoa powder, dark
1 tbsp. of goji berries

Freshly brewed coffee

INSTRUCTIONS
1. Mix together the flaxseeds, cream & cocoa & coffee.
2. Season with goji berries.
3. Cook inside your Air Fryer at 325°F/160°C for 5 minutes until warm.
4. Serve!

895. CHOCOLATE CHEESECAKE

Prep & Cook Time: 60 minutes | Servings: 4

INGREDIENTS

4 oz. of cream cheese
½ oz. of heavy cream

1 tsp. of sugar glycerite
1 tsp. of sugar

1 oz. of chocolate chips

INSTRUCTIONS
1. Combine all the ingredients except the chocolate to a thick consistency.
2. Fold in the chocolate chips.
3. Cook inside your Air Fryer at 325°F/160°C for 30 minutes.
4. Serve!

896. CRUSTY

Prep & Cook Time: 40 minutes | Servings: 3

INGREDIENTS

2 cups of flour
4 tsp. of melted butter

2 large eggs
½ tsp. of salt

INSTRUCTIONS
1. Mix together the flour & butter.
2. Add in the eggs & salt & combine well to form a dough ball.
3. Place the dough between two pieces of parchment paper. Roll out to 10" by 16" & ¼ inch thick.
4. Place inside your Air Fryer and cook at 375°F/190°C for 30 minutes.
5. Serve.

897. CHOCOLATE PEANUT BUTTER CUPS

Prep & Cook Time: 40 minutes | Servings: 2

INGREDIENTS

1 stick of butter

1 oz. / 1 cube of chocolate

5 tbsp. of sugar

1 tbsp. of heavy cream   4 tbsp. of peanut butter
INSTRUCTIONS
1. In a microwave, melt the butter & chocolate.
2. Add the sugar.
3. Stir in the cream & peanut butter.
4. Line the muffin tins. Fill the muffin cups.
5. Cook inside your Air Fryer and cook at 375°F/190°C for 30 minutes.
6. Serve!

898. MACAROON BITES
Prep & Cook Time: 30 minutes | Servings: 2

INGREDIENTS

4 egg whites   ½ tsp. of sugar   1 cup of coconut
½ tsp. of vanilla   4½ tsp. of water
INSTRUCTIONS
1. Preheat your Air Fryer to 375°F/190°C.
2. Combine the egg whites, liquids & coconut.
3. Put into the Air Fryer & reduce the heat to 325°F/160°C.
4. Bake for 15 minutes.
5. Serve!

899. CHOCO-BERRY FUDGE SAUCE
Prep & Cook Time: 15 minutes | Servings: 2

INGREDIENTS

4 oz. of cream cheese, softened   ¼ cup of sugar   1 tbsp. of raspberry syrup
1-3.5 oz. 90% of chocolate Lindt bar   ¼ cup of heavy cream
INSTRUCTIONS
1. Inside your Air Fryer, melt together the cream cheese & chocolate at 325°F/160°C for 5 minutes.
2. Open halfway and stir in the sugar.
3. Finish cooking and once cool, mix in the cream & syrup.
4. Serve!

900. CHOCO-COCONUT PUDDIN
Prep & Cook Time: 45 minutes | Servings: 1

INGREDIENTS

1 cup of coconut milk   ½ tsp. of sugar   1 tbsp. of water
2 tbsp. of cacao powder or organic cocoa ½ tbsp. of quality gelatin
INSTRUCTIONS
1. Inside your Air Fryer, combine the coconut milk, cocoa & sugar at 325°F/160°C for 30 minutes.
2. In a separate bowl, mix in the gelatin & water.
3. Add to the Air Fryer & stir until fully dissolved.
4. Pour into small dishes & refrigerate for 1 hour.
5. Serve!

901. STRAWBERRY DESSERT
Prep & Cook Time: 45 minutes | Servings: 1

INGREDIENTS

½ cup of strawberry preserves   2 cups of Greek Yogurt
½ cup of sugar   Ice cream maker
INSTRUCTIONS
1. In a food processor, purée the strawberries. Add the strawberry preserves.
2. Add the Greek yogurt & fully mix.
3. Cook inside your Air Fryer at 325°F/160°C for 30 minutes until baked.
4. Serve!

902. BERRY LAYER CAKE
Prep & Cook Time: 8 minutes | Servings: 1

INGREDIENTS

¼ lemon of pound cake   ½ tsp. of sugar   1 cup of mixed berries
¼ cup of whipping cream   Eighth tsp. of orange flavor
INSTRUCTIONS
1. Using a sharp knife, divide the lemon cake into small cubes.
2. Dice the strawberries.
3. Combine the whipping cream, sugar, & orange flavor.
4. Cook inside your Air Fryer at 325°F/160°C for 2 minutes until warm.
5. Layer the fruit, cake & cream in a glass.
6. Serve!

903. CHOCOLATE PUDDING
Prep & Cook Time: 50 minutes | Servings: 1

INGREDIENTS

3 tbsp. of chia seeds   1 scoop of cocoa powder   ½ tsp. of honey
1 cup of milk   ¼ cup of fresh raspberries
INSTRUCTIONS
1. Mix together all of the ingredients in a large bowl.
2. Let it rest for 15 minutes but stir halfway through.
3. Stir it again & refrigerate for 30 minutes. Garnish with raspberries.
4. Place inside your Air Fryer at 325°F/160°C for 2 minutes until warm.
5. Serve!

904. CRANBERRY CREAM SURPRISE
Prep & Cook Time: 30 minutes | Servings: 1

INGREDIENTS

1 cup mashed cranberries   2 tsp. of natural cherry flavoring   1 cup of organic heavy cream
½ cup of sugar   2 tsp. of natural rum flavoring
INSTRUCTIONS
1. Combine the mashed cranberries, sugar, cherry & rum flavorings.
2. Cover & refrigerate for 20 minutes.

3.   Whip the heavy cream until soft peaks form.
4.   Layer the whipped cream & cranberry mixture.
5.   Top with fresh cranberries, mint leaves or grated dark chocolate.
6.   Place inside your Air Fryer at 325°F/160°C for 2 minutes until warm.
7.   Serve!

905. BANANA CHOCOLATE CAKE
Prep & Cook Time: 30 minutes | Servings: 10

INGREDIENTS

1 stick of softened butter
½ cup of sugar
1 egg
1 banana, mashed
2 tbsp. of maple syrup

2 cups of flour
¼ tsp. of anise star, ground
¼ tsp. of ground mace
¼ tsp. of ground cinnamon
¼ tsp. of crystallized ginger

½ tsp. of vanilla paste
Pinch of kosher salt
½ cup of cocoa powder

INSTRUCTIONS
1.   Beat together the softened butter & sugar to combine well.
2.   Mix together the egg, mashed banana & maple syrup using a whisk.
3.   Combine the two mixtures, stirring well until pale & creamy.
4.   Add in the flour, anise star, mace, cinnamon, crystallized ginger, vanilla paste, salt, & cocoa powder. Mix well to form the batter.
5.   Grease two cake pans with cooking spray.
6.   Transfer the batter into the cake pans & place them in the Air Fryer.
7.   Cook at 330°F for 30 minutes. Frost with chocolate glaze if desired

906. LEMON BUTTER POUND CAKE
Prep & Cook Time: 2 hours 20 minutes | Servings: 8

INGREDIENTS

1 stick of softened butter
1 cup of sugar
1 medium egg
1 ¼ cups of flour

1 tsp. of butter flavoring
1 tsp. of vanilla essence
Salt
¾ cup of milk

Grated zest of 1 medium-sized lemon
For the Glaze:
2 tbsp. of freshly squeezed lemon juice

INSTRUCTIONS:
1.   In a large bowl, use a creamer to mix together the butter & sugar. Fold in the egg & continue to stir.
2.   Add in the flour, butter flavoring, vanilla essence, & salt, combining everything well.
3.   Pour in the milk, followed by the lemon zest, & continue to mix.
4.   Lightly brush the inside of a cake pan with the melted butter.
5.   Pour the cake batter into the cake pan.
6.   Place the pan in the Air Fryer & bake at 350°F for 15 minutes.
7.   After removing it from the Air Fryer, run a knife around the edges of the cake to loosen it from the pan & transfer it to a serving plate.
8.   Leave it to cool completely.
9.   In the meantime, make the glaze by combining with the lemon juice.
10.   Pour the glaze over the cake & let it sit for a further 2 hours before serving

907. FRIED PINEAPPLE RINGS
Prep & Cook Time: 10 minutes | Servings: 6

INGREDIENTS

⅔ cup of flour
½ tsp. of baking powder
½ tsp. of baking soda
Pinch of kosher salt

½ cup of water
1 cup of rice milk
½ tsp. of ground cinnamon
¼ tsp. of ground anise star

½ tsp. of vanilla essence
4 tbsp. of sugar
¼ cup of flaked coconut
1 medium pineapple, peeled & sliced

INSTRUCTIONS
1.   Mix together all of the ingredients, minus the pineapple.
2.   Cover the pineapple slices with the batter.
3.   Place the slices in the Air Fryer & cook at 380°F for 6 - 8 minutes.
4.   Pour a drizzling of maple syrup over the pineapple & serve with a side of vanilla ice cream.

908. HAZELNUT BROWNIE CUPS
Prep & Cook Time: 30 minutes | Servings: 12

INGREDIENTS

6 oz. of chocolate chips
1 stick of butter, at room temperature
1 cup of sugar
2 large eggs

¼ cup of red wine
¼ tsp. of hazelnut extract
1 tsp. of pure vanilla extract
¾ cup of flour

2 tbsp. of cocoa powder
½ cup of ground hazelnuts
Pinch of kosher salt

INSTRUCTIONS
1.   Melt the butter & chocolate chips in a microwave.
2.   In a large bowl, combine the sugar, eggs, red wine, hazelnut & vanilla extract with a whisk. Pour in the chocolate mix.
3.   Add in the flour, cocoa powder, ground hazelnuts, & a pinch of kosher salt, continuing to stir until a creamy, smooth consistency is achieved.
4.   Take a muffin tin & place a cupcake liner in each cup. Spoon an equal amount of the batter into each one.
5.   Air bake at 360°F for 28 - 30 minutes, cooking in batches if necessary.
6.   Serve with a topping of ganache if desired

909. SWIRLED GERMAN CAKE
Prep & Cook Time: 25 minutes | Servings: 8

INGREDIENTS

1 cup of flour
1 tsp. of baking powder
1 cup of sugar
⅛ tsp. of salt

¼ tsp. of ground cinnamon
¼ tsp. of grated nutmeg
1 tsp. of orange zest
1 stick of butter, melted

2 eggs
1 tsp. of pure vanilla extract
¼ cup of milk
2 tbsp. of cocoa powder

INSTRUCTIONS:
1.   Take a round pan that is small enough to fit inside your Air Fryer & lightly grease the inside with oil.
2.   In a bowl, use an electric mixer to combine the flour, baking powder, sugar, salt, cinnamon, nutmeg, & orange zest.
3.   Fold in the butter, eggs, vanilla, & milk, incorporating everything well.
4.   Spoon a quarter-cup of the batter to the baking pan.
5.   Stir the cocoa powder into the rest of the batter.
6.   Use a spoon to drop small amounts of the brown batter into the white batter. Swirl them together with a knife.
7.   Place the pan in the Air Fryer & cook at 360°F for about 15 minutes.
8.   Remove the pan from the Air Fryer & leave to cool for roughly 10 minutes.

910. OATMEAL APPLE & PLUM CRUMBLE
Prep & Cook Time: 20 minutes | Servings: 6

INGREDIENTS

¼ lb. of plums, pitted & chopped
¼ lb. of Braeburn apples, cored &
chopped
1 tbsp. of fresh lemon juice
2 ½ oz. of sugar

1 tbsp. of honey
½ tsp. of ground mace
½ tsp. of vanilla paste
1 cup fresh cranberries
⅓ cup of oats

⅔ cup of flour
½ stick of butter, chilled
1 tbsp. cold water

INSTRUCTIONS
1. Coat the plums & apples with the lemon juice, sugar, honey, & ground mace.
2. Lightly coat the inside of a cake pan with cooking spray.
3. Pour the fruit mixture into the pan.
4. In a bowl, mix together all of the other ingredients, combining everything well.
5. Use a palette knife to spread this mixture evenly over the fruit.
6. Place the pan in the Air Fryer & air bake at 390°F for 20 minutes. Ensure the crumble is cooked through before serving.

911. CHOCOLATE CHIP COOKIES
Prep & Cook Time: 25 minutes | Servings: 9

INGREDIENTS

1 ¼ cup of flour
⅔ cup chocolate chips, or any kind of
baker's chocolate

⅓ cup of sugar
½ cup of butter
4 tbsp. of honey

1 tbsp. of milk
High quality cooking spray

INSTRUCTIONS
1. Set your Air Fryer to 320°F & allow to warm up for about 10 minutes.
2. In the meantime, in a large bowl, cream the butter to soften it.
3. Add in the sugar & combine to form a light & fluffy consistency.
4. Stir in the honey.
5. Gradually fold in the flour, incorporating it well.
6. If you are using baker's chocolate, use a rolling pin or a mallet to break it up & create chocolate chips.
7. Throw the chocolate into the bowl & mix well to ensure the chips are evenly distributed throughout the dough.
8. Finally, add in the milk & combine well.
9. Lightly spritz your Air Fryer basket with the cooking spray.
10. Transfer the cookie dough into the Air Fryer & cook for 20 minutes.
11. Slice into 9 cookies. Serve immediately. Alternatively, the cookies can be stored in an airtight container for up to 3 days.

912. HOMEMADE COCONUT BANANA TREAT
Prep & Cook Time: 20 minutes | Servings: 6

INGREDIENTS

2 tbsp. of coconut oil
¾ cup of breadcrumbs
2 tbsp. of sugar

½ tsp. of cinnamon powder
¼ tsp. of ground cloves
6 ripe bananas, peeled & halved

⅓ cup of flour
1 large egg, beaten

INSTRUCTIONS
1. Heat a skillet over a medium heat. Add in the coconut oil & the breadcrumbs & mix together for approximately 4 minutes.
2. Take the skillet off of the heat.
3. Add in the sugar, cinnamon, & cloves.
4. Cover all sides of the banana halves with the rice flour.
5. Dip each one in the beaten egg before coating them in the bread crumb mix.
6. Place the banana halves in the Air Fryer basket, taking care not to overlap them. Cook at 290°F for 10 minutes. You may need to complete this step in multiple batches.
7. Serve hot or at room temperature, topped with a sprinkling of flaked coconut if desired.

913. MINI STRAWBERRY PIES
Prep & Cook Time: 15 minutes | Servings: 8

INGREDIENTS

1 cup of sugar
¼ tsp. of ground cloves
⅛ tsp. of cinnamon powder

1 tsp. of vanilla extract
1 [12-oz.] can of biscuit dough
12 oz. of strawberry pie filling

¼ cup of butter, melted

INSTRUCTIONS
1. In a bowl, mix together the sugar, cloves, cinnamon, & vanilla.
2. With a rolling pin, roll each piece of the biscuit dough into a flat, round circle.
3. Spoon an equal amount of the strawberry pie filling onto the center of each biscuit.
4. Roll up the dough. Dip the biscuits into the melted butter & coat them with the sugar mixture.
5. Coat with a light brushing of non-stick cooking spray on all sides.
6. Transfer the cookies to the Air Fryer & bake them at 340°F for roughly 10 minutes, or until a golden-brown color is achieved.
7. Allow to cool for 5 minutes before serving.

914. COCONUT BROWNIES
Prep & Cook Time: 15 minutes | Servings: 8

INGREDIENTS

½ cup of coconut oil
2 oz. of dark chocolate
1 cup of sugar
2 ½ tbsp. of water
4 whisked eggs

¼ tsp. of ground cinnamon
½ tsp. of ground anise star
¼ tsp. of coconut extract
½ tsp. of vanilla extract
1 tbsp. of honey

½ cup of flour
½ cup of desiccated coconut
sugar, to dust

INSTRUCTIONS
1. Melt the coconut oil & dark chocolate in the microwave.
2. Combine with the sugar, water, eggs, cinnamon, anise, coconut extract, vanilla, & honey in a large bowl.
3. Stir in the flour & desiccated coconut. Incorporate everything well.
4. Lightly grease a baking dish with butter. Transfer the mixture to the dish.
5. Place the dish in the Air Fryer & bake at 355°F for 15 minutes.
6. Remove from the Air Fryer & allow to cool slightly.
7. Take care when taking it out of the baking dish. Slice it into squares.
8. Dust with sugar before serving.

915. BANANA & VANILLA PASTRY PUFFS
Prep & Cook Time: 15 minutes | Servings: 8

INGREDIENTS

1 packet [8-oz.] of dinner rolls
1 cup of milk

4 oz. of instant vanilla pudding
4 oz. of cream cheese, softened

2 bananas, peeled & sliced
1 egg, lightly beaten

INSTRUCTIONS
1. Roll out the crescent dinner rolls & slice each one into 8 squares.
2. Mix together the milk, pudding, & cream cheese using a whisk.
3. Scoop equal amounts of the mixture into the pastry squares. Add the banana slices on top.
4. Fold the squares around the filling, pressing down on the edges to seal them.
5. Apply a light brushing of the egg to each pastry puff before placing them in the Air Fryer.
6. Air bake at 355°F for 10 minutes.

916. DOUBLE CHOCOLATE CAKE

Prep & Cook Time: 45 minutes | Servings: 8

INGREDIENTS

½ cup of sugar
1 ¼ cups of flour
1 tsp. of baking powder
⅓ cup of cocoa powder
¼ tsp. of ground cloves

⅛ tsp. of freshly grated nutmeg
Pinch of table salt
1 egg
¼ cup of soda of your choice
¼ cup of milk

½ stick of butter, melted
2 oz. of bittersweet chocolate, melted
½ cup of hot water

INSTRUCTIONS

1. In a bowl, thoroughly combine the dry ingredients.
2. In another bowl, mix together the egg, soda, milk, butter, & chocolate.
3. Combine the two mixtures. Add in the water & stir well.
4. Take a cake pan that is small enough to fit inside your Air Fryer & transfer the mixture to the pan.
5. Place a sheet of foil on top & bake at 320°F for 35 minutes.
6. Take off the foil & bake for further 10 minutes.
7. Frost the cake with buttercream if desired before serving.

917. BANANA OATMEAL COOKIES

Prep & Cook Time: 20 minutes | Servings: 6

INGREDIENTS

2 cups of quick oats
¼ cup of milk

4 ripe bananas, mashed
¼ cup of coconut, shredded

INSTRUCTIONS

1. Pre-heat the Air Fryer to 350°F.
2. Combine all of the ingredients in a bowl.
3. Scoop equal amounts of the cookie dough onto a baking sheet & put it in the Air Fryer basket.
4. Bake the cookies for 15 minutes.

918. SUGAR BUTTER FRITTERS

Prep & Cook Time: 30 minutes | Servings: 16

INGREDIENTS

For the dough:
4 cups of flour
1 tsp. of salt
1 tsp. of sugar
3 tbsp. of butter, at room temperature

1 packet of instant yeast
1 ¼ cups of lukewarm water

For the Cakes:
1 cup of sugar
Pinch of cardamom
1 tsp. of cinnamon powder
1 stick of butter, melted

INSTRUCTIONS

1. Place all of the ingredients in a large bowl & combine well.
2. Add in the lukewarm water & mix until a soft, elastic dough forms.
3. Place the dough on a lightly floured surface & lay a greased sheet of aluminum foil on top of the dough. Refrigerate for 5 to 10 minutes.
4. Remove it from the refrigerator & divide it in two. Mold each half into a log & slice it into 20 pieces.
5. In a shallow bowl, combine the sugar, cardamom & cinnamon.
6. Coat the slices with a light brushing of melted butter & the sugar.
7. Spritz Air Fryer basket with cooking spray.
8. Transfer the slices to the Air Fryer & air fry at 360°F for roughly 10 minutes. Turn each slice once during the baking time.
9. Dust each slice with the sugar before serving.

919. PEAR & APPLE CRISP WITH WALNUTS

Prep & Cook Time: 25 minutes | Servings: 6

INGREDIENTS

½ lb. of apples, cored & chopped
½ lb. of pears, cored & chopped
1 cup of flour
1 cup of sugar

1 tbsp. of butter
1 tsp. of ground cinnamon
¼ tsp. of ground cloves
1 tsp. of vanilla extract

¼ cup of chopped walnuts
Whipped cream, to serve

INSTRUCTIONS

1. Lightly grease a baking pan & place the apples & pears inside and place the pan inside your Air Fryer.
2. Combine the rest of the ingredients, minus the walnuts & the whipped cream, until a course, crumbly texture is achieved.
3. Pour the mixture over the fruits & spread it evenly. Top with the chopped walnuts.
4. Air bake at 340°F for 20 minutes or until the top turns golden brown.
5. When cooked through, serve at room temperature with whipped cream.

920. SWEET & CRISP BANANAS

Prep & Cook Time: 20 minutes | Servings: 4

INGREDIENTS

4 ripe bananas, peeled & halved
1 tbsp. of oatmeal
1 tbsp. of cashew, crushed

1 egg, beaten
1 ½ tbsp. of coconut oil
¼ cup of flour

1 ½ tbsp. of sugar
½ cup of breadcrumbs

INSTRUCTIONS

1. Put the coconut oil in a saucepan & heat over a medium heat. Stir in the breadcrumbs & cook, stirring continuously, for 4 minutes.
2. Transfer the breadcrumbs to a bowl.
3. Add in the oatmeal & crushed cashew. Mix well.
4. Coat each of the banana halves in the corn flour, before dipping it in the beaten egg & lastly coating it with the breadcrumbs.
5. Put the coated banana halves in the Air Fryer basket. Season with the sugar.
6. Air fry at 350°F for 10 minutes.

921. SHORTBREAD FINGERS

Prep & Cook Time: 20 minutes | Servings: 10

INGREDIENTS

1 ½ cups of butter
1 cup of flour

¾ cup of sugar
Cooking spray

INSTRUCTIONS

1. Pre-heat your Air Fryer to 350°F.
2. In a bowl. combine the flour & sugar.
3. Cut each stick of butter into small chunks. Add the chunks into the flour & the sugar.
4. Blend the butter into the mixture to combine everything well.
5. Use your hands to knead the mixture, forming a smooth consistency.
6. Shape the mixture into 10 equal-sized finger shapes, marking them with the tines of a fork for decoration if desired.
7. Lightly spritz the Air Fryer basket with the cooking spray. Place the cookies inside, spacing them out well.

8. Bake the cookies for 12 minutes.
9. Let cool slightly before serving. Alternatively, you can store the cookies in an airtight container for up to 3 days.

922. COCONUT & BANANA CAKE

Prep & Cook Time: 1 hour 15 minutes | Servings: 5

INGREDIENTS

⅔ cup of sugar, shaved
⅔ cup of butter
3 eggs
1 ¼ cup of flour

1 ripe banana, mashed
½ tsp. of vanilla extract
⅛ tsp. of baking soda
Sea salt to taste

Topping Ingredients:
sugar to taste, shaved
Walnuts to taste, roughly chopped
Bananas to taste, sliced

INSTRUCTIONS

1. Pre-heat the Air Fryer to 360°F.
2. Mix together the flour, baking soda, & a pinch of sea salt.
3. In a separate bowl, combine the butter, vanilla extract & sugar using an electrical mixer or a blender, to achieve a fluffy consistency. Beat in the eggs one at a time.
4. Throw in half of the flour mixture & stir thoroughly. Add in the mashed banana & continue to mix. Lastly, throw in the remaining half of the flour mixture & combine until a smooth batter is formed.
5. Transfer the batter to a baking tray & top with the banana slices.
6. Scatter the chopped walnuts on top before dusting with the sugar
7. Place a sheet of foil over the tray & pierce several holes in it.
8. Put the covered tray in the Air Fryer. Cook for 48 minutes.
9. Decrease the temperature to 320°F, take off the foil, & allow to cook for an additional 10 minutes until golden brown.
10. Insert a skewer or toothpick in the center of the cake. If it comes out clean, the cake is ready.

923. ROASTED PUMPKIN SEEDS & CINNAMON

Prep & Cook Time: 35 minutes | Servings: 2

INGREDIENTS

1 cup pumpkin raw seeds
1 tbsp. of ground cinnamon

2 tbsp. of sugar
1 cup of water

1 tbsp. of olive oil

INSTRUCTIONS

1. In a frying pan, combine the pumpkin seeds, cinnamon & water.
2. Boil the mixture over a high heat for 2 - 3 minutes.
3. Pour out the water & place the seeds on a clean kitchen towel, allowing them to dry for 20 - 30 minutes.
4. In a bowl, mix together the sugar, dried seeds, a pinch of cinnamon & one tbsp. of olive oil.
5. Pre-heat the Air Fryer to 340°F.
6. Place the seed mixture in the Air Fryer basket & allow to cook for 15 minutes, shaking the basket periodically throughout.

924. PINEAPPLE STICKS

Prep & Cook Time: 20 minutes | Servings: 4

INGREDIENTS

½ fresh pineapple, cut into sticks
¼ cup desiccated coconut

INSTRUCTIONS

1. Pre-heat the Air Fryer to 400°F.
2. Coat the pineapple sticks in the desiccated coconut & put each one in the Air Fryer basket.
3. Air fry for 10 minutes.

925. SPONGE CAKE

Prep & Cook Time: 50 minutes | Servings: 8

INGREDIENTS

For the Cake:
9 oz. of sugar
9 oz. butter
3 eggs
9 oz. of flour
1 tsp. of vanilla extract

Zest of 1 lemon
1 tsp. of baking powder

For the Frosting:
Juice of 1 lemon
Zest of 1 lemon
1 tsp. yellow food coloring
7 oz. of sugar
4 egg whites

INSTRUCTIONS

1. Pre-heat your Air Fryer to 320°F.
2. Use an electric mixer to combine all of the cake ingredients.
3. Grease the insides of two round cake pans.
4. Pour an equal amount of the batter into each pan.
5. Place one pan in the Air Fryer & cook for 15 minutes, before repeating with the second pan.
6. In the meantime, mix together all of the frosting ingredients.
7. Allow the cakes to cool. Spread the frosting on top of one cake & stack the other cake on top.

926. APPLE WEDGES

Prep & Cook Time: 25 minutes | Servings: 4

INGREDIENTS

4 large apples
2 tbsp. of olive oil

½ cup of dried apricots, chopped
1 – 2 tbsp. of sugar

½ tsp. of ground cinnamon

INSTRUCTIONS

1. Peel the apples & slice them into eight wedges. Throw away the cores.
2. Coat the apple wedges with the oil.
3. Place each wedge in the Air Fryer & cook for 12 - 15 minutes at 350°F.
4. Add in the apricots & allow to cook for a further 3 minutes.
5. Stir together the sugar & cinnamon. Sprinkle this mixture over the cooked apples before serving.

927. CHOCOLATE LAVA CAKE

Prep & Cook Time: 20 minutes | Servings: 4

INGREDIENTS

1 cup of dark cocoa candy melts
1 stick butter
2 eggs
4 tbsp. of sugar

1 tbsp. of honey
4 tbsp. of flour
Pinch of kosher salt
Pinch of ground cloves

¼ tsp. of grated nutmeg
¼ tsp. of cinnamon powder

INSTRUCTIONS

1. Spritz the insides of four custard cups with cooking spray.
2. Melt the cocoa candy melts & butter in the microwave for 30 seconds to 1 minute.
3. In a large bowl, combine the eggs, sugar & honey with a whisk until frothy. Pour in the melted chocolate mix.
4. Throw in the rest of the ingredients & combine well with an electric mixer or a manual whisk.
5. Transfer equal portions of the mixture into the prepared custard cups.
6. Place in the Air Fryer & air bake at 350°F for 12 minutes.

7. Remove from the Air Fryer & allow to cool for 5 to 6 minutes.
8. Place each cup upside-down on a dessert plate & let the cake slide out. Serve with fruits & chocolate syrup if desired.

928. ENGLISH LEMON TARTS

Prep & Cook Time: 30 minutes | Servings: 4

INGREDIENTS

½ cup of butter
½ lb. of flour

2 tbsp. of sugar
1 large lemon, juiced & zested

2 tbsp. of lemon curd
Pinch of nutmeg

INSTRUCTIONS

1. In a large bowl, combine the butter, flour & sugar until a crumbly consistency is achieved.
2. Add in the lemon zest & juice, followed by a pinch of nutmeg. Continue to combine. If necessary, add a couple tbsp. of water to soften the dough.
3. Sprinkle the insides of a few small pastry tins with flour. Pour equal portions of the dough into each one & add sugar or lemon zest on top.
4. Pre-heat the Air Fryer to 360°F.
5. Place the lemon tarts inside the Air Fryer & allow to cook for 15 minutes.

929. BLUEBERRY PANCAKES

Prep & Cook Time: 20 minutes | Servings: 4

INGREDIENTS

½ tsp. of vanilla extract
2 tbsp. of honey
½ cup of blueberries

½ cup of sugar
2 cups + 2 tbsp. of flour
3 eggs, beaten

1 cup of milk
1 tsp. of baking powder
Salt

INSTRUCTIONS

1. Pre-heat the Air Fryer to 390°F.
2. In a bowl, mix together all of the dry ingredients.
3. Pour in the wet ingredients & combine with a whisk, ensuring the mixture becomes smooth.
4. Roll each blueberry in some flour to lightly coat it before folding it into the mixture. This is to ensure they do not change the color of the batter.
5. Coat the inside of a baking dish with a little oil or butter.
6. Spoon several equal amounts of the batter onto the baking dish, spreading them into pancake-shapes & ensuring to space them out well. This may have to be completed in two batches.
7. Place the dish in the Air Fryer & bake for about 10 minutes.

930. NEW ENGLAND PUMPKIN CAKE

Prep & Cook Time: 50 minutes | Servings: 4

INGREDIENTS

1 large egg
½ cup of skimmed milk
7 oz. of flour

2 tbsp. of sugar
5 oz. of pumpkin puree
Salt

Pinch of cinnamon [if desired]
Cooking spray

INSTRUCTIONS

1. Stir together the pumpkin puree & sugar in a bowl. Crack in the egg & combine using a whisk until smooth.
2. Add in the flour & salt, stirring constantly. Pour in the milk, ensuring to combine everything well.
3. Spritz a baking tin with cooking spray.
4. Transfer the batter to the baking tin.
5. Pre-heat the Air Fryer to 350°F.
6. Put the tin in the Air Fryer basket & bake for 15 minutes.

931. MIXED BERRY PUFFED PASTRY

Prep & Cook Time: 20 minutes | Servings: 3

INGREDIENTS

3 pastry dough sheets
½ cup of mixed berries, mashed

1 tbsp. of honey
2 tbsp. of cream cheese

3 tbsp. of chopped walnuts
¼ tsp. of vanilla extract

INSTRUCTIONS

1. Pre-heat your Air Fryer to 375°F.
2. Roll out the pastry sheets & spread the cream cheese over each one.
3. In a bowl, combine the berries, vanilla extract & honey.
4. Cover a baking sheet with parchment paper.
5. Spoon equal amounts of the berry mixture into the center of each sheet of pastry. Scatter the chopped walnuts on top.
6. Fold up the pastry around the filling & press down the edges with the back of a fork to seal them.
7. Transfer the baking sheet to the Air Fryer & cook for approximately 15 minutes.

932. CHERRY PIE

Prep & Cook Time: 35 minutes | Servings: 8

INGREDIENTS

1 tbsp. of milk
2 ready-made pie crusts

21 oz. of cherry pie filling
1 egg yolk

INSTRUCTIONS

1. Pre-heat the Air Fryer to 310°F.
2. Coat the inside of a pie pan with a little oil or butter & lay one of the pie crusts inside. Use a fork to pierce a few holes in the pastry.
3. Spread the pie filling evenly over the crust.
4. Slice the other crust into strips & place them on top of the pie filling to make the pie look more homemade.
5. Place in the Air Fryer & cook for 15 minutes.

933. APPLE PIE

Prep & Cook Time: 25 minutes | Servings: 7

INGREDIENTS

2 large apples
½ cup of flour

2 tbsp. of butter
1 tbsp. of sugar

½ tsp. of cinnamon

INSTRUCTIONS

1. Pre-heat the Air Fryer to 360°F
2. In a large bowl, combine the flour & butter. Pour in the sugar, continuing to mix.
3. Add in a few tbsp. of water & combine everything to create a smooth dough.
4. Grease the insides of a few small pastry tins with butter. Divide the dough between each tin & lay each portion flat inside.
5. Peel, core & dice up the apples. Put the diced apples on top of the pastry & top with a sprinkling of sugar & cinnamon.
6. Place the pastry tins in your Air Fryer & cook for 15 - 17 minutes.
7. Serve with whipped cream or ice cream if desired.

934. CHOCOLATE MOLTEN LAVA CAKE

Prep & Cook Time: 25 minutes | Servings: 4

INGREDIENTS

3 ½ oz. of butter, melted
3 ½ tbsp. of sugar

3 ½ oz. of chocolate, melted
1 ½ tbsp. of flour

2 eggs

INSTRUCTIONS
1. Pre-heat the Air Fryer to 375°F.
2. Grease four ramekins with a little butter.
3. Rigorously combine the eggs & butter before stirring in the melted chocolate.
4. Slowly fold in the flour.
5. Spoon an equal amount of the mixture into each ramekin.
6. Put them in the Air Fryer & cook for 10 minutes
7. Place the ramekins upside-down on plates & let the cakes fall out. Serve hot.

935. PINEAPPLE CAKE
Prep & Cook Time: 40 minutes | Servings: 4

INGREDIENTS
2 cups of flour
¼ lb. of butter
¼ cup of sugar

½ lb. of pineapple, chopped
½ cup of pineapple juice
1 oz. of dark chocolate, grated

1 large egg
2 tbsp. of skimmed milk

INSTRUCTIONS
1. Pre-heat the Air Fryer to 370°F.
2. Grease a cake tin with a little oil or butter.
3. In a bowl, combine the butter & flour to create a crumbly consistency.
4. Add in the sugar, diced pineapple, juice, & crushed dark chocolate & mix well.
5. In a separate bowl, combine the egg & milk. Add this mixture to the flour & stir well until a soft dough forms.
6. Pour the mixture into the cake tin & transfer to the Air Fryer.
7. Cook for 35 - 40 minutes.

936. GLAZED DONUTS
Prep & Cook Time: 25 minutes | Servings: 2 – 4

INGREDIENTS
1 can [8 oz.] of refrigerated croissant
dough

Cooking spray
1 can [16 oz.] of vanilla frosting

INSTRUCTIONS
1. Cut the croissant dough into 1-inch-round slices. Make a hole in the center of each one to create a donut.
2. Put the donuts in the Air Fryer basket, taking care not to overlap any, & spritz with cooking spray. You may need to cook everything in multiple batches.
3. Cook at 400°F for 2 minutes. Turn the donuts over & cook for another 3 minutes.
4. Place the rolls on a paper plate.
5. Microwave a half-cup of frosting for 30 seconds & pour a drizzling of the frosting over the donuts before serving.

937. APPLE DUMPLINGS
Prep & Cook Time: 40 minutes | Servings: 2

INGREDIENTS
2 tbsp. of sultanas
2 sheets of puff pastry

2 tbsp. of butter, melted
2 small apples

1 tbsp. of sugar

INSTRUCTIONS
1. Pre-heat your Air Fryer to 350°F
2. Peel the apples & remove the cores.
3. In a bowl, stir together the sugar & the sultanas.
4. Lay one apple on top of each pastry sheet & stuff the sugar & sultanas into the holes where the cores used to be.
5. Wrap the pastry around the apples, covering them completely.
6. Put them on a sheet of aluminum foil & coat each dumpling with a light brushing of melted butter
7. Transfer to the Air Fryer & bake for 25 minutes until a golden-brown color is achieved & the apples have softened inside.

938. BANANAS & ICE CREAM
Prep & Cook Time: 25 minutes | Servings: 2

INGREDIENTS
2 large bananas
1 tbsp. of butter

1 tbsp. of sugar
2 tbsp. of breadcrumbs

Vanilla ice cream for serving

INSTRUCTIONS
1. Place the butter in the Air Fryer basket & allow it to melt for 1 minute at 350°F.
2. Combine the sugar & breadcrumbs in a bowl.
3. Slice the bananas into 1-inch-round pieces. Drop them into the sugar mixture & coat them well.
4. Place the bananas in the Air Fryer & cook for 10 – 15 minutes.
5. Serve warm, with ice cream on the side if desired.

939. RASPBERRY MUFFINS
Prep & Cook Time: 35 minutes | Servings: 10

INGREDIENTS
1 egg
1 cup of flour coated raspberries
1 ½ cups of flour
½ cup of sugar

⅓ cup vegetable oil
2 tsp. of baking powder
Yogurt, as needed
1 tsp. of lemon zest

2 tbsp. of lemon juice
Pinch of sea salt

INSTRUCTIONS
1. Pre-heat the Air Fryer to 350°F
2. Place all of the dry ingredients in a bowl & combine well.
3. Beat the egg & pour it into a cup. Mix it with the oil & lemon juice. Add in the yogurt, to taste.
4. Mix together the dry & wet ingredients.
5. Add in the lemon zest & raspberries.
6. Coat the insides of 10 muffin tins with a little butter.
7. Spoon an equal amount of the mixture into each muffin tin.
8. Transfer to the Air Fryer, & cook for 10 minutes, in batches if necessary.

940. PECAN PIE
Prep & Cook Time: 1 hour 10 minutes | Servings: 4

INGREDIENTS
1x 8-inch pie dough
½ tsp. of cinnamon
¾ tsp. of vanilla extract
2 eggs

¾ cup maple syrup
⅛ tsp. of nutmeg
2 tbsp. of butter
1 tbsp. of butter, melted

2 tbsp. of sugar
½ cup of chopped pecans

INSTRUCTIONS
1. Pre-heat the Air Fryer to 370°F.

2. In a small bowl, coat the pecans in the melted butter.
3. Transfer the pecans to the Air Fryer & allow them to toast for about 10 minutes.
4. Put the pie dough in a greased pie pan & add the pecans on top.
5. In a bowl, mix together the rest of the ingredients. Pour this over the pecans.
6. Place the pan in the Air Fryer & bake for 25 minutes.

941. ORANGE CARROT CAKE

Prep & Cook Time: 30 minutes | Servings: 8

INGREDIENTS

2 large carrots, peeled & grated
1 ¾ cup of flour
¾ cup of sugar
2 eggs

10 tbsp. of olive oil
2 cups of sugar
1 tsp. of mixed spice
2 tbsp. of milk

4 tbsp. of melted butter
1 small orange, rind & juice

INSTRUCTIONS

1. Set the Air Fryer to 360°F & allow to heat up for 10 minutes.
2. Place a baking sheet inside the tin.
3. Combine the flour, sugar, grated carrots, & mixed spice.
4. Pour the milk, beaten eggs, & olive oil into the middle of the batter & mix well.
5. Pour the mixture in the tin, transfer to the Air Fryer & cook for 5 minutes.
6. Lower the heat to 320°F & allow to cook for an additional 5 minutes.
7. In the meantime, prepare the frosting by combining the melted butter, orange juice, rind, & sugar until a smooth consistency is achieved.
8. Remove the cake from the Air Fryer, allow it to cool for several minutes & add the frosting on top.

942. CHOCOLATE COOKIES

Prep & Cook Time: 30 minutes | Servings: 8

INGREDIENTS

3 oz. of sugar
4 oz. of butter

1 tbsp. of honey
6 oz. of flour

1 ½ tbsp. of milk
2 oz. of chocolate chips

INSTRUCTIONS

1. Pre-heat the Air Fryer to 350°F.
2. Mix together the sugar & butter using an electric mixer, until a fluffy texture is achieved.
3. Stir in the remaining ingredients, minus the chocolate chips.
4. Gradually fold in the chocolate chips.
5. Spoon equal portions of the mixture onto a lined baking sheet & flatten out each one with a spoon. Ensure the cookies are not touching.
6. Place in the Air Fryer & cook for 18 minutes.

943. BUTTER CAKE

Prep & Cook Time: 25 minutes | Servings: 2

INGREDIENTS

1 egg
1 ½ cup of flour
7 tbsp. of butter, at room temperature

6 tbsp. of milk
6 tbsp. of sugar
Pinch of sea salt

Cooking spray
Dusting of sugar to serve

INSTRUCTIONS

1. Pre-heat the Air Fryer to 360°F.
2. Spritz the inside of a small ring cake tin with cooking spray.
3. In a bowl, combine the butter & sugar using a whisk.
4. Stir in the egg & continue to mix everything until the mixture is smooth & fluffy.
5. Pour the flour through a sieve into the bowl.
6. Pour in the milk, before adding a pinch of salt, & combine once again to incorporate everything well.
7. Pour the batter into the tin & use the back of a spoon to make sure the surface is even.
8. Place in the Air Fryer & cook for 15 minutes.
9. Before removing it from the Air Fryer, ensure the cake is cooked through by inserting a toothpick into the center & checking that it comes out clean.
10. Allow the cake to cool & serve.

944. SWEDISH CHOCOLATE MUG CAKE

Prep & Cook Time: 15 minutes | Servings: 1

INGREDIENTS

1 tbsp. of cocoa powder
3 tbsp. of coconut oil

¼ cup of flour
3 tbsp. of whole milk

5 tbsp. of sugar

INSTRUCTIONS

1. In a bowl, stir together all of the ingredients to combine them completely.
2. Take a short, stout mug & pour the mixture into it.
3. Put the mug in your Air Fryer & cook for 10 minutes at 390°F.

945. DUNKY DOUGH DIPPERS & CHOCOLATE SAUCE

Prep & Cook Time: 45 minutes | Servings: 5

INGREDIENTS

¾ cup of sugar
1 lb. of bread dough

1 cup of heavy cream
12 oz. of chocolate chips

½ cup of butter, melted
2 tbsp. of vanilla extract

INSTRUCTIONS

1. Pre-heat the Air Fryer to 350°F.
2. Coat the inside of the basket with a little melted butter.
3. Halve & roll up the dough to create two 15-inch logs. Slice each log into 20 disks.
4. Halve each disk & twist it 3 or 4 times.
5. Lay out a cookie sheet & lay the twisted dough pieces on top. Brush the pieces with some more melted butter & sprinkle on the sugar.
6. Place the sheet in the Air Fryer & air fry for 5 minutes. Flip the dough twists over & brush the other side with more butter. Cook for an additional 3 minutes. It may be necessary to complete this step-in batches.
7. In the meantime, make the chocolate sauce. Firstly, put the heavy cream into a saucepan over the medium heat & allow to simmer.
8. Put the chocolate chips into a large bowl & add the simmering cream on top. Whisk the chocolate chips everything together until a smooth consistency is achieved. Stir in 2 tbsp. of the vanilla extract.
9. Transfer the baked cookies in a shallow dish, pour over the rest of the melted butter & sprinkle on the sugar.
10. Drizzle on the chocolate sauce before serving.

946. PEACH CRUMBLE

Prep & Cook Time: 35 minutes | Servings: 6

INGREDIENTS

1 ½ lb. peaches, peeled & chopped
2 tbsp. of lemon juice
1 cup of flour

1 tbsp. of water
½ cup of sugar
5 tbsp. cold butter

Pinch of sea salt

INSTRUCTIONS

1. Mash the peaches a little with a fork to achieve a lumpy consistency.
2. Add in two tbsp. of sugar & the lemon juice.
3. In a bowl, combine the flour, salt, & sugar. Throw in a tbsp. of water before adding in the cold butter, mixing until crumbly.
4. Grease the inside of a baking dish & arrange the berries at the bottom. Top with the crumbs.
5. Transfer the dish to the Air Fryer & air fry for 20 minutes at 390°F.

947. BANANA WALNUT CAKE
Prep & Cook Time: 55 minutes | Servings: 6

INGREDIENTS

16 oz. bananas, mashed
8 oz. of flour
6 oz. of sugar

3.5 oz. of walnuts, chopped
2.5 oz. of butter
2 eggs

¼ tsp. of baking soda

INSTRUCTIONS

1. Coat the inside of a baking dish with a little oil.
2. Pre-heat the Air Fryer at 355°F.
3. In a bowl combine the sugar, butter, egg, flour & soda using a whisk. Throw in the bananas & walnuts.
4. Transfer the mixture to the dish. Place the dish in the Air Fryer & cook for 10 minutes.
5. Reduce the heat to 330°F & cook for another 15 minutes. Serve hot

948. CHEESY LEMON CAKE
Prep & Cook Time: 60 minutes | Servings: 6

INGREDIENTS

17.5 oz. of ricotta cheese
5.4 oz. of sugar

3 eggs
3 tbsp. of flour

1 lemon, juiced & zested
2 tsp. of vanilla extract [optional]

INSTRUCTIONS

1. Pre-heat Air Fryer to 320°F.
2. Combine all of the ingredients until a creamy consistency is achieved.
3. Place the mixture in a cake tin.
4. Transfer the tin to the Air Fryer & cook the cakes for 25 minutes.
5. Remove the cake from the Air Fryer, allow to cool, & serve.

949. CHOCOLATE BROWNIES & CARAMEL SAUCE
Prep & Cook Time: 45 minutes | Servings: 4

INGREDIENTS

½ cup of butter
1 ¾ oz. of cooking chocolate
1 cup of sugar

2 medium eggs, beaten
1 cup of flour
2 tsp. of vanilla

2 tbsp. of water
⅔ cup of milk

INSTRUCTIONS

1. In a saucepan over a medium heat, melt the butter & chocolate together.
2. Take the saucepan off the heat & stir in the sugar, eggs, flour, & vanilla, combining everything well.
3. Pre-heat your Air Fryer to 350°F.
4. Coat the inside of a baking dish with a little butter. Transfer the batter to the dish & place inside the Air Fryer.
5. Bake for 15 minutes.
6. In the meantime, prepare the caramel sauce. In a small saucepan, slowly bring the water to a boil. Cook for around 3 minutes, until the mixture turns light brown.
7. Lower the heat & allow to cook for another two minutes. Gradually add in the rest of the butter. Take the saucepan off the heat & allow the caramel to cool.
8. When the brownies are ready, slice them into squares. Pour the caramel sauce on top & add on some sliced banana if desired before serving.

950. PUMPKIN CINNAMON PUDDING
Prep & Cook Time: 25 minutes | Servings: 4

INGREDIENTS

3 cups of pumpkin puree
3 tbsp. of honey
1 tbsp. of ginger

1 tbsp. of cinnamon
1 tsp. of clove
1 tsp. of nutmeg

1 cup of full-fat cream
2 eggs
1 cup of sugar

INSTRUCTIONS

1. Pre-heat your Air Fryer to 390°F.
2. In a bowl, stir all of the ingredients together to combine.
3. Grease the inside of a small baking dish.
4. Pour the mixture into the dish & transfer to the Air Fryer. Cook for 15 minutes. Serve with whipped cream if desired

951. BANANA WALNUT BREAD
Prep & Cook Time: 40 minutes | Servings: 1 loaf

INGREDIENTS

7 oz. of flour
¼ tsp. of baking powder
2.5 oz. of butter

5.5 oz. of sugar
2 medium eggs
14 oz. bananas, peeled

2.8 oz. chopped walnuts

INSTRUCTIONS

1. Pre-heat the Air Fryer to 350°F.
2. Take a baking tin small enough to fit inside the Air Fryer & grease the inside with butter.
3. Mix together the flour & the baking powder in a bowl.
4. In a separate bowl, beat together the sugar & butter until fluffy & pale. Gradually add in the flour & egg. Stir.
5. Throw in the walnuts & combine again.
6. Mash the bananas using a fork & transfer to the bowl. Mix once more, until everything is incorporated.
7. Pour the mixture into the tin, place inside the Air Fryer & cook for 10 minutes.

952. PEACH SLICES
Prep & Cook Time: 40 minutes | Servings: 4

INGREDIENTS

4 cups of peaches, sliced
2 – 3 tbsp. of sugar
2 tbsp. of flour

⅓ cup of oats
2 tbsp. of butter
¼ tsp. of vanilla extract

1 tsp. of cinnamon

INSTRUCTIONS

1. In a large bowl, combine the peach slices, sugar, vanilla extract, & cinnamon. Pour the mixture into a baking tin & place it in the Air Fryer.
2. Cook for 20 minutes on 290°F.
3. In the meantime, combine the oats, flour, & of butter in a separate bowl.
4. Once the peach slices cooked, pour the butter mixture on top of them.
5. Cook for an additional 10 minutes at 300 - 310°F.
6. Remove from the Air Fryer & allow to crisp up for 5 – 10. Serve with ice cream if desired.

953. VANILLA SOUFFLE

INGREDIENTS

¼ cup of flour
¼ cup of butter, softened
1 cup whole milk
¼ cup of sugar

2 tsp. of vanilla extract
1 vanilla bean
5 egg whites
4 egg yolks

1 oz. of sugar
1 tsp. of cream of tartar

INSTRUCTIONS

1. Mix together the flour & butter to create a smooth paste.
2. In a saucepan, heat up the milk. Add the ¼ cup of sugar & allow it to dissolve.
3. Put the vanilla bean in the mixture & bring it to a boil.
4. Pour in the flour-butter mixture. Beat the contents of the saucepan thoroughly with a wire whisk, removing all the lumps.
5. Reduce the heat & allow the mixture to simmer & thicken for a number of minutes.
6. Take the saucepan off the heat. Remove the vanilla bean & let the mixture cool for 10 minutes in an ice bath.
7. In the meantime, grease six 3-oz. ramekins or soufflé dishes with butter & add a sprinkling of sugar to each one.
8. In a separate bowl quickly, rigorously stir the egg yolks & vanilla extract together. Combine with the milk mixture.
9. In another bowl, beat the egg whites, 1 oz. of sugar & cream of tartar to form medium stiff peaks.
10. Fold the egg whites into the soufflé base. Transfer everything to the ramekins, smoothing the surfaces with a knife or the back of a spoon.
11. Pre-heat the Air Fryer to 330°F.
12. Put the ramekins in the cooking basket & cook for 14 – 16 minutes. You may need to complete this step in multiple batches.
13. Serve the soufflés topped with powdered sugar & with a side of chocolate sauce.

954. BUTTER MARSHMALLOW FLUFF TURNOVER

Prep & Cook Time: 35 minutes | Servings: 4

INGREDIENTS

4 sheets of filo pastry, defrosted
4 tbsp. of chunky peanut butter

4 tsp. of marshmallow fluff
2 oz. of butter, melted

Pinch of sea salt

INSTRUCTIONS

1. Pre-heat the Air Fryer to 360°F.
2. Roll out the pastry sheets. Coat one with a light brushing of butter.
3. Lay a second pastry sheet on top of the first one. Brush once again with butter. Repeat until all 4 sheets have been used.
4. Slice the filo layers into four strips, measuring roughly 3 inches x 12 inches.
5. Spread one tbsp. of peanut butter & one tsp. of marshmallow fluff on the underside of each pastry strip.
6. Take the tip of each sheet & fold it backwards over the filling, forming a triangle. Repeat this action in a zigzag manner until the filling is completely enclosed.
7. Seal the ends of each turnover with a light brushing of butter.
8. Put the turnovers in the Air Fryer basket & cook for 3 – 5 minutes, until they turn golden brown & puffy.
9. Sprinkle a little sea salt over each turnover before serving.

955. CHOCOLATE-COVERED MAPLE BACON

Prep & Cook Time: 25 minutes | Servings: 4

INGREDIENTS

8 slices of sugar-free bacon
1 tbsp. of granular sugar

⅓ cup of chocolate chips
1 tsp. of coconut oil

½ tsp. of maple extract

INSTRUCTIONS

1. Place the bacon in the Air Fryer's basket & add the sugar on top. Cook for six minutes at 350°F & turn the bacon over. Leave to cook another six minutes or until the bacon is sufficiently crispy.
2. Take the bacon out of the Air Fryer & leave it to cool.
3. Microwave the chocolate chips & coconut oil together for half a minute. Remove from the microwave & mix together before stirring in the maple extract.
4. Set the bacon flat on a piece of parchment paper & pour the mixture over. Allow to harden in the refrigerator for roughly five minutes before serving.

956. SUGAR PORK RINDS

Prep & Cook Time: 10 minutes | Servings: 2

INGREDIENTS

2 oz. of pork rinds
2 tsp. of butter, melted

¼ cup of sugar
½ tsp. of ground cinnamon

INSTRUCTIONS

1. Coat the rinds with the melted butter.
2. In a separate bowl, combine the sugar & cinnamon & pour over the pork rinds, ensuring the rinds are covered completely & evenly.
3. Transfer the pork rinds into the Air Fryer & cook at 400°F for five minutes.

957. TOASTED COCONUT FLAKES

Prep & Cook Time: 5 minutes | Servings: 1

INGREDIENTS

1 cup of coconut flakes
2 tsp. of coconut oil, melted

¼ cup of sugar
Salt

INSTRUCTIONS

1. In a large bowl, combine the coconut flakes, oil, sugar, & a pinch of salt, ensuring that the flakes are coated completely.
2. Place the coconut flakes in your Air Fryer & cook at 300°F for three minutes, giving the basket a good shake a few times throughout the cooking time. Fry until golden & serve.

958. BLACKBERRY CRISP

Prep & Cook Time: 18 minutes | Servings: 1

INGREDIENTS

2 tbsp. of lemon juice
⅓ cup of sugar

2 cups of blackberries
1 cup of crunchy granola

INSTRUCTIONS

1. In a bowl, combine the lemon juice, sugar, & blackberries. Transfer to a round baking dish about six inches in diameter & seal with aluminum foil.
2. Put the dish in the Air Fryer & leave to cook for twelve minutes at 350°F.
3. Take care when removing the dish from the Air Fryer. Give the blackberries another stir & top with the granola.
4. Return the dish to the Air Fryer & cook for an additional three minutes, this time at 320°F. Serve once the granola has turned brown & enjoy.

959. CHURROS

Prep & Cook Time: 15 minutes | Servings: 1

INGREDIENTS

½ cup of water
¼ cup of butter

½ cup of flour
3 eggs

2 ½ tsp. of sugar

INSTRUCTIONS

1. In a saucepan, bring the water & butter to a boil. Once it is bubbling, add the flour & mix to create a doughy consistency.
2. Remove from the heat, allow to cool, & crack the eggs into the saucepan. Blend with a hand mixer until the dough turns fluffy.

3. Transfer the dough into a piping bag.
4. Pre-heat the Air Fryer at 380°F.
5. Pipe the dough into the Air Fryer in several three-inch-long segments. Cook for ten minutes before removing from the Air Fryer & coating in the sugar.
6. Serve with a chocolate sauce of your choice.

960. PEANUT BUTTER COOKIES
Prep & Cook Time: 15 minutes | Servings: 1

INGREDIENTS

¼ tsp. of salt
4 tbsp. of sugar

½ cup peanut butter
1 egg

INSTRUCTIONS
1. Combine the salt, sugar, & peanut butter in a bowl, incorporating everything well. Break the egg over the mixture & mix to create a dough.
2. Flatten the dough using a rolling pin & cut into shapes with a knife or cookie cutter. Make a crisscross on the top of each cookie with a fork.
3. Pre-heat your Air Fryer at 360°F.
4. Once the Air Fryer has warmed up, put the cookies inside & leave to cook for ten minutes. Take care when taking them out & allow to cool before enjoying.

961. AVOCADO PUDDING
Prep & Cook Time: 5 minutes | Servings: 1

INGREDIENTS

Avocado
3 tsp. of liquid Sugar

1 tbsp. cocoa powder
4 tsp. of milk

¼ tsp. of vanilla extract

INSTRUCTIONS
1. Pre-heat your Air Fryer at 360°F.
2. Halve the avocado, twist to open, & scoop out the pit.
3. Spoon the flesh into a bowl & mash it with a fork. Throw in the Sugar, cocoa powder, milk, & vanilla extract, & combine everything with a hand mixer.
4. Transfer this mixture to the basket of your Air Fryer & cook for three minutes.

962. CHIA PUDDING
Prep & Cook Time: 10 minutes | Servings: 1

INGREDIENTS

1 cup of chia seeds
1 cup of coconut milk

1 tsp. of liquid Sugar
1 tbsp. of coconut oil

1 tsp. of butter

INSTRUCTIONS
1. Pre-heat the Air Fryer at 360°F.
2. In a bowl, gently combine the chia seeds with the milk & Sugar, before mixing the coconut oil & butter. Spoon seven equal-sized portions into seven ramekins & set these inside the Air Fryer.
3. Cook for four minutes. Take care when removing the ramekins from the Air Fryer & allow to cool for four minutes before serving.

963. BACON COOKIES
Prep & Cook Time: 15 minutes | Servings: 2

INGREDIENTS

¼ tsp. of ginger
¼ tsp. of baking soda

⅔ cup peanut butter
2 tbsp. of swerve

3 slices of bacon, cooked & chopped

INSTRUCTIONS
1. In a bowl, mix the ginger, baking soda, peanut butter, & Swerve together, making sure to combine everything well.
2. Stir in the chopped bacon.
3. With clean hands, shape the mixture into a cylinder & cut in six. Press down each slice into a cookie with your palm.
4. Pre-heat your Air Fryer at 350°F.
5. When the Air Fryer is warm, put the cookies inside & cook for seven minutes. Take care when taking them out of the Air Fryer & allow to cool before serving.

964. LOBSTER TAILS & WHITE WINE SAUCE
Prep & Cook Time: 10 minutes | Servings: 4

INGREDIENTS

4 lobster tails, shell cut from the top
½ onion, quartered
½ cup of butter
⅓ cup of white wine

¼ cup of honey
6 garlic cloves, crushed
1 tbsp. of lemon juice
1 tsp. of salt

Pepper
Lemon slices to season
2 tbsp. fresh parsley

INSTRUCTIONS
1. Whack the lobster tails inside your Air Fryer.
2. Combine the remaining ingredients inside a mixing bowl & pour them over the lobster tails.
3. Switch your Air Fryer to 'broil' mode and cook for 15 minutes at 350°F.
4. Serve warm.

965. BROILED LOBSTER TAILS
Prep & Cook Time: 16minutes | Servings: 4

INGREDIENTS

2 lobster tails, shell cut from the top ½
1 cup of butter, melted

½ tsp. of ground paprika
Salt

White pepper, to taste
1 lemon, juiced

INSTRUCTIONS
1. Whack the lobster tails inside your Air Fryer.
2. Combine the remaining ingredients inside a mixing bowl & pour them over the lobster tails.
3. Switch your Air Fryer to 'broil' mode and cook for 15 minutes at 350°F.
4. Serve warm.

966. CHEESECAKE DELUX
Prep & Cook Time: 30 minutes | Servings: 15

INGREDIENTS

1 lb. of cream cheese
½ tsp. of vanilla extract

1 cup of graham crackers, crumbled
2 tbsp. of butter

2 eggs
4 tbsp. of sugar

INSTRUCTIONS
1. Combine the crackers with the butter inside a mixing bowl.

2. Spread the cracker mix on the bottom of a lined cake pan.
3. Place the pan inside your Air Fryer & cook at 350°F for 5 minutes.
4. In another bowl, combine the sugar with cream cheese, eggs, vanilla. Whisk until fully combined.
5. Smoother the filling over the cracker crust.
6. Cook the cheesecake in your Air Fryer at 310°F for 13 minutes.
7. Leave the cake in the refrigerator for 3 hours.
8. Slice & serve!

967. MACAROONS
Prep & Cook Time: 20 minutes | Servings: 20

INGREDIENTS

2 tbsp. of sugar

2 cups of coconut, shredded
4 egg whites

1 tsp. of vanilla extract

INSTRUCTIONS
1. Combine the egg whites with the sugar in a mixing bowl.
2. Toss in the coconut & vanilla extract. Mix until fully combined.
3. Sculpt macaroon shapes using the mixture.
4. Place inside your Air Fryer & cook at 340°F for 7 minutes.
5. Let cool and serve cold.

968. ORANGE CAKE DELUX
Prep & Cook Time: 25 minutes | Servings: 12

INGREDIENTS

1 orange, peeled & cut quartered
1 tsp. of vanilla extract
6 eggs
3 tbsp. of orange zest

4 oz. of cream cheese
1 tsp. of baking powder
9 oz. of flour

1 oz. of sugar
3 oz. of yogurt

INSTRUCTIONS
1. Mix the oranges and break them down using a mixer.
2. Toss in 2 tablespoons of flour, sugar, eggs, baking powder & vanilla extract. Mix until fully combined.
3. Pour the mixture into two spring form pans.
4. Whack the pans inside your Air Fryer & cook at 330°F for 15 minutes
5. Combine the cheese with orange zest, yogurt & the rest of the sugar inside a mixing bowl. Stir well.
6. Put one cake layer on a plate and pour roughly half of the cream cheese mixture on top.
7. Add the remaining cake layer & top with the remaining cream cheese mixture. Smoother well.
8. Slice and serve into portions!

969. AMARETTO
Prep & Cook Time: 15 minutes | Servings: 12

INGREDIENTS

1 lb. of bread dough
1 cup of heavy cream

11 oz. of chocolate chips
1 cup of sugar

½ cup of butter, melted
1 tbsp. of amaretto liqueur

INSTRUCTIONS
1. Add a dusting of flour to the countertop and roll out the dough on top.
2. When rolled, cut the dough into around 20 slices. Cut each slice into two smaller slices.
3. Using a brush, coat each dough slice with butter & sprinkle with sugar.
4. Whack the slices inside your Air Fryer and fry at 350°F for 4 minutes.
5. When done, flip the slices and fry the other side for a further 2 minutes.
6. When fried, take the slices out of your Air Fryer and place them onto a plate to cool.
7. On the stove top, pour the heavy cream inside a skillet and cook on medium heat, adding the chocolate chips & stirring until the mixture is melted and fully combined. Add the liqueur and stir.
8. Pour the mixture into a bowl & serve the bread dippers with this sauce.

970. CARROT CAKE DELUX
Prep & Cook Time: 55 minutes | Servings: 6

INGREDIENTS

5 oz. of flour
¾ tsp. of baking powder
¼ tsp. of nutmeg, ground
½ tsp. of baking soda
½ tsp. of cinnamon powder

½ cup of sugar
⅓ cup of carrots, grated
⅓ cup of pecans, toasted & chopped.
¼ cup of pineapple juice
½ tsp. of allspice

1 egg
2 tbsp. of yogurt
4 tbsp. of sunflower oil
⅓ cup of coconut flakes, shredded
Cooking spray

INSTRUCTIONS
1. Combine the flour with the baking soda, salt, allspice, cinnamon & nutmeg. Mix until fully combined and place to the side.
2. Inside another bowl, mix the egg with the yogurt, sugar, pineapple juice, oil, carrots, pecans & coconut flakes. Combine well.
3. Pour the two mixtures together and mix until fully combined.
4. Pour this combined mixture into a greased spring form pan.
5. Place the pan inside your Air Fryer and cook at 320°F for 43 minutes.
6. When cooked, let the cake cool, cur and serve!

971. BANANA BREAD
Prep & Cook Time: 50 minutes | Servings: 6

INGREDIENTS

¾ cup of sugar
⅓ cup of butter
⅓ cup of milk
1 tsp. of vanilla extract 1 egg

3 bananas, mashed
2 tsp. of baking powder
1 ½ cups of flour
½ tsp. of baking soda

1 ½ tsp. of cream of tartar
Cooking spray

INSTRUCTIONS
1. Combine the cream of tartar, sugar, butter, egg, vanilla & bananas inside a mixing bowl until sully combined and place to the side.
2. Inside another bowl, combine the flour with the baking powder & the baking soda.
3. Then, pour the two mixtures together and combine them well.
4. Grease a cake pan with the cooking spray and place it inside your Air Fryer.
5. Pour the combined mixture into the pan and cook at 320°F for 45 minutes.
6. When cooked, take out the bread and let it cool down. Slice into portions and serve!

972. MOUNTAIN GRANOLA

Prep & Cook Time: 45 minutes | Servings: 4

INGREDIENTS

1 cup of coconut, desiccated
½ cup of almonds
½ cup of pecans, chopped.

1 tbsp. of sugar
½ cup of pumpkin seeds
½ cup of sunflower seeds

1 tbsp. of sunflower oil
2 tsp. of nutmeg, ground
1 tsp. of apple pie spice mix

INSTRUCTIONS

1. Combine the almonds, pecans, pumpkin seeds, sunflower seeds, coconut, nutmeg & apple pie mix inside a large mixing bowl.
2. On a medium heat, heat a pan with the oil inside on your stove top. Add the sugar and stir.
3. Pour this over the nuts inside the bowl and mix until fully combined.
4. Grease a baking sheet with butter and pour this nutty mixture on top.
5. Place inside your Air Fryer and cook at 300°F for 23 minutes.
6. When cooked, let the granola slab cool and cut into slices and serve!

973. PEARS & ESPRESSO CREAM

Prep & Cook Time: 40 minutes | Servings: 4

INGREDIENTS

4 pears, halved & cored
1 tbsp. of water
3 tbsp. of lemon juice
1 tbsp. of sugar

1 tbsp. of butter
For the cream:
1 cup of whipping cream

1 tbsp. of espresso, cold
1 cup of mascarpone
⅓ cup of sugar

INSTRUCTIONS

1. Combine the pears with the lemon juice, sugar, butter & water until fully combined.
2. Place the mixture inside your Air Fryer and cook at 360°F for 25 minutes.
3. In the meantime, combine the whipping cream with the mascarpone, sugar & espresso inside a mixing bowl.
4. Store this mixture inside your refrigerator to keep cool until the Air Fryer stops cooking.
5. When cooked, take the pears out of your Air Fryer and portion them onto plates. Top with the cool expresso mixture.
6. Serve!

974. PARMESAN MUFFINS

Prep & Cook Time: 20 minutes | Servings: 4

INGREDIENTS

3 oz. of almond milk
3 oz. of white flour
3 oz. of parmesan cheese, grated

2 eggs
2 tbsp. of olive oil
1 tbsp. of baking powder

A dash of Worcestershire sauce

INSTRUCTIONS

1. Inside a large mixing bowl, combine the eggs with the olive oil, milk, baking powder, flour, Worcestershire sauce & the parmesan. Stir well.
2. Grease a muffin pan and place it inside your Air Fryer.
3. Pour the mixture on top and spread it evenly. Cook at 320°F for 14 minutes.
4. When cooked, take out the muffins and let them cool.
5. Serve!

975. ANGEL FOOD CAKE

Prep & Cook Time: 40 minutes | Servings: 12

INGREDIENTS

¼ cup of butter, melted
1 cup of powdered erythritol

2 tsp. of strawberry extract
12 egg whites

1 tsp. of cream of tartar
A pinch of salt

INSTRUCTIONS

1. Preheat your Air Fryer at 380°F for 5 minutes.
2. In the meantime, combine the egg whites & cream of tartar. Whisk until fluffy peaks form.
3. Toss in the remaining ingredients except for the butter. Whisk until fully combined.
4. Pour the mixture inside a greased baking dish.
5. Place the dish inside your preheated Air Fryer and cook at 380°F for 30 minutes.
6. When cooked, take out, let cool and drizzle with some melted butter.

976. UPSIDE DOWN CAKE

Prep & Cook Time: 40 minutes | Servings: 9

INGREDIENTS

¼ cup of almond butter
¼ cup of sunflower oil
½ cup of walnuts, chopped
¾ cup & 2 tbsp. of coconut sugar

¾ cup of water
1 ½ tsp. of mixed spice
1 cup of plain flour
1 lemon, zest

2 tsp. of baking soda
1 tsp. of vinegar
3 baking apples, cored & sliced

INSTRUCTIONS

1. Preheat your Air Fryer at 380°F for 5 minutes.
2. Inside a mixing bowl, combine the almond butter & 3 tbsp. of sugar.
3. Grease a baking dish and pour the mixture inside.
4. Place the dish inside your Air Fryer.
5. Inside another bowl, mix the flour, remaining sugar and baking soda together. Toss in the mixed spice.
6. Inside another bowl, combine the oil, water, vinegar, & lemon zest. Toss in the chopped walnuts and stir well.
7. Mix both bowls together until fully combined. Arrange the apple slices on top.
8. Bake at 380°F for 30 minutes.

977. BLUEBERRY LEMON CAKE DELUX

Prep & Cook Time: 40 minutes | Servings: 4

INGREDIENTS

2 eggs
1 cup of blueberries
Zest from 1 lemon
Juice from 1 lemon

1 tsp. of vanilla
Brown sugar for coating
2 ½ cups of self-rising flour
½ cup of monk fruit

½ cup of cream
¼ cup of avocado oil

INSTRUCTIONS

1. Inside a mixing bowl, combine the wet ingredients together.
2. Add in the dry ingredients and stir until fully combined.
3. Grease a baking dish and place it inside your Air Fryer.
4. Pour in the mixture and cook at 330°F for 10 minutes.
5. When cooked, take out and let cool.
6. Cut inside portions and serve!

978. STRAWBERRY COBBLER

Prep & Cook Time: 30 minutes | Servings: 4

INGREDIENTS

2 tsp. of butter
1 ½ cup of strawberries
1 tsp. of sugar
1 tbsp. of butter

½ cup of flour
¼ cup of heavy whipping cream
1 tsp. of cornstarch
½ cup of water

½ tsp. of salt
¾ tsp. of baking powder

INSTRUCTIONS

1. Grease a baking dish with butter and place it inside your Air Fryer.
2. Into the dish add the water, cornstarch & sugar. Cook at 390°F for 8 minutes until a gooey mixture is formed.
3. Add the strawberries to the mixture. Stir well.
4. Inside a mixing bowl, combine the salt, baking powder, sugar & flour. Pour in the cream. Add a little butter.
5. Spoon the mixture on top of the strawberries.
6. Bake for 13 minutes at 390°F until golden brown.

979. CHOCOLATE SOUFFLE

Prep & Cook Time: 18 minutes | Servings: 2

INGREDIENTS

3 oz. of baking cooking chocolate
¼ cup of butter
2 eggs, yolks & whites separated

2 tbsp. of sugar
½ tsp. of vanilla extract
2 tbsp. of flour

1 tsp. of powdered sugar for dusting

INSTRUCTIONS

1. Inside a microwaveable proof bowl, combine the butter and chocolate. Place inside your microwave and cook for 1 ½ minutes until melted.
2. Remove the mixture from your microwave and stir until smooth.
3. Inside another bowl, add the egg yolks. Whisk well until fully combined.
4. Add in the sugar & vanilla extract. Again, whisk well.
5. Add in the chocolate mixture and mix until fully incorporated.
6. Toss in the flour and mix well.
7. This time, in a mixing bowl, add the egg whites and whisk until fluffy peaks are formed.
8. Fold the fluffy egg whites into the chocolate mixture and place to the side.
9. Grease two ramekins and sprinkle with sugar for taste.
10. Place the final mixture into the ramekins and smooth off the top to form a flat and even surface.
11. Place the ramekins inside your Air Fryer and bake at 330°F for 15 minutes.
12. When baked, take out carefully and let cool. Sprinkle with the powdered sugar and serve warm.

980. BLUEBERRY CRISP

Prep & Cook Time: 18 minutes | Servings: 1

INGREDIENTS

2 tbsp. of lemon juice
⅓ cup of sugar

2 cups of blackberries
1 cup of crunchy granola

INSTRUCTIONS

1. In a bowl, combine the lemon juice, sugar, & blueberries. Transfer to a round baking dish about six inches in diameter & seal with aluminum foil.
2. Put the dish in the Air Fryer & leave to cook for twelve minutes at 350°F.
3. Take care when removing the dish from the Air Fryer. Give the blackberries another stir & top with the granola.
4. Return the dish to the Air Fryer & cook for an additional three minutes, this time at 320°F. Serve once the granola has turned brown & enjoy.

981. WHITE CHOCOLATE CHURROS

Prep & Cook Time: 15 minutes | Servings: 1

INGREDIENTS

½ cup of water
¼ cup of butter

White chocolate sauce
½ cup of flour

3 eggs
2 ½ tsp. of sugar

INSTRUCTIONS

1. In a saucepan, bring the water & butter to a boil. Once it is bubbling, add the flour & mix to create a doughy consistency.
2. Remove from the heat, allow to cool, & crack the eggs into the saucepan. Blend with a hand mixer until the dough turns fluffy.
3. Transfer the dough into a piping bag.
4. Pre-heat the Air Fryer at 380°F.
5. Pipe the dough into the Air Fryer in several three-inch-long segments. Cook for ten minutes before removing from the Air Fryer & coating in the sugar.
6. Serve with the white chocolate sauce.

982. INSTANT COOKIES

Prep & Cook Time: 15 minutes | Servings: 1

INGREDIENTS

¼ tsp. of salt
4 tbsp. of sugar

½ cup peanut butter
1 egg

INSTRUCTIONS

1. Combine the salt, sugar, & peanut butter in a bowl, incorporating everything well. Break the egg over the mixture & mix to create a dough.
2. Flatten the dough using a rolling pin & cut into shapes with a knife or cookie cutter. Make a crisscross on the top of each cookie with a fork.
3. Pre-heat your Air Fryer at 360°F.
4. Once the Air Fryer has warmed up, put the cookies inside & leave to cook for ten minutes. Take care when taking them out & allow to cool before enjoying.

983. CUSTARD PUDDING

Prep & Cook Time: 5 minutes | Servings: 1

INGREDIENTS

1 cup of custard
3 tsp. of liquid Sugar

1 tbsp. cocoa powder
4 tsp. of milk

¼ tsp. of vanilla extract

INSTRUCTIONS

1. Pre-heat your Air Fryer at 360°F.

2. Throw in the Sugar, cocoa powder, milk, & vanilla extract, & combine everything with a hand mixer.
3. Transfer this mixture to the basket of your Air Fryer & cook for 3 minutes.
4. When cooked, top the pudding with the custard (hot or cold). Enjoy!

984. BISCUIT PUDDING
Prep & Cook Time: 10 minutes | Servings: 1

INGREDIENTS

1 large plain biscuit
1 cup of coconut milk

1 tsp. of sugar
1 tbsp. of coconut oil

1 tsp. of butter

INSTRUCTIONS

1. Pre-heat the Air Fryer at 360°F.
2. In a bowl, gently combine the biscuit with the milk & sugar, before mixing the coconut oil & butter. Spoon seven equal-sized portions into seven ramekins & set these inside the Air Fryer.
3. Cook for four minutes. Take care when removing the ramekins from the Air Fryer & allow to cool for four minutes before serving.

985. SUGAR COOKIES
Prep & Cook Time: 15 minutes | Servings: 2

INGREDIENTS

¼ tsp. of ginger
¼ tsp. of baking soda

⅔ cup peanut butter
2 tbsp. of swerve

1 broken cookie, plain
3 tsp. of sugar

INSTRUCTIONS

1. In a bowl, mix the ginger, baking soda, peanut butter, & sugar together, making sure to combine everything well.
2. Stir in the broken cookie.
3. With clean hands, shape the mixture into a cylinder & cut in six. Press down each slice into a cookie with your palm.
4. Pre-heat your Air Fryer at 350°F.
5. When the Air Fryer is warm, put the cookies inside & cook for seven minutes. Take care when taking them out of the Air Fryer & allow to cool before serving.

986. BISCUIT & WHITE WINE SAUCE
Prep & Cook Time: 10 minutes | Servings: 4

INGREDIENTS

4 plain biscuits
½ onion, quartered
½ cup of butter
⅓ cup of white wine

¼ cup of honey

Lemon slices to season

INSTRUCTIONS

1. Break the biscuits with your hand and whack them inside your Air Fryer.
2. Add in the remaining ingredients.
3. Air Fryer for 15 minutes at 350°F.
4. Serve warm.

987. SOGGY BISCUIT
Prep & Cook Time: 16minutes | Servings: 4

INGREDIENTS

4 large plain biscuits
1 cup of butter, melted

½ tsp. of ground paprika
Salt

White pepper, to taste
1 lemon, juiced

INSTRUCTIONS

1. Whack the biscuits inside your Air Fryer.
2. Add in the remaining ingredients.
3. Air Fry for 15 minutes at 350°F.
4. Serve warm.

988. CRACKER CAKE
Prep & Cook Time: 30 minutes | Servings: 15

INGREDIENTS

½ tsp. of vanilla extract
1 cup of graham crackers, crumbled

2 tbsp. of butter
2 eggs

4 tbsp. of sugar

INSTRUCTIONS

1. Combine the crackers with the butter inside a mixing bowl.
2. Spread the cracker mix on the bottom of a lined cake pan.
3. Place the pan inside your Air Fryer & cook at 350°F for 5 minutes.
4. In another bowl, combine the sugar with the eggs, vanilla. Whisk until fully combined.
5. Smother the filling over the cracker crust.
6. Cook the cake in your Air Fryer at 310°F for 13 minutes. Let cool.
7. Slice & serve!

989. COCONUT BOMBS
Prep & Cook Time: 20 minutes | Servings: 20

INGREDIENTS

2 tbsp. of sugar

2 cups of coconut, shredded
4 egg whites

1 tsp. of vanilla extract

INSTRUCTIONS

1. Combine the egg whites with the sugar in a mixing bowl.
2. Toss in the coconut & vanilla extract. Mix until fully combined.
3. Sculpt the mixture into round bomb shaped balls.
4. Whack inside your Air Fryer & cook at 340°F for 8 minutes.
5. Let cool and serve cold.

990. ZESTY CAKE
Prep & Cook Time: 25 minutes | Servings: 12

INGREDIENTS

1 lemon, peeled & cut quartered
1 tsp. of vanilla extract
6 eggs
3 tbsp. of orange zest

4 oz. of cream cheese
1 tsp. of baking powder
9 oz. of flour

1 oz. of sugar
3 oz. of yogurt

INSTRUCTIONS

1. Mix the lemons and break them down using a mixer.
2. Toss in 2 tablespoons of flour, sugar, eggs, baking powder & vanilla extract. Mix until fully combined.
3. Pour the mixture into two spring form pans.
4. Whack the pans inside your Air Fryer & cook at 330°F for 15 minutes.
5. Combine the cheese with lemon mix, yogurt & the rest of the sugar inside a mixing bowl. Stir well.
6. Put one cake layer on a plate and pour roughly half of the cream cheese mixture on top.
7. Add the remaining cake layer & top with the remaining cream cheese mixture. Smoother well.
8. Slice and serve into portions!

991. LOW-CARB BANG

Prep & Cook Time: 15 minutes | Servings: 12

INGREDIENTS

1 lb. of low-carb bread dough
1 cup of coconut cream

11 oz. of sugar free chocolate chips
1 cup of coconut powder

½ cup of ghee, melted
1 tbsp. of red wine

INSTRUCTIONS

1. Add a dusting of flour to the countertop and roll out the dough on top.
2. When rolled, cut the dough into around 20 slices. Cut each slice into two smaller slices.
3. Using a brush, coat each dough slice with ghee & sprinkle with coconut powder.
4. Whack the slices inside your Air Fryer and fry at 350°F for 4 minutes.
5. When done, flip the slices and fry the other side for a further 2 minutes.
6. When fried, take the slices out of your Air Fryer and place them on a plate to cool.
7. On the stove top, pour the coconut cream inside a skillet and cook on medium heat, adding the chocolate chips & stirring until the mixture is melted and fully combined. Add the red wine and stir.
8. Pour the mixture into a bowl & serve the bread dippers with this sauce.

992. BIG CAKE

Prep & Cook Time: 55 minutes | Servings: 6

INGREDIENTS

6 oz. of flour
¾ tsp. of baking powder
¼ tsp. of nutmeg, ground
½ tsp. of baking soda
½ tsp. of cinnamon powder

½ cup of sugar
⅓ cup of carrots, grated
⅓ cup of pecans, toasted & chopped.
¼ cup of pineapple juice
½ tsp. of allspice

1 egg
2 tbsp. of yogurt
4 tbsp. of sunflower oil
⅓ cup of coconut flakes, shredded
Cooking spray

INSTRUCTIONS

1. Combine the flour with the baking soda, salt, allspice, cinnamon & nutmeg. Mix until fully combined and place to the side.
2. Inside another bowl, mix the egg with the yogurt, sugar, pineapple juice, oil, carrots, pecans & coconut flakes. Combine well.
3. Pour the two mixtures together and mix until fully combined.
4. Pour this combined mixture into a greased spring form pan.
5. Place the pan inside your Air Fryer and cook at 320°F for 43 minutes.
6. When cooked, let the cake cool, cur and serve!

993. YOGURT BREAD

Prep & Cook Time: 50 minutes | Servings: 6

INGREDIENTS

¾ cup of sugar
⅓ cup of butter
⅓ cup of milk
1 tsp. of vanilla extract 1 egg

2 cups of plain yogurt
2 tsp. of baking powder
1 ½ cups of flour
½ tsp. of baking soda

1 ½ tsp. of cream of tartar
Cooking spray

INSTRUCTIONS

1. Combine the cream of tartar, sugar, butter, egg, vanilla & yogurt inside a mixing bowl until sully combined and place to the side.
2. Inside another bowl, combine the flour with the baking powder & the baking soda.
3. Then, pour the two mixtures together and combine them well.
4. Grease a cake pan with the cooking spray and place it inside your Air Fryer.
5. Pour the combined mixture into the pan and cook at 320°F for 45 minutes.
6. When cooked, take out the bread and let it cool down. Slice into portions and serve!

994. SWISS GRANOLA

Prep & Cook Time: 45 minutes | Servings: 4

INGREDIENTS

1 cup of coconut, desiccated
½ cup of almonds
½ cup of pecans, chopped.

1 tbsp. of sugar
½ cup of blackberries seeds
½ cup of blueberries seeds

1 tbsp. of sunflower oil
2 tsp. of nutmeg, ground
1 tsp. of apple pie spice mix

INSTRUCTIONS

1. Combine the almonds, pecans, blueberries, blackberries, coconut, nutmeg & apple pie mix inside a large mixing bowl.
2. On a medium heat, heat a pan with the oil inside on your stove top. Add the sugar and stir.
3. Pour this over the nuts inside the bowl and mix until fully combined.
4. Grease a baking sheet with butter and pour this nutty mixture on top.
5. Place inside your Air Fryer and cook at 300°F for 23 minutes.
6. When cooked, let the granola slab cool and cut into slices and serve!

995. BANANA ESPRESSO ON-THE-GO!

Prep & Cook Time: 40 minutes | Servings: 4

INGREDIENTS

2 bananas
1 tbsp. of water
3 tbsp. of lemon juice

1 tbsp. of sugar
1 tbsp. of butter
For the cream:

1 cup of whipping cream

1 tbsp. of espresso, cold
1 cup of mascarpone
⅓ cup of sugar
INSTRUCTIONS
1. Combine the bananas, lemon juice, sugar, butter & water until fully combined.
2. Place the mixture inside your Air Fryer and cook at 360°F for 25 minutes.
3. In the meantime, combine the whipping cream with the mascarpone, sugar & espresso inside a mixing bowl.
4. Store this mixture inside your refrigerator to keep cool until the Air Fryer stops cooking.
5. When cooked, take the pears out of your Air Fryer and portion them onto plates. Top with the cool expresso mixture.
6. Serve!

996. AMERICAN MUFFINS
Prep & Cook Time: 20 minutes | Servings: 4

INGREDIENTS

3 oz. of almond milk
3 oz. of white flour

3 oz. of American cheese, grated
2 eggs

2 tbsp. of olive oil
1 tbsp. of baking powder

INSTRUCTIONS
1. Inside a large mixing bowl, combine the eggs with the olive oil, milk, baking powder, flour & the parmesan. Stir well.
2. Grease a muffin pan and place it inside your Air Fryer.
3. Pour the mixture on top and spread it evenly. Cook at 320°F for 14 minutes.
4. When cooked, take out the muffins and let them cool.
5. Serve!

997. SCIENCE CAKE
Prep & Cook Time: 40 minutes | Servings: 12

INGREDIENTS

¼ cup of butter, melted
1 cup of powdered erythritol

2 tsp. of blueberry extract
10 egg whites

1 tsp. of big bang sauce
A pinch of salt

INSTRUCTIONS
1. Preheat your Air Fryer at 380°F for 5 minutes.
2. In the meantime, combine the egg whites & big bang sauce. Whisk until fluffy peaks form.
3. Toss in the remaining ingredients except for the butter. Whisk until fully combined.
4. Pour the mixture inside a greased baking dish.
5. Place the dish inside your preheated Air Fryer and cook at 380°F for 30 minutes.
6. When cooked, take out, let cool and drizzle with some melted butter.

998. UP-SIDE CAKE
Prep & Cook Time: 40 minutes | Servings: 9

INGREDIENTS

¼ cup of almond butter
¼ cup of sunflower oil
½ cup of walnuts, chopped
¾ cup & 2 tbsp. of coconut sugar

¾ cup of water
1 ½ tsp. of mixed spice
1 cup of plain flour
1 lemon, zest

2 tsp. of baking soda
1 tsp. of vinegar
3 baking apples, cored & sliced

INSTRUCTIONS
1. Preheat your Air Fryer at 380°F for 5 minutes.
2. Inside a mixing bowl, combine the almond butter & 3 tbsp. of sugar.
3. Grease a baking dish and pour the mixture inside.
4. Place the dish inside your Air Fryer.
5. Inside another bowl, mix the flour, remaining sugar and baking soda together. Toss in the mixed spice.
6. Inside another bowl, combine the oil, water, vinegar, & lemon zest. Toss in the chopped walnuts and stir well.
7. Mix both bowls together until fully combined. Arrange the apple slices on the bottom. Flip the cake.
8. Bake at 380°F for 30 minutes.

999. BENNY'S BLACKBERRY CAKE
Prep & Cook Time: 40 minutes | Servings: 4

INGREDIENTS

2 eggs
1 cup of blackberries
Zest from 1 lemon

Juice from 1 lemon
1 tsp. of vanilla
2 ½ cups of self-rising flour

½ cup of cream

INSTRUCTIONS
1. Inside a mixing bowl, combine the wet ingredients together.
2. Add in the dry ingredients and stir until fully combined.
3. Grease a baking dish and place it inside your Air Fryer.
4. Pour in the mixture and cook at 330°F for 10 minutes.
5. When cooked, take out and let cool.
6. Cut inside portions and serve!

1000. BLUEBERRY COBBLER
Prep & Cook Time: 30 minutes | Servings: 4

INGREDIENTS

2 tsp. of butter
1 ½ cup of blueberries
1 tsp. of sugar
1 tbsp. of butter

½ cup of flour
¼ cup of heavy whipping cream
1 tsp. of cornstarch
½ cup of water

½ tsp. of salt
¾ tsp. of baking powder

INSTRUCTIONS
1. Grease a baking dish with butter and place it inside your Air Fryer.
2. Into the dish add the water, cornstarch & sugar. Cook at 390°F for 8 minutes until a gooey mixture is formed.
3. Add the blueberries to the mixture. Stir well.
4. Inside a mixing bowl, combine the salt, baking powder, sugar & flour. Pour in the cream. Add a little butter.
5. Spoon the mixture on top of the blueberries.
6. Bake for 13 minutes at 390°F until golden brown.

1001. FRIED BANANA SLICES

Prep & Cook Time: 40 minutes | Servings: 4

INGREDIENTS

4 cups of bananas, sliced
2 – 3 tbsp. of sugar
2 tbsp. of flour

⅓ cup of oats
2 tbsp. of butter
¼ tsp. of vanilla extract

1 tsp. of cinnamon

INSTRUCTIONS

1. In a large bowl, combine the bananas slices, sugar, vanilla extract, & cinnamon. Pour the mixture into a baking tin & place it in the Air Fryer.
2. Cook for 20 minutes on 290°F.
3. In the meantime, combine the oats, flour, & of butter in a separate bowl.
4. Once the banana slices are cooked, pour the butter mixture on top of them.
5. Cook for an additional 10 minutes at 300 - 310°F.
6. Remove from the Air Fryer & allow to crisp up for 5 – 10. Serve with ice cream if desired.

COOKING NOTES

CATALOGUE OF NUTRITIONAL INFORMATION

This table provides detailed macronutrient information for each recipe. This information includes standard nutritional macros for calories, proteins, fats & carbs. There are 1001 entries representing a total of 1001 recipes featured in this book. Values are given in whole numbers for 1 serving or portion, unless otherwise stated.

RECIPE#	CALORIES	PROTEIN	FAT	CARBS
1	443	11	12	20
2	171	17	19	6
3	388	12	5	14
4	135	18	4	23
5	379	9	15	7
6	474	11	20	17
7	93	9	20	23
8	488	7	14	10
9	436	10	18	18
10	197	18	5	13
11	202	3	12	23
12	120	13	25	8
13	265	11	15	22
14	260	17	6	15
15	145	10	21	8
16	381	4	13	22
17	132	11	9	16
18	372	8	21	24
19	209	7	23	12
20	121	19	20	24
21	495	17	14	6
22	368	18	10	7
23	319	5	4	15
24	357	10	3	24
25	492	6	5	3
26	348	4	19	9
27	355	16	10	10
28	367	20	21	6
29	206	15	17	13
30	131	15	13	19
31	194	16	22	9
32	90	20	24	6
33	147	6	25	13
34	86	10	23	8
35	161	19	15	7
36	438	12	3	22
37	334	9	4	22
38	348	10	20	19
39	278	11	18	20
40	481	5	14	21
41	500	8	9	15
42	448	7	24	5
43	159	11	18	10
44	323	9	13	14
45	222	2	5	24
46	389	7	17	23
47	184	12	3	19
48	419	10	8	18
49	497	18	3	11
50	193	17	15	11
51	258	17	23	20
52	367	6	24	7
53	444	11	17	3
54	456	13	3	14
55	211	3	15	11
56	456	7	4	16
57	278	5	7	13
58	309	19	18	17
59	429	3	15	20
60	483	3	9	18
61	283	17	19	10
62	363	5	24	4
63	182	14	21	21
64	500	10	20	16
65	472	10	22	14
66	94	2	7	19
67	135	16	15	19
68	172	10	10	7
69	184	18	23	17
70	388	4	11	13
71	307	7	21	6
72	433	19	25	8
73	478	19	13	12
74	195	13	19	10
75	90	3	17	14
76	82	12	24	15
77	473	18	11	13
78	372	16	22	20
79	345	7	7	12
80	433	15	15	24
81	329	19	14	11
82	322	16	10	10
83	291	8	11	8
84	225	9	12	19
85	175	10	19	7
86	330	9	12	16
87	99	16	9	5
88	335	19	14	16
89	462	9	3	19
90	348	7	6	4
91	345	19	19	14
92	448	20	3	8
93	351	3	10	20
94	155	12	8	7
95	143	10	21	11
96	494	4	17	6
97	480	19	24	16
98	247	8	19	23
99	447	5	5	4
100	256	6	10	21
101	228	9	4	4
102	114	13	5	3
103	127	10	20	5
104	262	17	5	10
105	171	15	12	23
106	74	6	21	15
107	301	15	5	9
108	229	4	22	3
109	295	16	10	13
110	121	12	10	22
111	253	15	22	6
112	453	11	23	15
113	95	2	15	20
114	120	6	12	10
115	350	6	19	10
116	72	14	21	24
117	457	20	12	4
118	327	7	23	24
119	395	9	9	20
120	294	5	11	7
121	203	18	5	24
122	133	12	14	13
123	131	18	20	6
124	195	2	23	12
125	355	14	10	19
126	473	11	17	3
127	431	20	16	16
128	407	6	24	21
129	222	6	15	13
130	130	13	18	9
131	294	18	19	10
132	380	7	22	19
133	412	9	21	13
134	198	16	7	8
135	146	9	16	17
136	453	4	19	10
137	93	3	5	16
138	357	5	24	13
139	165	17	23	21
140	462	9	12	19
141	103	16	16	12
142	391	7	12	15
143	363	8	19	12
144	154	4	12	10
145	396	17	14	13
146	131	20	18	6
147	211	5	16	9

148	394	8	18	9	233	500	18	18	6
149	199	15	22	20	234	238	20	10	24
150	306	7	14	20	235	171	7	25	12
151	412	19	17	3	236	355	13	11	4
152	306	13	13	20	237	186	19	13	11
153	118	6	10	21	238	291	13	9	6
154	453	20	11	9	239	411	7	7	17
155	193	17	10	23	240	462	17	18	4
156	157	2	11	23	241	225	10	25	17
157	469	5	14	7	242	392	19	8	17
158	308	7	10	3	243	130	3	4	7
159	282	16	10	13	244	396	13	3	9
160	323	13	5	17	245	346	2	19	18
161	99	10	6	13	246	316	3	18	15
162	339	4	10	16	247	456	3	15	20
163	478	15	25	23	248	399	8	23	5
164	447	2	19	9	249	417	14	7	21
165	255	14	10	15	250	450	7	9	23
166	486	15	11	18	251	162	8	10	5
167	81	16	10	12	252	457	15	19	13
168	367	11	7	22	253	273	18	18	14
169	267	17	16	9	254	341	2	8	13
170	464	7	9	7	255	344	9	8	19
171	281	2	10	12	256	222	3	11	15
172	417	5	4	16	257	242	17	10	11
173	339	3	21	19	258	287	4	18	14
174	358	16	20	19	259	313	10	8	22
175	322	5	25	9	260	454	6	5	22
176	390	5	4	18	261	336	20	11	16
177	434	17	25	5	262	208	3	17	24
178	385	12	17	16	263	270	12	25	7
179	163	15	11	24	264	117	10	19	13
180	83	19	18	4	265	79	14	17	11
181	272	15	13	18	266	284	13	24	10
182	102	9	4	14	267	148	5	10	7
183	100	18	14	16	268	189	6	14	16
184	115	18	18	23	269	294	19	22	14
185	382	8	12	17	270	82	18	10	14
186	147	3	21	16	271	381	11	13	10
187	140	10	21	15	272	279	14	7	16
188	189	2	21	21	273	141	12	7	10
189	462	4	15	6	274	101	14	3	20
190	353	2	10	6	275	299	10	5	20
191	245	11	15	5	276	253	20	17	13
192	169	6	15	24	277	481	11	14	21
193	271	17	9	3	278	445	11	18	14
194	488	15	6	7	279	485	19	15	7
195	232	10	18	24	280	465	4	21	5
196	398	19	23	24	281	443	13	23	9
197	104	15	20	18	282	315	15	20	7
198	430	10	3	5	283	183	19	4	8
199	460	3	19	19	284	310	7	6	3
200	500	20	21	21	285	84	7	5	3
201	321	6	15	19	286	496	6	6	24
202	178	3	13	14	287	396	12	4	7
203	483	4	8	12	288	129	11	7	17
204	469	7	14	8	289	448	4	15	21
205	394	4	17	5	290	222	9	13	3
206	235	19	16	16	291	471	13	5	9
207	368	4	13	21	292	491	15	5	14
208	244	13	17	20	293	89	11	17	16
209	309	8	16	15	294	137	13	7	24
210	142	20	21	20	295	476	17	18	20
211	184	16	25	13	296	218	3	10	13
212	145	11	14	14	297	111	20	6	8
213	94	14	19	16	298	387	8	20	14
214	92	7	6	15	299	374	17	16	23
215	279	5	25	14	300	280	8	25	11
216	235	8	16	21	301	73	2	5	12
217	308	4	21	5	302	258	18	17	16
218	254	14	20	11	303	193	6	17	10
219	457	20	7	24	304	423	4	12	17
220	236	10	5	11	305	192	7	24	5
221	242	11	15	19	306	434	15	18	7
222	215	8	24	4	307	465	6	25	12
223	154	2	22	10	308	429	13	8	9
224	144	3	12	22	309	211	6	6	24
225	109	10	12	12	310	392	2	7	10
226	315	11	15	23	311	318	16	8	8
227	397	18	8	22	312	235	2	22	19
228	303	19	8	11	313	283	3	7	16
229	284	11	23	7	314	500	16	9	14
230	76	8	16	9	315	117	11	18	7
231	400	15	3	13	316	211	13	11	7
232	432	7	3	12	317	204	8	10	11

318	479	16	19	22	404	165	3	17	6
319	123	16	24	5	405	311	4	21	21
320	308	9	10	13	406	492	2	23	22
321	271	8	3	6	407	90	17	18	16
322	80	2	4	14	408	424	8	22	7
323	471	13	15	9	409	250	10	20	15
324	245	2	21	17	410	437	13	19	13
325	299	19	19	13	411	464	5	25	8
326	475	5	16	22	412	435	15	15	18
327	437	5	15	18	413	463	2	4	16
328	251	18	12	3	414	123	18	22	10
329	240	6	11	18	415	411	10	12	23
330	392	5	19	11	416	136	20	16	13
331	497	9	14	24	417	481	19	21	9
332	490	20	21	17	418	296	8	19	14
333	431	9	11	23	419	77	14	20	19
334	291	12	25	14	420	468	5	18	16
335	445	17	19	23	421	72	14	17	15
336	484	12	18	6	422	362	16	22	10
337	419	19	3	7	423	76	4	12	6
338	257	17	22	15	424	359	14	6	11
339	477	19	24	6	425	178	3	11	18
340	361	3	25	7	426	415	7	20	9
341	310	9	6	16	427	325	18	10	5
342	495	12	21	5	428	433	10	15	16
343	319	15	23	7	429	160	6	13	3
344	236	10	9	15	430	225	8	6	21
345	401	15	14	7	431	196	3	20	13
346	481	16	11	7	432	399	4	11	19
347	255	6	14	12	433	314	18	5	17
348	131	10	20	24	434	225	18	5	22
349	327	16	11	21	435	334	19	11	12
350	174	10	25	8	436	343	17	22	19
351	161	19	20	21	437	93	17	7	11
352	194	17	25	7	438	138	5	10	16
353	144	12	14	19	439	340	13	14	5
354	484	10	15	11	440	406	8	9	15
355	261	11	7	5	441	368	20	18	17
356	108	8	24	21	442	427	13	9	7
357	178	8	10	16	443	462	8	14	13
358	174	13	19	12	444	394	16	15	22
359	345	17	23	24	445	366	16	21	16
360	119	5	20	20	446	168	3	10	22
361	442	10	18	19	447	277	16	6	23
362	135	8	6	4	448	268	19	22	17
363	493	20	19	24	449	155	15	19	8
364	107	6	12	17	450	466	17	23	11
365	480	7	19	15	451	140	12	22	10
366	421	11	21	13	452	294	14	17	4
367	446	2	8	4	453	76	6	11	15
368	407	5	6	21	454	491	6	23	11
369	379	12	15	15	455	103	8	15	8
370	455	13	6	17	456	344	17	17	20
371	484	5	9	15	457	79	12	23	13
372	111	13	9	15	458	281	19	20	7
373	229	15	5	19	459	338	16	13	19
374	390	2	21	24	460	144	7	3	9
375	319	3	5	24	461	308	5	15	23
376	151	7	25	10	462	483	9	16	17
377	186	16	11	19	463	462	3	11	15
378	478	16	7	12	464	146	17	22	21
379	218	8	22	10	465	276	8	6	7
380	137	15	15	4	466	122	15	21	9
381	398	8	7	15	467	203	11	3	23
382	167	14	11	8	468	313	13	13	11
383	460	20	18	11	469	282	6	8	17
384	85	2	21	14	470	439	7	21	5
385	363	4	9	11	471	394	3	13	20
386	227	2	17	17	472	401	10	15	23
387	340	17	24	4	473	196	12	21	18
388	413	14	17	11	474	255	7	5	5
389	462	8	5	12	475	445	18	21	3
390	349	20	11	10	476	260	14	22	20
391	401	12	24	19	477	260	20	17	16
392	189	11	8	8	478	353	9	21	3
393	215	18	21	18	479	328	12	19	7
394	201	10	3	24	480	74	9	20	6
395	398	5	16	3	481	106	8	12	22
396	131	9	5	15	482	296	16	11	19
397	391	3	13	15	483	133	10	11	7
398	437	13	9	8	484	312	19	15	13
399	136	20	22	20	485	252	2	24	17
400	351	12	25	13	486	431	17	10	5
401	187	5	13	16	487	346	9	12	3
402	244	15	12	17	488	317	18	23	14
403	183	2	11	19	489	167	9	23	8

490	457	19	8	6	575	220	9	18	23
491	74	5	12	8	576	335	10	23	9
492	263	3	19	21	577	421	10	5	23
493	302	19	7	20	578	142	6	9	9
494	419	3	3	7	579	158	3	24	13
495	140	13	16	4	580	331	3	24	10
496	397	9	17	14	581	373	7	16	16
497	286	8	22	22	582	438	8	18	22
498	500	10	9	22	583	131	6	18	17
499	329	17	4	14	584	439	10	17	6
500	329	10	22	4	585	181	19	4	24
501	454	4	10	24	586	277	15	12	17
502	74	13	17	14	587	293	9	21	3
503	399	9	13	5	588	87	14	19	21
504	496	17	3	22	589	403	6	18	15
505	104	19	5	24	590	437	8	3	7
506	175	20	5	21	591	342	4	7	23
507	362	19	10	13	592	290	7	12	3
508	489	5	11	16	593	244	3	18	16
509	377	19	23	22	594	365	2	9	6
510	260	5	20	14	595	126	2	9	3
511	293	14	18	11	596	100	15	23	3
512	248	16	3	24	597	342	15	13	16
513	110	11	17	13	598	411	14	19	9
514	402	8	9	19	599	130	14	10	3
515	351	15	12	17	600	387	2	21	8
516	136	17	17	5	601	331	8	21	18
517	481	3	16	16	602	397	5	11	16
518	327	19	13	21	603	342	7	12	4
519	483	2	6	3	604	490	10	15	6
520	325	15	25	14	605	135	16	18	10
521	204	10	9	9	606	233	2	11	14
522	217	7	20	22	607	365	8	14	19
523	373	16	4	13	608	192	10	15	12
524	225	13	25	22	609	78	18	20	16
525	325	7	8	3	610	119	7	15	11
526	316	14	6	18	611	309	8	22	3
527	223	13	22	19	612	256	17	7	24
528	403	14	18	12	613	261	16	7	5
529	210	3	17	21	614	73	7	3	24
530	127	4	9	15	615	106	17	25	18
531	118	20	6	7	616	151	10	7	4
532	260	14	13	5	617	234	9	12	13
533	490	15	20	16	618	273	16	15	19
534	193	8	21	7	619	194	3	13	13
535	128	7	8	21	620	176	7	18	12
536	239	4	9	10	621	382	17	17	10
537	154	18	17	21	622	233	5	23	5
538	319	18	20	7	623	206	3	23	8
539	141	15	17	23	624	279	7	20	9
540	356	2	3	17	625	410	5	14	6
541	336	6	14	8	626	302	12	7	4
542	368	2	10	6	627	443	11	12	20
543	104	17	13	16	628	171	17	19	6
544	455	4	17	5	629	388	12	5	14
545	241	8	18	21	630	135	18	4	23
546	108	6	11	6	631	379	9	15	7
547	225	20	12	10	632	474	11	20	17
548	79	10	21	19	633	93	9	20	23
549	408	8	13	8	634	488	7	14	10
550	232	7	22	21	635	436	10	18	18
551	251	3	18	9	636	197	18	5	13
552	315	18	24	4	637	202	3	12	23
553	93	3	11	18	638	120	13	25	8
554	85	17	20	7	639	265	11	15	22
555	272	13	20	4	640	260	17	6	15
556	185	19	4	13	641	145	10	21	8
557	357	15	11	5	642	381	4	13	22
558	385	3	19	18	643	132	11	9	16
559	225	2	19	21	644	372	8	21	24
560	449	11	25	11	645	209	7	23	12
561	128	7	7	18	646	121	19	20	24
562	327	6	12	21	647	495	17	14	6
563	157	5	11	17	648	368	18	10	7
564	111	7	15	24	649	319	5	4	15
565	169	16	4	15	650	357	10	3	24
566	395	13	8	17	651	492	6	5	3
567	387	7	13	8	652	348	4	19	9
568	398	18	7	18	653	355	16	10	10
569	424	17	14	7	654	367	20	21	6
570	122	3	10	22	655	206	15	17	13
571	105	18	8	17	656	131	5	13	19
572	342	3	9	4	657	194	16	22	9
573	83	6	23	11	658	90	20	24	6
574	94	13	16	6	659	147	6	25	13

660	86	10	23	8	746	151	7	25	10
661	161	19	15	7	747	186	16	11	19
662	438	12	3	22	748	478	16	7	12
663	334	9	4	22	749	218	8	22	10
664	348	10	20	19	750	137	15	15	4
665	278	11	18	20	751	398	8	7	15
666	481	5	14	21	752	167	14	11	8
667	500	8	9	15	753	460	20	18	11
668	448	7	24	5	754	85	2	21	14
669	159	11	18	10	755	363	4	9	11
670	323	9	13	14	756	227	2	17	17
671	222	2	5	24	757	340	17	24	4
672	389	7	17	23	758	413	14	17	11
673	184	12	3	19	759	462	8	5	12
674	419	10	8	18	760	349	20	11	10
675	497	18	3	11	761	401	12	24	19
676	193	17	15	11	762	189	11	8	8
677	258	17	23	20	763	215	18	21	18
678	367	6	24	7	764	201	10	3	24
679	444	11	17	3	765	398	5	16	3
680	456	13	3	14	766	131	9	5	15
681	211	3	15	11	767	391	3	13	15
682	456	7	4	16	768	437	13	9	8
683	278	5	7	13	769	136	20	22	20
684	309	19	18	17	770	351	12	25	13
685	429	3	15	20	771	187	5	13	16
686	483	3	9	18	772	244	15	12	17
687	283	17	19	10	773	183	2	11	19
688	363	5	24	4	774	165	3	17	6
689	182	14	21	21	775	311	4	21	21
690	500	10	20	16	776	492	2	23	22
691	472	10	22	14	777	90	17	18	16
692	94	2	7	19	778	424	8	22	7
693	135	16	15	19	779	250	10	20	15
694	172	10	10	7	780	437	13	19	13
695	184	18	23	17	781	464	5	25	8
696	388	4	11	13	782	435	15	15	18
697	307	7	21	6	783	463	2	4	16
698	433	19	25	8	784	123	18	22	10
699	478	19	13	12	785	411	10	12	23
700	195	13	19	10	786	136	20	16	13
701	90	3	17	14	787	481	19	21	9
702	82	12	24	15	788	296	8	19	14
703	473	18	11	13	789	77	14	20	19
704	372	16	22	20	790	468	5	18	16
705	345	7	7	12	791	72	14	17	15
706	433	15	15	24	792	362	16	22	10
707	329	19	14	11	793	76	4	12	6
708	322	16	10	10	794	367	11	7	22
709	291	8	11	8	795	267	17	16	9
710	225	9	12	19	796	464	7	9	7
711	175	10	19	7	797	281	2	10	12
712	330	9	12	16	798	417	5	4	16
713	99	16	9	5	799	339	3	21	19
714	335	19	14	16	800	358	16	20	19
715	462	9	3	19	801	322	5	25	9
716	348	7	6	4	802	390	5	4	18
717	345	19	19	14	803	434	17	25	5
718	448	20	3	8	804	385	12	17	16
719	351	3	10	20	805	163	15	11	24
720	155	12	8	7	806	83	19	18	4
721	143	10	21	11	807	272	15	13	18
722	494	4	17	6	808	102	9	4	14
723	480	19	24	16	809	100	18	14	16
724	247	8	19	23	810	115	18	18	23
725	447	5	5	4	811	382	8	12	17
726	256	6	10	21	812	147	3	21	16
727	228	9	4	4	813	140	10	21	15
728	114	13	5	3	814	189	2	21	21
729	127	10	20	5	815	462	4	15	6
730	119	5	20	20	816	353	2	10	6
731	442	10	18	19	817	245	11	15	5
732	135	8	6	4	818	169	6	15	24
733	493	20	19	24	819	271	17	9	3
734	107	6	12	17	820	488	15	6	7
735	480	7	19	15	821	232	10	18	24
736	421	11	21	13	822	398	19	23	24
737	446	2	8	4	823	104	15	20	18
738	407	5	6	21	824	430	10	3	5
739	379	12	15	15	825	460	3	19	19
740	455	13	6	17	826	500	20	21	21
741	484	5	9	15	827	321	6	15	19
742	111	13	9	15	828	178	3	13	14
743	229	15	5	19	829	483	4	8	12
744	390	2	21	24	830	469	7	14	8
745	319	3	5	24	831	394	4	17	5

832	235	19	16	16
833	368	4	13	21
834	244	13	17	20
835	309	8	16	15
836	142	20	21	20
837	184	16	25	13
838	145	11	14	14
839	94	14	19	16
840	92	7	6	15
841	279	5	25	14
842	235	8	16	21
843	308	4	21	5
844	254	14	20	11
845	457	20	7	24
846	236	10	5	11
847	242	11	15	19
848	215	8	24	4
849	154	2	22	10
850	144	3	12	22
851	109	10	12	12
852	315	11	15	23
853	397	18	8	22
854	303	19	8	11
855	284	11	23	7
856	76	8	16	9
857	400	15	3	13
858	475	5	16	22
859	437	5	15	18
860	251	18	12	3
861	240	6	11	18
862	392	5	19	11
863	497	9	14	24
864	490	20	21	17
865	431	9	11	23
866	291	12	25	14
867	445	17	19	23
868	484	12	18	6
869	419	19	3	7
870	257	17	22	15
871	477	19	24	6
872	361	3	25	7
873	310	9	6	16
874	495	12	21	5
875	319	15	23	7
876	236	10	9	15
877	401	15	14	7
878	481	16	11	7
879	255	6	14	12
880	131	10	20	24
881	327	16	11	21
882	174	10	25	8
883	161	19	20	21
884	194	17	25	7
885	144	12	14	19
886	484	10	15	11
887	261	11	7	5
888	108	8	24	21
889	178	8	10	16
890	174	13	19	12
891	345	17	23	24
892	119	5	20	20
893	442	10	18	19
894	135	8	6	4
895	493	20	19	24
896	107	6	12	17
897	480	7	19	15
898	421	11	21	13
899	446	2	8	4
900	407	5	6	21
901	379	12	15	15
902	455	13	6	17
903	484	5	9	15
904	111	13	9	15
905	229	15	5	19
906	390	2	21	24
907	319	3	5	24
908	151	7	25	10
909	186	16	11	19
910	478	16	7	12
911	218	8	22	10
912	137	15	15	4
913	398	8	7	15
914	167	14	11	8
915	460	20	18	11
916	85	2	21	14
917	363	4	9	11
918	227	2	17	17
919	340	17	24	4
920	413	14	17	11
921	462	8	5	12
922	349	20	11	10
923	401	12	24	19
924	189	11	8	8
925	215	18	21	18
926	201	10	3	24
927	398	5	16	3
928	131	9	5	15
929	391	3	13	15
930	437	13	9	8
931	136	20	22	20
932	351	12	25	13
933	187	5	13	16
934	244	15	12	17
935	494	4	17	6
936	480	19	24	16
937	247	8	19	23
938	447	5	5	4
939	256	6	10	21
940	228	9	4	4
941	114	13	5	3
942	127	10	20	5
943	119	5	20	20
944	442	10	18	19
945	135	8	6	4
946	493	20	19	24
947	107	6	12	17
948	480	7	19	15
949	421	11	21	13
950	446	2	8	4
951	407	5	6	21
952	379	12	6	17
953	455	13	6	17
954	484	5	9	15
955	111	13	9	15
956	229	15	5	19
957	390	2	21	24
958	319	3	5	24
959	151	7	25	10
960	186	16	11	19
961	478	16	7	12
962	218	8	22	10
963	137	15	15	4
964	398	8	7	15
965	167	14	11	8
966	460	20	18	11
967	85	2	21	14
968	363	4	9	11
969	227	2	17	17
970	340	17	24	4
971	413	14	17	11
972	462	8	5	12
973	349	20	11	10
974	401	12	24	19
975	189	11	8	8
976	215	18	21	18
977	201	10	3	24
978	398	5	16	3
979	131	9	5	15
980	391	3	13	15
981	437	13	9	8
982	136	20	22	20
983	351	12	25	13
984	187	5	13	16
985	244	15	12	17
986	183	2	11	19
987	165	3	17	6
988	311	4	21	21
989	492	2	23	22
990	90	17	18	16
991	424	8	22	7
992	250	10	20	15
993	437	13	19	13
994	464	5	25	8
995	435	15	15	18
996	463	2	4	16
997	123	18	22	10
998	411	10	12	23
999	136	20	16	13
1000	481	19	21	9
1001	296	8	19	14

Printed in Great Britain
by Amazon